# THE CONSUMER IN AMERICAN SOCIETY: ADDITIONAL DIMENSIONS

# THE CONSUMER IN AMERICAN SOCIETY: ADDITIONAL DIMENSIONS

JACK L. TAYLOR, JR.
School of Business Administration
Portland State University

ARCH W. TROELSTRUP
Emeritus Professor

Former Director
Family Economics Program
Stephens College

**McGraw-Hill**
**Book Company**

New York
St. Louis
San Francisco
Düsseldorf
Johannesburg
Kuala Lumpur
London
Mexico
Montreal
New Delhi
Panama
Paris
São Paulo
Singapore
Sydney
Tokyo
Toronto

**Library of Congress Cataloging in Publication Date**

Taylor, Jack Lawrence, date comp.
The consumer in American society.

1. Consumer education—Addresses, essays, lectures.
I. Troelstrup, Archie William, date joint comp.
II. Title.
TX335.T38 640.73 73-23122
ISBN 0-07-062965-X

THE CONSUMER IN AMERICAN SOCIETY: ADDITIONAL DIMENSIONS



1234567890DODO7987654

This book was set in Zenith by Rocappi, Inc.
The editors were Jack R. Crutchfield and Annette Hall;
the designer was J. E. O'Connor;
the production supervisor was Sam Ratkewitch.
R. R. Donnelley & Sons was printer and binder.

To the Discerning Consumer / Buyer

# Contents

# Preface

Like the captain who "navigates by the seat of his pants," the consumer frequently finds that his decisions are too often based on intuition and experience. Instrumentation, course control, and other factors have both increased the knowledge and sophistication required of the ship's captain and, at the same time, decreased the role of experience and intuition allowed. Similarly, the consumer who makes decisions solely on the basis of experience and spur-of-the-moment intuitions may become the last relic of a bygone era.

The above analogy provides an insight into the present paradox of consumers. On the one hand the complexities of consumer transactions and large-scale business organizations provide an environment which is both confusing and frustrating. On the other hand, consumers are hearing about an increasing array of laws, organizations, and buying techniques which purportedly are to bring order out of chaos, to provide information for purchase problem solving, and to encourage informed consumer decision making. It is indeed a truism that in the past we spent much of our time, money, and energy learning how to earn a living and little on learning how to purchase our chosen life style. This book focuses on how to increase purchasing power, how to learn to be a discerning consumer, and how to use the consumer protection laws that protect our rights.

The selections in this book represent dimensions and facets of consumer knowledge which generally fall beyond textbook parameters. The articles are intended for undergraduate students, taking a course in consumer economics, personal finance, or consumer decision making. In addition the readings will provide the seasoned consumer with a rich sample of consumer literature, including a unique *Library Factfinder* directing the reader to current sources of consumer information. Our purpose is to provide additional insights, views, and concepts for the basic consumer subjects—to offer an additional level of understanding.

The book is divided into three general subject areas for convenience, although different aspects of specific consumer subjects are at times developed in several sections.

*Part 1,* "The Modern Consumer," establishes the relationship between the consumer and his environment; the selections illustrate that the diversity and dimensions of modern consumer roles require many types of knowledge and information.

*Part 2,* "The Purchase of a Life Style," samples the rich literature on money management, consumer credit, buying food, clothing management, the purchase of a home, family transportation, health care, insurance, and investments.

*Part 3,* "Consumer Protection," adds a decisive dimension to any discussion on the modern consumer and his purchasing. The readings in this section capture the dynamics, the excitement, the challenges, and the problems of the changing nature of consumer protection and buyer-seller relations. Selections on the role of government at the federal, state, and local levels and the international consumer movement are included.

We thank the more than 100 authors and publishers for the insightful articles which made this anthology possible. We are deeply indebted to our editors, Jack R. Crutchfield and Annette Hall of McGraw-Hill Book Company, for their skill and help in charting the final production of the manuscript. No work of this nature could emerge without the genuine interest of the individuals who have been generous in their counsel, who typed and proofread the manuscript. For their special role we thank them. We hope that the book will challenge, motivate, inform, and encourage all readers to further investigate the many dimensions of the consumer in American society.

*Jack L. Taylor, Jr.*

# Author–Title–Source Index

| AUTHOR | TITLE | SOURCE | READING NUMBER |
|---|---|---|---|
| Asam, Edward H.<br>Bucklin, Louis P. | "Nutrition Labeling for Canned Goods: A Study of Consumer Response" | *Journal of Marketing* | 46 |
| Belth, Joseph M. | "Deceptive Sales Practices in Life Insurance" | *Indiana Business Review* | 83 |
| Berens, John S. | "Consumer Costs in Product Failure" | *M.S.U. Business Topics* | 93 |
| Berry, Leonard L.<br>Maricle, Kenneth E. | "Consumption without Ownership: Marketing Opportunity for Today and Tomorrow" | *M.S.U. Business Review* | 9 |
| Bloom, Murray T. | "A New Way to Prevent Arguments over Money" | *McCall's* | 20 |
| Blum, Walter J. | "Is Estate Planning Still with It?" | *Taxes* | 86 |

**CORRELATION OF TAYLOR AND TROELSTRUP READINGS WITH CHAPTERS OF SELECTED PERSONAL FINANCE TEXT BOOKS**

| TEXT | CHAPTER NUMBER 1 | 2 | 3 | 4 | 5 | 6 | 7 | 8 | 9 | 10 | 11 | 12 | 13 | 14 |
|---|---|---|---|---|---|---|---|---|---|---|---|---|---|---|
| Troelstrup: **The Consumer in American Society, 5/e** | 1-8 | 9-17 | ← 18-23 → | | ← 24-36 → | | 37-51 | 52-56 | 57-61 | 62-71 | 72-78 | 79-82 | 83-87 | 88-91 |
| Cohen and Hanson: **Personal Finance, 4/e** | 18-22, 96 | 4,5,7,8 24,28 52-56, 95,98 | | 30,35, 36, 105 | 29-32, 34, 103 | | 84,85 | 81-83 | | 72-82, 100, 101 | 62-71 | 57-61, 90,92, 93,102 | 89 | |
| Donaldson and Pfahl: **Personal Finance** | 1,2,6, 18,19, 20 | 4,5, 8-10 12,13 21-28 62-71 | ← 31-36 → | | | 84,85 | 81-84 | 72-78 | | 57-61, 90,101, 105 | 89,96, 100 | | | |
| Bailard, Biehl, and Kaiser: **Personal Money Management** | 1,2,7,9 22,94 | 4-6, 10,12 13,105 | 100 | 62-71 | 72-79 | 81-83 | 18-20, 24-28 | | | 21,23, 31,36 | 30, 32-35, 103 | 57-61, 90,92, 93 | 91 | 84,85 |
| Phillips and Lane: **Personal Finance, 2/e** | 1,2 4-6, 8,9 | 10,12, 13, 24-28 | 31-35, 103 | 84,85 | | | | | | | | | | |
| | | | ← 18-23 → | | | | | | ← 37-56 → | | | | | |
| | | | | | | | | | 36,57, 58-61, 90 | 62-71 | 72-79 | | | 81-83 |
| Gordon and Lee: **Economics for Consumers, 6/e** | 1-4 72,95 | 5 | 6-8, 12 | 9,10 | 37-51 | 80,88 | 53 | 52 | 13,16 | 14,15, 17 | 79,92, 93,94 | 102, 103 | | 30-36 |

CHAPTER NUMBER

| TEXT | 15 | 16 | 17 | 18 | 19 | 20 | 21 | 22 | 23 | 24 | 25 | 26 | 27 | 28 |
|---|---|---|---|---|---|---|---|---|---|---|---|---|---|---|
| Troelstrup: **The Consumer in American Society, 5/e** | 92–95 | ← 96–105 | → | 106–108 | | | | | | | | | | |
| Cohen and Hanson: **Personal Finance, 4/e** | | | 86,87 | | | | | | | | | | | |
| Donalson and Pfahl: **Personal Finance** | | 91 | | | 86–88 | | | | | | | | | |
| Bailard, Biehl, and Kaiser: **Personal Money Management** | 96 | | | | 89 | | 80, 86–88 | | | | | | | |
| Phillips and Lane: **Personal Finance, 2/e** | 30,92 93, 96–101, 105 | | 80, 86–88 | | | | | | | | | | | |
| Gordon and Lee: **Economics for Consumers, 6/e** | 63,64 68,76 78 | 60, 65–67 70–83 | 18,19 21,33 | 20, 22–24, 26–28 | 57–59, 61, 62,90 | 82 | 69–71, 73–75, 81 | 84–87, 89,91 | 54–99 | 55–56 | | 29,98, 105 | 77,96, 97,100, 101 | |

1. Top row of numbers represents chapters in each of the texts.
2. Numbers in all other squares represent readings in Taylor and Troelstrup.

# Part One

# The Modern Consumer

To many the consumer has just recently been discovered. This is not true. The Mail Fraud Act of 1872, The Food and Drugs Act of 1906, The Federal Trade Commission Act of 1914, consumer cooperatives, the Consumer's Union, and the Wheeler-Lea Amendment to the FTC Act of 1938 are all evidences of earlier concern for the consumer.

If we define consumerism as the consumer's reaction to abnormal conditions associated with, or caused by, the act of consumption, the laws encated in recent times seem to be a reaction to *abnormal conditions* in the marketplace. Recent laws enacted include: Truth in Packaging, 1965; Wholesome Meat Act, 1967; Truth in Lending, 1968; and Fair Credit Reporting Act, 1970.

The recent concern with consumer problems centers on the fact that a greater number of consumers are striving to fill their discretionary wants. They not only have the discretionary money, but the discretionary time and energy to get what they want and to bring about change in abnormal conditions in the relation between buyer and seller—that is, caveat emptor to caveat venditor.

Too frequently the study of the consumer is viewed along quite narrow lines. For example, personal finance, consumer economics, or some other specific consumer subject area is discussed without reference to the fact that the consumer in society, consumer decision making advertising; and money, marital happiness and democracy in home management, need to be "blended" together. The literature frequently does not place much emphasis on the impact of consumer actions on the totality of personal management.

Accordingly, the selections included in Part One show the magnitude of the consumer role in our society and how it relates to all aspects of the purchase of a life style.

# The Consumer in Our Society

Reading 1

## Competition as a Process of Adjustment

**Thomas A. Slaudt**
**Donald A. Taylor**

*Equilibrium is simply that state which exists when the conflicts are resolved.*

The environment in which the firm functions has been characterized as competitive, free enterprise, and market oriented. These terms are frequently used, and much lip service is given to the desirability of the organizational forms and patterns of action they represent. Everyone has some notion of what these mean, but the intricacy of the mechanisms through which society fulfills its needs and desires is not generally conveyed by them. Too frequently *competition* signifies a haphazard, unorganized approach to the economic affairs of society, one in which something akin to a "law of the jungle" prevails. In reality, competition is an intricate, delicately balanced system through which society satisfies its needs and desires.

Many analyses have been made of the degree of competition existing in the economy. For the most part they have been concerned with the number of buyers and sellers, their size, and the relative concentrations of power held by them. These studies are concerned with the *structure* of competition. And although very useful for certain purposes they fail to provide an insight into the actions that firms engage in when they are competitive. One definition of competition is a rivalry between two or more for the patronage of another. This definition treats competition as a form of *behavior* rather than as the *structure* of the behaving units. Our concern is then with what the rivals do. It is these actions that constitute the market affairs of the firm and the intensity of competition which will exist.

### THE NEED FOR ADJUSTMENT

Any society in which there is a division of labor must engage in a process of adjustment. So important, in fact, is the division of labor that some define marketing as "the set of activities that make possible (and in turn are made neces-

From *A Managerial Introduction to Marketing*, 2d ed., © 1970, pp. 4–6. Reprinted by permission of Prentice-Hall, Inc., Englewood Cliffs, N.J.

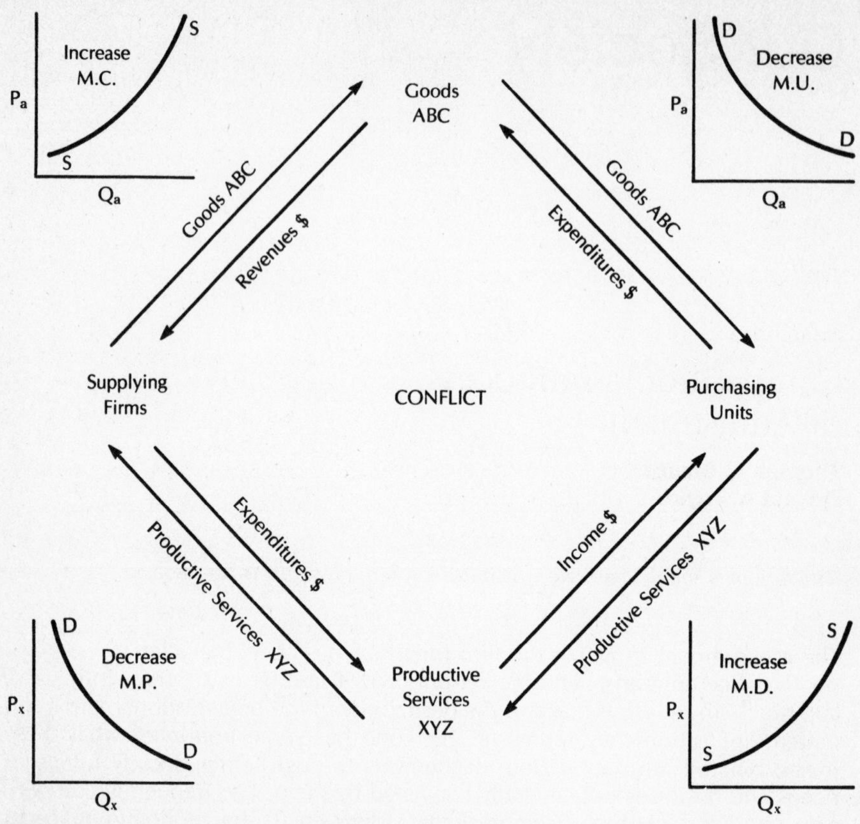


**Figure 1** A marginal diagram of the economy.

sary by) the intricate division of labor that characterizes our economy."[1] Any society in which the work is broken down into minute parts requires some system "to guide the choices economic specialists make among alternative uses of their resources and to exchange among them the goods and services they produce."[2] To simplify the explanation let us think of society as made up of a large number of supplying firms and an even larger number of purchasing units. It is the responsibility of the supplying firms to deliver to the purchasing units that standard of living they wish to enjoy and have the capacity to command. In a number of ways the purchasing unit must adjust to the supplying firm. Rarely do we buy just exactly what we want. For us to be able to do so would require a production-to-order economy, with all of the diseconomies such a scheme would entail. Fortunately we ordinarily enjoy the shopping experience of seeking out those things that we, at the time, think will satisfy us most. Supplying firms do however make many adjustments to satisfy purchasing units. This is evident in the parade of new products made available each year and in the wide variety of any single item marketed at any given time. The actions each supplying firm engages in to make appropriate adjustments are the responsibility of its management, and the actions of all firms, the substance of *competition.*

[1]Reavis Cox, *Distribution in a High-Level Economy* (Englewood Cliffs, N.J.: Prentice-Hall, Inc., 1965), p. 14.
[2]*Ibid.*, p. 14.

What kind of system guides "the choices economic specialists make among alternative uses of their resources . . . to exchange among them the goods and services they produce"? One approach is that of the economist. In equilibrium analyses the economist has tried to describe the results of the adjustment actions taken by the supplying firms and the purchasing units. In Figure 1 a set of relationships between supplying firms and purchasing units is recognized. The relationships are expressed in flows quantified in both real and monetary terms. The quantities are based upon hypothesized relationships between prices and quantities, with psychological forces expressed in the utility and productivity curves assumed. Underlying the entire analysis is a system of conflict; conflict between firms as they vie for the purchasing units' patronage; conflict between supplying firms and purchasing units as they negotiate along the demand curves; and conflict between purchasing units as they bid for scarce resources in the market place. Equilibrium is simply that state which exists when the conflicts are resolved. It is a tight theoretical treatment of the way purchasing units and supplying firms adjust to each other. The major limitation to this description of adjustment is that it describes a result and fails to provide an insight into the actions taken to resolve the conflicts.

Reading 2

# The Free Market and Other Myths

**Ralph Nader**

*There is no list of the ten most wanted corporations.*

The management of power in a complex society is built around institutions. In our country, the most enduring, coordinated, and generic manager of power is the corporate institution. Controlling great wealth and metabolized by the most fungible of factors—the dollar—the modern corporation possesses a formidable unity of motivation and action with great stamina. Much of what passes as governmental power is derivative of corporate power whose advocacy or sufferance defines much of the direction and deployment of government activity. The federal government is replete with supportive programs—subsidies, research, contracts, tax privileges, protections from competition—which flow regularly into the corporate mission of profit and sales maximization. So much of government resources is allocated and so much government authority is utilized to transfer public wealth into corporate coffers that Washington can be fairly described as a bustling bazaar of accounts receivable for industry-commerce.

It is important to recognize the multiple approaches to power which characterize the modern corporation, particularly the top two hundred companies that lead the economy. With limited liability for its owners and diffused responsibility of officers and directors, the corporation derives its strength at the outset from what it *gets,* not from what it *receives.* Its inherently acquisitive nature permits easy justification for wide discretion as to when and how to use or not to use the many permutations of its power. Critical impacts on other people and

From *Business and Society Review/Innovation,* Summer 1972, no. 2, pp. 29–33.

institutions proceed both from the use and nonuse of corporate power. How clear have been the consequences, for example, of the historic nonuse of insurance industry leverage vis-à-vis the auto industry's hazardous vehicle designs.

The nonuse of legitimate power has rarely been popularly evaluated for accountability. So many direct or indirect corporate impacts are of this order. Introducing the internal combustion engine early in the century for mass production in automobiles did not cause much of an air pollution problem. Year after year of rising automotive production with 100 million motor vehicles on the road, the same engine becomes a health menace to Americans. Inaction in 1910 and inaction in 1970 toward the same engine type are completely different displays of corporate behavior. Different magnitudes of hazards to health and property and greatly enhanced industrial capability produce vastly different ethical conclusions. As Alfred North Whitehead wrote: "Duty arises from our potential control over the course of events. Where attainable knowledge could have changed the issue, ignorance has the guilt of vice."

## CORPORATE RESILIENCE

Our legal system has just begun to trundle after the massively tortious impact of willful defaults in preventing known destructions of people's rights. For decades, with compliant regularity, the law has permitted so narrow an evaluation of corporate performance—balance-sheet performance—that wide areas of industrial depredations have escaped the law entirely. Historically, many of our country's struggles have been challenges of the corporate power to define the area of its accountability. This was true of the Populist and Progressive movements as well as the challenges of organized labor and the regulatory state of the New Deal. Against these and lesser buffetings, the corporation, with its peerless resiliency of bending now and consolidating later, prevailed only to increase its power.

The corporate institution proved relentless to its adversaries, including the regulatory state, through an impressive variety of stratagems. How else could zoning and urban renewal have become such intimate adjuncts to corporate renewal and enrichment? How else could a progressive income tax become a mechanism of transferring corporate risk and cost through innumerable loopholes to the individual taxpayer or transforming the corporate income tax into a private sales tax? How else to explain the web of procedural obstacles, such as the tyrannical standing requirements that blocked people from access to their own government? How else, indeed, to explain the staggering violence of corporate pollution against innocent people's property and health with virtual impunity? How else to explain an electoral process which year after year puts a greater premium on wealth and corporate indentures?

In no clearer fashion has the corporation held the law at bay than in the latter's paralysis toward the corporate crime wave. Crime statistics almost wholly ignore corporate or business crime; there is no list of the ten most wanted corporations; the law affords no means of regularly collecting data on corporate crime; and much corporate criminal behavior (such as pollution) has not been made a crime because of corporate opposition. For example, willful and knowing violations of auto, tire, radiation, and gas pipeline safety standards are *not* considered crimes under the relevant statutes—even if lives are lost as a result. The legal process requires courage, not routine duty, by officials to enforce the laws against such outrages. The law is much more comfortable sentencing a telephone coin box thief to five years than sentencing a billion-dollar price-fixing executive to six weeks in jail. It would not be unrealistic to conclude that corporate economic, product, and environmental crimes dwarf other crimes in damage to health, safety, and property, in confiscation or theft of other people's moneys, and in control of the agencies which are supposed to stop this crime and fraud. And it all goes on year after year by blue-chip corporate recidivists. Why? It is easy to answer—power.

## THE LACK OF INDIVIDUAL RESPONSIBILITY

But that is the beginning, not the end, of understanding. It is relational power—related to the amount of goods and services and workers employed in a community or about the country. For as long as the corporate mission is production and employment, the law has treated with laxness industrial-commercial damage to consumer-citizens as the "price of progress," or as limited deviations from the norm, or as indifference, instead of willful in motivation, and therefore insignificant. The retention of the slave mentality which says that the master who does not beat his slave is compassionate can be disastrous in a technological society that can destroy itself domestically by its own inadvertence or knowing indifference. The fact that Chairman James Roche of General Motors does not want his company to have a carcinogenic or genetic effect on the American population has little to do with the enormous damage of GM's plant and vehicle pollution which he and his company are starving of known or knowable remedies. Mr. Roche may privately plead insufficient authority to apply GM's huge resources to its environmental pollution, but he cannot justify his refusal to initiate as a leader. The excuse that there is a diffusion of power in a corporation and no locus of specific responsibility has long been a preconceived strategy of insulating company leaders from having to make such decisions.

Indeed, the entire corporate mechanism is patterned to insulate officials from specific accountability. This pattern is being increasingly refined. Delaware, the nation's corporate Reno for easy chartering of the biggest corporations, now permits corporate officials to be reimbursed by their company even for criminal fines. Rarely is the law invoked against corporate violence, but when it is, the prosecutional penalty or equitable remedy is applied to the corporate shell and not to those officials who make corporate policy. It is almost axiomatic that irresponsibility toward public interests becomes institutionalized whenever the making of decisions is so estranged from any accountability for their discernible consequences.

## THE PUBLIC SUFFERS

Further, the *style* of violence and fraud that flow from corporate activities enhances their perpetuation without countercorrection. Unsafely designed automobiles, pollution, harmful food additives, and other contaminants embody a silent kind of violence with indeterminate, unpredictable incidence per victim. That impact does not provoke immediate sensory response of pain or anguish directed at the source of the harm. Such harm does not depend on its motivation for its impact. And it does not come in the anthropomorphic form that is apparently so necessary to motivate action. Corporate-induced violence illustrates in compelling fashion the biological obsolescence of human beings toward machine, chemical, or other injurious exposures emanating from the technology of corporate groups. Our sensory apparatus, adapted to cruder and older forms of visible hazards, cannot detect carbon monoxide or radiation until it is too late. Soon, this widening gap between the obsolete mechanisms of man's physiology and the multiple, cumulative impacts of his technology may mark the confines of the struggle for planetary survival—even should peace between nations prevail. The mind of man must abstract what is happening more rapidly, for the body of man provides few early alert signals.

For decades the myth of the market's invisible hand was thought to work adequately to maximize consumer values. During the past generation, a new theory of self-correcting mechanisms—countervailing powers or economic pluralism—gained acceptance. One power bloc, it is said, substantially curbs the excesses of another power bloc, whether they be big sellers, big buyers, big unions, big government, or the collective feedback of ultimate consumers. Both these theories had an intellectual neatness to them that mesmerized many academic analysts into avoiding the arduous task of testing them against empirical reality. This is not to say that both theories have no connection with reality. The inescapable question is how much reality. Both types of political economy, and they do overlap in concept, can be driven toward their limits for justice only by the daily vigilance of advocacy equal to the distorting or suppressive forces.

A burgeoning technology is giving corporations more power than they choose to exercise responsibly. Witness, for example, the domestic chemical and biological warfare called, too charitably, pollution. Concentration of economic power develops momentums of abuse in political, social, educational, and union areas. Laws and antitrust and regulatory frameworks have been symbols rather than arms of democratic governing, while the corporate regulatees control the public regulators. The victims are the citizens, in terms of harm to their health, safety, incomes, and freedom.

There must be an end to official secrecy surrounding corporate crimes and incompetence that weights the taxpayer with corporate socialism. What is needed is systematic government assembling of data on corporate behavior so that long-enacted laws can be enforced and new policies forged. Reading business periodicals and relying on *Fortune's* 500 information provide entirely too casual a data base for antitrust policy planning and enforcement. A thorough data base would put an end to the restrictive association of "crime" to street crime while extending doctrinaire permissiveness and anarchy to corporate crimes of the rich.

## UNDERMINING SOCIETY'S VALUES

If radicalism is defined as a force against basic value systems of a society, then the corporate state is the chief protagonist. The ideals of the society run contrary to the behavior of the present political economy. Many Americans, if apprised of how Union Carbide operates here and abroad in producing pollution and job hazards, would disagree strenuously with that company's recent advertisement which arrogantly boasts: "When they look at us, they see a little of you. . . . And it's all quite simple. Overseas, we're you."

All this is not to declare that the noncorporate society is innocent. But a society's compassion tends to rot from the top down, and the exemplary power of the propertied institutions in either direction cannot be overemphasized in either the moral or depraved tone set for other groups and individuals. It was of lesser consequence, perhaps, when corporations adhered to narrower lasts. Now, however, corporate involvement pervades every interstice of our society. Companies are deep in the dossier-credit, city-building, drug, medical, computer-intelligence, military, and educational industries. The most intimate functions of government, including education, health, and military theater contracting, are engaging companies, and with these engagements come the parochial value system and insulation of the corporate structure. These are not temporary involvements but permanent presences. They point to the old Roman adage—"Whatever touches us all should be decided by all."

## WHEREIN LIES CHANGE?

The central question, then, is what changes are necessary to direct corporate resources toward respecting the values and pleas that are beyond the balance sheet's morality? And what are the instruments to achieve these changes? One alternative is a deconcentration of corporate power in two principal ways: thorough antitrust action and the federal chartering of corporations to rewrite the compact between the corporation and its creator—the state—which has been virtually unchanged for a century. In point of fact, the charter can make the grant of corporate status conditional on a responsiveness to well-defined public interests and a social accounting of corporate performance. The charter can establish structural receptiveness to official accountability, detailed disclosure, and rights of access by the various constituencies including victims. Other democratizing forces are possible—the use of routine government procurement in stimulating innovation such as less-polluting vehicles, consumer class actions, campaign financing reform, surcharging polluters, disclosure of more product and service information to consumers, and other basic changes to attenuate irresponsible uses of power. New technologies which permit smaller plant size without sacrificing efficiencies seriously undermine the conventional wisdom that efficiency requires giant corporations.

But even solid structural changes have a way of concentrating old power in new forms sooner or later unless there is a continual assertion and defense of individual rights and responsibilities within the corporate institution itself. Like the medieval peasants who never knew they were serfs, scientists, engineers, accountants, lawyers, physicians, and other corporate-employed professionals rarely realize the extent of their disenfranchisement inside their company government because their roles are defined so narrowly for them. These professionals are usually the first to know the consequences of corporate policies, but they do not have the protected rights vis-à-vis management to exert their professional missions. (Actually, the blue-collar unionized laborer has far more contracted rights with management.) They cannot muster the strength to blow the whistle when their company acts in ways clearly injurious to the public's well-being. So millions of defective cars roll off the production line, drugs are huckstered and food additives sold without adequate testing, tenants' and sharecroppers' rights are overridden by absentee management, the health of miners is depleted by companies which receive tax depletion allowances, and those inside the companies stay silent or actively promote and defend such acts or defaults. The professional employees who would speak out anticipate the consequences and do nothing. As long as the internal authority of the corporation remains unchallenged, any external pressures will have minimal and temporary impact. It is just this absence of internal rights that partly explains the successful resistance of the corporation to external disciplinary attempts. The other insulating factor is the absence of legal responsibility on the part of officers and management officials for corporate impacts. Even in the most personally oriented legal sanctions for investor protection administered by the Securities and Exchange Commission, only a handful of stock exchange and brokerage house officials—all relatively low-level—felt the arm of the law in the midst of recent manipulation, illegalities, and self-dealing which for dollar sums made the debacle of the twenties small by comparison.

Thus, against the growing sensitivity about corporate predations, willful or negligent, there is more than routine attention to be attached to the proposed, later rejected, code revisions affecting corporate officials by the National Commission on Reform of Federal Criminal Laws. These proposals would permit imposition of accountability for corporate conduct and law compliance on the individuals responsible for such company decisions. The entire range of legal sanctions against both the corporate structure and its officials has to be reconsidered, as the Commission has begun to do, beyond just simple civil-criminal fines toward a more flexible array of civil-criminal sanctions tailored to maximum deterrence. Suspension of corporate managers and board members, temporary bans on corporate advertising because of deceptive practices, required publication of violations to inform consumers who have been harmed or deceived by culpable conduct, and imposition of environmental bankruptcy for a company continually contaminating its neighbors' environment are some suggestions that may effectively deter illegal behavior.

Together with such internal changes, the emergence of full-time, independent corporate monitors, staffed by lawyers and other skilled professionals in Washington and state capitals, would have lasting effect. Such citizens' firms would simply invoke powerful strategies of citizenship against industrial and commercial abuses and advocate in forums of decision-making programs for necessary change.

The modern corporation is the engine of the world's largest production machine. If it is to be more than a mindless, parochial juggernaut, the hands of diverse human values and trusteeships for future generations must be exerted on the steering wheel. There should no longer be victims without representation. In any *just* legal system, a victim would have the right to decide with others the behavior of the perpetrator and his recompense. The corporate framework cannot be wished away or simply placed in a different crucible—such as government—and result in an equitable deployment of its resources and creativity. If it did not exist, the corporate entity would have to be invented in some form to collect capital, retain labor, and generate the outputs. As the consequences of corporate neglect mount more visibly, the popularization of the corporate condition through initiatory democratic rights, coupled with remedies and representation both on and within the corporation, are sure to become pivotal public issues in the coming decade.

**Reading 3**

# The Hart Antitrust Bill

**Senate Antitrust and Monopoly Subcommittee**

*. . . there are millions of consumers who will testify that corporate bigness is not necessarily related to product quality, although bigness is indeed related to inflated prices.*

Senator Philip A. Hart (D-Mich) tomorrow will introduce a bill—years in the making—to break up existing monopoly and oligopoly power in the United States.

Commenting on the bill, Hart urged a strong and immediate effort to break

From the Office of the Senate Antitrust and Monopoly Subcommittee, press release, Washington, D.C., Sunday, July 23, 1973.

up giantism. Otherwise, he said, inflation and unemployment will flourish and product quality will continue to deteriorate.

"Unless competition is restored to the economy," Hart warned, "we are headed toward a society dominated by a few corporate giants with an army of government clerks as their listless watchdogs."

The bill is aimed at corporate giants with big labor and government bureaucracy as secondary targets.

Hart, chairman of the Antitrust and Monopoly Subcommittee, would set up an Industrial Reorganization Commission and give it tough new monopoly-busting powers for its 15-year life.

The commission would give priority attention to seven industries:

**1** Chemicals and drugs
**2** Electronic computing and communication equipment
**3** Electrical machinery and equipment
**4** Energy
**5** Iron and steel
**6** Motor vehicles
**7** Nonferrous metals

"These industries," Hart explained, "are the ones with the greatest impact on the total economy."

The Hart Antitrust Bill would bring two important new wrinkles to antitrust enforcement:

- Trustbusters would no longer have to rely on evidence that defendant firms intended to create monopolies to control prices or to exclude competitors.
- The antitrust enforcement system for the first time would be geared to deal with the mechanics of dismantling monopolies—a necessary second step that the present system has trouble managing.

Hart explained:

"The law of monopolization developed under Section 2 of the old Sherman Act requires a showing that a defendant has power to set artificially high prices or exclude competition plus something more—'an element of intent'.

"But intent need not be proven under this bill. If corporate actions are harmful to society, they should be stopped whether the harm was intended or not.

"Secondly, *whether* an oligopoly ought be broken up is often easier than deciding *how* it should be broken up. This takes the kind of staff rarely available to district judges. The antitrust enforcement organization that we intend would have that staff."

Under the bill, a company or companies are presumed to have monopoly power if:

**1** The average rate of return on net worth for any corporation exceeds 15 percent for five consecutive years of the seven years preceding the complaint, or

**2** If there has been no substantial price competition among two or more corporations in any product line for three consecutive years of the preceding five, or

**3** If any four corporations account for 50 percent or more of sales for a product or industry in any year of the most recent three years.

Firms operating under any of the above conditions would be liable to the charge that they possess monopoly power unless they can explain their way out.

A firm could escape sanctions by showing that its unusually high profit levels were due to patent rights or its size was necessary for efficiency.

Cases would be tried by an Industrial Reorganization Court set up to handle nothing but cases brought by the commission. Decisions would be appealed directly to the Supreme Court.

Hart's subcommittee has been conducting economic concentration hearings off and on since 1964 and the Hart bill is the product of 11 volumes of testimony.

The hearings have been largely sedate and scholarly and have attracted little attention except in academic circles.

Besides attacking corporate giantism, the bill reaches big labor by requiring IRC study of the effects on competition of "collective bargaining practices" of our major industries. The commission is directed to come back to Congress with appropriate legislative recommendations.

As for government, Hart said that the market policing power of real competition will relieve the need for burgeoning regulatory bureaucracies.

Hart said that the bill was based on the "old-fashioned notion that honest competition is far more protective of the consumer interest than all the regulatory bureaucracies ever devised."

Corporate giantism, he said, is responsible for much of the nation's inflation problem because when only a few companies control a market, prices tend to be pegged more to the profit needs of the manufacturers than to the financial comfort of the consumer.

"What's more," said Hart, "there are millions of consumers who will testify that corporate bigness is not necessarily related to good product quality, although bigness is indeed often related to inflated prices.

"Certainly, I don't propose that we return to being a nation of small shopkeepers and backyard manufacturers. But at this moment two-thirds of the nation's manufacturing assets are held by 200 corporations.

"If we are going to rely on competition to give the consumer good value, then competition must be encouraged. But it cannot flourish if the number of competitors is constantly diminishing.

"We have tried some of the sweeter-tasting potions in the anti-inflation medicine cabinet and they have availed little. Now it is time for some stronger stuff, even if it is a little bitter going down."

Reading 4

# What Is Consumerism?

**Du Pont Context**

*Consumerism is concerned with the rights of the consumer to safety, to be informed, to choose, and to be heard.*

## SENATOR CHARLES H. PERCY

### (R., Ill.)

To me, the consumer movement represents a broad public reaction against bureaucratic neglect and corporate disregard of the public.

It is a repudiation of misleading advertising, empty warranties and guarantees, deceptive packaging, anti-competitive conduct, unfair pricing and bait-and-switch merchandising.

It is a check on sham, misrepresentation, deceit and fraud. And it is a control against monopolistic behavior by some corporations and the abuse of authority or discretion by certain agencies of government.

The fight for consumer protection is a battle for quality in goods and services, for fairness in advertising and promotion, for honesty in the marketplace. In its broadest sense, I believe that the consumer movement amounts to a yearning for an improved quality of life—for an America that works again, for people, products and governmental institutions that support the society rather than tear it apart. It is an affirmation of the interest of the many over the interest of the few, of a broader public interest over special interests.

What's good for the consumer is good for business. Most businessmen know this and build their businesses on this philosophy. And there is no better foundation than insuring that the product or service produced is worthy of public acceptance.

## SIDNEY MARGOLIUS

### Author and Columnist on Consumer Affairs

If I had to define the common denominator in the many aspects of this movement, I would define it as a protest and attempt to solve the problem of waste and diversion of family—and thus national—resources from urgent public needs. The protest often centers on waste which occurs because of poor design and undependable or unsuitable quality, or wastefully high marketing costs.

## JAMES BISHOP, JR.

### Deputy Bureau Chief—*Newsweek*
### Washington, D.C.

"Consumerism" is neither the creature of the "radic lib" nor a passing fad. America's newest "ism", conservative at bottom, represents the strong grass-roots demand for a new marketing ethic in America—an ethic which seeks

From *Du Pont Context*, Wilmington, De., 19898, E. I. Du Pont de Nemours & Company (Inc.), vol. 2, no. 1, 1973, pp. 1-3.

nothing less for every American than a secure physical environment and a just economic one.

Because millions of Americans have been exposed to such futures for decades by advertising, their expectations are high—so are their frustrations and, lately, their fears.

The widespread discovery of hazards has destroyed the 20th Century myth that the consumer is an omniscient, sovereign king who can protect himself in the bewildering marketplace of 1973.

By codifying the rights of every individual to truth, health and safety in the marketplace, the forces of consumerism are also signalling to industry the existence of a highly profitable new future—one in which profit will be based on performance, quality and disclosure. In sum, consumerism will be a major new form of competition for the rest of the century.

## SEN. WARREN G. MAGNUSON

### (D., Wash.)

"Consumerism" is a word used to describe the phenomenon whereby purchasers of goods and services are trying to attain a marketing system which makes the consumer sovereign—which guarantees to him *the right to safety, the right to be informed, the right to choose,* and *the right to be heard.*

Consumerism is based upon that basic tenet of the free enterprise system which says that the consumer (rather than government) should control, through rational purchasing decisions in the marketplace, which goods and services are produced. But consumerism looks to government to control producers who would interfere with rational choice and thereby destroy the free enterprise system.

For example, "consumerism" asks that government require producers to make products which do not contain hidden dangers; it asks that government require producers to give consumers certain information; it asks that government adjust the laws so producers live up to their warranties and other promises; it asks that government facilitate the settlement of disputes between consumers and producers; and, where necessary, it asks that government require the production of certain products that would not be available to the consumer but for such governmental requirements.

## DAVID A. AAKER

### Associate Professor of Business (University of California, Berkeley) and Author on Consumerism

Consumerism is an evolving set of activities of government, business, independent organizations, and concerned consumers that are designed to protect the rights of consumers. It is an evolving, dynamic movement with an enlarging scope and changing spokesmen and issues. It is action oriented and therefore more than an analysis of problems.

The activities are not confined to consumer activists. Indeed, government and business are involved in developing and implementing innovations which are part of consumerism today.

Consumerism is concerned with the rights of the consumer to safety, to be informed, to choose and to be heard. Although the meaning of these four rights has been broadened considerably and their focus altered since President Kennedy put them forth in 1962, they still form the core motivation for consumerism activity. A fifth right must be added, however: the right to an environment which will enhance and not detract from various life styles.

### LEO BOGART

**Executive Vice President and General Manager**
**Bureau of Advertising, American Newspaper Publishers Association**

Consumerism is a catchword in current vogue among marketers to describe a variety of distinct phenomena. These include (1) the *long-term evolution* of a more sophisticated and better educated buying public; (2) *public skepticism* about business practices, a reflection of deeper malaise with all established institutions in the aftermath of the Vietnam war; (3) *organized activism* (led by a handful of articulate advocates with a following among university students) to correct product deficiencies and advertising claims, and (4) *legislative moves* to increase consumer protection and an intensification of actions by government regulatory agencies.

### ROBERT E. BROOKER

**Chairman of the National Business Council for Consumer Affairs**

When the President formed the National Business Council for Consumer Affairs, we concluded that the answer to the problems that arise with consumers was *to provide goods or services which meet the consumer's expectations.*

In other words, *a consumer is one who uses goods or services to satisfy his needs.* Consumerism is the system, which may be either voluntary or regulated, which hopes to assure the consumer of being satisfied according to his expectations at the time the goods were acquired or the services contracted.

It is our feeling on the Council that it is the responsibility of business to satisfy the consumer's expectations on a *voluntary basis* by providing standards of performance which are fair and understandable to the consumer.

### HERBERT S. DENENBERG

**Pennsylvania Insurance Commissioner**

Consumerism is not merely putting safety into cars or taking fat out of hot dogs. It is much more than improving the physical environment, creating safer products, and protecting the public from fraud and other consumer abuses.

Consumerism should have more basic purposes. Consumerism should aim for government and institutions "of, by, and for the people" instead of government and institutions "of, by, and for special interest groups."

Consumerism has been focused on some of the obvious symptoms of lack of responsiveness to the public interest. But consumerism is moving toward a more fundamental definition which is in fact a reaffirmation of our basic democratic concepts: Consumerism seeks to give representation to all interests, especially the individual buyer, consumer, and citizen who now has no adequate voice in the power structure.

## BETTY FURNESS

### Former Special Assistant to President Johnson for Consumer Affairs

"Consumerism" is a word originally coined by industry to make the burgeoning consumer movement sound like a dangerous threat. Business loved the word. Consumer advocates didn't, but they were too busy doing their work to bother about it.

Today, the movement by any other name would smell as sweet. We'll take the title.

*Consumerism is an effort to put the buyer on an equal footing with the seller.* Consumers want to know what they're buying. What they're eating. How long a product will last. What it will and will not do. Whether it will be safe for them and/or the environment.

*That's* consumerism.

Consumers do not want to be manipulated, hornswoggled or lied to. They want truth, not just in lending, labeling and packaging, but in everything in the whole vast, bewildering marketplace.

## ERMA ANGEVINE

### Executive Director, Consumer Federation of America

Industry spokesmen coined the word "consumerism." It's their label for the rising tide of consumer self-awareness. It vaguely implies some philosophical connection with communism, socialism, or other "ism." Actually, we have no philosophy—except that "the *sole aim of production is consumption*" (Adam Smith). Because the word (consumerism) has no meaning, I abhor it.

This consumer self-awareness rose in the early New Deal days, ebbed during World War II, and turned to flood with President Kennedy's historic statement of the rights of consumers.

Instead of debating "consumerism," let's discuss those real, meaningful matters that affect consumers.

Reading 5

# Consumerism, 1990—Adapting to Today's Values for Tomorrow's Imperatives

**Aaron S. Yohalem**

*Probably the most articulate expression of industry's social responsibility—embracing employees, stockholders, communities, and supplies—would be to respond imaginatively to consumer demands.*

Our technology and industrial performance has all too palpably lacked clear, resolved, and balanced social perspectives. It has lacked a critical sense of itself; lacked an awareness of the social context in which it operates and the social impact it necessarily generates. In many major areas of our economy we have had a kind of mindlessness for which we are paying high costs.

Thus far, we in industry have not even questioned, let alone attempted to direct or control our technology, production, and distribution with a view toward consciously maximizing the public weal while minimizing public risk. Not that individual companies have not been mindful of this defect, for they have. But insofar as industry-wide or business-wide consciousness is concerned, our performance has been nonexistent.

## LISTEN TO THE NEW WINDS

The traditional cost/benefit factor, the short- and long-term profit orientation are seen as motivation and the foundation of our economic system. But the myths of business-as-usual, and the market-will-right-itself simply will not suffice in the face of the consumerism of today, let alone 1990. Nor will our own long-term best interests, including our profitable well being, be served.

We in industry can anticipate, of course, that as we seek to adapt to changing values, the very process of adaptation will impact on those values and alter them, bringing about the need for still further industry readjustments. But the inexorable vigor of the consumer movement permits little room for leisurely contemplation on an optimum course of action. It is clear that if business does not get moving well ahead of the consumerism train, we shall see one of the biggest wrecks in our economic history.

The potential threat, in my view, is that corporate lethargy, married with political timidity, may procreate unworkable alterations in the economic system. This would needlessly frustrate the nation's existing capacity to meet totally legitimate consumer demands, as well as other national imperatives.

The existing system of free markets and open competition is not immutable. Although it excelled in meeting yesterday's demands for economic growth, and for abundance at reasonable prices, those achievements are widely regarded today as insufficient. Today's concern is increasingly with "quality of life." There is a disquieting lack of public confidence as to the capacity of the industrial system to add this new requirement.

From *A Look at Business in 1990*, U.S. Government Printing Office, Washington, D.C., November 1972, pp. 107–110.

To be sure, today's consumer shops for products and services with a flinty eye on the price tag. But that is only one consideration. Now the consumer is likely to ask questions about such matters as the safety of the product, completeness of the information provided about it, its performance, the recourse if it does not perform well, hiring practices of the manufacturer, pollution created in its manufacture or use, and its social relevance.

Surveys of consumer attitudes reflect the depth of these concerns. Over half the public approves of Ralph Nader, an eloquent symbol and summary of consumer aspirations. Two-thirds want Congressional legislation assuring consumers of better value.

Consider, also, the attitudes of today's students. Researcher Daniel Yankelovich, a specialist on the restless generation, notes that: "What is new is not the presence of a small group of radicals on the campus but the mushrooming growth of a much larger number of students who agree with the radicals' diagnosis of what is wrong with America, even though they do not endorse their tactics. This larger supportive group is estimated at a whopping two out of five college students."

Their overriding concern, and the growing concern of many of their parents, is that the country's institutions, especially its business institutions, are indifferent to social needs—and incapable of voluntary change. This concern is highly emotional, often not susceptible to intellectual argument. It has taken a totally *political* turn.

This development is also reflected in the society at large. In just the last eight years, more than two dozen federal consumer laws have been passed. But they fall far short of what consumer activists find desirable. Consequently, they are pressing aggressively and effectively for personal involvement and for reform through the judicial system.

So long as the business community retains any appearance of ignoring the revolution in consumer values, the consumerism train will gain speed, trip another series of political signals, and the consequences may tangle our economic tracks to the satisfaction of no one—with the exception of a handful of committed extremists. Probably the most articulate expression of industry's social responsibility—embracing employees, stockholders, communities, and suppliers—would be to respond imaginatively to consumer demands.

## NEED FOR CONSUMER-TREND ANALYSIS

This suggests to me the need for industry to study the new dimension of consumerism with the same scale of investment in time, money, research, and analysis that it devotes to a major new service or product line prior to its introduction. Individual corporations, in the interest of improving on the best of the competitive system, should:

- analyze the demographics of consumerism as they affect their specific operations
- define those areas where consumer segments are correct or misinformed
- make the adjustments necessary to meet legitimate complaints
- undertake the communication effort required to alert the public, and its elected leaders, to the adjustments made and to areas of public misunderstanding or misinformation.

This is not a simple assignment. I suggest the only choice is to grasp the nettle. The question we in the business community must ask ourselves is: Are we smart enough to see what is happening? Have we the will to work at it in a methodical, professional way? Particularly, do we have the good sense to open up our communication channels to listen to, and learn from, even the most militant of the groups who oppose everything we believe in?

Are we in business and industry prepared to question the eternal validity of the GNP? Will we sit still to consider the arguments of the ZPGers and the ZEGers—respectively, the Zero Population Growth and the Zero Economic Growth advocates? Will we be able to derive any insight from the concept of static growth as opposed to dynamic, purely one-dimensional, linear growth?

I trust the answer will be a positive one; it had best be.

It is essential to realize that consumerism has long ago ceased to have the circumscribed limits of customary marketing concerns. Consumerism has a far more comprehensive, sophisticated relevance to our society as a whole. Consumerism further encompasses such controversial issues as:

- The use of stockholder proxies to propose resolutions affecting corporate policy, including public representation on corporate boards
- How to determine, and who to charge for, the cost of "negative externalities," such as air or water pollution
- "Product performance insurance"—and its effect on freedom of choice and the living standards of the poor
- Meaningful methods for auditing the social accountability of business
- The role of advertising and other promotion forms as they affect society's best interests
- The social obligation of investors, individual and institutional
- "Nationalizing" private systems, or "commercializing" public systems or both
- And the federal chartering of publicly held corporations

I am trying to emphasize that the complexity and intensity of the consumer movement cannot be overestimated. It is only a part, if a large part, of a pervasive public concern with increasing the social responsibility of business. Consumerism will not just go away. Coming to grips with it will inevitably take the form of a new but operative aspect of management responsibility.

While this movement is not new to our nation, it has never enjoyed more favorable conditions for nurturing it to full and robust bloom. To underscore the point, consider an extreme example: Bangladesh, which is light years from any concern over slack-fill, unit pricing, or grade labeling. Its single consumer demand is at the first plateau of Maslow's tier of hierarchial values: survival. America's consumers, on the other hand, are concerning themselves with his highest plateau: self-actualization and spiritual or humanistic rather than material considerations.

The consumer movement is today riding a flood tide characterized by a fundamental shift in national attitudes toward legislation affecting private enterprise. Historically, government has sought to proscribe those things that institutions *cannot* do. Today, however, government increasingly seeks to circumscribe those things institutions can do.

Clearly, then, if industry wishes to affect the shape of consumer legislation, the time is now, not the '90s, to take an introspective look at business performance as against new consumer attitudes toward "quality of life." Will we have the wisdom to recognize that the dollars involved in rearguard movements and holding actions normally exceed those required to bring about solutions?

Industry cannot, nor should it, undertake all the initiatives in seeking a rapprochement among business, government, and the consumer movement.

Nor have I the naive hope that consumerists will ever be totally satisfied, which, indeed, would impede social progress. But I do believe, given the kind of industry-wide effort required, that the business community can introduce The Rule of Reason to the consumer-industry dialogue. It will not be possible for each of the diverse elements striving for a better consumer society to have its own aspirations fulfilled, *totally*. Each will have to succumb to the rule of reason and make some accommodation to the needs of others. This, after all, is the definition of society.

The rule of reason demands that all of the sectors involved listen with comprehension—not merely take turns talking. It demands that we seek, in our own self-interest, to share understanding of common problems so that we do not exhaust our energies on the impossible or, unwittingly, the undesirable. It demands, too, that we distinguish carefully between our own point of view and the genuine insight of others, and that all of us accept the democracy of man's frailties. It may behoove us to consider some of the role reversals that, if society is to be properly served by industry, might possibly occur.

While the public utterances of industry on the matters of consumerism are encouraging, words hardly constitute actuality. I am concerned with its performance; that it matches its words. More to the point, I am concerned that our performance responds to the demands and needs confronting us. Only with performance can we begin to build a credibility that is today sorely missing, but which is a necessary foundation for the future.

Along with our own corporate committees on the environment, minority employment, the cities and the like, we must make certain that we maintain in industry the most realistic kind of self-criticism. We need, in effect, to maintain some form of corporate counter-culture or sub-stratum thereof that will make its business the task of continuously keeping us disabused so the better to keep us on our toes and performing credibly.

Business necessarily has to become more involved socially and more responsive to business in society. Business must be able to detach itself from its own myopic traditions. It must seek out, not automatically reject, reasonable critics. It must anticipate, indeed provide, progressive leadership in the march of consumerism to the 1990s.

The question remains: Not, do we have the foresight to understand the future, but, do we have the courage to change it?

## Reading 6

# The Consumer—King or Vassal?

**Mary Bennett Peterson**

*. . . a case of both caveat emptor and caveat venditor.*

Who is sovereign in the marketplace—the consumer or the producer?

Jennifer Cross, author of "The Supermarket Trap," is clearly a member of the producer sovereignty school. She sees the consumer as a victim of high-powered advertising and finance, a pawn of Madison Avenue, Wall Street and the giant supermarket, food, drug and cosmetic industries.

The opposing school sees the consumer as the wielder of some $700 billion of after-tax disposable personal income, a savvy if sometimes fickle and arbitrary boss with economic life-and-death power over the nation's shops, factories, professions and all other businesses. Economists Ludwig von Mises and W. H. Hutt christened this one "consumer sovereignty."

A specialist on consumerism and the food industry, Miss Cross bemoans the rise of giants such as General Foods and Kraftco, Safeway and A&P. She worries about the "bewildering" proliferation of heavily advertised and fancy-packaged goods. She hails the day the cash registers rang "no sale," the day in 1966 when housewives in Denver, Phoenix, Van Nuys and elsewhere boycotted and picketed their local supermarkets.

What Miss Cross seems to ignore, however, is that size is a response to function, that mass production requires mass marketing (and vice versa). The giants are largely creatures of the consumer, and what the consumer can make, the consumer can destroy. Economist A. D. H. Kaplan of the Brookings Institution has been keeping tabs on some of the destroyed, including such now whittled giants as American Locomotive, American Woolen and American Molasses.

In addition to some 200 million individual consumers, we have several million business consumers who are natural—and just as bargain-conscious—allies of the individual consumer. The lower unit cost volume purchases of A&P, for example, make possible lower prices to the A&P shopper.

Miss Cross laments the big advertising budgets of the food giants, mentioning the $154 million spent by General Foods and the $65 million by Standard Brands in 1968 and arguing that such sums are wasteful of the consumer's dollar. But so is their function—mass marketing. Also, much consumer advertising is informational, telling of new products or new uses.

She would also impose restrictions on packaging and new product introduction. This could be done, she explains, "by Federal legislation or by setting up a legal government-industry cartel, with extensive consumer representation." But her charge of new product proliferation (from about 3,000 to about 8,000 items in the postwar period in a typical supermarket) is short-sighted. Certainly she does not appreciate that choice and competition are thereby strengthened.

Again, her proposal for restrictive Federal legislation makes one recall the farm legislation of the 1930s. These farm laws in effect require higher taxes to pay subsidies to farmers to restrict their acreage to achieve higher food prices. Miss Cross somehow believes these laws actually work for lower food prices.

Who is sovereign in the nation's supermarkets? The evidence would point to the consumer. But if the Government really takes over, it's likely the "supermarket trap" would spring shut against both the consumer and the producer—a case of both caveat emptor and caveat venditor.

Reading 7

# An Abundance of Critics

**The Wall Street Journal**

*"Corporations need critics to notify them of public concerns. . . ."*

American corporations are coming in for a lot of verbal assault these days, from environmentalists, consumer advocates, racial and sexual egalitarians and what have you.

As Mr. Shafer reported in this paper the other day, Ralph Nader now has five "public interest" assault teams at work preparing suits, complaints, critical studies and manifestos aimed at business and government. Other such groups are popping up under other leadership.

Some of the criticism is valid and will serve, if nothing else, to remind corporate executives of their public responsibilities. But there are dangers too.

One of the principal dangers is that the new climate of criticism will stimulate government to new regulation of corporations that won't serve the public interest at all but will in fact damage it. The nation's ailing railroads attest to how damaging to the public interest excessive regulation can become. It is possible that airlines are being herded down the same path.

Because the self-appointed critics are highly active and vocal it is easy for both business and government to get a distorted idea that there is heavy public support for the critics' claims. In fact, they can't possibly represent the broad constituencies they claim, such as "the public." They can only represent themselves and whoever happens to agree with them. On some issues, if the facts were clear, their supporters might be very few.

Very often, business executives, in effect, are being asked to give such claims more weight when they make decisions than other measures of public sentiment that are more reliable—most notably the market. In some cases the public interest groups are making claims on the corporations that are in conflict with claims made by people who represent more precise and legitimate constituencies, such as the corporation's workers or its shareholders. Such a conflict comes up, for example, when outside critics insist that a plant is a nuisance and should be shut down.

It should thus not be surprising that the attacks of the public interest groups sometimes are stoutly resisted.

There also is a danger that the public interest groups will attract participants who are not in the least public spirited but who are simply looking for new ways to attack what they call the Establishment. The motives of such people are often murky or irrational. At the violent extreme they plant bombs. They can hardly be expected to serve the public interest.

Still another danger is that as more and more people become critics fewer and fewer will bother with the problem-solving and productive work that must be done if any society is to remain viable. Henry Ford II, chairman of Ford Motor Co., recently noted that a lot of people—and he specifically cited politicians and journalists—are better at exposing problems than at understanding and solving them. If the public interest groups really want to make a contribution they should look for solutions as well as problems.

Whatever their imperfections, American corporations have evolved into remarkable machines for accomplishing tasks and generating wealth. They can be guided into whatever tasks society demands of them, whether it be producing TV sets or retraining the unemployed. But when the guidance is supplied by forces other than the market, corporate managers must carefully consider whether the forces represent a legitimate public demand. Otherwise they risk misallocation of economic resources.

Corporations need critics to notify them of public concerns outside those that can be expressed through the market. These concerns, about environment, job equality, safety standards and all else that goes to make up the general quality of life, are legitimate ones. But the critics should think carefully about what they want. In a system that responds as well as the American system does today, the chances are good they will get it.

## Reading 8

# Consumers Aren't All Angels Either

**Rose DeWolf**

*Consumers buy magazines, take them home and read them, then return them for a refund claiming their husband bought duplicates.*

Oh, I know whose side I'm on . . . I'm a consumer. I bow to no one in my antagonism to useless warranties, fraudulent claims, garbled instructions, hidden flaws, and ridiculous computers which threaten to have me arrested if I don't pay $0.00 right away. If I feel affronted, I can holler for Ralph Nader as loud as anyone.

And yet . . .

Every once in a while, much as I try to fight it, I feel a twinge of sympathy for merchants, manufacturers, and providers of service. Every once in a while, though I feel like a traitor, I want to jump up and say: "You know, consumers can be pretty rotten, too."

Consumers are not all angels. They include in their numbers those who would quite cheerfully cheat, steal, lie and/or behave with incredible stupidity. There, I've said it and I'm glad.

Take the "switchers," for example. Those are the people who take the price tag from a cheap item and put it on an expensive item before taking the expensive item to the salesclerk. They hope the clerk will be too busy to notice and will sell the goods at a "bargain" price the store hadn't really counted on.

Switchers are everywhere. I once saw this very dignified-looking gentleman craftily switch the lids on a jar of peanuts and a jar of cashews. The prices, you see, were stamped on the lids. The man intended to buy his cashews, quite literally, for "peanuts."

And I have seen a dear little housewife slip a pound of butter into an oleomargarine box, assuming that the check-out clerk would never check. She assumed wrong. All check-out clerks know that trick.

From *Du Pont Context*, Wilmington, De., 19898. E. I. Du Pont de Nemours & Company (Inc.), vol. 2, no. 1, 1973, pp. 9–10.

One time I merely mentioned the word "consumer" to a friend of mine who works for a supermarket and the poor guy went bananas. (On special, that week.)

"Consumers!" he wailed. "I'll tell you about consumers. They buy magazines, take them home and read them, then return them for a refund claiming their husband bought duplicates . . . they demand to get five cents back on the five-cents-back coupon without buying the product first . . . they finish off bars of candy or bottles of soda while they walk through the store and then don't mention it when it comes time to pay. . . ."

Did you know that baby food manufacturers deliberately seal their jars so they'll open with a loud "POP." That, says my friend, is so that a consumer who gets a jar that opens only with a little "poof" knows it has been opened before. Seems some mothers want to taste the food at the store to make sure little junior will like it, but then don't want to buy the jar they tasted.

Do you know why most cereal manufacturers don't give away prizes in the cereal boxes anymore? That's because so many women used to pry open the package, snitch the prize, and leave the unsalable torn box on the shelf. Nowadays, if you want to get that super-spy ring your kid has been crying for, you have to buy the box, clip the coupon, and send 25 cents in coin.

Suburban stores tell of women who "buy" a fancy dress on the Friday just before the Country Club dance and then return it ("I just changed my mind.") on Monday. They get indignant if the clerk says the dress looks as if it had been worn.

There are those who carry on loudly when the billing computer makes a mistake and claims they owe a bill they know they don't owe—but keep awfully quiet when the computer gives them credit they know they don't deserve. That makes it tougher for the store to straighten out the error.

Don't we all know people who brag about how they got the "whole car fixed" on the insurance of the guy who merely dented a fender?

My local laundryman claims that if he ever loses a shirt (Heaven forbid), it invariably turns out to be (a) "very expensive" and (b) "just purchased."

"How come I never lose last year's cheap shirt?" he asks. "No. Those are the ones I manage to return. Right?" He is skeptical.

There are, of course, those who cheat the stores even more forthrightly. Shoplifting is at an all-time high. Do you know why manufacturers often pack such little items as batteries, pencils and razor blades in plastic bubbles attached to huge pieces of cardboard? That's because the cardboard is larger than the average consumer's pocket where many batteries, pencils and razor blades used to just disappear.

People who deal with consumers sometimes lose patience with them not because the consumers are greedy or dishonest but because they sometimes simply cause problems for themselves.

A local weights and measures inspector told me of pulling a surprise raid on a local butcher shop where the butcher was suspected of resting his elbow on the scale while weighing meat. Did the consumers appreciate the inspector's arrival? They did not.

"They were angry because it was close to dinner time. They started yelling at me," the inspector said. "They said I was holding them up . . . they had to get home to start cooking. They called me a city hall drone. They said I was annoying the butcher who was their friend. Some friend!"

Consumers can be funny. Recently, a spokesman for a national meat canning company told a convention of food editors that consumers persist in sending an open can of meat back to the company to illustrate whatever complaint they're making. The fact is, that after days of travel in the unrefrigerated mail, the product *always* looks awful and smells worse. How can the company possibly tell if the complaint was justified in the first place?

Consumers complain about high food prices and then insist on buying every convenience food on the market. They yell about too loud commercials and then don't buy the products advertised on soft ones.

The government says motorists will be safer if their cars buzz until the safety belts are fastened. But car-buyers by the hordes are threatening dealers with mayhem unless the buzzers are unhooked. (The dealers are prohibited by law from complying.)

Consumers are just not always happy with what is being done *for* them. Frankly, I have to admit that *I* was a lot happier before packages of hot dogs had to admit right out in public that they contain ground-up cow's lips. Ycchh. Do we have to know *everything?*

I'm not trying to say that the fact that the consumer can be, in his turn, greedy, dishonest, unappreciative, and just plain stupid, in any way excuses commercial interests for being the same. As my mother used to say, "Two wrongs don't make a right."

Still, fair is fair and somebody had to speak out. And now that I have gotten that out of the way, I can get to all these complaint letters I'm preparing for Ralph, and Virginia, and my local office of Consumer Affairs.

# Consumer Decision Making and Advertising

Reading 9

## Consumption without Ownership: Marketing Opportunity for Today and Tomorrow

**Leonard L. Berry**
**Kenneth E. Maricle**

*The choices we make, consciously and subconsciously, determine to a large extent the charts of our lives.*

Recent years have witnessed a surging growth in lease/rental activity involving industrial goods and, to a lesser extent, consumer goods as well. Products currently rented or leased range from diapers to airlines, furniture suites to computers, dress shirts to automobiles. One husband in Kansas even leased his wife to a millionaire rancher. When an important prospect was scheduled to visit, another man, the head of a newly organized firm, filled his large, almost bare offices with rented paintings, desks, and office equipment, then brought in rented people to use the equipment at the appointed hour. He closed the deal and now the furnishings, equipment, and employees are his own.[1]

Indeed, a review of current reports on the accelerating growth and variety of lease/rental activity suggests that the time is rapidly approaching, if not already here, when one virtually could live a happy and productive life without owning anything more substantial than a toothbrush.[2]

The dynamic nature of the lease/rental field is illustrated by the following:

A number of major companies are entering the lease/rental field; for example, RCA (having purchased Hertz), Consolidated Foods (having acquired Abbey Rents), and Greyhound Corporation (having bought Boothe Leasing).

Industrial equipment leasing has grown to become a more than $10 billion industry annually.[3] While at the beginning of 1967 there were less than one dozen companies in computer leasing, by mid-1969 there were more than 100 in operation.[4]

Third-party lessors, such as finance companies, commercial banks, and firms solely engaged in leasing, are growing so fast that they now control about 30 percent of all leasing activity.[5]

The American Rental Association indicates that the approximately 10,000 rental stores in the United States do a gross business in excess of $1 billion a

From *MSU Business Topics*, Spring 1973, pp. 34–41. Reprinted by permission of the publisher, Division of Research, Graduate School of Business Administration, Michigan State University.

year, a figure that should rise to $3 billion or more by the late 1970s. During the last five years of the 1960s the industry grew at a rate of 20 percent per year.[6]

Although the rapid growth in the lease/rental field is most likely already recognized by the well-informed business executive, much of this activity to date has been in industrial goods; while this market should continue to grow substantially, current developments in consumer goods lease/rental activity probably represent no more than the "tip of the iceberg" in terms of the potential that lies ahead.

It is with regard to this opportunity in consumer goods that this article is directed. Specifically, our purpose is to go beyond existing literature that largely reports on what is occurring in the lease/rental field and explore some of the fundamental reasons related to our changing values as consumers that help explain why consumer goods lease/rental opportunity has come to be so imposing.[7]

A number of terms which apply to the central theme of this article need to be defined. *Lease/rental* refers to any form of contractual agreement between the user of a product and the owner wherein the user returns the product to the owner at the termination of the agreement. By custom, the term *lease* usually applies to long-term agreements extending over several months or more and the term *rental* to short-term agreements up to a month. Lease/rental will not be used to refer to what the authors call *pseudo-leases*, which are agreements wherein title passes to the lessee at the end of the lease in return for a nominal or less-than-market value payment.

*Ownership* refers to possession of legal title to property but does not necessarily imply either consumption or physical possession of the property. Within the scope of this article, ownership refers to personal property as opposed to real property.

*Consumption* refers to the act of using a part or the whole of the useful life of a product. Consumption of most products implies physical possession but does not necessarily imply holding legal title.

*Consumption without ownership* is a generic term describing all forms of consumption in which the consumer does not possess legal title to the product being consumed. Lease/rental agreements are devices which frequently lead to consumption without ownership but are not necessarily the only devices.

## THE MYTH OF OWNERSHIP

Traditionally there has been a tendency for consumer goods marketers and hence consumers to automatically link ownership with consumption. That is, if one needs a new shirt, stereo, or tennis racquet, the "natural" or "automatic" reaction has been, and to a large extent still is, to buy one. However, the consumer need not own to consume. A number of devices which make consumption possible can be identified, including but not confined to cash purchase, charge purchase, time-payment purchase, and revolving-credit purchase. Leasing and renting are simply other consumption devices used increasingly by both consumers and industrial users. Finding, making, borrowing, inheriting, and even stealing are also devices leading to consumption. Although some of these devices are legal and some are not, some are commercially feasible and some are not, and some involve user ownership and some do not, the crucial point is that it is not necessary for the consumer to own that which he consumes.

Ownership is a function of marketing. Although this function must be performed somewhere in the channel of distribution, it does not necessarily have to be performed by the end user or consumer. Textbook discussions of marketing functions make only indirect references to ownership (buying, selling, storing) rather than directly listing ownership as a function. This perhaps has contributed to a lack of clarity concerning the ownership concept.

Whether or not the consumption device itself makes use of ownership, one or more entities in the channel (not excluding the consumer) must perform the ownership function. As a test, the reader may examine each of the consumption devices just named and ask the question: Does ownership exist when this device is used? In every instance the answer is *yes*. Again, the point to be made is that ownership exists when consumption takes place, but does not necessarily have to rest with the consumer or user.

The labeling of ownership as a marketing function seems to us to be more than just an issue of semantics. If the marketer views ownership as a legitimate function of marketing, the next step of retaining ownership within the channel (instead of passing it on to the consumer or user as a means to increase customer satisfaction and gain competitive advantage) should become clearer as a strategic alternative. Indeed, this is already occurring.

An early example of this inherent "shiftability" of the ownership function took place in the Chrysler Corporation channel of distribution. The consumer-lessee leased an automobile from a lease dealer who in turn had leased his inventory from a subsidiary of the Chrysler Corporation. In effect, the incidence of ownership was shifted from the consumer all the way up the channel until it rested with the manufacturer.

To recapitulate, the traditional tendency for marketers and consumers to link consumption with ownership is a function of consumer firms largely having practiced a "transfer-of-title" approach to marketing for many years. That consumption requires ownership on the part of the consumer is a myth. In our changing society, there are a number of potentially attractive features to consumption without ownership.

## ATTRACTIONS OF CONSUMPTION WITHOUT OWNERSHIP

Among the possible attractions for consumers avoiding ownership are relief from the various burdens of ownership (some of which are getting heavier in our changing society), and the need to effect a better balance between our economic and ecological systems. It is true that considerable research is still needed to ascertain the relative roles and importance of these and other attractions to consumption without ownership.

### Burdens of Ownership

When the consumer buys he often assumes various burdens associated with owning that are more or less relieved when consuming and not owning. These burdens of ownership include the assumption of (1) risk concerning product style change and obsolescence; (2) risk concerning the making of an incorrect product selection; and (3) responsibility for maintaining, fixing, and moving the product. Still another burden of ownership relates to its non-recognition of sporadic product use.

### Product Style Change and Obsolescence

Just as a business firm might lease a computer, at least in part to avoid the risk of equipment obsolescence, so might the consumer consider renting for the same reason. In a magazine article it was pointed out that

> advantages of renting include insurance against obsolescence (you won't fret if next year's camera turns out to have a much better lens and exposure meter) and style changes (a $100-a-month rented mink won't be out of date).[8]

When the consumer buys, product obsolescence is *his* problem. When he rents or leases, it is by and large the marketer's problem. The marketer may well have already recouped his investment by this time and/or may recondition or refurbish the product or rent it again in its existing state at a lower rate.

In an era of rapid technological advance, increasingly diverse life styles, massive information accessibility, and high transcience,[9] protecting oneself from purchasing obsolescence is not a matter to be taken lightly. As Ferdinand F. Mauser said, "Use-value is realistic, for it relates to change; asset-ownership is absolutistic-ritualistic, for it is fixed and inflexible."[10]

### Incorrect Product Selection

When a consumer takes title to a piece of merchandise, he faces an awkward situation should he later decide that he made an incorrect choice. Depending on the circumstances, he may be able to return the product. Or the consumer may even attempt to sell the ill-chosen item. Often, however, he must live with his mistake and the anxiety that may accompany it. Another potentially attractive feature of the lease/rental device is that this characteristic of "finality" is more or less eliminated with consumer non-ownership (depending upon the contract).

Increasing post-decision flexibility on the part of the consumer by non-ownership would seem to have particular attraction in circumstances where the consumer is considering a substantial departure from past buying behavior; for example, switching to a Toyota from a history of buying American cars, switching to a metal tennis racquet after years of experience with wood, or switching to a bright red kitchen floor tile from one with a dull, grayish color.

By leasing the Toyota, the consumer gains experience with the product without being confined to it should the experience prove unsatisfactory. Even the tennis player who would most likely want to own his racquet might be inclined to rent a metal racquet for a month to determine if the departure from wood is, in actuality, warranted. The ability to return the red floor tile after six months could well be sufficient encouragement to prompt transactions that otherwise might not occur.

Whether the rental/leasing device is used for "trial-use" pursuant to eventual purchase or used as a continuing substitute for purchase, the misfortune of incorrect product selection should be minimized. Trial use allows for experience that should be helpful in making wise purchases at a later date. Lease/rental as a substitute for purchase allows post-transaction flexibility in making needed changes.

### Maintaining, Fixing, and Moving the Product

Aside from the assumption of risk relating to the possible obsolescence and incorrect selection of the product, ownership often saddles the consumer with responsibility for maintaining, repairing, and moving that which he buys.

Lawn mowers, for example, would not seem on the surface to be a "rentable" item, since they are required continually during the growing season and also for other reasons. Actually, however, they are one of the most popular rental items from rental stores. Some consumers rent rather than buy mowers and other garden equipment because the rented tools are usually sharpened and oiled at the rental store. When the work is done, one can return the tools in their existing condition.[11]

In other words, the rental agency, not the consumer, maintains the product.

Lease/rental often frees the consumer from concern about repairing malfunctioning products. If the product breaks down it is the owner who fixes it, not the user who is making rental/lease payment for working merchandise.

Freedom from repair responsibility can be attractive indeed in a society of complicated products that consumer/owners typically cannot fix for themselves. Thus, complex product breakdown normally results in interaction with a repair service, which can be inconvenient, expensive, and risky.

Finally, lease/rental can mean a reduction in the burdensome task of giving away, selling, or moving items should the consumer change residences. That is, the furniture lessee who is moving from Dallas to New York has the items picked up by the rental firm in Dallas before departing. As one mobile furniture lessee of everything from a bed to his lamps remarked, "It's new, it's colorful and I don't have to worry about carting it all over the world when I'm transferred."[12]

By offering relief from the burdens of maintaining, fixing, and moving products, lease/rental, in effect, offers convenience and other benefits in a society increasingly characterized by affluence, mobility, and a poverty of time.[13] Indeed, ownership often takes time. Mr. Mauser says it this way:

> The affluent masses of today ... seek to free time ... the factory is expected to produce the wherewithal for freeing time. Throwaway goods; leasing communally owned facilities (where maintenance and servicing responsibilities are assumed at centrally located places that are staffed by experts); highly processed goods such as frozen foods ... all of these developments help to free time. In essence, citizens provide themselves with time by shedding themselves of ownership responsibilities.[14]

The convenience factor in lease/rental has been reinforced in several recent studies conducted by Kenneth E. Maricle. In one, a study of the reasons why consumers lease cars, convenience emerged as a major determinant.[15] In the other, an investigation of home renting benefits and other issues, about 70 percent of the benefit responses of 149 home renters interviewed related to convenience.[16]

Alvin Toffler sums it up well:

> The rise of rentalism is a move away from lives based on having and it reflects the increase in doing and being. If the people of the future live faster than the people of the past, they must be far more flexible. They are like broken field runners—and it is hard to sidestep a tackle when loaded down with possessions. They want the advantages of affluence and the latest that technology has to offer, but not the responsibility that has, until now, accompanied the accumulation of possessions. They recognize that to survive among the uncertainties of rapid change they must learn to travel light.[17]

### Non-Recognition of Sporadic Product Use

Consumers often buy products that are destined for only sporadic use. The reader will probably be all too familiar with the mental picture of a middle class American household storage closet containing a toboggan, three tennis racquets, two baseball mitts, two shovels, one spreader, one hoe, three different types of shears, two bicycles, one tent, one Coleman stove, three canteens, and so forth. Undoubtedly, some of these items will be used continuously by our hypothetical household and non-ownership could well be more burdensome than ownership. Others of these items, however, probably will be used only intermittently and renting could well make sense, like the father who plays tennis once or twice a year with his son.

Ownership does not recognize intermittent use. The price tag is the same whether the product is used or not used by the consumer. In many instances, renting overcomes this burden of ownership, an advantage illustrated by the following statement from a "do it yourself" consumer.

> I've stopped buying power tools for my workshop; it doesn't make sense to tie up money in an electric saw or a sander or a fancy drill when I can rent one for occasional jobs.[18]

Because renting lends itself to sporadic product use, it is a particularly attractive consumption device for certain kinds of products; for example, convalescent equipment such as wheel chairs and hospital beds, party items, and recreational equipment. The one-way truck rental industry has grown so fast in recent years that concern has been expressed about oversupply.[19]

Importantly, because a number of consumers will typically subsidize the same rental product, the rental device makes possible the consumption of products that might otherwise remain beyond the financial reach of many households. The rentals of sail boats or beach-front houses are illustrations. It is perhaps not far-fetched to suggest that imaginative marketers, using lease/rental or some other non-ownership device, will develop offerings that allow the poorer segments of society to avoid numbing interest payments and yet participate more fully in the fruits of American affluence.

## ECOLOGICAL CONSIDERATIONS

Another impetus to accelerating consumption without ownership may well prove to be ecological considerations. Well publicized disclosures of recent years have awakened American society to the recognition that its economic system is out of balance with its ecological system. This imbalance is essentially the result of maximizing the short-run operation of the economic system at the expense of the long-run preservation of the environment. In Barry Commoner's terms:

> The course of environmental deterioration shows that as conventional capital has accumulated, for example, in the United States since 1946, the value of the biological capital has declined.[20]

Since profits are less important than breathing, concrete steps have been, are being, and will be taken to effect a better balance between our economic and ecological systems. Since consumer nonownership often implies "shared use" of the same product among various consumers, the ecology movement may come to stimulate communal use of certain kinds of property so as to reduce unnecessary production. As a theoretical example of this point, the reader may recall the lawn mower illustration previously cited. By means of the renting mechanism, a number of households would share the use (and the cost) of the same piece of equipment, instead of each household requiring its own purchased mower which might be idle most of the time. Such factors as the more durably made rental lawn mowers, the maintenance and repair expertise of the rental agency, the force of technological advance and product obsolescence, and others, all suggest the likelihood that fewer lawn mowers would have to be produced in a rental economy than in an ownership economy.

As Barry Commoner writes:

> the most serious effect of an environmental recovery program on the economic system would be generated by the ... requirement for the rational social use of productive capacity. This is best illustrated by the role of power production, which is an essential requirement for almost every economic activity .... This means that the allocation of power to a given productive activity, in turn, would need to be governed by a judgment of the expected social values to be derived per unit of power consumption invested in that particular product. Applied, let us say, to two automobile factories, this principle would favor the manufacturer who produced the more durable vehicle—since that would enhance the social value (such as potential miles of use) achieved per unit of power expended in the manufacturing process. This same principle would favor the production of returnable bottles over nonreturnable ones .... The general outcome would be a strong tendency to govern production according to the rational-use value of the final product rather than by the value added in the course of production.... In other words, the ecological imperative calls for the governance of productive processes by social thrift.[21]

## THE CHALLENGE TO CONSUMER OWNERSHIP

At a time when the various burdens of ownership are becoming heavier in an affluent, time-conscious, mobile society, several of the early bases for consumer ownership have declined markedly in significance. Specifically, consumers no longer have to assume ownership responsibilities to assure themselves of supplies of goods, as had been the case in earlier economies of scarcity. Abundance has taken over and, as it has done so, one of the cornerstones to private property has been eroded.[22]

Also, the increasing emphasis in contemporary society on people first, and things second, as the "Age of the People"[23] emerges, is whittling away at another cornerstone of private property: the direct relationship between social status and material possessions. Personal ownership of private property does not seem as essential as in the past. Increasingly, what matters is *use*.

This trend away from the perceived essentialness of consumer ownership is suggested in a variety of ways, not the least of which is the increasing percentage of new housing starts devoted to rental apartments in recent years. As late as in 1955, apartments accounted for only 8 percent of new housing starts; by 1961, the figure was 24 percent. In 1969, for the first time in the United States more building permits were issued for apartment construction than for private houses. Apartment living is particularly popular among young adults who, in the words of one authority, desire "minimum-involvement housing."[24] Mr. Mauser offers the enlarged scope of warranty activity as another indication that the consumer prefers having use-value and is not particularly interested in ownership responsibility.[25] The fact that the average car owner in the United States keeps his automobile only three and one-half years is suggestive to Mr. Toffler of the present invalidity to the notion that a major purchase has to be a permanent commitment.[26]

Traditional underpinnings to the perceived necessity for consumer ownership are being eroded at a time when the burdens of owning are becoming more severe and when American society is searching for practical means to effect better balance between its ecology and its economy. In the authors' view, this convergence of forces will stimulate a very substantial growth in consumption without ownership, with the leasing/rental mechanism being the prime consumption device. Consumer marketers increasingly will recognize ownership for what it actually is, a function of marketing, and will assume this function, rather than pass it on, for reasons of competitive strategy. Indeed, the present boom in industrial leasing is most likely a forerunner of what is ahead in consumer lease/rental. Readers knowledgeable about industrial leasing already will have noticed the similarity among the benefits for consumer lease/rental and the usual benefits noted for industrial equipment leasing—for example, conserving working capital, minimizing maintenance problems, and protecting against obsolescence.

While consumption without ownership is ripe for substantial expansion, *consumption with ownership* is not going to be eliminated, by any means. Not only are some products clearly not amenable to the lease/rental device (food, shampoo, ethical drugs) but, also, there are burdens to non-ownership, just as there are burdens to ownership. Most homeowners will probably continue to own, rather than rent, a set of pliers, for example, because to not do so could be extremely inconvenient. Other possible burdens of non-ownership would include greater total economic cost and loss of residual value of the asset. Nevertheless, for reasons we have cited, the authors predict that by 1980, consumer lease/rental activity will dwarf the already considerable beginnings of today.

## IMPACT ON MARKETING AND BUSINESS

Although the scope of this article prohibits a lengthy discussion of the probable impact of greatly expanded consumption without ownership on marketing and business practice, some of the more likely implications follow.

For industry, one implication of expanded consumption without ownership is increased investment in inventory, coupled with reduced turnover rates, greater need for storage, and the repeated handling of goods. Inventories of used products will need to be financed and viewed as revenue generating assets. Storage facilities will take on new operational importance and will require capabilities for repairing, renovating, reconstituting, and repackaging.

Heavier and more extended demands for capital will mean that firms must make different arrangements with financial institutions. Single-season notes will not suffice since businesses will need funds to finance inventories held throughout the useful life of products. One alternative will be for financial institutions to take a more active role in the channel of distribution and perform the ownership function as a channel member. Banks that have established leasing subsidiaries are now taking steps in this direction.

It should also be noted that as the financing of ownership moves back into the channel of distribution there will be a corresponding reduction in the demand for consumer credit.

### New Inventory Concepts

Another implication for businesses engaging in lease/rental activity is that the "inventory" account will become more than a passthrough control point. In some cases, inventory accounts will be divided into categories reflecting the age or remaining useful life of products. In general, new and more responsive internal controls will be needed. Profits will hinge on continued employment of inventory rather than on stockturn rates. Indeed, firms involved in lease/rental will need to learn the meaning of "occupancy ratios" and "percent of capacity" criteria that are already well known by airline and hotel executives, among others.

### Increased Emphasis on Product Quality

Upgraded product quality is another likely result of expanding consumption without ownership. One has only to visit the exhibits at American Rental Association conventions to discover that the number-one selling feature promoted by manufacturers selling to the rental trade is the durability and quality of their product line. Price, on the other hand, appears to be a relatively minor determinant for establishments renting on a day-to-day or weekly basis to a wide variety of customers. Indeed, it has been suggested that Sears' short-lived venture into the rental business was terminated by the lack of durability of their products which were built for occasional home use rather than the constant and hard use associated with renting.[27]

Also, products destined for the lease/rental market can be expected to be designed to better facilitate maintenance and service than have been many currently available products. Manufacturers of items as disparate as furniture and dress shirts probably will begin to think more in terms of such criteria as "easy access" and "replaceable parts" as they design their technologies of tomorrow.

Still another distinct possibility for lease/rental product strategy is an application similar to the now popular strategy of systems selling, that is, marketing coordinated solutions to the totality of the customer problem. Just as former lock companies have progressed to the selling of home protection systems, so can we increasingly expect to see the leasing of "turn-key" furniture and accessory ensembles, complete wardrobes, and packaged vacations.

### Salesman as Consultant

Related to the probable expansion in the leasing/renting of coordinated product systems will be an increased emphasis on the advisory role for the marketer. In some product areas the strategy of providing coordinated, total solutions to consumer problems and the long-term relationship with customers implied by leasing arrangements, should result in the conversion of salesmen into consultants-of-consumption. Thus, the furniture rental outlet would provide interior decorator service, clothing store representatives would be wardrobe consultants, and the travel service would, in effect, provide travel advice, coordination, and booking. As this conversion from more traditional selling functions to consulting functions takes place, some consumers will no doubt develop loyalty to advisors in much the same way as they do today to brands.

### Flexible Pricing

Pricing is another element of the marketing mix that will most likely be affected as consumption without ownership advances. While the price in a sale/purchase is static, a rental price can be dynamic.

The price of a product being sold is fixed and relates directly to the condition of the product at the time of sale. The subsequent condition of the product is the owner's problem and will not change the price. Each time the consumer makes a rental payment, however, he has in his possession a product belonging to someone else. It seems fair to suggest that more than a few aggressive lease/rental outlets will come to implement "flexible" pricing to better reflect the condition of the product at the time rental payments are made. That is, in certain circumstances, consumers will be granted price adjustments as lease/

rental products near the end of their useful life. Indeed, the flexibility inherent in non-sale pricing suggests that the price variable will often be strategically important as lease/rental competition intensifies.

## CONCLUSION

The authors have suggested some of the underlying reasons behind an increasingly significant development in marketing: consumption without ownership. We have indicated that ownership is a marketing function and can be assumed within the channel rather than passed on to the consumer. The fact that consumers commonly think of "buying" when in a consumption situation is largely a result of past marketing practice, and, therefore, is a behavioral tendency that can be altered with future marketing practice. Societal changes are causing various burdens of consumer ownership to become exceedingly heavy and the authors believe that more and more firms will see retention of ownership within the channel by means of the lease/rental device as an attractive competitive strategy. Ecological considerations also should serve to stimulate consumption without ownership because of its "shared-use" character. While leasing has been experiencing dramatic growth in recent years in the various industrial equipment markets, consumer markets should experience equally dramatic growth in the near future. Indeed, it is already beginning to happen, although the potential that remains is awesome: furniture, clothing, appliances, automobiles, recreational equipment, and shelter, as examples.

The vast market potential for consumer goods lease/rental activity is additionally enhanced by the erosion of some traditional needs for owning. Not only is owning no longer necessary to assure supply in conditions of scarcity, but the relationship between social status and material accumulation increasingly is a vulnerable one in our changing society.

Among the probable impacts of greatly expanded consumption without ownership on business and marketing practices are differing financing needs, operational changes in inventory management, upgraded product quality, more attention to maintenance and servicing requirements in product design, the marketing of lease/rental "packages," or "systems," increased emphasis on serving the consumer in advisory capacities, and more evidence of "dynamic" rather than "static" pricing.

Industries whose products are (1) expensive and complex, (2) seasonal or occasional in consumer-use patterns, or (3) an unproven departure from existing products will be among the first to feel the growing pressure to offer consumption without ownership. At the same time a growing number of individual firms will try to capitalize on the fad-like attraction of lease/rental marketing. These firms most likely will fail if they do not realize the ownership-burden concept that typically underlies this kind of consumption.

Just as user ownership is not necessary for consumption to take place, neither is the lease/rental device necessary for consumption without ownership. For example, in Montpellier, France, a promising experiment involving consumer use of public automobiles to relieve downtown congestion has already drawn inquiries from a number of other cities and countries.[28] In any event, regardless of what adjunctive non-ownership consumptive devices might be developed, it remains clear that substantive operational and conceptual changes must be made by many firms that have developed in a marketplace where title was delivered with possession. To ignore the potential of consumption without ownership is to assume the above average risk of all stand-pat companies: shrinking market share and falling profits.

## REFERENCES

1 "You Can Rent Almost Anything These Days," *Changing Times—The Kiplinger Magazine*, November 1971, p. 35.
2 See, for example, "Leasing: Where It's At," *Purchasing Magazine*, 28 May 1970, pp. 35-42; "Renting Almost Everything—A New Way of Life," *U.S. News and World Report*, 30 March 1970, pp. 47-48; "Dynamic Leasing Business," *Financial World*, 25 June 1969, pp. 9, 50-51; "The Growing Lure of Leasing," *Business Management*, January 1970, pp. 40-46.
3 "The Growing Lure of Leasing," p. 40; also see, Nick Farina, "Leasing Becoming Sharp Marketing Tool, Zises Says," *Industrial Marketing*, August 1970, p. 10.
4 "Dynamic Leasing Business," p. 9.
5 "A Threat to the Booming Leasing Business," *Business Week*, 4 September 1971, p. 42.
6 "Renting Almost Everything—A New Way of Life," p. 47; Sylvia Porter, "Rental Outlets Enjoying Boom," *The Denver Post*, 28 December 1969, p. 2L.
7 Several notable exceptions are Francis A. Babione, "The Role of Rentals in Demand Stimulation," *Michigan Business Review*, May 1964; and Ferdinand F. Mauser, "A Universe-in-Motion Approach to Marketing," in *Managerial Marketing: Perspectives and Viewpoints*, 3rd ed. Eugene J. Kelley and William Lazer, eds. (Homewood, Ill.: Richard D. Irwin, Inc., 1967).
8 "You Can Rent Almost Anything These Days," p. 36.
9 The term *transcience*, popularized by Toffler, refers to the rate that our relationships with things, places, people, organizations, and ideas turn over. See Alvin Toffler, *Future Shock* (New York: Random House, 1970), pp. 40-41.
10 Mauser, "A Universe-in-Motion Approach to Marketing," p. 51.
11 "You Can Rent Almost Anything These Days," p. 36.
12 "Young Folks On the Go Foster an Industry by Renting Furniture," *Wall Street Journal*, 24 April 1967, p. 1.
13 For a discussion of changing patterns of affluence, mobility, and time value see William Lazer, John E. Smallwood et al., "Consumer Environments and Life Styles of the Seventies," *MSU Business Topics*, Spring 1972, pp. 5-17.
14 Mauser, "A Universe-in-Motion Approach to Marketing," p. 51.
15 Kenneth E. Maricle, "An Analysis of Automobile Leasing" (Ph.D. diss., Arizona State University, 1970).
16 Kenneth E. Maricle and Michael R. Padbury, "The Concept of Ownership in a Changing Society," (paper presented at the annual meetings of the Southern Marketing Association, Washington, D.C., 9 November 1972).
17 Toffler, *Future Shock*, p. 58.
18 "Renting Almost Everything—A New Way of Life," p. 48.
19 See "Has One-way Truck Rental Hit a Dead End?" *Business Week*, 27 March 1971, pp. 44, 46.
20 Barry Commoner, "A Businessman's Primer on Ecology," *Business and Society Review*, Spring 1972, p. 50.
21 Ibid., p. 53.
22 Mauser, "A Universe-in-Motion Approach to Marketing," p. 50.
23 For a fuller discussion of this point see Leonard L. Berry, "Marketing Challenges In the Age of the People," *MSU Business Topics*, Winter 1972, pp. 7-13.
24 Professor Burnham Kelly, as quoted in Toffler, *Future Shock*, p. 56.
25 Mauser, "A Universe-in-Motion Approach to Marketing," p. 54.
26 Toffler, *Future Shock*, p. 56.
27 Edward A. Nyren, "Rentals: There's No Ceiling in Sight," *Printer's Ink*, 24 July 1964, p. 42.
28 "Co-op Cars," *Newsweek*, 13 September 1971, pp. 58-59.

Reading 10

# The Payoff for Intelligent Consumer Decision-making

**E. Scott Maynes**

*When individual consumers achieve better purchase terms by searching out and obtaining lower prices and/or better quality, their actions tend to exercise a disciplining effect on all sellers, inducing them to offer better goods on better terms to all buyers.*

My guess is that most consumers—including many who certainly could be characterized as "intelligent"—fail to appreciate sufficiently both the number and size of the "payoffs," that is, gains, which intelligent consumer decision-making can yield.

The first part of this article makes the case for effective consumer decision-making. The core of the article deals with the meaning, origin, and accessibility of such payoffs. Then the reader is introduced to some tentative operating rules for consumers and to a detailed example of how a particular payoff was achieved.

## WHY DECIDE COMPETENTLY?

The most compelling reason for devoting time and effort to the making of better decisions as consumers is that this is an important means of increasing purchasing power. There are two paths by which such increases may be achieved: (1) buying the same (or similar) product[1] at a lower price, or (2) for the same price, buying a better-performing or more durable product. It follows that possible payoffs will be determined by the extent of price and/or quality variation for a product within a given market.[2]

The issues of *Consumer Reports*—the monthly publication of Consumers Union, a consumer-controlled product-testing organization—disclose numerous instances where the prices of the most expensive item tested are two, three, or even four times as high as the price of the least expensive item, after adjustment for quality differences.

Particular examples of price-quality variation are not difficult to find in which there is substantial opportunity for consumer "profit." An economic explanation for the persistence of such price-quality variations is dealt with later in this article.

A second and unappreciated reason for seeking to make better consumer decisions is that the "earnings" or "savings" from such decisions are untaxed. Thus, a family with a $10,000 income and an assumed federal-state tax rate of $0.30 on the last dollar earned would have to receive $1.43 of pretax income to

[1]Here a "product" will be defined as the set of goods or services designed to fulfill the same purpose. The exact specification of "same purpose" is left to each consumer.

[2]The number of sellers in a "given market" will depend upon the kind and location of sellers a particular consumer is willing to deal with. This, in turn, will depend upon the "costs" (time, effort) of dealing with alternative sellers. For a general discussion of "costs," see p. 48.

From the *Journal of Home Economics*, vol. 61, February 1969, pp. 97–103, copyright by the American Home Economics Association, Washington, D.C.

increase its purchasing power by as much as the $1.00 "earned" by making a better consumer choice. ($1.43 x 0.70 = $1.00 = amount left after taxes.) In *dollar* terms the worth of such consumer "earnings" increases with income level and decreases with family size, while the subjective worth of each dollar thus "earned" presumably decreases with income and increases with family size.

A third advantage of investment in better consumer decision-making is that it is open to anyone. This is in happy contrast to the "greater earnings" route to increased purchasing power which is more accessible to persons with unusual skills and exceptional energy.

A fourth reason for considering alternatives in consumer purchases is defensive in nature: to avoid being bilked. Too many consumers fail to understand that the sellers' interest is not the consumers' interest and that neither an implied fiducial relationship between buyer and seller nor the discipline of markets (as they exist) is sufficient to ensure optimal outcomes from the consumer's point of view. To cite one specific point, many consumers in relying on salesmen for product information fail to recognize the bias in salesmen-provided information resulting from the fact that salesmen receive their income from selling their array of products and not for providing accurate consumer information.

A final reason for deciding well as a consumer is the social payoff. Consumers, no less than sellers, are propelled by self-interest. What will induce them to invest more time and effort in consumer decision-making is the expectation that *their own* purchasing power will be substantially increased.

Nonetheless, it is comforting to reflect that this is one of those too rare instances where individual and social interests overlap completely. When individual consumers achieve better purchase terms by searching out and obtaining lower prices and/or better quality, their actions tend to exercise a disciplining effect on all sellers, inducing them to offer better goods on better terms to all buyers.

## COSTS OF THE SEARCH

To obtain consumer payoffs the consumer must "search" directly or indirectly for information regarding the prices and qualities of goods in which he is interested. If a *search* is defined as "each attempt to secure information regarding the price and quality of a product," what then are the costs of a search?

In general, a *cost* is "anything which is undergone or foregone in order to attain a given end." When this definition is applied to a search, some kind of search costs are obvious and readily understood. Most searches, for instance, involve *direct money* costs, such as payments for telephone calls and gasoline for auto searches. *Direct, but subjective,* costs raise problems of valuation but not of recognition. Anyone with a family recognizes that shopping (searching) with young children is difficult. But how can a money value be assigned to such costs? The consumer must ask himself how much money—given his financial position and family situation—he would be willing to pay to do his shopping without children. No actual payment will be involved. What the individual is doing is placing a money equivalent on the distaste he attributes to shopping with children.

The *indirect* costs of a search consist of that which is foregone in order to undertake the search. They may be *objective* and readily valued. This would be the case when the head of a household gives up a day's pay in order to search for new housing in a different city. Or they may be *subjective*. This would be the case when someone gives up an afternoon's sailing in order to visit used-car lots. In this case the indirect subjective cost of the search is the dollar equivalent of the utility or subjective satisfactions which sailing would have yielded. The crucial idea in identifying indirect search costs is that the buyer should consider *only* the second-best activity: what he would have done had he not engaged in the search whose costs he is evaluating.

Someone may object: "But I enjoy shopping!" The objection is pertinent and introduces three additional observations. First, for those who like shopping the subjective costs of the search may be negative; that is, they are not costs at all in the usual sense. Second, both costs of the search and the gross payoff may include subjective elements. Consider an instance where by prudent shopping someone succeeds in reducing by $50 the price of a television set he wishes to buy. He may be so pleased with this outcome that the subjective value of *this* $50 exceeds the amount of utility he usually associates with $50. To correctly reckon the gross payoff, it would be necessary to add to the payoff the money equivalent of the extra satisfaction successful shopping afforded. Third, it may be difficult in calculating net payoffs to separate subjective gross payoffs from subjective costs of the search. In general, such a separation is unnecessary. But for correct mental calculations it is important not to count the same source of subjective satisfaction twice.

## WHERE ARE THE PAYOFFS?

The central question for any consumer contemplating a purchase is: How many searches should he make? The general answer: Keep making searches as long as the expected net payoff is positive, that is, as long as the expected additional savings from the search exceeds the expected total cost of that search. Like most general rules, it is answer-begging. And so we shall move on to progressively more specific analysis and recommendations.

At a somewhat more specific level, consumers will find it profitable to search further under the following conditions:

1 When an item looms relatively large in the long-run household budget
2 When the cost of the search is low
3 When the expected variation in price and/or quality is large

The second and third of these deserve further discussion.

## REDUCING THE COST OF THE SEARCH

Any source of product information which is available to the buyer in his own home greatly economizes on search costs. Three sources in particular commend themselves: *Consumer Reports*, a Sears, Roebuck or Montgomery Ward catalog, and the classified telephone directory.

*Consumer Reports*, mentioned earlier, facilitates the making of informed brand choices and also provides preliminary price information. The catalog of a large mail-order firm is, in my judgment, indispensable for obtaining information regarding a reasonable price for a vast array of products. Although the Sears, Roebuck and Montgomery Ward prices may not always be the lowest, they are usually in the bottom quarter of the price range. Finally, the yellow pages of the telephone book provide the most readily accessible list of sellers of any product, and the telephone provides the cheapest means of obtaining either preliminary or final price information.

The use of the telephone for obtaining price information raises the problem of accuracy of information. It is possible for the buyer to secure partial protection against false or incomplete information by asking for the name of the informant and declaring that he will not purchase if the information given turns out to be seriously incomplete or false.

A final means of economizing on search costs is to conduct a number of different searches on the same shopping expedition.

## DETERMINANTS OF PRICE AND QUALITY VARIATION

As suggested earlier, the existence of substantial price and quality variation raises the possibility of large consumer payoff. What, then, determines the extent of price-quality variation? A preliminary answer—to be developed below—is that price and/or quality variations are greatest where:

1 Sellers practice price discrimination
2 Product differentiation is substantial
3 Consumer ignorance is great
4 The number of sellers is large
5 Price-fixing by manufacturers or laws is minimal

### Price Discrimination

The practice of price discrimination results in substantial *within-brand* and *within-dealer* variation in prices. By definition, price discrimination is practiced when different purchasers are charged different prices for an identical good by a single seller. To be a valid example of price discrimination, the differences in prices charged should not be attributable to differences in selling costs.

For a seller to engage in price discrimination, two conditions must be met: (1) different customers (or the same customer at different times) must have differing urgencies of demand for his product; (2) there must exist barriers which prevent resale of his product from the customers charged the lower price to those charged the higher price. A classic example shows why price discrimination is profitable and lays bare the importance of the two conditions.

In the era prior to modern packaging a grocer would purchase tea by the barrel. Upon receiving a new shipment, the first move of the competent grocer was to divide its contents between one display case labeled "good" and a second proclaiming the tea to be "better." "Good" tea was priced at 30 cents a pound and "better" tea at 45 cents a pound. What made the purchasers of the higher-priced 45-cent tea willing to pay more was their naïve belief that either the "better" label really meant better or that price is a reliable guide to quality. For these purchasers the same invincible innocence killed any appetite for the cheaper tea, and thus prevented resale from the 30-cent purchasers to the 45-cent purchasers. Since the cost of posting the "better" sign was near zero, the added 15 cents per pound represented pure profit.

Differential transportation prices (lower fares for children, students, servicemen, round-trippers), physicians charging lower fees to those they identify as poor, lower prices charged in sales are all relevant examples of price discrimination.

In the examples above, price discrimination was undertaken at the initiative of the seller (perhaps excepting physicians' fees). It need not be. An enterprising consumer can induce a seller to practice price discrimination. When such a consumer asks, "What discount do you offer?" and actually succeeds in purchasing goods or services at prices which are genuinely lower than the usual prices, he has induced the seller to practice price discrimination. It will be profitable for the seller to do this as long as the additional receipts exceed the costs directly attributable to this sale *and* as long as he does not have to generalize the lower price to all his customers. The latter requirement will be invariably met in the case of a new car purchase where the vast variety of engines, accessories, and lines makes it almost impossible to say what *the* price of *the car* is. It will also be met wherever there is a trade-in since the value of the trade-in is so subjective that it is difficult to say whether a particular used item has been overvalued or undervalued.

Price discrimination, then, is a major source of price variation. Knowledge of its practice and the opportunity to induce sellers to engage in individual price discrimination favorable to them open up attractive possibilities for consumer profit.

### Product Differentiation

To abuse Gertrude Stein: A toothpaste is not a toothpaste is not a toothpaste. The point: for a variety of reasons, some real, some imagined, consumers may develop a strong preference for a particular brand (or seller) and be willing to pay more for it (him).

In the case of toothpaste, a successful advertising campaign may persuade some consumers that one brand performs better than its competitors, and hence they may be willing to pay a higher price for it. Alternatively, recognizing the value of a convenient location, they may be willing to pay more for a particular brand when they buy it at their neighborhood drugstore. Indeed, there are other reasons why they may be willing to pay more for *any* product at the local drugstore: they may like the druggist and salespeople and enjoy dealing with them; they may feel, rightly or wrongly, that they can count on the druggist's honesty and his knowledge of household medical needs.

All of these factors come under the heading of product differentiation. Successful product differentiation enables a particular brand (particular seller) to command a higher price than its (his) competitors. Product differentiation gives rise to within-brand, inter-brand, inter-dealer price variations.

Product differentiation works in the low-price direction as well as the high-price direction. Some stores successfully identify themselves as "low-cost" "discount" operations and appeal to consumers whose taste for service, decor, personal relations with the seller is less and whose desire for lower prices is greater.

The lesson for the intelligent consumer is that if he is willing to give up the factors which lead to product differentiation of a high-price, high-service variety he can frequently obtain the product itself at a lower price.

### Consumer Ignorance

The importance of consumer ignorance in explaining variations in prices and quality can scarcely be overemphasized. *If* consumers were capable of obtaining complete and valid price and quality information about all variants of the products they were interested in, relatively little price and quality variation would remain. Gone would be price discrimination based on the inability of consumers to compare prices and qualities. Gone would be the high prices resulting from "successful" advertising not grounded in reproducible fact. One brand of bleach, for instance, would no longer command 59 cents a gallon while other chemically identical bleaches are priced at 42 cents; or a well-known aspirin would no longer command 79 cents per 100 tablets while medically equivalent unbranded aspirin sells at 24 cents.

What would remain would be price variations arising from different treatment of objectively defined groups; for example, discounts offered to older people. Also remaining would be the product differentiation and associated price-quality variation arising from people's differing tastes for service, decor, durability, "frills."

Consumer ignorance may exist either because consumers cannot obtain or do not seek the relevant price-quality information.

Home economists, in particular, are acutely aware of the difficulty of comparing the quality of today's numerous and technically complex products. It is precisely because such judgments are so difficult to make that Consumers Union, the product-testing organization cited earlier, came into being and continues to flourish. And, unhappily, for most products it is necessary to make quality comparisions before making valid price comparisons.

The fact that consumers search little is attested by the results of consumer surveys. Why? I would speculate that exposure to formal courses in economics and the folklore of our "free enterprise" economy conspire to oversell people on the effectiveness of competition. People may misremember and misapply what they learned in their long-ago courses in economics. They may remember correctly that "*perfect* competition" yields a single, lowest price for any product. But they may forget that this result rests on a nonexistent world in which (1) there are a very large number of sellers and buyers of the same product, (2) products are undifferentiated, (3) consumers possess complete and accurate information about all products and prices, and (4) perfect mobility of resources exists. If and only if all these assumptions hold, one of the operating rules of the naïve consumer—that price is an indicator of quality—is correct. Ironically, in the world of perfect competition, the rule is superfluous.

Real life violates all these assumptions. As for the "many sellers" assumption, a consumer is unusual indeed if for a typical product he has as many as twenty *retail* sellers conveniently accessible to him. In fact, few products are undifferentiated to the extent that consumers are indifferent as to brands or sellers. We have argued earlier that consumers *cannot* possess complete and accurate information and are now arguing that a misplaced belief in the efficacy of our economic systems leads them to seek less price-quality information than they should. Finally, the costs—monetary and psychological—of moving resources from one usage to another make perfect mobility of resources highly improbable.

Also contributing to nonsearching by consumers is utter reliance on the integrity of the seller. We should first point out that retail sellers—like ordinary consumers—often lack the technical knowledge, the objectivity, and the inclination to evaluate a wide range of products. Second, even if they were able and wished to make objective appraisals of competing products, the giving of "honest advice" would often require them to act against their own financial self-interest and to recommend the product of a competitor. It seems naïve to expect a Ford dealer to recommend a Chevrolet, or vice versa. Even where a seller handles many brands of the same product, his judgment may tend to be corrupted by the size of the commission he receives from different brands. These considerations notwithstanding, it is probably true that many consumers do count on sellers for product advice.

The fact that consumers often do not seek and often cannot make valid price-quality comparisons means that high and low prices can coexist, and that high-priced sellers will not fully feel the effects of competition.

A historical trend worth noting is that both federal and state governments are gradually backing into positions where they will assume some—and increasing—responsibility for the facilitation of product comparisons. Truth-in-Packaging and Truth-in-Lending legislation as well as the setting of minimum standards of safety for drugs and cars are manifestations of this tendency. It appears, however, that a long time will elapse before the results of the product-testing which the National Bureau of Standards performs for the Federal Government will be made available to the citizenry—consumers —who elect and finance it.

### Where the Number of Sellers Is Larger

Given the current state of market research and the cost of such research to sellers, it is not surprising that there remains among sellers considerable ignorance as to prospective consumer reactions to prices and products. The Edsel fiasco provides a classic example. Given the ignorance regarding consumer reactions which this example dramatizes, it is but one step further to argue that the greater the number of sellers, the greater the variations in prices and qualities that sellers will put to the market test.

It is probably also correct that the larger the number of sellers, the greater will be their diversity with respect to costs as well as the kind and extent of product differentiation they seek and achieve. Hence, as the number of sellers increases, these factors will add to price and quality variation.

If our generalization about the effects of the number of sellers appears to contradict the earlier-learned notion that extensive competition yields a single price, it will be because the earlier generalization rested on the unrealistic assumption of perfect competition.

### Price-fixing

Successful price-fixing at the retail level, whether instituted by manufacturers, by law, or by collusive or quasi-collusive behavior on the part of retailers, reduces price variations and hence opportunities for consumer "profit." Since the impetus for price-fixing usually comes from the least efficient and hence most vulnerable retail sellers, the net result is to establish a higher average level of prices than would otherwise prevail.

In general, manufacturer enforcement of uniform retail prices has been effective only when the number of retail outlets is relatively small. Thus, Volkswagen has been fairly successful in maintaining its "suggested" price. General Electric on the other hand, with thousands of products and thousands of retailers to deal with, has been unsuccessful.

In the 1930's the historic failure of price-fixing by manufacturers, coupled with the Great Depression and the political influence of small retailers, led to wide-scale enactment of resale price maintenance legislation (erroneously labeled "Fair Trade" laws) which put the force of state and federal law behind price-fixing by manufacturers. In the postwar period these laws have been less and less effective under the combined assault of protracted prosperity, successful legal challenges, the introduction of house brands, and lackadaisical enforcement. In 1955 it was estimated that resale price maintenance laws covered 4 percent to 20 percent of total retail sales. Today the proportion is certainly smaller.

Local retailers can agree, explicitly or implicitly, to set a single price. But as above we can argue that such price agreements become increasingly difficult to enforce as the number of sellers increases. As numbers increase, it becomes increasingly likely that some seller will feel that *his* interests are not best served by a common price. It will also become increasingly difficult and costly for non-price-cutters to police conformity to the agreed price.

Further, such collusive price-setting is easier to initiate and to continue when the product in question is relatively "standard," for example, a car wash at an automated installation.

### Sales

Thus far, we have focused on factors giving rise to price variations at a given point in time. Sales give rise to price variations over time. A genuine "sale" occurs when a retailer's usual line of merchandise is sold at reduced prices. Many of the factors listed above account for sales, but there may be additional explanations. Our list includes:

**1** The seller overestimated the demand for a certain product.

**2** Price discrimination: The only way a particular seller can sell to price-conscious consumers is by reducing prices. He does this *after* he has already sold to his regular customers at regular prices. (Of course, the same consumer may be a "regular" customer for some products and a price-conscious customer for others.)

**3** Loss leaders: The seller reduces prices, even below cost, on certain products, in order to attract buyers to his store, then expects to sell other products at the usual (or higher) margin.

**4** Tradition: A sale is conducted at a regular, but traditional, time. Traditional sales may even be continued when economic conditions indicate otherwise.

## TENTATIVE OPERATING RULES FOR CONSUMERS

We have sought to be progressively more specific in analysis and recommendations. The climax of this process comes with the spelling out of "tentative operating rules" for consumers.

**1** Before purchasing, ask yourself whether the product of interest is subject to substantial variations in price and quality.
  - **a** For relatively objective information on this point, consult *Consumer Reports, Consumer Research Bulletin,* or specialized publications such as *Popular Photography.*
  - **b** If objective information is not available, ask yourself:
    - **1** Whether the prices of the product (or brand) *are fixed* by law, manufacturer, or retailers and how effective any price-fixing arrangements are. If they are effectively fixed (and the fixed price cannot be avoided by buying elsewhere), buy forthwith and waste no further effort.
    - **2** Whether the product is subject to *product differentiation* as a result of attributes of the individual seller (friendliness, reliability, background information he possesses), characteristics of the outlet (reliability, decor, extent of service, location), or presumed or real differences in quality. If yes, ask yourself how much you wish to pay for the factors giving rise to higher prices through product differentiation.
    - **3** Whether the product or brand is subject to *price discrimination.* The relevant question is whether there are classes of people who will buy the product only at reduced prices. As we know, price

discrimination will be practiced only when the seller does not have to generalize the lower price, that is, when the favored groups are kept separate through classification, ignorance, or some other device. If you expect price discrimination, ask whether you are a member of a favored group or how you can join such a group.

4 Whether *consumer ignorance* regarding prices and quality is "great." A subjective question such as this can only have a subjective answer. My suggestion would be that you consider whether you personally believe you can make valid comparisons of the prices and qualities of different brands. If not, expect substantial variations from this source.

2 While purchasing:
- **a** Deal in the market with the largest possible number of sellers.
- **b** Whenever there is a trade-in, always seek a particularly favorable price (that is, induce the seller to practice individual price discrimination).
- **c** Whenever the price of goods or services is $100 or more (set your own minimum), always contact at least three sellers. Search more if:
  - **1** You have reason to expect more than average price-quality variation, or
  - **2** The expected outlay is very high, or
  - **3** The costs of the search are relatively low.

These rules are neither final nor complete. They could not be. Consumer decisions are too complex. In addition, the discussion from which they were constructed did not deal in detail with such important matters as sources of product information or "negotiating the purchase."

These tentative operating rules are offered in the hope that they will provide the consumer with an orderly framework in which to seek better consumer payoffs.

Reading 11

# The Purchase of a New Car

**Arch Troelstrup**

*Don't accept list prices.*

**Situation**

Old 1967, 2-door sedan to trade-in.
New 1972, 4-door, V-8 engine, power steering, tinted windshield, air conditioning, deluxe wheel discs.

**Analysis of Offer**

| Dealer Receives | | | Dealer Pays (wholesale) † | |
|---|---|---|---|---|
| Cash: | Down payment | $ 100 | Basic car | $2,618 |
| | At delivery | 2,709 | Power steering | 88 |
| | | | Tinted windshield | 23 |
| Old Car: | Wholesale value | 577* | Air conditioning | 310 |
| | Total | $3,386 | Deluxe wheel discs | 20 |
| | | | Total | $3,059 |

Dealer's gross profit is $327 ($3,386 − $3,059)

**Purchaser's Invoice (list prices on sticker)**

| | |
|---|---|
| Basic car | $3,228 |
| Power steering | 113 |
| Tinted windshield | 30 |
| Air conditioning | 397 |
| Deluxe wheel discs | 26 |
| Total | $3,794 |

Less: Trade-in $985
Down payment 100 = $1,085

Equals: Cash to be paid by buyer at delivery = $2,709

**Lesson to learn**

Don't accept list prices

| | | |
|---|---|---|
| List price | $3,794 | |
| Dealer pays | 3,059 | |
| | $ 735 | Gross profit |

An informed consumer would pay about $410 less:

$3,386
3,059
$ 327

Dealer would be happy to receive $327 gross profit (your bargaining factor)

* NADA Used Car Guide, 2000 K St., N.W., Washington, D.C. 20006. (Also on newsstands)

† Wholesale prices from Your Price Authority Auto Blue Book, 161 Tehama St., San Francisco, Calif. 94103. (Newsstand price .75¢), *Edmunds' New Car Prices*, 295 Northern Blvd. Great Neck, N.Y. 11021 (Newsstand Price $1.50).

# Why Do People Shop?

**Edward M. Tauber**

*For many shoppers, bargaining is a degrading activity.*

The field of consumer behavior has experienced a dynamic period of growth over the past 10 years. It is frequently overlooked, however, that this broad area consists of three distinct activities: *shopping, buying,* and *consuming.* Considerable progress has been achieved in identifying the behavioral dimensions of buying, and a number of theories of buying behavior have been postulated. However, less is known about the determinants of consuming and shopping which are also of substantial theoretical and managerial importance.

This article attempts to encourage behavioral research and theory building concerning shopping behavior by presenting some exploratory research findings on the question of *why do people shop?*

Numerous writings have been directed to this question. For example, researchers have suggested that shopping is a function of the nature of the product,[1] the degree of perceived risk inherent in the product class,[2] and the level of knowledge or amount of information about alternatives.[3] All of these answers are directed at the question, "Why do people shop in *more* than one store?" (comparison shopping). Other authors have maintained that shopping is a function of location, product assortment, and store image.[4] Again, these are variables which help explain, "Why do people shop *where* they do?" (store patronage).

The question considered in this article is, "Why do people shop? (i.e., go to a store in the first place). The most obvious answer, "because they need to purchase something," can be a most deceptive one and reflects a marketing myopia which management has been cautioned to avoid—a product orientation. This answer considers only the products which people may purchase and is but a partial and insufficient basis for behavioral explanations. It implicitly assumes that the shopping motive is a simple function of the buying motive.

This article hypothesizes that peoples' motives for shopping are a function of many variables, *some* of which are unrelated to the actual buying of products. It is maintained that an understanding of shopping motives requires the consideration of satisfactions which shopping *activities* provide, as well as the utility obtained from the *merchandise* that may be purchased. If needs other than those associated with particular products motivate people to go to a store, the retailer should incorporate this information into his marketing strategy.

[1]Richard H. Holton, "The Distinction between Convenience Goods, Shopping Goods and Specialty Goods," *Journal of Marketing,* Vol. 22 (July, 1958), p. 56.

[2]Donald F. Cox, ed., *Risk Taking and Information Handling in Consumer Behavior* (Boston: Graduate School of Business Administration, Harvard University, 1967).

[3]John. A. Howard and Jagdish N. Sheth, *The Theory of Buyer Behavior* (New York: John Wiley and Sons, 1969), pp. 286–295; *and Louis P. Bucklin,* "Testing Propensities to Shop," *Journal of Marketing,* Vol. 30 (January, 1966), pp. 22–27.

[4]Louis P. Bucklin, "The Concept of Mass in Intra-Urban Shopping," *Journal of Marketing,* Vol. 31 (October, 1967), pp. 37–42.

From the *Journal of Marketing,* published by the American Marketing Association, vol. 36, October 1972.

## METHODOLOGY

An exploratory study was undertaken to determine some reasons why people shop. Individual in-depth interviews were conducted in the Los Angeles area with a convenience sample of 30 people, divided evenly between men and women. Ages of respondents ranged from 20 to 47. Rather than a direct approach in questioning subjects as to why they shop, respondents were asked to recall their most recent shopping trips (of any type), to discuss their activities while shopping, and what they enjoyed about the trip. After considerable probing along these lines, the discussion narrowed to how various types of shopping differed, the subject's preferences for these different types, and his or her reasons.

From the list of reported shopping activities and satisfactions, the author categorized the responses into a number of hypothesized motives for shopping, classified (ex post) as either personal or social. While exploratory research results can be evaluated only on the basis of face validity, some of these motives for shopping have been identified in previous studies. A number of these motives do not relate to purchasing interest.

## HYPOTHESIZED MOTIVES FOR SHOPPING

### Personal Motives

**Role Playing** Many activities are learned behaviors, traditionally expected or accepted as part of a certain position or role in society—mother, housewife, husband, or student. A person internalizes these behaviors as "required" and is motivated to participate in the expected activities. For example, grocery shopping is a customary activity of the housewife. Attempts to eliminate "food shopping" through home delivery and telephone order have to date been relatively unsuccessful. Apparently, *the process* of grocery shopping has positive utility for a large segment of women who view it as an integral part of their role.

**Diversion** Shopping can offer an opportunity for diversion from the routine of daily life and thus represents a form of recreation. It can provide free family entertainment which is available without the necessity of formal dress or preplanning. The common term "browsing" and the phenomenon of masses strolling through shopping centers reinforce the belief that shopping is a national pastime. Indoor shopping malls are in an advantageous position to encourage this activity through exhibits and other traffic-generating attractions that appeal to various family members.

**Self-gratification** Different emotional states or moods may be relevant for explaining why (and when) someone goes shopping. For example, a person may go to a store in search of diversion when he is bored or go in search of social contact when he feels lonely. Likewise, he may go to a store to buy "something nice" for himself when he is depressed. Several subjects in this study reported that often they alleviate depression by simply spending money on themselves. In this case, the shopping trip is motivated not by the expected utility of consuming, but by the utility of the buying *process* itself.

**Learning about New Trends** Products are intimately entwined in one's daily activities and often serve as symbols reflecting attitudes and life styles. An individual learns about trends and movements and the symbols that support them when he visits a store. Rich and Portis found that among department and discount store shoppers in New York and Cleveland, 30% said "seeing new items and getting new ideas" was the reason they enjoyed shopping.[5] Many people are interested in keeping informed about the latest trends in fashion, styling, or product innovations. While such learning may take place with or without a purchase, a certain segment of shoppers for each product category is more prone to buying new items. Stores which are trend-conscious may appeal to these innovators.[6]

**Physical Activity** An urban environment characterized by mass transportation and freeway driving provides little opportunity for individuals to exercise at a leisurely pace. Shopping can provide people with a considerable amount of exercise. Many retailers attempt to minimize the walking distance on their premises believing that shoppers perceive it to be an inconvenience. However, some shoppers apparently welcome the chance to walk in centers and malls that have been designed with internal thruways.

**Sensory Stimulation** Retail institutions provide many potential sensory benefits for shoppers. Customers browse through a store looking at the merchandise and at each other; they enjoy handling the merchandise, and are either trying it on or trying it out. Sound can also be important, since a "noisy" environment creates a different image than one which is characterized by silence or soft background music. Even scent may be relevant; for instance, stores may possess a distinctive odor of perfume or of prepared food. Structured surveys that attempt to measure why people shop may not detect such influences since shoppers infrequently recall these stimuli in a top-of-mind response. Nevertheless, the gestalt of the shopping environment may influence a consumer's decision to shop in a specific store or mall.

### Social Motives

**Social Experiences outside the Home** The marketplace has traditionally been a center of social activity. In a number of underdeveloped countries, the market still serves as a gathering place for a town's inhabitants. Many parts of the United States still have "market days," "county fairs," and "town squares" that offer a time and place for social interaction. In urban environments contemporary equivalents exist in sidewalk sales, auctions, and swap meets. In general, shopping can provide the opportunity for a social experience outside the home (e.g., seeking new acquaintances or meeting those of the opposite sex). Some shopping trips may result in direct encounters with friends (e.g., neighborhood women at a supermarket); on others the social contrast may be more indirect, as exemplified by the pastime of "people watching."

**Communication with Others Having a Similar Interest** Common interests are a major link in stimulating communication and association between individuals. Many hobbies center around products or services, such as boating, collecting stamps, car customizing, and home decorating. Stores that offer hobby-related goods serve as a focal point for people with similar interests to interact. People like to talk with others about their interests, and sales personnel are frequently sought to provide special information concerning the activity.

[5]Stuart V. Rich and Bernard Portis, "Clues for Action from Shopper Preferences," *Harvard Business Review*, Vol. 41 (March–April, 1963), p. 147.

[6]See Thomas S. Robertson, *Innovative Behavior and Communication* (New York: Holt, Rinehart, and Winston, Inc., 1971).

**Peer Group Attraction** The patronage of a store sometimes reflects a desire to be with one's peer group or a reference group to which one aspires to belong. For instance, record stores are common "hangouts" for teen-agers. Such stores provide a meeting place where members of a peer group may gather. This "shopping" attraction is not necessarily related to the motive of common interest since the gathering spot tends to change over time; in many cases the shopper may have limited interest in the product category and little intention to make a purchase. However, if group status is associated with one's knowledge of the category and nature of holdings (e.g., size of record collection), then peer group influence may motivate the person to "develop" an interest in the product.

**Status and Authority** Many shopping experiences provide the opportunity for an individual to command attention and respect. In few other activities can a person expect to be "waited on" without having to pay for this service. A person can attain a feeling of status and power in this limited "master-servant' relationship. The general concept of a store is an institution which *serves* the public.

Store personnel compete for the buyer's favor, especially in lines of merchandise where comparison shopping is likely (e.g., expensive clothes, durables). In such instances, shopping can be more enjoyable than buying. For some customers the enjoyment of this sense of power may considerably delay a purchase decision since it terminates the attention they are receiving.

**Pleasure of Bargaining** For many shoppers, bargaining is a degrading activity; haggling implies that one is "cheap." Others, however, appear to enjoy the process believing that with bargaining goods can be reduced to a more reasonable price.

In addition to this competition between buyer and seller, there also appears to be an implicit competition that occurs between buyers—a type of ego-centered buyer competition. An individual prides himself in his ability to make wise purchases or to obtain bargains.

In a face-to-face exchange with flexible prices, a perceived bargain would result when the buyer believes he has paid less for a product than others will have to pay the seller for the same merchandise. The presence of "fixed" labeled prices prevents the buyer from deriving satisfaction in this manner. To the extent that a person perceives himself as a wise shopper, he will seek bargains in fixed-price situations by looking at relative prices between stores (comparison shopping) or relative prices over time (special sales).

## IMPULSE SHOPPING

If the shopping motive is a function of only the buying motive, the decision to shop will occur when a person's need for particular goods becomes sufficiently strong for him to allocate time, money, and effort to visit a store. However, the multiplicity of hypothesized shopping motives suggests that a person may also go shopping when he needs attention, wants to be with peers, desires to meet people with similar interests, feels a need to exercise, or has leisure time. The foregoing discussion indicates that a person experiences a need and recognizes that shopping activities may satisfy that need. Yet, retailers often observe that not all of their customers' behavior is so well planned. In the same way that a person may walk down an aisle viewing merchandise and buying on impulse, he may also drive or walk down a street viewing stores and deciding to enter on impulse.

The likelihood of going shopping on impulse has probably increased over time with changes in the concept of convenience. Gravitationalists[7] and behaviorists[8] have traditionally evaluated a store's attraction power in terms of the number of potential customers within a given radius of a store, or from the viewpoint of the customer's convenience, distance (or time) traveled from his home to that store. However, Robarts suggests that a number of nonretail spatial attractors may also influence a shopper's store patronage decision: e.g., employment, social, religious, education, club, or recreational activities.[9] Thus, shopping convenience would be determined by "the spatial juxtapositions of the greatest number of retail and non-retail attractors."[10] Since many people spend relatively little time at home, a definition of convenience which uses the home as the focal point may be misleading. The existence of modern transportation and the availability of increasing amounts of discretionary time serve to expose people to many shopping clusters while in transit to their job, or social and recreational activities. This mobility increases exposure to new shopping alternatives and enhances opportunities for impulse shopping. The sight of a store may serve as a reminder to purchase needed items. On the other hand, impulse shopping may be prompted by one of the motives identified above with no planned purchase intended.

## SUMMARY AND IMPLICATIONS

It is important to recognize the distinction between the activities of shopping, buying, and consuming and to understand the behavioral determinants of each. A unified theory of shopper behavior does not presently exist. This exploratory study has sought to advance the development of such a theory by identifying a number of hypotheses concerning why people shop. Future research should attempt to quantify the relative importance of these motives (and others that might be discovered) for different types of shopping trips and within different defined shopper segments. If the findings reported here are verified, there are substantial implications for retail management.

If the shopping process offers benefits other than exposure to products, then retail innovations that attempt to reduce "shopping effort" (vending machines, mail order, or home delivery) may have a dim future for some product categories. Automatic vending of convenience goods, especially confectionary items and cigarettes, has had notable success, but efforts to market presold grocery items in this manner have not been successful.[11] In addition, in-home shopping by telephone or mail has never captured a large percentage of retail sales.

Retailers may find that these hypothesized shopping motives offer additional opportunities for market segmentation and store differentiation. Accord-

[7]See P. D. Converse, "New Laws of Retail Gravitation," *Journal of Marketing*, Vol. 14 (October, 1949), pp. 379-384.

[8]See David L. Huff, "Defining and Estimating a Trading Area," *Journal of Marketing*, Vol. 28 (July, 1964), pp. 34-38

[9]A. O. Robarts, "A Revised Look at Selected Determinants of Consumer Spatial Behavior," in *Proceedings*, Thirteenth Annual Conference, Association of Canadian Schools of Business (Summer, 1969).

[10]Same reference as footnote 9, p. 219

[11]See Charles R. Goeldner, "Automatic Selling, Will It Work," *Journal of Retailing*, Vol. 38 (Summer, 1962), pp. 41-46, 51-52

ing to Haley, "the benefits which people are seeking in consuming a given product are the basic reasons for the existence of true market segments."[12] Darden and Reynolds found significant differences in customer shopping orientation, verifying Stone's contention that some shoppers are largely concerned with buying (economic shopper), while others are more concerned with socializing (personalizing shopper).[13] Thus, shopper segments may be distinguished by their preferences for the alternative benefits they obtain from shopping.

In the search for differential advantage, product-related store benefits such as quality lines, low prices, and credit can be easily duplicated by the competition. To some extent, even new store locations can be matched by competitors establishing nearby branches. In the future, the ability to gain a distinct differential advantage may depend on catering to shopping motives that are not product related.

Levitt and others have urged firms to broadly define their business from the standpoint of the consumer benefits it provides.[14] Product-oriented retailers would probably define their business as "retail distribution," and emphasize the promotion and distribution of goods. However, the list of shopping motives identified above might suggest that many retailers would benefit by defining their business as being part of the social-recreational industry. As businesses which offer social and recreational appeal, retailers must acknowledge that they are competing directly for the consumer's time and money with other alternatives that provide similar benefits.

Reading 13

# It's Time to Cut Down on Advertising Waste

**Philip Kotler**
**Fred C. Allvine**
**Paul N. Bloom**

*The most drastic approach would be to nationalize culprit industries, reduce the number of brands in competition, and restrict advertising to largely informational purposes.*

A fundamental public policy question of the 1970s may well be: "Does advertising cost too much?" Like its 1930s cousin, "Does distribution cost too much?" it represents another point of concern about the marketing efficiency of an advanced industrial society.

[12]R. Haley, "Benefit Segmentation: A Decision-oriented Research Tool," *Journal of Marketing*, Vol. 32 (July, 1968), p. 31

[13]William Darden and Fred Reynolds, "Shopping Orientations and Product Usage Rates," *Journal of Marketing Research*, Vol. VIII (November, 1971), pp. 505–508; and G. Stone, "City Shoppers and Urban Identification: Observations on the Social Psychology of City Life," *The American Journal of Sociology* (July, 1954).

[14]Theodore Levitt, *Innovation in Marketing: New Perspectives for Profit and Growth* (New York: McGraw-Hill Book Company, 1962); and Peter F. Drucker, "What Is Business?" in *The Practice of Management* (New York: Harper and Row, Inc., 1954).

From *Business and Society Review/Innovation, Winter 72/73, no. 4., pp. 9–18.*

The question in the thirties was whether the wholesale-retail structure and margins of middlemen unduly increased costs to consumers. The question in the seventies is whether the substantial expenditures of business on advertising are all in the public interest. Has advertising become a social expense that produces not economic growth but simply shifts in brand shares that lead to very little overall gain for consumers?

Current annual advertising expenditures in the United States amount to $20 billion, or approximately 2 percent of the gross national product. If we add the $5-$10 billion spent on consumer and trade promotion, the total cost of informing and persuading buyers may well amount to 3 percent of GNP. Thus the consumer apparently pays about three cents on the dollar to support the cost of obtaining product information and promotion. This would not seem too excessive.

However, this figure conceals the high level of expenditures on advertising and sales promotion for particular consumer products and brands. Products which exhibit a high advertising-sales ratio include soaps (11%), perfumes and cosmetics (11%), and drugs (10%). Certain companies in these fields invest a considerable percentage of their sales revenue in advertising: J.B. Williams (36%-); Block Drug (30%); Noxel Corp. (30%); and Colgate-Palmolive (22%). Many brands of toiletries, cleaning agents, and cold remedies are essentially made up of a few pennies of ingredients, a few more pennies of packaging, and many pennies of advertising per unit sold. When it comes to launching a new consumer product nationally, a major company may budget $10 to $20 million for advertising and sales promotion alone in the first several months. This expenditure level is clearly out of the reach of smaller firms and leads to one frequent criticism of advertising—that it might constitute an absolute cost barrier to entry.

The issue of whether advertising costs too much is compounded by a host of other issues posed by critics of advertising, such as charges of manipulation, cultural pollution, and excessive materialism. It is no wonder that various watchdog measures exist and new proposals have recently emerged directed toward the regulation of advertising as a force in American life. The Wheeler-Lea Act of 1938 empowered the Federal Trade Commission to investigate cases of "unfair or deceptive acts or practices," thus laying the basis for governmental action in the area of false or misleading advertising. The Federal Communications Commission can regulate the amount of commercial minutes offered by broadcasters so that it does not become excessive. The Federal Trade Commission has recently sought power for affirmative disclosure (requiring advertisers to disclose negative as well as positive features of their product), substantiation (requiring advertisers to provide evidence for their positive claims), corrective advertising (requiring advertisers who are guilty of misrepresentation to develop and broadcast corrective advertising), and counteradvertising (permitting critics of a product to broadcast counterinformation). Clearly the question of regulating the content of advertising is reaching a quick boil.

Proposals to regulate the quantity of advertising expenditure have also appeared, although no proposal has yet received broad consideration and widespread backing. Consumer advocates such as Ralph Nader, some government trustbusters such as then assistant attorney general Donald F. Turner, and some respected economists such as Lee E. Preston and Leonard W. Weiss have recommended or raised the issue of direct regulation of advertising expenditures. This would add a new form of regulation to other measures designed to preserve competition such as limitations on price discrimination, exclusive dealing, and mergers and acquisitions. Furthermore, it would differ from previous efforts at advertising regulation that have dealt with the *content* of advertising rather than its quantity. It is time to evaluate various proposals for direct regulation of advertising expenditures.

In examining the merits of direct regulation, it must be remembered that direct regulation is only one of six possible means of attempting to discourage or reduce advertising.

## THE DIFFERENT APPROACHES

The most drastic approach would be to nationalize culprit industries, reduce the number of brands in competition, and restrict advertising to largely informational purposes. A less extreme measure would be to establish a regulatory agency (as in the case of utilities) with power to influence or control prices, marketing expenditures, and profits. A still less extreme approach would be structural reform in which a culprit industry is reorganized to make it more competitive, through such actions as divestiture of subsidiaries or of certain brands, and/or government assistance to smaller firms. Structural reform is the classic solution of antitrusters. Then there is industry self-regulation in which the companies in an industry undertake, with the explicit or implicit consent of the government, to reduce their promotional expenditures according to some scheme on which they can all agree and which satisfies the public interest. Finally, the mildest approach is consumer education whereby it is hoped that by supplying consumers with more factual information about products and product values, they will be less susceptible to "psychological appeals" and much current advertising would lose its impact.

While direct regulation may well outdo these other five approaches as the most effective overall means of limiting advertising, the other approaches also have value. It will be seen that different industries require different approaches.

As for direct regulation itself, there are four possible forms, each with particular advantages and disadvantages:

1. Direct limitation on advertising expenditures;
2. Economic penalties for advertising;
3. Economic incentives for reduced advertising; and
4. Reduced access to the media.

Each proposal is worth examining in detail.

## DIRECT LIMITATION ON ADVERTISING EXPENDITURES

The most direct way of regulating advertising expenditure is to establish a ceiling on absolute dollar expenditures, advertising expenditure increases, advertising-sales ratios, or some other variable. Specifically, three alternative types of limitation are possible.

The first is an advertising freeze, in which companies are not allowed to spend more (in absolute or percentage terms) than they are currently spending on advertising. To leave some flexibility, advertising expenditures may be frozen as a total for the company rather than by product line or brand. The second is an advertising growth ceiling in which companies are allowed to increase their annual advertising budget up to a certain amount or percentage. For example, companies may not be allowed to increase their advertising budgets by more than 2 percent a year. The third is an advertising reduction in which companies are required to trim advertising budgets by a specified amount or percent a year. For example, companies may be required to cut their advertising budget by at least 2 percent a year.

It is hard to conceive of circumstances that might justify any of these forms of direct limitation as a permanent measure across all industries. Take an advertising freeze, for example. Like a price freeze or a wage freeze, an advertising freeze could only be conceived as a temporary measure to meet a particular crisis. Suppose national advertising expenditures suddenly increased at a rate of 20 percent a year, mainly taking the form of internecine competition over market share rather than market growth. Suppose further that all participants were paying dearly but none could unilaterally avoid matching competitive levels of advertising. In this situation, a state of emergency, so to speak, might be declared and a ceiling placed on advertising expenditures.

All kinds of distortions could be expected during the period when such an advertising freeze was in effect. Companies launching new products would have to draw advertising funds away from their established products. They might increase other promotional expenditures, which would not be limited by law, but which are less effective than advertising. Small companies beginning to make inroads on a large competitor would suddenly find themselves unable to spend more money on advertising. Companies that would want to cut their advertising expenditures (perhaps because of overdemand) might not for fear that they could not increase their advertising expenditures later if needed.

If, instead of an advertising freeze, advertising was allowed to rise (or required to fall) by a certain amount or rate a year, further inequities would rise. If the regulated variable was advertising dollars, a small company could increase its budget by the same number of dollars as a company many times its size, a situation which might bring forth cries of inequity from the large companies. On the other hand, consider what would happen if the regulated variable was a percentage. If, for example, companies were allowed to increase their advertising expenditures by up to 2 percent, a company spending $10 million a year could spend another $200,000 but a company spending $1 million a year could only spend another $20,000. The large company could buy ten times as much additional advertising exposure as the smaller firm.

These economic objections to a limitation on advertising expenditures are substantial enough to warrant avoiding it as an across-the-board solution for all industries. On the other hand, it may make sense for the government to apply direct limitation under certain conditions in a specific industry. Consider an industry that is caught up in an escalating advertising war which does not affect primary demand but only brand demand. Assume that each company will match increases in competitors' expenditures but not decreases. If any competitor raises his advertising expenditures, the others will follow; but if anyone lowers his advertising expenditures, no one else would follow. Soon all the competitors will be saddled with high costs but would be prevented from stopping the advertising arms race because of the law against collusion! Into such an impasse the government might step and freeze advertising expenditures, thus bringing relief to the industry. This scenario is not unlike the actual experience of the cigarette industry in which advertising budgets kept growing until the government stepped in and ruled that after January 1, 1971, cigarette companies could no longer advertise on television, thus ending a very expensive contest and restoring healthy profits to the industry.

But even in this case, there may be less drastic solutions than placing a direct limit on total advertising. The use of economic disincentives or incentives, industry self-regulation, and consumer education may be more feasible. We would conclude that direct limitation of advertising expenditures should not normally be used as a first line of defense against advertising inflation.

## ECONOMIC PENALTIES

"Excessive" advertising expenditures may be effectively discouraged through the creation of economic disincentives. Companies remain free to spend what they wish on advertising but pay a price for doing this.

Economic disincentives can take two basic forms. The first in an advertising tax. A tax can be placed on all advertising expenditures or on advertising expenditures above a certain amount or percentage. Furthermore, the tax can be a straight tax or a progressive tax. The latter would fall harder on the larger advertisers. An argument advanced for a progressive tax is that large advertisers enjoy volume discounts, which give them a competitive advantage over small advertisers; the progressive tax would offset this advantage and make the contest over market share more clearly equal between the larger and smaller firms. Regardless of the features of the tax, it is interesting to note that several states in the United States and a few foreign countries have, or have considered, taxes on advertising. More interesting is the fact that their intention has been primarily to raise revenue, not to discourage "excessive" advertising.

The second form of economic disincentive is an income tax disallowance. At present in the United States, all advertising expenditure is treated as a current expense against sales revenue. Consequently, company profits are reduced exactly by the amount spent on advertising. Thus advertising expenditures cost a firm only 50 cents instead of a dollar because of the 50 percent tax on corporate income. This has led to the suggestion that the income tax treatment of advertising expense be tightened up. An extreme proposal is to disallow advertising altogether as a tax-deductible expense. This would be an unprecedented treatment of a normal business expense, placing it in the category of dividends or charitable contributions which come out of profits. A more modest proposal is to allow companies to expense only part of their current advertising expenditures. The underlying argument is that advertising expenditures build up an asset known as goodwill. This asset depreciates at a certain rate each year and this should be allowed as the expense portion of the expenditure. Goodwill depreciation is assumed to be less than normal annual advertising expenditures because of the carryover effect of these expenditures. The result of this tax treatment would be an increase in reported profits and corporate taxes. This type of proposal has already been enacted in Mexico, where advertisers are only allowed to deduct 60 percent of a year's advertising expenditures in that year, 15 percent in each of the next two years, and the final 10 percent in the fourth year.

Either form of economic disincentive—the advertising tax or the income tax disallowance—would probably have to be enacted on all all-industry basis. It would be hard to imagine requiring the detergent industry to pay a tax on advertising but not the auto industry. Such treatment would be declared unconstitutional as discriminatory legislation. It is more conceivable that the economic disincentive could apply to all industries but be varied by industry in the case of, say, a depreciation requirement. The depreciation rate for an industry would depend on how much advertising it devoted to long-run image building (a lower rate of depreciation) versus stimulating immediate sales (a higher rate of depreciation.)

Certain undesirable economic consequences could be expected as a result of penalizing advertising expenditures. First, there would be a tendency of companies to switch funds to nonregulated forms of promotion—such as games, trading stamps, consumer and trade deals. Presumably these other forms of promotion are less efficient or they would have already been freely adopted by the company. This will increase the cost of doing business. The nonregulated forms of promotion may increase in usage so much as to lead to proposals to expand the promotional coverage of the legislation. Horrendous definitional problems would be faced as to which expenditures are promotional. Are expenditures on a sales force promotional? If so, companies would be penalized for expanding their sales force. How much of packaging is promotional? Are trade show exhibitions, catalogs, business cards, stationery, and office landscaping promotional? The fact is that the modern company builds some promotion into almost everything it does and it would be extremely hard to draw such a line.

Second, an advertising tax would discriminate against companies which are advertising-intensive rather than sales force-intenseive. Take the two cosmetic manufacturers, Avon and Revlon. Avon relies almost exclusively on door-to-door sales to sell its products and has built a $760 million business. Revlon depends chiefly on mass media advertising and has built a $370 million business. A tax on advertising would severely discriminate against Revlon in this industry. This example could be multiplied a thousandfold, a fact which accounts for some of the strong resistance to the use of economic disincentives.

Third, corporations rarely end up as the actual payers of taxes. Instead, they shift part of the tax backward to suppliers and forward to consumers. The extent and direction of these shifts depend on the elasticities of demand and supply and the amount of competition. Some increase in prices to consumers could be expected, another weakness of economic disincentive proposals. In sum, economic disincentives are not normally the most desirable approach for discouraging "excessive" advertising expenditures.

## ECONOMIC INCENTIVES

Economic incentives to encourage the reduction of advertising are another possibility. No specific economic incentive schemes have been proposed to reduce advertising expenditures, although it is hard to conceive of possible proposals. For example, companies in an industry that manage to reduce their advertising expense in a particular year might be granted a tax credit equal to, say, half the reduced advertising expenditure. Or they might receive a special tax break if they manage to bring down their advertising expenses for a few years in a row.

Economic incentives, like economic disincentives, raise certain questions of efficiency and equity. Firms can be assumed to have a natural incentive to bring down the costs of advertising without requiring an added incentive. For every dollar they save that would have been wasted, they increase their profits by 50 cents. An extra incentive could conceivably tempt them to cut their advertising expenditures when they could productively increase them. That might lead to short-run gains and long-run losses. Those companies that cut their advertising expenditures for other reasons would receive an unnecessary reward under this proposal. In general, the establishment of economic incentives really does not seem to serve any purpose not already served by natural incentives.

## REDUCTION OF MEDIA AVAILABILITY

A fourth means of direct regulation would be government action to reduce the media time or space available to advertisers. An extreme form of this proposal would be the banning of certain products from some or all media. A precedent for this was the banning of cigarette commercials over television. There is talk about a similar television ban of commercials advertising alcoholic beverages and children's toys. Other media, such as newspapers, radio, magazines, and billboards might ban, or be asked to ban, certain products. But an outright media ban is apt to be prompted more by social and moral considerations related to the product than by concern over heavy advertising expenditures.

A less extreme form of regulation would be to require the media to reduce the time or space they allot to commercial messages. In many European countries, companies are allowed to advertise only during certain blocks of time on television and radio. The European television viewer is not subject to frequent commercial breaks that interrupt the continuity of programming. The result of reducing a particular medium's availability would be to push up the costs of using that medium and shift advertising to the less expensive media. Presumably this will decrease advertising efficiency, since advertisers would have made the shift freely had it been efficient. Furthermore, total advertising costs would not fall proportionately because of the higher levels of advertising costs per time or space unit. Companies that depended heavily on the "taxed" media would be harshly penalized and would probably bring suits charging discriminatory legislation. Under some circumstances, however, selective banning or reduction of allowable commercial time or space might be an effective answer to specific situations of excessive advertising.

Each of the four forms of direct regulation has a surprising number of potential dysfunctional consequences along with the intended goal of reducing advertising. Questions are raised about companies shifting their advertising funds into less productive promotional channels and media, the discriminatory impact of different measures on companies within an industry and between industries, the partial shift of the cost to the consumer, and the administrative costs of enforcement. What Gordon Tullock calls the high "social costs of reducing social cost" threatens to spoil attempts at all-encompassing regulation of advertising.

In short, it would make little sense to apply any of the approaches to direct regulation across-the-board to all industries because of these unwanted consequences. Nonetheless, some forms of direct regulations as well as some of the other broad approaches to limiting advertising mentioned earlier might be appropriate to specific industries. For example, it an industry's deficiency lay in providing inadequate information about its product, consumer education would be the appropriate remedy. An industry-by-industry rather than across-the-board approach is called for. The main need, therefore is for a means of identifying and ranking problem industries so that the worst offenders against the consumer could be singled out first by antitrust agencies.

## AUDITING MARKETING PERFORMANCE

Over the years, antitrusters have developed a set of structural, performance, and conduct criteria for identifying industries whose competitive performance may be questionable. The antitrusters' norm is the model of pure competition in which many companies are competing primarily on a price basis and without restriction as to output. Such a state of affairs should produce low prices, high output, and modest profits. Both consumers and firms would have high information and high mobility and this would prevent prices and profits from staying high for very long. The role of the government is to preserve and abet these conditions by breaking up barriers to entry and encouraging the free and full flow of information. The major beneficiary of the government's watchdog role is presumably the consumer.

Unfortunately, this view of the trustbuster's job and of the economic scene is somewhat archaic. It made a great deal of sense when people lacked the necessities of life and it was important to increase output and keep prices as low as possible. But the economy has become transformed into one of goods abundance with the key emphasis on goods variety to satisfy the desires of different market segments. Desires exist for products not only at various price levels but also with various features, styles, qualities, and benefits. Price has become only one consideration, and not normally the most important, in the buying decision of consumers. All the emphasis on price competition in antitrust circles seems to be the sign of a cultural lag in adjusting to new consumer conditions.

What then is the appropriate model for examining whether an industry is serving the interests of the modern consumer and how does advertising fit in? Our basic assumption is that an industry is serving its customers well when it develops product offerings for the major market segments at reasonable prices. By a major market segment we mean any sizable distinct group of potential customers seeking a particular value, or configuration of values, from a product class. In every market, there may be a "low-price segment," that is, a group of customers seeking a low-price version of the product without frills or built-in services. There may be a "salutory segment," that is, a group of customers seeking health and/or safety values in the product. There may be segments seeking a particular feature, convenience, style, or benefit from the product.

Many industries fall into a state of designing a product offering mainly geared to the majority segment. All the firms in the industry decide independently to go after the modal buyer, with the result that the modal buyer faces numerous brand choices while minority buyers find little or no product offering matched to their desires. There are examples aplenty. For years American automobile manufacturers offered only large cars to the American public; and it was only the availability of foreign cars that allowed the compact-car-buyer segment to achieve any satisfaction. American television networks tend to all go after the modal viewer during prime time, with the result that the modal viewer is frustrated by a large choice of fare, while the minority viewer cannot find any programs to his liking. The large oil companies charge the same for gasoline, and the low-price-gas seekers are served only by the independent stations and chains which charge a few cents less per gallon. The independents are under constant attack by the major companies because of the threat they pose to the uniform price structures. Even with such products as breakfast cereals and detergents, where brands proliferate, consumers are usually forced to pay for a highly advertised brand because little is offered in the way of a low-price, low-promoted alternative.

## QUESTIONS TO BE ANSWERED

Thus the first question to ask in a marketing performance audit of an industry is:

**1** *Are there adequate product offers for each major price and taste segment of the market?*

If firms shun the low-price segment of the market or some important taste segment and offer primarily heavily promoted, high-priced products, then the "marketing system" is failing to function properly since important segments of the market are not being served.

When this condition is found in a particular industry, there are two possible remedies. The most direct is to require existing companies to introduce a product version of the type missing from the marketplace. For example, the British Monopolies Commission required detergent manufacturers to introduce a similar quality, low-priced, low-promoted brand of detergent to satisfy the segment of the market that wanted such a brand. Thus there was no direct regulation of their advertising, but the hope was that consumers would find the low- and the high-priced brands comparable and switch to the former, thus reducing the magnitude and effectiveness of advertising. This solution is an intriguing one, although it raises difficult questions with respect to getting shelf space for the low-promoted brand and making sure, through policing, that it is equivalent to the high-price brand.

A less direct solution is breaking up existing companies or assisting new companies to enter the industry in the hope that some of them would freely move toward the undersatisfied segments of the market. Unfortunately, this movement is not inevitable. The addition of a few companies may bring down everyone's profits or bring down prices but may not lead to the creation of new product offerings for those who are neglected. Or this may take place but at a high cost to the financial health and economic efficiency of the industry. Yet structural reform is the major solution advocated by most antitrusters.

Suppose an industry satisfies this first criterion. Is it then free of consumer-oriented criticism? We would recommend a second criterion be reviewed.

**2** *Are consumers provided with relatively full information about the offer?*

It is conceivable that an industry provides adequate product offers for the major market segments but information is poor or misleading, leading to inefficient buying and a consequent loss in consumer welfare. Examples of this situation abound. Consumers continue to pay 50 to 100 percent more for highly advertised brands of aspirin because they have been led to believe the quality is better. One might argue that they are buying "confidence" and they find this premium worth paying. Nevertheless, if the brands are equal in quality, this fact should be disseminated. Consumers are poorly educated as to recognizing quality differences in clothes, appliances, and many other products. Studies show that consumers, in their lack of information, often take price to be an indicator of quality, and will pay more for identical items because of price differences, labels, or fancy packaging.

What can be done about markets lacking relatively full information? There are two general approaches. The first is to require or encourage manufacturers and retailers to provide more information to the consumer. There is a whole history of legislation and regulation in this area related to specific industries. Pure Food and Drug Act (1906, 1938, 1958), Wool Products Labeling Act (1939), Flammable Fabric Act (1953), Automobile Information Disclosure Act (1958), Fair Packaging and Labeling Act (1966), Federal Cigarette Labeling and Advertising Act (1967), and Consumer Credit Protection Act (1968). Recently, some retailers have been freely supplying more information to their customers by such means as unit-pricing, ingredient labeling, nutritional labeling, open dating (dating the freshness of a product), and so on. To the extent that these steps are taken voluntarily, there is less likelihood of new laws being passed.

The other approach available to the government is to take an active role in supplying consumer information or supporting established organizations, such as Consumer Union, which do. Ralph Nader and others have proposed that the government publish its evaluations of various brands reviewed in making selections for institutional purchasing. It has also been suggested that the government allot more funds to private consumer organizations for testing consumer products and reporting results. Still another suggestion is that public schools offer more courses in consumer education to prepare people to buy more intelligently.

Suppose an industry has product offerings for the major market segments and the major segments know about them and their characteristics. Is this industry then to be exempt from public criticism? There is another shortcoming which might exist: Are the industry's costs higher than they have to be? We are not talking about the case of inefficient companies which presumably will be eliminated by more efficient competitors. Rather, we are concerned about situations in which the whole industry accepts a good deal of social overhead and consumers end up paying the bill. This is, for example, a perennial problem in regulated industries. Since a public utility is entitled to a certain return on its investment, it can be looser with costs because the regulatory commissions will allow them rates to cover their costs. In competitive industries, the same phenomenon can happen when all the firms tacitly accept higher costs. One of these higher costs may be advertising, as when all competitors spend millions of dollars to create images for their brands, although the basic product is essentially a commodity. Most people cannot tell the difference, when blindfolded, between major brands of coffee, beer, or cigarettes, let alone sugar, salt, flour, and so on; yet millions of dollars are spent to create psychological differentiation. Consumers wind up paying for these costs, and the question is whether these costs are too high a price to pay. The possible negative impact of this advertising in manifold: It creates brand monopolies; leads to commercial clutter; exaggerates and distorts product facts; deepens materialistic outlooks; and causes higher prices. So the third criterion that we would suggest in evaluating industries from a consumer perspective is:

**3** *Are advertising costs reasonable in relation to the commodity status of the industry?*

Admittedly, this criterion must be refined and made operational before it can be of practical use. Products can be considered commodities if either their objective characteristics are identical or consumers cannot distinguish them when identifying marks are missing. For such products, the government may want to consider advertising costs as excessive when advertising/sales ratios exceed a certain level (somewhat arbitrarily determined). For such industries, many of the remedies discussed earlier may apply, such as direct limitation or regulation of advertising expenditures, media limitation or banning, industry self-regulation, and/or consumer education. As for structural reform, it is not clear that increasing the number of companies in the industry will bring down the level of advertising expenditure; if anything, it might increase the amount.

Even when an industry is satisfying consumer wants, supplying relatively full information, and not indulging in high cost practices, there is a further test of whether it is satisfactorily serving the customer's interests. The question should be asked:

**4** *Are rates of return in the industry competitive?*

Certain industries may stand out as enjoying above-average profits for a long period of time. There may be different explanations for this, some quite acceptable. The industry may have an unusual record of innovation, in which case high profits are a legitimate reward to a progressive industry. The industry may face unusually high risks, in which case high profits may be a legitimate return to cover the risks. Finally, the industry may be characterized by high barriers to entry, either in the form of high absolute cost barriers (the high cost of advertising, capital equipment, technology, etc.) or collusive barriers. In this case, the high profits are not legitimate and are an unjust tax on the consumers. Here the government may give strong consideration to measures that would reduce the barriers to entry, such as structural reform, or, if this is not feasible, to direct regulation of the industry.

If an industry emerged with a clean bill of health on these four criteria, there appears little reason to investigate it. The only remaining question is whether the industry will stay healthy or whether there are incipient trends that do not augur well for the future performance of the industry. So a fifth and final question should be asked:

**5** *Is the industry free of incipient trends toward monopoly?*

There is a widespread feeling in antitrust circles that the time to intervene in an industry is not when it has become an established monopoly but rather when the first signs appear. Underlying the incipience philosophy is the idea that the public will be saved the costs of the monopoly state and also the mammoth cost of trying to restore competition. As a result, there is a search for early indicators of future monopoly, such as increasing concentration, unduly rising prices, accelerating promotional expenditures, product line proliferation, declining innovation, or increasing vertical integration. All of these signs have to be operationally defined to make this fifth and final criterion usable.

## A RATING TECHNIQUE

Taken together, these five criteria provide a technique to identify and rank problem industries from a consumer perspective. The technique is shown in the table along with illustrative ratings of several consumer industries. The criteria are listed in rows and industries are listed in columns. An industry is assigned a 2 if it fully satisfies a suggested criterion; 1 if it partly satisfies the criterion; and 0 if it fails to satisfy the criterion. We will assume that all criteria have equal importance, although this can be modified. Since there are five questions, an examplary industry would receive a score of 10 and a poorly performing industry would receive a score of zero. Scores between zero and 10 suggest the rough level of marketing and social performance of the industry.

Using the subjective ratings of the authors, it appears that the bread industry performs well, while the aspirin, breakfast cereal, deodorant, and oil industries rank relatively low and should be, as some of them now are, logical candidates for government investigation of their marketing performance. For example, the breakfast cereal industry, currently under antitrust investigation, can be faulted for lacking low-price, low-promotion brands, and for having high advertising costs, high rates of return, and trends toward monopoly.

**Marketing Performance Audit of Several Consumer Industries**
(2 = Yes, 1 = Partially Yes, 0 = No)

| | Aspirin | Breakfast cereal | Deodorant | Oil | Automobile | Beer | Bread |
|---|---|---|---|---|---|---|---|
| **1** Are there adequate product offers? | 2 | 1 | 1 | 1 | 1 | 2 | 2 |
| **2** Are consumers given relatively full information? | 0 | 2 | 1 | 0 | 2 | 2 | 1 |
| **3** Are advertising costs reasonable? | 0 | 0 | 0 | 2 | 2 | 1 | 2 |
| **4** Are rates of return competitive? | 0 | 0 | 1 | 2 | 0 | 2 | 2 |
| **5** Are incipient monopoly trends absent? | 1 | 0 | 1 | 0 | 1 | 0 | 2 |
| | 3 | 3 | 4 | 5 | 6 | 7 | 9 |

While imperfect, this technique begins to point out the problem industries and the nature and seriousness of their deficiencies. The pattern of deficiencies in any given industry is usually unique and so requires measures tailored to it rather than application of gross, traditional antitrust remedies. As indicated earlier, each deficiency suggests one or more particular remedies: these might be some form of direct regulation or one of the other major approaches to limiting advertising outlined earlier, or a combination of measures. Hopefully, with further improvement and operationalization of these criteria, they can be employed to reveal the serious problem industries and to suggest the particular remedies that might bring about improvements in consumer welfare.

Reading 14

# FTC Makes Public Advertising Documentation Submitted by 11 Air Conditioner and 4 Electric Shaver Manufacturers

**FTC News**

*. . .substantiating documentation available to the public without comment . . . .*

The Federal Trade Commission announced today that the responses by 11 manufacturers of air conditioners and four manufacturers of electric shavers to the Commission's Order to File a Special Report, issued August 18, 1971, will be available for public inspection beginning Wednesday, February 16, at the FTC's Washington headquarters.

The responses will be available for public inspection at each of the Commission's 11 regional offices on Wednesday, February 23.

The responses represent the manufacturers' substantiation for advertising claims cited by the Commission in its order.

The manufacturers are:

***Air Conditioners***

Berg-Warner Corporation, Chicago, Ill.
Carrier Corporation, Syracuse, N.Y.
Chrysler Corporation, Highland Park, Mich.
City Investing Company, New York City
General Electric Company, New York City
McGraw-Edison Company, Elgin, Ill.
Raytheon Company, Lexington, Mass.
Trane Company, La Crosse, Wis.
Westinghouse Electric Corporation, Pittsburgh, Pa.
Whirlpool Corporation, Benton Harbor, Mich.
White Consolidated Industries, Cleveland, O.

***Electric Shavers***

North American Phillips Corporation, New York City
Schick Electric, Inc., Lancaster, Pa.
Sperry Rand Corporation, New York City
Sunbeam Corporation, Chicago, Ill.

Five copies of all documentation submitted by the manufacturers will be available for public inspection in Room 551 of the Commission Building, Sixth St. and Pennsylvania Ave., N.W., Washington, D.C., between the hours of 9 a.m. and 5 p.m. from Wednesday, February 16, through Tuesday, February 22. After that date the materials will be available in Room 130 of the Commission headquarters.

From *FTC News*, Washington, D.C., Feb. 15, 1972.

An index of the material submitted, containing the advertising claims, the FTC demand, and a listing of the substantiating documents has been prepared by the Commission staff and will be furnished, upon written request. The Commission will also provide, for the cost of reproduction, copies of the specific documents. Later, at a date to be announced, the documents may be purchased from the National Technical Information Service.

In issuing this announcement, the Commission emphasizes that it has not evaluated the material submitted in response to its Order. Rather, the Commission is simply making the substantiating documentation available to the public without comment, reserving the right to conduct investigations of the advertising claims if, upon future evaluation, the substantiating documents, or lack of them in particular cases, merit such action.

**Reading 15**

# FTC Order against Marketer of Cranberry Drink Provides for Corrective Ads; Bans False Claims

**FTC News**

*A violation of such an order may result in a civil penalty up to $5,000 per day being imposed upon the respondent.*

A consent order provisionally accepted by the Federal Trade Commission prohibits false nutritional claims by the manufacturer of Ocean Spray Cranberry Juice and contains a corrective advertising provision.

The agreed-to order cites Ocean Spray Cranberries, Inc., Hanson, Mass., and its advertising agency, Ted Bates & Co., Inc., 1515 Broadway, New York City.

The order requires that for a one-year period at least one out of every four advertisements for the product—or, alternatively, 25 percent of media expenditures (excluding production costs)—be devoted to the following advertising text:

> If you've wondered what some of our earlier advertising meant when we said Ocean Spray Cranberry Juice Cocktail has more food energy than orange juice or tomato juice, let us make it clear: we didn't mean vitamins and minerals. Food energy means calories. Nothing more.
>
> Food energy is important at breakfast since many of us may not get enough calories, or food energy, to get off to a good start. Ocean Spray Cranberry Juice Cocktail helps because it contains more food energy than most other breakfast drinks.
>
> And Ocean Spray Cranberry Juice Cocktail gives you and your family Vitamin C plus a great wake-up taste. It's . . . the other breakfast drink.

From FTC News, Washington, D.C., May 5, 1972.

Forbidden by the order are claims that any beverage made by Ocean Spray or, in the case of Ted Bates, any beverage which is advertised as a product made with cranberries:

- Contains as many or a greater variety or quantity of nutrients than orange or tomato juice or any other beverage, unless this is true. (This does not prohibit representations which merely propose using any such product in place of other beverages without assigning any nutritional reason).
- Has more "food energy" than any other beverage unless clear disclosure is made that this term refers to calories.
- Is a "juice" unless it consists entirely of natural or reconstituted single strength fruit juice with no water added. [This does not prohibit (1) the addition of any ingredient to sweeten, flavor, preserve, fortify with vitamins, minerals or other nutrients, or color, or the like, such fruit juice, (2) descriptions such as "juice cocktail" or "juice drink" connoting a diluted or modified single strength juice, or (3) any name approved by any federal agency having appropriate jurisdiction.]

The firms are charged in the complaint with falsely advertising that Ocean Spray Cranberry Juice Cocktail contains a greater variety and quantity of nutrients than orange or tomato juice, that it should be substituted for them at breakfast because it is more nutritious, and that it contains cranberry juice entirely.

The complaint and consent order will remain on the public record from May 5, 1972 through June 5, 1972. Comments from the public received during this period will become part of the public record. The FTC may withdraw its acceptance of the agreement after further consideration.

The consent order is for settlement purposes only and does not constitute an admission by the firms that they have violated the law. When issued by the Commission on a final basis, a consent order does carry the force of law with respect to future actions. A violation of such an order may result in a civil penalty up to $5,000 per day being imposed upon the respondent.

## Reading 16

# Commission Supports Counter-Advertising for Certain Types of Product Commercials

**FTC News**

*. . . licensees might make available on a regular basis five minute blocks of prime time for counter-advertisements . . . .*

The Federal Trade Commission announced today, in a statement submitted to the Federal Communications Commission, that it supports the concept of "counter-advertising", i.e., the right of access to the broadcast media for the purpose of expressing views and positions on controversial issues that are raised by commercial advertising.

From FTC News, Washington, D.C., 20580, Jan. 6, 1972.

The statement was submitted in response to the F.C.C.'s Notice of Inquiry concerning the Fairness Doctrine, particularly in response to Part III of the Inquiry, entitled "Access to the Broadcast Media as a result of Carriage of Product Commercials".

Counter-Advertising, in the F.T.C.'s view, would be an appropriate means of overcoming some of the shortcomings of the F.T.C.'s regulatory tools, and a suitable approach to some of the present failings of advertising which are now beyond the F.T.C.'s capacity. The Commission noted that certain identifiable kinds of advertising are particularly susceptible to, and particularly appropriate for, recognition and allowance of counter-advertising, because of characteristics that warrant some opportunity for challenge and debate. Identifiable categories, along with examples of each, are as follows:

- *Advertising asserting claims of product performance or characteristics that explicitly raise controversial issues of current public importance* Claims that products contribute to solving ecological problems, or that the advertiser is making special efforts to improve the environment generally.
- *Advertising stressing broad recurrent themes, affecting the purchase decision in a manner that implicitly raises controversial issues of current public importance* Food ads which may be *viewed as* encouraging poor nutritional habits, or detergent ads which may be viewed as contributing to water pollution.
- *Advertising claims that rest upon or rely upon scientific premises which are currently subject to controversy within the scientific community* Test-supported claims based on the opinions of some scientists but not others whose opposing views are based on different theories, different tests or studies, or doubts as to the validity of the tests used to support the opinions involved in the ad claims.
- *Advertising that is silent about negative aspects of the advertised product* Ad claims that a particular drug product cures various ailments when competing products with equivalent efficacy are available at substantially lower prices.

Stating that it is not essential that counter-advertising be presented in the 30 or 60 second spot format so frequently utilized for commercials, the FTC suggested that "licensees might make available on a regular basis five minute blocks of prime time for counter-advertisements directed at broad general issues raised by all advertising involving certain products, as a way of fulfilling this aspect of their public service responsibilities."

The Commission said it defers to the FCC concerning the precise methods of implementation, but urged that "the following points be embodied in any final plan:

**1** Adoption of rules that incorporate the guidelines expressed above, permitting effective access to the broadcast media for counter-advertisements. These rules should impose upon licensees an affirmative obligation to promote effective use of this expanded right of access.

**2** Open availability of one hundred percent of commercial time for anyone willing to pay the specified rates, regardless of whether the party seeking to buy the time wishes to advertise or 'counter' advertise. Given the great importance of product information, product sellers should not possess monopolistic control by licensees over the dissemination of such information, and licensees should not be permitted to discriminate against counter-advertisers willing to pay, solely on account of the content of their ideas.

3 Provision by licensees of a substantial amount of time, at no charge, for persons and groups that wish to respond to advertising like that described above but lack the funds to purchase available time slots. In light of the above discussion, it seems manifest that licensees should not limit access, for discussions of issues raised by product commercials, to those capable of meeting a price determined by the profitability of presenting one side of the issues involved. Providing such free access would greatly enhance the probability that advertising, a process largely made possible by licensees themselves, would fully and fairly contribute to a healthy American marketplace."

Reading 17

# FTC Challenges a Selling Method of Mail-Order Book, Record Clubs

**Morton C. Paulson**

*. . . negative options are "inherently unfair . . . ."*

Should the Government outlaw the method used by most book and record clubs to sell merchandise to members?

The Federal Trade Commission (FTC) has proposed a ban on the method, usually known as the "negative option." Under this method, a book club or other mail-order business notifies a customer that one or more items are available, and then ships the items to the person if he fails to return a card stating he's not interested. At hearings here last week, an FTC representative heard consumer-group spokesmen attack negative-option arrangements. Industry spokesmen defended them.

The FTC, in proposing the ban, said it believes that negative options are "inherently unfair" because they take advantage of customer forgetfulness, procrastination, or preoccupation.

The FTC also contends that negative options add to computerized-billing difficulties. A number of persons have complained that they were billed for items they failed to receive or did not order.

Sanford Cobb, president of the Association of American Publishers, Inc., told The National Observer that the elimination of negative options would be a "very serious" economic blow to book clubs and probably would put some out of business. He argues that book clubs foster intellectual development by offering discount prices and by making books readily available in areas not well served by bookstores. The negative option, he contends, is similar to banks' Christmas savings plans that pay no interest in that it imposes personal discipline, "which people are very willing to accept as a means of getting reading matter that they think they will want into their homes."

Couldn't the clubs do as well with positive options, under which nothing would be sent to members without an order? Mr. Cobb doesn't think so. "Mail-order experience indicates that the response, if there were an order card which had to be sent back to get the book, would be considerably lower."

From *The National Observer*, Nov. 11, 1970.

At the hearings, Robert R. Nathan testified as an economist for the publishers that book publishing is a "low-profit, high-risk" business in which "profits have declined progressively during the past three years." A survey of 70 publishers showed that book-club sales accounted for an average of 15 per cent of their income before income taxes in 1969. That percentage is "very significant" in view of the industry's thin profit margin, said Mr. Nathan.

Describing the negative option as "one of the cornerstones of our success," Warren Lynch, executive vice president of the 1,000,000-member Book-of-the-Month Club, Inc., said that the device is not used to exploit unwary customers, but rather to "keep unwanted merchandise *from* the subscriber" by giving him the opportunity to reject recommended books.

Some consumer-group spokesmen contend, however, that abolition of negative options would be in the public interest. "Clearly, deceptive, unreasonable practices make negative option the profitable success it appears to be only for companies—while at the same time unreasonably burdening unsuspecting consumers," said Doris E. Behre, president of the Virginia Citizens Consumer Council, Inc. "It is clear that business is capable of operating without negative option but chooses not to."

The Consumers Federation of America, the nation's largest congress of consumer organizations, did not present testimony, but the group favors the proposed FTC ban.

An alternative plan advanced by book and record sellers consists of a four-point voluntary code designed to modify or eliminate unfair selling practices. Subscribers to the code would agree to give their customers at least five days in which to make their choices. They would agree not to bill or dun a member for items he had returned, not received, or already paid for. And they would agree to make fuller disclosure of contractual terms.

# Money, Marital Happiness, and Democracy in Home Management

**Reading 18**

## Money Matters

**Gloria Guinness**

*Which would you rather have, love, health, or* money?

MONEY . . . .If I were ten years younger I would say love but just now I need a fur coat more than anything else" or "When I think of what that beast George is doing to me all I want is to have enough MONEY to get away from him." "Or the old girl who looked at me straight in the eye and said, "Don't you know that when poverty comes through the door love goes out the window?" Many complained about love and health being a rich man's privilege and more than one advised me to take my question to Elizabeth Taylor. Why Elizabeth Taylor? Because she has all three and it would be interesting to know which one she prefers.

Summing up their answers, I would say the MONEY came in the top winner, with love a good second and health a long way off. But to be fair, these were women who most probably had already had their good share of love during their lifetime and perhaps never enough money to satisfy their needs of fancies. They were also in what seemed to me magnificent health.

Then I went to the young. "How about it, what would you rather have, love, health or MONEY?" Most girls answered without hesitation, "Love." When asked why, the answer was uniform, love brings peace, liberty. No mention of sex or of men for that matter, which I found strangely depressing. So off I went to the young men. "Which would you rather have, love, health or MONEY?" Young men not being as quick as young girls took their time to answer, "Love? . . . Health? . . . MONEY? . . . I don't know, I guess none" or "Man, are you kidding? I only want to sing" or "That's my business" or "Why do you want to know? You think I go for acid?"

As you can see young men do not appreciate personal questions, so I went a step further back, to children. And that was lovely. The instant answer was "MONEY" and the reasons why, beautiful. "Well you see, my Mummy loves fast cars and my Daddy won't give her one, so if I had the money . . ." or "I would pay the dentist to take this brace away." "I could have my own television set." "I could buy clothes." "My Mummy has nothing to wear." "I want to have a dog of my own," said a little boy. "I want a horse," from a little girl. And from another little girl, "They always ask for MONEY when you go to Mass." And so it went

From *Harper's Bazaar.*

with money being the choice of most everyone, with the older people worried about admitting it, and the younger ones refusing to admit it and the little ones thrilled at the very thought of it. Thus, I came to the conclusion that MONEY is neither dirty nor evil. That money, to most people is a comfort, something to be thankful for. Something that we want all our lives, not only for ourselves, but mostly to keep others.

Reading 19

# Love and Money

**Eugenia Sheppard**

*It takes more courage to come out in favor of money.*

Once upon a time everybody wrote poems about love, but money has had lots more publicity lately.

Love is loaded with old-fashioned charm, but money, especially lots of money, is terribly contemporary.

Love is a fireplace with the logs blazing, but the fire sometimes goes out. Money is an air-conditioned house with great paintings on the wall and a Rolls Royce waiting at the door. It's also the instant plane ticket to get away from anybody or anything.

Love is a paper valentine, but money is a twenty-carat diamond, at the very least.

Love is a basic argument, but money is a circle of smiling faces that never say no.

Money used to be divided into old money and new money. Old money was tolerated as a kind of gift from heaven, but new money was frowned upon as vulgar.

Now, any kind of money gets by, and the only question asked is, "How much?" New money is no more brash than the psychedelic lights, the four-letter words, the slits, the see-throughs and the bosoms bursting out of décolletages in fashion.

It's an open secret to the rest of the world that American women are more pro-money than almost any of the others. They handle more money and more of them make it themselves. They are the world's most enthusiastic spenders.

When Frenchwomen get together the talk is still about their own or somebody else's loves or lovers. But with American women, the subject is the latest luxury or at least something with a price tag.

Most European men find American women too businesslike, even about love. From the preliminaries to the follow-through, they are as sure of what they want as if they had seen it in a catalogue and were ready to open their handbags and turn in the trading stamps.

When my grandmother really wanted to say no, she drove home the negative with "Not for love nor money." Even then she was admitting that love and money are equally powerful drives.

From *Harper's Bazaar*, February, 1969, pp. 91.

Frank as they are about most things, though, most women won't admit the power and importance of money in their lives.

Money is so important that it is easier to forgive a woman for being beautiful than for being rich. It's instinctive to be cruel to any woman who marries into lots of money. She couldn't possibly love him, could she?

Money is the thing. Money is modern. Money deserves the same kind of attention love has had, doesn't it? Why not even a special Money Day to balance St. Valentine's?

It sounds soulful to rave about love like the hippies and would-be hippies, who are actually air-borne through the world on other people's money.

It takes more courage to come out in favor of money.

Only a few brave women have ever spoken up candidly for money, and Mrs. Vincent Astor is the bravest. When a heckler at a meeting called out, "Hey there, Mrs. Astor, I hear you have lots of money," she smiled sweetly and answered, "Yes, isn't it nice?"

**Reading 20**

# A New Way to Prevent Arguments over Money

**Murray Teigh Bloom**

*"My mother taught me all the important things about money—like how to spend it fast."*

In the past few years psychologists, sociologists and economists have started paying serious attention to the family money process: Who pays the bills? Who is the real money decision maker? How much do wives know about the cost of running a car, of life insurance? How much do husbands know about the cost of food, of children's clothes? Why can some families manage to live better than others with the same income? These are some of the questions on which there is remarkably little hard information. Right now we know much more about rocks on the moon than about money decisions in the average American family.

To get some insight into what really takes place in family decision making about money, *McCall's* editors asked me to survey typical families around the country. With the help of the Family Service Association of America, I was able to select 25 families living in suburbia—in California, Colorado, Illinois, Ohio, Massachusetts, Connecticut, New York, Maryland and Georgia. All had children—generally two or three—and their incomes fell, mainly, into the $12,000-to-$20,000 range. In short, they were very much like millions of other American families. But I also included two couples who had narrowly skirted the edge of financial disaster and survived only with last-minute expert help. The educational range was great. One husband had a Ph.D. and one wife was a high-school dropout. (And because things are seldom what they seem when it comes to money, the dropout, whose husband earns considerably less than the Ph.D., was managing money better—and living better.)

From *McCall's*, September 1972.

The actual procedure was simple. Each husband and wife was asked to fill out identical questionnaires *separately.* Usually we put them at opposite ends of the room and told them not to ask each other for figures as they went along. The questionnaire asked how much money was coming in and how it was going out. The couples were asked about their attitudes toward money. And, finally, we asked them what they would do with money under certain conditions. The purpose was to see if each husband's and wife's assumptions were based on the same figures or widely disparate ones; to see if their attitudes were similar or different; and, finally, to see how each would react to changes in the family's financial status.

As we suspected they would, the results showed a great deal of misunderstanding between each married couple. When asked to give their husbands' take-home pay, 16 wives missed the actual amount by more than 10 percent, and only nine were fairly accurate. Twelve gave much higher figures. One Maryland woman thought her husband's take-home pay was $1,600 a month; it was $1,300. Another estimated $1,100 when it was really $950. Four wives estimated take-home pay too low; one thought it was only $675 when the true figure was $1,000. (In all cases, the actual figures emerged after the questionnaires were completed and the couples discussed the discrepancies that had become apparent.)

On the other hand, half the husbands had an unrealistically low impression of family food costs. Neil D of Atlanta thought his wife, Carole, spent about $120 a month for their family of five. The actual figure was $200. Louis C of Wheaton, Maryland, thought the food budget for his family of seven was $240 a month. His wife, Dolores, showed that it was $320. Seven husbands were too high. Arnold C of Denver believed the family food bill was $280 a month. His wife showed him that it was only $200 for two adults and three children.

Similarly, on clothing costs, most husbands gave estimates that were on average about 35 percent too low. Typical were the L's of Ohio. He thought she was spending $25 a month for clothing on their family of five. The true figure was $60. Only nine husbands gave clothing figures that were too high.

Twelve wives came quite close to estimating how much life insurance the husband carried. Curiously, most other wives underestimated—by an average of $20,000—the amount of their husbands' insurance. Barbara R of Rockville, Maryland, thought her husband, Paul, was insured for $30,000; he has $60,000. Four wives overestimated; Mary I of Littleton, Colorado, thought there was $100,000 of insurance on her husband's life, but discovered there is only $40,000 worth.

The closest agreement was on the questions of monthly mortgage or rental payments and on family installment payments. (Eight couples have no installment payments at all. On the question "Do installment payments make you nervous?" some 25 wives said "yes" with varying degrees of vehemence. Seventeen of the men agreed.)

On how much saving the families did, about half the couples were from 50 to 75 percent apart, with the wives generally the ones who were uninformed. One thought they were saving $60 a month when $120 was the actual amount. And only four couples were close in their estimates of how much they spent on entertainment. All the rest were incredibly far apart—at least 50 percent in most cases.

It was not surprising that such discrepancies on spending and saving were paralleled by widely differing *attitudes* toward money. The highest level of agreement was reached on "Do you ever quarrel about money?" Nearly all agreed they do "sometimes." Two said, "often." When husbands were asked to characterize their wives' attitudes toward money, the most frequent answer was "too easy-going," and a number of wives in turn called their husbands "too thrifty."

Most couples admitted they did not worry about money. But ten couples couldn't even agree on this question. One pair, Jerry and Ann K of Westchester, California, had the following exchange:

*Ann:* I worry when the paycheck comes in and there are bills to pay. I also worry when I go to buy something big.

*Jerry:* Well, I don't worry.

*Ann:* I know you don't. That's why we bought a color TV set at Christmas-time when we couldn't afford it. *That's* why I worry.

*Jerry:* Okay, so I'm an impulse buyer. You want me to be a worrier, too?

There was little agreement on "What was the most foolish thing you ever did with money since marriage?" Among the men, automotive blunders led the list: bad used cars, an unnecessary second car, expensive repairs for a foreign sports car. Next came mistakes in the stock market. (The only man who reported sizable winnings is a high-school dropout who cheerfully admits that his wife has all the money sense.) Among wives, the biggest mistakes concerned clothes, mainly their own. But one wife said it was the Pierre Cardin suit she bought her husband as a gift. Others listed big mistakes their husbands made: "bought an airplane," "bought a huge dog that eats more than the rest of the family."

When the 50 husbands and wives were asked to complete the sentence, "I worry about money when . . ." an interesting difference emerged. Mainly, wives' money worries concern here-and-now items: "panty hose that don't last,"rising taxes or food prices, a bounced check, a potential dental bill. Husbands for the most part worry when they look ahead—to nursing-home costs for aged parents, to the bills for their children's college education, to dim prospects for financial advancement or to the possibility of being physically disabled. Only rarely were any couples on the same track here. Joyce D wrote she worried about money "only when I don't have it." Across the room, her husband was answering the same question with, "when Joyce does have it."

"Do you expect your family financial situation to change much within the next five years?" While 23 men estimate they will be making an average of $5,000 more, only 13 of the women agree, and another eight wives don't expect *any* change. Even those who expect increased income foresee less improvement than their husbands do.

Fifteen couples do not keep any kind of budget, and among the rest the largely informal chore is divided equally: five husbands, five wives. Nearly all the couples have joint checking accounts with which most are reasonably satisfied. Bill paying is primarily the husband's responsibility in 16 families, with the wives doing it in eight.

"What's the most you would spend on your own, without discussing it with your spouse—apart from regular household expenditures?" Four wives thought their husbands wouldn't spend more than they did; two wives thought they would probably spend more on their own than their husbands would. But the overwhelming majority (19 wives) agreed that their husbands would spend far more on their own than they themselves would—anywhere from twice as much right up to two wives who felt it could be 100 times what they would spend. There was not too much disagreement from the husbands: Fifteen of them said they would spend much more without consulting their wives, somewhere between two to four times as much, than their wives would spend without consulting them.

One couple with a wide discrepancy on discretionary spending was encouraged to discuss it. Robbie A wasn't fazed when she learned her husband,

John, had written he would "spend any amount" without discussing it with her. "He's entitled, he makes it," she said. But John was genuinely shocked that Robbie had written she would spend up to $100 without asking him.

There was much more agreement between most husbands and wives on "What's the most sensible thing you ever did with money since marriage?" Eleven husbands and ten wives answered: buying their home. Five husbands wrote "buying stock," but only one wife agreed with that.

"It really hurts me to spend money on . . ." brought agreement as well. The leading category here was "cars." For men, next was "medical and dental expenses," followed by "entertainment" and "eating out." For wives, money spent on appliances was next. Then movies, particularly bad ones. But in later talks another category appeared on which there was considerable agreement: poor-quality items in general. Most couples felt that in the past few years the quality of products had deteriorated considerably.

"What would you do if you suddenly came into $10,000?" Most wives would put all or most of the money into savings or a large home. Husbands chose "reducing debts," as well as buying a larger home or more land.

One couple, Jim and Pat H of Smyrna, Georgia, did come into $10,000 unexpectedly when local land rezoning doubled the value of their modest home. They sold it, rented another—and adopted two children. Pat simultaneously listed the adoptions as "the most sensible thing" the H's did, but also wrote that *not* buying a new home was the most foolish thing they did.

What would they love to splurge on? Travel was first choice for both men and women. Several added: *without* the children, if possible.

With all this basic disagreement in money attitudes, with their many discrepancies on how they estimate their basic household expenses, the obvious conclusion must be that most husbands and wives just do not talk to each other about money.

I had been warned by Dr. Rober Ferber of the University of Illinois that getting couples to talk about money candidly was remarkably difficult. He and his research staff have been interviewing hundreds of young couples during the past few years. "Many assured us they'd be freer to talk about their sex lives than their money lives." I found men in particular reluctant to talk about money; several scheduled interviews had to be cancelled because the husbands refused to participate, even though their names would not be used. Psychiatrists encounter the same phenomenon. One of them writes: "My patients show far less resistance in relating hatred for their parents or in disclosing sexual perversions than in discussing money. It is as if they equated money with their inmost being."

A typically revealing instance took place one evening in Champaign, Illinois, when Lois and Bob W came to the local Family Service Association office to fill out the *McCall's* questionnaire. Since they were the first couple on my list, I was a trifle anxious. Bob, a warehouse manager, didn't help any when he looked up from the questionnaire and joked, "Y'know, if we get separated by having a fight over these answers, it's your responsibility." The W's, who have three children and have been married 14 years, had many discrepancies in their answers, but the one I was most curious about was that Lois did not think they were saving any money. Bob wrote they were saving $30 a month. He explained that his employer deducted $30 a month buy stock for him and he now had 15 shares worth about $550.

Lois looked at him wide-eyed. "This is great. Here I thought after 14 years I knew all about you: how you nearly froze your toes when you were a boy; how your mother can't resist shoe sales and now has 100 pairs. And now I find out you've been saving $30 a month and I never knew about it."

Nervously, I got set for a family battle right there, but Lois quickly reassured me. "Don't worry. I don't really *care* about money. I guess Bob didn't want me

### The Family-Money Questionnaire

**Following is a slightly condensed version of the questionnaire used in the accompanying article. Husbands and wives should answer these questions separately, in writing, and then compare answers. The discrepancies that turn up can open the way for useful discussion of family practices and attitudes concerning money.**

**1. Which of the following would best describe your attitude toward money?** a) too thrifty ______ b) too easygoing ______ c) too worrisome ______ d) other ______

**2. Which would describe your spouse's attitude?** ______

**3. In general, does it seem to you that you worry a great deal about money?** ______ **Does your spouse?** ______

**4. What money problem is the most frequent source of disagreement?** ______

**5. Do you think that you have a better money sense than your spouse?** ______

**6. If your family had to cut down sharply, where would you first cut expenditures?** ______ **Where would your spouse?** ______

**7. If you came into $10,000 suddenly, what would you do with it?** ______ **Your spouse?** ______

**8. What was the most foolish thing you ever did with money since marriage?** ______ **Your spouse?** ______

**9. What's the most you'd spend on your own, without discussing it with your spouse, apart from regular household expenditures?** ______
**What's the most your spouse would spend without talking it over with you?** ______

**10. What was the most sensible thing you ever did with money since marriage?** ______ **Your spouse?** ______

**11. What's your family's monthly take-home pay?** ______

**12. Approximately how much does your family spend per month for the following important budget items:** a) rent or mortgage-and-taxes ______ b) food ______ c) clothes ______ d) entertainment ______

**13. Do you feel that any of these is out of line?** ______ **Which one?** ______ **How much should it be?** ______

**14. How much does your family save a month, excluding insurance?** ______ **Do you think it's enough?** ______ **How much would you like to be able to save monthly out of your present income?** ______

**15. Has your attitude toward money changed since marriage?** ______ **If so, in what way?** ______ **Has your spouse's attitude toward money changed since marriage?** ______ **If so, in what way?** ______

**16. How much does your family pay out a month on installment debt for major appliances or a car?** ______ **Do you feel this is too much?** ______ **What would be a more comfortable figure for you?** ______ **Does installment buying in general make you feel uncomfortable or nervous?** ______

**17. How much life insurance does your family have?** ______ **If not, how much do you feel you should have at this stage?** ______

**18. Do you expect your financial situation will change much within the next five years?** ______ **If so, roughly how much more do you think will be added to the family income?** ______

**19. If you needed $1,000 quickly, to whom or where would you turn?** ______

**20. It really hurts to spend money on** ______

**21. You would really love to splurge on** ______

to know about the stock so I wouldn't bug him about it. Let's face it: I have absolutely no money sense at all and Bob has a good one and I trust him. He's the shopper in the family. When we got our new station wagon, he insisted on trying six different dealers. I'd have bought the first one we saw."

Like many of the other couples I interviewed, the W's went through an accommodation process that was not accompanied by much talking. Lois recalls it: "We used to have lots of arguments in the past about all the trivia I'd buy: he'd have cats about it. But gradually I've learned to control that crazy impulse."

At least four other couples had gone through a similar accommodation process. In Denver, Marilyn S said: "My mother taught me all the important things about money—like how to spend it fast. Now I'm beginning to learn how to hang on to it more." Don S smiled. "I used to be real tight with money and she was a real spendthrift. Now we've found a fairly happy medium, I think. We're both better than we used to be. That's marriage."

Accommodation was visible even in the marriage of Joyce and Jim D of Culver City, California, who had provided one of the most explosive interviews. Joyce admits freely, almost joyfully, that she has absolutely no money sense. "How could I? I'm in a constant state of urge—anything for myself. Me, Joyce, needs it all. For clothing, for everything . . . ." Yet when all the figures and attitudes were compared, it appeared that she too had learned to handle the family budget in a fairly realistic fashion. "Oh, you learn, you learn, all right," she said. "We probably talk a good fight, but generally we manage to work things out."

Not talking—or even arguing—about money is common in many marriages. One husband noted: "I think we talked about money maybe twenty minutes before we got married. We thought I was unromantic." His wife added, "In fact, we talked so little about money even *after* marriage that eighteen months later we had a terrible shock. It suddenly hit us we were spending eight hundred dollars a month and taking in only six hundred."

The obvious solution would seem to be that couples must learn to talk about money. Reuben Hill, professor of sociology at the University of Minnesota, found after a five-year study that "families who do most of the discussing in advance, who talk things over . . . who do more shopping around" are likely to have "a better chance of making their plans come about. Even when some unexpected emergency comes up, they can handle it because they know how they want to handle it in advance."

This would seem to be a great argument for open, equal discussion between husband and wife on all major money matters. But there is a catch—the dominance factor. Family power is a complicated question, but in most cases a strong impression emerges after seeing a husband and wife together. My own estimate of the 25 couples interviewed for this survey was that some 17 husbands were dominant; that four wives were dominant; and in four cases they seemed to be equal.

But dominance is not the only question. Equally important, experts now agree, is: *Who has the money sense in the family?* The simplest definition of money sense is *"the ability to handle money intelligently."* George Katona of the University of Michigan characterizes it as an intuitive sense of how to stay out of money troubles.

There is a certain vagueness here, but all 25 couples I interviewed seemed to know exactly what was meant when we asked them: "Which of you has a better money sense?"

Some 14 husbands said they had it—and in ten cases their wives agreed. Twelve wives said they had it—and in eight cases their husbands agreed. In two families, both husband and wife agree that neither has a money sense. One couple thought they had it equally.

What happens when the wife has the money sense, with the husband agreeing, but she is not dominant in that family? This was true in four cases. Three of these wives pay the bills; they also felt that there were many items their families could not afford at present. Three of the husbands think they can afford anything they really want.

Over the years these wives have come to make more and more money decisions; they are, in effect, able to exercise increasing veto power on husbandly impulses—to buy stocks, to buy a second car, to cut down on saving. The husband is still dominant, but . . .

As Frank V of Long Island puts it: "I make the strategic decisions and Sunny makes the tactical ones." His wife recalls: "I took over bill paying because I'm the most nervous about money. It's like the one who's most nervous about the baby's crying is the one who picks him up first. Well, when you pay the bills, and you're the most nervous about money, you acquire a kind of veto or *hold* power even on major decisions. Maybe as a result I've gotten less nervous; now I don't have to pay the bills right away. I *can* wait to the end of the month. Great improvement for me."

There was only one case of a wife dominating a husband whom both agreed had a better money sense. As it happened, Doris and William S were one of the two families I found with the help of Kal Waller, the president of the Consumer Credit Counseling Service of Metropolitan Cleveland. The CCCS, one of 140 similar agencies around the country, has helped some 7,500 families get out of severely crippling debt by counseling, rigid budgeting and getting creditors to allow debts to be paid off piecemeal. These nonprofit agencies, sponsored by credit grantors, unions and family agencies, have helped hundreds of thousands of families, keeping many of them from personal bankruptcy. Under CCCS guidance it took Doris and William S some 20 months of tight budgeting to work out from under their heavy debt load. Most of it was incurred by too-casual installment buying.

The other family Kal Waller found for me, Florence and Ned L, took three years to pay off an even greater debt load. I was particularly interested in families that had come through such a rough time because I wanted to see if it was possible for husbands and wives to acquire a money sense belatedly. Kal Waller thinks they can. He feels that all the families his agency has helped had acquired money sense as a result of their lengthy pay-out periods calling for rigid budgeting and self-control. As far as he knew, not one of the thousands of families that "graduated" had to come back a second time.

Based on my interviewing for this article as well as previous research, my impression is that family money matters should not be decided on a democratic everybody-has-one-vote basis. The parent with the active money sense should take charge—even if he or she is not the dominant one. In addition, in families where a parent with an active money sense is in charge of money decisions, there's a good chance that one or more of the children will somehow acquire this money sense in turn.

Sociologist Reuben Hill is inclined to agree. "Family participatory democracy in economics is a lot of hogwash," he told me. "Someone has to make decisions. In successful families, the one with the money sense can develop a leadership which is accepted."

I got further confirmation from Raeder Larson, a vastly experienced observer in family money battles. In the Minneapolis area he is the federal-court-appointed debtors' attorney for the Wage Earner Plan, which was created by

Congress in 1938. Under it, a hard-pressed family, overburdened with monthly payments, can ask the local federal court to protect it from garnishees and wage attachments while it makes court-assisted efforts to pay off the debts over a two- or three-year period. After helping more than 5,000 families through the painful process, Raeder Larson has come to these conclusions:

"In most marriages with growing children, one partner is usually dominant . . . .Very few marriages . . . involve a true equal partnership, at least on money. When the dominant partner can manage money well, the family seldom has serious financial problems, even during temporary layoffs or medical emergencies . . . If the dominant partner will not or cannot manage within the budgeted income available, the other partner is seldom able to improve matters. Financial counseling is theoretically helpful but seldom effective . . . .If neither partner has money-management ability, the situation is almost hopeless in modern society . . . ."

Reuben Hill is convinced, after an extensive study of three generations of some 312 Minneapolis-St. Paul families, that "good management patterns" are more frequently transmitted from generation to generation than poor management. He also found that the highest and likeliest form of this transmission was matrilinear—from grandmother to daughter to granddaughter.

Professor Hill thinks there should be training courses in money handling for all newly married couples: "Engaged and newly married couples are pretty much left to fend for themselves. Friends, kinsmen and even parents tend to respect the privacy of the newly married for several weeks after the ceremony . . . .Yet this is the period of maximum learning and emptiest of formal or informal programs of teaching and training." He is now seeking funds to set up a pilot program along these lines.

For most of us well into marriage, such programs are not going to be much help. What we *can* do is answer the questionnaire separately, as honestly as possible, and then compare. The truths, the discrepancies, the money sense that may—or may not—emerge, should provide some clues to good family money management.

**Reading 21**

# What Spending Money Reveals about You

**Theodore Issac Rubin, M.D.**

*Psychoanalytic help is almost always necessary to get to the roots of their money problems.*

Some people say—and believe—that "money is the root of all evil." That just isn't so. Money doesn't make people sick or corrupt. Sick people make sick or corrupt use of money, just as they do with other things in life.

Money represents time and energy. It is a medium of exchange and, as

From the *Ladies Home Journal*, October, 1970, pp. 44–45

such, it offers the possibility of enhancing human relations and communications. Unfortunately, as in other areas of human endeavor, constructive possibilities for using money can be displaced by destructive ones. So money has come to represent more than it should. To too many people, money has become highly symbolic. Everyday we hear expressions like: "I feel like two cents. . . . I feel like a million dollars. . . . Sound as a dollar. . . . Phony as a three-dollar bill."

In these expressions, the symbolic meanings attributed to money are clear. Sometimes, however, the meaning a person actually assigns to money exists on an unconscious level and the person is unaware of it.

How you feel about money, spend it, use it, etc., tells much about you. This is particularly true in marriage. Often the way a couple acts together in money situations reveals how they feel and relate to each other generally—a good deal of which they may not be aware of at all. Attitudes regarding money are very similar to those about sex, inasmuch as both usually reflect a great deal about how we relate to ourselves and to other people.

Let me describe the most common symbolic meaning of money. Bear in mind that these symbols can overlap: money can symbolize many things to the same person at the same time. Even more peculiarly, money can symbolize opposite values to the same person. Here, then, are some symbolic meanings of money that I have come across in clinical practice.

**1** Money is all that is evil, dirty, mysterious—even death itself—while poverty represents all that is good, clean, light and alive. I knew a man who felt this way but who, at the same time, also felt that money meant respectability and acceptability, while poverty stood for rejection and self-hate. He was in constant conflict about money. Without knowing why, such a person can fluctuate between great efforts to accumulate money and equally great efforts to fail financially in order to divest himself of every cent he worked hard to make.

**2** Money is knowledge, culture and expertise. People who believe this will repeatedly ask the richest man or woman they know for all kinds of advice on any subject, simply because they believe that to be rich is to be all-knowing. They will also strive for money of their own so that they, too, can acquire the instant wisdom that comes with money.

**3** Money is an antidote to self-hate, self-rejection and depression. Some people believe that money will give them self-esteem as well as an ability to relate successfully to others. Here money symbolizes the end of misery and the beginning of happiness. When it brings neither, the believer sometimes feels that he or she simply must get more money. When more money still doesn't solve the problem, the feeling of emptiness deepens. I have seen great depression ensue when people realize that money does not "bring" or "buy" what it is supposed to.

**4** Money means friendships with important people. Those who feel this way will display their money in expensive dress and possessions (such as jewelry, high-priced cars, furniture, etc.) in an attempt to impress and to attract the "right kind" of "important" people.

**5** Money is power, prestige and status. Here, too, ostentation with the aim of impressing others is often an attempt to hide underlying feelings of worthlessness. Some people will throw money around by overtipping or overspending just to show themselves and others that they "have arrived." But it doesn't work! These people are often shocked when they realize that money, however much they acquire, does not really change basic feelings of unworthiness, nor does it confer real self-confidence.

**6** Money is blood. As a result, spending money is like hemorrhaging or giving away vital pieces of one's self. People who feel this way are stingy people.

They can't spend money unless they are convinced they are getting the best deal possible. "Being taken," or getting the worst end of a bargain, can bring on terrible feelings of despair, even an urge to commit suicide. Usually people who can't spend money (assuming they have it to spend) can't spend emotions, either. They are very detached and constipated emotionally—as well as financially.

**7** Money is mastery, a manipulative tool that procures love or control over people. I have known parents who can't understand why their children do not love them even though they have given their children so much money. For these parents money equals love; they feel that the money-love they have given is as good as emotional love. Some women, to whom money equals love, will see their husbands' failure to love his family enough. If effect, these women are saying to their husbands, "If you loved me you would go out and earn more money for me."

**8** Money is the medium of exchange in a game called "Papa and the Little Girl." The husband gives his wife a weekly allowance. She is Little Girl, he is Papa. This stems from and enhances a dependency relationship in which he needs mastery and she needs to feel weak and protected. The husband may complain that his wife refuses to learn how to care for money, and the wife may complain that her husband won't treat her like an adult, but neither will take responsibility for changing until they examine and change their emotional outlook toward themselves and each other.

**9** Money is an emotional compartment. People who believe this never really share money, nor do they share emotions. They get married and maintain separate bank accounts—and usually separate emotional accounts, too.

**10** Money represents health and longevity. You hear people who believe this say, "Money buys the best medicine, the best doctors! . . . Imagine, John Smith died and he was actually a millionaire!" The belief behind these words is that money magically buys life and a way to cheat death.

**11** Money is nobility and an entree into a special circle of superhumans who live in a heaven on earth. It is often a big shock to people who believe this that human functions, limitations and problems exist and continue to exist no matter how much money they accumulate.

**12** Money is things—innumerable things, such as cars, clothes, appliances, houses, lawns—things that, if possessed, will replace a missing self and a missing sense of belonging.

**13** Money is a plaything, a child's toy. "I just love to handle money. I like the feel of it in my hand. I just like to jingle coins in my pocket. I just like to count money." Some thieves have this very childish feeling about money. They'll steal it to play with it, without actually valuing its buying power.

**14** Money is freedom. It makes work unnecessary and permits its possessor to spend his time as he wishes. This view of money may or may not be coupled with the belief that money equals longevity.

**15** Money is legitimacy. Some people believe that nothing really counts unless money is involved. A contract, for example, means nothing if money doesn't pass hands. A man who associates money with legitimacy may say that his son has accomplished nothing because he hasn't brought dollars into the home. Money becomes the symbol of accomplishment, and sometimes very great accomplishments are not recognized because they did not involve money.

**16** Money is rebirth. This attitude characterizes a person who feels that money is necessary before life can really start. A specific amount of money is usually meant, and at the moment that amount is possessed life is supposed to really begin. Needless to say, it seldom does.

Those are some of the most common values that money symbolizes. Sometimes, because of underlying emotional and personality problems, people are trapped by the symbolic use they make of money. Such people suffer from avarice, prostitution of self for money, spendthriftiness, chronic, sadistic exploitation of others, chronic indebtedness, gambling, economic failure, etc., and they need more than financial help. Psychoanalytic help is almost always necessary to get to the roots of their money problems.

## Reading 22

# Couple Shares Job, Household Chores

**Chicago Daily News**

*They want to avoid creating a work-and-home system that was just as structured as the old one.*

After 12 years of marriage and five children, Millie Stoll had it up to here with dirty dishes and laundry. Moreover, she says that she was having doubts about her identity.

"I wanted time for myself," said Mrs. Stoll, "to figure out who I am, not in relation to other people—and the kids—but just myself."

That was last September. Mrs. Stoll's husband, Andrew (Andy), remembers the crisis. "Millie got mad and walked out," he said. Her version is "I went away for a weekend just to think."

When she returned, Millie and Andy sat down and aired their individual complaints. Mrs. Stoll was irritated that when her husband offered to lend a hand, he said: "Let me help with your wash or your cooking."

"It's not my wash, it's our wash and our meals," she would snap back.

So Andy, 33 years old, and Millie, 30, divided the chores in their seven-room bungalow and the care of their five children, aged 2 to 10, on a nearly 50-50 basis.

The new role-sharing didn't work out satisfactorily. "I didn't get everything I wanted, but neither did Andy," said Mrs. Stoll.

Stoll's obvious complaint was that he was still working six days a week while taking on more work at home. A revision of the role-sharing was definitely called for.

The joint earning of a living was feasible for the Stolls because he (or rather, they) own a small glass company just three blocks from their home. Mrs. Stoll had helped out in the office from time to time since Andy and his father started the business 10 years ago. Millie and Andy had bought out the elder Stoll's interest in the business several months ago.

So, a few weeks ago the Stolls began a new venture in sharing. She runs the business one week while Andy is in full charge of the household, and the following week they switch. So far, both are happier than in the traditional husband-at-work, wife-at-home system or the brief-lived compromise attempt.

Mrs. Stoll refers to her week at the Stoll Glass Co. as "my week off." Stoll calls his week at home his week off. Both say they have found more time for themselves.

From the *St. Louis Post-Dispatch*, Apr. 16, 1972. Reprinted with permission from the Chicago Daily News/Sun-Times Service.

"I was tired of making heavy decisions every day and keeping four persons busy at the office," said Stoll.

Mrs. Stoll, in turn, in enjoying the challenge of learning the business. Her father-in-law has remained active in the business and she says that he has been especially helpful. She has found no resentment among the four men employees.

"I think it's a question of mutual respect and friendship," she said of the business operation. She uses the "we-have-a-problem" approach in seeking advice at the office. But she's trying to leave the business decisions in the office and not bring problems home to Andy who, after all, is slaving over a hot stove.

Stoll knew his way around a kitchen before the week-on, week-off switch began. Therefore, cooking is no problem. But after one week at home, he started working out a master plan of dividing chores among the children. He hopes to get the older children into a routine of doing their own laundry ("all you have to do is push buttons" on the washing machine, he reasons). Millie isn't convinced it will work, but she figures it is Andy's option to try.

Other chores are divided among all the members of the household on a rotating basis with each category of chores given a price tag. The division and payments are done at a Sunday night family council and Stoll figures that he is paying out $10 to $15 a week, less than he would have to pay a cleaning woman.

He and Mrs. Stoll collect equally with the children for carrying out garbage (25 cents a day), or keeping the front hall picked up (50 cents a week).

The children are in the process of being re-educated to take their compaints and request to dad, not mom, during his week of duty. The parents contend that there have been no problems with the children, but Andy overheard the older girls, Lisa, 10, and Teresa, 9, grumbling to each other that mother wasn't around much anymore.

One of the girls complained directly to her parents that "it used to be you together," but now father and mother are emphasizing their individuality.

Mrs. Stoll defends the shared responsibility at home, contending that all of us have to relate to different persons in adult life and children can learn early to deal with other persons, daddy included.

In the process of rearranging their lives, the Stolls have pondered the "who am I? What do I want from life?" questions. They are looking for the answers in their own way. Mrs. Stoll has become committed to the feminist movement and is helping to launch a NOW (National Organization for Women) chapter in Waukegan, Ill. She and a group of friends have rap sessions regularly and these, she says, helps her to "get my head on straight."

Stoll is into the same kind of self-assertiveness. He has become interested in Oasis, which is operated as the Midwest Center for Human Potential. The loosely-structured organization calls itself the third force and its followers emphasize human relations with an accent on love. Stoll also is into co-counseling, a kind of two-person, rap-and-advise sessions.

Stoll has more time for leisure pursuits during his "off" weeks, and he revels in it. He visited the Art Institute for the first time in his life and is again picking up photography, a onetime sometime hobby.

When Stoll want to be away from home during his "off" week he first asks his wife if she is willing to look after the children, if it is in the evening. Otherwise, he gets a babysitter.

Mrs. Stoll points out that although many couples could not work out a shared income-earning system such as theirs, they can use the Stoll's method of handling money. She explains that after the essentials—rent, groceries, insurance payments, etc. are covered—any money left over is "negotiated" between husband and wife.

She feels this is crucial for housewives who are not paid for their work and, therefore, are intimidated about insisting that their husbands' pay checks be shared. "Women think they are worthless because they don't earn a living," she said.

She also is developing a new attitude toward housework. She says that she felt guilty for years if the house wasn't exceptionally neat; that she had "failed" her husband by not having a showcase house and five happy, spotless children to greet him at the end of the day.

"That was unreal. And housework is a drag," she said resentfully.

Millie and Andy don't think they've arrived at Valhalla. They already have been confronted with some problems such as the children's resentment of less togetherness and mother's absence. They know that other unforeseen problems will come along. They want to avoid creating work-and-home system that is just as structured as the old one. But they want to try to find answers. And both think they are better persons in their newly-found individualism.

Reading 23

# Teach Your Kids the Value of Money

**Martha Patton**

*Set a lousy example.*

Some parents seem determined to ruin their children's chances of ever being solvent—let alone financially astute—adults.

After years of watching these "spoilers" at work, I feel I have a lot to offer new parents who would go the same route.

Routinely follow three or more of the following practices and I'll practically guarantee you an offspring who doesn't know the value of a dollar or how to manage one.

- Start with Christmas and birthdays. Set no limit to the number of presents you give your child. Fail to consider the amount he may receive from relatives and friends.
- *Be sure* your child is supplied with everything before either his age or stage would suggest it: a two-wheeler before he's old enough to ride in the street, a bedside radio or even his own TV before he's through with toys.
- *The minute* he expresses an interest in books run out and buy them instead of teaching your child the continuing pleasures of the public library—along with book ownership.
- *Get* your little girl a fur coat.
- *Rationalize* that what child's grandparents give him doesn't count.
- *Encourage* your teen-ager to be a fashion plate.
- *Make* sure your child has *new* books for school. Subtly suggest that the book exchange isn't quite "right" for your family.

From the *Chicago Daily News*, Sept. 26, 1970. Reprinted with permission from the Chicago Tribune-New York News Syndicate, Inc.

- *Stand by helplessly* while your teen-age son blows all his earnings and savings on a car, motorcycle or what-have-you. "*After all,* it's his money."
- *Let your child* wear you down in the battle over the junk that is pushed for Christmas. Peace at any price.
- *Be sure* the gifts you give are geared to win your child's affection and approval.
- *Let your children* charge on your accounts or, worse yet, on their own.
- *Live vicariously.* Give your child all those things you never had.
- *Get the children their own phone* even if there's no professional in the house who must have a clear line.
- *Send a child to an expensive camp* or private school when family money is tight and mother is home.
- *Equip him like a pro* for every sport he considers. (If he's good with a $5 dollar glove, just think what he'll do with one that costs $20.)
- Give him a "friend party" and a "family party" every birthday. Each with a full complement of presents.
- *Be sure* to pay him for routine family chores.
- *Give him the lessons* you wanted though he shows neither beginning or continued interest.
- *Never level with your kids* and simply tell them the family can't afford what they want.
- *Fall for the reasoning* "Mom and Dad have it, why can't I?" and leave little for the children to look forward to when they're your age.
- *Support* that big bearded boy forever, whether he remains in school or not.
- *Let your child quit a job* he wanted and accepted before his commitment is complete.
- *Encourage a teen-ager* not to work. "You have the rest of your life for that."
- *Assure your child*—without qualifying remarks about his responsibility for grades or financial contribution—that you will send him through college and even graduate school.
- *Give a teen-ager an allowance* long after he should be earning his own spending money.
- *Follow every fad. Be sure* that if dolls are the rage, your daughter has 14. Get that mini bike for your little boy.
- *Pay for good grades.* Accept grades below ability and continue privileges.
- *Fall for the reason* your minor gives for having his own car, his own apartment.
- *Get the family a color TV* so that your child can hold his own in the neighborhood.
- *Provide for every want,* leaving little incentive to earn.
- *Make no plans* with your child for a savings program.
- *Let your son or daughter take a car* to school and leave it in the lot all day. *This* even though car pool, school bus or public transportation is available.
- *Set a lousy example.*

# Part Two

# The Purchase of a Life Style

Once a household unit has specified its objectives in terms of needs and wants it must then develop a plan by which it hopes to accomplish them. This section deals with these planning and purchasing strategies.

The growing emergence of inflation has contributed to the increased emphasis which the consumer is placing on planning in money management, use of credit money, buying food, family clothing management, the purchase and operation of the family home, family transportation, the purchase of good health care and services, buying protection (insurance), buying investments, and expenditures for taxes and government services. An understanding of your wants and needs and the environmental factors which affect them, plus a realistic appraisal of your resources, provides a setting for intelligent decision making and effective personal management.

# Money Management, Consumer Credit, and Borrowing Money

Reading 24

## Consumption Budgets for Different Family Types

**U.S. Department of Labor**

How family consumption budgets that provide an equivalent level of living vary for urban families of different size and composition is shown in the following table.

**Annual *Consumption* Budgets for Selected Family Types, Urban United States, Autumn 1971 ***

| Family size, type and age | Lower level | Intermediate level | Higher level |
|---|---|---|---|
| Single person under 35 years | $2,040 | $3,020 | $4,180 |
| Husband and wife under 35 years: | | | |
| No children | 2,860 | 4,230 | 5,850 |
| 1 child under 6 | 3,620 | 5,350 | 7,400 |
| 2 children, older under 6 | 4,210 | 6,210 | 8,590 |
| Husband and wife, 35–54 years: | | | |
| 1 child, 6–15 years | 4,790 | 7,070 | 9,790 |
| 2 children, older 6–15 years † | 5,841 | 8,626 | 11,935 |
| 3 children, oldest 6–15 years | 6,780 | 10,010 | 13,840 |
| Husband and wife, 65 years and over ‡ | 3,176 | 4,484 | 6,592 |
| Single person, 65 years and over § | 1,747 | 2,466 | 3,626 |

* For details on estimating procedures, see "Revised Equivalence Scale," BLS Bulletin 1570-2.

† Estimates for the BLS 4-Person Family Budgets.

‡ Estimates for the BLS Retired Couple's Budgets.

§ Estimated by applying a ratio of 55 percent to the BLS Retired Couple's Budgets.

From News: U.S. Department of Labor, Office Information, Washington, D.C., 20210, p. 4.

Reading 25*

# A Divided Responsibility: Family Budget Plan

**Carl. F. Hawver**

*Budgeting need not be tedious or time-consuming.*

## FAMILY GOALS

People want many things from a marriage. As husband and wife they want to find happiness. As parents they want to give their children every possible advantage. And as a family unit they want to be financially independent—to enjoy a good standard of living, and a reasonable degree of economic security.

Family happiness depends largely on how successful people are in achieving these ambitions. The amount of income is not the most important factor. One need only read his daily paper to know that people with high incomes have family problems too. One key seems to be in planning family spending—in budgeting.

A family budget plan adds to the security of family relationships. It eliminates doubts, distrust, and baseless fears. It helps get the most from resources and still maintain a safeguard against emergencies. It helps people live more fully in the present even while they are preparing for the future.

## BUDGETING WITHOUT BOOKKEEPING

Budgeting is planning—not bookkeeping. Writing down every penny spent may be helpful in setting up a plan but is unnecessary after a Divided Responsibility Family Budget Plan is underway. If you hold to the plan you can forget the bookkeeping. Just keep the usual receipts and cancelled checks for tax and reference purposes.

### Family Budgeting

*Do not attempt to make your own personal budget conform exactly to the budget guide,* but do compare your budget with the Guide. If you are high in some areas, be sure there is a good reason. If there is, remember you must cut down in some other areas to make up for it. A budget is a specialized plan for a certain family. It should help them get the most out of their resources in terms of things that are important to them. That is why your budget will not be exactly like the Budget Guide, nor like anyone else's budget. The important thing is to plan your spending and savings so that your income will provide for your family the maximum of the things that are important to each of you.

## BUDGETING IS EASY AS ABC

**A** Figure your weekly cash needs and enter them in the proper column on the "Worksheet for Family Spending." Follow normal pattern as to who

* Readings 25, 26 and 27 are all related and should be read as a group.

From National Consumer Finance Association, Washington, D.C., 20036, 1969.

## WORKSHEET FOR FAMILY SPENDING
## DIVIDED RESPONSIBILITY PLAN

ee item-by-item explanation accompanying this worksheet.

o convert weekly figures into monthly figures, multiply by 4.33.

Name: ____________________ __________

Date: ______________________________

| ne o. | "HERS" | Col. #1 "Cash Weekly" | Col. #2 "Other Monthly" | Line No. | "HIS" | Col. #1 "Cash Weekly" | Col. #2 "Other Monthly" |
|---|---|---|---|---|---|---|---|
| . | **FOOD** | | | 51. | **SHELTER** | | |
| . | Grocery store | | | 52. | Rent or mortgage | | |
| . | Milk (if delivered) | | | 53. | Maintenance on home | | |
| . | Lunches for working wife | | | 54. | Property taxes | | |
| . | | | | 55. | Home insurance | | |
| . | | | | 56. | | | |
| . | Total | | | 57. | | | |
| . | **HOUSE OPERATION** | | | 58. | Total | | |
| . | Electricity | | | 59. | **TRANSPORTATION** | | |
| . | Gas | | | 60. | Auto pyts. (or saving for new car) | | |
| . | Heating fuel | | | 61. | Bus, taxi or train | | |
| . | Telephone | | | 62. | Gas & oil for car | | |
| . | Water | | | 63. | Auto tires & repair | | |
| . | Household help | | | 64. | Auto insurance | | |
| . | Furniture and equipment | | | 65. | | | |
| . | Personal allowance | | | 66. | | | |
| . | Children's allowances | | | 67. | Total | | |
| . | Newspapers & magazines | | | 68. | **PERSONAL** | | |
| . | Dues & fees | | | 69. | Personal allowance | | |
| . | Payments on old bills | | | 70. | Family entertainment | | |
| . | | | | 71. | Vacation fund | | |
| . | | | | 72. | Education | | |
| . | Total | | | 73. | Medicine & medical care | | |
| . | **CLOTHING** | | | 74. | All insurance (health, life, etc.) | | |
| . | Clothes for all family | | | 75. | Dues and fees | | |
| . | Cleaning & laundry | | | 76. | Income taxes not deducted | | |
| . | | | | 77. | Payments on old bills | | |
| . | Total | | | 78 | Lunches for working husband | | |
| . | **CONTRIBUTIONS** | | | 79. | | | |
| . | Churches | | | 80. | Total | | |
| . | Christmas gifts | | | 81. | **SAVINGS & INVESTMENTS** | | |
| . | Non-family gifts | | | 82. | Savings | | |
| . | Family gifts | | | 83. | Regular investments | | |
| . | Charities | | | 84. | Self-paid retirement plan | | |
| . | | | | 85. | | | |
| . | Total | | | 86. | Total | | |
| . | **SUMMARY: "HER" EXPENSE** | | | 87. | **SUMMARY: "HIS" EXPENSE** | | |
| . | Food | | | 88. | Shelter | | |
| . | House operation | | | 89. | Transportation | | |
| . | Clothing | | | 90. | Personal | | |
| . | Contributions | | | 91. | Savings and Investment | | |
| . | Total "HER" Expense | | | 92. | Total "HIS" expense | | |
| . | Total cash x 4.33 | | | 93. | Total cash x 4.33 | | |
| . | Total "HER" monthly expense | | | 94. | Total "HIS" monthly expense | | |
| . | Pay check for _____ days | | | 95. | Plus "HER" monthly expense | | |
| . | Other income | | | 96. | Average monthly expense | | |
| . | Average monthly income | | | 97. | Average monthly income | | |

spends what. Change the worksheet if necessary to fit your family's convenience.

**B** Figure your "other" needs on a monthly basis and enter them in the "other monthly" columns. Don't forget to include bills that come in less often than once a month, like insurance, taxes. Christmas bills, etc. Divide their annual totals by 12 and put in "other monthly" column. One good way to do this is to put your actual expenses for last month on a worksheet—put figures for the month before on another worksheet, keep on going back for 3 months, or 6 months, or a year, until you can get a reasonable monthly *average*.

**C** Total "His" and "Her" expenses together and compare with average monthly income. Cut back expenses if necessary to stay within income and still allow for regular savings programs.

After these three steps are taken, no books need be kept. The plan will take some adjusting at first, but soon it will fit the family pattern comfortably and help realize family goals. Then it will need no change until there is a change in income or in goals.

## THE CHECKING ACCOUNT

The budgeting family will find it easier to work their plan if they deposit all income in a checking account. Cash needs will be met by cashing weekly checks in the exact amount determined in the plan. All other money will remain in the checking account so it will be available when monthly (and less frequent) bills are to be paid.

## THE SAVINGS ACCOUNT

Arrangements should be made at the bank for an automatic transfer of the planned amount from the checking account to the savings account. This guarantees that the savings will grow and is far better than the old practice of putting in the savings account only what was left after all bills were paid. Somehow, there never seemed to be anything left.

## DIVIDING THE RESPONSIBLITY

The easiest way to follow your personalized budget is the Divided Responsibility Plan. In some households, the husband or the wife assumes all the responsibility for budgeting and spending all of the family income. Such a system, however, excludes others in the family from sharing this important family responsibility. Budgeting should be a family activity, shared with the children who are old enough to experience the financial realities of planning family spending.

Budgeting need not be tedious or time-consuming. Under the Divided Responsibility Plan, one month's record and a round table conference in which the entire family participates, can serve to budget income into broad categories of expenses and savings. The wife then assumes responsibility for spending the amounts budgeted for Food, House Operation, Clothing, and Contributions, while the husband handles the money for Shelter, Transportation, Personal Expense, and Savings and Investment.

As long as both can supply the needs of the family within the total amount allotted for their areas of responsibility, there need be no detailed record-keeping. When the amount allotted proves insufficient to meet the current or anticipated needs, however, a detailed account of all spending should be kept for a month or two (on Family Spending Worksheets) to determine where the plan is breaking down and what steps should be taken to bring spending back into line with income.

## CREDIT MANAGEMENT

Careful credit management demands that before a new credit obligation is assumed, the budget must be checked to be sure there will be money enough to make the necessary payments. If your net income is $600, for example, and you are considering a new car which will require a $50 a month payment, you will have to examine your normal spending pattern to see if you have a "surplus" of $50 so you can make your payments. If not, you may try to see if you can adjust your expenditures to provide such a surplus. If you can, you may decide to buy the new car. If not, try $25 payments and a cheaper car, or maybe you can't afford to take on any payments at all right now. Never sign up for credit payments of any kind until you have assured yourself you can handle them without sacrificing things that are more important to family living.

## ADJUST THE BUDGET FOR YOUR CONVENIENCE

A good budget is one that can be tailored to your own needs. If Hubby spends $10 a week for lunches, for example, there is no need for the wife to dole the money out each week: she just deducts $10 a week from "Her" food budget (line 2) and adds it to "His" budget (line 78). Make such other adjustments as are necessary to fit your budget plan to your family circumstances, using the blank spaces provided.

Reading 26

# Paycheck Control Sheet (PCC)

**National Consumer Finance Association**

*Remember that you normally will not spend in any one month all of the income received in that month.*

The Pay Check Control Sheet (PCC) should be used with the Family Budget Plan (FBP) worksheet which defines family goals on a monthly basis. This control sheet spells out the way each pay check should be allocated to meet the planned expenditures shown on the worksheet.

Remember that you normally will not *spend* in any one month *all* of the income received in that month. Your FBP worksheet calls for regular amounts to be set aside each month to build up funds from which future needs will be met.

From the National Consumer Finance Association, Washington, D.C., 20036.

These funds remain in the checking account until needed to pay bills that occur less often than once a month, such as: auto license plates, insurance, clothing, etc.

Note that there are *two* columns for each pay period. In the "PLAN" column show how you *plan* to spend every penny of each pay check. Thus the total of this column (line 44) should be the same as the amount of the pay check (line 45). Watch out for due dates of bills. If pay checks fall on the 10th and 24th and the gas bill is due the 15th, then the gas bill should be a planned expenditure for the check due the 10th.

In the second column enter the money actually *spent.* Amounts planned for *future* bills are not entered into the "spent" column until they are actually *spent.*

The following instructions will assist the family which is serious in its intent to make family income cover family goals:

**A** *Rate of pay check:* Insert at the head of each column the date each pay check will be received. If there are pay checks from more than one source, combine if they fall on the same day. Use a different column for each pay day.

**B** *HER cash (line 1):* From the FBP worksheet, transfer the *total* cash allotment for the wife *for the period covered by the pay check* (i.e., if pay check is every two weeks, use twice weekly amount shown on worksheet (in column #1, line 42; if pay check is semi-monthly, show half of monthly amount shown in column #2, line 42).

**C** *HER expenses (lines 2 through 21):* indicate in the "PLAN" column, from which pay check each item shown in column #2 of the worksheet will be allocated. Since you will be using only one spread sheet for each month, this means that you will be sure each item in column #2 of the worksheet will be put *somewhere* on the control sheet for each month.

**D** *Total HER (line 22):* The line 22 totals shown in *all* of the PLAN columns for the month, when added together, should equal the "Total HER Expense" shown in column #2, line 95 of the worksheet.

**E** *HIS cash (line 23):* From the FBP worksheet, transfer the *total* cash allotment for the husband *for the period covered by the pay check* (i.e., if pay check is every two weeks, use twice the weekly amount shown on the worksheet; if pay check is semi-monthly, show half of monthly amount; if weekly, show weekly amount).

**F** *HIS expenses (lines 24 through 42):* Indicate in the "PLAN" column, from which pay check each item shown in column #2 of the worksheet will be allocated. Since you will be using only one spread sheet for each month, this means that you will be sure each item in column #2 of the worksheet will be put *somewhere* on the control sheet for each month.

**G** *Total HIS (line 43):* The line 43 totals shown in all of the PLAN columns for the month, when added together, should equal the "Total HIS Expense" shown in column #2, line 94 of the worksheet.

**H** *Total HIS and HER (line 44):* The line 44 totals shown in *all* of the PLAN columns for the month, when added together, should equal the total of "Average monthly expense" shown in column #2, line 96 of the worksheet.

**I** *Pay check total (line 45):* The amount shown here should equal the amount shown in line 44, of each PLAN column.

**J** After you have filled out all the PLAN columns for the next 3 months cross check your monthly control sheet totals against the monthly worksheet totals to be sure they are the same.

**K** When each pay check comes in, write in the SPENT column, what is actually *spent.* Some items will be "allocated" in the 'PLAN" column but will be left in the checking account until needed for that planned expense.

**L** When you need to use money you have been "saving" check back to see how much you have entered in the PLAN columns but not yet entered in the SPENT columns.

Example: In January, February, March and April, the Smiths have put in the PLAN column, $20 each month for clothing, but they have *spent* none of this clothing money. In the first pay period of May, they add another $20, but they also spend $70 for spring clothes. They will then go *back* to the January column and put $20 in the SPENT column beside the $20 in the PLAN column for that month. This shows that the $20 set aside has now been spent. The same will be

**PAY CHECK CONTROL SHEET**
(A Family Spending Spread Sheet)

See reverse side for instructions MONTH:________ NAME:________

| Date of Pay Check → | | | | | | | | | | |
|---|---|---|---|---|---|---|---|---|---|---|
| | Plan | Spent | Plan | Spent | Plan | Spent | Plan | Spent | Plan | Spent |
| 1. HER cash | | | | | | | | | | |
| FOOD | | | | | | | | | | |
| 2. Milk (if delivered) | | | | | | | | | | |
| 3. | | | | | | | | | | |
| HOUSE OPERATION | | | | | | | | | | |
| 4. Electricity | | | | | | | | | | |
| 5. Gas | | | | | | | | | | |
| 6. Heat | | | | | | | | | | |
| 7. Telephone | | | | | | | | | | |
| 8. Water | | | | | | | | | | |
| 9. Help | | | | | | | | | | |
| 10. Furniture & equipment | | | | | | | | | | |
| 11. Dues & fees | | | | | | | | | | |
| 12. Old bills | | | | | | | | | | |
| 13. | | | | | | | | | | |
| CLOTHING | | | | | | | | | | |
| 14. Clothing for all family | | | | | | | | | | |
| 15. | | | | | | | | | | |
| CONTRIBUTIONS | | | | | | | | | | |
| 16. Church | | | | | | | | | | |
| 17. Xmas | | | | | | | | | | |
| 18. Non-family gifts | | | | | | | | | | |
| 19. Family gifts | | | | | | | | | | |
| 20. Charities | | | | | | | | | | |
| 21. | | | | | | | | | | |
| 22. Total HER | | | | | | | | | | |
| | | | | | | | | | | |
| 23. HIS cash | | | | | | | | | | |
| SHELTER | | | | | | | | | | |
| 24. Rent/mortgage | | | | | | | | | | |
| 25. Maintenance | | | | | | | | | | |
| 26. Home taxes | | | | | | | | | | |
| 27. Home insurance | | | | | | | | | | |
| 28. | | | | | | | | | | |
| TRANSPORTATION | | | | | | | | | | |
| 29. Auto payments | | | | | | | | | | |
| 30. Public transportation | | | | | | | | | | |
| 31. Gas & oil | | | | | | | | | | |
| 32. Car repair | | | | | | | | | | |
| 33. Car insurance | | | | | | | | | | |
| 34. | | | | | | | | | | |
| PERSONAL | | | | | | | | | | |
| 35. Vacation fund | | | | | | | | | | |
| 36. Education | | | | | | | | | | |
| 37. Medical care | | | | | | | | | | |
| 38. All insurance | | | | | | | | | | |
| 39. Dues & fees | | | | | | | | | | |
| 40. Old bills | | | | | | | | | | |
| 41. | | | | | | | | | | |
| SAVINGS & INV. | | | | | | | | | | |
| 42. | | | | | | | | | | |
| | | | | | | | | | | |
| 43. Total HIS | | | | | | | | | | |
| 44. Total HIS & HER | | | | | | | | | | |
| 45. Pay check total | | | | | | | | | | |

*Permission granted by the National Consumer Finance Association to reproduce the PCC chart.*

done for February and March. In the April column they will enter $10 to make up the balance of the $70 spent. Now the Smiths can tell at a glance that they have $30 left in their clothing budget ($10 for April and $20 for May).

Reading 27

# Future Goals Control Sheet (FGC)

**Carl F. Hawver**

*Families should "dream" together about what they would like to accomplish . . . .*

The Future Goals Control Sheet (FGC) is designed to be used with the Pay Check Control Sheet (PCC) and the Family Budget Plan (FBP) Worksheet. This control sheet helps the family achieve future goals by encouraging them, first, to establish such goals and, second, to develop a program to provide the money to pay for them.

Families should "dream" together about what they would like to accomplish in the future, then translate these dreams into reality by plotting them out on the Future Goals Control Sheet. Use the suggested items and blanks to identify your family goals. After the family decides what it *wants,* then the *cost* should be estimated as accurately as possible and the amount of *annual* savings needed should be figured.

The important thing is that such "future" needs should not be allowed to "sneak up" on a family. Families who plan ahead will be more likely to have their dreams realized—rather than shattered.

Each Future Goals Control Sheet is made up of several columns. For short term goals, each column represents a month, for longer range goals, each column represents a year. Either way, you can always tell at a glance how much money you have in each "goal" account.

## SHORT RANGE GOALS

Let's start with short range goals. These are the things you will need money for during the next year—like taxes, auto insurance premiums, annual vacations, etc. For example, suppose during the next calendar year you will need $150 for property taxes in March and another $150 in September. Opposite "taxes," (line 1) put $150 in the "goal" line under March and September. This tells you how much you will need and when. Next, put in the "plan" line the amount you will need to save each month to have *what* you need, *when* you need. If you are doing this on January 1, you had better set aside $50 in January and February and March to be able to pay the taxes due the end of March. Put $50 in the "plan" line for January and February and March. Then you will have 6 months (April through September) to save up the $150 you will need for taxes at the end of September. That will require only $25 a month. Enter this in the proper places. Enter other short term goals in the same manner.

This system will always tell you how much you have saved up for each

From the National Consumer Finance Association, Washington, D.C., 20036.

goal. When March comes and you spend the $150, just circle the $50 entered in January, February and March and the $150 March "goal" to show that this money has been spent and that goal met.

The money set aside for short term goals is usually kept in the family checking account. Amounts needed for various goals should be spaced out as much as possible so there will not be too much of a strain on any one month or any one pay check, since that must be the source of these set aside funds. Once the total needs for *all* goals are established, and are determined to be within pay

**FUTURE GOALS CONTROL SHEET**
**(A Family Goals Spread Sheet)**

See reverse side for instructions — NAME: ______________

| SHORT RANGE GOALS (Under 12 months) | G=Goal P=Plan | Jan | Feb | Mar | Apr | May | June | July | Aug | Sept | Oct | Nov | Dec |
|---|---|---|---|---|---|---|---|---|---|---|---|---|---|
| | G | | | | | | | | | | | | |
| 1. Taxes | P | | | | | | | | | | | | |
| | G | | | | | | | | | | | | |
| 2. Vacation | P | | | | | | | | | | | | |
| | G | | | | | | | | | | | | |
| 3. Home recreation equip. | P | | | | | | | | | | | | |
| | G | | | | | | | | | | | | |
| 4. Furniture | P | | | | | | | | | | | | |
| | G | | | | | | | | | | | | |
| 5. Minor appliances | P | | | | | | | | | | | | |
| | G | | | | | | | | | | | | |
| 6. Home insurance | P | | | | | | | | | | | | |
| | G | | | | | | | | | | | | |
| 7. Auto insurance | P | | | | | | | | | | | | |
| | G | | | | | | | | | | | | |
| 8. Personal insurance | P | | | | | | | | | | | | |
| | G | | | | | | | | | | | | |
| 9. Other insurance | P | | | | | | | | | | | | |
| | G | | | | | | | | | | | | |
| 10. Christmas expense | P | | | | | | | | | | | | |
| | G | | | | | | | | | | | | |
| 11. | P | | | | | | | | | | | | |
| | G | | | | | | | | | | | | |
| 12. | P | | | | | | | | | | | | |

| MIDDLE RANGE GOALS (1 through 5 years) | Mo. Av. | Total Each Year | | | | | | | | | | | |
|---|---|---|---|---|---|---|---|---|---|---|---|---|---|
| | | 19__ | 19__ | 19__ | 19__ | 19__ | 19__ | 19__ | 19__ | 19__ | 19__ | 19__ | 19__ |
| 13. Home improvement | | | | | | | | | | | | | |
| 14. Boat or other rec. equip. | | | | | | | | | | | | | |
| 15. HIS additional education | | | | | | | | | | | | | |
| 16. HER additional education | | | | | | | | | | | | | |
| 17. Automobile purchase | | | | | | | | | | | | | |
| 18. Special trip | | | | | | | | | | | | | |
| 19. Major appliances | | | | | | | | | | | | | |
| 20. | | | | | | | | | | | | | |
| 21. | | | | | | | | | | | | | |
| 22. | | | | | | | | | | | | | |

| LONG RANGE GOALS (Over 5 years) | Mo. Av. | Total Each Year | | | | | | | | | | | |
|---|---|---|---|---|---|---|---|---|---|---|---|---|---|
| | | 19__ | 19__ | 19__ | 19__ | 19__ | 19__ | 19__ | 19__ | 19__ | 19__ | 19__ | 19__ |
| 23. College for #1 | | | | | | | | | | | | | |
| 24. College for #2 | | | | | | | | | | | | | |
| 25. College for #3 | | | | | | | | | | | | | |
| 26. Other college | | | | | | | | | | | | | |
| 27. Purchase home | | | | | | | | | | | | | |
| 28. Wedding #1 girl | | | | | | | | | | | | | |
| 29. Wedding #2 girl | | | | | | | | | | | | | |
| 30. Other weddings | | | | | | | | | | | | | |
| 31. Retirement | | | | | | | | | | | | | |
| 32. | | | | | | | | | | | | | |

*Permission granted by the National Consumer Finance Association to reproduce the FGC chart.*

check possibilities, amounts must be transferred to the proper lines on the Pay Check Control Sheets. Money for longer term goals should be included in savings where they can draw interest.

## MIDDLE RANGE GOALS

Next let's look first at middle range goals. These are goals which will be reached in from one to five years. Included in this class would be the purchase of a new auto, adding a new room on the house, finishing a husband's or wife's education, etc.

Suppose you plan to add a new bedroom to the house when the twins are 6 (they are 2 now). It will cost $2,100 and you would like to do it in July. It's January 1 now. You have about 3½ years to raise the money—that's 42 months at $50 a month. First, you will enter $600 in the "plan" column of the Future Goals Control Sheet for each of the next 3 years (12 months at $50) and $300 for the fourth year (you want to start in July, remember?). Now you go back to your Pay Check Control Sheet and enter the $50 there for each month as "home improvement" (line 28). Next, add this $50 to the amount on the Family Budget Plan Worksheet which is automatically deducted each month for the savings account. Now you are in business, and when that important July rolls around, 3½ years from now, you will be ready—with the necessary cash.

## LONG RANGE GOALS

Long range goals are those which can be realized only after five years or more of planning. These would include buying a new home, a summer place, a nice wedding, college for the youngsters, retirement income, etc. For example, if your son is 8, and you expect him to graduate from high school at 18, you have 10 years to plan for his college expenses. If you think it will cost $2,500 a year for four years of college, that means you will need $10,000 or an average $1,000 a year for 10 years (excluding interest earned). That means *monthly* savings of about $83.33. If that amount is not realistic, then the family will have to readjust their goals. Perhaps $25 a month is all they can save. This would accumulate $3,000 (plus interest earned) in 10 years. This could be supplemented by family earnings *during* the boy's college years, and by the earnings of the boy himself. Indeed, if the control sheet shows that the family can save only $10 a month toward college, this would give the young man $1,200 to start and, knowing that he would need to earn part of his way, he could start his own college fund with a paper route or other earnings at an early age.

Remember that "goal" items should be entered "across the board" on the Future Goals Control Sheet, on the Pay Check Control Sheet, and on the Family Budget Plan Worksheet. Then you have built that goal into your total spending pattern and you will have the money when you need it.

Now, put on your thinking cap and start planning for the realization of the future goals most important to *your* family's happiness.

**Reading 28**

# Making Allowances: A Parents' Guide

**Grace W. Weinstein**

*You wouldn't expect a child to learn to read without having books. How can he learn to handle money if he doesn't have any?*

David Tenner, an eighth grader in the comfortable New Jersey suburb of Teaneck, gets an allowance of $1.25 a week, and he does not think it is enough. "I don't think parents have any idea what things cost now," he complains. "You can't even bowl two games a week on $1.25. I figured out that I could use $2.25. That would cover bowling and pizza and leave me 10 cents for extras."

Is he right? In order to find out what parents and children are actually doing about allowances, and to look for national patterns, *Money* recently surveyed allowance practices in 175 households across the country. We also talked individually to dozens of parents and children. Then, to find out what the experts think parents should do, we interviewed psychologists, teachers, principals and guidance counselors.

More than two-thirds of the parents in our sample give their children a regular allowance, usually weekly. We found a wide range within every age group, however: youngsters seven and under get from 20 cents to $2.50, teenagers 14 and 15 years old from 75 cents to $10. Geographically, we found southern parents most tightfisted, midwesterners most generous. For 11- to 15-year-olds, for instance, the averages were $2.77 in the Midwest, $2.67 in the West, $2.29 in the Northeast and $2.25 in the South.

Children generally spend about twice as much as they are given in allowance, according to the survey. The extra cash is usually money contributed by parents for lunches or bus fare, school supplies or music lessons. With older children, some of it comes from working around the house or on a part-time job.

With or without regular allowances, the children we surveyed do very nicely. Birthday and Christmas gifts and an occasional handout from a fond grandmother are pillars of many a youthful financial structure. When funds do run low, the children become downright resourceful. "John sells his toys," Mary Allan, a suburban New York City mother, says of her eleven-year-old son. "He used to collect the G.I. Joe dolls and clothes. Now he thinks he's too old for all that, so he has started selling them to his friend's younger brother."

The survey confirmed that parents have an extraordinary range of attitudes toward allowances, whether they give them or not. The professionals we consulted, however, were unanimous on most of the basic issues. What follow is a compendium of examples, parental opinions and expert advice on eight questions about allowances that puzzle many parents, beginning with the fundamental problem:

## SHOULD I GIVE AN ALLOWANCE AT ALL?

Eleven-year-old Carol Cochrane, one of David Tenner's neighbors in Teaneck, doesn't get an allowance. "What would I do with it?" she asks. "I get all the money I need from my father." A good many parents prefer to review each request as it comes up and see exactly where the money goes, which is hard to do when the child handles it all himself. Some simply don't like the negotiations involved in setting and supervising allowances. Stuart Walzer, a Beverly Hills lawyer who has four sons, takes things very casusally with the youngest, nine-year-old Lloyd. "If I want to get rid of him on Saturday," Walzer says, "I give him a dollar and tell him to go buy some candy." He explains: "I tried all the other things. I was very stern, very much for parental guidance, but I gave all that up years ago. I got so tired of hassling with them that I figured out the one I was really upsetting when I argued with them about money was me."

Other parents who do not give allowances have chosen that course because all else failed. "We used to give them allowances," says Sharon Chioni of Highland Park, Illinois, the wife of an engineer and mother of two sons, "but they didn't seem to follow through. They were supposed to hang up their clothes and pick up after themselves. I think we started giving them allowances when they were too young." A contrary view comes from Sibyl Saville of nearby Wilmette; she and her husband, a consultant for Illinois Bell Telephone, have five children. "As long as they are in school, it's our responsibility to see that they have money for food and other necessary expenses," she says. "An allowance teaches children that they have only so much a week to spend. It helps them learn to save. Each of our children was different in the way he handled money. Some were always saving for certain causes, but others—well, it was gone in a minute."

The experts agree that an allowance is a good idea. "It's a lot better to have an allowance system," the redoubtable Dr. Benjamin Spock has written, "than for a child to be begging for everything he wants, obliging the parents to decide each and every issue on its merits, which is hard work for even the most judicious adults." Many parents share the view of 91-year-old Sidonie Matsner Gruenberg, former head of the Child Study Association of America: "The only way for boys and girls to obtain constructive experience in the face of unavoidable financial dependence is by learning to use their share of the family income." She adds: "If we want our children to understand money as a very necessary tool in living, we will not keep this tool completely in our own hands, just because we are older and more experienced."

The beginner makes mistakes, but if given a chance, he should learn from those mistakes. The child who spends all of his allowance immediately, and then has to watch empty handed as the ice cream man goes by, will learn something about the value of saving for a specific purpose. That lesson remains unlearned if the mother supplies money each time the Good Humor bell rings. If the mother can bite her lip and not comment on the flimsiness of a purchase, the child will absorb another practical lesson. When a cheap, shoddy toy or gadge falls apart within a few days, the mother can mention, without reproach, that items in the price range tend to be poorly made. Sometimes, though, the lesson may not seem worth the cost. When 16-year-old Woody Alexander of Atlanta bought a shirt at a local boutique, it shrank to postage-stamp size on first washing. Now, once again, his parents buy most of his clothes.

Most parents who give regular pocket money do so because they hope that it will help their children learn these basic skills of money management. Some are not so sure. Marilyn Eichler, a Connecticut woman, gives her 13-year-old daughter a generous $5 a week, yet says: "I don't think anything is learned from an allowance. The only way to learn about money is through working for it. But the allowance does provide a certain necessary degree of independence for a child." That independence is important. The child who can join her friends for an after-school soda without asking for the money, the boy who can go bowling with his buddies, the youngster who can purchase a hair ribbon without explanations—all are assuming responsibility. As they learn what money can and cannot do, they become more mature.

## WHEN SHOULD IT START?

"I have never given my children a specific allowance because they never asked for it," said one physician who responded to our survey. But most parents don't wait for the kids to ask. The right time to begin is when the children start needing money on a more or less regular basis.

Nearly three-fourths of the parents we surveyed started allowances when their children were between five and eight. The exact timing depends on the child's needs and circumstances. The urban first grader who walks past a candy store each day to and from school can find uses for money earlier than the child in more rural surroundings. In city and suburb, though, sooner or later children find opportunities for spending money.

A good time to start a weekly allowance, then, is when you find yourself supplying money frequently for ice cream, bubble gum, baseball cards and other small needs and wants. You can even get your child used to the idea of an allowance gradually. When your preschooler starts asking for goodies each time he accompanies you on a shopping trip, give him a small sum of his own with the understanding that when it is spent, he gets no more.

## WHAT SHOULD THE ALLOWANCE COVER?

Comparing allowances is complicated because different families expect an allowance to cover different things. The ten-year-old who gets $2.50 a week and must buy his own school lunches probably has less disposable income than a classmate with 75 cents a week free and clear.

While most of our survey families feel that the child's recreational expenses should come out of his allowance, and a slightly smaller number agree that he should buy most of his own gifts, there is less agreement on the subject of lunch money. Many parents provide for lunches separately, perhaps because they fear that with a lump-sum allowance the child will eat inadequately while saving up for a special toy or game. Other parents, believing that children must learn through experience to allocate money for specific purposes, try to shut their eyes to occasional skimping on meals.

As always, parents find individual solutions to particular problems. When one Massachussetts sixth grader requested extra lunch money each day for special desserts, his parents decided instead to increase his weekly allowance by 50 cents. That left it up to him whether or not to augment his lunch. "Now he rarely buys the desserts he wanted so badly," he father notes. "He uses the money for other things, usually bowling." In making a choice, by allocating his limited funds to produce the greatest personal satisfaction available to him, this youngster has taken a step toward adulthood.

The path toward maturity is made more difficult by the problem of handling increasing expenses. "We find," says an Anaheim, Calif., housewife, "that our eleven-year-old's dollar allowance is not sufficient to cover her social activities, her ice skating, movies and scout outings. I resent passing out allowances every Saturday morning and then $2 for ice skating, $1.50 for a movie, etc." She and her husband are talking of increasing their daughter's allowance and then letting her budget it. Most child-development specialists agree that it is best to provide a larger allowance, covering such things as hobby materials and sports, school supplies and bus fare, to help the child learn about budgeting.

In families that use this approach, the allowance, and the responsibility, is usually increased gradually. A Tacoma, Wash., building contractor, for instance, reports: "We have a list set up that increases allowances each birthday, starting with 10 cents at age four up to $3.95 at 17 years." But sometimes the change can be abrupt. A Pennsylvania youngster, son of two psychologists, received $1 a week until his twelfth birthday last year, when he was jumped to $11 a week to provide for recreation, local transportation, school lunches, clothing and gifts.

## WHAT IS A REASONABLE AMOUNT?

Once a child gets past the preschool stage, when a few shiny pennies make him feel affluent, he starts to need more than that if he is to learn anything but frustration from having an allowance. Five and ten cent stores don't sell anything much any any more for 5 or 10 cents, or even a quarter. Sweets also have gone up. "A 5-cent candy bar costs 15 cents today," a Chicago advertising man says. "How can I expect my second grader to be satisfied with 10 cents a week?"

The one way to arrive at a sum that will satisfy both child and parent is to make a list of what the child actually spends money on each week, and then include in his allowance the expenditures that he is mature enough to handle. At the very beginning, with young children, the allowance should be purely discretionary money, enough to pay for an ice cream cone or a trinket.

This small amount for small children is "junk" money, in one father's words, for "the candy or toy we 'had' to buy every time we entered a store." As a youngster matures, his allowance can be increased to cover more of his needs. The child in the middle school years can gradually take responsibility for his school lunches, bowling, movies, etc. For teenagers, many families include money for at least some clothing. A little discretionary money should always be added to the earmarked amounts. A child learns nothing from an allowance that is completely allocated in advance.

Discretionary amounts, at every age, should be adequate and realistic. When her mother gave her a quarter to buy an ice cream cone not long age, an eight-year-old in the New York suburbs complained: "That's half my allowance." The 50 cents that had seemed a generous allowance for a third grader suddenly diminished in her parents' eyes.

Because different children have different needs, sometimes within the same family, some parents give a bigger allowance at the same age to, say, a highly social youngster than to a boy who plays baseball all the time or a girl who is always buried in a book. The experts have no easy answer to this one, but probably the fairer course is not to penalize a child who makes do with less than his brother or sister.

## SHOULD MY CHILD HELP DECIDE?

More than two-thirds of the parents who give allowances report that they review the amount at least once a year. Most discuss it with their children. Child-development authorities suggest that a regular review should always involve the child and should reveal whether the child is managing well and whether the amount is adequate as he grows.

Dr. Norman Handelman, a child psychologist, thinks that family discussion is most important: "The ground rules should be laid, and the expectations of both parent and child gotten out into the open. The context, rather than the money itself, is what's important—and open discussion between parent and child sets the right context."

When the children know that they have helped set the amount, they are less likely to carp about it afterward. Some parents, in fact, let the children decide. "We ask the children each fall what they think they need," reports Myrna Garfunkel, a New Jersey teacher and mother of two. "They've always been reasonable." Fourteen-year-old Joe now gets $1.50 a week, plus lunch money. Debbie, 11, gets 35 cents a week but has already told her parents that she will need more as she enters junior high school.

## SHOULD I RETAIN CONTROL OF SPENDING?

Almost two-thirds of the families in our survey said that they impose no restrictions on the way in which allowance money may be spent. But many of the same parents do provide what a Wellesley, Mass., father calls "strongly suggestive guidance." Some are selective. One Virginia mother of five, who puts no limitations on the way her 15-year-old son spends his $2.25 a week, does not allow an overweight daughter the same latitude; she is not permitted to buy candy.

While many parents feel that the allowance is best left free and uncontrolled, most drew the line at purchases they consider unacceptable—a switchblade knife, pornographic materials. Dr. Spock's view: "I don't think a parent should be so permissive about what a child can do with his allowance that he could regularly buy enough candy to rot his teeth or spend a couple of afternoons a week in movie theaters. In other words, a child should be able to use his allowance according to his taste as long as he stays within the laws of the land and the regulations of the family."

## SHOULD THE ALLOWANCE BE TIED TO BEHAVIOR, CHORES OR GRADES?

A Texas mother who works as a police sergeant sometimes withholds allowance as a disciplinary measure. She writes: "When a child grows up and goes to work, the money will not automatically come whether she earns it or not." A Jacksonville, Florida, teacher believes that pocket money should be unrelated to behavior but does not always act that way. She says: "I feel the allowance should be free and clear, with no interference from parents in how it is used. I dislike withholding it for punishment, but do so because it seems effective." Some parents compromise. "I give the allowances on Saturday morning, after I clean," says Sally Synn, a New Jersey mother and social worker. "If I can't get the vacuum through the mess on their floors, they pick up before they get the money. It's the only way to perserve my sanity."

These positions reflect fundamental, if sometimes unconscious, philosophical differences. A consulting school psychologist in a Connecticut suburb points out: "What the allowance means is tied in with the family's value system. People who hold to the Puritan work ethic see an allowance as a reward for good behavior and work performed; they see an allowance given independently of these things as permissive, spoiling the child. Other middle-class families are more likely to see an allowance as a learning tool, through which the child learns how to manage money. They also see it as a sensible way of handling the child's necessary expenses."

These opposing views are clearly represented in our sample. A Maryland minister asserted: "A work incentive is the basis of the allowance, to teach children how to earn, save, spend and be generous to others through a respect for, and wise use of, money." Needless to say, his twelve-year-old's $1 allowance is closely linked to the performance of household chores. But another family reports: "The allowance for our children is strictly for the purchase of things they want (usually toys). It is their portion of the family income and not the result of any work they have or have not done."

The experts favor the family-income theory. Sidonie Matsner Gruenberg told us emphatically: "Maintenance of a child costs thousands of dollars and an allowance is a small part of this cost. It should be treated the same as other costs. It should not be used for punishment, or reward, or to make him more considerate of his grandmother. It's just money." A child can be damaged emotionally if, in effect, his parents bribe him to be good or get better marks.

97% of our survey families expect their children to perform routine household chores. Some tie these chores to the allowance. A California forester reports: "Our girl, age seven, get 25 cents for setting the table for supper. Our boy, age five, gets 25 cents for emptying trash. As they grow older, both responsibilities and allowance will increase."

On the other hand, a bit more than half of our sample would agree with a West Hartford, Conn., teacher who wrote: "Household chores are done as a contribution to the family and are not paid for." The psychologists we interviewed agree that a child, as a member of the family, should be expected to help around the house without specific financial reward. They feel, though, that children should have the opportunity to earn extra money by performing special jobs around the house—as three-fourths of those in our sample do—as long as the jobs are the kind that an outsider might otherwise be hired to do.

Some parents pay their offspring only for special one-time projects, like cleaning out a year's accumulation of junk from basement or garage; others pay for regular chores, like mowing the lawn or shoveling snow, that are above and beyond normal household duties. If a child is to be given an outsider's opportunity to do a job, he should also have the outsider's opportunity to refuse. David Tenner, who doesn't think his allowance is big enough, does get $4 for mowing the family lawn. "I don't have any choice, though," he says. "I'd rather play instead."

## IF MY CHILD EARNS OUTSIDE INCOME, SHOULD HIS ALLOWANCE BE REDUCED?

By the time young people are in high school, more and more are earning money outside the house. In some families allowances are suspended when a child begins to earn consistently. The issue is complex: Do you penalize a child for having the initiative to seek a job? If you expect children to earn, should you penalize the child who needs all his spare time for study in order to do well in school?

96% of our sample families avoid these sticky questions by continuing the allowance. Chris March, 16, receives $10 a month. "Before we put him on an allowance," his mother says, "he was always needing something, always asking for money. Now he's learned that he can take care of some of his own needs. He does baby-sitting, tutors in math and teaches guitar. He's averaging $20 a week, but he gets his allowance no matter how much or how little he earns."

Above all, the experts' advice is that before you begin to think about specific sums, you should try to clarify your family's feelings about the uses and limits of money. Once you know what you believe an allowance is and what it is meant to accomplish, the other questions are easier to answer.

With the best of intentions, parents can easily make mistakes with allowances. Some school administrators told us that lower-middle-class families often give their children more pocket money than their more affluent neighbors do, perhaps by way of compensating for what they feel is their lesser social status. Our survey, however, showed little relation between family income and size of allowance.

Paents use overgenerous allowances to make up for other things: where both parents work, for example, the child will often be given a large allowance as recompense for their absence. None of this is a good idea. "Preadolescent children have a certain limited range of values," says Arthur Turkel, a New Jersey psychologist. "They don't know what to do with too much money. It only creates problems."

If too much money is bad, so is too little or none at all. Says one Long Island father: "You wouldn't expect a child to learn to read without having books. How can he learn to handle money if he doesn't have any?"

Reading 29

# Too Few Americans Go For Broke

**Dee Wedemeyer**

*There's nothing unique about going broke. Business and corporations fact it all the time—and declare bankruptcy. Individual Americans can do the same thing, through a relatively quick court proceeding—and many do.*

Two years ago, Irish emigrant Joseph Ridge thought the American dream had come true. Working overtime, he earned almost $15,000 a year. He was up-to-date on all his loan payments and his company was negotiating a new wage contract.

Then came a strike and the Phase I wage freeze and suddenly he and his family of eight children and his wife, Mary, were on welfare. The Ridges fell further and further behind on the payments. Finally, the seven-month strike ended, but so did the overtime. And Joe Ridge became one of about 180,000 persons who declare bankruptcy.

Although they are the least publicized bankrupts, the "Joe Ridges" are typical.

Research by the Brookings Institution in Washington shows the average individual bankrupt to be a blue-collar worker, about 40 years old earning about $130 a week, married 12 years with two children and carrying an average debt of about $5000. If he had not been in business previously, he owes the money to 12 creditors.

David Stanley, a senior fellow at Brookings and director of the research

From the *St. Louis Post-Dispatch*, July 2, 1972, Section 1-15E.

project, said that the average bankrupt could have gone along making his payments if some crisis had not occured—loss of overtime pay, birth of an extra child, medical bills or divorce.

Joe Ridge—not his real name but a real person who appeared in U.S. Bankruptcy Court in New York recently—fits into this category.

He emigrated from Ireland 17 years ago and began working for the New York Telephone Company immediately in an unskilled job as a frameman connecting underground wires with equipment in the central office.

When Ridge, 43, filed bankruptcy, he owed $5130 to two finance companies, a bank charge card, a department store and a mail order catalogue firm. An additional $200 owed to his employer is deducted from his salary at the rate of $10 each week and was not declared.

The Ridges did not go broke on high living. They live in a $112-a-month, three-bedroom apartment that is furnished with hand-me-downs from neighbors.

The five girls, ages 6 to 14, share one bedroom, sleeping on a twin bed and its trundle. Three boys share another room.

A big celebration for the Ridges was 11-year-old Geraldine's confirmation. They gave her $10 and took her out to dinner at a nearby Chinese restaurant.

On the day of their court appearance, Mary and Joseph appeared with their Legal Aid lawyer.

Joe, a meagerly built man, with faded red hair, took the stand first.

The judge was Roy A. Babitt, a veteran of more than seven years as a bankruptcy referee. He claimed he can easily spot a fraud. Babitt questioned Joe gently with standard questions.

"Do you own a car? Do you have a stamp or coin collection? Why did your income drop $4000? Do you have a bank account? How do you pay your bills? Are you due for an income tax refund?" the judge asked.

Ridge smiled about the income tax refund because even going bankrupt takes money. He paid $150 for the refund to Legal Aid—$50 for each standard filing fee that goes to the court and $50 more for the lawyer's miscellaneous expenses, including purchasing the bankruptcy petitions from a legal stationer for $5. If Ridge had filed without the help of a lawyer, the $50 fees, like his debts, could have been paid on the instalment plan.

Babbitt noticed that the Legal Aid lawyer had not exempted Ridge's pension fund from his assets and admonished the attorney for the oversight. Then he asked Mary the same questions.

"Did you ever own a car?"

"Yes. I sold it for $1," she said.

"Why only $1?" Babitt inquired.

"It wouldn't move," she said.

In 30 days, if no creditor has contested, the Ridges' debts are canceled. About two billion dollars in debts are discharged this way each year.

In open-and-shut cases like the Ridges', Babitt does not bother to appoint a trustee—usually a lawyer known to the court—to double check for assets. Other referees appoint a trustee in every case.

It would be the trustee's job to report these assets at another court session and administer their distribution to creditors. Sometimes the assets are so small they are abandoned to the debtor.

Some debts are never dischargable—taxes, alimony, child support, fines, debts incurred fraudulently or those resulting from intentional injuries to persons or property.

The Ridges did have one other alternative under the bankruptcy law—filing a wage earner's plan in which a court-appointed trustee administers, for a fee, an extended payment or partial payment plan. About 30,000 people in the United States file these plans each year. But it is out of the question for the Ridges. Without overtime, Joe has only earned $1800 so far this year and the prospects for higher wages don't look good.

"These are not bad people," Babitt said. "Bankruptcy is caused because they can't pay their bills. They've been told about the goodies. How can you tell them they can't have part of the goodies, too?

"Oh, you get deadbeats, sure, but you also get the fellow who has huge medical bills and a mongoloid child and then his wife gets sick. The tide of adversity has just swept him up," Babitt said.

Babitt said he believes bankruptcy is a form of rehabilitation for the honest bankrupt.

Other persons, including some poverty workers, have taken a more militant stand. One Washington civil rights worker has suggested that the best way for the poor to divide up the wealth a little more evenly is to run up large bills, then declare bankruptcy.

In fact, at hearings of the Commission on the Revision of the Bankruptcy Law, a lawyer testified that he was finding cases of persons running up bills, then filing bankruptcy.

According to the law, if this could be proved, the debts would not be dischargable. However, Judge Babitt pointed out that it is virtually impossible to prove.

"They can go out and buy television and bedroom sets to their heart's content," said Babitt. "Their creditors may be gulled, but they have been gulled by their own lack of business prudence. We recognize the frailites of people but the only brake, and I mean b-r-a-k-e, is that if they do, they better not do it for another six years and they better come back honestly."

Jan Slavicek, co-author of "The Layman's Guide to Bankruptcy," said he believes bankruptcy is a check against unscrupulous merchants who load up a customer with merchandise he can't afford. He estimates there are probably 20,000,000 persons in the United States who ought to declare bankruptcy.

"If you look at the American family as a business—a certain amount of money goes in, a certain amount goes out. If it were operated on business principles, half the families would declare bankruptcy today."

Slavicek said he believes more persons would declare bankruptcy if they only realized that it was a civil, not criminal, proceeding; that their credit will not be ruined forever, that it is not a drawn-out court procedure and that it does not necessarily mean the bankrupt has to give up everything he or she owns.

Most states exempt household furniture and clothes, though Florida has a law that exempts a man's underwear while his wife had to buy her own back from the court. Some states exempt automobiles.

Exemptions on homes vary from state to state. North Dakota protects a farm up to 160 acres and $40,000. South Carolina exempts only $1000 value.

Slavicek said that in some cases persons' credit could actually improve because they have become rare Americans—people without debts. They do, in fact, have a low repeater rate—about 2 percent—and a creditor has the assurance that bankruptcy can only be declared every six years. Sometimes credit purchasing can be done by making larger down payments.

"However, most persons after declaring bankruptcy don't want to ever hear of credit again," Slavicek said.

The Ridges have, in fact, sworn off credit, though she does regret the loss of the credit card because it came in handy for buying birthday presents when there was no cash available.

"But you know," said Mrs. Ridge, "this will be the first time since we were married we haven't had bills."

Reading 30

# Getting Out of Debt without Going Broke

**Changing Times**

*If your debts are still dragging you under, probably the only place you can get any real help is from the creditors themselves.*

Maybe it won't happen to you, but it does to many families who never thought it would. Suddenly they're in debt way over their heads and no relief in sight.

The problem has a way of sneaking up on the unwary. Many families tend to live right up to their income, often a bit beyond. Everything goes along okay until an emergency comes up, maybe a loss of income or some unplanned major expense. And all at once they're in the soup, can't pay their bills.

Could it happen to you? Here are some danger signals to watch out for. Any one of them might be a warning of financial distress ahead.

- You have no savings or don't have enough to tide you over a financial upset.
- You don't know what your living costs are. The money comes in, but you don't know where it goes.
- You often rob Peter to pay Paul. For example, you "borrow" the money saved for insurance premiums to buy something on impulse.
- You use a lot of credit. You've got charge accounts all over town, use several credit cards and pay the minimum on each account.
- You don't know what your debts come to. Maybe you've got some idea what your monthly payments are supposed to be, but you're pretty vague about the balance due.
- You postpone paying bills.
- You've begun to hear from your creditors.

Those are the danger signals, loud and clear. If they have already begun to show, now is the time to get cracking on the problem—before your creditors descend on you.

## HOW TO KEEP FROM GOING UNDER

Common sense dictates the first series of moves:

1 Let everyone in the family know that the money situation is tight and get them to help compile a detailed list of all expenses, including the mortgage payment, on a monthly basis.

2 List all your debts along with details: item for which you are paying, creditor, original amount, interest rate, finance charge, current balance, monthly payment, when payments are due. If you don't have this information, get it from the creditors.

3 Put down your family's total monthly net income. Do not include bonuses or occasional part-time earnings that can't be depended on.

4 Now subtract monthly living expenses from net income. This will show you how you would stand if you had no debts. Next, subtract the monthly payments you are supposed to be making to creditors.

You'll probably have to do this arithmetic for a few months to get the real picture of your situation. If you come out with a minus figure, you are obviously living beyond your means. Even if you get a surplus, you may still be headed for trouble if you are not saving something (instead of using the surplus for impulse buying) or if your debts, excluding home mortgage payments, eat up more than 20% of your take-home pay.

5 What you do now is tough but clear. You start shaving expenses. Likely areas of unwise spending are recreation, food, insurance and transportation. Many families spend too much for convenience—frequent meals out, heavy use of costly prepared foods, home delivery of eggs and dairy products. A second car used for running errands may be convenient, but it really pushes up transportation costs.

Okay, you've had what you consider a realistic look at your budget and pared it to the bone. What's cut should leave enough to pay your debts. But what if it doesn't?

## TIME FOR DRASTIC ACTION

Face it: If your debts are still dragging you under, probably the only place you can get any real help is from the creditors themselves. Difficult as it may be, you'll have to talk to each of them. But there's no point in seeing them until you have worked out a sensible plan of action that shows, in detail, how you can pay them off if they'll cooperate.

Consider the circumstances of the Jones family. Their current monthly payments on purchases and loans add up to $412.11. In addition, they have several overdue telephone, utility and other bills.

The Joneses have gone over their living costs and managed to cut them by $180. But that money applied to monthly payments doesn't put them into the black. They are still finding it extremely difficult to meet the remaining $232.11 in monthly payments.

Their next move is to figure out what would happen if they could get a reduction in payments, say by half. This, of course, would not cut the amount actually owed on each account but merely extend the time required to pay it off. There would be no sense in trying to reduce payments to the point where only the interest was being paid—they'd never get out of debt that way. Some secured loans can be cut, but others, such as those for a car, usually cannot be, though the lenders might consider refinancing the balance, probably at higher interest.

The Joneses' situation now looks like this:

| Creditor | Monthly payment | Proposed payment | Balance owed |
|---|---|---|---|
| Bank card | $32.00 | $16.00 | $810.30 |
| Store A | 22.00 | 11.00 | 460.62 |
| Store B | 22.00 | 11.00 | 396.20 |
| Store C | 25.00 | 12.50 | 136.02 |
| Loan A | 28.06 | 14.03 | 448.60 |
| Loan B | 38.76 | 19.38 | 158.16 |
| National card | 25.00 | 12.50 | 508.72 |
| Local card | 22.00 | 11.00 | 664.61 |
| Credit union* | 137.07 | 137.07 | 2,299.53 |
| Bank* | 60.22 | 60.22 | 700.64 |
| Phone | — | — | 75.83 |
| Utility | — | — | 80.05 |
| Other | — | — | 45.09 |
| Totals | $412.11 | $304.70 | $6,784.37 |

* Secured loans for cars.

(This is a simplified example. All payments are not normally reduced by the same percentage. The kind of debt, balance owed, whether the debt is secured and the policies of the creditor must be considered in determining each reduction.)

Cutting payments in half (except for the two car loans, which must be paid off at the current rate) reduces the monthly tab on debts to $304.70. That's not low enough if the Jones family is trying to get its payments down even more than the $180 they have managed to cut on their living expenses; they're still short of that mark by $124.70. Nor have they dealt with the $200 in overdue bills.

Car payments are the major drag, especially the big one of $137.07 a month for a new station wagon the wife uses. What to do about it? Mr. Jones might try to moonlight or his wife might look for a part-time job to cover those payments. But for various reasons neither of this solutions is practicable for the Joneses.

They feel they can get by with one car so they decide to sell the station wagon even though that means loss of money already paid. They figure they can get $2,000 for it. So after explaining the problem to the credit union that lent them the money, they sell the car and use the $2,000 to pay off most of the balance due. Then they get a consolidation loan of $500 from the credit union at an annual rate of 10% for 18 months. Monthly payments are $30. Of the $500, they use $300 to wipe out the remainder of the auto loan at the credit union and the other $200 to clean up the small bills.

At this point the Jones family has reduced their credit union payments by a hefty amount, cut transportation expenses—which came to $42 a month for insurance and operating costs on the station wagon—and trimmed total indebtedness from $6,784.37 to $4,783.87.

Monthly payments, according to the plan, would now be down to $197.63. That's easily taken care of by the $222 they have pared from their budget ($180 plus $42). In fact, that leaves about $24, which should be put into savings.

Everything now depends on whether the creditors are willing to agree to smaller monthly payments. This is the point at which the Joneses would begin calling on them in person.

If you find yourself in a situation similar to the Joneses, you should be quite open when you talk to your creditors. Explain why you have fallen behind on payments even if you must admit that you have been using credit too freely. Spell out how you intend to cut expenses.

To demonstrate your good faith, destroy all credit cards. Send the issuing companies a letter explaining why you did so and show copies of it to your creditors.

Some of the people you owe money to may be shocked, even angry, at your suggestion to cut your payments. If they resist, point out that the plan won't work unless everyone cooperates. Its failure might mean that you would have to go bankrupt and they'd stand to lose quite a bit that way. Sometimes a cooperating lender can help convince others to accept your plan. When a lender does agree to go along, be sure that no extra interest charges or fees are added to your indebtedness.

Getting out of debt this way is a long, hard task, and not a pleasant one. But you may have no other practical course open to you. If it works—and with persistence it will—you'll be in the clear, and much less likely to get into a similar fix again.

**Reading 31**

# Get a Consumer Bargain—Money

**Josephine Ripley**

*In shopping for credit, you should consider all possible sources and compare prices.*

There are some new consumer bargains today. Have you noticed?

Money is cheaper. It costs less to borrow now. For homes, cars, furniture, television sets, refrigerators, a vacation, perhaps. You name it.

Interest rates (or the annual percentage rate, to use the precise terminology) which have been sky high in recent years are coming down.

In fact, they are extremely low compared with what you have been paying.

You, Mr. and Mrs. Consumer, are in the driver's seat for a change. That is, you are in a position to drive a bargain—to shop for credit and be choosy.

Read the advertisements in the paper and see how popular you are.

Banks are begging you to borrow money. They are competing for your business, offering consumer loans at bargain rates.

One bank in the Greater Washington area recently ran spectacular, double-spread newspaper advertisement promising consumer loans at "reduced rates" for the next three months.

"We want your business," the bank stated bluntly.

Another bank threw down the gauntlet with this challenge in its ad: "Unless you have money to burn, why in the world should you pay more than 8 percent for a consumer loan?"

Still another featured its loan as "your best bargain," suggesting the consumer save money by borrowing to pay his bills with cash instead of putting them on a revolving charge account.

Their low-cost loan, the bank claimed in its advertisement, "gives you ready cash so you can avoid the high cost of the plastic world of credit cards." The annual percentage rate on revolving accounts is 18 percent.

So take your choice, consumers. Find your own bargain. Take your time. Money is plentiful. There is competition for business—your business.

Borrowing money is nothing new, of course. Consumers know the name of the game, but many of them don't know how to play it.

How should you shop for credit now that the shopping is good? Where can you go to borrow money? What questions should you ask when you apply for a loan?

What other charges are there, if any, in addition to the finance charge? What figures should you check before you sign a promissory note or an installment contract?

Should you take out credit life insurance when you borrow money? When is it desirable or necessary?

What is an "add-on" and what is a "discount" as applied to a loan?

These are questions which will be dealt with in this article.

But first—where and how can you borrow money? Suppose you want a cash loan. Or you want to finance a mortgage on your home. Or negotiate the purchase of a new car.

In shopping for credit, you should consider all possible sources and compare prices. That is, the price you pay for the use of the money you want to borrow.

• Your life insurance policy, for instance. You can borrow from the life insurance company on that. Here you will probably get the lowest annual percentage rate available. About 5 or 6 percent.

If you are a GI with a life-insurance policy issued by the federal government, you can borrow on that policy at an annual percentage rate of 4 percent.

Some people choose to borrow on their life insurance in order to pay cash for a purchase that would otherwise have been made on credit at a much higher annual percentage rate.

Also to be considered is the fact that money borrowed on a life insurance policy does not have to be paid back as long as the policy is in force, although interest must continue to be paid at regular intervals.

• A relative or friend might be glad to lend you money. After all, you could offer him a higher return on his money than he would get on a savings account, but a rate lower than you would have to pay if you borrowed from the bank.

• Then there is the credit union. Credit unions are consumer cooperative lending agencies, chartered by the state or federal government to make loans to members of the cooperative at a low annual percentage rate.

Credit unions not only handle small loans, but also engage in the financing of automobiles, durable goods, house trailers, boats, and so forth. Rates on secured loans range from an annual percentage rate of 9 to 12. Rates vary depending on the size of the credit union and the part of the country in which it is located.

These rates represent the total cost of the loan with no extras for service or other charges.

• Commercial banks. Banks are the biggest lenders of all. They have gone into the installment credit field in a major way in recent years. In fact, they now have the lion's share of the market in automobile financing. And you can usually get a slightly better rate on new car financing from banks today than from finance companies.

• Consumer finance companies. These companies charge a higher annual percentage rate than most lending institutions. They charge more because they will take higher risks. When you cannot get a loan from a bank because of your low credit standing, you can probably get it from a finance company.

These companies, by law, deal only in relatively small loans. Some companies may lend up to $1,000 while others may loan as much as $5,000, depending on the state small loan law.

To borrow $300 from such a finance company, you might pay an annual percentage rate of 36 percent.

Consumer loans at commercial banks may range from 8 to 13 in annual percentage rate. If your credit is good and the risk small, you might even bargain for a lower rate today. But this type of bargain might be found only in the District of Columbia where annual percentage rates are probably the lowest in the country at the present time.

The annual percentage rate on new cars today is running from 8 to 11 percent. The annual percentage rate on other types of loans—for the purchase of furniture, major appliances, jewelry, etc., is higher.

On furniture, rates would range from 18 to 22 on an annual percentage basis. On television sets and major appliances you would pay 20 to 22 percent on your loan.

These rates apply only to purchases in furniture stores or stores selling major appliances, not to department store purchases. Department stores have their own installment credit departments and handle their own financing. Some purchases are made on revolving credit accounts at an annual percentage fee of 18 percent.

Larger purchases are usually financed through the store's credit department on a closed-end account, with a definite deadline for payment.

## Reading 32

# It Pays to Shop for Cheapest Credit

**Morton C. Paulson**

*Americans often overpay for credit because they don't know how—or won't take the time—to shop for the best deal.*

Isabelle Warfield, a Salina, Kan., housewife (that's not her real name), searches out the best buy in town when she shops for beef, yarn, washing machines, and other items.

But not when she borrows money. Hence, she and her husband paid $32 more than necessary when they bought a color television set for Christmas.

Theirs isn't an uncommon story. Americans often overpay for credit because they don't know how—or won't take the time—to shop for the best deal. Moreover, surveys conducted for the National Commission on Consumer Finance found that many people still do not know that lenders are required to reveal financing costs under the Truth in Lending Act.

From *The National Observer*, February 3, 1973, p.3.

Such costs vary enormously. Interest rates range from as little as 5 per cent for a loan against a life-insurance policy to 40 per cent or more charged by some small-loan companies. A one-year, $1,000 loan could cost less than $55 in interest or more than $230.

## BASIC NOMENCLATURE

Families that have reasonably good ratings can almost always borrow at reasonable cost. And they can keep the cost at a minimum by shopping for the best deal. Before discussing some of the ways to do this, let's take a quick look at some basic finance-charge nomenclature:

There's the *monthly rate,* expressed as a percentage rate per month on the unpaid balance of a loan; the *add-on rate,* under which a finance charge is added to the face amount of a loan you are obligated to repay in instalments; the *discount rate,* under which the finance charge is deducted from the face amount of a loan to be repaid in instalments; the *discount-plus-fee rate,* under which the finance charge is deducted, the borrower is billed for a loan fee, and the full amount of the loan is repaid in instalments.

In addition to interest, many lenders charge loan fees of one kind or another, sometimes including the cost of life insurance on the borrower.

To minimize the confusion, Congress decreed in passing the Truth in Lending Act that interest must be stated in terms of true annual interest, or annual percentage rate. And on most loans the total cost of the financing must also be revealed.

The annual percentage rate is the yardstick by which the costs of all types of credit can be determined and compared. Essentially, the yardstick expresses the yearly cost of credit in percentage terms, but because of the numerous variables, the formulas for determining annual percentage rates can be complex.

## SOME EXAMPLES

To help understand how the various credit plans work, first consider a loan at simple or actual interest. A bank lends you, say, $1,000 for a year at 6 per cent. You have the use of the full face amount of the loan for a year and then you repay it in full, plus interest of $60. Your annual percentage rate, in the example, also would be 6 per cent.

Now suppose you borrow $1,000 for a year with a 6 per cent add-on charge. You typically would agree to repay $1,060 in monthly instalments over a year. But this time your annual percentage rate would be higher—10.9 per cent—because you had the full use of the face amount of the loan only for the first month.

If you obtain a loan or buy merchandise at a monthly rate of ¾ of 1 per cent of the unpaid balance, you are agreeing to an annual percentage rate of 9 per cent. A monthly rate of 1½ per cent, a very common rate on credit-card and revolving-charge-account balances, is the equivalent of an annual percentage rate of 18 per cent.

Finance-company rates are considerably higher. Typically their charges will be calculated as follows: 3 per cent per month on the first $150; 2 per cent per month on anything between $150 to $300; and 1 per cent per month on that part of a loan above $300. That translates into at least 30 per cent a year as an annual percentage rate.

It's often possible to get far better terms by shopping around or by using a different approach to borrowing. Here are some possibilities:

### Life-Insurance Loans

Almost all life-insurance policies that have a cash-in value permit the policyholder to borrow quickly any amount up to the cash-in value. The interest rate is 5 per cent as a rule, 6 per cent on a few loans.

A word of caution, though. If you borrow on life insurance and die before the money is repaid, the amount owed will be deducted from the face value of the policy before any payments are made to beneficiaries.

### Borrowing on a Savings Account

Yes, it's possible to get a bank loan using a savings account as collateral. The annual percentage rate usually will run about 9 to 10 per cent, but that will be somewhat offset by your savings account, which will continue to draw interest at 4 or 5 per cent. However, you will be required to keep an amount equal to the balance of the loan in the account until the obligation is fully paid.

### Credit-Union Loans

If your company, church, or other affiliation has a credit union, you can get favorable rates on loans by joining. These nonprofit organizations charge an annual percentage rate of between 8 per cent and 12 per cent. Their biggest lending volume is in personal loans, but credit unions sometimes also finance cars, boats, home improvements, and big appliances. The usual rates for car loans—12 per cent or as little as 8 per cent with a 25 per cent down payment—compares with 21 per cent or more charged by some finance companies.

### Bank Loans

Bank customers with good credit ratings usually can obtain personal instalment loans without cosigners, payable over one, two, or even three years. Rates, terms, and collateral requirements vary, but banks commonly charge 11.5 or 12 per cent annual percentage rate. Thus, a bank loan could be cheaper than, for instance, a department-store purchase financed by an 18-per cent revolving-credit account. And auto loans from a bank can be much cheaper than those arranged by a car dealer or obtained from a finance company.

By putting up collateral such as stocks, bonds, or mutual-fund shares, it may be possible to get a bank loan for as little as 6 per cent annual percentage rate.

Here are a few other things to keep in mind when borrowing. Along with the annual percentage rate, you should find out exactly how much the loan will cost you in dollars. You may be surprised by the high cost. Watch out for "balloon" clauses; you may find your last payment considerably higher than the rest. And beware of stores that claim to offer exceptionally low credit rates; the prices of their merchandise may have been raised to compensate for them.

One other thing: If you've been planning to buy a car, a house, or whatever on credit, the sooner you act the more money you may save; interest rates appear to be heading up.

Reading 33

# How to Find Out about Credit Reports

**Education Department, Credit Union National Association, Inc.**

*For the first time the law gives you a way to challenge what is said against you.*

Have you ever been turned down for a loan because of a credit report?

If you have, you may have wondered what to do. Thanks to a new law, effective April 25, 1971 (Title VI, PL 91-508), you can now demand to know what's in your credit file at a credit bureau.

There are two basic reasons why you might want to know: you've been denied for a loan because of a credit report; you're just curious about what credit people say about you.

Let's take the first case: you've been denied for a loan or the interest rate has been raised, because of a credit report. Denial of insurance or employment or an increase in insurance rates because of a credit report is also covered by the law. In all these cases, the user of the credit report (credit union, bank, other lender) *must let you know:* 1) that your loan (or insurance or employment) was denied; and 2) the name and address of the credit bureau making the credit report.

Then, you can go to the credit bureau and ask to see your file: there is no charge if you do this within 30 days. If you think there is an error in your file, you say so. The credit bureau will investigate the item and let you know the outcome. If you disagree with the outcome, you can file a written statement, disagreeing with the findings.

Now, let's say you are just curious: you can go to the credit bureau and get the same service. BUT, you may have to pay their normal fee for the information—the same fee they normally chrge a bank or credit union for the information.

## HOW DO I ARRANGE TO FIND OUT ABOUT MY CREDIT FILE?

Go to the local credit bureau in person (you can find it in the Yellow Pages under "Credit Reporting Agencies") and ask to see your file.

This can be handled over the telephone if you make an advance request, in writing.

During the interview you can be accompanied by your spouse or one other person.

## WHAT INFORMATION DOES THE CREDIT BUREAU HAVE TO GIVE ME?

The credit bureau must disclose all information in your file and the sources of that information. You must also be given the names of all persons who have received employment reports in the last two years, and persons given credit reports in the last six months.

Prepared by *Everybody's Money,* the credit union magazine for consumers, published by Credit Union National Association, Box 431, Madison, Wisconsin, 53701.

## HOW CAN I CORRECT AN ERROR IN MY FILE?

If you spot an error, ask the credit bureau to delete it. They will check it out.

If you disagree with the findings, file a written statement. If the credit bureau helps you prepare the statement, they may limit it to 100 words. When such a statement of dispute is filed, it must go along with any subsequent credit report containing the disputed information.

If an item is wrong and is deleted, or if it is disputed, the credit bureau must, at your request, inform all persons who have used your file for employment in the past two years, and those who got a credit report in the last six months.

## WHAT IF A CREDIT UNION GETS A REPORT ON ME?

If a credit union (or any other lender) gets a credit report on you and as a result turns down your loan, they must tell you so and give you the name and address of the credit reporting agency. If you are denied credit because of a credit report or credit information, the credit grantor (credit union, bank, etc.) must say so.

If they get credit information on you (other than a formal credit report) and deny your loan as a result, they must tell the nature of the information, but not the source, if they turn down your loan. If a credit bureau report is not involved, the credit grantor (credit union, etc.) must inform you that you have 60 days to request the reason for a loan turndown, if they have gotten credit information from someone else.

## HOW WILL I KNOW IF A CREDIT REPORT CAUSED ME TO LOSE A LOAN?

If a formal credit report was involved, you must be given the name and address of the credit bureau involved.

## WHAT IF I'M DENIED CREDIT FOR OTHER REASONS?

Let's say your credit union asks your bank or another credit union about your credit—and then turns down your loan. You can ask why. Credit unions may do this kind of thing seldom—but many banks and other lenders do it often. Whoever does it—the new law gives you the right to know the nature of the information on which the denial was based.

## HOW LONG DOES BAD INFORMATION STAY IN MY FILE?

It used to stay forever. Now, bankruptcy information stays for 14 years. Some other credit information stays for only 7 years.

Other personal information can be challenged by you and removed sooner—just contact your local credit bureau, see what information they have, and challenge anything you think is unfair or inaccurate. There may be a fee.

## WHAT KIND OF CREDIT IS COVERED BY THE NEW LAW?

Generally, all consumer credit—auto loans, home loans, etc.—is covered by the law. Farm, professional, and commercial loans are not covered.

**CAN JUST ANYONE GET CREDIT INFORMATION ON ME?**

No. It can go to you, to lenders, the government (if they are extending you credit or about to employ or insure you), or to a court (upon a court order).

The information sent to a governmental agency is limited to name, present and former addresses, and present and former employment. Lenders may receive all the information in your file.

Your credit union has always respected your confidence and the privacy of your credit transactions.

The new law requires all other lenders and credit agencies to give you the same consideration your credit union always has.

**WHAT CAN I DO IF I HAVE A COMPLAINT?**

Call the credit bureau, if you have a complaint about a credit report. Find out how much it costs to see your credit file. If you wish, your credit union will be glad to explain your rights under PL 91-508.

Once you have seen your credit file, make sure all is in order. If there are errors, challenge them—in writing. Make sure the credit bureau removes any items which you can demonstrate are wrong.

The intent of the law is to protect you against the use of inaccurate or outdated credit information. Now, if you are denied a loan because of an adverse credit report, you will know because you must be told about it. For the first time, the law gives you a way to challenge what's said against you.

Reading 34

# Court Strikes Down Some Rights of Creditors to Repossess

**Elizabeth M. Fowler**

*Parties whose rights are to be affected are entitled to be heard.*

Some years ago, Mrs. Rosa Washington got into a fight with her divorced husband, a local deputy sheriff in Pennsylvania, over the custody of their son. Her former husband obtained an order to seize the boy's clothes, furniture and toys.

Out of Mrs. Washington's bizarre experience—together with similar cases—the United States Supreme Court has fashioned an historic decision for consumer rights.

In a 4-to-3 decision by Justice Potter Stewart, the court recently struck down almost all existing state statutes governing the rights of creditors to repossess collateral—rights rooted in the 600-year-old common law doctrine of "replevin."

In simple terms, the court held that state laws cannot permit creditors to repossess collateral—whether an automobile, gas stove, or stereo set—without first giving notice and without providing a hearing.

Mrs. Washington's case was the most unusual of the five that the Supreme Court considered jointly, and Justice Stewart himself called it "bizarre." However, it was the battle of Margarita Fuentes against the Firestone Tire & Rubber Co. that was more typical and, indeed, received the court's fuller attention.

The facts in the case—Fuentes Vs. Florida—are simple. Mrs. Fuentes bought a gas stove and service contract from a local Firestone store and later bought a stereo set. To finance them she signed typical installment sales contracts.

Her total cost was about $500, plus $100 for the financing. For more than a year she paid regularly and owed only $200 when she got into a dispute with Firestone about servicing the stove. Then she refused to pay.

Firestone began an action against her in small claims court both for repossession of the stove and the stereo set and at the same time obtained a writ of replevin (repossession) which empowered the local sheriff to seize the goods.

Once a suit is filed, Florida law requires only the filling in of blanks on a form and submission of the seizure documents to the clerk of the court for signature. The same day the sheriff and a Firestone agent seized the stove and stereo from Mrs. Fuentes's home.

Her lawyer filed an action in U.S. District Court, in Florida, challenging the constitutionality of Florida's replevin statute. He stressed that it prejudged the case without giving her a hearing and thus violated the due process of law in the Fourteenth Amendment to the U.S. Constitution.

The lower court upheld the Florida law, and the case moved to the Supreme Court on appeal. There, the Fuentes case involving Florida law was joined with Rosa Washington's case and three others that challenged Pennsylvania's repossession law.

Justices Powell and Rehnquist had not joined the court when the cases were argued and did not participate in the decision.

What bothered the court was that the plaintiffs received no prior notice and were allowed "no opportunity whatever to challenge the issuance of the writ of replevin" until after the property was actually seized.

Under Florida law, the sheriff must keep the goods three days and during that time the defendants can reclaim them but must post a bond equal to double the value of the goods. If he cannot afford that or refuses, the property goes to the creditor who sought the writ, pending final judgement, of course, final judgement can take time.

Justice Stewart stressed the rights for due process of law, quoting a previous decision that "parties whose rights are to be affected are entitled to be heard; and in order that they may enjoy the right they must be notified."

In its conclusion the court made clear it did not question the power of a state to seize goods "before a final judgement to protect creditors so long as these creditors have tested their claim through the process of a prior hearing."

It also said that states had the right to make quick seizures without hearings where necessary for the public interest such as to collect taxes, help a war effort, protect the public from the disaster of a bank failure and to protect from misbranded drugs or contaminated food. "These situations, however, must be truly unusual," the court said.

Reading 35

# Introduction of the Fair Credit Billing Act

**Congressional Record**

*The credit card revolution has been a mixed blessing for the consumer.*

## S. 652—INTRODUCTION OF THE FAIR CREDIT BILLING ACT

*Mr. Proxmire.* Mr. President, I introduce a bill to be known as the Fair Credit Billing Act, and ask that it be appropriately referred.

*The President pro tempore.* The bill will be received and appropriately referred.

The bill (S. 652) to amend the Truth in Lending Act to protect consumers against careless and unfair billing practices, and for other purposes, introduced by Mr. Proxmire, was received, read twice by its title, and referred to the Committee on Banking, Housing and Urban Affairs.

*Mr. Proxmire.* Mr. President, following the passage of the Truth in Lending Act in 1968, the Congress has made great strides in consumer protection legislation. Last year, for example, the President signed into law legislation I introduced to control the unsolicited mailing of credit cards and protect consumers from inaccurate or misleading credit reports. These legislative victories indicate that at long last the voice of the consumer is beginning to be heard in the halls of Congress.

In order to build upon the achievements of past Congresses, I am today introducing on behalf of myself and Senator Brooke, a *Fair Credit Billing Act* to protect consumers from unfair or careless billing practices. The legislation is introduced in the form of an amendment to the Truth in Lending Act and would be administered by the Federal Reserve Board which has done such an outstanding job in consumer credit regulation. The bill addresses itself to numerous complaints I have received about billing practices and the use of credit cards. Many of these complaints are undoubtedly a reflection of the rapid growth of credit cards and revolving credit plans used by major creditors across the country.

## THE CREDIT CARD REVOLUTION

The use of credit cards has been truly phenomenal. It has been estimated that there are well over 300 million credit cards in circulation today. The Federal Reserve Board reports that the total amount of credit owed by consumers on their credit cards as of June 30, 1970, was $14.7 billion, up $2 billion from the year before. Of this amount, $3 billion was owed to commercial bank credit card plans, $1.6 billion to oil companies, $9.8 billion to retail stores, and $300 million on other credit card plans. Commercial bank penetration into the credit card field has been particularly impressive. Commercial banks more than tripled their outstanding credit volume on bank credit cards from 1968 to 1970. During 1970, more than $5.3 billion in sales were made on bank credit cards alone. It is

From the *Congressional Record*, vol. 17, Feb. 8, 1971, no. 13, Senate pp. 1–2.

clear that credit cards are playing an increasingly important role in the consumer's family budget.

The credit card revolution has been a mixed blessing for the consumer. It is perhaps inevitable that our consumer protection laws have lagged behind the rapidly changing developments in the use of credit. The consumer has been harassed and intimidated by computer written dunning letters; he has been shortchanged by tricky billing practices which result in interest rates far above the legal usury ceilings; he is being given less and less time to pay his bills before incurring a finance charge; and he is forced to subsidize the credit card system whenever he pays cash instead of using a credit card.

## TWELVE POINT CONSUMER PROGRAM: PROPOSED BILL OF CONSUMER RIGHTS

Mr. President, in order to redress these and other abuses, I have prepared a 12-point program to strengthen the rights of the consumer in credit card and billing transactions. These provisions constitute a bill of rights for the consumer when he deals in credit. They insure that the consumer will be dealt with fairly and equitably by the credit grantor.

Here are the 12 provisions:

One, creditors are required to investigate and answer inquiries about billing errors within 30 days, or otherwise forfeit the amount in dispute;

Two, creditors cannot threaten a consumer with an adverse credit rating while a billing dispute is being investigated. Whenever a consumer disputes a bill, the creditor must also send him a copy of any adverse report made to a credit reporting agency and must inform the agency that the amount in question is disputed by the consumer;

Three, creditors who operate revolving credit plans must mail out their monthly statements at least 21 days prior to the time the consumer must make a payment in order to avoid a finance charge;

Four, creditors are prohibited from using the so-called previous balance system on their revolving charge accounts. Under this system, consumers do not receive credit for any partial payments they might make during the month;

Five, creditors are prohibited from imposing a minimum charge on their revolving charge accounts;

Six, banks are prohibited from using the funds in their customer's checking account in order to satisfy a credit card debt;

Seven, creditors must credit payments on revolving charge accounts on the date the payment is received;

Eight, creditors must promptly credit consumers with any excess payments they might make on their revolving charge account, and refund any excess payments if requested;

Nine, consumers are given the same legal rights and defenses against the issuer of a credit card that they would have against the merchant honoring the card in the event of any dispute;

Ten, merchants and other retailers are permitted to offer a cash discount to consumers who pay cash in lieu of using a credit card notwithstanding any agreement to the contrary between the merchant and the issuer of the credit card;

Eleven, creditors are required to disclose on their monthly bills a brief description of all of the items purchased during the month together with the merchant or store involved;

Twelve, creditors must disclose on their monthly billing statements an address and telephone number to be used by consumers in the event they have any questions concerning the accuracy of the bill.

Mr. President, these protections do not by any manner or means exhaust the areas of concern in the consumer credit field. No attempt has been made to regulate the maxiumum rates which creditors can charge: nor does the bill attempt to prohibit deceptive or harassing collection practices; finally, there is no attempt to alter the general pattern of legal remedies available to creditors with respect to consumer credit transactions. Nonetheless, these provisions do cover most of the complaints which consumers have voiced about current billing practices. These complaints have been made to Members of Congress, to the Federal Trade Commission, to the National Commission on Consumer Finance, and to the President's Special Assistant for Consumer Affairs. I am hopeful that the Fair Credit Billing Act will go a long way toward relieving the consumer's legitimate grievances with respect to creditor billing practices.

## CORRECTION OF BILLING ERRORS

Mr. President, the main provisions of the legislation are to be found in a new chapter IV which would be added to the Truth in Lending Act. Section 161 of this chapter deals with the correction of billing errors. Under this section, Creditors are required to acknowledge consumer inquiries about billing errors within 10 days and to respond affirmatively to the inquiry within 30 days. By the end of the 30-day period, the creditor must either correct the consumer's account, or explain to him why the original bill was correct, after having conducted an investigation. If the creditor does not meet these requirements, he forfeits the amount in dispute. Moreover, if the consumer can prove that the amount in dispute actually is an error of the creditors, the consumer can collect three times the amount of the error plus attorney's fees and any actual damages sustained by the consumer.

This provision is designed as a remedy for a situation which is becoming all too familiar. By now, almost everyone has had the frustrating and often degrading experience of attempting to resolve a billing error. It often takes months and even years to break through the chain of computers which are seemingly oblivious of consumer complaints. The penalty provisions of this section are designed to provide creditors with an incentive to respond promptly and affirmatively to consumer billing inquiries.

Certainly it should not be beyond the ingenuity of the American business system to respond to billing inquiries within 30 days. If computers can be programed to write dunning letters, they can also be programed to contain their rhetoric until a human being has investigated a customer's specific complaint. Struggling to resolve a billing error is perhaps not the most important problem faced by consumers. Nevertheless, a protracted battle over a billing error can be extremely annoying and burdensome. Many consumers simply give up rather than subject themselves to further harassment. This provision is designed to restore the consumer's faith that he can indeed change the system if he makes an effort to do so.

## CREDIT REPORTS

In a related provision, the bill also regulates communications between a creditor and a credit reporting agency whenever a billing dispute is involved. First of all, whenever a consumer makes a written inquiry challenging an item on his bill, the creditor is prohibited from threatening his credit rating until he actually conducts an investigation and explains to the consumer why he believes the bill to be correct. This will prevent creditors from intimidating consumers into paying an unjust bill simply to avoid the possibility of an adverse credit rating.

Second, whenever a bill is in dispute, a creditor cannot communicate any adverse information about the nonpayment of the bill unless he also sends a copy of the report to the consumer. This provision is designed to let the consumer know that the creditor is placing adverse information in his credit file. The consumer then has the right under the Fair Credit Reporting Act to contact his credit reporting agency, and to correct any inaccurate or misleading information. If the dispute still cannot be resolved, the credit reporting agency must then enter the consumer's version of the dispute in its file and report the consumer's side of the story to all subsequent users of the information.

Third, a creditor cannot report a disputed account as delinquent unless he also informs the credit reporting agency that the account is in dispute and furnishes the agency with a brief version of the consumer's contentions. Moreover, he must report any subsequent change in the status of the account to the credit reporting agency. For example, if the creditor subsequently discovers that he is in error, he must communicate this fact to the credit reporting agency.

These provisions are designed to protect not only consumers but other creditors from the consequences of inaccurate or misleading credit information. Certainly everyone has a stake in an accurate credit reporting system. My objective is not to disrupt the free flow of legitimate credit information, but rather to insure that the information is as accurate as possible.

A creditor should certainly not be permitted to secretly blackball a consumer over a disputed bill. Why should consumers have to spend sleepless nights worrying that their credit rating may be adversely affected because of a dispute they are having with a recalcitrant merchant?

## THE SHRINKING BILLING PERIOD

A third provision of the legislation regulation regulates the so-called shrinking billing period. It requires that creditors mail out their bills at least 21 days before payment is due in order to avoid the imposition of a finance charge.

While most creditors theoretically give the consumer 30 days to pay his bills in order to avoid a finance charge, in actual practice, the consumer is given much less time. Some creditors take as much as a week or even 2 weeks before mailing out their monthly bills. When this delay is added to the time required by the mails, the consumer often has only a few days to pay a bill before being socked with a finance charge. Since many consumers are in the habit of paying their bills on a monthly basis rather than weekly or daily, they have often been lulled into incurring a finance charge.

Other creditors have deliberately chosen to contract the payment period to 25 days even though they are on a monthly billing cycle. The effect of this is to give the consumer far fewer days to pay his bill before incurring a finance charge. While the so-called shrinking billing period might provide more revenue to the creditor, it is basically unfair to the consumer. If the consumer is given an option to avoid a finance charge by paying cash within a specified period of time, it should be a meaningful option and one which he can exercise with ordinary standards of due care. I believe the 21-day rule strikes a reasonable balance between the creditor and the consumer. For those creditors on a monthly billing cycle, it gives them approximately 9 full days to close their books and mail out their monthly statements. At the same time, the consumer is given a reasonable period of time to exercise his option.

## BILLING SYSTEMS

A fourth provision of the legislation would prohibit the so-called previous balance system on revolving charge accounts and require the use of the so-called adjusted balance system. Under the previous balance system, consumers are given no credit for any partial payments they might make during the current payment period. For example, if a consumer had an opening balance of $100 and made a partial payment of $90, a creditor using the previous balance system would charge the consumer 1½ percent of the $100 balance, or $1.50. When the $1.50 finance charge is compared to the $10 actually owing, the annual interest rate works out to 180 percent. In effect, the consumer is paying interest on the money he has already paid back to the creditor. I estimate that consumers are paying an extra two hundred million a year in finance charges because of the previous balance system.

On the other hand, a store using the adjusted balance method would give the consumer credit for the partial payment and charge him only on the remaining balance. This system is far more equitable since it gives the consumer credit for the payments he has made. Moreover, it gives the consumer a positive incentive for paying back his bills since his finance charge is reduced accordingly. By way of contrast, a consumer would have no incentive for making a partial payment under the opening balance system, since he would pay the same finance charge anyway. Thus the opening balance system can encourage excessive consumer indebtedness.

Congress was well aware of the differences between the adjusted balance system and the previous balance system when it passed the truth-in-lending law. Although both systems disclose the same annual percentage rate, it is obvious that the adjusted balance method results in a far lower finance charge to consumers. Nevertheless, it proved to be impossible to come up with a method for reflecting the differences in the various billing systems in the disclosure of an annual percentage rate. Congress therefore required that creditors disclose their monthly rates and their annual equivalents while at the same time disclosing their methods for arriving at the balance upon which the finance charge is assessed. These disclosures have made many consumers aware of the basic inequity of the previous balance system. No doubt many members of the Senate have received letters from their constituents protesting that the previous balance system is illegal or usurious.

While the Truth-in-Lending Act adopted a disclosure approach, it is obvious that full justice cannot be done unless the various billing systems are subject to some form of regulation. The Fair Credit Billing Act therefore requires that creditors must use the adjusted balance method on their revolving charge accounts whenever the consumer is given an option to avoid a finance charge by paying his account in full within a specified period of time. In other words, if he is given an option, it must be a meaningful option and one not hedged with tricky restrictions. A creditor would not be prevented however from basing his finance charge on the average daily amount of credit actually used by the consumer computed from the time of each extension of credit to each payment. Under this system the consumer would, of course, have no option to avoid a finance charge. He would be charged in exact proportion to the number of days of credit actually used. In effect, there would be no free period.

## MINIMUM FINANCE CHARGES OUTLAWED

A fifth provision of the legislation would prohibit the imposition of minimum finance charges on revolving credit plans. Under the Truth-in-Lending Act, any minimum finance charge in excess of $0.50 must be reflected in the annual percentage rate. This has made it possible for creditors to impose a minimum finance charge of $0.50 or less without reflecting it in the annual percentage rate. While it certainly is not the intent of the Truth-in-Lending Act to authorize the imposition of such charges, some creditors have used the law as an excuse to institute a minimum finance charge.

The use of minimum finance charges is unfair to the consumer because it subjects them to astronomical interest rates. For example, if a consumer has a balance of $10 in his revolving charge account, he could be subjected to a minimum finance charge of $0.50. This comes to 5 percent a month, or 60 percent a year. If he had a $5 balance, the annual percentage rate would come to 120 percent.

Creditors have attempted to justify the minimum finance charge by arguing that they have certain fixed costs in connection with the mailing of a bill, and that they are entitled to recover these costs in the finance charge. If this argument is valid, then one wonders why creditors do not impose the same $0.50 minimum finance charge on those customers who pay their bills within the specified period of time, since the same fixed costs are involved on all monthly bills.

The practical effect of the minimum finance charge is to single out a particular group of customers for the payment of a fixed charge supposedly connected with the mailing of a monthly statement. These consumers are those who have low credit balances and cannot afford to pay them in full. They are the very ones who live the closest to poverty and who can least afford to pay interest rates of 120 percent or higher. As presently operated, the minimum finance charge is thus basically unfair and discriminatory. It hits only the poor and not the rich or affluent.

## PROTECTION OF CHECKING ACCOUNTS

A sixth provision of the legislation would prohibit creditors from using funds on deposit as an offset against a credit card debt. For example, the terms of a bank credit card plan often permit the bank issuing the credit card to use any funds which the cardholder might have on deposit with that bank as an offset against the consumer's indebtedness. This permits the bank to obtain payment without any recourse to the courts. It permits the bank to collect a debt even though the consumer may have a legally valid reason for not paying. It nullifies whatever bargaining power the consumer might have by threatening to withhold payment in order to obtain satisfaction on a merchandise dispute.

The use of offsets are quite similar to wage assignments which have been prohibited by most of the 50 States. A wage assignment permits a creditor to attach a debtor's wages without any legal recourse to the courts. It has proved to be abusive and overly harsh on consumers and has been properly outlawed by most of the States. There is no reason why offsets should not be similarly prohibited.

Nothing in the legislation would prohibit a bank from attaching the funds in its customer's account under the general garnishment law of the State, provided that such remedies were available to creditors generally

## CREDITING PAYMENTS WHEN RECEIVED

A seventh provision of the legislation would require creditors to credit consumers with making payment on their revolving charge accounts on the date the payment is actually received by the creditor. Some creditors apparently delay the posting of a customer's payment until several days after the actual receipt thereof. Under these circumstances, it is possible for a consumer to incur a finance charge, even though he has sent his payment within the specified period of time. This is not fair to the consumer and should be prohibited. If the consumer makes a payment, he ought to get credit for it on the date the funds are actually received by the creditor. The consumer has no control over how long it takes the creditor to post the payment to his books.

## CREDITING EXCESS PAYMENTS

An eighth provision of the legislation governs the treatment of excess payments. Whenever a consumer makes an excess payment on his revolving charge account, he must be credited promptly with that amount.

If he has other bills outstanding, the excess payment must be used to offset the amount of those bills. If at the end of the month he has an outstanding credit balance, the creditor must disclose the balance to him and indicate that he has an option to request a cash refund of part or all of the outstanding credit balance.

While I believe that most legitimate creditors already follow these procedures, consumers do need to be protected from the few unscrupulous creditors who might seek to appropriate excess payments for their own uses.

## LEGAL RIGHTS OF CREDIT CARD USERS

A ninth provision of the legislation would give credit card customers the same rights and defenses against the issuer of a credit card that they would have against a merchant or other seller in any transaction arising out of the use of that credit card. For example, if a consumer buys a TV set directly from a merchant on credit and the TV set does not work, the consumer can withhold payment until the merchant honors his warranty. Should the merchant sue to enforce payment, the consumer can defend against such a suit by claiming a breach of warranty.

On the other hand, should the same consumer purchase the same TV set from the same merchant by using a bank credit card, the bank can legally require the consumer to pay notwithstanding his legitimate dispute with the merchant. This is because the bank is either a holder in due course or a cash lender. Under the former theory, a holder in due course is entitled to enforce payment on any installment note purchased by him, notwithstanding any dispute the consumer may have with the seller of the note. While this doctrine would be nullified by a proposed FTC regulation, there is some doubt that it would extend to transactions covering banks.

Under the second theory, a bank can be held to be a cash lender with respect to any purchases made by a consumer through the use of a bank credit card. The courts have generally given cash lenders the right to collect on their loans, even though the borrower may have a legitimate dispute with a merchant from whom goods were purchased with the proceeds of the loan. The rights of cash lenders would not be affected by the proposed FTC regulation although they would be circumscribed by the proposed legislation if the loan was pursuant to a credit card plan.

This provision will provide an incentive to commercial banks to be more selective in choosing the merchants authorized to honor bank credit cards. It will also prevent a gradual erosion of a consumer's basic legal rights as the use of bank credit cards begins to replace direct credit arrangements between the merchant and the consumer. The inclusion of a third party such as a bank or a credit card company should not be permitted to weaken the traditional rights and defenses which a consumer might have in any retail transaction entered into directly with a merchant.

## CASH DISCOUNT PERMITTED

A 10th provision of the legislation would enable merchants to offer a cash discount of up to 5 percent to those buyers who like to pay cash rather than use a credit card. The discount may be offered notwithstanding any agreement to the contrary with a bank or other credit card company which prohibits the offering of such a discount. Such discounts would also be exempted from the disclosure requirements of the Truth-in-Lending Act, thereby facilitating their use.

Many banks have sought to promote the widespread use of their credit card by prohibiting merchants from offering a cash discount. This prohibition is basically unfair both to merchants and to cash buyers, and should be nullified by public policy. Since the bank charges the merchant a discount of 3 or 4 percent in connection with credit card transactions, the merchant has an obvious incentive to avoid the payment of such a discount by offering the consumer a similar discount in return for prompt payment by cash. The cash buyer likewise benefits from such a discount since he is charged a lower price.

There has been much dispute as to whether the payment of a discount to a bank or a credit card company causes merchants to raise their retail prices. Regardless of whether prices are raised directly because of discounts paid by the merchant, there is no denying that these discounts are an element of cost and must ultimately be reflected in the prices charged. Thus those consumers who pay cash are in effect helping to subsidize those who buy on credit. I hope that the incentives offered by this legislation will induce more merchants into offering the cash buyer a discount, thereby removing this source of inequity.

Should a merchant offer a cash discount, he must offer it to all prospective buyers whether or not they have credit cards, and must clearly and conspicuously disclose its availability pursuant to regulations of the Federal Reserve Board. This is to insure that all cash buyers receive the benefit of the discount, and not just those who happen to have a credit card or are inclined to request such a discount.

## DISCLOSURES ON MONTHLY STATEMENTS

An 11th provision of the legislation strengthens the Truth-in-Lending Act by requiring creditors to include on their monthly billing statements a brief description of all of the items purchased during the billing period together with an identification of the merchant or vendor involved. The existing Truth-in-Lending Act does not require the disclosure of the merchant or vendor. Moreover, the act waives the requirement for a brief description of the items purchased if a copy of such transaction were previously furnished to the consumer. Most credit card plans give the consumer a copy of the sales draft at the point of the transaction. By so doing, the credit card issuer is not required to provide a brief description of such items on his monthly bill. Thus, unless the consumer saves all of the sales drafts during the month, and makes a laborious comparison of the amounts with the amounts listed on the bill, he would have no way of checking the accuracy of the bill.

By requiring a fuller description of each credit transaction on the monthly statement, the consumer is thus given more information about his transactions. Hopefully, such disclosures will help detect billing errors and reduce fraud losses.

## TELEPHONE CONTACT

A 12th provision of the legislation require creditors to list on their monthly billing statements an address and telephone number which the consumer can use if he has any questions about an item appearing on his bill. This provision is designed to facilitate communications between a consumer and a creditor over an alleged billing error. I also believe the Congress should give serious consideration to requiring that creditors list the name of a real person whose job it is to receive consumer complaints about billing errors. While this requirement may prove to be infeasible, it certainly would go a long way towards humanizing the billing system and reducing the level of consumer frustration.

Mr. President, many provisions of the proposed legislation are contained in a proposed FTC trade regulation. The FTC had originally planned to hold hearings on this trade regulation in late January. However, at my request the FTC has decided to postpone the hearings in order that Congress might consider a legislative approach to the problem.

I believe that a legislative solution is desirable for two reasons: one, legislation passed by Congress would clearly extend to commercial banks whereas there is some doubt that banks can be included under the FTC regulations since they are specifically exempt from the FTC Act; and two, a legislative solution can avoid the narrow and restrictive definition of interstate commerce which has limited the jurisdiction of the Federal Trade Commission. Moreover, since the Truth in Lending Act and amendments thereto are founded in part upon the general monetary powers of the Congress, a case can be made for extending the provisions of the act to credit transactions which are purely intrastate in character.

In addition, the proposed legislation goes considerably beyond the FTC regulation in a number of respects including regulation of billing systems, the authorization of treble damage suits against nonresponsive creditors, the incentives provided for cash discounts, and the subjecting of credit card issuers to the rights and defenses of credit card holders.

Mr. President, I am hopeful that the Committee on Banking, Housing and Urban Affairs to which this legislation will be referred can hold prompt and thorough hearings on this important legislation. Undoubtedly, some of the provisions may need to be refined as the committee gains additional information during the course of the hearings. I am hopeful that representatives of the credit industry and consumer advocates will come forward with their ideas for a sound and workable statute.

## S. 652

*Be it enacted, etc.,* That this Act may be cited as the "Fair Credit Billing Act."

Sec. 2. Section 127 of the Truth in Lending Act (15 U.S.C. 1637) is amended—

(1) by adding at the end of subsection (a) a new paragraph as follows:

(8) The protection provided by section 161 to an obligor under any such account in the event of an erroneous billing:

(2) by amending subsection (b) (2) to read as follows:

(2) The amount and date of each extension of credit during the period, the vendors and/or creditors involved, and, if a purchase was involved, a brief identification of the goods or services purchased:

(3) by adding at the end of subsection (b) new paragraphs as follows:

(11) The right of the obligor and the obligations of the creditor under section 161 in the event the obligor believes there is an error in the statement of his account and gives written notice thereof to the creditor;

(12) The address and telephone number to be used as a contact between the obligor and the creditor for the purpose of receiving requests by the obligor to correct mistakes or make adjustments to the obligor's billing statement.

Sec. 3. The Truth in Lending Act (15 U.S.C. 1601 1655) is amended by adding at the end thereof a new chapter as follows:

## CHAPTER 4 CREDIT BILLING

Sec.
161 Correction of billing errors.
162 Regulation of credit reports.
163 Length of billing period.
164 Credit for partial payments.
165 Prohibition of minimum charges.
166 Prohibition of offsets.
167 Crediting payments on date of receipt.
168 Crediting excess payments.
169 Rights of credit card customers.
170 Use of cash discounts.
171 Civil penalties.

## §161 CORRECTION OF BILLING ERRORS

(a) If a creditor, having transmitted to an obligor a statement of the obligor's account in connection with an extension of consumer credit, receives a written notice from the obligor in which the obligor—

(1) directs the attention of the creditor to an amount shown in the statement as owing from the obligor, which the obligor believes to be in error in whole or in part, or seeks additional clarification with respect to such statement.

(2) indicates the amount (if any) by which the amount shown in the statement is greater or less than the sum believed to be owing to the creditor by the obligor, and

(3) sets forth the reasons of the obligor for the belief that the bill is in error or requires additional clarification, the creditor shall—

(A) not later than ten days after the receipt of the notice, send a written acknowledgement thereof to the obligor, and

(B) not later than thirty days after the receipt of the notice and prior to taking any action to collect the amount, or any part thereof, believed to be in error—

(i) make appropriate corrections in the account of the obligor and transmit to the obligor a statement of his account which has been revised so as to show the corrections, or

(ii) send a written explanation to the obligor setting forth the reasons why the creditor believes the account of the obligor was correctly shown in the statement together with copies of documentary evidence of the obligor's indebtedness after having conducted an investigation in response to the obligor's written notice.

(b) creditor, having received a notice from an obligor as provided in subsection (a), who fails to comply with the requirements of that section—

(1) Forfeits any right to collect from the obligor the amount shown in any statement of the obligor's account which the obligor believes to be in error and has specified in such notice in the manner prescribed in clause (2) of such subsection, including any finance charge or other charge imposed by the creditor in connection with the amount so specified; and

(2) if such amount is in fact an error, is liable to the obligor in an amount equal to the sum of—

(A) the actual damages sustained by the obligor as a result of the failure of the creditor to comply with such section;

(B) $100 or three times the amount referred to in paragraph (1), whichever is the greater; and

(C) in the case of any successful action to enforce the foregoing liability, the costs of the action together with a reasonable attorney's fee as determined by the court.

## §162 REGULATION OF CREDIT REPORTS

(a) After receiving a notice from an obligor as provided in section 161, a creditor may not directly or indirectly threaten the obligor with consequences adverse to his credit rating or credit standing until the creditor has met the requirements of section 161 and allowed the obligor thirty days thereafter to make payment.

(b) Any creditor who reports adverse credit information concerning a disputed amount allegedly owed by the obligor in connection with a consumer credit transaction to a consumer reporting agency, as defined in section 603 (f) of this Act, or to any other third party shall first notify the obligor of the name and address of the parties to whom such information is reported together with a copy of the report.

(c) A creditor may not report as delinquent the account of an obligor to a consumer reporting agency after receiving a notice from the obligor as provided in section 161 without also reporting that the account is in dispute and furnishing a brief description of the obligor's contention. A creditor shall report any subsequent disposition of any such disputed account to any consumer reporting agency to whom it has previously reported the account as delinquent.

## §163 LENGTH OF BILLING PERIOD

Where a creditor operates an open-end credit plan under the terms of which an obligor has the option of avoiding the payment of a finance charge by paying the outstanding balance in full within a specified period of time, a finance charge may not be imposed unless a statement of the outstanding balance upon which the finance charge for that period is based is mailed at least twenty-one days prior to the date by which payment must be made in order to avoid imposition of that finance charge.

## §164 CREDIT FOR PARTIAL PAYMENTS

Any creditor who operates an open-end credit plan under which the obligor has the option of avoiding the imposition of a finance charge by paying the opening balance in his account in full within a specified period of time shall compute the finance charge by applying a periodic rate or rates to the amount represented by the opening balance reduced by an amount equal to all payments and other adjustments received and credited to the obligor's account during such period.

## §165 PROHIBITION OF MINIMUM CHARGES

No creditor who operates an open-end credit plan shall impose a minimum finance charge on the periodic billing statement.

## §166 PROHIBITION OF OFFSETS

Notwithstanding any agreement to the contrary, no credit card issuer shall offset a cardholder's indebtedness against funds of the cardholder held on deposit with the card issuer. This section does not annul the right under State law of a card issuer to attach funds of a cardholder held on deposit with the card issuer if that remedy is available to creditors generally.

## §167 CREDITING PAYMENTS ON DATE OF RECEIPT

Any creditor who operates an open-end credit plan shall credit payments to an obligor's account based on the date of actual receipt of such payment by the creditor or his agent.

## §168 CREDITING EXCESS PAYMENTS

Whenever an obligor transmits funds to a creditor in excess of the total balance due on an open-end credit account, the creditor shall promptly refund the amount of payment in excess of such balance or promptly credit such excess amount to the obligor's account. If an obligor has an outstanding credit balance at the close of any billing period, the creditor shall disclose, on the periodic billing statement immediately following such period, that the obligor is entitled upon request to a prompt refund of any credit balance. Any creditor receiving such a request shall promptly refund the amount of the credit balance requested by the obligor.

## §169 RIGHTS OF CREDIT CUSTOMERS

A card issuer who has issued a credit card to a cardholder shall be subject to all claims and defenses arising out of any transaction in which the credit card is used as a method of payment or extension of credit.

## §170 USE OF CASH DISCOUNTS

(a) With respect to a credit card which may be used for extensions of credit in sales transactions in which the seller may be a person other than the card issuer, the card issuer may not, by contract or otherwise, prohibit such sellers from offering a discount to a cardholder to induce payment in cash rather than the use of a credit card.

(b) With respect to any sales transaction, any discount not in excess of 5 per centum offered by the seller for the purpose of inducing the payment of cash at the time of the transaction rather than the use of credit shall not constitute a finance charge as defined under section 106 provided such a discount is offered to all prospective buyers and its availability is disclosed to all prospective buyers clearly and conspicuously in accordance with regulations prescribed by the Board.

## §171 CIVIL PENALTIES

Any person who fails to comply with any requirements imposed under this chapter (except for section 161) with respect to any consumer is liable to that consumer in an amount equal to the sum of—

(1) any actual damages sustained by the consumer as a result of the failure;

(2) punitive damages of $100 or such greater amount as the court may allow; and

(3) in the case of any successful action to enforce any liabiltiy under this section, the costs of the action together with reasonable attorney's fees as determined by the court.

Sec. 4. This Act takes effect upon the expiration of one hundred and eighty days after the date of its enactment.

## Reading 36

# Beware the Pitfalls in the Fine Print

**Jean Carper**

*Many disclaimer clauses must be taken seriously.*

Not long ago, a couple in an Eastern state signed a contract for $2500 to have their big old house renovated. Three weeks later, their contractor died, and the work was never begun. Nevertheless, the couple received notice from a finance company demanding the $2500 in monthly payments.

The couple wrote, explaining the situation, and thought no more about it. Two months later, a sheriff notified them that the finance company had foreclosed on the house and would put it up for auction—unless they produced the cash to cover the contract plus legal fees. They sought help in every direction, but could not raise the money. Thus, incredibly—to pay for a job never done—their house was auctioned off. Worth perhaps $30,000, it was bought, by an officer of the finance company, for $20,000.

From the *Family Weekly*, April, 12, 1970.

In another case, a 56-year-old widow bought automobile insurance from a company recommended by her insurance agent. Her policy was canceled the following year with no explanation. Three years later, she received a letter ordering her to pay the state $291.49, because she was liable for claims against this now-defunct company that had once insured her car.

How are such things possible? The explanation is: *"fine print."* It appears on installment contracts, insurance policies, credit cards, on almost any legal document you sign. And its potential for disaster cannot be underestimated.

Here are the most insidious problem-makers to watch out for:

- *Waiver of defenses* The fine-print clause that ensnared the couple who lost their home was buried in their contract in the seemingly innocuous words: "We agree not to assert against any assignee hereof any claim or defense which we may have against the contractor." This meant that when the contract was sold to a finance company (the assignee), the couple waived their rights to take up with the latter any complaints that they might have had against the contractor. In short, they agreed to pay the finance company *regardless*—even if the work was not completed or even begun.

Nearly every credit contract sold to banks or finance companies contains such a *waiver-of-defenses* clause. In most states, the consumer has no way around it, except to do business with reputable companies which will make good no matter what the legal technicalities. So unfair is this clause that several states have outlawed it in certain types of consumer contracts. Many authorities believe it should be outlawed nationwide.

- *Contingent liability* The widow who was later forced to help pay the insurance company's outstanding claims had been a high-risk driver and unable to get a policy with old, established companies. Her agent directed her to one of the "assessable mutual" companies which specialize in high-risk drivers. In most of these policies, the catch is a bit of verbiage which makes the policyholder a part owner of the company and responsible for its debts. The statement reads: "Each member shall assume a contingent liability equal to, and in addition to, the premium provided by this policy." If the company fails, policyholders therefore can be assessed by the state to help pay outstanding claims.
- *Written notification* A New York woman lost a credit card. She reported the loss immediately by phone, and a few days later made written confirmation. Meanwhile, however, someone charged $685 worth on her card. She refused to pay, arguing that she had notified the company immediately. She lost the case in court because the fine print on her card required *written* notice. "It is unfortunate that she did not immediately send a telegram," the judge remarked.

Some credit-card companies allow phoned notice. But fine print can make you liable to many firms—at least up to the limit of $50 set by a newly passed law—until they receive written notice of card loss. Meanwhile, losses from the unauthorized use of credit cards are currently estimated at more than $100 million a year.

- *Confession of judgment* This fine-print clause dupes millions of Americans a year into signing away important rights. It works this way: A Pennsylvania man bought $250 worth of carpeting, agreeing to pay the dealer in monthly payments. After installation, the customer found that his floors had been damaged, and the ends of the carpet were frayed. He felt he had been cheated, and refused to make his first payment. Whereupon the finance company holding the contract got a court order requiring him to pay; otherwise his property would be attached to satisfy the debt. (In another state his wages might have been garnisheed.) There was no trial, no chance for the buyer to defend himself; he had signed a contract containing a confession-of-judgment clause, waiving his right to a court hearing by agreeing, *in advance,* to the charge.

This clause is found in all kinds of contracts—rental leases, installment contracts, notes—and reads in effect: "If I fail to make payments when due, I irrevocably appoint any attorney of any court of record to confess judgment in favor of the seller against me for the amount due." It makes possible unbelievable exploitation, especially among the poor. In Cook County (Chicago) alone, every year, more than $22 million worth of debts are collected through confession of judgment. It is an abominable clause. Some persons have been successful in striking it out before signing contracts.

- *Pre-existing health condition* In applying for health insurance, a California man inadvertently failed to note on his application that he had a record of high blood pressure. Later, after he suffered a heart attack, the insurance company denied him payment for $5000 worth of medical bills. The company claimed that there was evidence of heart disease before the policy was taken out. Therefore, under the fine-print pre-existing-health-condition clause, it was not obligated to pay.

Found in individual (usually not in group) health and accident policies, this clause typically *excepts* from coverage any bodily disease that originated prior to a date specified in the policy. The key word is "originated." If it can be proved that you had the disease—even unknown to you—prior to taking out the policy, you may be stuck, even though you were not asked for your complete medical history. However, in most states, an insurance company must honor the claim if a policy has been in effect either two years or three, unless you have knowingly concealed information.

When applying for accident or health insurance, don't hide previous illnesses or visits to doctors. Answer every question. Otherwise, a company can allege fraud and refuse to honor your claim. If you have a medical condition, a rider will probably be attached to the policy, excluding coverage for that condition—or allowing it, at a higher premium. If a policy does not make such provisions, the company may be relying on after-the-claim investigation and the pre-existing-condition clause for its own protection. (If you have any doubts about a policy or a company, check with your state's department of insurance.)

- *Liability waivers* On a flight from Buenos Aires to New York, a woman's suitcase, which had been checked, was lost. It contained a mink stole, plus other items, worth $900. The owner assumed that the airline would be fully responsible. But the airline paid her only $165 for the loss. Her ticket contained fine print limiting company liability to $7.50 per pound on international flights; if she had wanted additional coverage, she should have taken out insurance.

Such disclaimers of liability occur on any number of documents—from hotel-room and restaurant signs to baggage checks and rental leases. The fine print characteristically reads: "We are not responsible for any loss . . .," or "Our liability is limited to . . ." Many disclaimer clauses must be taken seriously. For example, household-moving companies, in their contracts, hold to a maximum liability of 60 cents a pound for each item. On the other hand, as Prof. Monroe H. Freedman, of George Washington University Law School, says: "Many disclaimers are legally meaningless, and are put there mostly to discourage lawsuits. There must be thousands of people who have had their cars damaged in parking lots who have been discouraged from pressing for compensation because the attendant said, 'Read the back of your claim stub. It says right there we're not responsible.' "

Courts are taking an increasingly dim view of fine-print liability disclaimers. One U.S. district court ruled that the "lilliputian typography" on the back of an airline ticket was not adequate notification of liability to the holder. A California court upheld an injured patients' right to sue a hospital for malpractice, even though on admittance he signed a contract absolving the hospital of liability for negligence.

Under a barrage of criticism and legal reform, some companies are simplifying the fine print, enlarging it, and putting necessary information in more conspicuous places where you are likely to find it. Courts are increasingly striking down rigid fine-print interpretations and siding with the consumer in fine-print disputes. Legislators are trying to abolish or modify a number of unfair fine-print clauses which are unconscionably weighted against the buyer.

Despite this increased protection, you must still exercise extreme caution. Read the fine print in any contract, and make sure you understand it. Don't let a finger-drumming salesman tell you that the fine print isn't important. It is, or it wouldn't be there.

# Buying Food

**Reading 37**

## How Three Families Buy Their Food

**Business Week**

*"My friends kid me because I can tell you the price of most everything in the store and whether its up a cent or down a cent."*

What is the first thing you do in the morning? How do you feel when you get up? When do you eat breakfast? What is the first thing you want to eat?

Such questions are being fired at some 4,000 American households as part of a major new approach to market research in the food business. In the past, Market Research Corp. of America, which conducts the industry's biggest continuing piece of market research, measured American eating habits and brand preferences. A study undertaken every five years, the National Menu Census is financed by General Mills, General Foods, Pillsbury, Campbell Soup, and a host of other food giants who pay up to $125,000 each for the full report.

This year for the first time, MRCA, a subsidiary of Computing & Software, Inc., is going one step further and exploring the consumer psychology behind American food habits and why people eat what they eat. The popular buzzword is "psychographics."

### Changing Lifestyles

As Norman Friedmann, president of C&S, explains it: "More and more women are working, and today's kids are increasingly mobile. This could mean that we are seeing a breakup of the family institution and the big, old-fashioned family dinner. Fast-food operations are thriving. This probably has something to do with the higher rate of working mothers, which means a bigger family income that permits more eating out. We are also seeing a boom in convenience foods, which obviously ties in with this. What our study will try to get at is the depth and degree of these trends, and just how much our changing lifestyles are affecting our foodstyles and how we eat."

MRCA's new lifestyle analysis grew out of some of the bits and pieces of psychographics that emerged from other past studies. One MRCA client, for instance, found that a vegetable that it sold was being used as the main course instead of a side helping. "This changed the company's entire advertising outlook," say Edgar W. Nelson, the C&S vice-president responsible for market research activities.

From *Business Week*, Nov. 25, 1972, pp 86–90.

The survey will not be completed until February, but will begin yielding its first preliminary results in January. Until then, the psychological and economic reasons that underlie today's changes in eating habits are indicated by three representative families interviewed by *Business Week*.

## THE HENRICHS: $50 A MONTH

The aroma from two steaming loaves of banana bread fills the tri-level home that Ted Henrichs, 39, built near Crownpoint, Ind., 15 years ago. His 36-year-old wife, Shirley, is putting some hamburger on the stove, as the two boys, Mark, 11, and Danny, eight, sit at a breakfast nook, poring over their homework. While 13-year-old Tammy puts plates on the dinner table overlooking their patio and garden beyond, six-year-old Lisa watches her mother prepare one of Lisa's favorites: tacos. "My husband wanted stuffed cabbage," Mrs. Henrichs tells a visitor, "but the kids voted for tacos."

Shirley Henrichs runs her household on $14,000 a year from her job as a parttime nurse and her husband's job as an instrument repairman. She spends only about $600 of that, or about $50 a month, on food. On this particular late afternoon, she jots down in her National Menu Census diary French taco seasoning mix, Imperial margarine, and Amigos tortillas. Because the Henrichs house sits on 10 acres of land, the diary entry for vegetables usually reads "homegrown" or at least "home canned." Each fall, she puts up green beans, peppers, pickles, beets, sauerkraut, peaches, and cherries. She also makes jellies and preserves out of strawberries, cherries, grapes, and blueberries. "In the summer, we never buy a tomato or green bean," she says. "So you can guess how much we save. My husband helps with the canning, and the kids haul vegetables from the garden."

### Shopping List

When Mrs. Henrichs does go shopping—usually at a Jewel store 10 minutes from her home—she buys in large quantities. This might include as many as 15 boxes of cereal (Wheaties, Cheerios, Ricechex), 25 lb. of flour (Robin Hood), 10 pounds of sugar (G&W). When she shops for meat, she may pick up a whole side of beef for 70¢ per lb.

Though she occasionally buys convenience foods such as Pillsbury mashed potatoes or Chef Boy-Ar-Dee canned ravioli, convenience foods do not take up much space in her cupboard. "I prefer to make things from scratch," she says. In the same way, frozen foods only rarely go into her grocery cart. Purchased vegetables are canned. "My husband doesn't like the taste of frozen vegetables," she says. Nor does she buy snack foods or cola drinks. However, Mrs. Henrichs does buy Jays potato chips, Fritos, and Jiff peanut butter.

She uses coupons for products that she would normally buy but seldom for products with which she is unfamiliar. Yet she does not head automatically for a brand name. "If I like a national brand better, I'll buy it. But if a store's brand is cheaper, and if I like it, I'll buy that." However, the children are more influenced by TV advertising. "They may say, 'Let's try this'—mostly cereal. If I buy it, someone will always eat it. But the other day, they saw on TV some packaged canned pudding for lunches. It was the highest-priced stuff I've ever seen—around 60¢. I took the children to the store and showed them how, for the same money, I could buy six boxes of pudding, and each box would serve the entire family. I told them that if we made the pudding ourselves, they could have the joy of making it, which they like to do. Not once did they ask to buy it again."

### Menus

A typical Henrichs day begins with a family breakfast of dried cereal with sugar and milk, and possibly toast with margarine and strawberry jam. Mr. and Mrs. Henrichs usually drink Folger's coffee with sugar, and either cream, Pet milk, or Coffeemate.

The noon meal for the kids and Mr. Henrichs is usually a sack lunch with a salami or lunch meat sandwich, fruit, and some cookies or a slice of cake. For dinner, the family might sit down to tacos, stuffed cabbage, or chopped sirloin with chili sauce, potato salad (either homemade or once in a while from the delicatessen), celery strips, Motts applesauce, and pineapple, toasted garlic bread, milk for everyone, and then coffee for the parents.

The family eats out about three times a month. "We usually take a poll to see where the kids want to go," says Mrs. Henrichs, "and you know where that usually is—Burger King or McDonald's. Maybe once a month, we'll have a nice meal in a restaurant." Now that the children are older, "we're eating out more than we did before," she adds. "It isn't that we have more money. I guess they just get tired of eating Mom's cooking." If there were just her husband and herself, Mrs. Henrichs says she would prepare such things as stroganoff more often. "But the little ones," she notes wistfully, "don't like everything mixed together."

## THE ARNOLDS: $90 A MONTH

Twenty-five-year-old Fred Arnold and his wife, Dianne, 27, live on a skintight budget. As a millhand at Bethlehem Steel in Los Angeles, Arnold earns about $5,200 a year. Yet the Arnolds, who have three children—three-year-old John, one-year-old Fred, and daughter Sandy, four months—are paying $150 a month in taxes and mortgage payments for their small, two-bedroom house in South Gate, a working-class industrial area 10 mi. southeast of downtown Los Angeles. They are spending $105 a month for the new grey 1972 Dodge Polara that sits in the driveway. They are also laying out $90 a month on food, 20% of Arnold's average monthly salary of $433.

"We just love to eat," says Dianne Arnold, "and I've never felt I had to scrimp on food." The Arnolds eat meat two or three times a day. Hamburger appears on the dinner table three times a week. Pork, steak, roast, and chicken fill out the week's menu. "I used to economize by buying whole chickens," Mrs. Arnold says. "But with small children, I worry about the tiny bones." So now she buys breasts and wings.

### Priorities

"Both my husband and I have cooked since childhood and pride ourselves on home-cooking," Mrs. Arnold says. It is not unusual for either of them to spend up to four hours on such fixings as stew, chili, spaghetti sauce, or vegetable soup. When they make chili, the Arnolds use dried beans, which take three hours to cook, instead of canned beans, which can be warmed in a few minutes. Vegetables are almost always fresh with one exception: corn. They prefer the taste of frozen corn.

"My friends kid me," Mrs. Arnold says, "because I can tell you the price of most everything in the store and whether it's up a cent or down a cent." She does most of her shopping just four blocks from home at Lucky's. Rib steak, she claims, goes for 35¢ a lb. less at Lucky's than at a nearby Ralph's. For produce, she drives an extra five miles to McCoy's, where apples go for 10¢ a lb. vs. 29¢ at

Lucky's. Mrs. Arnold prefers Wyler's dry soup mix to Campbell's because it "not only tastes better but sells for 9¢ to 10¢ a package compared with 17¢ and up for a can." She also watches for sales and goes heavily toward lower-priced, private-label items. "Harvest Day and Lady Lee green beans at 19¢ a can," she claims, "are just as good as Del Monte at 25¢ or Green Giant at 26¢."

Yet taste and quality often take priority over price. The family uses Imperial margarine at 42¢ a lb., because "it tastes good." The Arnolds buy only Armour Gold Star canned hams, even though a five-pounder runs $7.79. Another treat at least once every two months: sirloin tip roast from a butcher at $1.59 a lb., instead of shoulder cut from the grocery store at $1.19.

### Luxuries

In the same way, the Arnolds indulge their taste for Italian deli groceries—she is of Italian ancestry and he, Portuguese. Once a week they take a 30-minute drive to an Italian deli for green olives at 40¢ a half pint and salami at $1.79 a lb. Arnold has a salami sandwich in his brown bag almost daily. The family also buys Ronzoni manicotti at 65¢ a dozen at the deli. "We tried the grocery store brand, La Rosa, at 40¢ a dozen but they broke apart in cooking," she says. "I'd rather buy the more expensive brand if it's going to taste or cook better."

Both the Arnolds have a pronounced prejudice against canned and packaged convenience foods. "I don't cook from scratch just to save money," Mrs. Arnold stresses. "We love to cook and hate the way most things taste out of a can. Most of our friends can't understand that." Not that the Arnolds will not give convenience foods a try. In recent months, they sampled Hunt-Wesson's Skillet Dinners and General Mills' Hamburger Helper. "But we haven't found much that we like," says Arnold.

One convenience that Mrs. Arnold does like is Shasta and other soda pop in aluminum, pull-tab cans. "I hate returnable bottles," she says. "They're just too much trouble to take back." She figures that she spends an extra 15¢ for every three cans of soda pop she buys—a nickel more for the pop and a dime for throwaway containers.

Since the children eat a lot of breakfast cereal, Mrs. Arnold tries to stay clear of the sugar-coated brands, but concedes that she gives in. "My kids will only eat Fruit Loops and Trix. If I give them shredded wheat or oatmeal, I just have to throw it out." Just the other day, her three-year-old insisted on buying General Mills Frankenberry because he wanted the monster prize inside the box. He had heard about the new cereal on television.

Family dining-out is limited to a stop every two weeks on payday at a neighborhood McDonald's. "We've tried Colonel Sanders chicken twice in the five years we've been married," says Dianne Arnold. "I just happen to like my own fried chicken much better."

## THE ANTHONYS: $120 A MONTH

"I detest spending time in a supermarket," says 45-year-old Alice Anthony, a Livingston (N.J.) housewife. "I limit my weekly shopping trip to one hour, and if I forget something, we usually just do without for the rest of the week. Convenience stores are too expensive—even for small, odd items."

Though her 51-year-old husband, Charles, earns $25,000 a year as corporate research coordinator at M&T Chemical Co., in Rahway (N.J.), Mrs. Anthony is fairly frugal in her buying. She holds her food budget for her family of four to $120 a month, only $25 more than she spent in 1969, when food prices were lower and fewer nonfood items went into her shopping cart. In fact, the only regular addition to her shopping list over the last half-dozen years is a 5-lb. bag of Kennel Ration dogfood, that she began buying last month for her family's newly adopted, eight-week-old beagle, Nugget.

### Penny-wise

A few month ago, Mrs. Anthony switched to an A&P store after its conversion to discount WEO ("Where Economy Originates"), but quickly returned to her old haunt, Shop-Rite in Livingston. She finds prices there "a few pennies cheaper." She also prefers Shop-Rite private-label items, which make up a big proportion of her groceries—especially, coffee, frozen vegetables, and orange juice. Yet she stresses: "I cook what the family likes, not particularly what's the cheapest."

Her husband and long-legged, 10-year-old twin boys, Eric and Stewart, like hearty meals and plain fare: chicken, pork chops, hamburger, roast beef. "We have chicken more than anything else—often twice a week," says Mrs. Anthony, who catalogues at least half a dozen chicken recipes, including barbecued chicken, chicken cacciatore. Oriental chicken with soy souce, and plain, baked chicken. "I used to buy clams and other seafood," she says. "This was for myself, since no one else in the family likes it, but now it's just too expensive"—at as much as $3.29 a lb., for instance, for scallops.

Like the Arnolds of Los Angeles, the Anthonys make dinner almost a ritual. "The whole family is together," says Mrs. Anthony. "We like to have long conversations with the children and find out what everyone's been doing all day." And the spacious, colonial dining room with its expensive, handmade cherry table is conducive to lesiurely, comfortable dining.

Stewart, who has a flair for cooking, often whips up an apple pie or even a beef stew on a rainy Saturday afternoon. "If he's baking, he never uses a mix," says Mrs. Anthony. "He hates them. Eric, on the other hand, will dabble with cooking, but he's usually in it just to lick the bowl."

### Daily Fare

While Charles Anthony eats lunch 20 mi. away at work, both boys streak home at noontime to their large, two-story brick house, which is situated in one of New Jersey's leafier and better-heeled suburban communities. Usually awaiting them is Shop-Rite or Campbell's vegetable soup and tuna fish sandwiches, along with their ever-ready beagle pup. "For a while there, we had a run on peanut butter sandwiches," says their mother, "but when Eric got his braces this summer, it quickly turned to tuna fish. And we're still on that binge."

Breakfasts at the Anthonys are usually hearty, especially on weekends. Added to the usual juice, cereal, eggs, and coffee are Danish pastry, bacon or ham, peaches, oranges, or other fresh fruit. "We have no real brand preference when it comes to cereal." Mrs. Anthony says. "We buy any brand, depending on what kind of toy is inside or which coupons I've picked up."

While several of Mrs. Anthony's friends have recently gone back to work "and probably eat out more now," she has no plans to do either. "If we do eat out," says Anthony, "it's usually at a nice restaurant."

For those little food emergencies that crop up, Mrs. Anthony keeps her freezer well fortified. This week it is stuffed with two large homemade casseroles (turkey tetrazzini and sausage and shrimp), frozen peach preserves, pork chops, ham, chicken, roast beef, chicken breasts, beef stew, three large bags of frozen Shop-Rite string beans, corn, and peas, and some odds and ends—including some of Stewart's cookies.

Reading 38

# The Body Builders: How They Work

**Giant Food Stores**

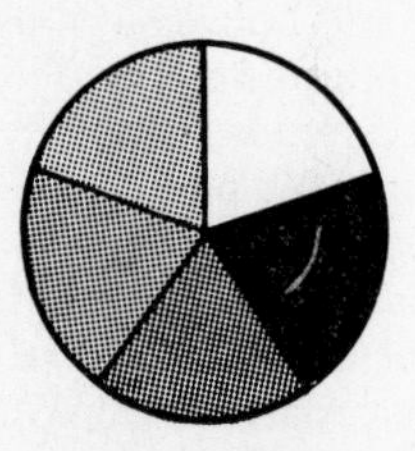

## THE SYMBOL

The circular symbol (above) shown on packages and posters tells you there is nutritional information provided. Look for it on posters and products.

## THE BODY BUILDERS: HOW THEY WORK

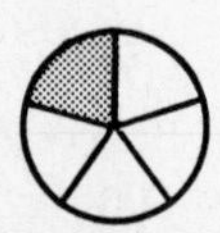

### Protein

The body's main building material, repairs body tissue and helps fight infection.

Sources: High quality protein: Meat, fish, poultry, eggs and dairy products. Lesser quality: Nuts, soybeans, cereal grains, peas and beans, which when combined with animal proteins and other foods, i.e. milk, make a meal of high quality.

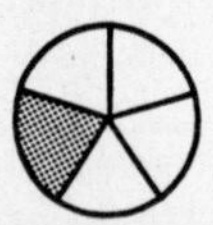

### Vitamins

Are essential to the functioning of the body. They are easily destroyed by light, air and heat. Often lost during improper cooking or storage.

**Vitamin A:** Protects against night blindness, helps to resist infection. Sources: Egg yolk, liver, milk fat, green and yellow vegetables.

**B Vitamins:** Thiamin, riboflavin and niacin help body tissues to function. Sources: Liver, whole grains, yeast, unpolished rice.

From the Giant Food Stores, Giant Food, Inc., P.O. Box 1804, Washington, D.C., 20013.

**Vitamin C:** Is not stored in the body and must be included in the daily diet. It is essential for healthy skin, gums, blood vessels, bones and teeth.

Sources: Oranges, lemons, grapefruit, tomatoes, Brussels sprouts, raw cabbage.

**Vitamin D:** Is not plentiful in foods. It is manufactured by the sun's rays shining on our skin.

Sources: sunshine, vitamin D fortified milk, fish liver oil, vitamin supplements.

**Minerals**

Play a vital part in the structure and metabolism of the body. Minerals may be lost by refining of grains or prolonged cooking of vegetables in a lot of water.

**Calcium:** Part of bones and teeth. Is needed for healthy skin and blood clotting. Helps regulate nerves and muscles.

Sources: milk and cheese.

**Iron:** Needed for healthy red blood.

Sources: Egg yolk, liver, prunes, raisins, green leafy vegetables.

**Carbohydrates and Fats:**

Supply energy for life processes, such as heart beat and all movement. This energy is measured in *calories*. Fats are needed for cell growth, and carbohydrates help the body use other nutrients. Too few calories result in weight loss, and a lack of fats produces nervous irritabilty and vitamin deficiencies.

**Carbohydrates:** Sources are fruits, grains, starchy vegetables.

**Fats:** Concentrated sources are butter, margarine, vegetable oil, cream and salad dressing.

Reading 39

# Nutrition Labeling: Proposed Criteria for Food Label Information Panel

**Charles C. Edwards**

*The information produced from the tests of nutrition labeling, comments from consumers and nutritionists, and the limited data available before the current programs were initiated strongly support the consumers' interest in nutrition labeling.*

The increasing number of processed and formulated foods makes it difficult for consumers to identify the nutritional qualities of the products they purchase. The White House Conference of Food, Nutrition, and Health recommended that the Food and Drug Administration consider the development of a system for identifying the nutritional qualities of food: "Every manufacturer should be encouraged to provide truthful nutritional information to consumers about his products to enable them to follow recommended dietary regimens." Many consumer groups have also requested that uniform nutrition labeling be placed on all foods.

## PROPOSED RULE MAKING

The Food and Drug Administration has accepted the recommendation to develop nutrition labeling for packaged food. Initial activities have been directed toward the development of formats of nutrition labeling which could be evaluated by appropriate consumer testing.

Prior to the White House Conference little had been done on evaluating nutrition labeling as a means of consumer education and information on nutrition and good diet. Improved labeling of foods for special dietary use had been generally recommended by dietitians, and the medical profession had called for fat labeling as an aid to persons on modified fat diets. However, no consumer data were available on the format or detail of nutrition labels or on food classes to be covered.

In 1970, Dr. David Call of Cornell University produced a study report based on questionnaires sent to all members of the American Institute of Nutrition. His report indicated that these professional nutritionists had no specific preference for systems of listing nutrients, but a majority felt that vitamins and minerals should be based on a standard such as the Recommended Daily Allowances (RDA) of the National Academy of Sciences-National Research Council (NAS-NRC). Dr. Call concluded generally that the majority (over 80 percent) of the professional nutritionists think that there should be more nutrition information on food labels, but the group was divided as to what information and what format should be used.

In October 1970, the *"Chain Store Age"* (a trade magazine) published the results of a study in which consumers were exposed to products with full disclosure of nutrition content. Control groups were exposed to products without nutrition information. *In this study* the nutrition information was presented in percentages for both major and minor nutrients and calories were also listed.

From the *Federal Register*, vol. 37, no. 62, Mar. 30, 1972, pp. 6493–6497.

This study indicated that "the type of full disclosure labeling investigated does have an effect of moving customers in the direction of greater purchasing of the full disclosure brands." It was pointed out that the shifts were small. However, in some cases and in certain age groups, the purchase of labeled brands increased by over 10 percent, and brands without nutrition labeling decreased in sales. Younger customers and those with annual incomes under $10,000 were more responsive to the labeling.

Based on the limited information provided by these studies, the Food and Drug Administration developed a working draft outlining various approaches to nutrition labeling. In June 1970, the preliminary drafts were evaluated for scientific correctness by members of the Food and Nutrition Board of the NAS-NRC, representatives selected from the American Dietetic Association, and professional nutritionists selected from the American Institute of Nutrition. The comments from these individuals were carefully evaluated, and a new working draft suggesting six alternate approaches to nutrition labeling was prepared. In August 1970, these alternative labeling systems were sent to a number of professional nutrition groups, consumer groups, food industry associations, home economists, and dietitians. In October 1970 comments on the various labeling systems had been received from all of the individuals and groups contacted by the agency. A trade association requested that the Consumer Research Institute, a private nonprofit research group, assist by carrying out consumer testing of labeling systems which the agency determined were suitable for further study. The agency accepted this support, as it provided a means for immediately beginning to evaluate nutrition labeling.

On the basis of the comments received and of the information available from the few earlier studies, the agency prepared a final working paper including the three basic labeling alternatives which had received the strongest support from the various groups and which appeared to be technically feasible. These three labeling systems had several common features. All nutrition information was presented in terms of a portion, expressed as a household measure, or in units easily identified as a usual serving. All nutrition statements were based on the Recommended Dietary Allowances (RDA) established by the Food and Nutrition Board, National Academy of Sciences-National Research Council. Information on the amount of caloric, fat, protein, and carbohydrate content was presented in all systems. Protein content was also expressed in terms of the percentage contributed toward the RDA protein allowances, and, for the purpose of labeling, the adult protein level of 65 grams was selected as the standard. For practical purposes, a single set of values for the vitamins and minerals to be stated on the labels was compiled from the extensive list of values established by the Food and Nutrition Board, and the following seven nutrients were selected to appear on nutrition labeling: Vitamin A, vitamin C, thiamin (vitamin $B_1$), riboflavin (vitamin $B_2$), niacin, calcium, and iron. As a means of telling the consumer the nutritional value of the product, the vitamin and mineral content was presented as a percentage of the RDA.

The three labeling alternatives differed in the format used for presenting the percentage of RDA for the seven nutrients. The three formats proposed for testing were: A numerical statement of the percent of the RDA, the percent of the RDA expressed as adjectives, and the percent of the RDA expressed as units with 10 units equal to 100 percent of the RDA. The units in the third format could be represented numerically or pictorially.

The testing was designed to answer the basic questions of how to present the information on (1) vitamins, minerals, and protein in relation to nutrient allowances, and (2) whether to provide a complete labeling format on every labeled product or only information on the nutrients present in the product. The testing also sought an indication of consumer support for nutrition labeling and understanding and use of nutrition labeling. The specific questions addressed were as follows:

**1** Is there strong consumer support for nutrition labeling when examples of labels are actually available for review?

**2** What type of labeling format is most acceptable to consumers and results in changing consumer performance?

**3** What aspects of nutrition labeling (calories, protein, fat and carbohydrates, and vitamins and minerals) raises maximum consumer response? Is the combination most effective?

**4** Do consumers react better to complete listing of nutrients or to listings which include only those nutrients present in significant amounts?

Consumer Research Institute (CRI) carries out its test in two phases. They developed a protocol for studying the three labeling alternatives in terms of consumer understanding and use. The final protocol was completed in May 1971, and field studies with an independent research group were started in June 1971 and completed in September 1971. CRI also developed a large consumer questionnaire study which was initiated in January 1972 and completed in February 1972. The questionnaires were sent to three population groups: 2,000 consumers selected to represent the American population (U.S. probability sample), 2,000 consumers identified as low income, and 600 consumers identified as "under educated" (having no high school education).

During the development of the alternatives, a number of food chains expressed interest in studying consumer reaction to nutrition labeling. Following a series of preliminary discussions, five chains agreed to carry out in-store tests involving one of the labeling alternatives developed by FDA. These in-store tests included not only evaluation of the consumer response to individual labeling but also consumer acceptance of nutrition labeling.

The evaluation of the food chain tests has been divided into two parts: (1) The store evaluation composed of consumer responses, and (2) a formal consumer evaluation being conducted in each area by Drs. Daniel Padberg and David Call of Cornell University, Ithaca, N.Y., under contract to the Food and Drug Administration. This evaluation has attempted to identify the consumers' response and understanding of nutrition labeling, to evaluate the consumer interest in nutrition factors, and to obtain some measure of nonuse benefits expressed by consumers. A second phase of the contract with Cornell University was designed to provide more detailed information on the specific formats for nutrition labeling and on consumer understanding of how nutrition labeling related to developing a good diet.

At the present time most, but not all, of the evaluation studies are complete. Preliminary results have been sent to the Food and Drug Administration. The results of the tests completed and evaluated provide strong support for the concept of nutrition labeling.

The first phase of the CRI activities was designed to answer questions on how nutrition labeling affected purchasing patterns and which labeling format had the greatest effect. In addition, a questionnaire was developed to evaluate changes in consumers' attitude toward nutrition, and their understanding of nutrition before and after the labeling study. The study was conducted in 950 educated middle-class households in Connecticut and Georgia who, as part of the panel, did grocery shopping at home using a catalog of food items. The preliminary results were presented at a public meeting on December 7, 1971. The conclusions stated by CRI were as follows:

**1** Nutrient information was used by the consumers observed in this study. This is demonstrated by the fact that their purchase patterns changed after the introduction of nutrient labeling.

**2** In situations where a product or brand has a real nutritional advantage over its competitors, there was a major change in that product's share of the market.

**3** The consumers' attitudes toward nutrition were found to be rather high before the introduction of nutrition labeling. The changes in attitude were positive but small, since the consumers in the test panel already had very positive attitudes about nutrition.

**4** There was a considerable increase in the consumers' knowledge of nutrition, especially in their awareness of vitamins and minerals.

**5** All three formats for communicating the amount of RDA (numerical percent, adjective representation, and numerically or pictorially represented units) are understood and used equally well. It would not appear that any of the three has a major advantage over the others among the educated and affluent in our society.

**6** No differences in consumer reaction were found between listing all nutrients and listing only those nutrients present.

**7** The fact that listing of protein, fat, and carbohydrates in percent composition is useful to the consumer was indicated by changes in purchase behavior.

The second phase of the CRI studies was completed in early February 1972, and a preliminary report was provided to FDA on February 25, 1972. This phase of the study sought to determine (1) whether the quantity of nutrients should be communicated by numerical percent, adjectives, or numerical or pictorial representation of units and (2) whether all key nutrients or only those present in the food should be listed. (The phrase "all key nutrients" refers to the five vitamins and two minerals included as the basic information in all labeling formats.) Questionnaires sent through the mail were used to determine the answers to both of these questions. In addition face-to-face interviews were conducted in studying the first question.

With reference to the first question, the questionnaires were evaluated to determine which nutrient labeling format was most intelligible to the consumer. Attention focused on the consumers' ability to detect differences between two products as well as to select the more nutritious of these products. Over 80 percent of those in the national sample were able to perceive differences between products with each of the three formats, and almost 80 percent could select the more nutritious product with each of the formats. In the lower income groups, approximately 77 percent perceived differences with the numerical percent and numerically or pictorially represented units, but only 70 percent perceived differences with the adjectives. In selecting the more nutritious product, the lower income group did best with the numerical percent and numerical or pictorial units (about 70 percent correct). Only 66 percent of the lower income group was able to select correctly on the basis of adjectives.

In a face-to-face survey of 600 low income consumers with no high school education, approximately *90* percent of all those surveyed were able to perceive differences and to make the correct choice of a more nutritious product using any of the formats. The higher percent of positive responses is associated with the abilities of the interviewer to motivate the person being questioned. As the low income, less educated groups were considered most likely to be confused by nutrition labeling, they were asked to indicate which labeling format they felt they would be able to use best. Approximately 50 percent of the sample indicated that the numerical percent was best, about 33 percent preferred adjectives, and about 16 percent selected pictorial units. (Numerical representation of units was not used in the face-to-face interviews). Expression in numerical percent was preferred by the majority, because it was considered more exact and easier to use. Adjectives were considered vague and confusing, and pictorial units were considered too silly or childish. Thirty people conducted the interviews. Of these, 24 felt the numerical percent was the easiest for consumers to use.

The questionnaires were also evaluated to determine whether all nutrients or only those present should be listed. The percent of persons making the correct choice and perceiving differences between products was slightly better when the label contained only the nutrients present instead of when all seven nutrients in the labeling format were listed with zero content indicated for those nutrients not in the product. Among the low income group, 77 percent perceived differences when only nutrients present were listed, and about 73 percent perceived differences when all nutrients were listed. In the national sample, a similar difference was observed, with almost 86 percent perceiving a difference with only nutrients present listed and about 82 percent when all nutrients were listed. No attempt was made to evaluate the educational benefit which might be associated with the more complete disclosure.

In considering whether information on the fat, protein, and carbohydrate content should be listed, consumer purchase patterns from the first phase of the CRI study were evaluated to see if presenting this information would improve consumer understanding. In two product classes where fat and caloric differences between products were significant (imitation cheese spread (6 percent fat) versus cheese spread (20-25 percent fat) and salad dressing (65 calories per portion) versus mayonnaise (180 calories per portion)), consumers began purchasing more of the products with lower fat and caloric content.

Two of the five food chains conducting nutrition labeling tests have submitted preliminary reports. In both cases the results were primarily based on consumer interest and response via mail and telephone, although one chain also completed a general questionnaire among consumers in their stores. In one of these two tests the majority of consumers who responded in the first 2 months of the labeling test (approximately 800 letters) asked that nutrition labeling be continued. Of 3,000 consumers questioned in that test, 62.4 percent were aware of the test and over 75 percent were interested in having nutrition labeling. The second food chain's report shows that the consumer letter response during the early stages of the test was more limited than the response to the first chain's test. This may be because the second test involved much less total promotion, concentrated on in-store activities, and involved fewer labeled products. Out of several hundred letters from consumers, only three opposed nutrition labeling. Those objected because of anticipated price increases resulting from the labeling. Most consumers expressed strong support for the nutrition labeling. The other three chains did not start their studies until after December 1971 and no reports are available. Each of these chains plans some evaluation.

The preliminary report from the Cornell University evaluation covered only the two completed chain tests. The questionnaires were carried out in the stores. Demographic information was obtained so that the relationship of education, income, and racial group to perception and understanding of the purpose of nutrition labeling could be determined. Preliminary results indicate that perception of the labels was correlated to education and income. In the test by the first food chain, 35.7 percent of those interviewed were aware of the labels after 2 weeks. In the second chain test, which involved few labeled products and less promotion, only 20 percent of the persons questioned had seen the label. Almost 90 percent of those questioned in the first test understood the purpose of nutrition labeling. A preliminary test was given to a random sample of customers before the labeling study started. Seventy percent of the persons tested gave correct answers when asked specific questions concerning which of several products provided the most of specific nutrients. Twenty weeks later, 80 percent of the persons asked were able to give correct answers to the identical questions. The 10-percent increase in correct answers is significant.

Of particular interest was the consumers' concern with nonuse benefits associated with nutrition labels. Consumers were asked if they felt the following benefits would result from nutrition labeling.

**1** Nutrition information for food products will increase consumer confidence in the food industry.

**2** If manufacturers have to show nutrition information, they will try harder to make their products nutritious.

**3** Nutrition labels encourage advertising that will promote consumer education.

**4** More information indicates a greater concern for consumer welfare.

**5** Consumers have the right to know the nutrition value of food products on the market.

The results averaged from the two tests studied thus far indicate that 87.9 percent of all persons interviewed agreed that these nonuse benefits would occur with the use of nutrition labeling. In addition, 97.6 percent of all those interviewed agreed that it was the consumers' right to have nutrition information on food products on the market.

The information produced from the tests of nutrition labeling, comments from consumers and nutritionists, and the limited data available before the current programs were initiated strongly support the consumers' interest in nutrition labeling. The information provided in the various labeling formats was used by consumers. The questionnaire studies indicated that consumers, including those with low incomes and with less than a high school education, were able to understand and use nutrition labeling. The studies also indicated that the numerical percent format is more acceptable to the low-income segment of the population, even though all three formats used in the studies were understood and used by consumers.

In relation to the use of complete listing of the seven nutrients on each label, the slight reduction in the number of persons able to understand and use the labeling has been considered in relation to the education benefits associated with the more complete labeling. It has been suggested that, when a complete listing of nutrients is required, products that do not contain any of the vitamins or minerals or protein are made to appear very inferior. It does not appear reasonable to require the complete listing on products such as vegetable oils and fruits like apples and pears. These products would not have nutrients added under usual circumstances and thus can not have their nutrient levels improved like most formulated products. However, it is possible that some consumers may falsely believe that products with no information on vitamins and minerals are good sources. In order to prevent such misunderstanding, manufacturers would be offered the option of listing the vitamins and minerals which shall be required as part of nutrition information or of stating that the food contains no significant quantities of the vitamins and minerals. After evaluating the information available at the present time, the Commissioner proposes to establish regulations governing nutrition labeling for packaged food products. While all of the issues associated with nutrition labeling have not been definitively resolved, the completed studies have provided the answers to the basic questions. The strong consumer interest in nutrition labeling and the evidence that consumers are able to understand and use nutrition labeling indicate that such a proposal is timely.

While the information obtained thus far in the tests suggests that consumers can utilize the individual nutrient labeling systems, there is no evidence supporting the view that each food company should develop its own nutrition labeling procedure. It is important that a single nutrition labeling guide be established and followed by the food industry. A proliferation of different approaches would lead to consumer confusion and reduce the potential educational benefits of nutrition labeling. As indicated in the notice on nutrition labeling in the *Federal Register* of November 19, 1971 (36 F.R. 22078), if different types of nutrition labeling resulting in consumer confusion are used, FDA will be obligated to take regulatory action or to seek new statutory authority to control nutrition labeling.

The Commissioner has concluded, on the basis of the information available at the present time, that nutrition labeling should be based on the following general criteria:

Listing protein in terms of both the amount present in the product and a percent of the RDA offers consumers maximum information. Concern has been expressed that protein quality should be incorporated into this statement. Such a protein quality factor could be established by requiring that any protein with a quality less than that of casein must reduce the claimed contribution by the factor obtained by dividing 100 into the protein quality of the protein expressed as a percent of the quality of casein as determined in standard protein evaluation tests and then multiplying the actual protein content by this factor. This calculation would give the amount of protein to be used in determining the percent RDA for the protein. A lower limit could also be set for any statement relating to protein quality; for example, no protein with a quality less than 50 percent of casein could be stated on the label in terms of the percent RDA. This approach offers maximum information but is complicated both for the manufacturer and for the consumer. Comment is particularly requested on this question.

The Commissioner also requests that comments be provided by interested groups and individuals on whether it would be most useful to consumers for protein, carbohydrate, and fat content to be stated by percent, by weight, or by grams per portion.

The Commissioner is aware that there is variation in the natural nutrient content of food products. In developing a nutrition labeling system, it is therefore important that the manufacturer be permitted a sufficient tolerance so that he may provide useful nutrition information on the label without incurring excess costs for quality control which will result in a significant increase in prices to the consumer. However, consumers will expect that the nutrition labels will honestly represent the product. By using a percentage of the RDA expressed in increments of 5 to 10 percent, some of the variation in products can be accommodated. In addition, for the purposes of nutrition labeling, the statement will be considered in compliance if at least 80 percent of the product in the package meets or exceeds the claimed nutrient levels, and if no sample of the product will have a nutrient content less than 80 percent of the nutrient claim.

Finally, manufacturers frequently ask where to print nutrition labeling and other related information which is not required on the principal display panel. It is important that such information appear in a uniform location so that consumers will have it readily available. Uniformity in displaying such information will make it more easily found and read by consumers under normal conditions of purchase and use. For a number of years canners have utilized an information panel for serving sizes and other pertinent information concerning the contents of a can. Breakfast cereal manufacturers have primarily utilized one panel for nutrition information. An information panel, as well as the principal display panel, is a suitable location for nutrition information. The Commissioner therefore proposes *to define the information panel as that part of the label* immediately to the right of the principal display panel. If the package has alternate display panels the information panel may appear to the right of either. If the top of the container is the principal display panel, and there is no alternate principal display panel, the information panel is any part of the label adjacent to the top.

Therefore, pursuant to provisions of the Federal Food, Drug, and Cosmetic Act (secs. 201, 403, 701, 52 Stat. 1040-42 as amended, 1047-48 as amended, 1055-56 as amended by 70 Stat. 919 and 72 Stat. 948; 21 U.S.C. 321, 343, 371) and under authority delegated to him (21 CFR 2.120), the Commissioner proposes to amend Part 1 by adding the following two new sections:

## 1.3d Food Labeling: Information Panel

**(a)** The term "information panel" as it applies to packaged food means that part of the label immediately to the right of the principal display panel. If the package has an alternate principal display panel, the information panel is immediately to the right of either principal display panel. If the top of the container is a principal display panel and the package has no alternate principal display panel, the information panel is any panel adjacent to the principal display panel.

**(b)** All information required to appear on the label of any package of food pursuant to §§ 1.8a, 1.8c, 1.10, or Part 125 of this chapter shall appear either on the principal display panel or on the information panel unless otherwise specified by regulations in this chapter.

**(c)** All nutrition information appearing on the label of any package of food shall comply with § 1.16 and shall appear either on the principal display or on the information panel unless otherwise specified by regulations in this chapter.

**(d)** All information required on the principal display panel or the information panel pursuant to this section must appear on the label with the prominence and conspicuousness required by section 403(f) of the Federal Food, Drug, and Cosmetic Act and § 1.9, but in no case may the letters be less than 1/16 inch in height. The requirements for conspicuousness and legibility shall include the specifications of § 1.8b(h) (1) and (2).

**(e)** All information required on the principal display panel or on the information panel pursuant to this section shall appear on the same panel unless there is insufficient space. If there is insufficient space for all of this information to appear on a single panel it may be divided between these two panels, except that the information required pursuant to any given section or part must all appear on the same panel.

### 1.16 Food: Nutrition Labeling

**(a)** Nutrition information relating to a packaged food may be included on the label of the product provided that it conforms to the requirements of this section.

**(b)** All nutrient quantities including vitamins, minerals, calories, protein, fats, and carbohydrates shall be declared in relation to the average or usual serving expressed in common household measurements or in terms of a unit which is easily identified as an average or usual serving. The weight of the serving may also be expressed in grams. The declaration shall contain the following items:

**(1)** The heading shall be "Nutrition Information."

**(2)** A statement of the serving size shall be given.

**(3)** A statement of the caloric content per serving shall be expressed to the nearest 5-calorie increment.

**(4)** A statement of the number of grams of protein, fat, and available carbohydrates per serving shall be expressed to the nearest gram.

**(5)** A statement of the amounts per serving of the vitamins and minerals listed in paragraph (c) of this section shall be expressed in percentages of the Recommended Dietary Allowances (RDA) as stated in paragraph (d) of this section. The percentages are expressed in 10-percent increments, except that 5-percent increments may be used up to the 20-percent level. Nutrients present in an amount comprising less than 5 percent of the RDA shall be considered insignificant and will be so listed under the RDA percentage. However, if a product does not contain at least 5 percent of the RDA for any of the vitamins or minerals listed in paragraph (c) of this section, the statement, "Contains no significant quantities of vitamins and minerals," may be used in place of the complete listing of the vitamins and minerals required in paragraph (c) of this section. The listing shall follow the order given in paragraph (c) of this section.

**(6)** A statement of the amount of protein present per serving shall be expressed as a percentage of the 65-gram RDA. The percentages are expressed in 10-percent increments, except that 5-percent increments may be used up to the 20-percent level. Protein present in an amount less than 5 percent of the RDA shall be considered insignificant. In such cases, the amount of protein will be represented either as 0 percent of the RDA or by the words "none" or "insignificant," whichever is appropriate. However, if a product contains no protein, the protein expressed as a percent of the RDA need not be listed.

**(c)** In the case of vitamins and minerals, the label declaration must contain information on vitamin A, vitamin C, thiamin, riboflavin, niacin, calcium, and iron and may contain information on any of the other vitamins and minerals listed in paragraph (d) of this section.

**(d)** For the purposes of nutrition labeling, the following daily amounts of vitamins and minerals are the standard Recommended Daily Allowances (RDA):

Vitamin A, 5,000 International Units.
Vitamin D, 400 International Units.
Vitamin E, 30 International Units.
Ascorbic Acid (Vitamin C), 60 milligrams.
Thiamin (Vitamin $B_1$), 1.5 milligrams.
Riboflavin (Vitamin $B_2$), 1.7 milligrams.
Niacin, 20 milligrams.
Vitamin $B_6$, 2 milligrams.
Folacin (Folic acid), 0.4 milligram.
Vitamin $B_{12}$, 6 micrograms.
Biotin, 0.3 milligram.

Pantothenic Acid, 10 milligrams.
Calcium, 1,000 milligrams.
Phosphorus, 1,000 milligrams.
Iron, 18 milligrams.
Iodine, 0.15 milligram.
Zinc, 15 milligrams.
Magnesium, 400 milligrams.
Copper, 2 milligrams.

These nutrient levels have been adopted by the Food and Drug Administration from information in a report of the Food and Nutrition Board, National Academy of Sciences-National Research Council, "Recommended Dietary Allowances," Seventh Edition, 1968.

**(e)** A statement may be included offering additional information upon written request to a specified address. Any such additional labeling shall comply with all the requirements of Part 1 and, if applicable, Part 125 of this chapter.

**(f)** The location of the nutrition information on the label shall be in compliance with § 1.8d.

Interested persons may, within 90 days after publication hereof in the *Federal Register,* file with the Hearing Clerk, Department of Health, Education, and Welfare, Room 6-88, 5600 Fishers Lane, Rockville, Md. 20852, written comments (preferably in quintuplicate) regarding this proposal. Comments may be accompanied by a memorandum or brief in support thereof. Received comments may be seen in the above office during working hours, Monday through Friday.

Reading 40

# Standards for Meat and Poultry Products—A Consumer Reference List

**U.S.D.A., Consumer and Marketing Service**

*Chopped ham—Must contain fresh, cured, or smoked ham, along with certain specified kinds of curing agents and seasonings.*

To be labeled with a particular name—such as "All Beef Franks" or "Chicken Soup"—a Federally inspected meat or poultry product must be approved by the U.S. Department of Agriculture as meeting specific product requirements. Following are products for which percentages of meat, poultry, or other ingredients have been established. (This list does not include all products for which requirements have been set, nor does it necessarily include all requirements for those products that are listed.)

## RED MEAT PRODUCTS

(All percentages of meat are on the basis of fresh uncooked weight unless otherwise indicated.)

From the Consumer and Marketing Services,—85, USDA, February 1971.

- Barbecued meats—Weight of meat when barbecued can't exceed 70% of the fresh uncooked meat. Must have barbecued (crusted) appearance and be prepared over burning or smoldering hardwood or its sawdust.
- Barbecue sauce with meat—At least 35% meat (cooked basis).
- Beans with bacon in sauce—At least 12% bacon.
- Beans with frankfurters in sauce—At least 20% franks.
- Beans with ham in sauce—At least 12% ham (cooked basis).
- Beans with meat balls in sauce—At least 20% meatballs.
- Beef and dumplings with gravy or beef and gravy with dumplings—At least 25% beef.
- Beef burgundy—At least 50% beef.
- Beef sauce with beef and mushrooms—At least 25% beef and 7% mushrooms.
- Beef sausage (raw)—No more than 30% fat.
- Beef stroganoff—At least 45% fresh uncooked beef or 30% cooked beef, and at least 10% sour cream or a "gourmet" combination of at least 7.5% sour cream and 5% wine.
- Beef with barbecue sauce—At least 50% beef (cooked basis).
- Beef with gravy—At least 50% beef (cooked basis). / Gravy with beef—At least 35% beef (cooked basis).
- Breaded steaks, chops, etc.—Breading can't exceed 30% of finished product weight.
- Breakfast sausage—No more than 50% fat.
- Brunswick stew—At least 25% meat.
- Burritos—At least 15% meat.
- Cabbage rolls—At least 12% meat.
- Cannelloni with meat and sauce—At least 10% meat.
- Capelletti with meat in sauce—At least 12% meat.
- Chili con carne—At least 40% meat.
- Chili con carne with beans—At least 25% meat.
- Chili hot dog sauce with meat—At least 6% meat.
- Chili hot dog with meat—At least 40% meat in chili.
- Chili macaroni—At least 16% meat.
- Chili pie—At least 20% meat.
- Chili sauce with meat—At least 6% meat.
- Chop suey (American style) with macaroni and meat—At least 25% meat.
- Chop suey vegetables with meat—At least 12% meat.
- Chow mein vegetables with meat—At least 12% meat.
- Condensed, creamed dried beef or chipped beef—At least 18% dried or chipped beef (figured on reconstituted total content).
- Corned beef and cabbage—At least 25% corned beef.
- Corn dog—Must meet standards for frankfurters and batter can't exceed the weight of the frank.
- Cream cheese with chipped beef (sandwich spread)—At least 12% meat.
- Croquettes—At least 35% meat.
- Curried sauce with beef and rice (casserole)—At least 35% beef (figured on beef and sauce part only).
- Deviled ham—No more than 35% fat.
- Egg foo young with meat—At least 12% meat.
- Egg rolls with meat—At least 10% meat.
- Enchilada with meat—At least 15% meat.
- Frankfurters, bologna, other cooked sausage—May contain meat and meat by-products; no more than 30% fat, 10% added water, and 2% corn syrup; no more than 15% poultry unless its presence is reflected in product name; no more than 3.5% cereals and nonfat dry milk, with product name showing that

they're added. / "all meat"—Only muscle tissue with natural amounts of fat; no by-products, cereal, or binders. / "all beef"—Only meat of beef animals.

- Fried rice with meat—At least 10% meat.
- Fritters—At least 35% meat.
- Frozen breakfasts—At least 15% meat (cooked basis).
- Frozen dinners—At least 25% meat or meat food product (cooked basis, figured on total meal minus appetizer, bread and dessert).
- Frozen entrees: meat and one vegetable—At least 50% meat (cooked basis) /meat, gravy or sauce, and one vegetable—At least 30% meat (cooked basis)
- Goulash—At least 25% meat.
- Gravies—At least 25% meat stock or broth, or at least 6% meat.
- Ham-canned—Limited to 8% total weight gain after processing; if gain is up to 8%, must be labeled "ham, with natural juices"; if between 8% and 10%, must be labeled "ham-water added-with juices".
- Ham-not canned—Must not weigh more after processing than the fresh ham weighs before curing and smoking; if contains up to 10% added weight, must be labeled "ham-water added"; if more than 10%, must be labeled "imitation ham".
- Ham a la king—At least 20% ham (cooked basis).
- Ham and cheese spread—At least 25% ham (cooked basis).
- Hamburger or ground beef—No more than 30% fat; no extenders.
- Ham chowder—At least 10% ham (cooked basis).
- Ham croquettes—At least 35% ham (cooked basis).
- Ham salad—At least 35% ham (cooked basis).
- Ham spread—At least 50% ham.
- Hash—At least 35% meat (cooked basis).
- High meat baby foods—At least 30% meat.
- Lasagna with meat and sauce—At least 12% meat.
- Lima beans with ham or bacon in sauce—At least 12% ham or cooked bacon.
- Liver sausage, liver loaf, liver paste, liver cheese, liver pudding, liver spread, and similar liver products—At least 30% liver.
- Macaroni and beef in tomato sauce—At least 12% beef.
- Macaroni salad with ham or beef—At least 12% meat (cooked basis).
- Manicotti (containing meat filling)—At least 10% meat.
- Meat balls—No more than 12% extenders (cereal, etc.).
- Meat balls in sauce—At least 50% meat balls.
- Meat casseroles—At least 25% fresh uncooked meat or 18% cooked meat.
- Meat pies—At least 25% meat.
- Meat ravioli—At least 10% meat in ravioli, minus the sauce.
- Meat salads—At least 35% meat (cooked basis).
- Meat taco filling—At least 40% meat.
- Meat tacos—At least 15% meat.
- Meat turnovers—At least 25% meat.
- Omelet with bacon—At least 12% bacon (cooked basis).
- Omelet with ham—At least 18% ham (cooked basis).
- Pate de foie—At least 30% liver.
- Pepper steaks—At least 30% beef (cooked basis).
- Pizza sauce with sausage—At least 6% sausage.
- Pizza with meat—At least 15% meat.
- Pizza with sausage—At least 12% sausage (cooked basis) or 10% dry sausage, such as pepperoni.
- Pork sausage—Not more than 50% fat.

- Pork with barbecue sauce—At least 50% pork (cooked basis).
- Pork with dressing and gravy—At least 30% pork (cooked basis) / pork and dressing—At least 50% pork (cooked basis).
- Sandwiches (containing meat)—At least 35% meat.
- Sauce with meat or meat sauce—At least 6% meat.
- Sauerbrauten—At least 50% meat (cooked basis).
- Sauerkraut balls with meat—At least 30% meat.
- Sauerkraut with wieners and juice—At least 20% wieners.
- Scalloped potatoes and ham—At least 20% ham (cooked basis).
- Scallopine—At least 35% meat (cooked basis).
- Scrapple—At least 40% meat and/or meat by-products.
- Spaghetti sauce and meat balls—At least 35% meat balls (cooked basis).
- Spaghetti sauce with meat—At least 6% meat.
- Spaghetti with meat and sauce—At least 12% meat.
- Spaghetti with meat balls and sauce—At least 12% meat.
- Spanish rice with beef or ham—At least 20% beef or ham (cooked basis).
- Stews (beef, lamb, and the like)—At least 25% meat.
- Stuffed cabbage with meat in sauce—At least 12% meat.
- Stuffed peppers with meat in sauce—At least 12% meat.
- Sukiyaki—At least 30% meat.
- Sweet and sour pork or beef—At least 25% fresh uncooked meat or 16% cooked meat, and at least 16% fruit.
- Swiss steak with gravy—At least 50% meat (cooked basis). /Gravy and swiss steak—At least 35% meat (cooked basis).
- Tamale pies—At least 20% meat.
- Tamales—At least 25% meat.
- Tamales with sauce—(or with gravy)—At least 20% meat.
- Taquitos—At least 15% meat.
- Tongue spread—At least 50% tongue.
- Tortellini with meat—At least 10% meat.
- Veal birds—At least 60% meat and not more than 40% stuffing.
- Veal cordon bleu—At least 60% veal, 5% ham, and containing Swiss, Gruyere or Mozzarella cheese.
- Veal fricassee—At least 40% meat.
- Veal parmagiana—At least 40% breaded meat product in sauce.
- Veal steaks—Can be chopped, shaped, cubed, frozen. Beef can be added with product name shown as "veal steaks, beef added, chopped, shaped, and cubed." No more than 20% beef or must be labeled "veal and beef steak, chopped, shaped and cubed." No more than 30% fat.

## POULTRY PRODUCTS

(All percentages of poultry—chicken, turkey, or other kinds of poultry—are on cooked deboned basis unless otherwise indicated.)

- Breaded poultry—No more than 30% breading.
- Canned boned poultry:

--boned (kind), solid pack—At least 95% poultry meat, skin and fat.
--boned (kind)—At least 90% poultry meat, skin and fat.
--boned (kind), with broth—At least 80% poultry meat, skin and fat.
--boned (kind), with specified percentage of broth—At least 50% poultry meat, skin and fat.

- Chicken cacciatore—At least 20% chicken meat, or 40% with bone.
- Chicken croquettes—At least 25% chicken meat.

- Chopped poultry with broth (baby food)—At least 43% poultry meat, with skin, fat, and seasoning.
- Creamed poultry—At least 20% poultry meat.
- Poultry a la king—At least 20% poultry meat.
- Poultry barbecue—At least 40% poultry meat.
- Poultry burgers—100% poultry meat, with skin and fat.
- Poultry chop suey—At least 4% poultry meat. /chop suey with poultry—At least 2% poultry meat.
- Poultry chow mein, without noodles—At least 4% poultry meat.
- Poultry dinners—At least 18% poultry meat.
- Poultry fricassee—At least 20% poultry meat.
- Poultry fricassee of wings—At least 40% poultry meat (cooked basis, with bone).
- Poultry hash—At least 30% poultry meat.
- Poultry noodles or dumplings—At least 15% poultry meat, or 30% with bone. /noodles or dumplings with poultry—At least 6% poultry meat.
- Poultry pies—At least 14% poultry meat.
- Poultry ravioli—At least 2% poultry meat.
- Poultry rolls—Binding agents limited to 3% in cooked roll.
- Poultry salad—At least 25% poultry meat.
- Poultry soup—At least 2% poultry meat.
- Poultry stew—At least 12% poultry meat.
- Poultry stroganoff—At least 30% poultry meat.
- Poultry tamales—At least 6% poultry meat.
- Poultry tetrazzini—At least 15% poultry meat.
- Poultry with gravy—At least 35% poultry meat. /gravy with poultry—At least 15% poultry meat.
- Sliced poultry with gravy—At least 35% poultry.

## COMPLETE STANDARDS OF IDENTITY

These currently exist for three meat products. These standards *require specific ingredients* to be present as follows:

- Corned beef hash—Must contain at least 35% beef (cooked basis). Also must contain potatoes (either fresh, dehydrated, cooked dehydrated, or a mixture of these types), curing agents, and seasonings. May be made with certain optional ingredients such as onions, garlic, beef broth, or beef fat. May not contain more than 15% fat nor more than 72% moisture.
- Chopped ham—Must contain fresh, cured, or smoked ham, along with certain specified kinds of curing agents and seasonings. May also contain certain optional ingredients in specified amounts, including finely chopped ham shank meat, dehydrated onions, dehydrated garlic, corn syrup, other chemical substances as permitted in the Federal standard, and not more than 3% water to dissolve the curing agents.
- Oleomargarine or margarine—Must contain either the rendered fat, oil, or stearin derived from cattle, sheep, swine, or goats; or a vegetable food fat, oil, or stearin; or a combination of these two classes of ingredients in a specified proportion. Must contain—individually or in combination—pasteurized cream, cow's milk, skim milk, a combination of nonfat dry milk and water or finely ground soybeans and water. May contain optional ingredients specified in the standard, including butter, salt, artificial coloring, vitamins A and D, and permitted chemical substances. Fat in finished product may not exceed 80%. Label must indicate whether product is from animal or vegtable origin or both.

**Reading 41**

# M-Men Battle Shifty Scales That Bilk Public

**August Gribbin**

*M-Men step up efforts against short-weighting on meat and food.*

It hardly seems worth bothering about. You pay $1.68 at the supermarket for a 12-ounce Delmonico steak, and it's really only 11½ ounces. Your loss: 7 cents. You buy a 65-cent package of cheese, and instead of 12 ounces you get 11. Your loss: 5 cents.

Pennies, nickels, and dimes. Hardly worth bothering about—until you discover that short-weighting, deliberate or accidental, bilks consumers of an estimated $6 billion a year. That's $6 billion, and mostly on food purchases.

Shorting is widespread. It's most prevalent on food but is common on gasoline, home fuel oil, firewood, packaged hardware supplies, and pills. Difficult to control, short-weighting nonetheless is getting increasing attention by budget-conscious consumers and "M-Men"—state weights-and-measures officers charged with seeing that scales, meters, and other measuring devices are accurate.

Last month, a three-day investigation of meat sales in Wichita by Sedgwick County lawyer Dave Calvert turned up evidence that at least 30 per cent of meat checked in each of 11 stores was short-weighted. In Tennessee, officials began a surprise Saturday testing program last month. Reports Matt Jennings, head of the state's marketing division:

"The results have been astounding. Already we've seen pre-packaged steaks short-weighted to the tune of 31 cents. The average shortage of a batch of steaks in a store I won't name was 27 cents per steak. It wasn't an accident."

A personal shopping tour in the Washington, D.C., area by this reporter on a Saturday, when short-weighting increases sharply, turned up instances of shorting on rolled turkey roasts, packaged fresh string beans, and seedless grapes. The test weighing was done on official state scales and supervised by Maryland M-men. Confronted by the fact, a Maryland store manager countered:

"All weight errors are human errors. Sure. We had a three-fourths of an ounce error in meat because a girl unused to handling the scales used it that day. A completely isolated error. We have more overweights than underweights and this incident is not worth reporting in any story."

Maybe. But Maryland law states that a shortage or overage of one-eighth of an ounce on any item is illegal. Inspectors sent to the store found a significant number of short-weighted roasts and stopped sale of the meat until clerks reweighed it and priced it properly.

It is true that most short-weighting is caused by carelessness, according to weights-and-measures men. But Leland Gordon, economist and director of the Weights and Measures Research Center at Denison University in Granville, Ohio, points out that whatever the reason, the consumer still gets clipped.

In a 252-page survey titled *Weights and Measures for the Consumer,* Mr. Gordon relates the experience of Arkansas officials who checked numerous

From the *National Observer,* 1970, p. 1.

one-pound cans of vegetables and found that none contained 16 ounces of vegetables; net contents varied from 9⅛ to 11⅜ ounces.

Mr. Gordon also tells of Pennsylvania investigators who discovered that 15.5 per cent of all prepackaged food items they checked were short-weighted and that some chain stores consistently were shorting on 25 per cent of the packages checked. He says that Tennessee inspectors found 61 per cent of 118 stores they surveyed were shorting on meat.

All 45 states that require M-men to check packages as well as scales have reported finding illegal shortages in foods. Mr. Gordon's estimate or the national incidence of short-weighted packaged foods goes as high as 34 per cent.

Mr. Gordon, identifies 48 ways shorting can occur at the meat counter—excluding the method of a buxom Pennsylvania lass whose bust depressed the weighing tray each time she used the scales.

Leaving ice, water, paper, pencils, or other items on the weighing plate will boost the meat price. Propping up a corner of the scales with a folded matchbook, gristle scraps, or with a sheaf or crush of wrapping paper will make it read higher.

Many scales can be adjusted manually to register more than they should. Even the combination scales used in large supermarkets—the scales that weigh, compute unit price, and print labels to affix to wrapped packages—have control knobs that can make the scales "read fast."

But the biggest single cause of short weight is failure to allow for the weight of the container.

"I was told always to put paper on the weighing tray before adding the meat," recalls a man who worked behind the counter in a New York store. "I was told always to watch the customer to see if he watched the scales, and if she was distracted, I was told to boost the weight a trifle." The National Consumers Union of Chicago, a citizens group, reports it has letters from store clerks who say essentially the same thing.

Clarence Adamy, president of the National Association of Food Chains, pooh-poohs the idea that short-weighting is a problem.

"We're talking about tenths of an ounce here. You never find greater errors. . . .Weights-and-measures investigators are in our stores five, six times a week, every single week. Once in awhile they list a citation for some sin as they did two weeks ago when they weighed 300 packages in a Midwestern city and finally found one [that was] a tenth-of-an-ounce off. All the harassed store manager can do about that is cuss and comply."

Nonetheless, C. O. Cottom, Michigan's supervisor of weights and measures, complains it is months between store checks and that lack of funds and staff keeps his office from checking more often. Yet he and all measurement men insist short weighting goes up when the rate of checking goes down.

In many places, M-men are practically powerless. Five states do not require packages to be inspected and don't encourage the checks Mr. Adamy says are common. Officers in eight states cannot order sales stopped as Maryland officials did with the turkey roasts. In 10 states M-men can't seize items to be used for evidence.

Weights-and-measures officials in just 16 states can prosecute repeated violators, and they won 1,572 convictions last year. But consumer organizations say the good is undone by the states' generally lenient policy of "educating" offenders by issuing warnings and giving even repeated offenders explanations of the law rather than taking them to court.

**Reading 42**

# Major Food Companies Move toward Nutrition and Natural Ingredients

**Food Processing**

*Nutritive content of foods appears to be more important to a growing number of consumers than texture, color, and long shelf-life.*

The old saw that "you can't sell nutrition" seems to be out of date. Natural food stores, organic groceries, and other special outlets are rapidly being supplemented by special sections of chain stores and drug stores.

Because organic, natural, and "health" foods (more about the distinctions later) are rapidly becoming more than a fad, major food companies are taking a long hard look at this growing market. These new-old foods are more than Crunchy Granola and carrot juice—they can be, and hopefully will be, solidly formulated foods, carefully processed only as much as absolutely necessary, with a sharp eye to maximum nutrition. Nutritive content of foods appears to be more important to a growing number of consumers than texture, color, and long shelf-life.

Of the numerous new products fitting within the "natural" or nutritious food image entering the market, a large number were developed by large commercial companies. Within the last year:

**1** Ralston-Purina entered California test markets with a line of cereal and high-protein breakfast items, snack chips, and high-protein drinks.

**2** Pillsbury introduced a group on unbleached flours and flour blends designed for the home bread baker.

**3** Miles Laboratories entered test markets with some excellent ersatz breakfast meats, formed from vegetable proteins, under their Morningstar Farms label, which reads, in part, "no cholesterol, no animal fats".

Other major companies that are currently active in the special foods market include General Mills with their "Chono" egg substitute, Sunshine Biscuit Co. (wheat sesame crackers) and A. E. Staley's Wagner Foods division (sunflower kernels). The number of stores specializing in "natural foods" has increased to over 3000 (from 1200 in 1968), not counting the growing number of supermarket chains and drugstores featuring "natural" or organic foods.

Last February, the Massachusetts Institute of Technology followed Harvard and Yale by opening a dining room featuring organic foods—serving whole wheat macaroni, lentil stews, fresh vegetables and fruits, and raw peanuts and seeds. Young people are educating their tastes differently than previous generations, with the flavors of soybeans and the textures of whole grain cereals becoming highly acceptable.

Nutritious snack foods may soon be "in"; and consumers may learn more about storing foods, making additives less necessary. When consumers see what happens to their own home-baked bread after two days, they may become less critical of bakery bread, and understand why a loaf doesn't stay soft and tasty at the end of a week. Price may become less a stumbling-block also. Consumers of

From *Food Processing*, October 1972, pp. 14–15.

organic foods are accustomed to paying a premium for their concept of nutrition.

The question of identifying a "natural" food, an "organic" food, or a "health" food cannot be answered using an unequivocable criterion or any easy-to-apply test.

Defined by the Rodale organization, an organic food is one grown without the use of chemical fertilizers, herbicides, or pesticides on land free from their residues, and processed, minimally, without chemical additives. How do you know if your 69¢ per lb carrots are really organically produced? You don't. Bills proposed by Representative Edward Koch (N.Y.) and Senator Alan Cranston (Cal.) would define organic foods (roughly by the Rodale definition) and require that FDA set standards for advertising, labeling, and distributing organic foods.

Natural foods are less clearly defined. Roughly, they would be foods containing the maximum possible of nutritive substances in a raw food, carefully processed to retain the nutritive substances. Refining and processing such as bleaching and polishing are kept at a minimum. Chemical additives, and ingredients not from natural sources are avoided, and trace elements are retained. Natural foods require careful technology, as the "safety factor" of certain additives is removed, and salmonella, shigella and botulism is just as harmful whether it comes from a natural food or a highly-but-carelessly processed one.

"Health" foods are even less well defined. There appears to be even more extravagant claims made for "health" foods—some justified and many not. Certain ingredients appear more often in health foods, although these same ingredients appear frequently in natural foods, too. These ingredients run the gamut from those that are good, highly nutritious foods to specialty items whose virtues are reminiscent of snake-oil cure-alls. A food processor that puts ginseng on a food label is "ripping off" his consumers.

## "HEALTHY" INGREDIENTS—WHAT'S GOOD ABOUT THEM AND WHERE DO YOU FIND THEM

### Sweeteners:

High on the list of a food faddist's requirements (as differentiated from the list of an organic dieter's list) is "raw sugar" or turbinado. (Raw sugar does not exist in the U.S.; it is too filthy.) Turbinado is sugar processed just to the point of bleaching—or bleached, with some of the molasses added back. It doesn't have any appreciable nutrients, except pure carbohydrate. However, some sweeteners contribute appreciable amounts of Vitamin B and minerals. Honey (100 grams) contains 20 mg calcium, 10 mcg thiamin, and 70 mcg riboflavin. One hundred grams of light molasses contributes 80 mg sodium, 165 mg calcium, 70 mcg thiamin, 60 mcg riboflavin, and other minerals (average values, varies widely). Honey and molasses can be troublesome from a handling standpoint; however, on the positive side, the invert content adds humectant qualities to baked foods.

### Grains, Fruits, Nuts:

Some of the "good guy" ingredients include the soybean, sesame seed, sunflower seed, safflower, dried fruits (raisins, dates, figs, apricots), peanuts and other nuts. Grains are preferred ground in whole and relatively untreated, and some strong points are made for sprouted rye, wheat, and soy for use in salads and breads.

**Fats:**

Without becoming involved in the polyunsaturated controversy, 90 score butter no longer appears to be the benchmark of quality it once was, as more people look to liquid oils. Unfortunately there appears to be a widespread belief that certain oils are more "fattening" than others. A recent *Newsday* article inaccurately mentioned that olive oils shouldn't be used as they are too "rich".

**Flavors:**

Carob (St. John's Bread) appears prominently in "organic" confections. It has a flavor similar to chocolate, and is used in confectionery coatings and beverages. Natural vanilla beans are used in "organic" ice creams, as are fruit purees of all natural composition. Sea Salt is used on snacks, contributing trace minerals.

Reading 43

# Vitamin Poisoning Threat to Children

**Norman Mark**

*Pals is advertised as a necessary ingredient to joining a huge in-group.*

Erin Shelton, now age five, said that Captain Kangaroo had told him that vitamins make a little boy grow big and strong. He wanted to grow big and strong real fast. That's why Erin ate 40 Pals Vitamins with iron on Sept. 10.

Erin's mother, Nancy, speaking by telephone from her home in Overland Park, Kan., told the rest of the story: "I don't know if Captain Kangaroo ever said that, but that's what Erin thought he said, and that's why we bought Pals."

The Sheltons were preparing to go on a church-sponsored camping trip, and Nancy and Erin had just returned from shopping. Nancy was busy unpacking five bags of groceries and didn't see Erin take the bottle of Pals. Later, she found the nearly empty bottle.

Now, she reflects, "I feel that God led me to that bottle. Otherwise, my child would be dead right now."

At that moment, Erin had become a victim of vitamin poisoning, which continues to be a largely unknown danger and yet is still the second largest cause of poisoning of children under age five (aspirin poisonings are the most common).

Erin suffered from both Vitamin A and iron poisoning. About 40 pills will start the Vitamin A poison symptoms and as few as 25 vitamin pills with iron can give you iron poisoning, the most deadly of all.

According to Dr. Frederick H. Lovejoy, Executive Secretary of the Boston Poison Information Center, iron is the most dangerous because an overdose can cause diarrhea, blood in the stools, vomiting and possible shock and coma.

An overdose of Vitamin A, according to Dr. Lovejoy, "will cause vomiting, irritability, poor appetite and structural changes in bones, and it will also increase intracranial pressures resulting in a bulging front (top of the head)."

From the *St. Louis Post-Dispatch*, Apr. 16, 1973, p. 12G. Reprinted with permission from the Chicago Daily News.

Yet within most children's shows today and saturated throughout each Saturday morning television schedule are advertisements for vitamins.

A child can hear, "yabba dabba doo. Flintstone vitamins are good to chew," or, "how do you know when you're grown up to the taste of Chocks?"

The 4-year-old can see Bugs Bunny Vitamins sold by Porky Pig, who says, "tastes g-g-g-great." There are even chocolate Zestabs, which look like M & M candies. Pals is advertised as a necessary ingredient to joining a huge in-group.

Of course, Pals and other vitamins have labels warning parents to keep the pills out of children's reach. But Erin was 4½ then and he couldn't read the label.

Nancy Shelton is an intelligent mother and she knew that it was wrong for Erin to swallow 40 pills. She didn't know how wrong.

Nancy, whose husband is part-owner of a sporting goods store in Kansas City, called the local poison control center and they warned that Erin must vomit immediately. The longer an overdose of iron stays in the body, the more likely it is to irritate the lower intestines and this can cause horrible bleeding.

Then Mrs. Shelton was told to take her son to the University of Kansas Medical Center. She moved slowly through rush hour traffic with her progressively sicker child, a hellish trip that took a very long 30 minutes.

In the hospital, Erin became one of the more than 3400 reported cases of vitamin poisoning among under-five year olds each year. An additional 370 children suffer from the more serious iron poisoning.

Erin's stomach was pumped, he was given intravenous fluid and taken to the intensive care section where he hovered between life and death for two days.

Stop to think of that for a moment. Less than an hour before, Mrs. Shelton had been planning a church camping trip. Now her son was close to death.

In two days, Erin was out of intensive care and, a day later, he returned home, where he celebrated his fifth birthday on March 1. He's a healthy child now.

Mrs. Shelton says, "It's horrible, really horrible, something we'll never forget.

"What's really awful is that the manufacturers are not trying to sell those vitamins on the level of the parent. They want to make it seem as if vitamins are almost like candy to children."

A spokesman for the Federal Communications Commission, which could ban such ads, told me, "with this particular problem, we eagerly follow the Food and Drug Administration and the Federal Trade Commission."

On Nov. 10, action for children's television, a group of concerned parents, asked the FTC to ban vitamin ads on children's TV shows. The FTC staff is still studying that request.

The Food and Drug Administration has labeled vitamins as food, rather than as a drug. The FDA spokesman promised to call me back with information about what action the FDA is taking. He has not called back.

A spokeswoman for Bristol-Meyers Co., distributors of Pals, told me, "no decision has been made as yet" on putting better caps on Pals bottles, about inserting stern warnings in the Pals TV commercials or about not advertising vitamins during children's TV shows.

A Columbia Broadcasting System spokesman maintained that Captain Kangaroo never said what Erin thought he had said. CBS also said that vitamin commercials are directed at mothers.

So the buckpassing continues, and each day more Erins are rushed to hospitals to be treated for vomiting, diarrhea and painful internal bleeding.

Reading 44

# Health Foods: Fact or Fakery?

**Everybody's Money**

*Many of our foods do contain lots of additives, emulsifiers, preservatives, and stabilizers. Some are known to be harmful.*

With all the talk about our food being stuffed with chemicals and empty calories, it's no wonder many people are switching from conventional foods to "health foods." By eating these foods, "health food" enthusiasts claim we will grow healthier, become immune to disease, cleanse our bodies and return to nature.

Few of us would argue with the virtue of those claims, but how truthful are they?

"Health foods," say the believers, are generally defined as those foods that give good health because of their superior nutritive value. Within the "health food" category are organic and natural foods. Organic foods are grown without use of manufactured chemical fertilizers or pesticides. Natural foods refer to those that aren't treated with preservatives, emulsifiers, artificial flavorings and colorings. Not all organic foods are natural foods, and vice versa.

Much controversy centers around the loose definitions used to describe "health foods." Nutritionists, for example, say all foods are "health foods." The Food and Drug Administration is expected to announce specific definitions for these terms shortly.

The Federal Trade Commission is also supposed to be drawing up definitions for "health foods." Recently the commission ruled that "Sugar in the Raw," a "health food" favorite, couldn't be advertised as higher in nutrition than other sugar.

The nutritional superiority of "health foods" is a popular claim, however. A spokesman for Rodale Press, publishers of *Organic Gardening and Farming,* told us that " 'health foods' generally are and can be nutritionally superior" to conventional foods. The condition of the soil, he says, can make "health foods" more nutritious than other foods. Those who dispute the nutritional qualities of "health food," he says, are "tied to food companies" and can't criticize the products that are produced.

Food scientists disagree that "health foods" have more nutrition than conventional foods. Dr. Ruth Leverton, science advisor in the U.S. Department of Agriculture, advises against "making the decision to eat health foods on a nutritional basis." She, like most other food experts, agrees that "health foods" offer no more nutrition than conventional foods. Mary Mennes, associate professor of food science at the University of Wisconsin-Madison and co-chairman of an ad hoc food facts committee on "health foods," says "research done so far has not been able to demonstrate any difference" between commercially and organically grown foods.

"Health food" enthusiasts blame commercial fertilizers for robbing our food of nutrients. Manure and compost are used as alternatives to chemical fertilizers. The true "health food" believer doesn't use pesticides, either.

Reprinted with permission from the Autumn 1972 issue of *Everybody's Money*, pp. 4–6, the credit union magazine for consumers, published by Credit Union National Association, Inc., P.O. Box 341, Madison, Wisconsin, 53701.

Food scientists argue that plants don't distinguish between organic or chemical fertilizers. "The fact that they are grown in a different fashion doesn't mean they are more nutritious," says Mrs. Mennes. The food experts say nutrients in a plant are based on its genetic nature. "Every plant needs certain nutrients," says Mrs. Mennes, "if it doesn't have them, the plant won't grow." Says Dr. Leverton, "No amount of organic fertilizer will make an apple high in vitamin C."

The same arguments apply to claims made by "health food" believers that our soil is worn out, depleting our food of necessary nutrients. Food doesn't grow in depleted soil, the food experts say. Or if it does, there is a small yield.

There also is the question of how much food would be available without commercial fertilizers. The USDA has said that the land currently farmed could support only 40 percent of the U.S. population if fertilizers weren't added to the soil. Not using pesticides would cut down food production even more.

The USDA agrees that most soil can use additions of compost and manure, but sees some dangers in their usage. Composts and manure can contain unhealthy bacteria, such as salmonella, says the USDA. Composts, says Mrs. Mennes, must be built properly to be safe and sanitary. She recommends that organic food growers contact an agricultural extension office for instructions on how to build a compost.

The chemicals used during processing are deplored by "health food" believers too. Food experts find this argument tougher to dispel. Many of our foods do contain lots of additives, emulsifiers, preservatives, and stabilizers. Some are known to be harmful. But scientists generally agree that only the amount consumed may be harmful, not the substances themselves.

Modern science has its advantages, too. Mrs. Mennes uses the example of raw milk, a popular "health food." Without pasteurizing, she says, milk can carry bacteria. Mrs. Mennes also wonders about the cleanliness of "organic" produce. Many food stores use open bins to display their "health" vegetables and fruits. This can invite insect and rodent filth, she says. If you buy "organic" produce, Mrs. Mennes recommends washing it before eating to get the soil bacteria off.

"Health food" enthusiasts, says Mrs. Mennes, have a "hang-up on the word *chemical.*" She lists some purposes of chemicals in foods: to prevent mold, keep food from becoming rancid, improve nutrition (vitamins A and D added to milk), stabilize food and enhance flavor. The "health food" people, she says, give the word *chemical* a "destructive connotation."

One claim that few people will argue is that "health foods" taste fresher. Food experts haven't been able to dispute the freshness claim, says a spokesman for Rodale Press. "Health foods" often do taste fresher because of the proximity of farmer to buyer. Unlike conventional foods, they are picked only when ripe and sold within a few days afterward.

Overprocessing of food is another worry of the "health food" group. It's true, for example, that substantial nutrients are lost in the milling of flour for bread and bakery goods. "Health foods" such as brown rice and cook-before-you-eat cereals, says Mrs. Mennes, are tasty and nutritive. But, she says, the conventional grains are as nutritive as those labeled "organic." Dr. Leverton agrees that grain mixtures are "perfectly legitimate" as diet supplements.

"Health food" enthusiasts, says Dr. Leverton, often limit their diet and their need for all nutrients. "Health foods" are many times eaten to the exclusion of other foods, denying the body of nutrients from the four basic food categories. People who eat only "health foods" don't get the variety of food necessary for a healthy, balanced diet, says Dr. Leverton.

The macrobiotic diet is an example. With this regimen, brown rice and vegetables are often the only foods eaten. The American Medical Association Council on Foods and Nutrition has warned against the diet, noting that several people have died from it. Says Mrs. Mennes, " 'health foods' are not an alternative to processed foods."

The cost of "health foods" is considerably higher than for conventional foods. Mrs. Mennes recently compared "health food" and regular food prices. She gives these differences: organic honey, 98 cents a pound, conventional, 58 cents; yellow corn meal .395 cents a pound compared to .155 cents a pound for regular; organic long grain rice 55 cents a pound, 23 cents more than conventional.

Aside from the higher prices, there is no way of knowing if the more expensive foods are really organic, says Mrs. Mennes. The problem is that many conventional foods have been falsely labeled and sold as "health foods." And says the USDA, it is possible for foods grown organically to be "contaminated" by pesticide residues carried from one farm to another by air and water.

Robert Rodale, editor of *Organic Gardening and Farming,* is as concerned about the misrepresentation of "health foods" as the food scientists. He estimates that fully half of the food sold is unworthy of the "organic" label. The USDA says that much more food is being sold as "health food" than is being grown. To help combat this abuse, Rodale has begun a certification seal for foods grown organically. Foods are tested by a laboratory to make sure there are no pesticide and additive residues on the food. There are about 100 certified farms in California alone. Representative Edward Koch of New York has asked for a national certification program for "health foods." His legislation would not only provide a definition for "health foods" but would establish a government inspection and certification program.

Asked by *Everybody's Money* if misrepresentation of "health foods" has curtailed their sale, Rodale Press said people are "looking at where foods are coming from."

That recommendation, of course, isn't always possible. Robert Rodale admits that the only way to really know what you're buying is to grow your own "health foods."

In conclusion, there are no special benefits to be gained from eating "health foods." However, they can be fun additions to your diet. And if you grow your own, you'll know you're getting the real thing—and for much less cost.

Reading 45

# An Open-Dating Glossary

**Consumer Reports**

*After the freshness date, food will remain edible but will gradually lose quality.*

The vocabulary of food dating has not been universally agreed on, but the following definitions are recognized by experts in the field.

## PACK DATE

The day the food was manufactured, processed, or packaged. It tells you how old the food is when you buy it but not whether it is too old to trust.

## SHELF LIFE

The length of time after the pack date during which a food will retain its best quality if stored under proper temperature and humidity conditions.

## PULL DATE

The last day a retail store should offer the food for sale, provided it has been stored and handled properly, but not the last day it can be eaten without loss of quality. To allow for a reasonable period of home storage, the pull date should be considerably earlier than the end of the shelf life.

## FRESHNESS DATE

The last day you can definitely expect the food to be at its best. Good manufacturing practice would set this date earlier than the end of shelf life to allow for normal variations in home-storage conditions. After the freshness date, food will remain edible but will gradually lose quality.

## EXPIRATION DATE

The last day the food may be acceptable for intended use. After expiration, for example, milk may begin tasting sour, and baby formula may begin losing a significant amount of vitamin potency.

## SHELF-DISPLAY DATE

The date the store puts food on display. Clerks would stamp this date on packages along with the price. It tells nothing about shelf life but is intended to help stores rotate stock and people at home to use up older foods first. Some supermarkets are putting this date on fresh meat and poultry packaged by the store.

From Consumer Reports, June 1972, p. 393.

Reading 46

# Nutrition Labeling for Canned Goods: A Study of Consumer Response

**Edward H. Asam**
**Louis P. Bucklin**

*Thus, it was hypothesized that if consumers perceive nutrition labels as useful in making purchase decisions, they will rate brands carrying such information more favorably than brands that do not provide this information.*

Although federally established grades for many food products have existed for some time, nutrition values have not typically been built into the standards despite knowledge of widespread dietary deficiencies.[1] For basic canned goods—with which this study is concerned—grading has been based upon color, uniformity, blemishes, clearness of the liquid, and, in some instances, toughness and flavor. The amount of vitamins, proteins, fats, carbohydrates, and even calories has historically been ignored. Nor has such information been voluntarily placed on cans by the packers.

However, with the publication of the Department of Health, Education, and Welfare, "Proposed Criteria for Food Label Information Panel," in the March, 1972 Federal Register,[2] the absence of such information appears to be at an end. The proposal calls for an information panel on each food label; food manufacturers would furnish statistics on the amount of vitamins, proteins, fats, carbohydrates, and calories contained in the contents of the package. Although the proposal contains numerous controversial elements, two are of specific interest. The first is the voluntary nature of the requirements, and the second is the so-called 80-80 rule.

The voluntary aspect of the proposal is that it requests all food manufacturers to place this information on the label. Officials of the Food and Drug Administration believe that existing law does not make mandatory regulations possible in this area. They noted that such legislation may be in the offing, although Senator Schweiker of Pennsylvania, author of such a bill, suggested that "legislation may not be needed if the nutritional labeling standards set by your industry are good enough."[3]

The 80-80 rule calls for a program in which 80% of the units in a given lot would equal or exceed the nutrient levels stated on an information panel while none of the remaining units would fall below 80% of these values. This plan is more restrictive than a possible alternative rule calling for labels with average industry nutrition values. The latter would result in similar nutrient levels being posted upon all cans of the same generic product. Data would be obtained from representative samples of industry output.

While imposition of the 80-80 rule would provide more precise informa-

[1] Andrea F. Schoenfeld, "Nutrition Report/FDA's Proposal for Guideline Signals New Approach to U.S. Diet," *National Journal*, Vol. 2 (October 31, 1970), pp. 2399-2400.

[2] 37 F.R., pp. 6493-6497.

[3] "FDA Proposed Compliance Policy for Nutritional Labeling Hit," *Food Chemical News* (April 17, 1972), pp. 29-39, at p. 38.

Reprinted from the *Journal of Marketing*, published by the American Marketing Association, vol. 37, April 1973, pp. 32-37.

tion to consumers, it poses unique problems for canners. Most basic canned products (fruits, vegetables) are "natural" foods in the sense that they are processed without the addition of any new nutritional elements. Because of wide variations in growing conditions, each lot of canned product differs from others in terms of its specific nutritional content. To meet the 80-80 rule, canners believe that they would either be forced to lower dramatically the nutrition ratings on their labels (reducing some elements to zero) or to test and label each lot separately. The latter procedure is regarded as extremely costly, both in terms of test charges and the requirement to make continuous label changes.

These problems place canners in a position different from other food processors who create new types of packaged foods such as breakfast cereals or salad dressings, and who are free to employ many different natural and artificial ingredients. For the latter, the 80-80 rule seems reasonable. Assuming, as most canners appear to believe, that their industry preserves as many nutrients as possible with today's technology, the issue of the appropriateness of the 80-80 rule is less clear.

The findings of this study relate to the question of the type of labeling rule to be employed and to the voluntary nature of a nutrient labeling policy for canned goods. Specifically, the authors were interested in whether nutritional labels with average industry values would be "good enough." Would they be noted by consumers and affect their choices in any way? If consumers were largely indifferent to this information, then there would be scant pressure from the market to cause firms to provide such data on a voluntary basis. Such a result would suggest that new legislation establishing mandatory labeling would be required to make this information uniformly available and that other regulatory approaches, possibly encompassing the 80-80 rule, should be considered so as to make nutrition play a greater role in consumer decision processes.

## RESEARCH DESIGN

Resources to conduct an extended study of actual purchases were, unfortunately, not available. Consequently, although questionnaires were employed to develop the data, the experimenters wished to avoid securing biased information from consumers who were believed to have a yea-say response bias on issues of this type. Therefore, a quasi-laboratory research design was used, based upon Cardozo's proposal that ". . . marketers may be able to maximize customers' evaluation of their products by communicating the proper amount of (positive and accurate) information. . . ."[4]

Cardozo used a laboratory shopping environment and examined the relationship between customer effort and product quality ratings. He concluded that the examination of useful information by buyers led to a higher evaluation of the product purchased compared with circumstances where limited information was provided. He noted, however, that where too much information was provided, and product selection becomes complex, buyers skim or reject the messages. Cardozo surmised that this led to the same low levels of product evaluation that would exist if no information were provided.[5] Thus, it was hypothesized that if consumers perceive nutrition labels as useful in making pur-

[4]Richard N. Cardozo, "Customer Satisfaction: Laboratory Study and Marketing Action," in *Reflections on Progress in Marketing,* L. George Smith, ed. (Chicago: American Marketing Association, 1964), pp. 283-289, at p. 286.

[5]Same reference as footnote 4, at pp. 286-287.

chase decisions, they will rate brands carrying such information more favorably than brands that do not provide this information.

Brands of canned peas were selected for study because they are a widely used product. The researchers were aware of no major factors that might create extraordinarily different perceptions of one brand versus another. Shopper perceptions were obtained by interviewing patrons outside the supermarkets in which they were about to shop.

The effect of nutrition labels upon shopper attitude was ascertained by varying the degree of nutritional information contained on the label of the can. As shown in Table 1, the minimal description provided a simple promotional statement certifying quality. At a slightly higher level, a listing of the major nutrient components, and the extent to which the product was high or low in them, was provided. The third treatment divulged the major nutrients in the canned peas and the amounts by appropriate unit. The last description listed all nutritional components, including trace materials.

To disguise the research interest in nutrition, the information panels were attached to cans of peas bearing four different brand names and prices. Two were brands of major packers and were priced the highest. Two unknown names were selected to represent the private-brand element of the market. These brands were priced a few pennies below the national brands. Simulated rather than actual private brand names were used to avoid possible confounding of test results with the supermarket location in which the interviews were conducted. For example, an unknown bias might accrue to the rating of A&P's brand among shoppers who regularly visit this chain. Four locations adjacent to

**Table 1 Variations in Nutritional Information Provided on Labels of Canned Peas**

| Level | Label statement | | Ingredients |
|---|---|---|---|
| Level I | Sweet and Succulent<br>Picked at Their Prime<br>A Tasty Part of Any Meal | | Ingredients: Whole Medium Peas, Sugar, Salt, and Water |
| Level II | High in Energy<br>High in Protein<br>High in Iron<br>High in Thiamin<br>Low in Fat | | Ingredients: Whole Medium Peas, Sugar, Salt, and Water |
| Level III | Each Three-Ounce Serving of these Peas Contains:<br>Energy value<br>Protein<br>Carbohydrate<br>Fat<br>Moisture | <br><br>80 calories<br>46 grams<br>15.0 grams<br>0.4 grams<br>79 percent | Ingredients: Whole Medium Peas, Sugar, Salt, and Water |
| Level IV | Each Three-Ounce Serving of these Peas Contains:<br>Energy value<br>Protein<br>Carbohydrate<br>Fat<br>Moisture<br>Ash | <br><br>80 calories<br>46 grams<br>15.0 grams<br>0.4 grams<br>79 percent<br>1.0 grams | Plus: Calcium—25 mg., Phosphorus—67 mg., Iron—1.7 mg., Sodium—206 mg., Potassium—96 mg., Vitamin A—469 units, Thiamin—0.1 mg., Riboflavin—0.06 mg., Niacin—1.0 mg., Ascorbic Acid—8 mg., Magnesium—25 mg. Ingredients: Whole Medium Peas, Sugar, Salt, and Water |

*Source:* Bernice K. Watt and Annabel L. Merrill, *Composition of Foods: Raw-Processed-Prepared,* Agriculture Handbook No. 8 (Washington, D.C.: U.S. Department of Agriculture, Agricultural Research Service, Consumer and Food Economics Research Division, December, 1963).

different supermarket chains were employed, and 50 shoppers were interviewed in each, for a total sample size of 200 subjects.

A Latin Square experimental design was used to evaluate the results with respect to the four nutritional labels, four brands, and four store sites. This design is suitable where the effect of a single experimental variable (nutritional labeling in the present case) does not interact with the control variables (brand/price and store/site). Although this was a moot assumption in the present case, no basis could be found to suspect an interaction in the design, and the Latin Square was deemed suitable.

The experimental design is shown in Figure 1. Each nutritional level treatment was rotated so that it was associated with every brand, and the order of presenting the brands was similarly varied. Shoppers at any one site saw only one nutritional treatment applied to a given brand. Cell values were the mean responses by 50 shoppers associated with the brand/nutritional level combination.

## MEASURES OF MARKET RESPONSE

The dependent variables in this study were shopper perceptions and purchase preferences for the different brands/prices and associated nutrition labels. Interest was focused on how shoppers appraised the quality of the brand. It was felt that the concepts of *taste, tenderness,* and *wholesomeness* would tap the various dimensions of quality. Since these were highly specific factors, it was believed that a more general, comprehensive measure would also be useful. The term *liking* was viewed as expressing this more inclusive construct.

Since it was presumed that most canned goods brands possess a high cross elasticity of demand, the term *good buy* was used to measure the role of price. A nine-point scale using bi-polar adjectives was used to assess each brand/nutritional level combination on the above dimensions.

*Purchase preferences* were also measured by having each shopper rank the four brands shown to her (each, of course, with a different nutritional label) in the order that she would buy them if given the opportunity.

**Figure 1** Experimental design for four levels of nutritional information, I-IV on food labels.

| Brand and price | Stores A | B | C | D |
|---|---|---|---|---|
| Private 1 21 ¢ | III | IV | I | II |
| Private 2 22 ¢ | II | III | IV | I |
| Major 1 25 ¢ | I | II | III | IV |
| Major 2 26 ¢ | IV | I | II | III |

## POWER OF THE TEST

Since the research was attempting to determine the degree to which different nutritional labels affect shoppers' brand perceptions, the power of the experimental design to detect such effects is of particular importance. What, then, are the chances of the Latin Square design of discovering an effect attributable to the label treatments? In order to answer this, knowledge is required regarding the extent of variation that exists in consumer attitudes for canned food, and how much of this might be due to brand/price and store/site variables. This information was not available prior to the test.

It is possible, however, to build upon some assumptions. First, the researchers estimated that most of the differences in attitudes toward canned peas are probably tied to brand/price perception and that this may account for 50% of the total variance. If the nutritional labeling treatments were to meaningfully affect market choices, it was believed they would have to be at least 25% as important as brand differences, and, therefore, would have to account for approximately 12.5% of the total variance in consumer attitudes toward the brand.

If the above assumptions are correct, the remaining portion of the variance would be due to attitudinal differences resulting from patronage at the four store/sites and to factors unexplained by the test. Because the store/sites chosen varied by both locale and ownership, it seemed likely the sample would be comprised of consumers who were heterogeneous on various demographic and socioeconomic criteria. At the outset, it was believed that the variation introduced in this manner might account for 25% of the total—possibly as low as 12.5%—resulting in a range for the unexplained variance of from 12.5% to 25%.

Assuming that differences among attribute scale values must have less than a 10% chance of being due to random fluctuations to be significant (i.e., alpha = .10), the power of the 4x4 Latin Square design was found to range from 68% in the worst case postulated to almost 90% in the best.[6] That is, given the magnitude of the types of effects hypothesized, the test has better than two chances out of three of detecting what was regarded as a meaningful market impact of nutritional labeling.

## RESULTS

In analyzing the data derived from the Latin Square design, the sums of squares for the brands, stores, and treatments were computed. The significance of possible differences in these three variance estimates were evaluated by means of the F-ratio (df. 3,6). This evaluation revealed that nine of the eighteen independent variables (three for each attitude measure) were significant at the 10% level or better. Of these, four reflected differences in the brand/price variable, three related to the store/site factor, and two were attributable to nutritional labeling. Detailed ANOVA computations are presented in Table 2.

Table 3 shows the results for nutrition labeling in greater detail. Scores found in the first five columns derive from a nine-point scale. Buying preferences were based upon rank, with the least desirable of the four alternatives present given a weight of one. Each number in the table represents the mean score registered for the attribute at a specific level of nutritional information.

[6]Jacob Cohen, *Statistical Power Analysis for the Behavioral Sciences* (New York: Academic Press, 1969), pp. 277-281, 405

**Table 2 ANOVA Results for Test Scores of Selected Consumer Attitudes toward Different Nutrition Information, Brand/Price and Store/Location**

| Attitude | Source effect | df. | Sum of squares | Mean square | F-ratio |
|---|---|---|---|---|---|
| Tender | Nutrition | 3 | 0.7595 | 0.2532 | 5.90* |
| | Brand/price | 3 | 1.8429 | 0.6143 | 14.32* |
| | Store/location | 3 | 1.9301 | 0.6434 | 15.00* |
| | Error | 6 | 0.2575 | 0.0429 | |
| Wholesome | Nutrition | 3 | 0.5577 | 0.1859 | 9.44* |
| | Brand/price | 3 | 0.0867 | 0.0289 | 1.47 |
| | Store/location | 3 | 0.8649 | 0.2883 | 14.63* |
| | Error | 6 | 0.1179 | 0.0197 | |
| Taste | Nutrition | 3 | 0.1449 | 0.0483 | 0.89 |
| | Brand/price | 3 | 0.7209 | 0.2403 | 4.43* |
| | Store/location | 3 | 0.9673 | 0.3224 | 5.95* |
| | Error | 6 | 0.3252 | 0.0542 | |
| Liking | Nutrition | 3 | 0.2942 | 0.0981 | 1.21 |
| | Brand/price | 3 | 0.0398 | 0.0133 | 0.16 |
| | Store/location | 3 | 0.0238 | 0.0079 | 0.10 |
| | Error | 6 | 0.4882 | 0.0814 | |
| Good buy | Nutrition | 3 | 0.6957 | 0.2319 | 1.68 |
| | Brand/price | 3 | 14.9181 | 4.9727 | 36.09* |
| | Store/location | 3 | 0.2875 | 0.0958 | 0.70 |
| | Error | 6 | 0.8266 | 0.1378 | |
| Preference (rank order) | Nutrition | 3 | 0.3418 | 0.1139 | 1.41 |
| | Brand/price | 3 | 1.0778 | 0.3593 | 4.46* |
| | Store/location | 3 | 0.0 | 0.0 | 0.0 |
| | Error | 6 | 0.4836 | 0.0806 | |

*Critical F(3, 6): alpha (.10) = 3.29. Asterisks indicate all F-ratios above this level.

**Table 3 Mean Scores for Attitudes and Preference Scales for Four Different Levels of Nutritional Information on Can Labels**

| Nutritional treatment | Scale | | | | | |
|---|---|---|---|---|---|---|
| | Like | Good buy | Tasty | Tender* | Whole-some* | Prefer-ence |
| Level I | 4.73 | 4.88 | 5.05 | 5.78 | 4.86 | 2.47 |
| Level II | 4.49 | 4.38 | 4.87 | 5.39 | 4.90 | 2.28 |
| Level III | 4.63 | 4.71 | 4.87 | 5.65 | 5.13 | 2.55 |
| Level IV | 4.86 | 4.91 | 5.07 | 5.99 | 5.32 | 2.69 |

*F-ratio (df. 3, 6) shows chance of difference among means due to random factors to be .10 or less.

For example, Level III mean scores are derived from the diagonal cells of the Latin Square matrix of Figure 1.

The table shows that nutritional labeling clearly improved consumer perception of the quality attributes of "wholesomeness" and, to a lesser extent, "tender." Some nutritional information effects on the ratings of other attributes appear likely, although these were not statistically significant. A rather consistent pattern exists throughout the table. The Level II information appears to have the smallest effect, whereas higher evaluations were associated with Levels III and IV which provided relatively detailed nutritional information. Interestingly, responses to Level I, which employed only promotional terms such as "sweet and succulent," were comparable, in most instances, to those of Level IV.

## CONCLUSIONS

In attempting to reach conclusions, it must be remembered that the data were collected from a small sector of the total population. They deal directly with but a single product and have relevance to only a limited number of possible shopper attitudes. The possibility of interactions among the variables is moot, and other label designs might conceivably have been more informative. Although these results must be interpreted with caution, their implications appear to be as follows:

**1** Vague nutrition labels which state the presence of elements in loose terms, such as high and low, are not apt to have any effect upon consumer choice patterns.

**2** More detailed nutrition labels containing average industry values may be used by some consumers and may affect their perception of product quality and the ordering of preferred items.

**3** Promotional terms used by canners, such as "sweet and succulent," will provide some consumers with a feeling of quality assurance comparable to that of more detailed nutrition labels.

**4** Despite the fact that some consumers might use the labels, promotional efforts by canners are likely to obscure the effect of this use on either industry or individual canner sales volume.

These findings suggest that at least some consumer interests would be served by the provision of a labeling program with detailed information and that it be federally mandated to insure complete compliance. Similarly it appears that, if Senator Schweiker's criticism of "good enough" requires such a program to have a meaningful impact upon the nutritional intake of consumers, the average industry values are unlikely to suffice. The interest shown by some sample members in labels with greater detail suggests that it would be useful to determine if the 80-80 rule, with its greater precision, might create more consumer concern.

That the 80-80 rule would meet this criterion of "good enough" is not, however, a necessary conclusion nor one that can be made from this research. Indeed, if anything, the findings suggest that additional studies be conducted before such a rule is arbitrarily adopted, since it may not be any better than the average industry values and conceivably might be worse.

Additional research must necessarily be aimed at understanding the impact of this information upon general awareness of nutrition and menu choice as opposed to consumer decisions among similar types of canned foods. If the effect of the 80-80 rule were principally to initiate consumer search among canned peas to find the lot with the lowest calories or highest vitamin C, then the inability of the industry to improve these qualities precludes any major net nutritional gains for the nation as a whole. Under these conditions the 80-80 rule may not be worth the cost. Contrarily, if use of the 80-80 rule with canned goods were to result in a heightened consumer awareness of nutrition and greater effort to improve menu selection among *different* kinds of products, then this type of program would be desirable.

This broader concern of menu choice suggests that the focus of further research on nutrition labeling for all products might be advantageously moved from just measuring the extent of consumer shift among similar types of food products. It should, instead, examine the impact of labels upon consumer use of nutrition as a factor in meal planning. In addition, the interaction between nutrition labels and other diet information, e.g., from television "commercials," should be evaluated in order to consider the role of labeling in conjunction with other types of programs that can alter current consumption patterns.

Reading 47

# Chemicals in Food Draw Increasing Attention

**Arthur E. Rowse**

*When coverage occurs, it is often too brief or superficial to be useful to consumers.*

The story of food additives won't go away. Public interest in it rose to a high pitch last week as a Senate subcommittee conducted three days of hearings on the matter.

The hearings were conducted by Senator Gaylord Nelson (D-Wis.)

*At issue were two bills.* One is the Food Protection Act (S.3163); the other is S.76. The former seeks to broaden the authority of the Food and Drug Administration to regulate food additives and would require the government to set nutritional standards for food. The aim is to eliminate use of unsafe, untested and unnecessary chemicals in food products.

The second bill seeks primarily to broaden coverage of the Delaney section of the present law banning use of any additives which have been shown to cause cancer in animals or humans. The bill would also ban additives linked to mutagenic (hereditary) and teratogenic (birth defect) changes.

*The main problem addressed by the committee and witnesses* was how the federal government should regulate use of additives so as to protect human health and yet not stifle genuine advances in food processing and packaging . . .

*For individual consumers,* however, such public airings of expert testimony can provide clues for immediate guidance in shopping and using today's food products . . .The widely acknowledged inadequacy of governmental response to the public health problems puts additional pressure on private citizens to take matters into their own hands within the obvious limits of such action.

There are three basic alternatives open to consumers:

- *Dismissing the problem* by relying completely on the judgments of government and industry officials,
- *Using all available public information as a daily guide* to shopping and use of foods containing potentially harmful chemicals, or
- *Seeking to completely avoid all processed foods* by returning to so-called natural and organic food items.

*Scarcity of pertinent and useful information* is the most limiting factor for individuals. The daily news outlets, the principal sources of such information for the average person, have generally neglected the story. . . .When coverage occurs, it is often too brief or superficial to be useful to consumers.

From *Consumer Newsweek,* Issue #50, weekly newspaper, Washington, D.C., Consumer News, Inc., 813 National Press Bldg., 20004.

*More significant is the lack of scientific literature.* Even when the government has the will to act, it may not have sufficient data to support the action. Acceptable testing procedures are so stringent and time-consuming that the answers to serious questions are often subject to long delays.

*Adding to the difficulties are the conflicts of interest,* some unavoidable and some deliberate in product testing. Several witnesses at the hearings cited the prevalence of industry representatives on scientific reviewing boards used by the Food and Drug Administration and other government agencies. Making matters worse is the fact that the FDA usually adopts the decisions of such panels without change.

*A case in point is MSG (monosodium glutamate),* the makes-you-want-more flavoring found in many prepared foods.

*Numerous scientific studies have linked MSG to brain damage* in small animals. Dr. John W. Olney, associate professor of psychiatry at the Washington University School of Medicine in St. Louis, described such tests in detail in 1969 at earlier Senate hearings. Largely as a result of his testimony, baby food manufacturers voluntarily agreed to stop adding it to processed products for infants and small children.

*Last week, Olney presented an even stronger indictment of MSG.* He referred to 17 studies indicating harmful side effects, including one showing fetal lesions in pregnant mice.

*"Yet," said Olney, "MSG remains on the GRAS* (Generally Recognized As Safe) *list today to be used freely in any foods,* in any amounts and for any age group. How is this explained?

*The main reason,* said Olney, was the conclusion of an advisory subcommittee of the *National Academy of Science* that Olney's own test on monkeys was irrelevant. The subcommittee recommended that no regulatory action be taken.

The Academy based its findings on two new studies contending that primates are not susceptible to MSG-induced brain damage. Shortly after the Academy issued its report, a third study appeared to add new evidence to support the same conclusion.

*But Olney became suspicious* of what he called "the rapid-fire development of negative primate data in multiple laboratories and an NAS subcommittee embracing these data to exonerate a toxic food additive. . ." He said the entire performance "had too many characteristics of an industry-arranged white-wash."

*He blamed "a high degree of industry bias and poor qualifications"* of the NAS panel. He proceeded to describe the close ties of the laboratories to both industry and government groups through previous contracts. He said a majority of subcommittee members "had almost no qualifications in the area of scientific specialization where they should have been most competent, in the area of neuropathology." He listed a number of subcommittee members who were or had been working for industry.

*Olney said he described the "messy situation"* because it "exemplifies much of what is wrong with our current system for evaluating the safety of food additives and establishing policy decisions pertaining to them . . ."

He pointed to "a group of individuals who maintain close ties with the food and drug industries, individuals who are highly regarded by those industries as 'food protection authorities' and who function as a team prepared to swing into action whenever a food safety issue arises.

"Some members of the team specialize in generating made-to-order evidence, while other members are asked (by FDA through NAS) to evaluate the evidence. Quality of evidence is not an issue . . .none would seriously question the quality of a teammate's evidence . . ."

*This was the way the three laboratories and the NAS subcommittee came to their conclusions about the use of MSG in food,* said Olney. "Their performance," he said, "was a travesty on science but provides an excellent example of how an industry dominated 'food protection' system works."

Olney strongly supported the two Senate bills under consideration.

*Olney's views about NAS and the Senate bills were seconded* by Dr. Samuel Epstein of Case-Western Reserve Medical School in Cleveland. He said the "system of checks and balances essential to the democratic process is largely absent from FDA regulatory practice. . . The concept of matching benefit against risk has been often applied by the FDA to maximize short-term benefits to industry, even though this may entail minimal benefits and maximal risks to the consumer."

*Several witnesses questioned the use of nitrites and nitrates,* which are used primarily for coloring purposes in meat products such as hot dogs . . .

Strong criticism of these chemicals was contained in a 31-page report of the House Committee on Government Operations last month. In the report, "Regulation of Food Additives—Nitrites and Nitrates" (House Report No. 92-1338 dated August 15, 1972), the Committee concluded that:

*Both substances "pose a potential danger to public health"* and the FDA had not taken effective action to limit their use as additives. In fact, said the report, regulations of both the FDA and the Department of Agriculture allow "unnecessary residues" of these substances in meat and fish.

*Numerous tests have shown that sodium nitrite* combines with other substances in the stomach to form chemicals that are carcinogenic (cancer-producing). In a 78-page report submitted to the Senate subcommittee, Dale Hattis, a graduate student in genetics at Stanford University Medical School, charged the FDA with refusing to comply "with its plain legal mandate to protect the public against fish products adulterated with sodium nitrite even though the FDA, as early as 1948, took the position . . .that the substance is *'poisonous and deleterious . . .and not required in the manufacture of any food* subject to the jurisdiction of the Food, Drug, and Cosmetic Act.' "

Nitrites and nitrates are labeled on most food products containing them.

*But there is no way for the buyer to know* which of many food colorings he may be consuming. Anita Johnson of the Health Research Group said Red No. 2, a coal-tar dye used in many food products, had caused cancer in rats and birth defects in chickens in low concentrations.

Another witness, Michael F. Jacobson of the Center for Science in the Public Interest, was particularly critical of the use of *BHA (butylated hydroxyanisole) and BHT (butylated hydroxytoluene),* antioxidants which are used to retard spoilage in food containing oil.

He cited the case of a woman who suffered mysterious tingling and facial swelling, apparently because of consuming BHT in dehydrated potatoes and corn flakes on different days. He said that although neither BHA nor BHT were apparently serious hazards, according to available evidence, neither additive is necessary because other substances can serve the same purpose. He said more testing was needed.

Meanwhile, he offered a list of food products showing which ones contain the substances and which do not. His data follows:

*Among liquid shortenings,* he said, both BHA and BHT are present in Crisco and Safeway's Nu-made, but they are not present in Wesson oils.

*Among solid shortenings,* Spry had both but Crisco had neither.

*Among nut products,* Planters had neither, but Fishers and Virginia brands indicated they contained BHA.

*Among potato chips,* Jay's and Wise showed none on labels, while Lays and Sunshine listed both BHA and BHT.

Reading 48

# Universal Product Code

**Food Processing**

*The code essentially adopts presently used case codes, identifies the manufacturer, and identifies the product.*

A code symbol identifying each individual food processor and each item within a manufacturer's complete product line will become an integral part of the packaging/identification of all food products within the next two years. Universal Product Code, a system developed by an organization composed of the Grocery Manufacturers of America and six other major trade associations, is rapidly approaching reality. This program will permit complete identification for computerized automation of product handling from manufacturer through distribution channels through supermarket registers using fully automatic electronic scanners.

Although ongoing U.S. and European supermarket test programs have shown that the most dramatic advantages accrue to the supermarket—65% quicker checkout, instantaneous inventory/reorder information, and elimination of expensive in-store price marking—a unified system should also benefit food processors in following product flow right through to the all-important retail purchase.

The Universal Product Code (UPC) system uses 10 digits: the first 5 are assigned by a central agency to identify the manufacturer, and the second 5 are assigned by the manufacturer to each of the items in his line. For automatic electronic scanning purposes, the 10-digit numeric code takes the form of a standard symbol that can be preprinted on each package.

UPC is not a date or batch code and does not identify plant, line, formula, or special process. The code essentially adopts presently used case codes, identifies the manufacturer, and identifies the product. The symbol representing the code will indicate that a package contains, as an example, breakfast cereal with an 11 oz weight produced by XYZ company or a 16 oz can of sliced, yellow, cling peaches packed by ABC company or one-half gallon of low-fat milk from DEF dairy.

Work on UPC started in mid 1970, after almost 40 years of theoretical discussions and evaluations, and is sponsored by seven major trade associations: Grocery Manufacturers of America, National Association of Food Chains, Super Market Institute, Co-operative Food Distributors of America, National Association of Convenience Stores, National Association of Retail Grocers of the U.S., and National-American Wholesale Grocers' Association. Cost studies and tests

From *Food Processing,* no. 34, January 1973, p. F13.

are coordinated by McKinsey & Co. Thirty-three equipment companies are represented on the committee for symbol development and selection.

## CODE SYMBOL

Final symbol selection is scheduled for March 30, 1973. Codes can be numeric, alphabetical, alphanumeric, or symbolic such as bar, bullseye, radial spokes, colors, etc. Equipment companies have proposed various code symbols that they consider best suited for scanning by their equipment and that will, in their estimation, best fulfill the need with least problems. 7 symbols have been proposed and are being tested either in-store (2) or by Battelle Labs (5). Only one of the symbols will be known as the UPC symbol.

The symbol can be affixed to the package in many ways. The most efficient and the one with the least or in effect no cost is to design the symbol into the label and/or printing. This will work exceptionally well on cartons such as cereal boxes, TV dinners, frozen foods, and crackers. Another possibility is to have pressure sensitive printed symbols that can be affixed to the container. Still another possibility is to have the symbol printed on the container but not as part of the label.

A decision will have to be made as to where the symbol application will be made. Projected costs of applying the code—estimate only—is $5.10/M to apply at the retail level and $0.325/M to apply at the manufacturer's level. It would appear obvious from these projected figures that the majority of the codes will be affixed by the manufacturer regardless of who actually absorbs the cost.

## SCANNERS

Two types of scanners are currently being tested. One is a fixed scanner which is built into the check-out counter and over which the package with the symbol is passed. The other is a hand held scanner which is passed over the symbol on the package. Both scanners perform basically the same function of identifying the symbol for the computer.

The fixed scanner has been in test in a Kroger store in Ohio for several months and in stores in Switzerland. The hand scanner is being tested in a Safeway store in California. With the fixed scanner, which is located at the end of the checkout counter conveyor belt, the cashier takes the package from the belt, passes it over the scanner and in the same motion places the package in bags for the customer. The scanner transmits the symbol identification to the computer which then transmits price information to a window above the checkstand so that the customer can verify the price being charged.

Affixing the symbol is complicated by the multiple types of packages passing through grocery channels. Of the 123 billion units sold through stores in 1969, exclusive of meats and produce, 36% were paper-board containers, 14.6% glass and plastic jars and bottles, 29.4% cans and aerosol, and 20.0% flexible packaging materials. Produce and meats result in special problems in that each package has a different weight and consequently a different total price. Codes, of necessity, will have to be printed in the store and affixed manually or by label application machines.

## BENEFITS

Manufacturers, working with the retailer, will be able to develop much more sophisticated market test data when introducing new products. Pricing, advertising, couponing, store placement, point of purchase material, and numerous other marketing variables can be tried and the data collected at will—hourly, daily, weekly—and for each change. Promotions or marketing changes for established products will likewise lend themselves to study and instant replay of results.

In the tests at the Kroger store, the number of checkout counters were reduced from 6 regular checkout lines plus one express to 4 electronic/scanner registers plus one express line or a reduction of approximately ⅓. In talking to customers of the store, they reported less waiting with the reduced number of registers. Kroger reports no equipment problems and no adverse customer reactions.

One of the problems of coupons is misuse. With the new system, much better control of couponing will be available to the manufacturer. Coupons can be printed with the actual symbol for the item covered by the coupon. As coupons are tendered to the cashier she can pass them over the scanner which will in turn ask the computer if the item was actually purchased rather than taking the customers word or searching the bagged groceries to determine purchase.

Probable distribution approach in the future will have consumer packages packed in tray pack corrugated or shrink wrapped cases (Green Giant now uses shrink wrap on 85% of their volume), for direct shelf stocking at the store. Pricing will be affixed to the shelf for the customers information. In addition, portable optional scanners may be placed at various points in the store for the consumers usage.

## Reading 49

# Difficult Recipe—A Food Price Rollback Would Not Be Simple

**John A. Prestbo**

*Another factor in rising food prices is that the food industry is simply inefficient.*

It won't be easy getting food prices back where the President wants them.

This is the almost unanimous view of people in the food industry as concern mounts over soaring prices for beef, pork, some fresh vegetables and a wide range of other food products.

The administration has moved fast to try to calm the uproar. Hearings into the causes of the increases have been scheduled, Treasury Secretary John Connally has been "jawboning" with supermarket executives, (some of whom have agreed to hold the line on meat prices), and the Internal Revenue Service has been alerted to watch closely the profit margins of grocery stores and meat packers. Mr. Nixon has lashed out at the food industry's "middle-men" as the prime villains.

From *The Wall Street Journal*, Apr. 3, 1973. Reprinted with permission of *The Wall Street Journal*, 

But finding ways to handle food prices won't be an easy task for the administration's inflation fighters. Experts base this judgment on the sprawling nature of the U.S. food industry and the many factors that have brought retail prices to their present levels.

## "NO ATTRACTIVE OPTIONS"

"There aren't really any easy or attractive options," concedes one official of the Cost of Living Council, which oversees Phase 2. "If there were, we'd have taken them already."

Everyone agrees food prices are climbing painfully fast. Beef prices rose 3% in January and 4% more in February. The average retail price for beef is a record $1.15 a pound, 14 cents higher than a year ago. Pork prices climbed a whopping 9.3% last month. At the produce counter, cucumber prices jumped 22.6% in February, green peppers rose 17.8% and lettuce increased 13.8% from January levels.

The basic factor is that demand exceeds supply. The corn blight two years ago caused ranchers and feeders to cut their herds, so not as many cattle as planned came to market this winter to satisfy consumers' taste for beef. Hog farmers intentionally cut back to compensate for their price-depressing overproduction of a couple of years ago. Bad growing conditions and other factors are crimping some produce supplies.

A momentary break is in sight. Cattle and hog prices have been declining in recent weeks as more animals have been brought to market and as consumers have switched to chicken, eggs and other substitutes. These declines should begin showing up at retail this month. Fresh produce generally becomes less expensive in the spring, and this year should be no exception. But economists warn that demand for beef, pork and produce will get stronger as the economy picks up momentum, so even a temporary slack in supplies could send prices shooting back up again.

## BIG AND INEFFICIENT

Because of the nature of the food industry, the increases in the prices of raw food—which aren't regulated by Phase 2 at all—are magnified by the time they reach the consumer. The food industry is the nation's biggest, moving at retail nearly $120 billion of foodstuffs and related products a year. It is also among the nation's most inefficient industries in getting its products to where people can buy them. Some items change hands a dozen times before reaching a grocery shelf; by comparison, auto makers sell their cars to dealers who in turn sell them to consumers.

Each of the many layers of middlemen—from country grain elevators to processors to wholesalers to retailers—must earn a profit. Not an exorbitant profit that can be rooted out and controlled by Phase 2, but just a run-of-the-mill gross profit of, say, 5%. But even that's enough to turn a tiny increase in the price of a raw food into runaway inflation by the time the consumer pays for it.

Suppose, for example, a raw food that a processor buys goes up two cents a pound to 52 cents. Disregarding the value a processor may add to the product, a 5% profit on top of the extra two cents boosts his price to 54.6 cents from 52.5 cents. The regional distributor likewise passes along the two-cent increase and adds 5% of the larger amount. The local distributor and the retailer follow suit. Eventually, what started out as a 4% price increase ends up as a 15% jump at the check-out counter. And no single middleman can truthfully be charged with gouging the consumer.

## MR. GRAYSON'S PROPOSAL

The illustration is greatly simplified, of course, but under *Phase 2 food prices have been allowed to balloon in such a fashion.* Partly for that reason, the "middleman's" share of the retail food dollar rose to 60.3% in February from 59.9% in January. Over a longer period, the trend shows up even more dramatically. The prices that farmers get for their foodstuffs average only 7% higher than 20 years ago, while wholesale prices have increased 22% and average retail prices are up 44%. The *average annual food bill for U.S. families rose $21 last year [1972],* the government estimates, and all but $1 of the gain went to the middlemen.

C. Jackson Grayson Jr., the Price Commission chairman, says that one action his group might take is to require a strict dollars-and-cents pass-through of any price increases of raw foods. That would mean a two-cent increase at the farm would still be two cents at the supermarket. The effect would be to shrink the profit margins of each middleman every time a price increase was passed along.

Not surprisingly, middlemen don't think highly of that suggestion. "The administrative costs alone would be enough to raise prices," asserts a spokesman for the National Association of Food Chains. "Take beef—if carcasses went up a penny a pound, how much of that should be allocated to hamburger and how much to porterhouse?" An official of Jewel Cos., the Chicago-based supermarket concern, says, "Supermarkets generally make only 1% profit on sales, which means that consumers would save only 40 cents on a $40 grocery order if we made no profit at all. Is that a big enough deal to warrant such a drastic action?

The simpler solution of freezing all food prices everywhere except the farm also is being discussed in Washington, but it, too, has drawbacks. "An absolute clamp-down on retail prices eventually will lead to black markets as items disappear one by one from grocery stores," contends the trade group spokesman. Henry B. Arthur, a Harvard Business School professor who has observed the food industry for several decades, says, "Price ceilings won't be effective for very long without rationing, and frankly I don't think we're that bad off yet."

Washington's war on the middleman can bog down for a variety of other reasons as well.

One is that food prices are buoyed by the government's own policies, which Phase 2 controllers can't easily change. One of these is the import quotas on beef, sugar and other commodities, which boost domestic prices. C. Fred Bergsten of the Brookings Institution calculates that import quotas cost consumers about $500 million a year extra on dairy products, a like amount for sugar and about $300 million for meat.

Various farm subsidies, commodity price supports and payments for keeping some land out of production are other examples of governmental programs that work at cross purposes with Phase 2. These payments are expected to rise sharply this year, mainly to keep farmers from growing an unneeded glut of corn.

Another factor in rising food prices is that the food industry is simply inefficient. "The food industry still operates much as it did 30 years ago," says Gordon F. Bloom, a marketing lecturer at Massachusetts Institute of Technology and a former food retailing executive. "I don't say that individual companies aren't efficient; in fact, there isn't much room for many of them to improve. But the industry itself is still geared to a slower-paced world of corner grocery stores."

Mr. Bloom has just written a book full of examples of this. He notes, for example, that most stores have to hire stock boys to mark the price on each item because the industry can't agree on pre-marking procedures. High-paid driver-salesmen from bakeries come to a store each day to pick up the old bread and put out the new, while minimum-wage stock boys watch.

He also notes the food industry has two "standard" sized pallets for carrying shipments, with one considerably bigger than the other. "As a result, we have the ridiculous scene of a truck delivering a shipment on one size pallet to a wholesaler's warehouse that can handle only the other size," Mr. Bloom says. "Everything else in that warehouse may be automated to the hilt, but on the loading dock they have to lift boxes from one pallet to another by hand."

Because the food industry is so labor-intensive in many ways, it's particularly vulnerable to wage increases. The average hourly labor cost for marketing food products has increased 66% in the last 10 years, and this is reflected in higher retail prices. Rising labor and other overhead costs at every layer of middleman are the main reason that falling prices for agricultural products aren't always passed along fully to consumers.

Consumer tastes also play a role in boosting food prices, and these aren't easily changed by Phase 2 controllers, either. The continuing growing demand for convenience foods, for instance, increases prices to pay for the research and development and labor costs that go into them.

"There are probably 10 different ways we can buy potatoes now, besides in a 10-pound bag, all the way from potato chips to au gratin," says the Jewel official in Chicago. "People like this variety well enough that they'll pay for it, but make no mistake, they do pay extra."

Sometimes things consumers don't want also push prices higher than they otherwise might be. Retailers and meat packers say they could save scads of money—some of which would be passed on to the consumer, they say—if steaks and roasts were cut and packaged at the packing plant, frozen and shipped to stores for sale in freezer cases. This would eliminate the need for butchers in stores. But housewives are wary of buying frozen meat, so the practice hasn't been widely adopted.

Needham Packing Co. tried it, and failed miserably, a few years ago and concluded it might take years for housewives to get over their frozen meat phobia. "They won't buy it frozen in the store, but they'll take a fresh cut home and put it in their own freezer," sighs Jerry Kozney, Needham president.

Reading 50

# The Effect of Unit-Pricing on Choices of Brand and Size in Economic Shopping

**Michael J. Houston**

*Unit price, as a choice criterion to use in economic shopping, can be calculated in any store.*

Most consumer research has been concerned with how knowledge of consumer behavior patterns can direct the firm in the development of marketing strategy and policies. However, relatively little research has investigated how policies of the firm can be beneficial to the consumer in his buying behavior.[1] This article examines unit-pricing as a potential aid to consumers. It reports a study designed to determine the effect of unit-pricing on the ability of consumers to choose the most economical brand and size in a product class.

Unit-pricing, a retail pricing policy, is designed to aid primarily the economy-minded consumer—that consumer who is interested in minimizing the cost of a single purchase or set of purchases without regard to quality. Its benefits seem to exist primarily in the purchase of grocery items. When a good is unit-priced, its price is expressed in terms of the cost per unit of measure of the product in addition to its total price. For example, with unit-pricing a consumer would know that a ten-ounce container of instant coffee priced at $1.65 costs 16.5 per ounce.

The numerous brands and sizes of grocery items now available to the consumer often make it difficult for her to determine the lowest unit-cost item in a product class. Therefore, unit-pricing should enable the value-conscious shopper to better determine the item with the lowest unit-price.

## RESEARCH DESIGN AND PROCEDURES

The study reported here was conducted over a two-day period in a midwestern town of 15,000-20,000 people during the fall of 1970. Outlets of three major supermarket chains operate in the town.

Every grocery item in Store A is marked according to its actual price as well as its unit-price. The two remaining stores use a combination of pricing procedures: "per item" pricing where only the price for the individual item is marked, and multiple-pricing—the "two for 49 cents" variety. Although Stores B and C use both procedures to some degree, Store B tends to emphasize "per item" pricing, while Store C tends to emphasize multiple pricing.

A sample of 53 housewives was chosen for the study. The researcher initially contacted three housewives and asked them to participate in the study. They were also asked to find other participants who, in turn, found additional subjects. As a result, a portion of the sample was composed of a small church

[1]David T. Kollat, James F. Engel, and Roger D. Blackwell, "Current Problems in Consumer Behavior Research," *Journal of Marketing Research,* Vol. 7 (August, 1970), pp. 327-332.

Reprinted from *The Journal of Marketing,* published by the American Marketing Association, vol. 36, July 1972, pp. 51-59.

group and a small neighborhood group. Other than the small neighborhood group, the subjects represented a rather wide geographical area of the community.

The subjects were randomly assigned to one of three groups, and each group was assigned to one of the stores. Eighteen shoppers were assigned to both Stores A and B, while seventeen were assigned to Store C. The random assignment was intended to control for differences in store familiarity between subjects.

Members of each group were sent to their respective stores on an individual basis and instructed to purchase items from a list of fourteen product classes (Table 1). The same list of instructions (Table 2) was given to each subject prior to her departure and reviewed orally with the researcher. Each subject was instructed to buy the most economical brand and size in each product class without regard to her personal preferences or beliefs concerning differences in qual-

**Table 1 Worksheet for Participants**

Name ____________________
Date ____________________
Name & location of
store surveyed ____________________
____________________
____________________
Time entered store ____________________
Time survey completed ____________________

| Category | Choice (brand, size, quantity) | Brand | Remarks (optional) |
|---|---|---|---|
| Toilet tissue (2 ply) | | | |
| Apple sauce | | | |
| Canned peaches | | | |
| Canned peas | | | |
| Canned tuna | | | |
| Chunk cheddar cheese | | | |
| Granulated sugar | | | |
| Instant coffee (not freeze-dried) | | | |
| Liquid dishwashing detergent | | | |
| Low calorie soda | | | |
| Mayonnaise | | | |
| Peanut butter (smooth) | | | |
| Paper towel | | | |
| Potato chips (unflavored, unruffled) | | | |

**Table 2 Instructions to Participants**

On the sheet of paper you now have there is a list of 14 grocery items often purchased by consumers. What I would like you to do is go to the local ______________ supermarket and purchase these items with the money being provided you. Before you go, however, there are some instructions that I want you to follow in your shopping.

1 In buying each item make the most economical purchase. Buy the size and brand that gives you the best buy for your money. Forget about quality. Do not purchase the brand or size you usually buy unless you feel it is the most economical.

2 Some items will require more time than others in determining the most economical buy. But, in any event, do not spend more than five minutes in shopping for any one item. This is very important.

3 Before leaving for the store, rewrite the list of items on another sheet of paper. Use this second list as your shopping list.

4 Please note the time you entered the store and the time you left the store.

5 Purchase the items in the order given on the list. Make your purchases individually. Please *do not* talk or confer with anyone about your purchases when you are making them.

6 Upon completing your shopping, return with the items and any change to this room.

7 On the original list of items, please fill in the necessary information in the upper right hand corner and the brand, size, quantity, and price for each item.

8 Place the completed list in your shopping bag and return the items and change to the designated person.

ity between brands. Unless specified on the list of product classes, subjects were to give no consideration to variations within a product class such as differences in color, ingredients, etc. Although unit-price was not specifically pointed out as the criterion to use in choosing the most economical brand and size, the instructions attempted to eliminate all other choice criteria. Hopefully, their effect was, thus, minimized.

Each shopper was given the same list of product classes; however, the order of the classes was randomized for each individual. Each shopper was instructed to purchase the items in the order appearing on the worksheet. These procedures were designed to prevent any order effects. Subjects were allowed to keep four of the purchased items as a payment for their participation. However, they were not given this information until after they had made their purchases. In addition, a contribution was made to the treasury of the church group.

Unknown to the subjects, a price-checker was sent to each store to determine unit-prices of all brands and sizes in each product class. The price-checker reported that all of the most economical items (except as noted below) seemed to be in sufficient stock.

The purpose of the above design was to measure at stores using alternative pricing procedures the absolute frequency with which an item other than the minimum unit-price item was chosen and the resulting monetary differences between the items. Since two of the stores used a mixture of pricing procedures, the "treatment" levels in the analysis should be considered the three stores, since they are mutually exclusive alternatives. However, a comparison of the effect of a unit-pricing policy (existing in one clear-cut case) versus an alternative system using a mixture of price-reporting techniques (existing at both of the other stores) is being made.

Two dependent variables were used in the analysis: (1) The absolute frequency with which the chosen item did not correspond with the minimum unit-price item for each individual; and (2) The monetary difference for each individual between her actual choices and the lowest unit-price alternatives.

The following hypotheses were tested in this study:

**1** The frequency with which the items chosen at Store A do not correspond with the minimum unit-price items is significantly smaller than at Stores B and C.

**2** The resulting monetary differences between the items chosen and the minimum unit-price items at Store A are significantly smaller than those at Stores B and C.

## DATA ANALYSIS

### Frequency of Noncorresponding Choices

In order to test the first hypothesis, the frequency with which an item chosen in a product class did not correspond to the minimum unit-price item for that product class was computed for each individual. One product class (granulated sugar) was dropped from the analysis when it was reported that one of the stores did not have it in stock that day.

Analysis of variance was performed on the results to test for significant differences between the stores.[2] The results of the analysis are summarized in Table 3. A significant difference in the effects of the three stores on the extent to which the minimum unit-price item is chosen is evident. Individual comparisons of means using t-tests showed the mean number of noncorresponding choices per individual at Store A, the unit-pricing outlet, to be significantly lower than those at both Stores A and B ($p < .01$).[3] The existence of unit pricing at Store A has significantly reduced the extent to which a brand and size other than the minimum unit-price band and size is chosen.

### Dollar Differences

While unit pricing does seem to reduce the number of errors made, this result will acquire more meaning if it also means a substantial reduction of monetary differences. To compute the dollar differences resulting from choices other than the minimum unit-price item, the following procedure was used for each individual. For each nonminimum unit-price choice made by the shopper, the price difference between that item and the minimum unit-price item was computed on a per-unit basis. This margin was then multiplied by the quantity purchased

**Table 3 Analysis of Variance for Frequency of Noncorresponding Choices**

| Source of variation | d.f. | M.S. | F |
|---|---|---|---|
| Between stores | 2 | 20.30 | 7.3* |
| Within stores | 50 | 2.78 | |

| Store A | Store B | Store C |
|---|---|---|
| $n = 18$ | $n = 18$ | $n = 17$ |
| $\bar{x} = 4.71$ | $\bar{x} = 6.71$ | $\bar{x} = 6.35$ |
| $s = 1.32$ | $s = 1.90$ | $s = 1.73$ |

*$p < .01$.

[2] Allen E. Edwards, *Experimental Designs in Psychological Research,* Third Edition (New York: Holt, Rinehart, and Winston, 1968).

[3] James L. Bruning and B. L. Kintz, *Computational Handbook of Statistics* (Glenview: Scott, Foresman and Co., 1968).

**Table 4 Analysis of Variance for Dollar Differences**

| Source of variation | d.f. | M.S. | F |
|---|---|---|---|
| Between stores | 2 | 10,330 | 18.85* |
| Within stores | 50 | 548 | |

| Store A | Store B | Store C |
|---|---|---|
| $\bar{x}$ = 36¢ | $\bar{x}$ = 54¢ | $\bar{x}$ = 84¢ |
| s = 14.0 | s = 28.8 | s = 24.9 |

*$p < .001$.

to give the *dollar difference on the quantity bought.* Dollar differences for each item were summed to give the total dollar difference for the individual. For example, consider an individual who made two errors on coffee and dishwashing detergent. Assume she bought 10 ounces of coffee at 18 cents per ounce, and the minimum unit-price brand and size sold for 14 cents per ounce. Therefore, a monetary difference of 40 cents exists on the quantity of coffee bought. Similarly, if a consumer paid 15 cents per pint (16 ounces) for 64 ounces of dishwashing detergent and the "best buy" sold for 12 cents per pint, then a 12-cent difference exists on the quantity of detergent bought. The total dollar difference for this individual is, therefore, 52 cents.

Computing each participant's dollar difference as described above, the one-way analysis of variance and individual comparison of means were performed on the results. The results of the analysis are summarized in Table 4. A significant F-ratio was computed, showing that differences in dollar deviations across stores did exist.[4] The comparison of means showed the mean dollar difference at Store A to be significantly lower than the mean at Store B ($p < .05$) and significantly lower than the mean at Store C ($p < .01$).[5] Unit pricing, therefore, has reduced the dollar differences resulting from choices other than the minimum unit-price brand and size.

An interesting result, which did not occur in the analysis of frequency scores, occurred in the analysis of monetary differences. A significant difference between the mean values at Store B (emphasis on "per item" pricing) and Store C (emphasis on multiple pricing) was found to exist ($p < .001$). In fact, the difference (30¢) between Stores B and C is substantially greater than the difference (18¢) between stores A and B.

Perhaps, it is more difficult to determine the minimum unit price under multiple pricing procedures. However, a better explanation may be that when a choice other than the minimum unit-price item is made, the resulting dollar difference on the quantity bought is compounded by the fact that multiple units of the item are purchased. In any event, multiple pricing procedures do not seem well suited to the needs of the economic shopper.

## SUMMARY AND CONCLUSIONS

Unit price, as a choice criterion to use in economic shopping, can be calculated at any store. However, stores can vary in the amount of information they provide regarding unit price. The purpose of this study was to determine if a pricing system that provided the unit price for each item in a product class was benefi-

[4]Same reference as footnote 2.
[5]Same reference as footnote 3.

cial to value-conscious consumers. That is, if consumers wish to shop for the most economical brand, does a unit-pricing system facilitate the purchase decision? The investigation was not designed to measure the extent to which unit pricing is desired or actually used by consumers in a natural setting. Therefore, any conclusions probably apply only to the value-conscious consumer.

If minimum unit price is accepted as the appropriate choice criterion to use in economic shopping, two conclusions are evident from the results of the study. First, the consumer is better able to determine the most economical item in a product class at stores with unit pricing than at stores using alternative forms of price-reporting that provide less information regarding unit price. Second, when an item is chosen other than the minimum unit-price item, the total dollar difference between the chosen items and the minimum unit-price items is reduced significantly when unit-pricing information is provided.

The results of this study indicate that further research is needed that varies the type of consumer involved. For instance, consumers with different shopping orientations (e.g., brand-loyal shoppers) could be given the same shopping tasks in order to observe their choice behavior under a unit-pricing system. A similar design in which consumers are segmented on selected socioeconomic variables (especially, level of education) could also be employed.

Reading 51

# How New Food Labeling Affects the Consumer

**The National Observer**

*The FDA regulations also include stringent prohibitions on foods designated for special dietary use.*

As an aggressive champion of consumer interests, the Food and Drug Administration (FDA) has a record that has been spotty. But the Federal agency showed some new teeth last week as it announced a set of sweeping changes in food labeling along with sharp restrictions on vitamin and mineral products. FDA Commissioner Charles Edwards boasted that the 12-part program represented "the most significant change in food labeling since food labeling began."

For once, consumer groups and the food-processing and distribution industry, who have been engaged in a relatively quiet but intense debate on the subject for years, tended to agree. "The most significant step for consumers and the food industry in a quarter of a century," declared George W. Koch, president of the Grocery Manufacturers of America, which represents about 85 per cent of the manufacturers whose products are sold in supermarkets. And Dr. Jean Mayer of Harvard, a leading nutritionist, called the FDA program "a major first step."

From *The National Observer*, Jan. 27, 1973, p.10.

## MAJOR ELEMENTS

Among the major elements of that first step, the following will mean the most to American consumers:

- The appearance of canned and packaged foods in your supermarket will be significantly different, with some of the first changes showing up as soon as next summer when some Del Monte products get new labels. By the end of 1974, FDA Commissioner Edwards predicts, 90 per cent of all packaged food will carry the new labels, nearly all of them the result of competitive pressure rather than Government regulation.
- The new labels will be uniform, clearly describe the size and number of servings in the package, and list the caloric, protein, carbohydrate, and fat content. In addition, the new labels will list the percentage of the U.S. Recommended Daily Allowance (RDA) of protein, vitamins, and minerals.
- When a food manufacturer claims that his product is "enriched" or "fortified" he'll have to put up or shut up—either list the full nutrients on the label or withdraw his claim.
- For the first time, food manufacturers will be able to list on the label the cholesterol, fat, and fatty-acid contents of their products, a step the FDA emphasized should not be interpreted as taking sides in the debate over whether such substances increase the risk of heart disease.
- Forget the term Minimum Daily Requirement (MDR) and remember its successor, Recommended Daily Allowance, which nearly doubles the suggested daily intake of various vitamins and minerals for children and adults.
- Depending on the amount of vitamins and minerals a food product contains over and above the RDA, the Food and Drug Administration can classify it as an ordinary food, a special dietary food, or a drug intended for treating disease. Some breakfast cereals containing large amounts of vitamins will be affected.
- In keeping with a recommendation by the 1969 White House Conference on Food, Nutrition, and Health, the word "imitation" won't be appearing in labels with nearly the frequency it now does, but will be required whenever a food is nutritionally inferior.

The FDA regulations also include stringent prohibitions on foods designated for "special dietary use," including a prohibition on claims that the product can by itself prevent, treat, or cure disease; the label may not imply that a diet of ordinary foods cannot supply adequate nutrients; claims are forbidden that transportation, storage, or cooking of foods may result in inadequate or deficient diet; also disallowed are claims that such nonnutritive ingredients as rutin, para-aminobenzoic acid, and other similar ingredients have nutritional value.

The one segment of the processed-foods industry most adversely affected by the regulations will be the health-foods industry. Max Huberman of Youngstown, Ohio, the president of the National Nutritional Foods Association, complains that the FDA regulations will unduly "restrict" him and his associates. "We applaud the Government efforts to list the contents of food," says Huberman. "We've been the ones mainly decrying the use of unhealthful additives in food. We're the conscience of the $125 billion processed-foods industry, though we represent only 1 per cent of it."

David King, a former congressman who now serves as legislative counsel for the National Foods Association, argues that the proposed regulations deny consumers the right to take vitamins and minerals that are safe and wholesome.

"What alarms us most," says King, "is that dietary supplements can't exceed 150 per cent of the Recommended Daily Allowance. If they do they must be called drugs, and this puts the health-food industry at the mercy of a FDA panel which deals with over-the-counter drugs."

Within the food-processing industry, on the other hand, the reaction to the FDA regulations was generally favorable. Richard G. Landis, president of the huge Del Monte Corp., called the guidelines "realistic and workable," and pointed out that his company has already geared up voluntarily to use the nutritional labels. At General Mills, a spokesman expressed "strong approval" of the labeling program, and predicted that it "shouldn't cost the consumer anything extra because we are constantly running tests and samples of our food products, and frequently changing our labels and packages."

## 'NO IMMEDIATE IMPACT'

Grocery Manufacturers president George Koch, however, predicted that the new labeling procedures would require price hikes, even if they are months and years away. "There will be no immediate impact on consumer prices," Koch said, "but it will ultimately have an effect." He declined to predict how much of an effect.

Among the consumer advocates who applauded the new FDA regulations were Virginia Knauer, assistant to the President for consumer affairs, and Mrs. Knauer's predecessor in the post, Esther Peterson. "There can be little doubt that these regulations will have a profound, perhaps revolutionary, effect on the supermarket and the way shoppers buy food," said Mrs. Knauer. Mrs. Peterson, now a consumer consultant for a large Washington, D.C., food chain, called the proposals "a great step ahead. It makes a fine historical culmination of giving the consumer more information."

One of the loudest critics of the FDA rules, Rep. Benjamin Rosenthal of New York, complained that they don't give the consumer enough information. "This program is built on the quicksand of those two oft-discredited concepts—voluntary compliance and self-regulation," Rosenthal said. "It has no teeth, no incentive, and no guts."

# Family Clothing Management

Reading 52

## What Will Happen to the Gray Flannel Suit?

**Moira Johnston**

*International costume will probably express the new set of values now being altered to fit the post-industrial age.*

As the American frontier spread westward, settlers pulled a sameness of dress across the land as they moved from one cleared patch of ground to the next. On this continent there never have been the centuries of isolation needed to develop richly individual regional dress. Today, the drab clothes of the West are universal, dulling the brilliant saffrons, batiks, and indigo of other cultures.

At first, standardized Western dress—essentially the suit—spread around the world as a prime symbol of progress and industrialization. The 19th century British suit brought clothes to the greatest separation of the sexes ever—with men, upright phallic symbols and women, glorified tea cozies. Now the development of an international dress parallels the supranationalizing of the world politically and economically—the direction many futurists see as the only way to go. The world of the future will undoubtedly be influenced by Asian and African cultures that, in spite of the suit, still have some color and sensuality left to feed into the sartorial melting pot. But, essentially, nations will have to lose themselves in the larger idiom. International costume will probably express the new set of values now being altered to fit the post-industrial age. The traditional Western ethic, like its clothes, will probably be too old fashioned to work. The earth's ecological crisis is already forcing a compromise between the manipulated, architectural shapes of the West and the natural flow and fatalism of Eastern robes.

But will humans ever be willing—or able—to give up altogether the little differences, the nuances that continue to make every person, town, city, nation, and civilization visually distinctive? Will history, with its ego-building tales of territorial victories and gorgeous ethnic costume be a threat to a globalizing world? I don't think so. For humans haven't changed much. At times of upheaval, people have always clutched traditional clothes like a security blanket, giving volatile emotions something familiar to focus on . . . to hold on to. People have always found the confidence to face the future in the clothes of the past. And though forms will change, universal principles of dress will continue.

From the *Journal of Home Economics*, vol. 64, November 1972, pp.28–33, copyright by the American Home Economics Association, Washington, D.C.

## HISTORIC IDENTITY

This persistence of historic identity in the face of change struck me last year in Europe. All the young people of both sexes in America, England, and France were wearing essentially the same costume—flared pants, long skinny knit sweaters or shirts, and wide leather belts. They had all responded to one of the most basic universals—the compulsion to identify with what seems admirable. It's the dynamic force that has spread the business suit around the world and puts small boys into cowboy hats. It's the force that ties the army, the school, the team, the office, the nation together visually. And it is the force that has made bell bottoms, belts, and knit tops—originally an American style—an international uniform of the young.

But in each country at the time of my visit something was spontaneously changing the effect. And that something was history. In the States, the outfit was raw, like the frontier. It was a direct and dishevelled challenge to the impeccable dress of the establishment. Minimal wardrobes of jeans and shirts, worn until they fell apart, were a sacrificial purge of parents' overstuffed closets. The young were wearing like a hair shirt the accumulated guilt of a rich society. They'd gone back to the honest clothes, the cooperative effort, the closeness to the earth of their own frontier, and with jeans, boots, and belts slung on like Western gunbelts, were throwing this earlier image of America back in the faces of parents who had apparently lost sight of the founding values. And girls with masculine hip-slung belts and no brassieres were belligerently deemphasizing the ancient fertile image of lavish breasts and hips and defined waists, groping for a redefinition of sex roles.

Last year, in France, I saw a different trend in dress. The sleekness of the cut and fit, the sophistication of the colors, and the elegance of the belt lifted the look beyond social comment and revolt to the French tradition of taste and fashion. The spirit of the 18th century salons was alive and well on the Boulevard St. Germaine. There was still more concern for refinement than for raw innovation. The tight top and pants that left no confusion about sex and the polished buckle that weighted the belt down in front like a sassy fertility girdle showed that the French young were not involved in Women's Lib. They were still using clothes to play the old seductive roles and to advertise to the world that France still cares about keeping up appearances.

In England, the fluid shirts and pants of both sexes were just a base for the romantic flow of long hair, long capes, rich blue and maroon velvets that gave any group of young people queueing up for a rock concert the appearance of a medieval procession. The English young have been left hanging without the confident identity the empire gave their parents. In a search for alternatives, the English youth had dipped unconsciously into their own medieval past. Their low-slung belts were worn like sword belts.

In all three countries, clothes seemed a dynamic assertion of nationalism, of individuality, in the face of what seems an irresistible tide of global uniformity. I see this urge to resist a collective image even within San Francisco where little microcultures manifest themselves in the Ivy League suits of bankers; in the hand-decorated levis of a Berkeley student; in the white gloves and British tweed suits of the ladies; in the trousers of the black school boys whose mothers won't let them wear jeans because jeans "look poor"; in the lacquered beehive hairdos and toreador pants; and in the calico sacks of adolescent earth mothers. Beyond the uniform of slacks, knits, and belts is this seemingly chaotic range of styles. But this is just the kind of clue that indicates we are in the midst of a social revolution that is very big and very deep. What we're seeing on our streets, what San Francisco (which gave birth to the costumes of counterculture and student activists) is experiencing, is the chaotic period that some futurists consider inevitable as people respond to change at different speeds.

## A GLANCE BACKWARD

But the chaos falls into order if we look back into history, for history shows us patterns that seem to repeat themselves at times of transition. I have detected three forces that motivate people in their manner of dress. Some cling to tradition, hanging on to the old ways of dressing. Others hunt desperately for alternatives to what seems a bankrupt present and uncertain future. These persons search through the past, grab at mystical cults, the dress of other cultures, and escape into fantasy. But a third force, the future, pushes through spontaneously. And most of us become schizophrenic trying to integrate in our style of dress all the conflicting forces of our society. We tend to end up with the kind of ambiguous statement Dinah Shore made on television last season in her long midi skirts, split up the front, revealing hot pants. It was an assertion of female dependency and seduction fighting it out with liberation before our eyes. This confusion of clinging, escape, and change always leads to extravagant and exciting periods of dress such as we have today.

One of the earliest, biggest changes in dress took place when men shifted from hunting to farming. Men had always hunted and had always worn furs and skins. At the time, farming didn't seem much of an improvement. Settled towns were vulnerable, and the whole way of life lacked the old excitement and stimulation of the hunt. Men now had woven fabrics and rectangles of wool and linen. But they were reluctant to give up their skins. So they went to the enormous trouble of making a fake fleece that combined both. They took loosely woven cloth and pulled tufts of real sheep or goat wool through it in horizontal rows, creating a shaggy cloth called "kaunakes." It had the look, feel, smell, and bulk of the real thing but used the new technology of weaving, too. It helped them get through the neolithic transition.

Compare that with the popularity of fake furs today. The postwar prestige of mink stoles shows that fur has continued as a prime status symbol. And although the killing of animals to drape women in pelts is beginning to seem immoral, downright primitive, and a threat to the balance of nature, the need for the status associations of fur is so strong that a technology that can produce a moonsuit bends its talents to duplicating leopard, lamb, and chinchilla in manmade fibers. They are our kaunakes. In the same way, the new plastics are meant to be poured, molded, and bonded, but we are emotionally unready to leave weaving behind. So we go to the excruciating trouble of spinning polyester threads and weaving simulations of the cotton, linen, and wool the neolithic farmwoman was weaving 10,000 years ago. It is still difficult for us to feel affection for a vinyl tunic. Thus we accept the new only in the guise of the old.

## ROME AND THE TOGA

Looking back through history, we see that another great and painful point of transition occurred with the decline of Rome. The end of Rome was the end of the classical world and the end of the domination of the earliest civilizations ringing the Mediterranean. The state religions and bureaucracy had become hollow and impersonal, and people searched desperately for a way out of the emptiness. They imported mystical religions from the East, dressing one cult in complete Persian regalia. The Christian sect hid in catacombs and took on the humble tunics of the servant class to look like "the servants of the Lord," and often replaced the toga with the rectangular pallium wrap that had become a symbol of asceticism. As they began to gain strength and courage, they wore their clothes as a form of defiance against decadent Romans who were finding their escapes in makeup and jewels, blond wigs, lovers, silks, and astrology. Officials, feeling the threat, imposed the toga with renewed vigor. For centuries, the toga had been the visible symbol that had rallied Romans and motivated them to greatness. The establishment felt that to lose the toga—the pride of every citizen—was to lose the fiber of Rome. Augustus tried to force its wearing by law. Consuls and officials throughout the empire paraded the toga with increasing determination. And the toga grew bigger, more complicated, more visibly impressive—like a monumental arch. But all that the insistence achieved was more alienation, for as the toga became more elaborate, working men could scarcely afford it, could not work in it, and, without servants, could not even put it on. They stored their togas away in chests, bringing them out only for ceremonial occasions, and by the 4th century A.D. stopped wearing the toga altogether. No longer a live garment, the toga had shrunk to little more than a jeweled ceremonial scarf.

While the toga was weakening, the clothes of the future were creeping in—the wool cloaks and bright plaids of the barbarians of the northern frontier. Roman women were importing blond German hair for their wigs. Soldiers were adopting the barbarian trouser. These trends, I think, are valid clues to the end of the Roman Empire. For the power to influence dress has always pulsed out from the centers of political, economic, and cultural power. And the appearance in Rome of barbarian dress meant that there had been a subtle shift of power from Rome to the North and to the struggling new religion. Christian robes and barbarian pants show that the impressive facade of Rome had begun to crack several centuries before historians admit to the fall of Rome. And reviewing it now, I get a strong sense of *déjà vu.*

## TRANSITION IN THE MIDDLE AGES

In the 14th and 15th centuries, we come to another transition that might compare with our own. Call it Renaissance, Reformation, Age of Science and Reason, or what-have-you . . . it was a shift from the otherworldly superstition of the medieval soul, from volatile emotions and fears held in check by costumed spectacle, and religion made real by church statues carved in the fashionable clothes of the day. The transition then was a shift to the outer-directed, rational humanism of the Industrial Age.

It grew out of the gloom of dark European forests and the specter of death. Towns were replacing castles, guns had made armor obsolete, trade was replacing war; and the Black Death had wiped out what little confidence remained after the disasters of the Crusades, which had undermined the strength of the Church. The old way was failing, and people tried to hold on to it a little longer.

The Church, one of the pillars of the Middle Ages, increased its production of ceremonial vestments, for threatened symbols tend spontaneously to reassert themselves before they give up. Capes and chasubles reached a peak of elaboration, as gold and silk embroideries turned them into works of art, countering the secular threat of the Renaissance.

The old gear of the knight was dragged out, exaggerated and distorted, and paraded up and down the land in public ceremonials that turned the waning

Middle Ages into a poignant Mardi Gras. Never have so many fountains spewed so much wine nor have so many birds flown out of so many room-sized pies. The knight's old heraldic motifs, which had identified and rallied him in battle, were blown up like supergraphics and spilled over into everything—wives' dresses, servants' clothes, banners, pennons, canopies, stockings.

Parti-color, the old divisions of color in the coat-of-arms that identified the families that had married into the knight's family, now turned up in men's hose, with one leg green, the other red-and-yellow stripes. The skin-protecting underwear of the knight came out from under the armor as doublet and hose that now dressed shoemakers and merchants. And knights in great suits of plate armor, engraved and polished to a dazzle, were hoisted up on plumed and caparisoned horses at tournaments that turned war into flamboyant ritual. The new armor was more impressive than the old coats of mail, but it was no longer functional for war. It grew heavier and more awkward, and gradually clanked into retirement, much as the toga had faded into retirement. And as the business suit may do in the future. For when garments lose their vital function and become ceremonial, we're headed for a new way of dressing.

Despite all this glorification of knightly symbols, the Renaissance was pushing through. There was a new interest in man, new wealth, great social competition. And after centuries of medieval robes that enshrouded the figure, the desire to display man was becoming irresistible. Hose and doublet fitted like skin, and display became more and more extravagant as heraldry, fantasy, and Renaissance ego and wealth fused together. Loose medieval sleeves grew into huge trailing sleeves that swept back like butterfly wings. Poulaine shoes stretched out to ridiculous lengths, and modest veils stretched out on yard-high pointed hennins and flaunted from the tips like banners. There were tournaments, masked balls, ceremonial entries in which diplomats paraded into cities with huge retinues all dressed in cloth-of-gold.

But not all the lavish display could keep the Renaissance from emerging. In fact much of the ostentation *was* Renaissance. But the spectacle gave people something reassuring on which to focus wild emotions during the transition.

I do believe strongly in the social functions of clothes. They communicate, motivate, attract or separate, show discipline or rebellion. And though these fantastic clothes of the 14th and 15th centuries had moved from function, in the utilitarian sense, to a ritual role, they were still working hard to control the chaos that was always hovering.

## THE INFLUENCE TODAY

I think clothes are doing the same things today. I see the power to influence clothes pulsing out now from colleges, communes, and the street; from the working class; from Blacks; from England, California, Peking, shifting from the establishment here as Rome shifted from its bureaucrats. I see our traditional institutions—municipal governments and IBM—fighting like Augustus to hold the line on our toga—the business suit—with rules and regulations that restrict long hair and jeans at work. I see the President of the United States reverting to 19th century palace guard uniforms for the White House guard. I see the suit becoming a hollow shell as men lose faith in the complex ethic of work, technological progress, manipulation of nature, utilitarianism, and material success the suit has symbolized. They toss it aside as disaffected Romans did the toga and search for alternatives. Today we see strung-out hair, Indian headbands, donkey beads, amulets, embroidered vests, and knitted ponchos. Will any of them prove to be the barbaric plaids and Christian palliums of our future? The three forces—tradition, escape, and the future—are all here keeping each other in balance, helping us through to a new age.

Look back on the last 5 years: First, the young people of this continent joined in a massive migration from reality, with drugs, clothes, and music that broke all the rules their daddies played by. Young people involved their senses in color and texture, something Galileo warned us against over 300 years ago. They stripped the structure out of clothes—the unnatural silhouettes that were one of the best ways the West had of showing how well it could twist nature to new forms. Rather than working life away, the young celebrated it in outrageous costumes. They aimed in every way at what has now been called the "new naturalism," and expressed it all with clothes—their desire to get back to the land and nature; to take the artificiality out of relations between the sexes; to return to tribal community; to let themselves be moved by feeling rather than reason; to find more pleasure in display of found objects such as feathers and shells than in possessions such as stocks and country clubs.

At first youth looked absurd, because our eyes simply could not accept a way of dressing that was not scrubbed, neat, plain, and practical. But gradually their way began to take on a coherence and pattern of its own.

Then, some women over 25 began tentatively to try out the new styles, occasionally wearing pantsuits to cocktail parties and accepting the soft bras that turned breasts from architectural monuments back into mammary glands. Men toyed with color and pattern in ties and shirts. On this continent people began to understand that the suit was not essential to social and business functioning; that drab colors and hampering skirts were not instinctive; that men had been *men* in past cultures in plumes, wigs, and blazing jewels. A new idea was groping for expression in clothes.

The threat was real, and the establishment had to respond, as it always does. The reaction set in several seasons ago. Fashion proclaimed a return to the conservative suit and to the madras and seersucker sports coat of the fifties. In women's clothes, the garments that could be considered American classics—blazers, pleated skirts, shirtwaist dresses, plaid coats—were revived. The thirties and forties were shaken out and paraded again.

As in the 15th century, the symbols of the old order were exaggerated: wide-lapeled, pinch-waisted suits became parodies. President Nixon and his aides—on their visit to China—sold the American way with an impenetrable wall of dark worsted. The draggy skirts, come-hither red lips, and frizzled hair of pre-Women's-Lib days were being flounced around.

"The party's over," and "sanity returns," the reports said. And *Women's Wear Daily* recorded the colors of the cashmere sweater sets Jackie Onassis had bought.

## A LOOK AHEAD

But if I have a premise about clothes, it's that they are the outward expression of the inner condition. If this is so, then the party is *not* over. For, though the conservative reaction dominates fashion right now, even its intensity proves the threat is still there. Clothes are still saying "loud and clear" that the dress of the Western world has been profoundly changed, as survival forces us to soften our commitment to progress at any cost. Jeans, symbol of alienation from the business suit, are now the most coveted garment in the world. Levis sell for $90 on the Russian black market. Organic forms wake a slumbering need for contact with nature's rich vocabulary of pattern and sense pleasure. Ancient status symbols—rare furs, jewels, and gold—are under attack as a squandering of the earth's resources. And now that pants, bodyshirts, and miniskirts have given women the freedom and pride of body that Christian morality denied them, will they go back willingly to constriction and limitations?

It may be, as some students of counterculture claim, that by avoiding the business suit and its obligations, youth avoids the rites of passage into manhood and clings to adolescence. But unless the adult world begins to look more appealing, will the young give up the jeans and shirts they were raised in?

Hippie dress or Levi's, though, have not taken over the world, but they are the cutting edge of revolution, going to excess as revolutionary dress always does to make its point. The extremes may already be past, and even the passion for jeans could subside.

But the shabby trousers that rallied the "sans-culottes" of the French Revolution were cleaned up after the revolution and have been with us ever since. Homespun Christian robes have had more power in the long run than the toga. Obviously we cannot say for certain what's ahead. All we do know is that in our time the young caught the vibrations of a new idea first and expressed it in their own way. And I, for one, think the idea is here to stay. I believe that despite closetsful of somber suits all across the land today, by the end of this decade, the business suit will be something we will look back on with nostalgia and amusement.

Reading 53

# Clothing and Self-Concept of Adolescents[1]

**Carolyn Humphrey**
**Mary Klaasen**
**Anna M. Creekmore**

*Clothing has previously been studied in relation to social insecurity rather than instability of self-concept.*

In the socialization process which leads to the development of the concept of self, clothing is believed to play a significant role *(1)*. Many think it to be an expression of self and a factor in social adjustment *(2)*. Research has shown that individuals differ in the ways they value, see, and use clothing and that these differences are related to social and psychological variables, particularly to feelings of insecurity *(3,4,5)*.

Social psychologists view man chiefly as a product of society rather than the result of biological determinants, but they vary in their views about the dimensions of self-concept and the stability of that concept. McGehee *(6)* defined self-concept as a "social product . . . consisting of the system of cultural meanings an individual has about himself." In other words, the self-concept is

[1]Michigan Agricultural Experiment Station Journal Article No. 5205.

From the *Journal of Home Economics*, vol. 63, April 1971, pp. 246-250, copyright by the American Home Economics Association, Washington, D.C.

what an individual thinks he is. If this concept includes all the beliefs the individual holds concerning the kind of person he is, then the valuation he places on himself is also a part of his self-concept. This idea of worth as a part of the concept of self defines the qualitative level of the concept, or self-esteem. Another dimension investigators have defined is the stability-instability continuum which is reflected in the firmness with which an individual holds to what he thinks he is at one point in time and over time.

## QUESTIONS INVESTIGATED IN THE STUDY

This study was primarily concerned with relationships between the two dimensions of self-concept—self-esteem and instability—and the various ways in which clothing is used by adolescents. Do teenagers with high self-esteem use clothing in a different way from those with low esteem? Are there differences between those who are unsure of themselves or less stable in their feelings about themselves and those who are more sure or more stable?

Clothing has previously been studied in relation to social insecurity rather than instability of self-concept. Each of the studies reviewed supports in some measure the idea that socially secure individuals may use clothing for self-expression, while those who are less secure may use clothing as a means of coping with social situations *(3,4,5)*. Since both insecurity and instability of self-concept are related to feelings about self in social situations, there appears to be some similarity between the two variables. Therefore, expectations were that individuals with stable self-concepts would use clothing in different ways than those with less stability.

## METHODOLOGY

### Measures

Scales developed and tested by Creekmore *(7)* and further refined by Brady *(4)* and other similar measures of clothing variables were analyzed for content and statements which were then categorized into eight clothing uses. These uses were:

- **Aesthetic**—use of clothing to achieve a pleasing or beautiful appearance. Neatness in dress is included as a part of appearance.
- **Approval**—use of clothing to attain a feeling of belongingness or acceptance by others in a particular role—indicates a willingness to conform.
- **Attention**—use of clothing to gain status or prestige. The attention sought may be either socially approved or disapproved, depending on the reference group.
- **Comfort**—use of clothing to achieve comfort relative to temperature as well as physical response to certain textures and tightness or looseness of garments.
- **Dependence**—indication of sensitivity to influence of clothing on moods, emotions, and feelings.
- **Interest**—willingness to give attention to clothing—to investigate, manipulate, or experiment with putting together the parts of a costume.
- **Management**—the thoughtful and careful use of resources, including the use of time, money, and energy in planning, buying, and using clothing. This can be an economic aspect of clothing usage.
- **Modesty**—the use of inconspicuous clothing—conservative in design, color, fit, and body exposure.

Although the clothing inventory was treated as one measure for purposes of administration, it was composed of eight scales of eleven statements each. Each of the items described a concrete situation on which the subject rated himself from one to five according to whether he "never" or "always" behaved in the manner given in the item.

The scales were pretested three times and item analyses computed to determine which statements discriminated best between high and low scorers. After each pretest, statements were dropped or revised in an effort to improve the reliability of the measures. No attempt was made to validate the scales beyond the judgmental assessment of a group of six clothing specialists. Subsequent analyses of the scales, using Hoyt's method of estimating reliability *(8)*, resulted in acceptable reliability coefficients for five of the eight scales. Those scales with coefficients somewhat below the acceptable level (below .70) were management, comfort, and aesthetics. The lowest had a reliability coefficient of .46 for girls and .58 for boys *(9)*.

Investigators have proposed several operational definitions of stability-instability. Brownfain *(10)*, in his analysis of self-concept, identified three types of variablity of self-concept: (1) level of self-evaluation, referred to as self-esteem in this study; (2) affective discrepancy, the amount of discrepancy occurring in the self-evaluation at one point in time; and (3) temporal discrepancy, the amount of discrepancy over a period of time.

A modified version of Brownfain's Self-Rating Inventory *(10)* was used to measure the three facets of self-concept—self-esteem, affective discrepancy, and temporal discrepancy. With this measure, each subject rated himself on twenty self-descriptive words; once as he saw himself positively and once, negatively. Each time he was instructed to compare himself with the other students in his school. One week later he rated himself again on the same two scales. The self-ratings and their definitions were *(11)*:

> **1** "Positive Self"—a rating of himself slanted positively. Here the subject gives himself the benefit of every reasonable doubt while still conceiving of this self-picture as believable. This is the self as he hopes he is.
>
> **2** "Negative Self"—a rating of himself slanted negatively. Here the subject denies himself the benefit of every reasonable doubt while still conceiving of this as a believable self-picture. This is the self as he fears he is.

The positive self-rating minus the negative self-rating from the first contact comprised the score for the affective discrepancy (instability of self-concept at one point in time). The difference between the first negative rating and the second negative rating determined the score for the temporal discrepancy (instability over time). Since McGehee *(6)* found the negative self-rating to be a better discriminator for level of self-concept or self-esteem than the positive self-rating, the first negative self-rating was selected as the measure of self-esteem.

### Procedures

The subjects, 270 girls and 250 boys, comprised approximately one-third of the students attending the only high school in a midwestern industrial city of approximately 15,000 population. Due to scheduling problems, a random sample was not possible. Instead, the students from six study hall periods containing sophomores, juniors, and seniors were the sample.

Data were obtained in two sessions, one week apart. During the first session, the subjects completed the clothing inventory, negative self-rating, and positive self-rating portions of the questionnaire. The section on demographic data (including questions about age, grade, and social-class position of the main wage-earner) and the second positive and negative self-ratings were administered during the second session. Two hundred potential subjects had to be dropped from the study because of absences from school on one of the data collection days or because of inadequate information on essential portions of their questionnaires.

Analysis of the biographical data revealed that the subjects ranged from 13 through 19 years of age, with 84 percent of the boys and 90 percent of the girls in the 15 to 17 age bracket. Sixteen percent of the girls and 26 percent of the boys were on the honor roll. Forty-one percent of the boys and 50 percent of the girls were in the fourth, or next-to-the-lowest social-class, position according to Hollingshead's two factor index based on occupation and education *(12)*.

## FINDINGS AND DISCUSSION

Pearson product moment correlation coefficients revealed that some clothing uses were significantly related to self-esteem, but none of the eight was related to either of the measures of instability (Table 1). Although the coefficients do not reflect strong relationships between the variables, they are statistically significant, indicating that the relationships are not the result of the operation of chance, thus offering minimal evidence to support the hypotheses. Specifically, for the boys self-esteem was positively related to the aesthetic and attention uses of clothing and for the girls to aesthetic, attention, interest, and management uses. The findings indicate that the boys and girls to whom these uses were important tended to have higher levels of self-esteem or more positive feelings about self. However, two of the relationships, aesthetic and management, may be questioned on the basis of the somewhat inadequate reliability coefficients for these clothing measures. Since the attention and the interest scales had adequate reliability coefficients, it is safe to say that both the boys and girls with higher self-esteem scores used clothing to attract attention to themselves. The girls with more self-esteem enjoyed experimenting with clothing and were more interested in it than were girls with less self-esteem.

Since none of the clothing uses was significantly related to either affective or temporal discrepancy, one cannot say on the basis of the simple correlations that students with highly unstable self-concepts used clothing in ways that differed from those with more stable self-concepts (Table 1). Nevertheless, the negative direction of the majority of the coefficients resulting from the correlations between both types of instability and the clothing uses suggests that greater personal insecurity was reflected in slightly lower scores on many of the clothing uses.

When the interrelationships between the three facets of the self-concept were determined by simple correlations, self-esteem was negatively related to both affective discrepancy (−.76 for boys, −.69 for girls) and temporal discrepancy (−.19 for boys, −.27 for girls), and affective and temporal discrepancies were positively related to each other (.23 for boys, .24 for girls). Since self-esteem and the two types of instability were strongly related in the negative direction and since self-esteem was positively related to four of the clothing uses, expectations were that relationships between either of the discrepancy measures and clothing uses would be generally negative in character, as was shown by simple correlation coefficients given in Table 1.

**Table 1 The Correlations between Clothing Uses and Self-Esteem and Two Types of Instability of Self-Concept**

| | | Instability of self-concept | |
|---|---|---|---|
| Clothing uses | Self-esteem | Affective discrepancy | Temporal discrepancy |
| Aesthetic | | | |
| Boys | .24* | .00 | .00 |
| Girls | .22* | −.05 | −.03 |
| Approval | | | |
| Boys | .04 | −.01 | .07 |
| Girls | −.04 | −.01 | −.10 |
| Attention | | | |
| Boys | .17† | −.08 | .00 |
| Girls | .16† | .00 | −.05 |
| Comfort | | | |
| Boys | .00 | .11 | .03 |
| Girls | .06 | −.02 | .13 |
| Dependence | | | |
| Boys | .05 | −.03 | .00 |
| Girls | .05 | .03 | −.01 |
| Interest | | | |
| Boys | .11 | −.01 | −.02 |
| Girls | .17† | .01 | −.02 |
| Management | | | |
| Boys | .07 | .07 | −.05 |
| Girls | .24* | −.01 | −.08 |
| Modesty | | | |
| Boys | .09 | .00 | −.07 |
| Girls | .08 | −.05 | −.05 |

*Significant at .01 level
†Significant at .05 level

Further analyses of the data were made, using partial correlation techniques, to determine whether the significant relationships found between clothing and self-esteem would hold when the effects of other variables were removed. The simple correlation coefficients revealed that the family social-class position was significantly related only to the management of clothing for the girls. However, when the effect of social-class variability was removed statistically, the significant relationships between variables reported in Table 2 remained, with the coefficients being substantially the same size.

The results from the partial correlations gave interesting and confusing information about the relationships. Self-esteem, with the effects of both affective and temporal discrepancies removed statistically, continued to be significantly related to the aesthetic and attention uses of clothing for both boys and girls and to management and interest in clothing for the girls. These coefficients were generally as high as those resulting from the simple correlations, indicating self-esteem to be the strongest factor in the relationship.

Surprising results occurred when the self-esteem variable was removed from the relationships between clothing uses and the affective and the temporal discrepancies. The affective discrepancy was shown to be positively and significantly related to three of the same clothing uses as was self-esteem. However, the aesthetic use relationship for girls was lost and a positive relationship between concern for comfort for boys was added (Table 2).

These results indicated that the unstable or insecure individuals of both sexes (at one point in time) were more interested in buying and care of clothing

**Table 2 The Correlations between Clothing Uses and Self-Esteem with the Effects of Affective and Temporal Discrepancies Removed and the Relationships between Clothing Uses and Affective and Temporal Discrepancies with the Effects of Self-Esteem Removed**

| Clothing uses | Self-esteem | | Self-esteem removed | |
|---|---|---|---|---|
| | Affective removed | Temporal removed | Affective | Temporal |
| Aesthetic | | | | |
| Boys | .35* | .25* | .26* | .05 |
| Girls | .25* | .22* | .12 | .03 |
| Approval | | | | |
| Boys | .04 | .05 | .02 | .08 |
| Girls | −.06 | −.07 | −.05 | −.11 |
| Attention | | | | |
| Boys | .16† | .17† | .06 | .04 |
| Girls | .21* | .16† | .14 | .00 |
| Comfort | | | | |
| Boys | .11 | .01 | .16* | .03 |
| Girls | .06 | .10 | .02 | .16* |
| Dependence | | | | |
| Boys | .05 | .05 | .01 | .01 |
| Girls | .09 | .05 | .09 | .00 |
| Interest | | | | |
| Boys | .14 | .11 | .09 | .00 |
| Girls | .23* | .17† | .16† | .03 |
| Management | | | | |
| Boys | .17† | .06 | .17† | −.04 |
| Girls | .31* | .23* | .20* | −.01 |
| Modesty | | | | |
| Boys | .14 | .08 | .10 | −.05 |
| Girls | .06 | .07 | .00 | −.03 |

*Significant at .01 level
†Significant at .05 level

than were the more stable. Unstable boys also appeared concerned about the appearance and comfort of their clothing, while the insecure girls spent much more time in experimenting with parts of costumes. The most unstable girls (discrepancy over time) were significantly concerned only with comfort in clothing.

The fact that positive relationships were found between both self-esteem level and instability and some of the same clothing uses suggests that clothing functions in different ways for individuals with different psychological characteristics. In a theory developed by Maslow *(13)*, variations of human behavior are explained in terms of relative satisfactions of basic needs. Maslow not only holds that individuals who are striving to satisfy needs may use an activity or behavior as a means of coping with a situation but also that those whose needs are generally satisfied may exhibit the same behavior as a means of self-expression.

Using Maslow's framework as a starting point, Creekmore *(7)* investigated the relationships between striving for satisfaction of basic needs and common ways in which college girls used clothing. She found that five of the eight needs related positively to some clothing uses and negatively to others. An analysis of the relationships seemed to indicate that the clothing variables closely resembling aesthetic concerns, conformity, attention seeking, and modesty in clothes in this study could be a means of self-expression when a need was satisfied but a means to an end when a need was relatively unsatisfied.

The findings of this study seem to support Creekmore's proposition *(7)* that clothing is used both as a means of coping with environmental situations and a means of self-expression, since the boys and girls with high self-esteem were concerned with the same clothing uses as those with high instability at one point in time. Certain of the uses of clothing—concern for clothing aesthetics for the boys, experimental interest for girls, and concern for selection and care of clothing for both—were related positively to both level of self-esteem and amount of instability of self-concept at one point in time. The implication of these findings is that clothing can reflect either the adolescent's feelings of self-worth or his feelings of insecurity.

## SUMMARY

Eight ways in which high school boys and girls use clothing were related to two dimensions of self-concept, self-esteem and instability. A questionnaire comprised of eight separate scales was used to measure the clothing uses. A modified version of Brownfain's Self-Rating Inventory *(10)* was used to measure the three aspects of self-concept—self-esteem, affective instability, and temporal instability.

Simple correlation coefficients indicated that the boys and girls with higher levels of self-esteem were concerned with a pleasing appearance and were unafraid to draw attention to themselves through their use of clothing. The girls with higher self-esteem enjoyed experimenting with parts of costumes and were concerned with selection and care of clothing.

The self-esteem variable was negatively related to both types of instability of self-concept. Partial correlations revealed self-esteem to be the strongest factor in the relationships between self-concept and clothing uses. Instability of self-concept at one point in time was related more often to clothing uses than was instability over time. However, both types of instability were significantly and positively related to one or more specific uses of clothing regardless of the strong negative relationship between self-esteem and instability.

The partial correlation coefficients, although low in numerical value, indicated the reported relationships to be firm between self-esteem and specific clothing uses. In addition, they revealed that both boys and girls with unstable self-concepts were concerned with management of clothing; that unstable boys were concerned about a pleasing appearance as well as comfort in their clothes; and that unstable girls also enjoyed experimenting with costume parts.

The conclusion that a particular use of clothing reflects both feelings of self-worth and feelings of insecurity for adolescents, supports to some extent propositions from previous research which state that clothing may be a means of self-expression or a means of coping with social milieu.

Given the dual function of clothing, it should be noted that predicting the personal characteristics of an individual on the basis of clothing alone, without other supporting information, can lead to erroneous assumptions about the individual.

## REFERENCES

1 Stone, G. P. Appearance and Self. In *Dress, Adornment, and the Social Order.* Edited by M. E. Roach and J. B. Eicher. New York: John Wiley and Sons, Inc., 1965, pp. 216–245.

2 Stiles, L. P. Clothing and Social Interaction of Four-Year-Old Children. Unpublished master's thesis, University of North Carolina at Greensboro, 1967.

3 Lapitsky, M. Clothing Values and Their Relation to General Values and to Social Security and Insecurity. Unpublished doctoral dissertation, The Pennsylvania State University, 1961.
4 Brady, B. L. Clothing Behavior: Refinement of a Measure and Relationships with Social Security and Insecurity for a Group of College Women. Unpublished master's thesis, The Pennsylvania State University, 1963.
5 Dickey, L. E. Projection of the Self through Judgments of Clothed-Figures and Its Relationship to Self-Esteem, Security-Insecurity and to Selected Clothing Behaviors, Unpublished doctoral dissertation, The Pennsylvania State University, 1967.
6 McGehee, T. P. The Stability of the Self-Concept and Self-Esteem. Unpublished doctoral dissertation, Michigan State University, 1956.
7 Creekmore, A. M. Clothing Behaviors and Their Relation to General Values and to the Striving for Basic Needs. Unpublished doctoral dissertation, The Pennsylvania State University, 1963.
8 Hoyt, C. J., and Krishnaiah, P. R. Estimation of test reliability by analysis of variance technique. *J. Experimental Educ.,* Vol. 28 (March 1960), pp. 257-279.
9 Fetterman, N. I. An Analysis of the Creekmore Scales of Eight Clothing Variables. Unpublished master's thesis, Michigan State University, 1968.
10 Brownfain, J. J. Stability of the self-concept as a dimension of personality. *J. Abnormal & Soc. Psychol.,* Vol. 47 (1952), pp. 597-606.
11 Silver, A. W. The Self Concept: Its Relationship to Parental and Peer Acceptance. Unpublished doctoral dissertation, Michigan State University, 1957, p. 36.
12 Hollingshead, A. B. *Two Factor Index of Social Position.* New Haven, Conn.: Yale University, 1957.
13 Maslow, A. *Toward a Psychology of Being.* Princeton, N. J.: D. Van Nostrand Co., Inc., 1962.

Reading 54

# What's in a Label?

**Nancy B. Conklyn**

*Prior to July 1972, many garment manufacturers did not disclose any care instructions to prospective purchasers.*

> FLAMMABLE
>
> (Does not meet U.S. Dept. of Commerce Standard DOC FF 3-71.) Should not be worn near sources of fire.

Have you seen this label on items of children's sleepwear this fall? Sleepwear in sizes 0-6X, manufactured after July 29, 1972, must be "prominently, permanently, and conspicuously" labeled with this warning *unless* they meet the specifications for flame retardancy set up by the Department of Commerce. Sleepwear manufactured after July 29, 1973, must be flame retardant; the cautionary label option will no longer be available.

## CAUTION—MOST FABRICS WILL BURN

Most textile fibers and fabrics are combustible because they are made from organic compounds. Some fabrics, more than others, are exposed to the hazards of fire. For example, fabrics used in children's sleepwear are potentially dangerous because children wearing such garments may be near sources of fire. Recent investigations show that sleepwear is involved in a high percentage of apparel burn accidents; children under six frequently are victims. For this reason, the Children's Sleepwear Flammability Standard was established by the Federal Trade Commission.

The year between July 1972 and July 1973 is intended to give the industry time to solve the problems of installing new production methods and processes so that enough flame retardant fabric can be produced to meet the rising demand. In the meantime, stores may have children's sleepwear with: (a) *no flammability identification* (manufactured prior to July 1972), (b) *warning labels* (manufactured after July 1972 from the same types of fabrics previously used), (c) *labels identifying flame retardant properties* (manufactured from fabrics that meet U. S. Department of Commerce Standard DOC FF 3-71).

**From *Consumer Close-Ups*, Consumer Economics & Public Policy. Reprinted with permission of the New York State College of Human Ecology, a statutory college of the State University, Cornell University, Ithaca, New York.**

## CHILDREN'S SLEEPWEAR—PERMANENT CARE LABELS

All textile apparel including children's sleepwear, manufactured after July 1972, must carry permanently attached care labels. In addition, if special care is needed to protect flame retardant garments from agents or treatments that are known to cause deterioration of their flame resistance, they must be labeled with precautionary instructions. By law, flame retardant characteristics must remain through 50 launderings.

MW Machine Wash Warm
Tumble Dry

100% Cotton
PENN-PREST
FLAME RETARDANT FABRIC
To Retain Flame Retardancy Properties
Do Not Use Soap, Bleach, Low or Non-Phosphate Detergent. Do Not Send to Commercial Laundry.

## OTHER APPAREL—PERMANENT CARE LABELS

Prior to July 1972, many garment manufacturers did not disclose any care instructions to prospective purchasers. Or when such information was supplied, it usually was in the form of detachable labels or tags which were misplaced easily. For this reason, the Federal Trade Commission established the Care Labeling Rule for textile wearing apparel. In announcing the rule, the FTC noted that the "technological advances which have occurred in the apparel and cleaning industries have had a significant effect on the care process. The large number of products on the market, each with different care performance characteristics, has made it almost impossible for consumers to be informed about any one product, much less the entire range of products. As a result, the traditional source of care information, personal experience based on trial and error, no longer meets the needs of consumers."

*Permanently attached care labels must disclose fully, clearly and thoroughly regular care and maintenance* for the ordinary use and enjoyment of the item. Care instructions given must apply to all components of the product. Both domestic and imported garments are covered by the rule. Instructions for washing, ironing, drying, bleaching, drycleaning and any other procedures needed to care for a particular article must be given. Spot care information is not required. Use of promotional language such as "never needs ironing" or "easy care" is prohibited, since such phrases do not tell if ironing is possible, nor define what constitutes "easy" care. Care labels must warn consumers if usual methods seem to apply, but do not. For example, white goods that are not bleachable and items that cannot be drycleaned, must be so labeled.

The Care Labeling Rule mandates the use of word descriptions on the label; symbols may not be used unless accompanied by words. The labels must be easy to locate on the garment; they must remain legible through washings and/or drycleanings, and must stay attached to the garment.

*Exemptions from the Care Labeling legislation are:* headwear, handwear, and footwear except some sheer hosiery products and those that color bleed; apparel which requires no care, as disposable products; fur and leather items; and purely decorative and ornamental items. Completely washable items intended to retail for $3.00 or less, or items whose utility and/or appearance would substantially be impaired by a permanently affixed label, may be exempted by special petition to the Federal Trade Commission. Items that have been exempted to date include: white and colored underpants and undershorts except those containing wool; baby bibs; diapers; men's work aprons; collar overlays as on choir robes; handkerchiefs and ties.

*Consumer protection* is the objective of the new labeling legislation. Shoppers have a RIGHT to expect to find labels relating to care and flammability of children's sleepwear attached properly to the apparel. It is the RESPONSIBILITY of consumers to study these labels, understand their purpose and follow their instructions.

## REFERENCES

Federal Trade Commission. "Trade Regulation Rule Including a Statement of Its Basis and Purpose. Care Labeling of Textile Wearing Apparel. Effective July 3, 1972." December 1971. (Mimeograph)

Federal Trade Commission. "Children's Sleepwear, Notice of Standard." Federal Register, Vol. 36, No. 146, July 29, 1971.

Reading 55

# Hearings on Children's Flammable Sleepwear

**Nancy L. Ross**

*The figure of 175,000 clothing-burn injuries and 4,000 deaths is often contested.*

The young Iowa housewife testified yesterday that her 3-year-old daughter had suffered third degree burns over 50 per cent of her body when her cotton nightgown caught fire as she played with a cigarette lighter. Today, after 30 operations costing more than $25,000, she remains disfigured for life; most of both ears are missing, as is one finger, and her neck and chest are a mass of scar tissue.

Mrs. Dennis Brehm of Des Moines was testifying at a Commerce Department hearing on proposed amendments to the Standard for the Flammability of Children's Sleepwear, and had brought her daughter Elizabeth, now 5, with her.

"Torture, gentlemen, is watching your child try to walk again and hearing

From the *Washington Post*, Feb. 25, 1972.

her scream in pain with each step." Mrs. Brehm said. "Or to hear her scream for five solid days when she lost chest grafts and lay there with that area raw, or to hear her scream in pain every time her dressings were changed.

". . . All her suffering was unnecessary, her injuries need never have occurred if the garment industry had thought her life, her well-being was worth the few cents necessary to have flameproofed the nightgown she was wearing."

Mrs. Brehm noted that flameproofing standards are not yet in effect although Congress passed the law requiring them five years ago, three years before her daughter's injury.

The largely male audience of fiber, textile and garment manufacturers squirmed restlessly and sighed. When the young mother suggested non-fire resistent children's garments should have a skull and crossbones on the label, there were snickers.

They had heard such stories before. And tragic as they may be, some manufacturers believe their numbers are exaggerated. The figure of 175,000 clothing-burn injuries and 4,000 deaths is often contested. They seemed far more interested in their negotiations with the Commerce Department board which promulgated the standard than in hearing Mrs. Brehm and consumer advocates.

A histrionic presentation by Herman Glaser of the American Trial Lawyers Association turned the snickers to outright laughter at one point. Glaser's argument repeatedly mentioned the name of a manufacturer who, in his opinion, had solved the problem of flammable fabrics. Yet when Richard O. Simpson, Deputy Assistant Secretary of Commerce for product standards, asked Glaser if that manufacturer's fabric could pass the standards set, the lawyer replied he didn't know. The audience laughed heartily.

The Flammable Fabrics Act was passed by Congress in 1953. Standards for children's sleepwear up to size 6X were finally established in 1971, and are due to go into effect in mid-1973. Some segments of the industry are now trying to reopen the discussion on the grounds that the standards are not reasonable, technologically practicable or appropriate. Their amendments would, critics claim, dilute the present standards.

Cost to the manufacturer and ultimately to the consumer combined with consumer indifference and inexactitude of test methods were the reasons most often given to change the standards. Speaking as the chairman of the American Apparel Manufacturers Association, Roger Wilson called for, among other changes, elimination of negative labeling (saying a garment was not flame-retardant), elimination of sizes 0 to 1 on the grounds that infants up to 9 or 10 months are not subject to unreasonable fire hazards, and revision of many technical aspects of testing.

On the subject of flammable fabrics, Wilson said, "It has been oversimplified and our technological capacity greatly exaggerated." Then he added, "We don't want to get off the hook. We want to comply with a standard that makes compliance possible and assures that a genuinely good producer, who is exercising sound process control techniques, will not suffer severe economic loss."

He also proposed advancing the mandatory compliance date to April 1, 1973, four months ahead of schedule. This, said Wilson, would enable manufacturers to have flame-retardant sleepwear on the market by fall 1973 when the heaviest buying season occurs. Though he denied it, several other witnesses accused Wilson of trying to make a deal in advancing the date in exchange for substantial concessions.

Leonard Smith, representing Cotton, Inc., a Raleigh, N.C., organization for the promotion of cotton, said his group alone is spending a million dollars a year on research and development of flame-retardant fabrics, but the present sleepwear standards are resulting in "only minor gains in safety." Though tubular cotton knits account for about 70 percent of children's sleepwear, Smith called for exemption of knits from the standards. He reasoned that knits fit close to the body and therefore are less susceptible to accidental ignition.

David A. Swankin, Washington director of Consumer's Union, observed that 75 out of the 76 samples of children's sleepwear tested by his organization failed the flammability standards. He therefore urged the standards be tightened, not loosened.

The lone sample which passed CU's test was purchased at Sears, Roebuck & Co. The firm's nation merchandising manager for infants' sleepwear, Ira Quint, had previously testified that Sears had experienced "very disappointingly low consumer acceptance" to flame retardant garments. Customers thought it unnecessary because of the rarity of accidents involving sleepware and the belief that most are the fault of negligent parents. Quint said customers would not pay extra for safety garments unless convinced of the necessity. He urged a stronger safety education campaign.

Reading 56

# While Federal Regulators Fiddled, Flaming Fabrics Killed 6,000 People

**August Gribbin**

*Clothing burns, which mostly victimize the young and the elderly, inflict heavy financial loss and psychological damage as well as severe physical pain.*

"She was helping me. She leaned over to remove a piece of French toast from a skillet. Her pajama sleeve brushed the skillet, and she ignited, literally ignited. And in getting the fire out of her hair and protecting her ear and face, I sacrificed her right arm."

Thus Mrs. Robert Root of State College, Pa., describes how her daughter Kathy, 9, recently received third-degree burns to her arm in a clothing fire. It was a type of fire that probably would not have occurred had several laws passed by Congress, some as long as 17 years ago, been fully implemented.

But the regulations against marketing flammable fabrics are minimal. The Commerce Department is only now getting ready to issue the first regulating *proposal* under 1967 laws empowering the department to set standards to minimize or eliminate the type of accident that maimed Kathy.

The House has just received a Senate-passed bill giving even more power and money to use in eliminating flammable fabrics. Passage by the House is uncertain. But according to Richard J. Medalie, a lawyer and former adjunct professor of administrative law at Georgetown University Law Centers, the dangers from flammable fabrics will not decrease even if the proposals eventually become law. He says:

"The textiles industry is dragging its feet and it has, I think, exercised considerable influence within those sluggish agencies responsible for formulating

From *The National Observer*, Oct. 5, 1970, p. 1.

needed flammable-fabric standards and in enforcing them." Mr. Medalie is a member of an investigative team that recently prepared a social report on Federal safety legislation for the National Commission of Product Safety.

There is even doubt about just when the first regulation proposals under the 1967 law will be made.

"Barring acts of God or a public enemy, we should get out the proposed standard on children's sleepwear in October," says William M. Segall, assistant director of the Commerce Department's Office of Textiles. The standard will ban certain kinds and sizes of sleepwear that can catch fire.

Mr. Segall has made such forecasts before, and now he adds: "I'm merely speculating, but when we come out with the standard it will be just a proposal. I envision delays after that. A final standard is some time away."

When it does take effect, that standard will come down hardest on cotton and rayon goods. These ubiquitous cloths make the most flammable garments, especially when the fabrics are loosely woven or worked into pile finishes. They also are the easiest to fireproof.

Linens burn rapidly. Wool and many man-made fibers resist fire better, while some of the newest fabrics defy the fiercest flame.

Delays and industry-sought exemptions have plagued practically every effort to deal with the flammable-fabrics problem. The problem is major; since Congress asked for tough fabric standards in 1967, an estimated 400,000 persons have been injured and 6,000 killed in accidents similar to Kathy Root's.

Yet statistics do not tell the story. Clothing burns, which mostly victimize the young and the elderly, inflict heavy financial loss and psychological damage as well as severe physical pain.

Kathy's parents spent more than $1,000 for the month Kathy was in the hospital fighting a severe staph infection caused by her burns.

"We haven't even started with a plastic surgeon yet," her mother says. "We've been told to be prepared for terrific costs there. But oh—it's terrible to see a child in pain. Removing dressings is incredible. Parents can't stand to see that very often. Kathy was in terrible shape from it; she went into shock once."

Dr. Gilbert Barkim, a Silver Spring, Md., pediatrician and allergist, declares: "Often when you see burned kids wheeled into the hospital, you feel like hiding your eyes and walking away. There's comparatively little you can do. And performing plastic surgery on burns is one of the least rewarding forms of surgery."

The effort to regulate use of flammable fabrics began in 1953. Then, shortly after 20 persons wearing sweaters made of a new fabric were seared within a few days, Congress passed the original Flammable Fabrics Act.

The act outlawed these "torch" sweaters and other "highly flammable apparel." The Commerce department decided to judge whether a garment was highly flammable by submitting it to a "four-second burn test" devised by the textile industry.

Just before the law was to take effect in July 1954, the industry won an amendment that softened the law and the standard. The amendment made it possible to market 250,000,000 yards of sheer organdies, tulles, and georgettes, which otherwise would have been banned.

The modified standard still prevails. Although some 54,000 persons have burned to death in clothing fires since 1953, the Federal Trade Commission (FTC) has never found that the fabric involved in a fatality has violated the standard.

In 1967, Congress passed the purportedly tough amendments to the Flammable Fabrics Act. The amendments expanded the law to cover all fabrics—

those used in beds, upholstery, drapes, and the like—not just the cloth in garments. They authorized the Department of Commerce to create tougher standards, and they established stiffer penalties for knowingly violating the act.

According to Mr. Medalie and others, the amendments also provide for delay. They give the industry, which stoutly opposes regulation, a large say in actions taken to regulate it.

They split the standards-making and the enforcing operations among four agencies: the Departments of Commerce and of Health, Education, and Welfare; the FTC; and the National Bureau of Standards, which is a Commerce Department agency. The split has caused confusion.

Besides, Congress waited nearly a year before voting funds to implement the act and the agencies involved have been tardy in using available funds.

The amendments stipulate a one-year wait between the time final standards are promulgated and the time they take effect. Mr. Segall, the Office of Textiles official, explains why:

"You may know that in 1967 I was an industry lobbyist. At one point we were seeking protection for manufacturers' inventories, so if a standard were slapped on us, we wouldn't be left with stores of unsold goods. We asked for provisions in the proposed amendments that would give special exemptions for inventories. If not that, we wanted a one-year delay before announced standards would take effect. Somebody goofed. We got both."

Because the manufacturers got both, it is now possible and legal for them to build huge stockpiles of goods between the time a final standard is announced and the time it takes effect. Marketers are permitted to sell stockpiled fabrics and clothes for as long as they wish after the standards take effect.

The Senate-passed bill now in the House will not speed up standards making; it simply stipulates that once the Department of Commerce sets standards, the manufacturers will have to test the fabrics before marketing them and certify that the goods qualify as safe. Presently, no premarketing tests are required. The new proposals also would increase civil and legal penalties for violations.

The textile industry objects to the bill, which constitutes amendments to the basic 1953 law. Speaking for the National Cotton Council, the American Textile Manufacturers Institute, the Northern Textile Association, and the American Apparel Manufacturers Association, George S. Buck, Jr., has called the amendments "premature, unfair, and impractical."

He says they are "police-state procedures, and they will impede progress toward greater safety." Mr. Buck adds: "We won't invite useful co-operation at the point of a gun."

If and when the industry is forced to make sleepwear and other cotton and rayon garments fireproof, it will use chemicals that have been available for 14 years. They are variations of a substance created for the Army in 1955 by two Department of Agriculture scientists.

Cotton and rayon treated with the compounds can withstand the flames of a blow-torch without catching fire. They can be washed almost for the life of the garment without losing their antiflame protection.

Since 1955, several companies have come up with additional flame-proofing alternatives: fibers of glass, asbestos, modacrylics, and a special nylon that won't burn and will resist heat. There is a chemical used in the space program that enables a sheet of paper sprayed with it to resist burning in temperatures as high as 2,200 degrees.

The special report to the National Commission of Product Safety declares: "Indeed, progress is so great that the largest barrier to achieving the application of technological solutions (to the flammable fabrics problem) is not want of knowledge, but cost—both in real terms and in the minds of conservative marketers."

Officials at such involved companies as DuPont, American Viscose, Hooper Chemical Corp., CIBA Corp., a New York City chemical company, and Owens-Corning Fiberglas Corp. all declare that real costs for using their fibers or treatments would come down appreciably if the textile makers created a large demand for their products.

Despite current costs and the problems old-line textile makers attribute to the new fibers and fire-retarding chemicals, the Federal Government is making considerable use of most of the products in its own operations. So is American business. And several large marketers, such as J.C. Penney, and especially Sears, Roebuck, have been test marketing flame-proof garments.

Last year Sears sold two items of flame-proof apparel. In its 1970 Christmas catalog, it is offering six items. Prices for these clothes, mostly pajamas for youngsters, range from 42 cents to a dollar more than comparable garments that have not been fireproofed.

# A Home for Your Family

Reading 57

## The Rocky Road to Home Warranties

**Business Week**

*The toughest problem of all may be to persuade homebuilders to take part in a warranty program.*

In late 1971, Robert La Vigna, a regional supervisor for Avco Financial Services, Inc., bought a new $44,000 house in New City, N.Y., which carried a one-year warranty from the builder. In the first six months, the heating system refused to function, the floor in the den sank 3 in., the foundation slab cracked, and the driveway "erupted and collapsed." The builder sent several men to look at the defects, but none of them was fixed to La Vigna's satisfaction. When the year was up, he suddenly found it impossible to contact the builder except through his attorney, who denied further responsibility. When La Vigna appealed to the savings and loan association that had given him his mortgage, he discovered that the S & L's lawyer was the same one used by the builder. Now, frustrated and angry, he is fixing the defects at his own expense.

Jay A. Salmanson, an engineer with the National Aeronautics & Space Administration, is only a little better off. When he arranged to buy a $44,900 townhouse in Montgomery County, Md., last year, he noticed that the insulation was being improperly installed, that there were fewer lighting fixtures than promised, and that some were misplaced. He eventually collected $3,500 in compensation from the local electric company and an offer from the builder to buy the house back at cost. Salmanson refused because the house had risen $12,000 in value. But 130 of his neighbors are now suing both the builder and the utility company because of similar problems.

### TEN-YEAR PACKAGE

These and similar cases of consumers' complaints—plus the threat of federal legislation—are behind a top-priority drive for a national warranty program by the 70,000-member National Assn. of Home Builders. In recent months, the NAHB has given wide publicity to a proposal that would provide a 10-year warranty-and-insurance package covering major structural elements: For the first two years, the builder would correct defects, then they would be remedied under an insurance policy. "It's hard to conceive of the thing's not being a success," says NAHB President George C. Martin, a Louisville (Ky.) builder.

From *Business Week*, July 28, 1973, pp. 49–50.

But the NAHB plan has met opposition from within its own ranks. The Council of Housing Producers, 15 of the country's largest builders who produce about 1% of the country's new housing (and who are also all NAHB members), believes warranties should cover more than structural defects. "The average buyer isn't complaining about those," says Edward Cortese, a vice-president of Levitt & Sons, Inc. "He wants the builder to take care of things like illfitting doors and sloppy painting." As a result, the council is pressing for a year's coverage of workmanship—a stand that has already delayed the NAHB's plans.

Part of the council's attitude stems from recent housing horror stories in which big builders have come off badly. Kaufman & Broad, the Larwin Group, and Levitt have all been the subject of bad publicity over the quality of their homes, though they have taken steps to correct the faults. More important, a constant stream of complaints against small homebuilders has added steam to the warranty movement.

## LEGISLATION THREAT

So has the prospect of federal legislation. Last year, a three-year warranty plus a builder's performance bond for all homes sold with government-insured mortgages (about 20% of the annual output) was under active consideration as part of the housing bill that died at the end of the Congressional session. This year, Senator Charles H. Percy (R-Ill.) has introduced a bill that also includes a three-year warranty, though it is not given much chance of immediate passage. In addition, Senator Philip A. Hart (D-Mich.) has introduced a truth-in-housing bill that requires builders to tell prospective buyers of any defects. He is offering his bill "more as a vehicle to launch a dialogue than as a solution" to the problems of poor construction.

To try to head off legislation, the NAHB initiated a crash program in January to develop a national warranty scheme. It hired Eugene A. Gulledge, former commissioner of the Federal Housing Administration and an ex-president of the NAHB, to make a study of the subject.

Gulledge's suggested plan, the one publicized by the NAHB, was based on a scheme that has operated in Britain since 1936. His proposed 10-year warranty-and-insurance package would cost the builder $50 per home, a sum that would presumably be passed on to the buyer in the price of the house. Part of the money would go to operate a national Insured Home Warranty Council to set standards, register builders, inspect new houses "five or six times" during construction, and arbitration procedures for builders and buyers. The rest of the $50 fee would be the insurance premium.

In his haste to disarm critics, Martin won approval of the principle of a voluntary warranty scheme from his executive and finance committees in April and from 700 members of his board of directors in May. By last month, four NAHB committees were hard at work to meet Martin's timetable: a program that could actually be operating in two or three states, one of them probably Florida, by October.

## OPPOSITION

The rash of publicity and the news that NAHB might have to spend up to $2-million to implement the scheme led the Council of Housing Producers to intervene. A council delegation spent five hours with Martin and other NAHB officials in Washington, complaining about the exposure a mere plan was being given and pointing out that faulty workmanship, not structural defects, is the consumers' main complaint. "We cleared up a lot of our concerns," says Rene A. Henry, Jr., the council's executive secretary. Specifically, the NAHB's working committees will be calling on experts from the big builders for advice.

Though Martin now talks of including workmanship under warranties, agreement on details is still a long way off, and there are other problems. One is to compile a list of which first-year defects should be covered and to what extent—a monumental task since the average house contains some 3,000 components. Another is insurance: Should the NAHB set up its own insurance company, as Martin believes, or use an established casualty carrier, some of which are interested?

The toughest problem of all may be to persuade homebuilders to take part in a warranty program. "Our ranks contain a lot of rugged individuals who just don't think we need such a plan," says Martin candidly. One such company is New Jersey-based Leisure Technology Corp., which builds in seven states. "I don't know whether there really can be any kind of warranty that's going to serve the needs of the various builders and the needs of the various buyers," says Frank Edelstein, corporate marketing vice-president. His company won't participate.

Nonetheless, the NAHB is pushing forward to present a finished warranty plan at the annual meeting in New Orleans on Sept. 20. "The scheme could be operational by January of 1976," says NAHB Executive Vice-President Nathaniel H. Rogg, Martin's top staff man. "We are very hopeful that we will meet our date."

## Reading 58

# Home Improvements for Love or Money

**William B. Mead**

*By adjusting your personal preferences to those of the marketplace, you can make improvements that increase your comfort without costing you a heavy penalty when the house is sold.*

Two houses on a pleasant block in Holyoke, Mass., were sold within the past three years. They were similar in age, style and size, but one had a large backyard swimming pool and a finished third floor with bedroom and bath. So the house with pool brought top dollar compared with its unimproved neighbor, right?

Wrong. Mr. and Mrs. Francis T. Martin Jr. bought the house with the pool for $30,500. Twenty months later, Mr. and Mrs. John E. Dowd paid $38,000 for their house, which, like the Martins', has five bedrooms and two and a half baths, but no pool and an unfinished third floor. "When we bought the house we never even saw the pool," Mrs. Martin said. "It was covered with snow." Mrs. Dowd said she and her husband were attracted by the spacious rooms of their house and by the neighborhood.

From *Money*, January 1973, pp. 24–27.

The experience of the two Holyoke families is not unusual. Many homeowners incorrectly assume that the money they spend on improvements will be returned, perhaps even with a profit, when they sell the house. In fact, that is rarely true. On average, a dollar spent on remodeling adds only about 50¢ to the resale price of the house. Some improvements add nothing at all.

"Adding onto an old house is very expensive, and the costs are not fully recoverable," says Richard A. Bowler, a Holyoke appraiser with a national reputation in his field. "The best buck you can spend is on a newer house with the space and amenities you're seeking." Bowler's opinion is shared by many experts, including Milton J. Francis, director of the appraisal and mortgage risk division of the U.S. Department of Housing and Urban Development. For the family wishing to improve its housing in the most economical way, Bowler and Francis have a simple recommendation: move.

Still, Americans spent $7.4 billion last year on home improvements, and it would be wrong to judge that money ill spent. Most people improve their houses for reasons of comfort, convenience and status, not as an investment. Unlike most new houses, an improvement can be tailored to your needs. Moreover, staying in a choice location instead of moving elsewhere may more than justify the high cost of remodeling, and no beady-eyed appraiser can put a dollar sign on your personal taste or satisfaction.

That is not to say that improvements have no resale value. But the family that considers home improvement partly as an investment in the eventual sale price should proceed carefully. By adjusting your personal preferences to those of the marketplace, you can make improvements that increase your comfort without costing you a heavy penalty when the house is sold. Appraisers, contractors and real estate agents generally agree on four axioms that everyone should consider before remodeling:

- The quality of the neighborhood is by far the most important factor in the sale price of your house. If the average neighborhood price is $35,000 and your house cost you $30,000, you may recoup most of a $5,000 remodeling job. But $10,000 worth of improvements would not be such a good investment because the buyer seeking a $40,000 house will be looking in a neighborhood of $40,000 houses. That does not mean you can let your house deteriorate, expecting neighborhood values to sell it for you. A rundown house in any neighborhood tends to sit on the market, as unwanted as the fat kid on the block basketball team.
- An improvement should be appropriate to the house and the neighborhood. Wallace W. Kidwell, vice president of Thomas J. Owen & Son, Inc., a leading appraisal firm in Washington, D.C., says homeowners often overlook this point. "People go bananas," Kidwell says. "In a $30,000 or $40,000 house, they'll put a kitchen that fits a $70,000 house. The improvement should fit the house in degree of luxury." It also should fit the neighborhood architectural style, no matter how plain. An avant-garde addition may win an architectural medal, but in a neighborhood of ordinary split levels it may bring less on resale than would a more conventional design.
- With few exceptions, any improvement costs more than it would have had it been built into the house at the start. Compared with original construction, an added room costs about twice as much per square foot. Even remodeling jobs done within the existing walls exact a premium. If you convert a bedroom niche into a bathroom, it will cost about half again as much as it would have to install that bath when the house was built. Remodeling a kitchen or adding a fireplace costs at least 20% more than doing the same job as part of the original construction. The eventual buyer of the house, of course, will not pay

that premium; to him, a room is a room. Indeed, if your improvement is not carefully designed, it may produce an odd floor plan that will make your return on the improvement even smaller than it would have been otherwise. If you add a family room for $8,000, you can presume it would have cost the original builder of your house only $4,000. Unpleasant as it may be to take a 50% loss, if that room adds $4,000 to the sale price of your house, you have done as well as you can expect. Converting a porch or a breezeway into a family room costs about 40% less than building the same room from scratch and will probably yield the same price on resale; it is thus a better investment. Of course, the margin of loss can be cut drastically, or even eliminated, if you make an improvement yourself. But do it well, because a shoddy do-it-yourself job may cut the price of your house by the amount it would cost to do it over again professionally.

## WHAT YOU SPEND ISN'T WHAT YOU GET

A thorough kitchen remodeling costs $4,000 to $7,000. It will help sell the house when you move, but you'll get back only $1,000 to $3,000. A first-floor powder room costs $600 to $2,500; remodeling an upstairs bathroom costs $1,000 to $3,000. Neither returns more than half what you pay.

Central air conditioning costs $1,000 to $4,000, depending on whether ductwork must be added. Except in the far North it is perhaps your best buy: it returns $1,000 to $2,000. Room air conditioners cost $100 to $300 each; they are worth little or nothing when you sell.

Adding a first-floor family room costs $5,000 to $10,000 and usually helps sell the house. But it is unlikely to add more than half its cost to the eventual resale price.

An unfinished basement can be transformed into an attractive recreation room for $1,200 to $2,400. But basement rec rooms are out of vogue; they're worth only $500 to $1,000 when you sell.

To some buyers, a swimming pool is more bother than boon; your investment of $3,000 to $10,000 may go down the drain.

A good driveway costs about $1 per square foot. An ordinary straight drive is less than half as expensive as an elaborate U-shaped one, which can cost $1,000 to $3,000. At resale, the difference between plain and fancy is only $300 to $500.

Conventional landscaping keeps the value of your property up. A lavish touch can increase outlays by at least $500—often much more—but it raises the resale value very little, or not at all.

Experts agree that there are several reasons why home improvements cost so much more than original construction. John J. Heyn, a former builder, is now president of the National Home Inspection Service, a firm that checks out for prospective buyers how well a house is constructed. He says that because remodeling contracts are for much smaller amounts than house-building contracts, remodelers usually get a 100% markup while a contractor building a house gets only 10% to 20%. There are other factors. Often a contractor must bid on a room addition, for example, without knowing what hidden pipes, wiring or masonry he may run into in a wall that must be removed. So he will bid high, just to be safe. If you know your house thoroughly, inside and out, you may get a lower bid by guaranteeing in advance that the job will not require major changes in plumbing or wiring. Many contractors also add a bit to their bid to compensate for the inconvenience of having to work while you and your family are in residence. You may save something by agreeing to take your vacation while the job is being completed, it you know the contractor well enough to trust him in your house while you are away. But stay in touch, because if the contractor encounters an unexpected problem he may be able to deal with it relatively cheaply if you will agree to modify your specifications.

- The more visible an improvement, the more likely it is to increase the value of the house. "The way a house looks when a buyer walks in is usually what sells it," says Ann Brehm, a real estate broker in Scarsdale, New York. "Most people go by the surface." As a result, some substantial but prosaic improvements add virtually nothing to the sale price: replacing galvanized water pipes with copper, for example, or boosting the electrical wiring capacity. Even so there is also little return on some visible exterior improvements, like adding storm windows, applying aluminum siding or replacing an asphalt roof with tile or cedar shingles. The average buyer expects a house to have windows, siding and a roof and is unlikely to pay extra for high quality. Appraisers have difficulty accounting for this reluctance, since storm windows reduce heating bills and aluminum siding saves on maintenance, but they agree that it is the rule.

Wisely or not, the average buyer considers installations of this kind maintenance, not improvement. Experts agree that maintenance is important to the resale price, but only to keep it from dropping below the neighborhood norm. If the exterior paint is peeling, you may be penalized $1,000 or so on resale. An aluminum or vinyl siding job costs three to four times as much as repainting, but it does little more to keep up the resale price. So a siding job is worthwhile only if you stay put long enough to benefit from the saving on maintenance. Do not expect the buyer to pay you the money he will save by not painting every few years.

In general, improvements that pay off the best are popular ones that can be made at a cost not much greater than that of original construction. The cost penalty varies, but it can be estimated in advance. So can the degree of popularity, by checking whether the feature you are considering is a local "builder's item," one commonly included in new housing of the same price range in your area. Builders are the couturiers of housing fashion, and features they are pushing would probably help sell your house too.

The most dependably popular jobs are kitchen and bath remodeling, because they appeal strongly to housewives. They are also the projects most often undertaken by homeowners. According to an annual survey conducted by a Northwestern University business statistician for Home Improvements, a trade magazine, Americans spent $1.64 billion last year on their kitchens and $330 million of their bathrooms. Although they are superb sales promoters, kitchen and bath remodeling jobs rarely add more than 25% to 50% of their cost to the sale price.

Every house has a kitchen and at least one bath, so those tend to be taken for granted. Central air conditioning, however, is a feature many houses lack, so it is an exception to the rule—it often pays its way. Window and wall units do not, illustrating the principle that an improvement should not look like something tacked on as an afterthought.

Like skirts, housing fashions have their ups and downs. Although they are relatively inexpensive, basement recreation rooms are no longer sought after. Appraisers say that these days most people simply do not like to spend their leisure hours underground. Family rooms at ground level are more expensive but also far more popular with most buyers. Screened porches went out with cardboard fans, but patios are fashionable. Styles also vary from city to city, sometimes in mysterious ways. Considering the climate, one can readily understand why swimming pools are popular in southern California, but garages? "Out here, you must have at least a carport," says William W. Abelmann, a prominent Glendale, Calif., appraiser and past president of the 17,000-member Society of Real Estate Appraisers. In the suburbs of Los Angeles, Washington and Chicago, many buyers consider a first-floor lavatory a necessity. But that is not true, for example, in Raleigh, North Carolina. If they are behind in plumbing fashions, though, the people of Raleigh are trend setters in outdoor leisure. They prefer wooden decks to the patios that remain in vogue elsewhere in the country.

Outdoor improvements are usually riskier investments than indoor ones, perhaps reflecting the fact that shelter is the basic function of any house. A patio is likely to help sell your house but unlikely to return more than half its cost. Storage sheds and barbecue grills are even worse investments. A driveway is important and worth maintaining well, but an elaborate U-shaped drive adds little to resale value. It may make parking more convenient, but to most buyers a driveway is a driveway, as mundane as siding or roofing. Bedraggled landscaping may make your house a pariah on the market, but it is not economically worthwhile to do more than keep the grass green and maintain enough trees and bushes to make sure that your yard stays abreast of neighboring ones.

Indeed, expensive shrubbery may even repel some buyers, since many men would rather spend their weekends golfing than pruning. Some other improvements similarly limit the number of prospective buyers. A finished third floor, with bedrooms and bath, appeals only to a large family. The housewife who does not need the space may view it as a burden—more stairs to climb and rooms to clean. Although family rooms are popular, they are risky if tailored to a particular motif. Your paneled bar may be worthless to the buyer who pines for his own billiard parlor. A garage converted to a family room may add or detract; many buyers consider automotive shelter more valuable than an extra room.

If a remodeling job has improved your house both visually and functionally, you can probably depend on inflation to make up some of the cost before you sell. Housing prices are marching smartly forward, and Francis of HUD says they appear locked in "a steadily inflationary spiral." The pattern differs from city to city, and housing values have declined in a few localities with heavy unemployment, but in some areas—certain suburbs of Washington, for example—housing prices appear to be increasing by 10% or more a year. That does not mean that the passage of time will allow you to turn a profit on a remodeling job, but it does give you some economic elbowroom. If you paid $30,000 for your house five years ago and expect to live there another five years, and if similar houses in your neighborhood are selling for $35,000 already, an expensive remodeling job is easier to justify. The upward trend in prices may more than make up for the cost of remodeling, and until you finally sell your house you will have the benefit of the improvements.

Any improvement will probably boost your property tax. When the contractor gets his permit, the details are automatically forwarded to the assessor's office. You must also consider capital-gains taxes. In determining the difference between what you paid for your house and what you got for it on resale, you value improvements at what you paid for them. You may include upgrading, from a room addition to replacement of wooden storm windows with modern metal ones. (Movable appliances like a refrigerator or stove may not be included, nor may painting and decorating.) If you sold your house for more than your investment in it, this formula is to your advantage: it does not discount your home-improvement dollars. For example, if you bought your house for

$40,000, spent $10,000 improving it and sold it for $50,000 ten years later, you pay no capital-gains tax, even though inflation may have been more important that improvements in boosting the sale price. Even if you sell for more than your total investment, you can postpone paying any capital-gains tax by using the proceeds to buy another house within a year, or within 18 months if you are building a new house. But there is another, less agreeable housing provision that few people know about. If you overimprove and get less for your house than you invested in it, the Internal Revenue Service will not help you absorb the loss. Unlike a loss on stocks or bonds, a capital loss on your residence cannot be deducted.

Although appraisers and real estate men agree that it is wise to work out in advance the economic consequences of any planned improvement, they acknowledge that any housing sale is a one-on-one proposition. A single buyer's tastes may vary widely from the norm. "The women make the market, and that's what drives us male appraisers crazy," says Charles M. Hartsock, manager of real estate appraisal for Cameron-Brown Co., a leading Raleigh mortgage banking house.

The most chancy improvement of all is perhaps a swimming pool. In southern California and Florida, a pool will usually help sell your house and return maybe 50¢ of each dollar spent on it. The same may be true elsewhere in the country in expensive neighborhoods where pools are prevalent. But in most of the U.S., a swimming pool will add little or nothing to the sale price, particularly if it is the only one on the block. It may even scare off buyers. Hartsock says many buyers consider pools a bother and fear little children may fall in and drown. "You get three months of pleasure and twelve months of maintenance," Hartsock says. "And the woman is afraid that pool will bring all the neighborhood kids over."

When Bill Cosby, the entertainer, rented a house in Los Angeles last year while filming his television series, it came with a swimming pool, no doubt a plus from the landlord's viewpoint. Not so to Mrs. Cosby, who arrived later, after school closed for the summer, bringing the children, aged 3, 5 and 7. Fearing one might fall in, Mrs. Cosby had the pool sealed over with a removable rigid plastic cover at a cost of about $3,000. To the Cosbys, the pool cover, not the pool, was the improvement.

## Reading 59

# Some Private Pools Drain Wallets

**Patricia F. Bode**

*Inefficient or disreputable pool builders soak consumers throughout the country every year, especially when families lose their cool during a hot spell and rush into a contract.*

A big hole behind their Scottsdale, Ariz., home was all that Jack and Linda Elkinton had to show for their $3,000 payment to a Phoenix swimming-pool builder, who went out of business shortly after taking their money last year.

The Elkintons decided to go ahead with the pool so their five children

From the *National Observer*, July 28, 1973, p. 8.

could use it. Elkinton, who manages a grocery store, obtained a second personal loan and paid an additional $4,000 to swimming-pool contractors. "This has been a hardship, a really painful experience," says Mrs. Elkinton.

Mrs. Earl Payne of nearby Phoenix says her swimming pool has been "the biggest headache I've ever had." The out-of-business Phoenix contractor also left the Paynes high and dry. It cost them an extra $2,000 to get other contractors to convert the hole in their yard into a pool. A last-minute hardship was discovery that improperly installed electrical wiring would have to be reinstalled at a cost of $400. This month the Paynes finally dived in—15 months behind schedule.

Homeowners in metropolitan Phoenix have encountered so many problems with backyard pools that a citizens' group was formed two years ago to pressure recalcitrant companies and government officials. Called Sink or Swim (SOS), the group was organized by Dean Anderson of Tempe, a retired Army master sergeant who says he still gets four or five new complaints every week. Anderson formed SOS when a national pool company neglected to fix his own pool, which leaked so badly it had to be rebuilt three times.

Inefficient or disreputable pool builders soak consumers throughout the country every year, especially when families lose their cool during a hot spell and rush into a contract.

The backyard pool boom and its accompanying problems are no longer confined to California and Florida. Homeowners throughout the Northeast and Southeast are also buying pools, usually metal framework models with vinyl liners that are installed above ground or only partly in the ground. The liner, like a giant envelope full of water, rests on a bed of sand.

## MIDDLE CLASS TOO

Vinyl-lined pools usually cost several hundred dollars less than permanent cement pools of similar size. The average price for all types of medium-size pools (less than 20 by 40 feet) is $5,278, according to the National Swimming Pool Institute, a trade association.

No longer are pools the playthings of just the rich. "Swimming pools have turned from a luxury item to almost a necessity in Southern California. More and more middle-income people, especially those living in the large subdivisions and tract areas in Orange County and the San Fernando Valley, are having pools built into their homes," observes Dale Sekovich, consumer-protection specialist in the Los Angeles office of the Federal Trade Commission (FTC).

Consumers are likely to get into hot water even when dealing with established companies, Sekovich warns, because many "stretch themselves too thin" as orders pour in. "Instead of everybody getting good service, everybody gets mediocre service," he contends, noting that out of hundreds of new pool owners, he has talked with only one or two whose pools were completed on time.

Once completed, pools often leak, crack, or show other signs of shoddy workmanship, Sekovich says, recalling a complaint last week from a woman who said a bucket had been cemented into the bottom of her pool.

Hurried, poor-quality construction is a frustrating problem. But consumers are likely to get into much deeper water by dealing with fly-by-night operators who probably won't even be around to hear about deficiencies in the completed pool. FTC officials warn that these companies often use bait-and-switch tactics to sell their products at inflated prices.

For example, a consumer may be intrigued by an advertisement, often placed in a newspaper's TV section, picturing an above-ground swimming pool "completely installed" and "fully guaranteed" for prices varying from $375 to $895.

But if the prospective buyer calls a salesman, he is likely to discover the pool company doesn't think much of its advertised special. Typically, the salesman plays down the economy model as too cheap for the consumer's taste and pressures him to contract for a deluxe model. The buyer is likely to pay from $4,000 to $5,000 for a pool that's worth much less.

Merle Dowd, director of special projects for the National Swimming Pool Institute in Washington, D.C., believes there are one or two unscrupulous dealers "in every community between here and Chicago." Dowd says his 1,700 members are anxious to see the end of the marginal operations he says give all pool dealers a bad name. He warns consumers to scrutinize ads and avoid contracting with companies who seem to misrepresent their products. For example, low-cost pools usually can accommodate only one or two swimmers comfortably but advertisements often picture many more enjoying the pool.

The Federal Trade Commission is investigating bait-and-switch tactics, false advertising, and truth-in-lending violations in several cities and has recently issued complaints against two companies, Shangri-La Industries in northern Ohio and Southern States Distributing Co., which has sold pools throughout the Southeast.

## WATCH THOSE GUARANTEES

The guarantee is one of several matters that consumers should consider carefully when buying a pool. Read the contract to ascertain exactly what equipment is warranted and who will stand good for defects. Vinyl liners often are guaranteed for 10 years, but only on a pro rata basis for a replacement purchased from the same manufacturer.

"People act like these contracts are written in stone," Sekovich observes, recommending buyers read contracts carefully and then write in provisions to protect themselves.

Often a buyer doesn't realize that he has contracted for unexpected construction costs that might be caused by rock or a high water table. Often the contract waives the builder's responsibility for underground utilities: If workers break a sewer line, the homeowner must pay.

## AVOID PRESSURE TACTICIANS

Never sign a contract under pressure. If you are doing business with a reputable company, that "once-in-a-lifetime" deal should still be available next week.

Never sign a blank contract. Salesmen sometimes draw up a handwritten version, then ask for a signature on another blank sheet on which the handwritten text will be typed. You have little protection if the typing results in changes in prices or other terms.

Check with your local Better Business Bureau and governmental contractor-licensing agency before signing with a company. Determine whether the firm has an established place of business in your area. Ask for the names of former customers to check performance.

Investigate local building codes and ordinances; they may change some of your pool plans. Make sure the pool builder will bear the expense of compliance, and if not, consider costs you may face. In Chicago, for example, it costs $150 just to apply to the zoning board for a permit.

If you approach a pool purchase carefully, take your time, and deal with reputable companies who sell quality products, you're likely to wind up with a good pool that will mean hours of healthy recreation for your family. In the Northeast or Midwest, the next few months may be the best time to shop for bargains as the summer rush dwindles. In warmer climates, you usually can get the best buys during the winter.

Reading 60

# About Your Home

**Office of the District Attorney, Multnomah County, Oregon**

*Protect yourself by demanding the seller's references and checking them out.*

## A HOME SELLING GENERALLY

A home sale is one where the salesman comes to your home either personally or by means of a telephone. Usually the product is one you would ordinarily not think of purchasing if you were in a store. One of the drawbacks of this method is that there must be an extremely high commission, sometimes as much as 500%, on each sale to pay for the time of the salesman individually calling in your home and the cost of legal and cancellation fees. This is one situation where you should follow certain rules so that you will not be cheated.

Never sign the contract on the day the person visits your home or while he's in your home for the first time. Make them come back the next day to close the sale. That gives you time to see if you really want the product and to check the contract over. It also gives you a chance to compare the product and the price at local stores to see if you are getting proper value for your money. Most important, it allows you to cool down to see if you really want the item. The salesman will frequently try some phony gimmick, such as a "gift" or "discount" to close the deal the first day. They will tell you that you cannot get the bargain price if you don't sign today. Don't believe it—it is seldom true. An additional problem you might have with this type of sale is getting service. Where do you go? Even if it's a national brand, it's difficult to get servicing when the servicing center is several hundred miles away. This is one reason for going to one of your many reputable local merchants.

The following are some of the gimmicks used in this type of selling:

**1** The salesman tells you he's conducting a survey or a questionnaire.
**2** The salesman wants to discuss home economics.
**3** The salesman wants to use your home as a model.
**4** The salesman wants to obtain names from you of other persons so that he can give you the product he sells at a very low price. This is against the law.
**5** The salesman conducts a contest and you are to receive a gift or free sample.

From Consumer Protection Handbook, Multnomah County District Attorney, Portland, Oregon, pp. 9–16.

**6** The salesman solicits your business for an interview by phone or mail. Beware of the salesman who wants both the husband and the wife at home at the same time. They do that so that they can get both signatures on the contract.

In addition to the remedies which apply to all sales, the buyer may cancel a home solicitation sale until midnight of the third business day after the day he signs an agreement. The buyer may cancel for any reason including changing his mind. The three-day period does not begin to run until the buyer signs an agreement containing certain specific language. This language must be in the wording described by law in a certain size and form. If the agreement does not contain this information, the three days continue to run until the buyer gets the information in the proper form. If you cancel a home sale, you must do so by sending a written notification in the mail to the seller at his business address. The notice must tell him you intend to cancel the obligation. If the seller fails to perform all the obligations placed upon him by the home solicitation sales laws, the buyer may keep possession of any goods delivered until the seller returns down payments or trade-in goods to which the buyer is entitled. The buyer must use reasonable care in order to protect the goods from damage. If the seller fails to pick up the goods from the buyer within 20 days of cancellation, they become the property of the buyer. This law does not apply to *cash* sales in an amount of $50 or less.

## B ALUMINUM SIDING

The first problem is the illegal "Use your home as a model" technique. You are told that they will use your home as a model to look at and thereby you are allowed siding, supposedly for a greatly reduced price. It really turns out to be a lot more than you would pay for a good siding job from a reputable dealer. Remember that siding is particularly subject to varying values. You must know exactly what brands and what particular grade or model is used to know if you are getting a bargain. Again, in these cases, never have any work done on your home without checking references, checking with your local consumer protection agencies and consulting with your attorney. Work done on your home can affect the ownership of your home by way of a lien.

The second basic problem is the "lowball" and the lien. After the siding has been put on your home, the final cost may be several times the "lowball" estimate. Then you are told if you don't pay for it there will be a lien put on your home and foreclosure on it. Then your house will be sold to pay for the siding. Anytime you are threatened by anyone in this way, you should call your local district attorney immediately.

## C REPAIRS OR HOME IMPROVEMENTS

One of the most important things you must do to protect yourself from fraud is wait until all the work is done to your satisfaction before paying any money at all. Never pay even a down payment for purchase of material and so on, because, if you do, you cannot count on the person ever coming back. If the contractor does not like this arrangement, don't hire him. There are a lot of people who take down payments and do just a little bit of work and never return.

To protect yourself when hiring someone to make repairs or improvements follow these steps:

1. Ask for three persons who have recently hired the "contractor" and call them about the quality of his work.
2. Get three competitive bids so you can figure out the fair value of the work to be performed.
3. Make out a small written contract which specifies
   - **a** Labor costs
   - **b** Material costs
   - **c** Exact quality of materials
   - **d** Completion date (with a penalty clause for the contractor's failure to finish on time).
4. Get the contractor's bank (commercial account) references and permission to talk to his banker. (It is nice to know where his assets are located if he later cheats you or damages your property). (It is also nice to know if his account has been garnished in the last year).
5. Finally, make no payment (not even a small down payment) until the work is completed to your satisfaction. (If you get a notice of a materialman's lien during the work phase, make your check out to the contractor and materialman and get a receipt from both before you give them your check.)

## D CHARITY DONATIONS

It has come to pass that the charity donations scheme is well-used by many fast-stepping crooks. Everything is used from under-privileged children to research for major diseases to religions, etc. Many times they play on your desire not to be prejudiced against racial or religious minorities. Any small gifts or donations you may wish to make should be looked into in detail. Always check with your local consumer protection agency, Better Business Bureau and United Good Neighbors and City License Department to determine whether it is a bona fide charity.

## E CORRESPONDENCE SCHOOLS

Besides the problems mentioned in this handbook under Trade Schools, the most important thing to remember regarding correspondence schools is that you send your money away to a distant state. It may then become impossible to sue that school if the course is not what they lead you to believe or they did not complete their part of the contract. Therefore, you should talk to someone locally who has had satisfaction with that school and check out every school you plan on attending through the Oregon State Department of Higher Education Licensing Section. They will tell you whether the school is licensed and whether it is reputable. One of the best safeguards is to ask for and check local references of satisfied students. Remember also that the course may not qualify you for employment as their advertisements promise. Therefore, check with local companies to see if they will accept graduates of that particular school. And, finally, call your district attorney's office.

## F ENCYCLOPEDIAS

There have been many problems in the sale of encyclopedias by the door-to-door vendor. Use comparative shopping to make sure the set of encyclopedias is comparable in value to those on sale in your local stores. Don't be fooled by any sort of phony research or surveys or advertising programs or free gifts, etc., used in connection with this kind of sale. The basic approach is to make you feel that unless you have the set of encyclopedias you are depriving your children of necessary educational tools. Your emotions will take care of the rest. Remember that to make a sale, the seller must make it look as if it is going to cost you a very small amount of money. It never turns out to be a small amount of money, because somewhere in there is a hidden gimmick to pay for the entire set of encyclopedias plus a large salesman's commission.

## G EXTERMINATORS

Deceptive trade practices in this field are conducted with a phony inspector and have been prosecuted successfully in Oregon as obtaining money by false pretenses, a felony. Carefully check the credentials of any person who states he is a city, county, state or fire department inspector. If there is any doubt, always check by calling the alleged inspector's office, and look the number up yourself since he may give you a phony number to one of his confederates.

## H FLOATING PHOTOGRAPHERS

It is important to seek a company that is reputable. The floating, or fly-by-night, photographers are usually in a position where they can be disreputable but fly before they're caught. Some of the gimmicks are to:

**1** Get your name on a contract you later find is more expensive, or
**2** Greatly misrepresent the contract, or
**3** Prey upon your feelings and desires to have pictures of your children over a period of years, or
**4** Use various psychological approaches, like shaming you into getting photographs of your children for their grandparents. Before you hire anyone for photographic work, get references from satisfied customers. Then compare the cost.

## I FAKE SALES

State law prohibits fake and fraudulent sales. It is against the law to advertise something as a sale item when in fact the price has not been reduced for the sale. It is also against the law to make a transaction appear to be a sale when in fact the item is purchased by someone representing the company.

## J FIRE ALARMS

Fire alarms might save someone's life. They are on sale at several stores and door-to-door. Before you purchase any of these items you should check and compare as you should with all purchases to make sure you are really getting the price and quality you want. Furthermore, you should be wary of the sales approach which tries to scare you by showing you pictures of burned children and quoting unpleasant facts. This practice of scaring you, bringing your family together in the same room and using the wife's fears to pressure the husband's sales resistance, even if done in a sweet and subtle manner, is psychologically a very deceptive practice. Therefore, you must watch for subtle scare tactics, high pressure and misrepresentation as to the value and use of the item. Companies can make as much as 500% profit on these items. Beware of so-called "approval" or "certification" by local fire department authorities.

Always compare the product at several stores and with other brands. Don't let the salesman do the comparing for you because he will tell you all the reasons why you shouldn't buy another product or at another store.

## K FRAUDULENT INSPECTORS

Official government inspectors are not allowed to give referrals to businessmen. They are also not allowed to look the other way if there is a violation of law. One of the main gimmicks used is to make you feel that your wiring or furnace is in violation of the law but they will overlook it if you get it corrected quickly. And then they suggest someone who will do it. It is always a scheme. Call your district attorney.

## L FURNACES

One of the oldest door-to-door schemes is the unwanted or unneeded sale or repair of air conditioners, air filtering systems, vent cleaning, furnace cleaning and other furnace related items. Be careful of the phony inspector. Always delay purchase of any air filtering equipment, etc., for at least one day. Then call your district attorney and Better Business Bureau to check the reputation of the seller's company.

An old scheme is to tear down your furnace and then refuse to put it back together. You are told that it would be too dangerous for this furnace to continue working. If someone comes in and tries to take your furnace apart, call the district attorney's office, get their license number, etc.

## M HOME PARTIES

The concept of selling products by home parties is not necessarily a deceptive practice. It allows the salesman or woman to market a product at a lower per person cost since the customer does not have to be contacted individually. However, there are many companies that take advantage of the home party business and use this approach to sell people things they don't really wish to buy. These "forced sales" are done by group and social pressure, and phony discounts and gifts. One thing to remember: "Never buy on the same day of your party." Even if that means you miss out on a bonus, a free gift or crush someone's feelings. Delay one day. It is important that you check out the products very carefully and compare values with those products sold in stores. Then if you like the home sale product, buy it.

## N MAIL ORDER HOUSES

The problem with ordering from a catalog or an advertisement in a magazine is that you send your money to a distant state having "faith" that the company will deliver the goods as promised and that the goods will work as advertised. Don't rely on the reputation of the magazine, because they may not be responsible for their advertizers. Some mail order houses have gone out of business leaving a trail of many unfilled orders behind them. A protection in this particular situation is "COD." You can, at least, be sure that you have a package delivered to your door, regardless of its contents. It will likely be what you ordered. That's one protection. Once you get delivery of the article, you may find that it fails to live up to the advertised promises. Avoid that problem by checking before you order with Better Business Bureaus in the state where the mail order house is located as well as your local Better Business Bureau to see if there are any complaints. You can also check with the postal inspectors because they receive many complaints based upon undelivered or poor quality goods.

You should also check a local store when you are ordering a brand name item. The chances are excellent that it is cheaper locally and you'll have a greater chance of redress through a local distributor. You may also ask around to see if someone has ever dealt with that mail order company to see if they are reputable.

## O REFERRAL SALES

Under 1971 Consumer Protection Laws it is illegal to use referral sales. Therefore, if someone tells you that you can earn future commissions, gifts or any compensations in exchange for submitting names to him, even if it is far removed from the sale, it is against the law. Beware of a seller who tries to tell you his product will cost you little or nothing if he can get the names of some of your friends who will be given a demonstration of the product.

## P REPAIRS—AUTO AND TELEVISION

1 Free estimate. What is a "free estimate"? They may take your auto apart for nothing but charge you to put it back together again. This is particularly true in the transmission field. Be very careful of this and don't look at a free estimate with your eyes closed.
2 While your appliance is in the repair shop, nothing prevents a deceptive repairman from replacing perfectly good parts with older parts. You would never find it out. To increase profits any repairman may:
   a Replace parts that do not need to be repaired.
   b Build in problems to crop up later.
   c Steal good parts and replace them with older ones.
   d Use your item, car or television, etc., for his own personal use while it is in the shop, telling you it must be delayed for certain parts, etc.
   e Switch complete components, i.e., inside a television set chassis put an older or cheaper brand that fits.
   f Charge you and not fix the item at all.
   g Repair items without your authorization.

In regard to (f) and (g), if you try to sue or refuse to pay, they may file a mechanic's lien forcing you to pay to get your item back. Then if you get a judgment against them, they may have no assets available to satisfy your judgment.

Call your district attorney if any of these are used on you. You should also check with your attorney. It used to be too costly to sue in these situations. Luckily, a new law now makes just about any contract action where deception or breach of warranty is involved practical. You should have a witness with you when ordering repairs so that no repairs will be done contrary to your instructions. Also, get the agreement in writing. Even though you must rely on the mechanic's judgment as to repairs needed, he must ask you before he exceeds your repair instruction. If he doesn't do this, it is a deceptive trade practice. Therefore, don't pay for unauthorized work until you have talked to the district attorney's office. When you have repairs done you might check to see if they were really accomplished as your bill states. Here's a tip—ask for and check references of people who have been satisfied by this repairman before you hire him.

## Q SENIOR CITIZENS

Cheaters know that identification and prosecution, either civilly or criminally, is less likely by senior citizens because their faculties are diminished. A rule for senior citizens: Always have a close friend or relative check out the deal and wait a few days before parting with any money or signing a contract. Ask someone who is out in the business world to look at it for you. Call your local district attorney's office or consumer protection office. You should also have a family attorney. You will be surprised how many attorneys do free work for persons who are on limited income. Please don't equate asking for information with loss of pride.

Schemes to be particularly aware of are:

1. Phony home repairs.
2. Overcharging for repair work.
3. Receiving down payments on contracts and failing to perform further.
4. Convincing you that work is needed to be done, when in fact it is not.

## R SEWING MACHINES

What is true of door-to-door sales of vacuum cleaners and fire alarms is also true of door-to-door sales of sewing machines. Compare the machine with those in the stores to see if the price is right.

Never finance with a company selling door-to-door until you check another source of financing the purchase. Check credit unions, banks and other finance companies for a better interest rate. Also, watch out for the free machine with a five-year service gimmick. The cost of the machine is included in the cost of the service. Use comparative shopping and delay one day before signing a contract.

## S TALENT SCOUTS

There are a great many artist and music schools soliciting new talent. Basically, there are two problems: First, you must find out whether the school or course offers you any value. Just because it is advertised extensively doesn't mean it is a reputable company. Check out the particular school with some of the local art or music schools. Also check with Better Business Bureaus and your district attorney's office. Furthermore, you should check every school with the Department of Higher Education Licensing Section.

The second problem is this: Many of the schools offer you a talent test and surprisingly enough it shows you have a great talent worthy of development. Although it is flattering to you, check with more than one source before you decide to develop your talent or a child's talent. If you send your money away or sign a contract—look out!

## T TELEPHONE SALES

Telephone sales are usually tied to a "junky" free gift or "phony" contest schemes. There is always a promotional fee of some kind. Normally, someone will come to your home to collect the fee. Under Oregon law the person soliciting business on the phone must within the first 30 seconds of conversation:

1 Give their name.
2 Give the name of the company.
3 State the purpose of the call.

The purpose of the call is to make a sale if a sale is made at any time thereafter. If they did not do this and later make a sale, you may cancel the contract. Additionally, in contracts over $50 or where a credit purchase is made, the buyer must be given notice that he has three days in which to cancel any contract entered into as a result of the door-to-door sale, even where the sale began over the phone. Those three days do not start until the buyer actually gets the notice in the written form prescribed by law. Because telephone solicitations have been a source of deception for many years, there is a lot of law built up on the subject, and if you will contact your attorney, you may find that you have a good chance of being successful in suing for deceptive trade practice. See Deceptive Trade Practices, Chapter 744, Section 13, Oregon Laws 1971, which section allows you a minimum of $200 damages or actual damages if they are greater than $200. The court is also authorized to award attorney fees and punitive damages in appropriate cases.

## U UPHOLSTERY/CARPET WORK

There is a lot of variance in the quality of materials in carpeting and upholstery. Remember the old "rug merchant" jokes? People claim to be experts when in fact they are not. Protect yourself by demanding the seller's references and checking them out. Talk to satisfied customers and ask them a few questions. Remember, merchandise may be switched on you from the store to your home. It may look like the same but it may be a different quality. Take someone with you who knows about upholstery and carpeting. There is a lot of garbage that looks like quality merchandise. Watch out for a "lowball" estimate that turns into a much higher purchase price.

## V VACUUM CLEANERS

There have been a lot of articles written about the comparative values of vacuum cleaners purchased at home or in the store. Your best protection is to really compare and check with consumer report magazines and go from store to store to decide just what is the best value. We have had many complaints about fraudulent misrepresentation as to the value or prior ownership in this business and the sewing machine field. Be very careful. Compare—don't sign anything the first day.

## Reading 61

# Facts to Know about Leases

**Sidney Margolius**

*Verbal promises are hard to prove.*

You should settle beforehand these points in particular:

**1** Any restriction on occupancy other than by yourself and your immediate family you may want to make.

**2** Any restrictions on alterations you may want to make, and an understanding regarding which kind of improvements or fixtures you add become the property of the landlord when you move. For example, are built-in bookcases or additional electrical fixtures to become the property of the landlord?

**3** What your responsibilities are, and those of the landlord, for any needed repairs and, in general, for keeping the property and fixtures in good condition. For example, who is responsible for painting and for making ordinary repairs like fixing the plumbing?

**4** Are you allowed to assign the lease or sublet if you want to move or will be away temporarily? Will you need the landlord's consent? Must it be in writing? What are the conditions for obtaining such consent? If your subtenant does not pay the rent, will you still be liable?

**5** On what day is the rent due each month, and do you have any days of grace (permitting you to be late a number of days if necessary)?

**6** What regulations governing fire insurance and garbage disposal are you required to observe?

**7** Are you or the landlord responsible for any harm or damage to you, your family, guests, or your property caused by falling plaster, burst steam pipes or other defects in the building? Many lease forms exempt the landlord from any responsibility if not caused by his negligence, and from liability for any loss of your possessions stored in a storage room, or for any accident you may suffer in a laundry room or other common facility. In that case you may want to carry your own liability and property insurance.

**8** Any redecorating or new equipment which the landlord agrees to provide if you rent the place should be listed in writing and made part of the lease. Verbal promises are hard to prove.

**9** What services will the landlord provide, such as heat, electric current, gas, garbage removal, etc.? Are these enumerated in the lease?

**10** If you default on your obligations under the lease, are you liable for any additional charges such as landlord's legal expenses or his costs of preparing the premises for rerental?

**11** Does the lease provide for renewal at your choice at the end of the term, and if so, at what rental?

**12** Are you required to put up a deposit as security; for example, a month's rent? This is often a sore point between landlords and tenants because usually landlords do not want to pay interest on these deposits. Too, at the end of the lease landlords often keep part and sometimes even all of the security. The justification usually advanced is that the money withheld represents the cost of restoring or repairing the premises after occupancy. Take note, in the form you will be asked to sign, what potential reasons may be listed for withholding your deposit.

From The New Adult Guide to Independent Living, 1968, pp. 21–22.

# Family Transportation

Reading 62

## Cost of Operating an Automobile: A Ten-Year Average

- Standard Size
- Compact Size
- Subcompact Size

**L. L. Liston**
**C. L. Gauthier**

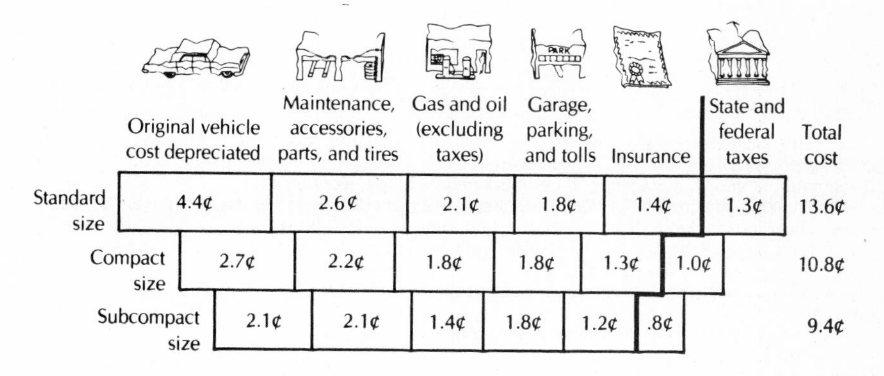


**Figure 1** A suburban based operation, cents per mile.

From the U.S. Department of Transportation, Federal Highway Administration, Office of Highway Planning, Highway Statistics Div., Washington, D.C., April 1972, pp. 9–11.

**Table 1 Estimated Cost of Operating a Standard Size 1972 Model Automobile***

(Total Cost in Dollars, Cost per Mile in Cents)

| Item | First year (14,500 miles) | | Second year (13,000 miles) | | Totals and averages for ten years (100,000 miles) | |
|---|---|---|---|---|---|---|
| | Total cost | Cost per mile | Total cost | Cost per mile | Total cost | Cost per mile |
| Costs excluding taxes: | | | | | | |
| Depreciation | 1,226.00 | 8.46 | 900.00 | 6.92 | 4,379.00 | 4.38 |
| Repairs and maintenance | 81.84 | .56 | 115.37 | .89 | 2,146.91 | 2.14 |
| Replacement tires | 17.90 | .12 | 16.05 | .12 | 399.85 | .40 |
| Accessories | 3.21 | .02 | 3.08 | .02 | 52.18 | .05 |
| Gasoline | 286.75 | 1.98 | 257.16 | 1.98 | 1,977.96 | 1.98 |
| Oil | 11.25 | .08 | 11.25 | .09 | 118.50 | .12 |
| Insurance† | 164.00 | 1.13 | 156.00 | 1.20 | 1,350.00 | 1.35 |
| Garaging, parking, tolls, etc. | 208.36 | 1.44 | 199.22 | 1.53 | 1,809.40 | 1.81 |
| Total | 1,999.31 | 13.79 | 1,658.13 | 12.75 | 12,233.80 | 12.23 |
| Taxes and fees: | | | | | | |
| State: | | | | | | |
| Gasoline | 74.62 | .51 | 66.92 | .52 | 514.71 | .51 |
| Registration | 30.00 | .21 | 30.00 | .23 | 300.00 | .30 |
| Titling | 177.15 | 1.22 | - | - | 177.15 | .18 |
| Subtotal | 281.77 | 1.94 | 96.92 | .75 | 991.86 | .99 |
| Federal: | | | | | | |
| Gasoline | 42.64 | .30 | 38.24 | .30 | 294.12 | .30 |
| Oil‡ | .22 | - | .22 | - | 2.37 | - |
| Tires | 1.38 | .01 | 1.24 | .01 | 30.80 | .03 |
| Subtotal | 44.24 | .31 | 39.70 | .31 | 327.29 | .33 |
| Total taxes | 326.01 | 2.25 | 136.62 | 1.06 | 1,319.15 | 1.32 |
| Total of all costs | 2,325.32 | 16.04 | 1,794.75 | 13.81 | 13,552.95 | 13.55 |

*This estimates covers the total costs of a fully equipped, medium priced, standard size, 4-door sedan, purchased for $4,379, operated 100,000 miles over a 10-year period, then scrapped. Baltimore area prices, considered to be in the middle range, were used.

†Previous editions of this study used insurance rates designated for Baltimore city. The rates shown above are for the Baltimore suburbs, and consequently are less than the rates presented in the previous study. If the Baltimore city rates had been used in this study, the insurance costs would have been higher. (For example, the first year would have been $232).

‡Where costs per mile were computed to be less than 1/20 cent, a dash (-) appears in the column.

*Source:* Office of Highway Planning Highway Statistics Division

From the U.S. Department of Transportation, Federal Highway Administration, Office of Highway Planning, Highway Statistics Div., Washington, D.C., April 1972, pp. 9–11.

**Table 2 Estimated Cost of Operating a Compact Size 1972 Model Automobile***

(Total Costs in Dollars, Costs per Mile in Cents)

| Item | First year (14,500 miles) | | Second year (13,000 miles) | | Totals and averages for ten years (100,000 miles) | |
|---|---|---|---|---|---|---|
| | Total cost | Cost per mile | Total cost | Cost per mile | Total cost | Cost per mile |
| Costs excluding taxes: | | | | | | |
| Depreciation | 674.00 | 4.65 | 519.00 | 3.99 | 2,696.00 | 2.70 |
| Repairs and maintenance | 79.41 | .55 | 107.14 | .83 | 1,784.50 | 1.79 |
| Replacement tires | 15.30 | .11 | 13.71 | .11 | 341.77 | .34 |
| Accessories | 3.21 | .02 | 3.08 | .02 | 52.18 | .05 |
| Gasoline | 244.25 | 1.68 | 218.97 | 1.69 | 1,684.48 | 1.68 |
| Oil | 10.50 | .07 | 10.50 | .08 | 113.25 | .11 |
| Insurance | 155.00 | 1.07 | 147.00 | 1.13 | 1,299.00 | 1.30 |
| Garaging, parking, tolls, etc. | 208.36 | 1.44 | 199.22 | 1.53 | 1,809.40 | 1.81 |
| Total | 1,390.03 | 9.59 | 1,218.62 | 9.38 | 9,780.58 | 9.78 |
| Taxes and fees: | | | | | | |
| State: | | | | | | |
| Gasoline | 63.56 | .44 | 56.98 | .44 | 438.34 | .44 |
| Registration | 20.00 | .14 | 20.00 | .15 | 200.00 | .20 |
| Titling | 109.86 | .75 | - | - | 109.86 | .11 |
| Subtotal | 193.42 | 1.33 | 76.98 | .59 | 748.20 | .75 |
| Federal: | | | | | | |
| Gasoline | 36.32 | .25 | 32.56 | .25 | 250.48 | .25 |
| Oil† | .21 | - | .21 | - | 2.27 | - |
| Tires | 1.17 | .01 | 1.05 | .01 | 26.07 | .03 |
| Subtotal | 37.70 | .26 | 33.82 | .26 | 278.82 | .28 |
| Total taxes | 231.12 | 1.59 | 110.80 | .85 | 1,027.02 | 1.03 |
| Total of all costs | 1,621.15 | 11.18 | 1,329.42 | 10.23 | 10,807.60 | 10.81 |

*This estimate covers the total costs of a medium priced, compact size, 2-door sedan, purchased for $2,696, operated 100,000 miles over a 10-year period, then scrapped. Baltimore area prices, considered to be in the middle range, were used.

†Where costs per mile were computed to be less than 1/20 cent, a dash (-) appears in the column.

*Source:* Office of Highway Planning Highway Statistics Division

**Table 3 Estimated Cost of Operating a Subcompact Size 1972 Model Automobile***

(Total Costs in Dollars, Costs per Mile in Cents)

| Item | First year (14,500 miles) | | Second year (13,000 miles) | | Totals and averages for ten years (100,000 miles) | |
|---|---|---|---|---|---|---|
| | Total cost | Cost per mile | Total cost | Cost per mile | Total cost | Cost per mile |
| Costs excluding taxes: | | | | | | |
| Depreciation | 310.00 | 2.14 | 285.00 | 2.19 | 2,064.00 | 2.07 |
| Repairs and maintenance | 76.15 | .53 | 114.59 | .88 | 1,775.71 | 1.78 |
| Replacement tires | 13.98 | .10 | 12.53 | .10 | 312.29 | .31 |
| Accessories | 3.21 | .02 | 3.08 | .02 | 52.18 | .05 |
| Gasoline | 181.84 | 1.25 | 163.02 | 1.25 | 1,255.15 | 1.25 |
| Oil | 10.50 | .07 | 9.75 | .08 | 103.50 | .10 |
| Insurance | 145.00 | 1.00 | 140.00 | 1.08 | 1,251.00 | 1.25 |
| Garaging, parking, tolls, etc. | 208.36 | 1.44 | 199.22 | 1.53 | 1,809.40 | 1.81 |
| Total | 949.04 | 6.55 | 927.19 | 7.13 | 8,623.23 | 8.62 |
| Taxes and fees: | | | | | | |
| State: | | | | | | |
| Gasoline | 47.32 | .33 | 42.42 | .33 | 326.62 | .33 |
| Registration | 20.00 | .14 | 20.00 | .15 | 200.00 | .20 |
| Titling | 84.57 | .58 | - | - | 84.57 | .08 |
| Subtotal | 151.89 | 1.05 | 62.42 | .48 | 611.19 | .61 |
| Federal: | | | | | | |
| Gasoline | 27.04 | .18 | 24.24 | .19 | 186.64 | .19 |
| Oil† | .21 | - | .19 | - | 2.07 | - |
| Tires | .94 | .01 | .84 | .01 | 20.90 | .02 |
| Subtotal | 28.19 | .19 | 25.27 | .20 | 209.61 | .21 |
| Total taxes | 180.08 | 1.24 | 87.69 | .68 | 820.80 | .82 |
| Total of all costs | 1,129.12 | 7.79 | 1,014.88 | 7.81 | 9,444.03 | 9.44 |

*This estimate covers the total costs of a low priced, subcompact size, 2-door sedan, purchased for $2,064, operated 100,000 miles over a 10-year period, then scrapped. Baltimore area prices, considered to be in the middle range, were used. Since cost data for American made subcompacts does not exist past the second year, only the first, second, and estimated ten-year totals are shown.

†Where costs per mile were computed to be less than 1/20 cent, a dash (-) appears in the column.

*Source:* Office of Highway Planning Highway Statistics Division

Reading 63

# How Sam Marshall Makes Out with His Deal

**Peter Vanderwicken***

*The car's "sticker" price—the one posted on the window—has nothing to do with its actual price.*

By a wide margin, automobile dealers are the businessmen Americans distrust most. Used-car dealers have long been popular targets for suspicion and scorn (and wry jokes), but in recent years public antipathy has engulfed new-car dealers as well. According to a recent Gallup poll, Americans have five times as much confidence in an undertaker, and even three times as much in a plumber, as they do in a car dealer.

Most car buyers are so mystified by the industry's arcane pricing system that they cannot help wondering whether they got "a good deal" on their costly new Belchfire Brougham. Their wrath is rising over dealers' sales tactics, some examples of which are among the sleaziest to be found in American commerce. Most of all, dealers have become targets for consumers' ire about the poor quality of the automobiles they buy. With every report of defects, recalls, pollution, and lack of safety—especially on top of the soaring aggravations and cost of repairs—car buyers tend naturally to direct most of their frustration at their closest contact with the industry: the man who sold them their car.

A good deal of this public obloquy is fully merited—but much of it is not, and probably results simply from a monumental lack of public understanding of how an automobile dealership operates. Despite a flood of magazines, books, brochures, and advertisements about automobiles, even including the latest wholesale price lists in paperback at the corner drugstore, most people have a vastly exaggerated notion of a car dealer's profits, and too little patience with his often valid excuses for poor service.

Dealers do, after all, have their own real problems. Many a new-car owner, driving home with an empty wallet and dark suspicions, might be surprised to learn how few of his dollars will end up in the dealer's profit account. The average car dealer earns less than 1 percent on his volume, a minuscule margin far below that of most other retailers—and of Ford or General Motors. The owner unhappily paying a $140 bill for a brake relining might be less upset if he knew that few dealers make a profit on their service business, and that many consider servicing an albatross hung around their necks by the manufacturers. Many of the public's other complaints can be resolved only in Detroit. But the manufacturers, under heavy criticism themselves, have been only too anxious to let their dealers take a lot of the heat.

## COMPETITION AT THE "STORE"

There are 30,100 dealers in the U.S. franchised by manufacturers to sell one or more makes of new cars. Most car dealerships are quite small businesses; the

*Research associate: Varian Ayers Knisely

From *Fortune*, December 1972, pp. 120–130.

average dealer last year sold 331 new cars and 265 used cars and had a sales volume of $2,100,000. His sales included $320,000 in service and parts, and the average dealership netted $18,000.

But the averages encompass many thousands of small rural dealerships that sell only a few cars a year. Increasingly, dealerships in urban and suburban areas are becoming large, complex, and highly competitive businesses. One of the better of these is the Ford dealership run by Samuel L. Marshall in Mayfield Heights, Ohio, a Cleveland suburb. Last year Marshall's "deal" or "store" (as they call it in the industry) sold 2,171 new cars and trucks, 1,681 used cars and trucks, and $1,110,000 worth of service and parts. Marshall Motor Co. had a total volume of $10,194,000 and after-tax profits of $37,800. Its profit margin was only 0.4 percent—lower than average, partly because Marshall spends more on service for his customers than most dealers do.

This year, with the automobile business doing exceptionally well, Marshall's dealership should earn about $97,500 on a volume of some $13 million. That would provide a 14 percent return on its net worth and a profit margin of 0.8 percent—much better than last year. Many dealers include their finance, insurance, and leasing activities in the dealership's figures, and these highly profitable services raise their profit margin substantially. Marshall, however, runs each as a separate company in which he is the majority stockholder, and only the earnings from his insurance operations are consolidated with his dealership's figures. This year he will earn about $21,000 from commissions on the sale of life and disability insurance to customers who are financing cars.

The finance company will earn about $20,000 this year on receivables of $1,300,000. It handles about a third of Marshall's credit sales (the rest are financed by Ford Motor Credit Co., or by local banks). The fast-growing leasing operation tries to gross $25 a month on each of the 1,000 cars it has on lease, and it will earn about $50,000 this year.

Sam Marshall, sixty-four, fails utterly to fit the common image of the brash, sport-jacketed, high-pressure car dealer. He is a white-haired, pipe-smoking, genial, and relaxed man who acts like the family doctor and dresses like a banker. Marshall laughs a lot, often at himself, and seems to derive more joy from his work than from the wealth it has brought him. "I have been thinking about what are the qualities of a good dealer," he said recently. "Some would define him as one who makes a lot of money. Others would define him as making a satisfactory return on investment, having good relations with customers and employees, and being happy in his work. That is my definition. Regardless of what arises, I enjoy what I am doing."

Marshall has homes in Shaker Heights and in Florida. Two of his children are in college, and a third recently graduated from St. Francis College in Biddeford, Maine. Sam and his wife are health-food fans and often drive to a farm forty miles from Cleveland to buy organic vegetables and untreated meats. They used to own show horses, and Sam has recently become a photography enthusiast. He has a reputation for generously and quietly supporting a long list of private charities.

He began working in a garage full time while still in high school and then, managing two years of college at night, he sold used cars. By 1931, at the age of twenty-three, he was sales manager of a Cleveland Heights Ford dealership. It was deeply in debt, and the owner offered the agency to Marshall if he could keep it out of bankruptcy court. By 1939 Marshall had paid off the debts and owned the deal. During World War II he was also salesman, mechanic, and floor scrubber (after closing, with the lights out so he wouldn't be seen). In 1964 he moved the expanding operation eleven miles farther east of Cleveland to a new building in Mayfield Heights, an affluent and growing suburb close to Shaker Heights.

## IN THE SHOWROOM AT 9:00 P.M.

With his Ford dealership as a base, Marshall has built a diversified personal fortune. He has been, but is no longer, owner or partner in a half dozen other dealerships. He has interests in Cleveland real estate and thirty-three oil wells, and is currently seeking a dealership in Florida. Mostly "as a toy," Marshall runs a small Fiat dealership as a branch up the street from his Ford store. It sells about 200 cars a year and its figures are consolidated into the company totals. By now, the net worth of Marshall Motor Co. (of which Marshall owns 91 percent) is $679,000, and Marshall himself has a personal net worth of more than $2 million.

Marshall's entire operation reflects a carefully defined business philosophy. The customer is always right, he feels, and he spends $25,000 a year on free service to customers' cars. He is frequently in the service department when it opens at 7:30 A.M. to hear customers' complaints, and he often stays in the showroom to greet buyers until it closes; on Mondays and Thursdays closing time is 9:00 P.M.

His high standards inspire loyalty from both customers and employees; many customers say they "always come here," and fifteen of Marshall's ninety employees have been with him for more than twenty-five years. The Marshall store has the informal atmosphere of a closely knit small business, but his sophisticated financial controls would do credit to a much larger enterprise.

Marshall's dealership is much better managed than most. Nearly all of his eleven supervisors were trained by Marshall himself. Each earns over $30,000 a year, including a bonus based on profits; several also have minority interests in the dealership or Marshall's other companies. Marshall himself takes $51,700 a year out of his business, in a variety of ways. He pays himself a salary of $24,000, and last year gave himself a bonus of $10,000. In addition, he received $1,300 in dividends from the dealership and $7,400 in salaries and dividends from his finance and leasing companies. As the dealership's landlord (many dealers own their deal's buildings and land), he received its annual rent of $78,000, but paid out $69,000 of that on a mortgage.

## THE MYSTERY OF PRICE

Nothing about the automobile arouses more confusion and distrust than the way in which it is priced. More myths abound about dealers' seemingly mysterious—and presumably highly profitable—pricing methods than about any other aspect of the dealer's business. The result is to leave most customers feeling at best anxious and uncertain, at worst simply cheated. "I don't believe that more than 15 percent of the new-car buyers are at peace with themselves on the way home, and think they got a good deal," says Marshall. "That is the tragedy of this business."

Part of the problem is that so many variables are involved. Pricing is affected by the value of the used car traded in, the options ordered on the new car, even the season of the year. A lot of confusion about pricing arises from customers' widespread reluctance to recognize just how little their used car is worth. New cars can lose a third of their value in the first year. Dents that seem minor to an owner sharply reduce a car's value. Seasonal variations have an important impact on prices; a used station wagon can be worth $300 more in April than in December. Small cars keep their value better than larger cars. A year-old compact, in consequence, might well have the same trade-in value as a year-old full-size model that originally cost $3,000 more.

Most sellers estimate the trade-in value of their car by reading used-car ads in newspapers—which, of course, list *retail* prices. Dealers pay wholesale prices for trade-ins; the difference, usually $350 or so, is eaten up by reconditioning, transportation, and overhead. The result is that people frequently believe that their used car is worth at least $350 more than it really is, and insist that they be credited with its retail value as a trade-in. The salesman is then forced to resort to the "highball"—he allows the retail value on the used car and tries to make up the dealer's loss by bargaining for a higher price on the new car.

Once the allowance for the trade-in has been set, three other factors determine the price of a new car: the dealer's wholesale cost, his minimum markup, and whatever additional amount above the minimum the salesman can extract from the customer. The car's "sticker" price—the one pasted on the window—has nothing to do with its actual price.

The sticker price does, however, provide a clue to the dealer's cost. On small cars (such as Ford's Pinto and Chevy's Vega) the sticker price is 17 percent higher than dealer cost, on intermediates (Torino and Chevelle) it is 20 to 21 percent higher, and on full-size and luxury cars 24 to 25 percent higher. The sticker also marks up the dealer's cost of most options—such as radio, air conditioning, or power steering—by 17 to 24 percent.

But what the sticker price does not reveal is the amount of the dealer's own markup—i.e., the gross margin that covers his costs and his profit. It is this figure

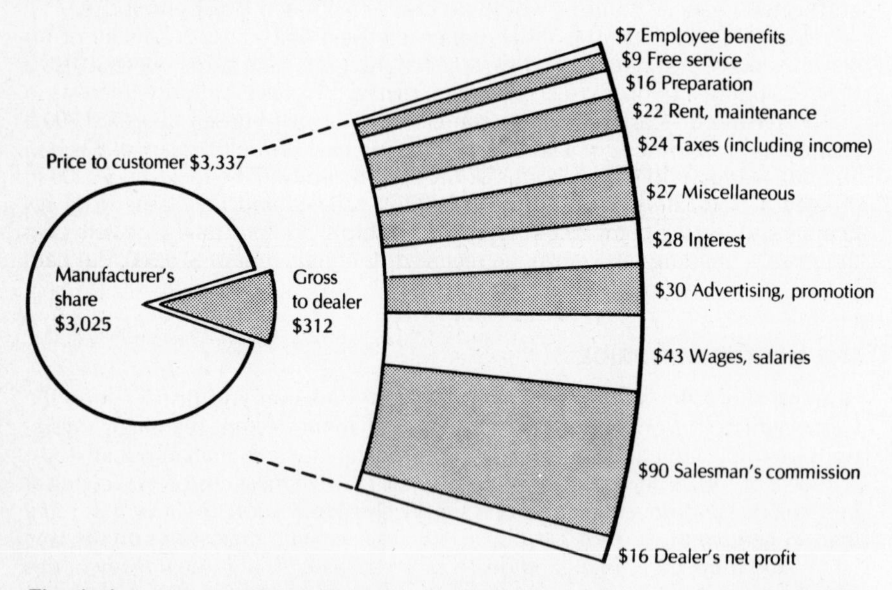


**The dealer gets very little on the money a customer pays for a car. The chart breaks down Sam Marshall's expenses and profit on a typical sale. The buyer pays Marshall $3,337 for a car for which Marshall has paid Ford $3,025. His gross margin, then, averages $312 (which here includes a "holdback" of 2 percent of the wholesale price rebated by Ford to the dealer at year-end, and a $55 service fee).**

**Marshall's biggest expense is the salesman's commissions: 35 percent of the gross margin (less the service fee). Financing his loan on the car while he carries it in stock costs Marshall $28, and he spends $30 on local advertising for every car he sells. After all his expenses, including his own salary and bonus, Marshall's dealership earns a $16 profit on each car. Marshall can double that by arranging financing for the buyer and selling life and disability insurance to go with it.**

that determines his minimum selling price. The margin varies among dealers, among regions (it is highest in California), and even by season (prices tend to be firmer in the autumn when demand for new models is strong).

Marshall's own minimum gross margin is $200, plus a $55 service charge that covers extra expenses such as changing a car's tires or adding power steering to clinch a deal. That $255 is his normal markup—the amount he customarily adds to the factory cost of any car, regardless of its price. The total of his cost and his markup represents the lowest price at which he will sell the car. For example, the typical car costs Marshall about $3,000 wholesale. He will sell that car for no less than $3,255 (plus transportation charges and taxes).

He does have some additional sources of revenue from each car sold, but these are not added to his minimum gross margin or to his selling price. He receives a 2 percent rebate from Ford at the end of the year on each car he has sold during the year. In addition, he gets $25 per car from Ford for pre-delivery service; Marshall counts this sum as a reduction of his service expense and does not include it as part of his gross income from the individual car. Although Marshall's markup remains the same regardless of the cost of a car, the amount he actually realizes will vary because the 2 percent rebate returns more on a large than a small car.

## DETROIT WANTS VOLUME

How much more than his minimum price he receives on any car depends, of course, on the respective bargaining abilities of the salesman and the customer. But his average gross margin of about 9 percent on the actual price of a car is well below the 25 percent or more that is usual for retailers of consumer durable goods. Says Marshall: "Our low margins reflect the manufacturer's constant clamor for volume. But the manufacturer sure as hell gets his, volume or no volume."

When one of Marshall's salesmen agrees on a price with a customer, he takes the contract to Nicholas W. Monda, fifty-six, the vice president and general manager, or to Charles L. Price, thirty-eight, the sales manager, for approval. No salesman is permitted to commit the agency to a deal; each contract must be approved by Monda or Price. The salesman reads off the model and the options the customer has ordered, and the manager, using a list of wholesale prices, "costs out" the car.

After totting up the wholesale cost of the car and the options on an adding machine, Monda or Price adds the dealer's minimum gross of $255, transportation charges (which vary by location and model), and taxes. That is the car's real price. If the customer has agreed to pay more, the dealership will profit. If he has not agreed to pay that much, the agency may reject the deal. If, however, sales are currently running above budget and overhead can be spread over a larger number of units, Monda or Price might agree to shave the minimum gross and accept the deal. In either case, contrary to one of the most common myths about automobiles, the dealership gets no separate markup whatever—and therefore no added profit—on the options.

What counts is the total price. Since the salesman receives a commission on whatever the dealer gets, he has a strong incentive to get all he can from the buyer. Every car salesman has his own story of losing a sale on a $6,000 car because another dealer offered a price $5 or $10 lower. Competition keeps the real price of most cars quite close to their wholesale cost and far below their presumptive list prices.

Financing provides an additional source of profit to the dealer. About two-thirds of all cars are bought on credit, and competition among finance companies for dealers' business is keen. To get business, they pay dealers a "finance reserve" (actually a sales commission or kickback). In much of the country this reserve can be as high as 10 percent of the amount financed—e.g., $300 on a $3,000 financing. Dealers in these areas might then sell cars for close to the wholesale cost and make up their loss through the finance reserve.

## THE CREAM FROM CREDIT

In Ohio, a state law limits the "finance reserve" to 2 percent and the interest rate to 8 percent, discounted in advance. Marshall's current normal interest rate is 6½ percent discounted (i.e:, about 12 percent simple interest). The 2 percent finance reserve brings in $60 on a $3,000 loan. For that sum, Marshall's staff has to handle all the paper work for the loan. But on the half of the sales for which it arranges the financing, the reserve enables Marshall to double his net profit on the entire deal at no additional cost to the buyer. Marshall also offers his customers life and disability insurance covering the amount of their loans. The $80 commission on a $2,000 policy nearly doubles his profit again.

Last year more than half of Marshall's net profit on new-car sales was derived from finance reserves and insurance commissions. Even including those and Ford's 2 percent rebate, however, gross revenues averaged only $350 per car, and the dealership netted only $35 on every new car it sold.

Since many people believe that a dealer's net profit on a car runs well over $100, Marshall's customers are really better bargainers than they think. They are misled mostly by the great gulf between the sticker price and the true price. Rather than filling the buyers with glee, the gap seems instead to leave them anxious, resentful, and feeling somehow *had.* The sticker, says Marshall, is "a phony list price and nothing more than a pure fiction."

He would reduce the sticker price for all models to 15 percent above dealer's cost. That would still leave dealers $100 to $125 of bargaining room above the wholesale price and their average margin. Dealers' profits would not be affected, and buyers might be far more confident that they were paying only a fair and competitive price for their car. "Distrust would go out the window," Marshall believes. "Money differences would no longer be the deciding factor in a purchase; it would be a question of service. Then the best dealers would make the most money."

Detroit, on the other hand, argues that the sticker price is a reasonable ceiling. Ford claims that reducing it would lead to "marketing chaos and customer outrage." In fact, however, the wide gap between the sticker prices and the prices that buyers actually pay is already creating a considerable amount of customer outrage.

The excessive sticker price is also the basis for much of the dubious advertising that confuses the public. Many dealers advertise discounts. "Discounts from what?" asks Marshall—nearly everybody gets a large discount from the sticker price. Some dealers advertise that they will sell anyone a car at "$100 over cost." But "cost" usually adds about $250 to a car's wholesale price, so "$100 over cost" really means $350 more than wholesale—much more than most buyers actually pay. Such advertising, says Marshall, "has done more than any other single factor to destroy the image of the dealer."

## A $5 MISUNDERSTANDING

There is no doubt also that the automobile industry's sales tactics leave a lot to be desired. The manufacturers have made some efforts to weed out the most dishonest dealers, but too many unsavory practices and too much outright thievery still persist. For example, an elderly couple recently came into Marshall's dealership with a tale of woe. They had previously bought their cars at Marshall's but, having little to fill their time, they had decided to shop at other dealers. One salesman took the keys to their car, ostensibly to have the vehicle appraised. The salesman then demanded $5 to return their keys after they declined to sign a blank purchase contract. They paid him and left (and bought a car from Marshall).

Marshall prevents such dishonesty at his store by tough rules and constant admonitions to his employees. By paying well he is able to attract better than average salesmen and hold them to high standards of conduct. Salesmen are guaranteed $8,400 a year against commissions of 35 percent of the dealer's gross (excluding his preparation charge) on every car they sell; the usual commission in the Cleveland area is 25 to 30 percent. The sixteen salesmen average $14,000 a year, and one earns $24,000. Chuck Price, a former radio disk jockey who has been Marshall's sales manager since 1969, monitors the salesmen by scrutinizing contracts and interviewing customers.

## SPIFF MONEY AND PURPLE PINTOS

Price also puts a considerable amount of money and effort into incentives for salesmen. In a typical month he distributes about $4,000 in cash and merchandise. "The salesmen need to be excited," he explains. His most effective incentive is cash, which is disbursed in an astonishing variety of ways. Every month he pays out $1,050 in crisp new bills in what he calls "spiff money"—small cash bonuses for the salesmen.

One regular bonus, paid immediately whenever a salesman sells a car, is based on an improvised game of dice. The salesman rolls, and for every spot that comes up he gets up to $10, depending on the rate that Price has set at random for that day. A recent Thunderbird golf tournament, held on a slow Friday afternoon and open to all salesmen who'd sold a Thunderbird in the previous month, offered a top prize of $175—and dinner on the house for all.

At a recent early-morning sales meeting, Price pointed to an expensive color television set and said, "The man who sells the most [leftover] 1972 cars this month gets one just like it." Then he jolted the salesmen awake. "It's going to be a big day today, so get up off your asses. You might find some money under them." The salesmen leaped up and searched under their chairs to find the $5 and $10 bills that Price had hidden there earlier.

Price also thinks up schemes for motivating the customers to buy from Marshall. Wacky promotions help, and one last year was unusually offbeat. "We got twenty pink and twenty purple Pintos and jammed them all into the showroom," Price says. "The salesmen joked about it, but every customer came in with a smile. That is a nice way to start with a customer."

Such devices counter the feeling most people have that buying a car has become just a periodic chore. John Skinner, who has been a salesman at Marshall's since 1936 and whose customers buy from him year after year, says, "It used to be a big thing to buy a car. People would dress up. The ladies would wear white gloves and the men would have on ties and suits. It isn't like that anymore."

## "WE CAN GET RID OF ALMOST ANYTHING"

Marshall needs to sell 191 new cars a month to break even, and Price usually orders 250 from Ford, including fifteen to twenty for fleet buyers. The average car is in inventory thirty days before it is sold. Quick turnover is important to a dealer; the instant a car leaves the factory, he is billed for it, and must begin paying interest on it. This "floor-plan" interest is one of Marshall's biggest single expenses ($72,000 last year).

The manufacturers all establish a "planning volume," or sales quota, for each dealer, and the dealer is expected to meet it. If he does not order enough cars, the factory may simply send him the cars to fill his quota—a practice that arouses bitter complaints from many dealers. The quotas and unwanted shipments have provided much of the ammunition for the Ford Dealers Alliance, a group constituting about 16 percent of Ford's 5,600 dealers, which seeks to reduce factory control over dealers.

Price is phlegmatic about both quotas and shipments. Ford has just raised Marshall's planning volume by 47 percent, to 2,670 cars next year, but that is 330 cars less than Marshall's internal budget calls for, and Price is confident he can sell them all. As for unwanted cars, he says, "The factory does send us cars we don't want, but they don't load us up. We can get rid of almost anything they give us."

Marshall maintains an inventory of 100 to 120 used cars. lined up in four rows on its lot. The "creampuffs" or "straight cars" (clean-looking cars in good condition) are placed up front and the "budget buggies" and "junkers" are kept in back. Most have been received as trade-ins on new cars, but Mike Tozzi, the used-car manager, also buys cars at auctions and some from other dealers.

Marshall reconditions and resells on its lot about two-thirds of the cars that are accepted as trades—those in the best condition. The other third are sold to wholesalers and will wind up on used-car lots in downtown Cleveland or in the South.

When the dealership accepts a used car as a trade-in, its margin of profit is highly dependent upon Tozzi's appraisal. If he prices it too high, the dealership risks losing money on both the new and used cars. If he makes too low an appraisal, he risks losing the new-car sale to another dealer. In any case, Marshall will not know whether it made a profit on the entire deal until it sells the used car—often weeks after the new car is delivered to the customer. Since the used-car market is highly competitive, profit margins are slim even in the best of times. Last year, on sales of $1,584,000, Marshall's used-car department earned $9,900—an average of only $6 a car.

## TROUBLE IN THE BACK END

Nothing creates more anger among motorists than the difficulty of keeping their cars running properly. The federal Office of Consumer Affairs receives more complaints about servicing problems with automobiles than it gets on any other subject. The primary interest of both manufacturers and dealers is, of course, to sell more cars, and there is considerable evidence that they have, until recently, shown too little concern for keeping them running. Many dealers wish their franchise did not require them to operate a service shop, which they call "the back end." The general manager of a Dodge dealership down the street from Marshall holds a typical view. "We've never been able to break even on the back end," he says, "and if we could operate just in new-car sales we'd jump at the chance."

The operating costs of a service department are enormous. Marshall's back shop occupies more than half the space in his building. A large expense comes from the twelve or so cars taken daily as free "loaners" by customers whose own cars are being repaired. The thirty mechanics in the Ford and Fiat service departments and body shop, all members of the machinists' union, are guaranteed $190 a week; their pay ranges from $11,000 to $18,000 a year. Four service writers check in cars from customers and diagnose their problems. A control tower, staffed by two people, keeps track of all work and makes telephone appointments for service. The parts department, manned by six men, maintains an inventory of 12,000 items with a total value of $150,000. The Fiat branch has its own parts inventory worth $35,000.

## REPAIRS CAN RUIN A DAY

On an average day, a hundred cars are repaired in the service area and body shop. Many are there because of a manufacturer's recall campaign. Marshall recently had three simultaneous recalls going on, involving several thousand cars, and the campaigns are an increasing and unprofitable annoyance. Dealers contend that the manufacturers fail to reimburse them adequately for the considerable overhead involved.

The service department's high overhead, in fact, wipes out the savings from volume and efficiency. All told, Marshall's service, parts, and body-shop operations last year brought in $1,110,000, including $450,000 from parts sales. Marshall lost $10,000 on the business.

Understandably, Marshall insists that the cost of repairs is not excessive. "What the public doesn't realize," he says, "is that by paying a TV repairman $15 for a house call, you absorb the overhead. You supply the heat and the electricity. Yet his hourly charge is more than ours (which is $12.50), and we have to provide facilities, thousands of dollars in parts inventory, and free service loaners—all of this is included in our hourly rate." What people really object to, he thinks, is not the cost but the failure to get the job done right. "You can forget cost but not bad workmanship. That is what disturbs people."

Marshall tries hard to keep his service department's standards high. He pays bonuses to the mechanics who provoke the fewest complaints or "comebacks" (a return visit for the same problem). Two inspectors—inspectors are rarely found in dealers' service departments—check every job and test-drive every car after it has been repaired. Service manager Robert McHugh regularly sends every mechanic in the shop to a service school for refresher courses. Every year, six mechanics are sent to a two-day course in air-conditioner repairs. All the mechanics attend a monthly dinner discussion of general service problems.

In addition to all that, says Marshall, he talks to the mechanics. "I talk about what happens to a frustrated customer. His day can be ruined, it can upset his family. Why? What right do you have to do that? The mechanics will listen."

## CLOUDS OF PUFFERY

Many dealers explain their poor service by saying they are unable to find mechanics. There is a shortage of trained mechanics, largely because the automobile industry, until two years ago, made little effort to attract men to the job or to train them. But McHugh has no trouble finding them. He keeps in touch with the proprietors of local mechanics' schools, and he has more applicants than he can hire. For their part, the mechanics seem to have nothing but praise for Marshall's emphasis on quality. Like everyone else, mechanics do take pride in their work—when they know the management cares. "This is the best shop I ever worked," says Bill Warner, who proudly claims he does all the dirtiest engine repairs.

Faced with mounting consumer outrage, Detroit has recently begun spewing forth clouds of puffery about its efforts to improve service. Chrysler, for example, has appointed a vice president for consumer affairs. American Motors has set up a "buyer protection plan." Ford has created a customer-service division and has been heavily advertising a "no unhappy owners" program.

American Motors' program is much the best. It features free loaner cars for customers whose cars break down and, for $149, a plan that pays all service and repair charges for two years. Ford's new program essentially tells customers who are dissatisfied with a dealer's service to contact Ford's district service representative—who bounces the complaint right back to the dealer. And while the program includes prizes for mechanics who get good grades on customers' questionnaires, it excludes completely the men who prepare new cars for delivery, and are best able to prevent many complaints from arising.

Clearly, the manufacturers' programs are aimed in the wrong direction. They try to alleviate the effects of poor quality after the car has been sold. The manufacturers would do better to make greater efforts to build the cars right in the first place. Detroit has lately been lauding its quality control, but there is little evidence of it in the product.

Joseph Sallay, who began as a mechanic with Marshall in 1933 and is now a service inspector, says that "twenty-five years ago if a customer was given a paint job like today, he'd say 'stick it.' The new cars come in here with everything wrong—the lights every which way, the wheels out of line. We almost have to rebuild them." Sam Marshall makes the same point more delicately: "I believe that a certain percentage of automobiles made today are not put together properly, and this percentage is too high."

The industry's pay structure for mechanics also tends to encourage hasty and careless workmanship. Mechanics are paid according to "flat-rate manuals," which are published by each manufacturer. The manuals list a standard time for the completion of each repair job (e.g., 1.9 hours for a front-end alignment). If a mechanic completes the job in less than the standard time, he is nonetheless paid for the full time. He can begin another job and, in effect, be paid for two jobs at once. If he needs more time, however, he is not paid for it, and the temptation is great to leave the job undone or complete it improperly.

Many of the bitterest customer complaints concern the inadequacy of the manufacturers' warranties—which, incredibly, have been reduced. Faced with soaring warranty costs, the auto makers two years ago cut their guarantees from five years or 50,000 miles on some parts to twelve months or 12,000 miles on the entire car. The public, says Marshall, plainly thinks that twelve months is too short a warranty on an automobile. He absorbs $25,000 a year in customers' repairs that be believes should be—but are not—covered by Ford's warranty. Most dealers will charge their customers for such work, but all dealers have been absorbing a lot of public wrath over service that actually ought to be aimed at the manufacturers.

## KEEP THE CUSTOMERS HAPPY

To discover his customers' attitudes. Marshall some years ago arranged to have a telephone call made to the owners of cars that had been brought in for service. Each interview is taped, transcribed, and sent daily to Marshall. Every complaint is followed up, and most are corrected at Marshall's expense. One woman recently complained of squeaky brakes, even after they had been checked. Marshall sent the report to McHugh, with a note: "Call and discuss her problem (or ours)." When she was called back, the woman said her brakes had stopped squeaking and that she was satisfied with the service.

The surveying is expensive—it costs $10,000 a year—but Marshall thinks it is essential to keep his customers happy. "Voluntary involvement is the only way we can show the public that we are concerned," he says. "Just because we are ignorant of complaints doesn't mean they aren't there. Unless we can satisfy our customers we won't stay in business—and won't deserve to."

Reading 64

# Yes, There is a Best Time to Trade Your Car

**Changing Times**

*By the end of the fifth year, the car has lost about 84% of its original value.*

Whenever you trade in your old car for a new one, there's always someone ready with the upsetting news that you chose the wrong time. Now, finally, here is someone who is qualified and willing to tell you the right time in terms of economical, dependable transportation.

The advice comes from Runzheimer and Co., Inc., a management consultant firm that specializes in business travel expenses for hundreds of major corporations. At the request of *Changing Times,* R. E. Runzheimer Jr., company president, studied the problems of the individual owner, instead of those of large companies, with their fleets of autos, that he normally deals with.

Runzheimer reduced the issue to three principal factors: depreciation; maintenance and repairs; tires. Gas and oil, he feels, are relatively constant provided the car is well maintained. Other costs, such as license plates, insurance and taxes, which do not vary much by car age on a national average, are left out of the equation.

The figuring was done for a fully equipped standard-sized car, a Chevrolet Impala or Ford Galaxie, bought new at a cost of $4,150, about 90% of list price. For typical nonbusiness use Runzheimer estimated 12,000 miles a year. Specific costs for smaller cars would be lower, but the general reasoning still would apply.

The answer he came up with: The best time to trade is early in the fourth year of ownership. Alternately, you can keep the car through five full years. Here are the details:

## DEPRECIATION

This is a major cost, as you can see from the current figures: a 35% drop in value the first year; 17% the second year; 13% the third year and 11% the fourth year. By the end of the fifth year, the car has lost about 84% of its original value.

Because of the new federal laws requiring true mileage on odometers, car dealers can no longer legally set back the mileage on used cars. So even with

Reprinted by permission from *Changing Times*, The Kiplinger Magazine, May 1973, p. 16.

moderate mileage dealers will be dropping allowances further—$75 off for 48,000 miles (four years at 12,000 miles a year) and $100 off for 60,000 miles (five years at 12,000).

## MAINTENANCE AND REPAIRS

Runzheimer assumes that you are not going to encounter any unusual costs, such as the major repair of an automobile transmission. Estimated costs: $42 the first year; $96 the second year; $162 the third year; $226 the fourth year and $251 the fifth year. Beyond that, the averages tell him, costs will rise sharply because of what he refers to as "capricious maintenance"—unexpected and expensive repairs.

## TIRES

These will have to be replaced in the second year, after about 20,000 to 22,000 miles. Provided you choose the same tires—four first-line belted bias plies, which are original equipment on most cars—the cost would be about $160, figuring a discount that you can usually get. If you keep the car through the fourth year, you will have to replace them again. If you decide to keep it through the fifth year, you will have to buy two tires to hold you until you can unload the car.

Taking all these figures into account, the average annual cost comes to $1,032 for four years, $978 for five years. This breaks down to $1,495 in the first year; $962 the second year; $752 the third year; $918 the fourth year; $763 the fifth year.

Naturally, this doesn't consider the extreme cases—the owner whose transmission goes bad at 32,000 miles, or the lucky driver whose car never needs any work. The former is best off unloading that dog and swallowing his loss; the latter may live happily with his car for a long time.

Nor does it involve the somewhat ailing car, shod with cheap tires, that is used as a second or third car in a family. The formula applies to dependable transportation. It also does not include the seldom-driven, exceptionally clean auto.

Beyond this, Runzheimer has four simple money-saving suggestions: Buy a smaller car, if practical, and you'll scale down all your costs; at the start of the fourth year ask your mechanic to predict what your car may need and then decide what to do with it; plan ahead on tires, so you don't trade away too much good rubber. The biggest lesson: Buying brand-new cars is very expensive. Look for a good, clean year-old car with 12,000 miles on it, or a two-year-old with 24,000 miles. They're hard to find, but they hold big savings for you if you do.

Reading 65

# The Tire Swap Game

**Money**

*Before driving out of the showroom, a buyer should be sure that the tires meet the specifications for the car.*

Buying a new car is a gamble; even the most carefully chosen car can turn out to be a lemon for no apparent reason. Sometimes, however, the reason is all too plain. Officials of the National Highway Traffic Safety Administration, part of the Department of Transportation, say they have "numerous" reports that dealers have wittingly or unwittingly delivered cars with the original tires replaced by others that are undersized and unsafe. Tires that do not conform to safety standards can fail prematurely, causing dangerous blowouts. The buyer who requests special tires—steel-belted radials, for example, when they are not standard equipment—is particularly subject to being stuck with undersized tires.

A dealer caught selling a new car with tires that do not meet federal safety standards is subject to a fine whether the offense was intentional or not. But unless the dealer inadvertently put on the wrong tires and will replace them voluntarily, the buyer's only remedy is to prove to Traffic Safety Administration investigators that the car dealer supplied him with undersized equipment. That can be difficult if the bill of sale is missing or incomplete.

Before driving out of the showroom, a buyer should make sure that the tires meet the specifications for the car. If he has ordered the car with standard-equipment tires, he can simply check the numbers on the tire walls against those given in the owner's manual. If he has ordered special tires, however, the numbers may be different. In that case, he can compare the gross vehicle weight rating of the car, given in the owner's manual, with the total load capacity of all four tires—the sum of the capacity numbers marked on the sidewall of each tire. The gross vehicle weight rating should never be greater than the tires' maximum load-carrying capacity.

From *Money*, July 1973, p. 18.

**Reading 66**

# Consumer Protection for Used Auto Purchasers

**Oakland California Tribune**

*Minimum performance guarantees would be offered for each grade of automobile.*

There is little question but that the buying public in America today is flexing its muscles as never before. The old axiom "let the buyer beware" is rapidly giving way instead to one of "let the seller beware."

The public is insisting upon product quality and when it isn't forthcoming it is demanding protective legislation cracking down on the industries involved.

One problem is that the pendulum, on occasion, may swing too far. Overzealous consumerism can result in the imposition of quality standards which are so unrealistic that a particular business or industry can no longer function profitably.

The answer usually is agreeing upon a set of consumer standards which both the consumers and the affected industry can live with.

Just such an agreement seems to be in the works for protecting future purchasers of used cars in California. The unsophisticated used car buyer, short on mechanical expertise, has in the past had a most difficult time discerning whether he was buying a well-running, properly maintained trade-in or simply "someone else's troubles." He had little more to rely upon than a salesman's assurances.

Regulatory legislation has been under consideration in Sacramento for several years now. But most of the bills went too far, prohibiting a dealer from selling a mechanically unsound used car even if the purchaser was aware of the defects and was willing to undertake repairs himself.

Now, however, a joint government-industry panel has agreed upon tentative legislation which would offer adequate protections to both car buyers and sellers.

Under the proposal, all cars offered for sale would be graded by the dealers themselves—given either an "A," "B," "C," or "D" rating. Minimum performance guarantees would be offered for each grade of automobile.

For instance, an "A" grade would mean the car is unconditionally guaranteed for 30 days or 1,000 miles. The power train—engine, transmission and rear axle—would carry an additional 60 day or 2,000 mile warranty. A "B" car would carry a 30 day unconditional guarantee with no additional power train coverage. A "C" graded car would have a 30 day or 1,000 mile power train warranty only and a "D" car would be sold "as is," with no guarantees.

Obviously, prices would run in accordance with the guarantees offered. The buyer would have a more reliable means than simply kicking a tire of evaluating a contemplated used car purchase.

The proposed legislation would seem to serve the purposes of both the consumers and dealers. It has been deemed acceptable by the Independent Auto Dealers Association of California. The measure should get early attention when the legislature convenes next year.

From *Oakland California Tribune*, Dec. 18, 1972.

## Reading 67

# PSU Study Reveals Discrepancy in Car Repair Service

**Ellen Emry**

*"At four places mechanics took my wife for a 'test ride' before they gave her an estimate, but not one took ME for a ride."*

Girls, if you don't know the engine from the carburetor, you'd better learn.

That's the advice of Ron Peninger, a senior at Portland State University, who claims women pay more than men for car repairs. And Jim Foglio, another PSU senior, backs him up.

Both men have completed studies which suggest a woman can save herself money be sending a man to the garage when her car is out of joint. The investigations were made for a business course, Urban Consumerism, conducted at PSU by Prof. Jack Taylor Jr.

Ron got the idea for his study last summer when his own car was in need of repair. After taking it apart to detect the problem—a chipped tooth in one of the gears—Ron put the pieces back together so he and wife Carol could get diagnoses and cost estimates from local garages.

Both selected eight shops each, including new car dealerships, medium-sized garages and small garages. At every shop Ron or Carol complained of a "clunking sound," then asked for the lowest and highest repair cost figures.

Price estimates ranged from $22 to $250, the lowest at a small garage and the highest at one of the dealerships. Ron later made the repairs himself after buying a new part for $18.

Computing the cost figures, Ron discovered Carol was quoted estimates averaging more than 23 per cent higher than his. And even though labor was a fixed cost rather than an estimate, quoted prices for labor alone were almost 12 per cent higher for Carol than Ron.

Ron smiled as he commented, "At four places mechanics took my wife for a 'test ride' before they gave her an estimate, but not one took ME for a ride."

Jim Foglio and his wife Jane recently completed a similar study, this one concentrated in the Model Cities area of northeast Portland. Each drove into eight different shops, asking for a cost estimate on a 15,000 mile tune-up replacing spark plugs, points and condenser and setting the timing. Jane received written estimates averaging 17 per cent higher than her husband's. In addition, while none of the garages tried to sell Jim any extra product or service, three garages told his wife she needed such items as a distributor cap, rotor, coil, spark plug wires, or cleaning and adjustment of the carburetor.

"That was even after I stated specifically what repairs I wanted done," Jane emphasized. "And not one place listened to the engine or lifted the hood."

"If I were a single girl," her husband suggested, "I'd take my car to a diagnostic shop first, then check three or four garages for estimates. Before I took the lowest one, I'd call the Better Business Bureau to find out if they'd received any complaints about that shop."

Ron's suggestion for single girls was brief—"I'd find out something about the car—or find a man!"

From *The Oregonion*, Dec. 10, 1971, Sec. 2, p. 1.

Both studies reveal, however, that not only women but men too are victims of arbitrary pricing. Ron checked figures at two locations—Beaverton and north Portland—of a garage under the same franchise. The cost estimate for repairs and labor was $30 higher at the West Side outlet.

"The only thing that stops garages from installing unneeded parts is their integrity," said Ron.

"Even when the garage owners intend to do a good job, they can't control the apathy or dishonesty of their employes. Most work on a standard rate plus commission, which encourages them to do fast rather than thorough work. The type of compensation may be part of the problem."

Both students noted that many garages make profits from selling the car parts, charging list prices when parts stores may offer discount prices. "Spark plugs sell for 89 cents at the variety store, but the garage may mark them up to $1.25," Jim said. "And most places won't offer the service unless the customer buys parts there too."

Prof. Taylor pointed out the limitations of both studies. "We didn't have the money to get the hard evidence. But the studies aren't over—I hope to have $1,000 next year to actually get repairs done."

Taylor agreed with students Ron and Jim that such studies must go beyond indicating the problem to show the cause and suggest a cure. Ron thinks state and federal legislation may be needed. With the passage of the Consumer Protection Law last July, television repairmen must now be licensed, and mechanics may face similar controls in the future.

Jim wondered about state-run diagnostic centers, where customers could be assured of accurate estimates before taking their cars in garages for repair. "Garages should be inspected for proper equipment, too. Some shops substitute screwdrivers and wrenches for fancy equipment because installation of electronic devices for repair involves a major capital investment."

**Reading 68**

# How to Buy Tires Today

**Changing Times**

*Your choice of tire types should depend on two points: The amount of mileage you will put on the car before you sell it and the kind of driving you'll be doing.*

When federal tire-quality grading standards go into effect in 1974, some of the worry over buying the right tires should lift from your shoulders. You will at least have a base point from which you can judge.

The standards are concerned with three vital factors: traction, tread life and high-speed performance. All tires will be graded against "average" models, special tires designed by the government just for this purpose.

The grade of each tire will be imprinted on the sidewall so that you can tell easily whether the tires you are looking at will perform above or below the level

Reprinted by permission from *Changing Times*, The Kiplinger Magazine, April 1973, pp. 21–23.

of the "average" tires. That will be helpful. But it will not tell you some equally vital facts about which tires, regardless of their grade, will suit your comfort, your car and your driving needs. To arrive at the proper decision, then as now, you will need more information about the different kinds of tires, what goes into them and what they can or cannot do for you.

## DIFFERENT TIRES FOR DIFFERENT JOBS

Except for fancy sidewall designs, all tires look pretty much alike. Yet three completely different types are widely available, covering a broad range of prices and performance.

### Bias Ply

These were the standard tires for many years. As the illustration on the next page shows, the carcass of the tire is formed by crossing the plies, or layers, of fabric at an angle, commonly 35° to 36° in most passenger tires. The construction is relatively simple. This means that you can buy them fairly cheaply and be assured of having a type that has proved its worth over the years.

The fabric itself is important, too. Polyester has largely replaced rayon and is used in a huge number of tires today. It is stronger than rayon and is not affected by moisture or oils. Because polyester is being used in such volume, the price is low, which means you can buy tires made of this material at reasonable cost.

Nylon, once used only in expensive tires, is produced today in such quantity that tires made of it can be among the best buys around. It has the greatest tensile strength of the three fabrics, yet it has plenty of stretch, which gives a comfortable ride. Tires of this material do take on temporary flat spots when left standing overnight, so you must get accustomed to a mild thumping noise until the tires warm with a few miles of driving.

### Belted Bias Ply

This is the tire that has replaced the bias-ply tire as original equipment on most new cars. The switch was made for two good reasons: They last longer than conventional bias plies, and they stick to the road better on corners and during braking. As the illustration on the next page shows, this tire starts with a normal bias-ply construction and then has a belt of fabric added around its circumference. The belt is what makes the tire better. It holds the tread firm, keeping it from squirming and wearing itself out on the pavement as you drive. This also aids traction. However, the belts do tend to give a firmer ride over rough city streets.

The plies of most such tires these days are made of polyester because it is economical and easy to work with. Nylon gives a slightly softer ride, according to tire engineers, but nylon belted tires are harder to make because nylon is easily stretched and the belt material is not.

The belts may be made of rayon, fiber glass or steel strands coated with brass. All are effective. Rayon is the easiest to work with and so tires with rayon belts are usually the cheapest to buy. Fiber glass belts are the standard today, and—after some early problems were overcome—have proved effective and durable. Steel wire belts are the newest design feature. Steel has the lowest stretch of all and so keeps the tread the firmest as well as the most resistant to road damage. But it is expensive to buy and produce, so tires with steel belts cost more than the others.

On the horizon is a new belt fabric called Fiber B, developed by DuPont.

Engineers say that it is not only durable but five or six times stronger than steel by weight. Despite its strength, it is flexible and therefore is said to give a soft ride. You may hear a good deal about it in the future.

### Radial

Radial tires are not just different; they offer some significant advantages. The illustration shows how different the construction is. The fabric for the body of the tire is laid on from bead to bead (the edge of the tire that fits against the wheel). A belt is laid around the circumference. Radials work even better than belted bias plies. Mileage in the 40,000 to 50,000 range isn't unusual, and there is so little rolling resistance on the highway that drivers usually find their gasoline mileage improves. On curves, where other tires tip a bit so that some tread contact with the road is lost, the sidewalls of these bulge sideways but the tread stays firmly planted. Many are made of polyester with steel belts. Others are of rayon and steel or rayon and rayon. They have three principal drawbacks: Some people find that the low-speed ride is harsh, although it is exceptionally smooth at 50 mph or above; the tires do not resist sidewall bruising as well as bias or belted bias plies; and they are more expensive than other kinds.

## THE TIRES YOU'LL NEED

You may think of buying tires only when you need replacements. But the first time you actually buy them for a car is when you order the machine from the dealer. The least expensive cars usually are offered with bias-ply tires as standard. You can order either belted bias plies or radials at additional cost. Belted bias plies are generally standard on medium-priced cars, with radials as an option. You will see radials as standard equipment on a number of higher-priced cars from Detroit this year. (They have been on some European cars for years.) Sometimes you can make a better deal on the tires through a tire dealer, rather than the car dealer, by swapping the tires from your new car and paying some extra cash.

Your choice of tire types should depend on two points: The amount of mileage you will put on the car before you sell it and the kind of driving you'll be doing.

### Low Mileage, Low Speed

Unless you plan to drive a lot, radials are an expensive luxury. Cars used primarily for commuting or suburban shopping can do with far less—bias-ply tires for subcompacts and some of the lighter compact cars and belted bias plies for

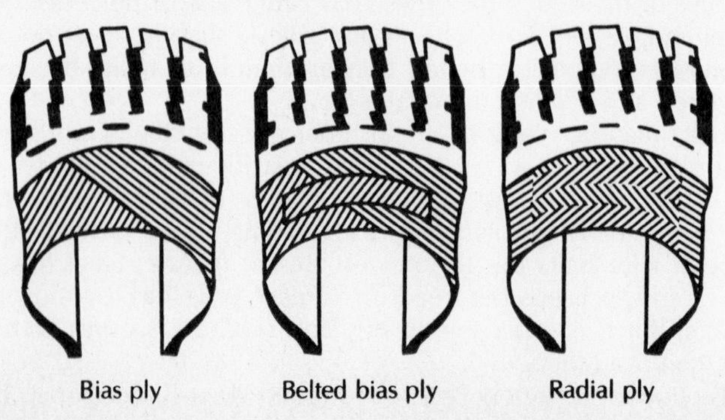

most intermediate-sized models. Low-speed driving and the typical low mileage in such use don't wear them out very fast.

### High Mileage, High Speed

For a car that you are going to keep a long time, 50,000 miles or more, or one in which you'll be doing a great deal of high-speed driving, it's best to start with tires at least one grade better than original equipment. You'll pay more, but the extra wear should more than compensate for the additional expense.

## REPLACING WORN TREADS

All tires now have "wear bars" molded into the tread. When there is less than 1/16 of an inch of tread left, the bars appear as a solid band going across the tire.

### Who Really Makes It?

**You can identify the manufacturer of any tire sold in this country through the first two code letters following "DOT" imprinted on the sidewall. If you prefer one brand over another, the list below will help you sort them out. Bear in mind, however, that many private-label tires are made to the specifications of the retailers and are not necessarily the same as those the manufacturer sells under his own name.**

|  |  |
|---|---|
| Armstrong | CE, CF, CH, CV |
| Cooper | UP, UT |
| Dayton | HX, HY |
| Denman | DY |
| Dunlop | DA, DB, DC, DD, DE, DF, DH, DJ, DK, DL, DM, DN, DP, DU |
| Firestone | VA, VB, VC, VD, VE, VF, VH, VJ, VK, VL, VM, VN, VP, VT, VV, VW, VX, VY, WA, WB, WC, WD, WF, WH, WJ |
| Gates | BW, BX, BY |
| General | AA, AB, AC, AD, AE, AF, AH |
| B. F. Goodrich | BA, BB, BC, BD, BF, BH, BJ, BK, BL, BM, BN, BP |
| Goodyear | MA, MB, MC, MD, ME, MF, MH, MJ, MK, ML, MM, MN, MP, MT, MU, MV, MW, MX, MY, NA, NB, NC, ND, NE, NF, NH, NJ, NK, NL, NM, NN, NP, NT, NU, NV, NW, NX, NY, PA, PB, PC, PD, PE, PF |
| Lee | JA, JB, JC, JD, JE, JF, JH, JJ, JK, JL, JM, JN, JP, JT, JU, JV, JW, JX, JY, KA, KB, KC, KD, KE, KF, KH, KJ, KK, KL, KM, KN, KP, KT, KU, KV, KW, KX, KY, LA, LB, LC, LD, LE, LF |
| Mansfield | WL |
| McCreary | CY |
| Michelin | FF, FH, FJ, FK, FL, FM, FN, FP, FT, FU, FV, FW, FX, FY, HA, HB, HC, HD, HE, HF, HH, HJ, HK, HL, HM, HN, HP |
| Mohawk | CA, CB, CC |
| Pennsylvania | WK |
| Seiberling | AV |
| Uniroyal | AJ, AK, AL, AM, AN, AP, AU, LH, LJ, LK, LL, LM, LN, LP, LT, LU |

When the bars show in two or more adjacent grooves, it is time to replace the tire. At this stage they hydroplane more easily on wet roads and puncture and skid more readily.

If you need just one tire, you should buy the same size and type that is on your car now. A different size could create dangerous handling problems. The new tire, along with the best of the old ones, should then be mounted on the rear axle on conventional rear-wheel-drive cars. All responsible authorities—including the federal government, industry groups and the major manufacturers—now say that this is the best place to put the best tires. Failures at the rear wheels cause greater problems and more severe accidents.

If you need two tires—which is the way a majority of people buy replacements today—you have some choice. You can, for example, begin the switch from bias plies to belted bias plies. The belted tires should be put on the rear axle to minimize any handling problems. You should check the sizes against the charts that every tire dealer has to make sure that those you pick are compatible with the ones already on the car. If you switch to radials, you must put them on all four wheels. Using only two radials is dangerous.

If you need four tires, you should simply decide how much mileage and traction you want and buy accordingly. And when you buy four, you often can make an excellent deal with only a little bargaining.

## THE PRICE YOU PAY

All tires sold in this country must pass five basic government tests—high speed, endurance, strength, bead unseating, physical dimensions—and must have certain required labeling. All can be considered safe, but that doesn't mean they are equal in performance.

Among the five major U.S. manufacturers—Firestone, General, Goodrich, Goodyear and Uniroyal—the tire-for-tire differences are generally small. But put them together with their subsidiaries, the independent companies and the huge number of private-label brands and you have a tremendous range of price and quality. Price differences are obvious between a basic bias-ply tire and a radial, which takes far more labor and material. The differences between two tires of the same type can be subtle. One that is substantially cheaper probably has less tread, and the compound from which it is made probably contains less expensive ingredients.

While there are plenty of bargains, particularly at sales where you must buy two or more tires, you basically get what you pay for. No matter what a salesman may try to tell you, few if any inexpensive tires will wear or perform as well as higher-priced ones. Don't forget that the guarantee is part of what you are paying for. You should understand its provisions. Mileage, for example, is usually on a pro rata basis. So if your 40,000-mile tire wears out after 30,000 miles, you are given a credit for 10,000 miles toward the purchase of a new tire.

Before you leave the store, make sure that the seller registers your name and address against the serial numbers on your new tires. That way the manufacturer can get in touch with you if a hidden flaw is discovered.

Reading 69

# Auto Insurance: The Road to Reform

**Consumer Reports**

*The time has come for consumers to unite in a crusade for auto-insurance reform.*

Automobile insurance is by now probably the most thoroughly studied of all consumer problems. The verdict of investigators from the insurance industry, government, the legal profession and consumer groups is unanimous. Something must be done to make insurance do a better job of paying the cost of highway injuries. Something must be done to stop the runaway price of insurance. Something must be done to make sure the right kind of insurance is available to every car owner, and at a fair price.

The time has come for consumers to unite in a crusade for auto-insurance reform. Everyone else is getting into the act. The three major auto-insurance industry trade groups are sponsoring plans. Even the American Trial Lawyers Association, traditional foe of any change that might detract from the fees its members earn by representing accident victims, has drafted legislation in the name of reform. Actually, it's a last-ditch effort to patch up the present liability-insurance system.

Reform is already under way in Puerto Rico, where a government-run plan insures every accident victim for his full medical expenses and a modest amount of wages while he's disabled. Massachusetts inaugurated this year a compulsory medical and wage-loss policy and eliminated most liability claims for less than $2000 of injury expenses.

Many states are now debating reforms based on three pioneering plans: The Keeton-O'Connell Plan, the American Insurance Association Plan (developed by one group of insurance companies), and the New York State Plan. All three would de-emphasize the role played by liability insurance, and the AIA Plan would do away with it entirely. Legislation patterned on the AIA Plan has a good chance of adoption this year in Minnesota.

Meanwhile, Senator Philip A. Hart has introduced in Congress a bill that would require every state to adopt a uniform kind of automobile insurance embodying principal features of the three preceding plans and some additional features contributed by the Senator himself. The Hart Plan contains much that consumers can support, although some important details remain to be worked out. Still awaited (as this issue goes to press) is the recommendation for insurance reform being developed by the Secretary of Transportation as the product of a study ordered by Congress.

There is no single, perfect plan. Some students of the problem even doubt that the system of privately sold insurance can be salvaged. They look toward government insurance. Certainly, the problem is made less critical by state-administered health-insurance and medical-care plans in those countries that have them. Then, at least, there is never a question of availability of medical care for all victims regardless of ability to pay and regardless of whether they are victims of automobile accidents, other accidents or illness.

CU believes that this country's automobile insurance should be revamped with a view to the universal health insurance that appears to be somewhere on

From *Consumer Reports*, April 1971, pp. 223–226.

the horizon. With that in mind, we present on page 261 a 14-point set of objectives that we think are required in a reform designed in the best interests of consumers as policyholders and as claimants.

To place those objectives in an understandable framework, let's first take a look at what's gone wrong with the present system.

At issue is liability insurance and the legal doctrine that makes it necessary. The law says a motorist whose bad driving kills or injures someone or damages his property must pay for the damage. Bad driving, the law says, includes not only recklessness but also carelessness. Almost everybody makes mistakes behind the wheel, and sometimes mistakes cause accidents costing many thousands of dollars in medical bills and lost wages. Liability insurance is designed to protect the financial assets of car owners from those possibly overwhelming obligations to people they may injure. The insurance company pays what its policyholder would otherwise have to pay his victims.

Society invents laws for a purpose. One idea behind liability law is to deter people from carelessly hurting other people. Automobile insurance, though, relieves individual motorists of heavy financial penalty by spreading the risk among all insured motorists. Little or no financial risk means little or no deterrent to carelessness. But the liability doctrine of deterrence wasn't very sound anyway. The instinct for survival is doubtless a far stronger incentive to safe driving.

The main social purpose of liability law is to see that innocent victims are paid their losses. Hence, every state either compels or puts heavy pressure on car owners to buy automobile insurance. One of the intolerable things about it is that the system works out unfairly. People with minor losses tend to be overpaid, while people with severe losses are likely to be underpaid. Here are some things a Department of Transportation study found out about seriously injured traffic victims who collected on liability-insurance claims:

People who suffered less than $500 injury costs collected an average of four times their losses.

People who suffered from $10,000 to $25,000 injury costs collected an average of half their losses.

People who suffered more than $25,000 injury costs collected an average of only about 15 per cent of their losses.

The study counted only the kinds of costs that took money from the victims' pockets; it made no estimate of the costs of pain and suffering. Insurance payments were measured after subtracting lawyers' fees, which cost victims an average of 25 per cent of their benefits.

Only about 45 per cent of seriously injured people in auto accidents collect any money from liability insurance. There is obviously no such right of payment for victims of one-car accidents or for those whose careless driving led to their own injury. Most state laws call for no liability payment if both drivers made mistakes. There is no auto-insurance liability payment, either, where no one is to blame for the accident or where a defective car or a defective highway is to blame. There is many a crash that embroils its victims in deadlocked argument over who was to blame.

Other kinds of insurance help to fill the gap in accident expenses left when there is no liability claim or when liability insurance underpays. But the Department of Transportation study found again that those most severely hurt are often left in financial straits. When a highway accident takes more than $10,000 from the victim's pocket, only three victims in 10 recover more than half their losses—and that's counting payments from sick-leave plans, social security, collision coverage and so forth.

## RISING PREMIUMS

The steeply rising cost of automobile insurance makes the poor delivery of its benefits all the more deplorable. In the 10 years to 1970, Senator Hart has noted, premiums went up faster than even the soaring cost of car repairs and medical care.

Automobile liability insurance fails to put the money where it's most needed. About 56 cents of every dollar spent on liability insurance pays for insurance-company expenses and lawyers' fees. Half the remaining 44 cents pays claims for pain and suffering, as opposed to actual out-of-pocket expenses. An additional 8 cents pays for expenses already covered by other kinds of insurance. That leaves about 14 cents to pay for medical costs and lost wages that otherwise would not be recovered by the victim.

In short, what has come to be called the fault system of auto insurance has broken down; yet law and public policy force almost all car owners to buy fault insurance from private companies. Besides misdirecting consumer expenditures, the fault system puts a heavy and costly burden on the time and facilities of the civil courts. Those who must pursue their claims in court sometimes wait as long as five years for a verdict, and the average claim takes 16 months to settle. The delay and uncertainty of liability-insurance benefits throws part of the medical cost of auto accidents on the shoulders of the general public through higher taxes and higher hospital bills.

Worst off are the victims. The Department of Transportation study translated hardship into numbers. When serious injury occurs on the highway, 5 per cent of the stricken households have to send other members of the family out to work; 3 per cent have to move to cheaper housing; 20 per cent have to take money from savings or the sale of property; 12 per cent miss debt payments.

---

## THE GOALS OF AUTO-INSURANCE REFORM

*In CU's view, the following 14 objectives should be met by any reform plan.*

**1** Medical care. All people injured in car accidents should receive, at first mainly from private insurance but soon, we hope, from a Federal health plan, the expenses of complete medical care, including rehabilitation. Automobile medical-insurance benefits, like other medical insurance, should be paid to all who are hurt, regardless of who caused the accident, including drunk drivers and drugged drivers. Such people must be kept from driving. But depriving them of medical care won't keep them off the road; it will only visit hardships upon their families.

*Do the major reform plans meet this objective?*

*Keeton-O'Connell Plan*—No, it limits no-fault benefits to $10,000 per person.
*American Insurance Association Plan*—Yes.
*New York State Plan*—Yes.
*Hart Plan*—Yes.

**2** Wage replacement. All disabled victims who cannot work should receive the equivalent of their take-home pay, their earning capacity if they are students or unemployed, or their services to their families—all such payments to be limited to an amount adequate to sustain a decent standard of living in their community. No one should receive more money than he was taking home before being injured, however. Social security pays some wage loss already to disabled persons. It should be expanded to do the full job.

*Do the major reform plans meet this objective?*

*Keeton-O'Connell Plan*—No, it limits wage replacement to $750 per month and counts that as part of the $10,000 maximum no-fault benefits.

*American Insurance Association Plan*—No, it limits wage replacement to $750 per month but does pay it indefinitely.

*New York State Plan*—Yes, it goes beyond the objective by paying unlimited wage losses.

*Hart Plan*—No, it limits wage replacement to a total of $30,000 but does provide up to $1000 per month, enough for an adequate living standard at present price levels.

**3** Periodic payment. Auto-accident-insurance benefits should be paid to victims month by month as expenses and wage lossess occur.

*Do the major reform plans meet this objective?* Yes.

**4** Other insurance. Auto insurance should take care of paying only what less-costly insurance plans do not cover. Most plans, including social security, group hospital and medical policies, Blue Cross, and individual health policies now return a far larger percentage of the premium to the policyholders than auto insurance does.

*Do the major reform plans meet this objective?*

*Keeton-O'Connell Plan*—Partly. Though it does away with duplicate payments for the same loss, it might leave automobile insurance as the primary source of benefits, at least until there is a government health-insurance system.

*American Insurance Association Plan*—No. Same as Keeton-O'Connell.

*New York State Plan*—Yes.

*Hart Plan*—Yes.

**5** Group auto policies. State laws and administrative rules obstructing the sale of group automobile insurance should be overruled by Federal law. Many states have been persuaded by auto-insurance agents to hamper group sales and such mass-marketing devices as insurance for a company's employees on the payroll-deduction plan.

*Do the major reform plans meet this objective?*

*Keeton-O'Connell Plan*—No. But the plan itself would encourage group selling.

*American Insurance Association Plan*—No. Same as Keeton-O'Connell.

*New York State Plan*—Yes, in that New York has no law against group insurance.

*Hart Plan*—Yes.

**6** Cancellation. Auto-insurance policies must be noncancelable, guaranteed renewable, and available in the open market to all eligible consumers. Everyone licensed to drive or able to register a car should be eligible as long as he pays the premiums. The situation now is that 14 per cent of motorists have had their insurance canceled, and when one company cancels, others tend not to accept you. From 8 to 10 per cent of car owners must now buy through assigned-risk plans because no company will deal with them voluntarily; yet an eight-state analysis of assigned-risk policyholders found that 53 per cent of them has had no accidents or convictions for traffic violations. The price of being an assigned risk is very high—sometimes double the standard rate. In most states the most insurance you can buy as an assigned risk is the minimum liability coverage required by the state.

*Do the major reform plans meet this objective?*

*Keeton-O'Connell Plan*—No.
*American Insurance Association Plan*—No.
*New York State Plan*—No.
*Hart Plan*—Yes.

**7** Pain and suffering. The number of claims for pain and suffering should be greatly curtailed, leaving only the most serious ones. Most such claims today are paid to victims of minor injuries rather than to the seriously hurt. The average person with medical expenses of less than $100 and with a lawyer to press his claim receives six times his loss. With the elimination of petty claims for pain and suffering, the insurance system might be able to pay, in addition to out-of-pocket losses, at least some compensation to seriously disfigured and permanently disabled victims. Preferably, every such victim should be paid. If that makes insurance too costly, it may be necessary to preserve his right to sue a negligent driver.

*Do the major reform plans meet this objective?*

*Keeton-O'Connell Plan*—Yes, by means of a $5000-deductible liability claim against a faulty driver.
*American Insurance Association Plan*—No.
*New York State Plan*—No.
*Hart Plan*—Yes, by means of a liability claim against a faulty driver for permanent disability and disfigurement.

**8** Property damage. Damage done by automobiles to property other than automobiles should be repaired with money from the car-owner's automobile insurance even if the accident was not his fault.

*Do the major reform plans meet this objective?*

Yes, except that the Hart Plan makes such coverage optional.

**9** Compulsory coverage. Every car owner should have to carry the basic no-fault automobile insurance. Companies could offer all kinds of optional extra coverages: higher benefits for pain and suffering, higher wage benefits, etc.

*Do the major reform plans meet this objective?* Yes.

**10** Automobile damage. The consumer should have three choices of automobile damage insurance: 1) no collision insurance, 2) today's type of collision insurance, which pays for damage regardless of fault, 3) insurance that pays damage done to his car if the driver of another car caused the accident. The third choice should be offered in fairness to owners of cars with too little value to merit full collision insurance. Collision premium rates should be scaled, as some companies scale them now, to encourage construction of damage-resistant cars. Fire, theft and comprehensive insurance should be optional, as now.

*Do the major reform plans meet this objective?*

*Keeton-O'Connell Plan*—Yes, it originated the three-choice idea.

*American Insurance Association Plan*—No. It offers full collision insurance or nothing.

*New York State Plan*—No. Same as AIA.

*Hart Plan*—No. Same as AIA. But this is the only plan that would require premiums based on damageability of the car.

**11** Premium rates. They must be held down and, if possible, reduced. A system that pays benefits without attempting to establish blame can redirect to premium savings or improved benefits at least 25 per cent of the cost of today's liability insurance. Elimination of automobile-insurance payments for losses already covered by cheaper insurance will cut the premium further. Elimination of pain-and-suffering claims for minor injuries will cut costs even more.

*Do the major reform plans meet this objective?* Yes, all claim to. But there is disagreement on the savings. The Keeton-O'Connell Plan puts a $10,000 limit on no-fault medical and wage benefits because its actuary could not otherwise foresee reduced premiums.

**12** Price comparisons. The driver-rating system should be standardized. A person's age, sex, where he lives, the car he drives, and how much he uses his car do appear to have a real bearing on his chances of having an accident. With no-fault insurance, companies should also design their rates around the size of the family, its other insurance and its income—in other words, those factors that would determine compensation in the event of an injury-causing accident. The important thing is for each company to use the same rating standards, including identical geographic rate zones. Companies should compete on the basic price from which all rates would be figured by percentage increases or decreases. Shoppers would then find it relatively easy to compare prices.

*Do the major reform plans meet this objective?*

*Keeton-O'Connell Plan*—No.

*American Insurance Association Plan*—No.

*New York State Plan*—No.

*Hart Plan*—Yes. It originated the idea.

**13** Claims service. Insurance companies should report regularly to a Government agency their claims-paying practices, and the agency should publish data indicating how well each company satisfies its claims. CU's recent survey of claims experiences showed significant differences in the way companies handled their claims (CONSUMER REPORTS, June 1970). Full knowledge of the quality of a company's service is essential to the consumer's rational choice of a company.

*Do the major reform plans meet this objective?*

*Keeton-O'Connell Plan*—No.

*American Insurance Association Plan*—No.

*New York State Plan*—No.

*Hart Plan*—Yes. It originated the idea.

**14** Industry regulation. Automobile insurance should be regulated by a Federal agency instead of by each individual state. It would be appropriate for the motoring public to finance the agency with a tax on insurance policies. Present law exempting insurance companies from the antitrust laws should be repealed. Prices should be regulated by the market under surveillance of the new Federal agency. Few states can hire the professional staffs needed to cope with their regulatory obligations. A single Federal agency could afford highly competent attorneys, accountants and actuaries and could use their services efficiently in the public interest. The American population is mobile. It travels on interstate highways, and it changes residence frequently from state to state. Americans need uniform motor-vehicle laws and uniform automobile insurance.

*Do the major reform plans meet this objective?*

*Keeton-O'Connell Plan*—No.
*American Insurance Association Plan*—Does not specify.
*New York State Plan*—No.
*Hart Plan*—No. Insurance regulation would remain with the states in consultation with a Federal administrator.

Reading 70

# Highway Robbery

**Time**

*If their persuasive salesmanship fails, they sometimes tack on unauthorized replacement orders.*

- When Mrs. James Hogsed drove into a service station in Georgia, an attendant pushed the front of her car, told her that she had a bad shock absorber and that "if I had to stop suddenly, I might break a tie rod." She paid $29.90 for a new shock absorber, plus $5 for labor. Later, her father-in-law, a mechanic, inspected the old shock and told her that it was not only in perfect condition but that she had paid twice what she should have for the unneeded replacement.
- Reporters from the *Wall Street Journal* had a defective rotor installed in an otherwise perfect car and took the car to several Dallas auto repair shops. The one mechanic who fixed only the rotor charged $1. Six others made unnecessary repairs, one charging $54.60 for his services. Two other mechanics wanted the car left for even more expensive repairs, and one suggested a $130 valve job.

These examples of auto repair swindles have a familiar ring to most Americans. They are typical of the many detailed by Attorney Donald A. Randall and Journalist Arthur P. Glickman in their new book *The Great American Auto Repair Robbery*, which will be published later this month by Charterhouse Books Inc. As the authors describe it, the auto repair industry is fraught with deceit at every level, from gas station attendants who surreptitiously puncture tires with a screwdriver to insurance estimators who take kickbacks from body shops to steer business their way. In a modern version of highway robbery, the authors contend, the owners of the 90 million registered automobiles in the U.S. are bilked out of $8 billion to $10 billion a year—or about $1 of every $3 that they spend to keep their cars running.

Randall, especially, knows whereof he writes: he was director of a four-year investigation of the auto repair racket for the U.S. Senate Subcommittee on Antitrust and Monopoly. In that position he discovered that auto mechanics are, as often as not, incompetent hacks. None of the 50 states requires that automobile mechanics be licensed, says Randall, although "persons engaged in less life-and-death-related professions such as beauticians, barbers, and real estate agents generally must pass proficiency tests and be licensed in order to practice their trades."

The authors even have a word of caution about the professional-looking service managers who greet drivers at the entrance to the service department of auto dealerships: they are often paid by commission and thus have powerful incentive to recommend unneeded repairs. If their persuasive salesmanship fails, they sometimes tack on unauthorized replacement orders. Many garages also make use of "flat-rate manuals" that list labor charges based on highly inflated estimates of the time it takes to do each job. If the repairs are finished in half the stipulated time, the fee remains the same—and the garage may hold the car against a "mechanic's lien" if the owner refuses to pay.

To minimize the chances of being swindled, Randall and Glickman suggest that motorists carefully follow the routine maintenance procedures outlined in the owner's manuals; that should lessen the need for major repairs. If such repairs become necessary, owners should avoid the repair services operated by new car dealers and franchise specialty shops in favor of long-established independent garages and individual mechanics who have proven their reliability.

Taking such precautions might have paid off for William Jeffrey Faren of Torrance, Calif. A few days after the springs and brakes on his 1965 Mustang had been repaired (for $523) at a shop operated by one of the largest tire companies in the nation, he lost control of his car on a curve. The state trooper who investigated the accident concluded that "The brake bands were not seated ... All four wheel cylinders for the brakes were leaking and it appears that some fluid other than the normal brake fluid was used ... A pinhole leak was found in the 'Mag' wheel,* which should have been detected during the mounting. This leak was probably a vital factor in the accident." Faren, unfortunately, was in no position to take legal action against the repair shop. He was killed in the crash.

*The supposedly airtight metal rim on which a tire is mounted.

Reading 71

# The "No Fault" System: How It Works

**U.S. News & World Report**

*Payments are made to the policyholder by his own insurance company. . . .*

No fault auto insurance is intended to speed settlements after an accident by doing away with the need to decide who was legally responsible before payments are made to victims.

Though there are variations in the no-fault system, its general framework is this:

- Each motorist carries liability insurance to cover medical payments and income losses resulting from an accident affecting himself and any passengers in his car. Payments are made to the policyholder by his own insurance company—not, as at present, by the insurance company of the driver held to be at fault.
- The right to sue for intangible damages, such as "pain and suffering," is eliminated in most no-fault plans until after hospital and medical bills go above a certain amount. Then an individual can hire a lawyer and sue for a larger sum if he suffers physical injuries greater than the policy provides.
- Present no-fault plans generally apply to bodily-injury claims for car drivers, passengers, and pedestrians. Plans adopted in Florida and Delaware go a step further in paying for some damages to vehicles or other property.



Reprinted from *U.S. News & World Report*, July 2, 1971, p. 22.

# Buying Good Health Care and Services

Reading 72

## Medical Care Policy: A Dose of Competition

**W. Lee Hoskins**

*Hence, some difficult decisions or choices must be made as to not only the amount of resources devoted to medical care, but also how they are to be employed.*

Although doctors long ago abandoned the practice of bloodletting, Americans claim they are still being bled by the medical sector—through their wallets. As the cost of getting ill continues to rise at an unprecedented rate, the cry that Government bind the wound has reached new decibel levels. Thus, Congress is currently sifting through a host of palliatives designed to provide medical care on the basis of "need" rather than ability to pay (see table).

Government programs that attempt to achieve this goal by simply injecting massive doses of dollars into the veins of the existing medical care systems may be, at best, inefficient, and, at worst, self-defeating. The underlying issue at stake is the ability of the medical care industry as it currently operates to deliver the increased level of services that may be demanded under Government-financed programs or insurance. Success in achieving more or better medical care for every American and the cost to society will depend crucially upon the impact of the program selected on the organization of the medical care delivery system.

**Major Congressional Proposals for a Healthier Nation**

| Human security program |
| --- |
| A national health insurance plan financed partly from Social Security taxes and partly from general revenues, the Human Security Program would insure all citizens comprehensive health care by 1973. The plan would require no minimum fees or deductibles, and the benefits would run the gamut from preventive care to home nursing care. Cost estimates range anywhere from $53 billion to $60 billion by 1974. Employees would pay a 1 per cent payroll tax on their income up to $15,000 annually, and a 3.5 per cent tax would be levied on employers. The Federal Government would match the employer's portion from general revenues. The Government would finance and administer the program, but services would still be provided by the private sector. |
| **Medicredit** |
| A program of income tax credit for private health insurance, Medicredit would be based on the individual's tax liability. The program could provide tax credit anywhere from 0 to |

From *Business Review*, Federal Reserve Bank of Philadelphia, September 1971, pp. 3–12.

100 per cent, thereby virtually guaranteeing health care which is free to the poor and paid by the Federal Government. Under this plan, the Medicare program would not be altered, but the Medicaid program would be eliminated. Private insurance plans would have to meet certain standards to qualify for the program, and individuals (except the poor) would have to pay deductibles. The cost to the Federal Government is estimated at $4.5 billion.

**National Health Insurance and Health Services Improvement Act**

This plan encompasses a program of health care for the entire population similar to the present program for the elderly, but with coverage provided by private carriers. Contributions of .7 per cent each would be made by both employers and employees, with a matching contribution by the Federal Government of .7 per cent. In 1973, this percentage would increase to 2 per cent for all and 3 per cent by 1975. Subscribers would be entitled to 90 days' hospital care, post-hospital care, all physician-related services, with appropriate deductibles and coinsurance. As in the Human Security Program, these taxes would be levied only upon the first $15,000 of earnings of employees and on the total payroll of employers. The estimated cost to the Federal Government by 1975 is $68.1 billion.

Individuals can avoid the Government plan by purchasing an approved private health insurance plan. The contribution of the poor would be assumed by the Federal Government.

**Administration's Health Plan**

**1** The main thrust of this plan is passage of the National Insurance Standards Act, which requires employers to provide their employees with insurance covering up to $50,000 of medical expenses for each worker and each family member. Effective in 1973, employers would initially assume 65 per cent of the insurance cost, increasing to 75 per cent by 1976. Employers' payments would be tax deductible. Beneficiaries would be required to pay 25 percent of the costs up to $5,000, plus certain other deductibles. The plan would pay the remaining full costs of care from $5,000 to $50,000.

**2** The second focus would be on the Family Health Insurance Program for low-income families, which would replace a portion of the existing Federal-state Medicaid program. The maximum eligibility ceiling would be $5,000 for a family of four. Families of four with income below $3,000 would have their medical costs completely assumed by the Federal Government. Families with incomes between $3,000 and $5,000 would have to make individual contributions on a graduated scale for items like deductibles.

**3** Premiums paid by the elderly for doctor-bill coverage under Medicare's Part B would be financed through Social Security payroll taxes. This would force a rise in the Social Security wage base to $9,800 a year. (It currently is $7,800.)

**4** The development of health maintenance programs—groups of doctors furnishing prepaid health care with emphasis on service outside of the hospital—would be given impetus. An estimated $45 million, an increase of $43 million, will be sought for this. Both of the above programs must offer their beneficiaries the option of receiving care from these health maintenance organizations. These programs would be the key step to reorganizing the health care delivery system.

**5** The program also seeks to promote the formation of more family health centers in the urban ghettos and to instigate a HEW commission to study the rising cost of malpractice insurance.

**6** Increased grants to medical schools will be given, the size of which will be determined by the number of graduating students. Also grants to students from low-income families would be increased.

The overall plan calls for $80 million in additional appropriations in the fiscal year beginning July 1.

**National Health Care Act**

The National Health Care Act proposes a program of health insurance which would be jointly financed by private payments, tax deductions, and the Government. State-assigned risk pools would cover the poor. Services provided include physicians' service and visits, nursing-home care, and some dental care. Cost to the Federal Government for the first year is estimated to be $3.3 billion.

## MEDICAL CARE AND SCARCITY

Health policymakers are faced with an indomitable fact of life that has marked man's trek through time—scarcity. There are, and always have been, an unlimited number of competing uses to which man can devote his limited resources. Hence, even the wealthiest of nations cannot have all it wants of everything. Choices must be made. The problem of obtaining more or better medical care is painful testimony to this pervasive and inescapable fact. Society simply does not have the resources to take all known steps to prevent or cure illness and postpone death while continuing to meet the claims of housing, food, and pursuit of "the good life." Moreover, classifying particular economic goods such as housing, food, or medical care as "needs" does not alter the fact that the world in which we live is one of too few resources relative to our desires.

"Needs" are not readily observable absolutes, nor are they costless to satisfy. Consequently, the problem society faces is to determine the *level* of medical "needs" or wants it is willing to pay for. In other words, what are we willing to give up for more or better medical care? To say we are willing to supply all that is "needed," while laudable, is misleading. At some point, society will find that additional resources are more valuable in other areas, such as poverty or education programs, than in medical care. Further complicating the issue is how best to use those resources that are devoted to medical care. For example, more resources placed in hospital capacity mean less available for out-patient care, drugs, dental services, or training of doctors. Hence, some difficult decisions or choices must be made as to not only the amount of resources devoted to medical care, but also how they are to be employed. Scarcity is a tough and unfeeling taskmaster.

Yet, the problem posed by scarcity is effectively dealt with daily in most areas of our economy. Why does it seem to reach crisis proportion in the medical sector? An important part of the answer can be found in the crippling of the market system usually employed to resolve scarcity difficulties.

### The Crippled Hand

The U.S. economy relies primarily on private incentives and consumer wants expressed through competitive market forces to settle problems posed by a world of too few resources. The underlying notion behind this form of economic organization is simply that individuals in their role as consumers and producers, by attempting to make themselves better off, end up putting their *privately* owned resources to uses most highly valued by *society* as a whole. That is, resources automatically would be put to socially desirable uses and in the appropriate amounts. This notion works surprisingly well in a market-oriented economy when markets are open to all comers and are allowed to respond to competitive forces. All the information and incentives needed to make the system work are guided by the "invisible hand" of the market.[1]

[1]The process works this way. Competitive prices are signals which direct the flow of resources to uses most highly valued by society as a whole. And consumers play the dominant role in determining which uses are most highly valued by bidding up the prices of goods they prefer more of relative to those they prefer less of. As a result, relative market prices reflect the taste and desires, or values, consumers attach to having additional units of each good. This information about society's tastes and desires is essential, for it tells producers where to direct resources.

Profit-seeking producers are important cogs in the workings of the system. Noticing a change in relative market prices (or anticipating one), a sharp-eyed producer bids resources away from the lower valued uses and directs them to the production of goods and

The medical care system, for the most part, is shielded from this process, and market forces are severely crippled. Despite the fact that about 60 per cent of the funds paid out for health and medical care are private expenditures made in a market situation, the market signals yielded are confused and often go unheeded. Little *information* is generated on the most economically productive combination of medical resources (doctors, nurses, and hospitals). For example, since neither doctors nor hospitals openly compete on price, charges vary for similar services. Among other things, this lack of competition hides information about the most efficient methods, hospitals, and doctors.

Moreover, much of the *incentive* for efficiently combining these resources is weak or nonexistent. Hospitals are rarely "for-profit" institutions, which means they may lack the incentive to respond to a profitable situation, such as demands by consumers in a particular area for more hospital beds. In addition, hospitals are rarely selected on the basis of costs by a patient, since he is usually hospitalized where his doctor is affiliated. And last, an individual covered by some form of third-party payment (private health insurance or government program) has little incentive to shop for price among doctors and hospitals since the insurer is paying the bill.

### Treating the Poor

Further complicating the problem of dealing with scarcity is the issue of the poor. Even if the medical care delivery system functioned as a competitive market, a family's income would still be crucial in determining the amount and quality of care received. Since the rewards in a free-enterprise system are unevenly distributed among individuals, some people may lack the funds to purchase the level of care (either through insurance or from out-of-pocket expenditures) that society deems they ought to have. And as medical costs continue to soar (see "Footing the Medical Care Bill" in this issue), this problem is exacerbated. Hence, some means of insuring that the poorer members of society (or those with large medical bills relative to their incomes) receive this level of care is required.

## THE FIRST ATTEMPT

The Federal Government's first large-scale attempt to cope with the medical care dilemma took the form of the Medicaid and Medicare programs. Medicare and Medicaid are aimed respectively at the old, whose medical demands are large, and at low-income members of society. Since 1966, these two programs have injected billions of dollars into the medical system each year. Yet, the hue and cry about "inadequate" care continues, in part because these programs did nothing to improve the organization and operation of the medical system.

---

services for which consumers have expressed a desire (or can be expected to desire). His incentive to do this is an increase in wealth. But, as production expands, a point will be reached where the additional resources are going to cost the producer more than they can add to his return. He will stop producing goods which use these resources before that point is reached, if he is interested in achieving the largest return possible. This return will be kept to a minimum by competition (or the threat of it) from other producers. Hence, market prices provide producers with both the necessary information and incentive to insure that resources flow to uses most highly valued by society. And, as a consequence, any rearrangement of society's output would leave it worse off, providing that the current distribution of wealth is acceptable, competitive markets prevail, and that individuals bear the consequences of their actions.

Moreover, these national programs suffer from an underlying flaw which could easily lead to a deterioration in the care they attempt to provide.

### Some Side Effects

The Medicare and Medicaid programs were simply grafted on to the existing medical care delivery system. These programs did nothing to reorganize or improve the efficiency of that system, while at the same time, they expanded the demands placed on it.[2] As a result, many observers have placed a good portion of the blame for the recent rapid rise in medical costs on the doorstep of the Medicare-Medicaid programs.

People making use of these programs are clearly benefitting. However, the fate of others is less certain. To the extent that the jump in medical prices is caused by Medicare and Medicaid, people outside these programs must pay more than they would had there been no Government program. These people may seek less or lower quality medical care. In addition, in areas where hospital beds are relatively scarce, a larger proportion of hospital care goes to those covered under Medicare than goes to the rest of the population. Hence, the young may receive less hospital care in these areas than they would if there had been no such programs.[3] Nor have the increased expenditures noticeably made access to care any easier for those in ghetto and rural areas where medical services are hard to come by.

### The Split Decision

Perhaps even more disturbing is the fact that these national programs suffer from an underlying flaw. The decision about how much care people want or demand is separated from the decision on the amount to be supplied or financed through the programs.

Supply and demand decisions pose a problem if they are split up because individuals behave differently when making choice decisions through *groups* (governments) than when making *private* decisions.[4] For example, if a national health program or insurance scheme is financed through Government, as the Medicare-Medicaid programs are, an individual citizen is involved in a "group" choice on the amount of medical services to finance through Government. Higher levels of medical care then imply higher taxes for individuals. The gains (more or better medical care) are weighed against the costs (higher taxes) by the individual through his Congressional Representative and a *specific* level of care is set for a *specific* dollar amount in taxes. Medical care on the supply side is in no sense "free."

But if the decision on the demand side to use medical care is an individual one where a good deal of care is offered "free" (or at nominal charges) after joining the program, then individuals would attempt to obtain more or better

[2]There is evidence that both the quality and quantity of hospital care demanded because of these programs has increased. Since the inception of these programs, there has been a doubling in the rate of increase in real inputs per patient-day, which indicates people choose higher quality service when hospital bills are paid for them. See J. P. Newhouse and V. Taylor, "The Insurance Subsidy in Hospital Insurance," *Journal of Business* (October, 1970), p. 453. In addition, the hospital admission rate per 1,000 people covered under Medicare alone has risen 8.5 per cent over the past four years.

[3]M. S. Feldstein, "Econometric Model of the Medical System," *Quarterly Journal of Economics* (February, 1971), p. 9.

[4]For the development and analysis of this problem in Britain's National Health Service, see J. M. Buchanan, "The Inconsistencies of the National Health Service," Occasional Paper 7 (Institute of Economic Affairs, Ltd., Great Britain, 1964), pp. 3-23.

quality medical care than they indicated they were willing to pay for through the group or Government decision. This behavior is perfectly consistent. Even under a Government program, the amount or quality of medical care people actually seek is a private decision or choice. They weigh the added benefits from more service against the added cost. But since the added cost is essentially zero or minimal to *them* once they have joined the program, people seek more or better quality medical care than they would if each had to pay for it out of his own pocket.

A simple analogy would be a luncheon in which a group of people agree to split the bill. Each person has an incentive to order a more expensive lunch than the next fellow, since everyone in the group will bear part of the added cost. As a result, the total bill is likely to be larger than if each had agreed to pay for his own lunch separately.

It could be argued that a lower price or cost of "needed" care will not induce an individual to purchase more of it. It is certainly true that for some types of medical care, price will have little effect on the *amount* people seek. It is doubtful that a lower price would have much influence on the number of broken limbs repaired or slashed arteries stitched. But it may have a considerable impact on whether the more expensive hospitals or doctors are selected. Thus, for medical care as a whole, price or cost does have an impact on the amount and quality sought. People want ("need") more or better medical care when the price to them is lower.

The outcome of splitting the supply and demand decision is that the actual Government expenditures run far in excess of the planned amounts. (In 1969, actual Federal expenditures for Medicaid alone were 50 per cent greater than the estimated cost.) At some point the group decisionmakers—Congress—will try to limit the overruns, since they imply even higher taxes. The first attempt to do so under the Medicare-Medicaid programs took the form of tighter administrative controls. Now there is a proposal under consideration by Congress to extend these controls to doctors' fees, limiting increases to the rate of increase in Social Security benefits. The likely outcome of such controls would be a breakdown in the quality of service.[5] Doctors may refuse to treat patients covered under Government programs or give less time to them. A similar result may occur if hospital charges are also directly controlled.

## NEW DIRECTIONS

The experience with Medicare and Medicaid suggests that new medical or health care proposals must prescribe something more potent than dollar injections if efficiency and "adequate" care for all are to be achieved. Two problems must be faced. First, the financial mechanism or "insurance" scheme designed to make medical care available to the poor (or any other group) must get around the problem of the split decision. Second, some provision must be made for insuring greater efficiency in the operation of the medical care delivery system or market.

[5]The British experience demonstrates this point. In 1965, over 70 per cent of Britain's family doctors threatened to resign pending the outcome of negotiations with the Minister of Health. Hospitals were crowded, and there were lengthy delays in obtaining treatment, except in emergency cases. Moreover, the number of new entrants to the medical profession became fewer, while British doctors continued to emigrate (Buchanan, *op. cit.*).

## Financing Medical Care

One way to skirt the problem of the split decision associated with national health plans is to have Government make both the supply and demand decision for a *portion* of medical care. Government could choose the total amount it wishes to finance (a supply decision) and hand out "health vouchers" totaling to that amount (a demand decision) to the poor. There would be no cost overruns, hence, no incentive to curtail or control services. The size of the voucher, of course, could differ over location, age, and income group. Additional medical care (or insurance for additional care) would then be a *private* choice on *both* the demand and supply sides.

Moreover, there are a number of ways to couple a voucher scheme with insurance programs to induce people to seek out the lower cost producers of medical care. One method would be to set the voucher equal to the cost of an "acceptable" benefits plan, based on *average* hospital charges. Next, allow the vouchers to be "cashed" only with insurance companies that rank hospitals according to expense. Let the voucher holder choose how expensive a hospital he will use in case of illness. Those who select hospitals classed above the average in charges would have to pay something over and above their voucher for the insurance. However, people choosing hospitals classed below average in charges could apply the unused portion of their voucher to dental care or optician services. (A cash refund might provide even greater incentive to seek the lower cost facilities.) Unlike current medical insurance programs, either public or private, this plan provides some built-in incentive to seek the lower cost hospitals.[6] "Deductibles" and "coinsurance" features, which tend to make people cost-conscious when purchasing medical care, can also be woven into a voucher or subsidy plan.

While this type of voucher or subsidy system would help those covered, it is not likely to lead to any basic changes in the organization of the medical care delivery system. Yet it is the organization and operation of the medical care system that play an important part in determining how much of a subsidy or voucher is required to achieve a particular level of medical care.

## Towards a More Competitive System

There are several ways to reorganize or coordinate medical care delivery in order to serve the consumer better and keep cost under control. One method would entail a streamlining of the present system by medical planners. An alternative approach would rely on increasing competitive forces to tailor medical care delivery. It may be the case that a combination of these two methods may serve us best.

One method of bringing the cutting edge of competition to bear more heavily on the operation and organization of the medical care system is to adopt measures which permit and encourage "for-profit" institutions or corporations. While such measures may not be workable under all circumstances because of the nature of the product and its relationship to human life, maximal

[6]A number of other variations on this scheme can be employed. For example, the voucher could be used just for catastrophic illness or injury insurance which would come into effect after some amount, say 10 per cent of a family's income, is spent for medical care. For development of these plans and others, see J. P. Newhouse and V. Taylor, "How Shall We Pay for Hospital Care?" *Public Interest* (Spring, 1971), pp. 78–92; M. S. Feldstein, "A New Approach to National Health Insurance," *Public Interest* (Spring, 1971), pp. 93–105; R. Eilers, "Postpayment Medical Expense Coverage: A Proposed Salvation for Insured and Insurer," *Medical Care* (May-June, 1969), pp. 191–208.

extension of market forces would further the goal of a more efficient health care delivery system.

The seeds for bringing medicine to the marketplace are already planted—prepaid group practice plans.[7] Prepaid group plans differ from ordinary health insurance in that they provide the hospitals, doctors, and laboratory services for a fixed yearly fee (which is paid monthly) rather than simply paying the bills when certain types of sickness or injury occurs. More importantly, these plans have a vested interest in keeping you healthy rather than just paying your bills. The healthier a member is, the less he will use the facilities, hence, the smaller the cost to the organization.

The organization takes on the responsibility of *insuring* medical care for members and suffers the consequences of failing to keep members healthy. Doctors are paid salaries and are provided with monetary incentives to use the facilities and treatment techniques efficiently. If revenues are more than costs at year's end, they can receive a bonus. Moreover, they spend all their time practicing medicine rather than engaging in billing, worrying about patient's financial status, gearing treatment to fit the type of insurance coverage he has, and hiring and supervising office personnel. There is no incentive for needless surgery or medication, since doctors are paid salaries. Moreover, such organizations have built-in incentives to uncover and fire incompetent doctors, since they can serve only to raise costs.[8]

Prepaid group plans are just one form of medical service organization that could develop in a more competitive atmosphere. It takes little imagination to visualize the many forms this model for reform might take, if given the chance. Large corporations, with stockholders to undertake the risk, might develop in the medical care field. These organizations could easily extend the program on a nationwide scale, providing insurance, doctors, hospitals, and laboratory service for its members any place in the nation or world.

The competition between several of these "medical corporations" in addition to that from doctors in private practice and independent hospitals would keep continual downward pressure on costs and lead to attempts to extend services to more people. One method of obtaining more customers is advertising. And advertising can benefit the consumers since it often is an important source of information for comparing price and quality—information that is sadly lacking in today's medical system.

The advantage of a competitive marketplace is not that a particular type or form of organization will develop but, rather, that it generates the information and incentive for altering organizations to meet the changing demands of society. The forces of a competitive marketplace are wedded to flexibility and variety, rather than to a particular structure.

Moreover, there is nothing inherently immutable about the existing organization of the medical system. Other "necessities" of life, such as food, clothing, and shelter, are provided by profit-motivated enterprise in a competitive environment. Finally, much of the impetus for a national health scheme comes from Government's desire to finance medical expenditures for those too poor to do so. Achievement of this goal through an appropriate national insurance or financing program would remove a major objection to a competitive marketplace for medical care.

[7]The Kaiser Foundation Plan in California and the Health Insurance Plan of Greater New York are the two most well-known prepaid group practices.

[8]For a comprehensive discussion of prepaid group practice plans, see E. K. Faltermayer, "Better Care at Less Cost without Miracles," *Fortune* (January, 1970), p. 80f.

But if a more competitive medical system is to thrive, many of the laws and practices which thwart its development must be eliminated. There are currently 22 states which prohibit or greatly limit the role of prepayment group practice organizations. And at least one state legislature is considering a proposal to outlaw proprietary or "for-profit" hospitals. Moreover, restrictive licensing practices can prevent doctors from delegating many tasks to competent assistants. This delegation would enable doctors to organize and deliver medical care more efficiently. In addition, current licensing procedures give professional medical societies the power to discipline doctors who introduce more competitive methods, such as advertising and price cutting, into their practices and to control entry into the profession. Some believe tight control over entry to the profession is responsible for the "doctor shortage" and is the most important area for reform.[9] Eliminating these legal obstacles to competition in the medical industry would be a step in the direction of increased efficiency in the organization and operation of the system. An efficient system would mean more or better care without increased expenditures.

## MORE "HEALTH" PER DOLLAR

Improving the efficiency of the medical care system is not sought for its own sake. The more efficiently this industry is organized, the better it would serve the

[9]In concern over the quality of medical care, almost every state government requires prospective practitioners to obtain a license. State medical examining boards set the requirements for a license. These requirements are practically the same as those of the American Medical Association, which through its affiliated local medical societies plays a large role in the selection of the state examining boards. In effect, government has given the medical profession power to set standards and police the actions of its members. This power also extends to medical school training standards, since in most states a condition for obtaining a license is graduation from an "approved" (by the American Medical Association) medical school. Moreover, actions by doctors such as advertising, openly competing on prices, and organizing prepayment group practice plans can be, and have been, restricted in the name of quality control. While this power might be used to raise the quality of doctors, it can also be employed as a device to raise or protect incomes of existing practitioners by restricting entry to the profession and policing actions of recalcitrant members.

These actions, to the extent that they are employed, tend to reduce the effectiveness of market forces in allocating medical resources. Nor is it clear that they insure high-quality care. Licensure only indicates a man's competence at the time he takes the examination and tells little about his competence a quarter century later. Moreover, it may limit the number of practitioners available, which means some people may do without medical care, take home remedies, or seek advice of untrained people. Any relevant measure of medical care quality ought to include the impact of any reduction in the amount of care for the society as a whole. If licensure does improve the quality of medical care, it does so only for those who have access to the care.

One way around the problem posed by licensure is certification. Universities certify a level of quality when they grant doctorates, masters, and bachelors degrees to physicists, chemists, engineers, and others in professional and scientific groups. And some members of these groups do deal with life-and-death situations. Astronauts trust their lives with the engineers and physicists that send them millions of miles into space. Other unlicensed scientific personnel insure the food and water we consume will not kill us. The threat of law suits and competitive pressure from rival firms tends to eliminate potentially dangerous incompetents from responsible positions. For discussions of how the American Medical Association exerts its control and monopoly returns in medicine, see M. Friedman, *Capitalism and Freedom* (Chicago: University of Chicago Press, 1963), pp. 149–160; M. Friedman and S. Kuznets, *Income from Independent Professional Practice* (New York: National Bureau of Economic Research, 1945); R. Kessel, "AMA and the Supply of Physicians," *Law and Contemporary Problems* (Spring, 1970), pp. 267–283. Elton Rayack, *Professional Power and American Medicine* (New York: World Publishing Company, 1967).

sick. Greater efficiency also implies more resources available for helping the poor obtain medical care. Perhaps even more important over the long haul would be the resources released for preventing or reducing the incidences of those very ills that confound doctors and doctoring and account for so much sickness and death in America—heart and kidney disease, alcohol and drug abuse, and cancer.

With all the demands on the consumer's dollar for better housing, education, nutrition, and safety programs (all of which may have substantial health benefits), policy-makers must take a long, hard look at alternative ways of achieving a healthier society if they are interested in getting the most "health" per dollar spent.

**Reading 73**

# National Health Insurance: The Next Attack on Medical Costs

**Changing Times**

*Make no mistake about it: Some form of NHI (National Health Insurance) is coming.*

With doctors' fees rising twice as fast as other prices, hospital costs increasing about 15% every year and out total medical bill in 1975 expected to be twice what it was in 1968, the soaring cost of health care has reached the crisis stage.

Eventually—perhaps soon—there will be near-revolutionary changes in both how you get your medical care and how you pay for it. Many believe these changes will come in some form of national health insurance, some scheme for providing comprehensive health coverage to all Americans regardless of income.

Several such proposals were brought before the last Congress but not acted upon. The same ideas doubtless will be reintroduced in the Congress convening this month. The table with this article shows the main features of the plans offered so far. Whatever form national health insurance eventually takes, it probably will embody ideas drawn from those plans.

As you can see, none of the schemes adds up to anything as drastic as "a government takeover of medicine." Some would substitute government insurance for the private health insurance we know today. More doctors might work for a salary or in group practices instead of for fees in individual practice, but they would retain their right to practice privately, too.

Nor would the plans mean "free medical care" except for those at the very bottom of the economic ladder. For the relatively affluent, the direct and indirect costs could be considerable—more in some cases than they pay now.

Two of the five proposals follow a social-insurance or compulsory payroll-tax approach and call for change in the way care is provided. Two others rely on the voluntary purchase of subsidized private coverage and leave the present health-care system largely unchanged. The fifth, introduced by Sen. Jacob Javits of New York, has elements of both approaches. It would allow people to choose between government health insurance and private coverage.

## THE SOCIAL-INSURANCE VIEWPOINT

Advocates of the compulsory payroll-tax approach contend that Americans are receiving far less than full value for their health-care outlays. They point out that the U.S., the sole remaining industrialized nation without some form of NHI, spends more money and a larger share of its resources for health purposes than any other country, yet lags behind 15 in infant mortality, 17 in male life expectancy and 10 in female.

The main reason for this disparity, social-insurance proponents believe, is that health care is organized, delivered and financed in outmoded and inadequate ways. Hospitals, for example, commonly are paid on a cost-plus basis by third parties—the government, Blue Cross and insurance companies—and thus have little incentive to reduce costs through efficiencies. Doctors are commonly paid on an uncontrolled fee-for-service basis, instead of receiving a set fee, a salary or so much per patient.

Backers of the Kennedy and Griffiths bills, introduced by Sen. Edward Kennedy of Massachusetts and Rep. Martha Griffiths of Michigan, claim that a more efficient system would pare the nation's health bill by more than 14 billion dollars a year. On that theory, these two proposals go beyond simply finding a new way to finance the bills. They envision basic changes in the way medical care is provided.

The Griffiths NHI plan would have the government enter into contracts with medical groups and hospitals to provide health services on a per-person basis, with a predetermined amount taking care of a family's total health-care needs. It is hoped that this would promote flexibility in the assignment of patients to the most appropriate accommodations—at home, in a nursing home or in a hospital.

The Kennedy bill would provide funds for the development of prepaid group-practice arrangements and for increasing the supply of physicians and paramedical personnel. Fee-for-service payments, while not encouraged, would be permitted under the Kennedy proposal. Hospitals would have budgets arrived at through negotiation, and experimentation in new forms of care would be encouraged.

One of the most controversial aspects of both bills is that they would eliminate private health insurance. The reasoning is that it is an unnecessary and overly expensive link between patient and care. It hasn't really worked very well, the critics charge, pointing out that although some 170,000,000 Americans have some insurance coverage, many get woefully inadequate benefits—$20 a day for hospitalization in many instances.

Furthermore, the industry does not market a truly comprehensive policy. To obtain blanket family protection now, a government economist figures you'd have to buy several policies: a medical and hospital plan, a dental care plan and a hypothetical drug plan at a combined cost of $1,000 to $1,200 a year. And this package probably still would not include nursing home care, private-duty nursing and other services.

**These Are the Principal Plans That Have Been Proposed**

| The proposal | What you pay | What you get | How it's run | How it's financed |
|---|---|---|---|---|
| | | **Social-insurance approach** | | |
| Health Security Program<br>*(Kennedy bill)*<br>Backed by the Committee of 100 for National Health Insurance (UAW) | Minimal cost for lowest income earners; up to $315 a year for those earning $15,000 or more. | Comprehensive health benefits for all U.S. citizens and residents, the major initial exclusion being dental services for adults (to be covered later). Limitations on drugs and nursing home and mental health care. Benefits would be available without cost-sharing on the part of the insured. | By HEW through a federal board, and regional, subregional and local offices. | Tax of 3.5% of employers' payrolls, 2.1% of individual income up to $15,000 and general tax revenues equal to 40% of total program costs. According to sponsors, program would cover 70% or 57 billion dollars of health-care costs in fiscal 1974, first full year of operation. HEW estimates costs considerably higher by then—77 billion dollars. Would absorb medicare, but medicaid could continue to provide noncovered benefits. |
| National Health Insurance Act<br>*(Griffiths bill)*<br>Backed by the AFL-CIO | Minimal cost for lowest-income earners; up to $150 a year (by 1975) for those earning $15,000 or more. | Comprehensive health benefits for all persons residing in the U.S. one year or longer, the major exclusion being dental care for adults. Patient cost of physician, dentist and other ambulatory services $2 per visit after first visit. Maximum annual cost of $50 for individuals, $100 for families. | By a federal board composed of HEW officials and nongovernment members, regional groups and advisory bodies. | Taxes equal to 7% of the nation's total payroll: a 1% tax on employes, 3% on employers and the balance from general tax revenues. Maximum earnings to be taxed: $15,000, adjusted upward as wages increase. Sponsors put the cost at 56.2 billion dollars by 1974, the first full year of operation. Would absorb medicare and medicaid. |

| The proposal | What you pay | What you get | How it's run | How it's financed |
|---|---|---|---|---|
| | | **Combination** | | |
| National Health Insurance and Health Services Improvement Act of 1970<br><br>*(Javits bill)* | Minimal cost for lowest-income earners; up to $495 a year for those earning $15,000 or more. If employer provides adequate alternative plan, employe would pay no more than 25% of cost. Employe may "elect out" of government plan by buying qualified private coverage. | Would expand medicare hospital and medical benefits and make this coverage available, to all in two stages: aged citizens and aliens with five years' residence, widows 60 and over and widowers 62 and over by July 1971, all others by July 1973. | By HEW or, under contract with HEW, by state governments. Claims would be processed by private companies or by quasi-government organizations. | Employers, employes and general tax revenues initially would each contribute 0.7% of covered payroll; this would rise to 2% by 1973 and to 3.3% by 1975—to a total of roughly 10%. The tax would be levied on the first $15,000 of earnings for employes and on the total payroll of employers. HEW estimates the 1975 cost at approximately 66.4 billion dollars. Plan would absorb medicaid. |

**These Are the Principal Plans That Have Been Proposed *(Continued)***

| The proposal | What you pay | What you get | How it's run | How it's financed |
|---|---|---|---|---|
| | | **Private-insurance approaches** | | |
| Medicredit<br><br>*(Fulton-Broyhill bill)*<br><br>Backed by the American Medical Association | Coverage would be provided at no charge for those who pay $300 or less income tax. Graded scale of tax credits from 98% for tax liability of $301 to 10% when taxes exceed $1,300. | Would be offered on a voluntary basis to everyone under 65. Minimum benefits would include medical services, hospitalization up to 60 days, and optional benefits including catastrophic illness, all subject to cost-sharing and deductibles, which would be waived for the poor. | By a federal advisory board (including HEW, IRS and other members appointed by the President), which would establish standards for use by state insurance departments in approving private health insurance plans. | Would be financed from federal general tax revenues. The AMA estimates that the 1970 net cost of basic benefits, excluding optional protection, would have been 8 billion dollars; HEW sets it considerably higher—at approximately 15 billion dollars. Plan would absorb medicaid. |
| Pettengill-Aetna Proposal<br><br>*(not introduced as bill in 91st Congress)*<br><br>Embodies approach favored by a number of health insurers. | The poor would pay nothing, the near poor and uninsurables would pay part of premium costs. No exact figures are available. | The poor, near poor and uninsurables under age 65 could elect to receive state minimum benefits to be specified in federal law and to include ambulatory and institutional care. Catastrophic medical expense coverage would gradually be extended to all, starting with the poor. | By the states through statewide insurance pools administered by an insurance company selected by each state with the approval of the federal government. | Premiums paid by the near poor and uninsurables for minimum uniform health benefits would go into state insurance pools. Deficits would be made up by the state and federal governments. The catastrophic medical expense portion would be financed out of federal and state general revenues. Estimates of cost are not available. Plan would absorb medicaid. |

## THE PRIVATE-INSURANCE VIEWPOINT

The position of the AMA and the health insurance industry can be summed up in the recurring admonition: "Don't throw out the baby with the bath water." Many insurance executives admit that change is inevitable and, to a degree, warranted. They insist, however, that you don't scrap a system that has registered solid accomplishments just because it isn't perfect—especially if you aren't sure that what would replace it is any better, or even as good.

The counter arguments begin with the thesis that it has always been national policy to give the private approach a fair trial before turning to the government. A number of organizations are formulating their own NHI plans.

Daniel Pettengill, vice-president of Aetna Life & Casualty, has presented his company's version of NHI to Congress. Though its benefits are extremely limited, it would provide minimum protection to the poor, near poor and uninsurables and eventually give some assistance to others with extraordinarily high medical charges. The Health Insurance Association of America has committed its more than 300 member companies to the improvement of health care and is preparing its own scheme.

Backers of this approach also challenge the cost estimates of social-insurance plans. Medicare is more expensive than anticipated. Will the costs of the more far-reaching NHI plans really be at the estimated levels? Opponents doubt it. They have much greater faith in private health insurance companies operating under government regulation than in government running the whole show.

Finally, advocates of the private approach agree that money alone won't do the job. We now have a shortage of about 50,000 physicians. Estimates are that if the medical school output were doubled now, it would take 20 years to catch up with present demand, which under NHI would be bound to increase. After college, medical school, internship, residency and perhaps military service, the average doctor is in his thirties before he starts to earn any money. If doctors' pay is controlled by the government, critics ask, how many would go through that grind without the lure of $45,000 a year or so by the middle years?

Medicredit, introduced by Reps. Richard Fulton of Tennessee and Joel Broyhill of Virginia, would pay full insurance premiums for people who owe $300 or less in taxes. For those with more income, a sliding scale of tax credits would be given to help pay premiums.

## THE MIDDLE GROUND: BEST BET

Make no mistake about it: Some form of NHI is coming. Some observers say it might take as long as five to seven years. Others think the 92nd Congress will not only start the job but finish it. Regardless of timing, these are the prospects:

- No proposal is going to survive the legislative process intact. The Senate-House conference committee on medicare had to resolve over 500 differences before the bill was finally approved.
- Since Congress thrives on compromise, the proposal enacted will probably more closely resemble the Javits plan than any other. The administration is also readying a plan similar in some respects to this proposal.
- One way or another, you'll continue to pay plenty for medical care. Don't be deceived by the maximum direct costs in the table. "General revenues" mean taxes, too—and those taxes will be paid by you and your employer.

Reading 74

# Comparison of Six National Health Proposals

**Allen Ferguson, Jr.**

*. . . no one of them is likely to pass in its present form.*

## ANALYSIS OF SIX PROPOSALS

The six proposals analysed in the following section provide a representative sample of national health proposals. It should be remembered that they are all subject to change, and no one of them is likely to pass in its present form. However, elements from many of these plans, as well as others, will undoubtedly be combined to form a national health proposal that will eventually be put into effect. Various aspects of the proposal are presented and evaluated here in order to give the reader a concrete idea of the *kinds* of plan that are being proposed.

From *National Health Proposals, The Neighborhood Health Center and the Poor*, Seminar Program. Monogram Series 2, University Extension, Berkeley, California, 94720, pp. 19–20.

**Comparison of Six National Health Proposals**

| Criteria | Least change ← | | | | | → Most change |
|---|---|---|---|---|---|---|
| | **Long** | **Nixon** | **AMA** | **Javits** | **Kennedy** | **MCHR** |
| Coverage | Some employees (compulsory). | Most employees and some poor (compulsory). | All residents (voluntary). | All residents (compulsory). | All residents (compulsory); some provision for visitors. | All residents and visitors (compulsory). |
| | **Long** | **Nixon** | **AMA** | **Javits** | **Kennedy** | **MCHR** |
| Benefits | Catastrophic illness only. | Unlimited hospital & physician visits (excluding psych) for employees. Limited hospital & physician visits for poor. Some additional benefits. | Limited hospital & unlimited physician visits (including psych) & catastrophic. | Limited hospital & unlimited physician & some eye, ear, dental & drugs. | Unlimited hospital & physician & some psych, drugs, dental, eye, & supportive services. | Unlimited hospital & physician, psych, drugs, dental, eye, transportation, outreach and other. |
| | **Long** | **AMA** | **Javits** | **Nixon** | **Kennedy, MCHR** | |
| Expenses to Patient | Patient pays all expenses up to $2,000 per year. | Substantial coinsurance, deductibles for everyone plus premium charge for nonpoor. | Substantial coinsurance & deductibles. | Substantial coinsurance, deductibles, & premium charges with relief for poor. | No direct expense to patient. | |
| | **AMA** | **Nixon** | **Long** | **Javits, Kennedy** | **MCHR** | |
| Financing mechanism | Federal income tax credit for those who buy insurance. | Employers & employees purchase private policies; Government purchases policies for poor. | Added Social Security tax pays. | Combination of added Social Security tax & Federal general revenues. | New progressive national health tax on wealth. | |

**Comparison of Six National Health Proposals**

| Criteria | Least change ← | | | → Most change |
|---|---|---|---|---|
| | **Long, AMA** | **Nixon, Javits** | **Kennedy** | **MCHR** |
| Payment to Providers | Fees for covered services only. | Fees for covered services or capitation prepayment to new delivery organizations. | Capitation prepayment to providers in or out of new delivery organizations, & fees for covered services as long as funds last. | Communities receive capitation amount. Local health councils distribute funds to providers on salary basis. |

| Criteria | **AMA** | **Long** | **Nixon** | **Javits** | **Kennedy** | **MCHR** |
|---|---|---|---|---|---|---|
| Cost Control | No provision. | Standardized Medicare rates. | Some regulation of insurance rates; encouragement of capitation prepayment. | Required efficiency of fiscal intermediaries; Payment to providers of "appropriate" (HEW approved) fees; encouragement of capitation prepayment. | Prospective budgets for institutions; elimination of private insurance policies & fiscal intermediaries, limit on drug prices. | Elimination of private health insurers; elimination of profit making and excessive salaries. |

| Criteria | **AMA** | **Long** | **Nixon** | **Javits** | **Kennedy** | **MCHR** |
|---|---|---|---|---|---|---|
| Role of Private Enterprise | Reliance on private health insurers (profit-making or nonprofit) & private practitioners. | Reliance on private fiscal intermediaries (usually nonprofit) & traditional providers. | Possibility of increased role for private delivery organizations. Reliance on private health insurers. | Possibility of increased role for private delivery organizations. Reliance on private fiscal intermediaries. Place for private insurers. | New delivery organizations must be nonprofit but may subcontract with profit-making providers. Possibility of private fiscal intermediaries. | Health care publically funded & delivered; prohibition of profit making. |

| Criteria | Least change ◄ | | | | ► Most change | |
|---|---|---|---|---|---|---|
| | **AMA** | **Long** | **Nixon** | **Javits** | **Kennedy** | **MCHR** |
| Administration | Limited Federal guidelines; mostly left to private insurers & state insurance depts. | Social Security Administration & fiscal intermediaries. | Department of HEW; Social Security Administration; new Federal agency for insurance; state insurance depts.; state health agencies; private insurance. | Department of HEW, fiscal intermediaries & private insurers meeting Federal standards. | New Presidentially appointed board in HEW with regional & local subdivisions. | New national, regional & local elected boards of consumers & health workers. |
| | **Long, AMA, Nixon, Javits** | | **Kennedy** | | **MCHR** | |
| Consumer Input | No provision. | | Consumer majority on appointed advisory boards at national, regional & local levels. | | A $2/3$ majority of consumers on policy-making boards at all levels. | |
| | **Long** | **AMA** | **Nixon** | **Javits** | **Kennedy** | **MCHR** |
| Quality of Care | No provision. | Peer review only. | Standards of providers reviewed by new professional review organizations. | National licensing standards & continuing education requirements for practitioners. Specialty standards for specialists. | National licensing & continuing educational standards for practitioners. National standards for hospitals, nursing homes, etc. Power to enforce additional regulations. | National licensing & continuing educational standards for practitioners. New quality review boards of consumers & professionals at all levels. |

**Comparison of Six National Health Proposals**

| Criteria | Least change ◄ | | | ► Most change |
|---|---|---|---|---|
| | **Long, AMA** | **Nixon, Javits** | **Kennedy** | **MCHR** |
| Effect on Organization & Delivery | No provision for change. | Start-up support of new group practice & similar organizations (ambulatory & inpatient). Limited provision to increase resources. Little government power to make changes. | Direct support of new group practice organizations (ambulatory or ambulatory & inpatient); strong incentives for professionals to join. Continuing funds to increase & redistribute resources. Government power to make changes. | Direct support of community centers (ambulatory) and back-up hospitals. Continuing funds for increasing & redistributing resources. Team medicine and personal care. Power of consumer-worker boards to make changes. |

| Criteria | **Long** | **Nixon** | **AMA, Javits** | **Kennedy** | **MCHR** |
|---|---|---|---|---|---|
| System for the Poor | Poor people not covered. | Not all poor people covered. Inferior benefits & separate financing system for poor. Means testing required for poor. | Same benefits & financing system for poor & nonpoor, but high coinsurance & deductibles with no relief for the poor. | Same benefits & financing system for poor & nonpoor. No out-of-pocket expense for covered services. | Same benefits & financing system for poor & nonpoor. No out-of-pocket expenses for health care. Tax structure would partly redistribute wealth. |

## Reading 75

# Groping Through the Maze of Mail Order Insurance Policies

**Edward J. Gorin**

*One company advertised it had the highest rating ever given by a certain insurance rating service. When checked, that proved to be true, except that the highest rating was the worst a company could get.*

"I thought I was the picture of health until I woke up staring at a hospital wall."

That's the way the message begins in a recent newspaper ad from the National Home Life Assurance Co., the one that pays Art Linkletter $50,000 a year to endorse its policy.

Bill Martin, a fictitious character, is being quoted from his hospital bed.

"And then it struck me that bills were piling up at home, too. The mortgage. Car payment. Groceries. Telephone. Electricity, gas, heat, all the day-in, day-out expenses. How could I pay all the bills?"

Then Bill's wife, Mary, smiles and reminds him that he has a policy with National Home. Bill had forgotten to send the quarter to put the policy into effect, but good old Mary had remembered.

"Bless my smart wife," says Bill. Now he'll collect $1,000 a month for the two months he'll be hospitalized.

The ad also tells you, if you read closely, that Bill wouldn't have gotten anywhere near $2,000 if he had stayed in the hospital for five days and spent the next seven weeks recuperating at home.

In that case he would have received $166.65—$33.33 a day for each day he was hospitalized—and nothing for the time spent at home.

It also tells you, if you look closely, that if Bill had been hospitalized for illness instead of injury and had remained in the hospital for just five days he would have received nothing.

In case of illness, the ad says, the payment of $33.33 a day doesn't begin until after the fifth day of hospitalization.

Bill does say that his paycheck will be coming for a few more weeks, but he wonders what he would have done after that, without his National Home Policy.

There are about 800 companies in the nation selling direct-mail supplemental hospital insurance. The consumer supposedly saves some money by dealing direct with the company rather than through an agent.

You don't need a medical examination. No illness you had before the policy becomes effective is covered for two years after that date, whether you knew about the illness or not.

Most policies say they can't be canceled by the company and rates can't be raised. Some will tell you that the policy can't be canceled by the company or premiums increased unless the company cancels the policies or increases the premiums of everyone in the state.

The similarities end here. Premiums vary sharply, as do benefits. Exclusions may be few or many.

The National Home policy—or one National Home policy, because many

From *The Record*, Hackensack, New Jersey, 1973.

have been offered—excluded payment for hospitalization as a result of an act of war, mental disease, use of alcohol or narcotics, or pregnancy (available for extra premium), and for care in a government hospital.

The policy has no limits. It will pay the $33.33 a day for the rest of your life—assuming you spend the rest of your life in a hospital.

Compare this to the policy offered by Commercial Travelers Mutual Insurance Co. of Utica, N.Y.

The policy advertises benefits of $200 per week, which comes out to $28.57 per day. The premium is higher than National Home—$72 a year compared to $64.20—but coverage begins on the first day of hospitalization for both illness and injury.

However, the policy has a limit of a year for each occurrence, a maximum of $10,400, while National Home places no time limit on benefits.

Now compare both of these to the "$25,000 Family Protection Plan" being offered to Stern Bros. credit card holders. It pays $25,000 cash to your family if you meet with accidental death.

It also provides $600 cash a month—$20 a day—for a full year while you're hospitalized for an injury, and $300 a month—$10 a day—for each day of hospitalization after the first year, for life—if necessary.

The premium is $42 a year. Payments begin on the first day of hospitalization. Exclusions? Here's what the advertisement says:

"Are there any exceptions? To help keep you cost low, these logical exclusions are made: an act of war, military service, speed contests, professional athletics, motorcycling, hernia, suicide or self-inflicted injury, intoxication, illegal use of narcotics, illegal occupation, injury and death covered under Workman's Compensation, and confinement in mental institutions or U.S. Government hospitals."

If you read fast, skimmed the headlines, and didn't pay close attention, you still may not realize that this is an accident policy only. It never quite says that it doesn't cover illness, and if you haven't noted that coverages for accident and injury aren't followed by the word illness, you may sign up without ever realizing it.

This is the main argument that insurance commissioners have with these types of insurance. The benefits are thrown at you in big headlines, while the negative aspects of the policies are hidden or ignored.

Dr. Herbert S. Denenberg, the Pennsylvania insurance commissioner who started the nationwide hard look at these ads, says there are better alternatives.

"Blue Cross will return 95 cents or better on the dollar," he said. "It has a more efficient marketing system."

Some of the profit-making companies are returning only 30 to 60 cents on the dollar, he said, and none ever tell you in their ads just what kind of profit margin they have.

"The public would be better served if all these little companies returning only 30 or 40 cents would go out of business," Denenberg said.

Denenberg has forced the direct-mail companies to file copies of the ads with him at the time of their use, and he directs changes in the ads.

It may take the form of merely repositioning paragraphs on a page to make the exclusions more obvious, or it may take the form of word changes.

One company advertised it had the highest rating ever given by a certain insurance rating service, Denenberg said. When he checked, that proved to be true, except that the highest rating was the worst a company could get.

Denenberg is planning a shopper's guide to health and accident insurance

**Five Health Insurance Policies: A Comparison**

This chart compares five mail order health insurance policies that were brought to the attention of *The Record* by its readers.

These companies represent a sampling of what is available on the market and how much policies may differ.

| Company | Advertised benefit claim | Total maximum benefit | Daily benefit | Illness coverage begins | Pre-existing conditions covered after | Annual premium, age 35 |
|---|---|---|---|---|---|---|
| National Home (Art Linkletter) | $1,000 month | Unlimited | $33.33 | 6th day | Two years | $64.20 |
| Physicians Mutual (Doctors Hospital Plan) | None | $5,000 | $14.28 | First day | One year | $47.40 |
| Stern's (Beneficial Standard) | $25,000 | Unlimited | $20 first year, $10 afterward | Not covered | Not covered | $42.00 |
| Commercial Travelers | $200 week | $10,400 | $28.57 | First day | Two years | $72.00 |
| American Express (Fireman's Fund) | $36 day | 500 days | $30 day plus $6 day in lump sum on discharge | First day | Two years if treated in year prior to policy, but one year if no treatment needed for 12 consecutive months after policy | $75.60 |

like the one he has issued for life and auto insurance, but he says it's difficult because the policies differ so widely that they are hard to compare.

He is thinking of making companies standardize their contracts or even include a form cover sheet with 20 questions about the policy to make them easier for the buyer to compare.

In the meantime, he is working on forcing companies to make their policies more readable so the average person, who must work without an agent to explain things, will be able to understand what he's buying.

The New Jersey Insurance Department has issued a booklet called "The Stop and Look Approach in Buying Mail Order Accident and Health Insurance," available free from the department at the State House Annex, Trenton, N.J.

The booklet tells what questions to ask about the policies to be better able to compare them. The key among them is whether the company is licensed in New Jersey. If it isn't, there's little the state can do to help you if you later have a problem.

When you're looking at the big numbers in the policy for monthly or yearly benefits, the booklet says, keep in mind that only one hospital stay in 50 lasts as long as a month, and more than half of the hospital stays for persons under 65 end within five days.

## Reading 76

# A Price Guide to Prescription Drugs

**Consumer Reports**

*Your physician will save you money on some drugs by prescibing the generic name instead.*

The prices listed below for 94 prescription drugs and four nonprescription insulin preparations can serve as a point of reference in your own drug shopping, especially for frequently refilled medications. Although a typical pharmacy stocks up to 5000 prescription items, the drugs listed account for about 40 per cent of all prescriptions filled by the 178-store Osco Drug, Inc., chain. The prices, derived from those displayed in the Chicago area, range around 35 per cent below a national average. According to Osco, most of its Chicago stores offer such pharmacy services as the maintenance of a record of your previous prescriptions and a bank credit card charge account, and, without publicizing the fact, some stores also provide after-hours service in case of emergency. The prices do not include delivery.

Where prescriptions or wholesale quantities are standardized at some measure other than 100, the price shown is that of the standard quantity. Whenever practical, however, the price is given for quantities of 100 in order to simplify comparisons. Osco's price per unit of most drugs listed is the same regardless of quantity. Thus, to determine the price of 30 tablets, multiply the listed price per 100 by 0.3.

Most of the drugs listed are brand names. Your physician may be able to save you money on some drugs by prescribing the generic name instead. (The pharmacist isn't allowed to substitute a generic for a brand name.) Where reliable generic versions are available, they are identified in parentheses. Generic drug listings are starred (*).

Ask your physician to write on a piece of paper separate from the prescription itself the name of the drug, the strength (50mg, for instance) and the quantity. Given that information, pharmacies should be willing to quote a price over the telephone. Those that refuse may not be worth patronizing.

| Drug name | Quantity | Price |
|---|---|---|
| Achromycin V 250mg (tetracycline HCL) | 100 | $6.00 |
| Actifed C Expectorant | 4 oz. | 1.79 |
| Actifed Syrup | 4 oz. | 1.59 |
| Actifed Tablets | 100 | 5.50 |
| Afrin Spray | 15cc | 1.69 |
| Aldomet Tablets | 100 | 6.95 |
| *Ampicillin 250mg | 12 | 2.28 |
| Atromid S | 100 | 7.40 |
| Azo Gantrisin .5Gm | 100 | 4.90 |
| Benadryl Kapseals 50mg (diphenhydramine HCL) | 100 | 3.80 |
| Benadryl Elixir (diphenhydramine HCL) | 4 oz. | .99 |
| Benylin Expectorant | 4 oz. | 1.19 |
| Butazolidin 100mg | 100 | 8.50 |
| Butazolidin Alka | 100 | 8.80 |
| Combid Spansule | 100 | 14.50 |
| Coumadin 5mg | 100 | 4.90 |
| Darvon 65mg | 100 | 7.95 |
| Darvon Compound 65mg | 100 | 7.95 |
| DBI-TD Capsules | 100 | 10.27 |
| Demulen (all dosages) | month | 1.59 |
| Diabinese 250mg | 100 | 8.50 |
| Dilantin Kapseals 100mg | 100 | 1.49 |
| Dimetapp Elixir | 4 oz. | 1.49 |
| Dimetapp Tablets | 100 | 9.80 |
| Diupres 250mg | 100 | 6.49 |
| Diuril 500mg (chlorothiazide) | 100 | 5.90 |
| Donnatal Elixir | 4 oz. | .99 |
| Donnatal Tablets | 100 | 1.69 |
| Dyazide | 100 | 8.25 |
| Elavil 25mg | 100 | 8.90 |
| Enovid E | month | 1.59 |
| Equanil 400mg (meprobamate) | 100 | 8.00 |
| Erythrocin 250mg (erythromycin) | 12 | 2.40 |
| Flagyl 250mg | 100 | 16.50 |
| Gantanol .5Gm | 100 | 6.90 |
| Gantrisin .5Gm (sulfisoxazole) | 100 | 3.60 |
| Hydrodiuril 25mg | 100 | 4.40 |
| Hydrodiuril 50mg | 100 | 5.90 |
| Hygroton 50mg | 100 | 8.00 |
| Ilosone 250mg (erythromycin) | 12 | 3.36 |
| Ilosone Susp. 125mg (erythromycin) | 60cc | 2.49 |
| Indocin 25mg | 100 | 7.97 |

| Drug name | Quantity | Price |
|---|---|---|
| Insulin Lilly U-40 (all types) | 10cc | .99 |
| Insulin Lilly U-80 (all types) | 10cc | 1.89 |
| Insulin Squibb U-40 (all types) | 10cc | .89 |
| Insulin Squibb U-80 (all types) | 10cc | 1.79 |
| Lanoxin .25mg | 100 | 1.00 |
| Lasix 40mg | 100 | 9.00 |
| Librax | 100 | 7.20 |
| Librium 5mg | 100 | 5.70 |
| Librium 10mg | 100 | 6.40 |
| Lomotil | 100 | 8.30 |
| *Meprobamate 400mg | 100 | 3.00 |
| Mycolog Cream | 15Gm | 3.89 |
| *Nitroglycerin (all dosages) | 100 | .89 |
| Norinyl 2mg | month | 1.79 |
| Norinyl (all other dosages) | month | 1.59 |
| Norlestrin (all dosages) | month | 1.59 |
| Oracon | month | 1.59 |
| Orinase | 100 | 6.99 |
| Ornade Spansule | 100 | 10.67 |
| Ortho-Novum SQ | month | 1.69 |
| Ortho-Novum 2mg | month | 1.79 |
| Ortho-Novum (all other dosages) | month | 1.59 |
| Ovral | month | 1.59 |
| Ovulen (all dosages) | month | 1.59 |
| *Penicillin G 400,000 units | 100 | 3.00 |
| Pentids 400 (penicillin G potassium) | 100 | 10.50 |
| Pentids Susp. 400 (penicillin G potassium) | 100cc | 2.59 |
| Peritrate 10mg (pentaerythritol tetranitrate) | 100 | 3.00 |
| Peritrate 20mg (pentaerythritol tetranitrate) | 100 | 3.78 |
| Peritrate SA 80 (pentaerythritol tetranitrate) | 100 | 7.70 |
| Phenergan Expectorant with codeine | 4 oz. | 1.29 |
| Phenergan VC Expectorant with codeine | 4 oz. | 1.79 |
| *Phenobarbital (all dosages) | 100 | .89 |
| Polycillin 250mg (ampicillin trihydrate) | 12 | 3.24 |
| Polycillin Susp. 125mg (ampicillin trihydrate) | 100cc | 4.49 |
| *Prednisone 5mg | 100 | .99 |
| Premarin 1.25 | 100 | 6.50 |
| Pro-Banthine | 100 | 4.88 |
| Proloid 1gr | 100 | 1.29 |
| Raudixin 50mg (rauwolfia serpentina) | 100 | 4.38 |
| *Reserpine .25mg | 100 | .99 |
| Ritalin 10mg | 100 | 7.13 |
| Ser-Ap-Es | 100 | 8.20 |
| Serpasil .25mg (reserpine) | 100 | 4.38 |
| Stelazine 2mg | 100 | 9.97 |
| Sumycin 250mg (tetracycline HCL) | 100 | 4.95 |
| Tandearil | 100 | 10.27 |

| Drug name | Quantity | Price |
|---|---|---|
| *Tetracycline 250mg | 100 | 2.99 |
| *Thyroid ½gr | 100 | .89 |
| *Thyroid 1gr | 100 | .89 |
| Tuss-Ornade Spansule | 100 | 11.77 |
| Valisone Cream | 15Gm | 2.79 |
| Valium 2mg | 100 | 7.00 |
| Valium 5mg | 100 | 8.68 |
| V-Cillin K 250mg (penicillin, phenoxymethyl potassium) | 16 | 1.84 |
| V-Cillin K Susp. 125 mg (penicillin, phenoxymethyl potassium) | 100cc | 1.99 |

Reading 77

# Few Nonprescription Drugs Effective

**Arthur E. Rowse**

*Of 22 vitamin or vitamin-mineral preparations, most were given only qualified support for claims made.*

Of 21 antihistamine products sold without prescription, only three are considered effective for any claim made on the list. Neo-Antergan Maleate Tablets were considered effective for hay fever, drug reactions and non-seasonal rhinitis. Neohetramine Hydrochloride Tablets were considered effective for relief of weeping eyes associated with colds, hay fever and nasal allergies. Nisaval Tablets were considered effective for prompt symptomatic relief in angioneurotic edema.

Found ineffective was Anahist for use against "allergies" because the term is too broad and the dosage too weak. All other products were rated only "possibly" or "probably" effective.

Of six products for the relief of menstrual problems, all were called either "possibly" or "probably" effective. The products are M-Minus 5 Tablets, Pre-Mens Tablets, Cardui Brand Tablets, Trendar Tablets, Pamphrin Tablets and Assure Tablets.

Of 22 vitamin or vitamin-mineral preparations, most were given only qualified support for claims made. The only item called effective by the medical panel was Syrup Calglucon for use in preventing calcium deficiency in childhood growth periods, but it was called ineffective for hyperirritability in infants.

Also called ineffective were Becaplets for "malnutrition" and "retarded growth," chiefly because the terms are too broad. Other products were called either "possibly" or "probably" effective for purposes claimed.

From *Consumer Newsweek*, Washington, D.C., May 29, 1972.

## NEED QUESTIONED FOR VITAMIN-MINERAL PRODUCTS

The medical panel evaluating vitamin and mineral preparations said it "does not recognize the need for vitamin supplementation in healthy individuals eating an adequate diet." It added, however:

"It does recognize the need for supplementation with single-vitamin preparations in certain segments of the population."

## FEW NONPRESCRIPTION DRUGS EFFECTIVE

It also said it recognizes "the lack of precise data on which rational formulation can be based."

Of 12 miscellaneous products, six were called effective. They included Johnson's Baby Lotion for helping "smooth and protect baby's delicate skin," Polysorb for relief of dry skin; Aeroplast spray-on plastic bandage, Rezifilm Surgical Spray Dressing and Scan Spray-on Wound Dressing.

Adjudged ineffective was Covicone Cream in protecting skin from poison ivy, allergens and contact dermatitis.

Five of 20 laxatives were called effective. They are Turicum Suspension, Doxan Tablets, Peri-Colace Syrup, Senokap and Dorbantyl. Others were partially effective.

Pragmatar Ointment was called effective for dandruff. But the claim that Visine gives "fast effective relief to red burning, irritated eyes . . . in just 60 seconds" was doubted.

Five sun screen agents are listed. They are Sun Stick, Sunswept Cream, Sun Bath Lotion and Cream, Sun Bath (Extra Protective Formula) Lotion and Cream and Sundare Lotion.

The first two and last were called "effective but . . ." should carry a warning about prolonged exposure. The report says Sun Bath's claim of "long-lasting suntan without burning, peeling" was not documented. It says Sun Bath's Protective Formula's claim that redheads, blonds and children can tan without burning or peeling is also not documented.

Nine vaginal contraceptives are declared highly, but not 100 per cent, effective. They include Lorophyn Jelly, Ramses Vaginal Jelly, Koromex Vaginal Cream, Lorophyn Suppositories, Immolin Cream-Jel, Lanesta Vaginal Gel, Emko Foam and New Improved Koromex Jelly.

None of the eight antibiotic preparations were called effective without qualification for any claim listed.

**Reading 78**

# Drug Prices Here Twice or Triple Those Paid by Foreigners

**Arthur E. Rowse**

*". . . it would be quite difficult to find a more glaring case of price discrimination against the American consumer than this one."*

New evidence is now available showing the degree to which American pharmaceutical firms overcharge ill people in this country, compared to what is charged for the same medicines to foreigners.

*In a speech scheduled for today* on the Senate floor, Senator Gaylord Nelson ( D-Wis.) lays out the full story in detail. Figures are from Justice Department data on wholesale prices of drugs under patent.

*Nelson cites a decision* by U.S. District Court Judge Sylvester Ryan, who found that the differences in price amount to illegal discrimination against residents of the United States. Similar data have been made public before by Nelson, who has been investigating the drug industry for six years.

"I think," says Nelson, "it would be quite difficult to find a more glaring case of price discrimination against the American consumer than this one." He says the information shows that drug companies "charge what the traffic will bear."

*The following are wholesale prices released by company,* with the overseas price listed first and the U.S. prices next:

*Bristol-Myers—Polycillin* (100 250-miligram capsules) $12.00, $18.20; (100 500-mg. caps) $17.00, $35.16; *Salutensin* (1,000 tablets) $35.00, $65.16.

*Travenol—Synthroid* (500 0.1-mg. tablets) $1.75, $4.47; (500 0.2-mg. tablets) $2.44, $6.28.

*Norwich Pharmaceutical Co.—Furadantin* (100 50-mg. tabs) $8.37, $12.08; (500 50-mg. tabs) $38.98, $56.25; (100 100-mg. tabs) $16.74, $24.17.

*Pfizer—Antivert* (500 tabs) $12.40, $16.96; *Diabinese* (1,000 tabs) $42.75, $67.64; (250 tabs) $10.60, $17.28.

*Ayerst Laboratories—Penbritin* (100 250-mg. tabs) $11.50, $18.18.

*Ortho Pharmaceutical Co.—Ortho-novum* (2-mg. dialpak) $54.72, $86.40; (1-mg.) $51.21, $77.04.

*American Hoechst—Lasix* (3,000 40-mg. tabs) $25.57, $31.37.

*Lakeside Laboratories—Mercuhydrin* (100 10cc vials) $63.24, $96.80; *Norpramin* (500 25-mg.) $11.40, $28.80; *Norpramin* (500 50-mg.) $17.50, $47.50.

*American Roche—Librium* (500 5-mg tabs) $16.65, $20.66; (500 10-mg.) $18.50, $26.78; *Valium* (500 2-mg.) $18.00, $26.69; (500 5-mg.) $21.00, $32.30; *Gantrisin* tabs $12.50, $20.24.

*Mallinkrodt—Dintensin and Dintensin-R* $20.00, $32.85.

*Dorsey-Triaminic* tabs $10.21, $13.80.

*A.H. Robins—Quinidex Extentabs* (250 tabs) $22.18, $26.67; *Dimetapp Extentabs* (500) $25.99, $31.25; *Robaxisal* (500 tabs) $19.40, $23.34; *Donnatal Extentabs* (500) $12.61, $15.17; *Donnazyme* (500 tabs) $12.65, $16.67.

*Lederle—Declomycin* (100 150-mg. caps) $13.19, $15.99; *Aristocort* (100 4-mg.) $7.82, $14.45.

From *Consumer Newsweek*, Issue 91, Washington, D.C., July 9, 1973, p. 3.

Reading 79

# Price Gaps between Brand and Generic Drugs Updated

**Arthur E. Rowse**

*The information shows virtually no change in the size or number of gaps between brand and generic prices.*

By now, there is no news in the fact that many people pay unnecessarily high prices for brand-name medicines which can be purchased for far less under simple generic terms.

But Senator Gaylord Nelson (D. Wis.), who has been conducting a running investigation of medical drugs for six years, has spelled the differences in current prices paid by druggists.

*The information shows virtually no change* in the size or number of gaps between brand and generic prices.

For example, said Nelson, the antihistamine ChlorTrimeton sells to druggists for $21.66 per 1,000 pills while the generic equivalent costs only $1.05 for the same quantity and quality.

For another, Peritrate, a heart drug, sells for $36.00 per 1,000 pills but costs only $1.75 generically.

*Nelson also cited a recent article* by Dr. Henry E. Simmons, recent director of the Food and Drug Administration's Bureau of Drugs, who confirmed that government tests showed no significant difference in quality between generic and branded drugs. Following are Nelson's price comparisons:

| Brand name, company, dosage form, and quantity | Brand name price | Generic price | Generic (official) name | Therapeutic category |
|---|---|---|---|---|
| Polycillin (Bristol): | | | | |
| 100 capsules, 250 mg | $14.85 | $4.70 | Ampicillin | Antibiotic. |
| 100 capsules 500 mg | 28.74 | 9.65 | do | Do. |
| Penbriten (Ayerst): | | | | |
| 100 capsules, 250 mg | 14.54 | 4.70 | do | Do. |
| 100 (2×50's) 500 mg | 24.92 | 9.65 | do | Do. |
| Pentids 400 (Squibb) 100 tablets. | 10.04 | 1.45 | Pencillin G | Do. |
| Pentids 800 (Squibb) 100 tablets. | 15.06 | 4.50 | do | Do. |
| Chlor-Trimeton (Schering) 1,000 tablets, 4 mg. | 21.66 | 1.05 | Chlorpheniramine (maleate). | Anthishistamine. |
| Teldrin (Smith, Kline, & French) 500 capsules, 8 mg. timed disintegration. | 24.25 | 3.20 | Chlorpheniramine | Do. |
| 500 capsules, 12 mg timed disintegration. | 32.50 | 4.00 | do | Do. |
| Benadryl (Parke, Davis): | | | | |
| 1,000 capsules, 25 mg | 18.68 | 4.85 | Diphenhydramine | Do. |
| 1,000 capsules, 50 mg. | 27.84 | 4.95 | do | Do. |
| Dilatin (Parke, Davis) 1,000 capsules, 1½ gr. | 15.85 | 4.95 | Diphenylhy-dantoin | Anticonvulsant. |
| Decadron (Merck, Sharpe & Dohme) 100 tablets, .75 mg. | 12.94 | 5.25 | Dexamethasone | Corticosteroid. |
| Dicumarol (Abbott) 1,000 tablets, 50 mg. | 21.28 | 6.85 | Bishydroxycoumarin | Anticoagulant. |
| Dramamine (Searle) 100 tablets, 50 mg. | 3.78 | .75 | Dimenhydrinate | Antiemetic. |
| Equanil (Wyeth): | | | | |
| 100 tablets, 400 mg | 7.06 | 1.05 | Meprobamate | Tranquilizer. |
| 1,000 tablets, 400 mg | 68.21 | 4.95 | do | Do. |

| Brand name, company, dosage form, and quantity | Brand name price | Generic price | Generic (official) name | Therapeutic category |
|---|---|---|---|---|
| Miltown (Carter-Wallace): | | | | |
| 100 tablets, 400 mg | 6.50 | 1.05 | do | Do. |
| 1,000 tablets, 400 mg | 61.20 | 4.95 | do | Do. |
| Feosol (SKF) 1,000 tablets | 11.00 | 1.95 | Ferrous sulphate | Antianemic. |
| Feosol Spansules (SKF) 500 capsules. | 21.25 | 4.80 | do | Do. |
| Nembutal (Abbott): | | | | |
| 1,000 capsules, ¾ gr | 13.07 | 4.50 | Pentobarbital | Sedative-hypnotic. |
| 1,000 capsules, 1½ gr | 19.24 | 5.85 | do | Do. |
| Gantrisin (Roche): 1,000 tablets, 0.5 gm. | 26.73 | 9.85 | Sulfisoxasole | Antiinfective. |
| Furadantin (Eaton): | | | | |
| 100 tablets, 50 mg | 10.26 | 2.50 | Nitrofurantoin | Antiinfective. |
| 100 tablets, 100 mg | 20.52 | 4.85 | do | Do. |
| Mandelamine (Warner-Chilcott) | | | | |
| 1,000 tablets, 0.25 gm | 18.00 | 4.50 | Methenamine mandelate. | Do. |
| 1,000 tablets, 0.5 gm | 36.00 | 6.70 | do | Do. |
| Noctec (Squibb): | | | | |
| 100 capsules, 3¾ gr | 2.97 | .85 | Chloral hydrate | Sedative-hypnotic. |
| 100—7½ gr | 5.00 | 1.25 | do | Do. |
| Erythrocin (Abbott): 100 tablets, 250 mg. | 17.39 | 6.70 | Erythromycin | Antibiotic. |
| Nydrazid (Squibb): 1,000 tablets, 100 mg. | 9.90 | 2.75 | Isoniazid | Antititubercular. |
| Peritrate (Warner-Chilcott): | | | | |
| 1,000 tablets, 10 mg | 27.00 | 1.65 | Pentaerythrito, tetranitrate. | Anitanginal. |
| 1,000 tablets, 20 mg | 36.00 | 1.75 | do | Do. |
| Peritrate with phenobarbital: | | | | |
| 1,000 tablets, 10 mg/15 mg | 29.70 | 1.65 | Pentaerythritoltetra-nitrate with phenobarbital. | Do. |
| 1,000 tablets, 20 mg/15 mg | 40.50 | 1.75 | do | Do. |

| Brand name, company, dosage form, and quantity | Brand name price | Generic price | Generic (official) name | Therapeutic category |
|---|---|---|---|---|
| Premarin (Ayerst): | | | | |
| 100 tablets, 0.625 mg | 4.08 | .35 | Conjugated estrogens | Estrogen. |
| 100 tablets, 2.5 mg | 12.97 | 3.95 | do | Do. |
| Premarin with methyltestosterone (Ayerst): | | | | |
| 100 tablets, 0.625 mg and 5 mg test. | 8.72 | 2.85 | Conjugated estrogens | Do. |
| 100 tablets, 1.25 mg and 10 mg test. | 15.40 | 4.45 | Plus testosterone | Do. |
| Pro-Banthine (Searle): 100 tablets, 15 mg. | 4.26 | 1.65 | Propantheline | Antispasmodic. |
| Pro-Banthine with phenobarbital. | 4.68 | 1.85 | Propantheline with phenobarbital. | Do. |
| Pyribenzamine (Ciba): | | | | |
| 100 tablets, 50 mg | 2.80 | .80 | Tripelennamine | Antihistamine. |
| 1,000 tablets, 50 mg | 27.16 | 3.45 | do | Do. |
| Serpasil (Ciba): 1,000 tablets, 0.25 mg | 39.50 | 1.35 | Reserpine | Antihypertensive. |
| Reserpoid (Upjohn): 1,000 tablets, 0.25 mg | 8.39 | 1.35 | do | Do. |
| Rau-sed (Squibb): 1,000 1,000 tablets, 0.25 mg | 10.86 | 1.35 | do | Do. |
| Sandril (Lilly): 1,000 tablets, 0.25 mg | 9.12 | 1.35 | do | Do. |
| Dexedrine (SKF): 1,000 tablets, 5 mg | 22.60 | 5.15 | Dextro-amphetamine sulfate. | Amphetamine. |
| Sudafed (Burroughs-Wellcome): 1,000 tablets, 60 mg | 32.67 | 7.90 | Pseudoephedrine | Bronchodilator. |

| Brand name, company, dosage form, and quantity | Brand name price | Generic price | Generic (official) name | Therapeutic category |
|---|---|---|---|---|
| Tedral (Warner-Chilcott): 1,000 tablets. | 32.85 | 3.75 | Combination of 130 mg theophylline, 24 mg ephedrine HCL, 8 mg phenobarbital. | Do. |
| Terramycin (Pfizer): 100 capsules, 250 mg. | 20.48 | 1.95 | Oxytetracycline | Antibiotic. |
| Tetracyn (Roerig): 100 capsules, 250 mg. | 3.86 | 1.20 | Tetracycline | Do. |
| 100 capsules, 500 mg | 7.50 | 2.25 | do | Do. |
| Achromycin V (Lederle): | | | | |
| 100 capsules, 250 ng. | 5.35 | 1.20 | do | Do. |
| 1,000 capsules, 250 mg | 52.02 | 7.95 | do | Do. |
| 100 capsules, 500 mg | 9.75 | 2.25 | do | Do. |
| V-Cillin K (Lilly): 100 tablets, 250 mg. | 8.95 | 2.60 | Potassium phenoxymethyl penicillin. | Do. |
| 1,000 (2 × 500), 250 mg | 75.00 | 23.50 | do | Do. |
| 100 tablets, 500 mg | 16.93 | 4.50 | do | Do. |
| Pen-Vee K (Wyeth): 100 tablets 250 mg | 10.47 | 2.60 | do | Do. |
| 100 tablets, 500 mg | 19.69 | 4.50 | do | Do. |

Average wholesale prices—1973 Red Book and supplement No. 1.

# Buying Protection, Social Security, Life Insurance and Annuities

Reading 80

## Funeral Societies—How They Help

**Changing Times**

*Also, because plans were discussed in advance, a family understands what is being done and they are better able to face death.*

For survivors, the death of a relative or friend is a time of sadness and often confusion. Few people know much about funeral traditions or burial laws, yet families under emotional stress must make business decisions quickly that can involve large sums of money. And the cost of dying keeps going up. In 1969 the average cost of an adult funeral was $926, and in 1971, $983. This year estimates are for a bill that runs over $1,000, and these amounts do not include vault, cemetery or crematorium expenses, a monument or marker, a fee for the clergyman or flowers.

Until recently few people seemed to give this inevitable problem much advance thought. Now there are signs that attitudes are changing. The growth of funeral or memorial societies, though their numbers are still small, indicates people are increasingly interested in making arrangements before death for simple, dignified funerals at reasonable cost. According to Bruce Bowman, president of the Funeral and Memorial Societies of Greater Washington, D.C., the primary work of these nonprofit organizations is to get people to talk, think and, most important, make agreements about death arrangements with next of kin. He points to the advantages of preplanning: Once you decide what you want, how to get it and what it will cost, survivors do not have to negotiate for a funeral. Also, because plans were discussed in advance, a family understands what is being done and they are better able to face death.

Organizers of memorial societies say there are several reasons why more people are enrolling. Saving money is certainly one incentive, perhaps the biggest. Dissatisfaction with elaborate funeral ceremonies causes many people to seek an alternative, and the cremation and anatomical donation programs encouraged by most funeral and memorial societies are attractive to the ecology-conscious and to humanitarians.

## THE SETUP OF THE SOCIETIES

Memorial groups may spring from an established organization, a church or religious fellowship, for instance, or a civic club or consumer cooperative. Whatever the source, reputable societies follow guidelines set by the Continental Association of Funeral and Memorial Societies. The association is a national clearinghouse for information and serves more than 100 societies with about 350,000 members.

Societies belonging to CAFMS follow an open-membership policy—no restrictions on race, creed, occupation or nationality. The groups are nondenominational, though some are organized by ministerial groups and many have offices in churches. The handful of churches and other religious organizations that sponsor funeral societies and restrict membership are not eligible for CAFMS.

Members manage their own societies, using volunteers to handle office duties and a board of directors to oversee business affairs, which may include contracts with funeral directors. Large organizations may hire part- or full-time secretaries to help maintain records and files.

The size of a society's membership can range from a small group with only a few families, say under 20, to organizations such as People's Memorial Association in Seattle, which has more than 40,000 members. The size of the area a society serves may vary, too. A single organization can serve an entire state or region; California, on the other hand, has a dozen groups within its borders.

For most memorial societies, major financial support comes from a one-time fee that is paid upon joining. The single payment for a family membership isn't higher than $20, and $10 is about average. The cost for individuals is usually half the family rate. No CAFMS-approved society charges annual dues, but some receive a "records charge"—an expense that is figured into funeral costs to help the society defray its expenses.

## THEY HELP IN DIFFERENT WAYS

All funeral and memorial groups want participants to choose arrangements that best suit their needs. For this reason, and because societies must conform to state and local laws, memorial groups work in different ways. Some limit services to advising and educating members on advance planning of death arrangements. Others also make or arrange for contracts on behalf of members with one or more funeral directors.

Generally, societies can help plan for disposing of a body by burial and cremation or anatomical donation, and advise members on cooperating funeral directors, cemeteries and crematoriums in the area. In addition, societies may provide information on planning to meet expenses and on funeral or memorial services appropriate to members' wishes. In most instances, societies issue membership cards and forms for recording information regarding death arrangements. Societies may request that copies of these forms be filed with their office or with a cooperating mortician.

The Memorial Society of New England is one society that limits its assistance to educating members because state laws in its region prohibit groups from contracting with a funeral home in advance of death. However, as part of its educational campaign, the society does provide information about funeral directors who have cooperated with members.

Usually, a society does not handle funerals for individual members. Instead, it makes arrangements with a funeral director, either in a formal contract or informal understanding, about the fees and services that are available. Members contact the funeral director on their own initiative to select the plans and costs they find most satisfactory. For example, the Maryland Suburban Memorial Society in Silver Spring has an agreement with a local funeral home giving members a choice of several cremation and burial plans. Prices range from $235 for cremation to $605 for a burial plan that includes embalming, casket, use of the chapel and a cemetery lot. Members are under no obligation to use any of the funeral plans and may change arrangements later if they wish.

## JOIN A SOCIETY OR PLAN ALONE?

Memorial societies agree that in some areas people may be able to arrange for simple services and economical rates themselves. But they say people are more likely to successfully plan and arrange in advance if they belong to a group that encourages them with the work.

If you're interested in finding a memorial society near you, check the white pages of the telephone directory for organization titles beginning with "Funeral" or "Memorial." The phone number may be for a private residence because some societies have offices in members' homes. Ask the society for information about the type of assistance it gives and its membership fee.

Unfortunately, some groups calling themselves memorial societies are not bona fide organizations. If an outfit asks for a fee much larger than the average or if it tries to sell you a funeral or cemetery lot, investigate carefully. Check with the Better Business Bureau or with CAFMS.

If you can't locate a nearby society, write to the Continental Association of Funeral and Memorial Societies [59 E. Van Buren St., Chicago, Ill., 60605], to find out whether a society serves your area or if a group is being formed. If you're interested in starting a society, the association will send information on how to go about it.

If you prefer to make prearrangements on your own, you must seek out and visit sympathetic funeral directors. Describe the type of services you want and emphasize that you're not willing to pay for services you don't want or need. If you check with your state's board of health about laws and regulations regarding embalming, cremation and other funeral practices first, you will be able to discuss these issues knowledgeably.

Whether you do the planning on your own or through a group, be sure to discuss the arrangements with your family. The best-made plans fall apart if you haven't clued next of kin to your ideas. Above all, discussing and planning death arrangements in advance means a family will get the help it wants at a time when the need is greatest.

Reading 81

# Life Insurance: How Costs Compare Company by Company

**Changing Times**

*One major problem always faced by insurance buyers is to sift out the net effect of premiums, cash values and dividends in some way that makes it possible to compare competing policies.*

When *Changing Times* first published the interest-adjusted costs of life insurance policies in March 1971, many people in the life insurance business protested vehemently.

Those cost comparisons demonstrated with hard figures that some companies charge more than others for basically identical insurance and that buyers can, therefore, save simply by shopping around. Although use of the interest-adjusted method for measuring costs had been recommended by a prestigious committee of life insurance experts, it was the first time that a national general-circulation publication applied the method to rank policy costs in a way that could be quickly understood by laymen.

The material for that initial compilation was obtained from the National Underwriter Co., an insurance trade publishing firm. This year, to update our rankings, the 50 companies with the largest amounts of ordinary insurance in force were contacted directly and asked to furnish 1973 data on their own $10,000 whole life policies. (Some top companies were excluded because they sell only to special groups.)

Of the 50 selected, only one—Western-Southern Life, Cincinnati, Ohio—refused to cooperate. This high rate of cooperation seems to indicate that insurance companies now more fully appreciate the public's need for cost-comparison facts.

The results of the survey begin on page 311. First, however, review a few fundamentals that will help you make better use of the rankings.

## THE TWO TYPES OF COVERAGE

Insurance companies sell two basic types of life insurance, term and cash value. The policies are modified in various ways, sometimes dressed up with fancy names, and joined in special combinations, but essentially you always get term, cash value or a package of the two. (Coming on the market soon will be a third type known as variable life, whose face amount and cash values will vary with the returns on a securities fund in which the premiums will be invested. For details, see *Changing Times,* January 1973.)

Term policies are sold for a specified period of one or more years, and the premiums rise each time you renew (to take account of the higher mortality risk). Most companies won't permit term insurance to be renewed past a certain age. Term policies accumulate no cash values in the usual sense.

In a cash value policy, the premium is fixed according to your age at time of purchase and usually doesn't change thereafter. For example, with a whole life policy you pay the same premium as long as you live. In a paid-up type of policy, premiums are payable only for a fixed number of years or until a prescribed age—65, 80, 85, etc.

When it charges a level premium, the company has to take into account that your mortality risk rises each year. To do that, it sets the premium high enough to exceed the cost of insuring your life during the early years and thereby builds up a fund for later years when the premium doesn't cover the full cost. It's that fund and the interest it earns that produce the cash values.

You can use the cash value of a policy as collateral for a loan from the insurance company or a lending institution. You can withdraw it in a lump sum, though, only if you surrender the policy. In that case, you may also use the money to buy the same amount of nonrenewable term for as long a period as the money will permit or a reduced amount of immediately paid-up cash value insurance.

A surprisingly large proportion of buyers do not retain their policies until death. One major company's figures, believed to be fairly typical of the business, show that about 25% let their policies lapse after one year (before most policies start accumulating cash values); 54% lapse or surrender their policies during the first ten years; and 70% terminate by the time they reach 60. About two out of five who surrender policies with cash values during the first 20 years take the term or reduced paid-up coverage instead of cash.

The rate and amount of cash value accumulation varies among policies and companies. Thus, an insurance buyer has to consider differences in both premiums and cash value schedules when comparing costs of policies. A third essential factor is the annual dividend paid on "participating" policies.

Dividends represent a refund of part of your annual premium. The amount depends on the company's current mortality, expense and investment experience. The agent can provide a schedule showing what dividends might be paid over the years. But those figures, unlike premiums and cash values, are *not* guaranteed. The company may pay more or less.

Because companies expect to pay dividends on participating policies, they charge a higher initial premium for them than for identical nonparticipating contracts. Eventually, the net payments—premiums minus dividends—of the participating policy may drop to and below the nonparticipating policy's premiums, but again that's not guaranteed. For that reason, participating and nonparticipating policies are ranked separately in the tables.

## THE OLD COST METHOD

One major problem always faced by insurance buyers is to sift out the net effect of premiums, cash values and dividends in some way that makes it possible to compare competing policies.

Insurance men have commonly compared policies by their "average surrendered net cost per $1,000" of face amount. But that formula, better known as the traditional net-cost method, can produce absurd results. Consider this illustration based on a $162.80 annual premium, $10,000 participating policy surrendered at the end of 20 years:

| | | |
|---|---|---|
| You pay out: | | |
| Premiums for 20 years | | $3,256.00 |
| You receive: | $1,046.00 | |
| Dividends for 20 years | | |
| Cash value at end of 20 years | $2,620.00 | |
| Total | $3,666.00 | |
| Subtract total from premiums: | | $3,666.00 |
| Cost of insurance for 20 years | | −$410.00 |
| Cost per $1,000 (divide by 10) | | −$41.00 |
| Cost per year per $1,000 (divide by 20) | | −$2.05 |

Notice that the cost is *negative.* The traditional net-cost formula in this instance would have you believe you can cash in the policy for $2,620 and come out without having paid a cent for 20 years of life protection. Only the company loses (to the tune of $410, or $20.50 a year), and yet companies are happy to sell such policies.

Obviously, the formula leaves some cost element out of the picture. The most significant factor omitted is interest. *When* you receive a fixed sum may be just as important as the amount. For example, these are the first three years' dividends on two policies. Which is the better way to buy?

| A | B |
|---|---|
| none | $10 |
| $20 | $18 |
| 30 | 22 |

Both pay a total of $50 for the first three years, and at first sight there doesn't seem to be any reason to choose one over the other. But if the dividends are compounded at 4% annually, as they would be if you put the cash each year into a 4% savings account, company B's policy emerges as the better deal. Adjusted for interest, it pays $51.54 against A's $50.80. Those interest differences widen after many years with the increase in dividends and the compounding of interest, and become a crucial cost factor.

Whether you actually deposit the dividends in a savings account or use them to reduce premiums or buy additional insurance doesn't matter. What really counts is that, in theory, you have the opportunity to earn interest on the money. Similarly, if one company charges a $200 annual premium and another only $180 for the same policy, the second company gives you a chance to earn interest on the $20 difference by putting the money into the bank each year.

That's why the interest-adjusted method of calculating policy costs was born.

## HOW THE NEW METHOD WORKS

Now see how adding interest to the traditional net-cost illustration changes the results:

| | | |
|---|---|---|
| You pay out: | | |
| Premiums for 20 years, at 4% compounded | | $5,041.75 |
| You receive: | | |
| Dividends for 20 years, at 4% compounded | $1,421.45 | |
| Cash value at end of 20 years | 2,620.00 | |
| Total | $4,041.45 | |
| Subtract total from premiums: | | 4,041.45 |
| Cost of insurance for 20 years | | $1,000.03 |
| Cost per $1,000 (divided by 10) | | $100.03 |
| Interest-adjusted cost per year per $1,000 | | $3.23 |

That final $3.23, the interest-adjusted cost, represents the amount that would have to be put away each year in a 4% account to accumulate to the $100.03 net cost of $1,000 of insurance protection for the 21-year period.

Don't confuse the interest-adjusted cost—or the traditional net cost illustrated earlier—with your actual out-of-pocket expense, which consists of the annual premium minus the annual dividend, if any. The interest-adjusted formula combines the premium, dividend and cash value data into a single cost *index*.

As you can see, there's nothing particularly mysterious about the new method. It merely cranks interest into the old formula to arrive at a more realistic index for comparing policies.

## IT, TOO, HAS WEAKNESSES

Although the interest-adjusted method constitutes a valuable improvement over present practice, certain drawbacks should be kept in mind.

- The formula assumes surrender of the policy, so it doesn't measure the cost of retaining a policy until the policyholder dies. Experts have been developing other, more sophisticated methods to evaluate the cost at death, raising the possibility that eventually life policies can be ranked by two formulas.
- Policies have to be compared at the same purchase age and for the same surrender period. A policy with a relatively low cost when issued at 25 and surrendered in ten years might show up with a high cost at 35 and twenty years.
- Each company sells a number of different variations of cash value policies, and you can't categorize its complete line by the cost of any one policy.
- Companies usually discount premiums for policies with higher face amounts. Thus, costs per $1,000 of coverage have to be matched against policies of the same size. (However, the *Changing Times* 1971 survey showed that the discounts often don't compensate for underlying cost differences among companies. Some of the insurers then were offering no-minimum-amount policies at less per $1,000 than comparable policies of other companies with minimums of $25,000 and more.)
- Applying different interest rates will produce different sets of interest-adjusted costs. The 4% rate employed for the tables was suggested by the committee mentioned at the beginning because it approximates the after-tax interest return likely to be attainable over a long period.

- Companies revise premium and dividend scales from time to time. It's not always safe to rely on a previous year's figures as a buying guide. Of course, the same can be said for using last year's prices of cars, bread or any other product.
- The interest-adjusted formula doesn't evaluate many peripheral cost factors, such as the rates at which cash values can be converted into paid-up or term insurance. For that matter, cost, however figured, is not the only factor to consider in buying insurance. Other matters, such as agent's service and pay-out methods, need to be explored, too.

Notwithstanding those qualifications, the formula represents enough of an advance for consumer-interest advocates to recommend that all companies be required to make public cost figures based on the interest-adjusted method or one similar to it.

Events appear to be moving in that direction, albeit very slowly. The Wisconsin insurance department this year ordered companies to provide prospective buyers in that state with a "surrender-value comparison index"—interest-adjusted costs—of the specific policies being considered. (It's up to the buyer to make his own comparisons by getting figures from several companies.) Other states are working on similar rules. The Pennsylvania Insurance Department has published interest-adjusted cost guides on companies selling there.

A special task force of the National Association of Insurance Commissioners is scheduled to meet this month to work on methods of comparing life insurance costs. And it was recently suggested in Congress that the federal government take the lead by imposing a national, uniform system of cost disclosure.

## HOW TO USE THESE TABLES

The companies are ranked according to the interest-adjusted cost per $1,000 of face amount of insurance, based on $10,000 whole life policies issued at ages 25, 35 and 45, surrendered at the end of ten and twenty years.

For companies that do not sell whole life, or not in the standard $10,000 amount, the closest comparable policy was selected. Massachusetts Mutual, Great-West Life, American United Life, Jefferson Standard (nonparticipating) and Provident Life and Accident policies are paid up at 95; Metropolitan's is paid up at 90; and Jefferson Standard's participating, John Hancock's and Prudential's are paid up at 85.

Some companies offer both participating and nonparticipating policies and are therefore represented twice.

Life of Virginia, Metropolitan, Prudential and State Farm automatically include with their policies a waiver-of-premium disability benefit that will pay premiums when the policyholder becomes disabled. Their interest-adjusted figures cover the *total* cost of the policy waiver combination because the policy cannot be purchased separately. Their interest-adjusted costs would be lower if the waiver, for which other companies charge an extra premium, were not included.

Some companies set premium rates according to your age at your last birthday while others use your nearest birthday. That difference might significantly affect your premium because rates increase with the buyer's age at time of purchase. Company practice on this point should be checked before contracting for a policy.

The insurance companies have been identified by their headquarters states to avoid confusion with other companies with similar names. You can usually find out whether any particular company sells in your area through the telephone listings of local agents.

Naturally, you need not limit yourself to the listed companies. Many others sell policies within the same cost range as the largest 50. You can make your own cost comparisons for nonlisted companies by asking the agents for interest-adjusted costs for the same type of policy covered in this survey. Many companies are reported to be calculating those cost figures in order to comply with Wisconsin state regulations.

**Bought by a man at age 25**

| Company | Interest-adjusted cost per $1,000 |
|---|---|
| *Participating policies surrendered at end of 10 years* | |
| Connecticut Mutual (Conn.) | $3.15 |
| Bankers Life (Iowa) | 3.22 |
| Northwestern Mutual (Wis.) | 3.63 |
| Provident Mutual (Pa.) | 3.77 |
| National Life (VT.) | 4.09 |
| Massachusetts Mutual (Mass.) | 4.25 |
| Mutual Benefit (N.J.) | 4.30 |
| Canada Life (Ont., Can.) | 4.34 |
| North American Life (Ont., Can.) | 4.57 |
| Confederation Life (Ont., Can.) | 4.59 |
| Guardian Life (N.Y.) | 4.66 |
| Phoenix Mutual (Conn.) | 4.79 |
| Sun Life (Que., Can.) | 4.79 |
| New York Life (N.Y.) | 4.84 |
| Great-West Life (Man., Can.) | 4.87 |
| State Mutual of America (Mass.) | 4.96 |
| New England Mutual (Mass.) | 4.99 |
| Nationwide Life (Ohio) | 5.01 |
| Penn Mutual (Pa.) | 5.03 |
| Home Life (N.Y.) | 5.06 |
| Jefferson Standard (N.C.) | 5.20 |
| Crown Life (Ont., Can.) | 5.23 |
| Prudential (N.J.) | 5.53 |
| Occidental Life (Cal.) | 5.57 |
| American United (Ind.) | 5.62 |
| Equitable Life (N.Y.) | 5.66 |
| Franklin Life (Ill.) | 5.66 |
| Mutual Life (N.Y.) | 5.70 |
| Manufacturers Life (Ont., Can.) | 5.71 |
| Lincoln National (Ind.) | 5.76 |
| State Farm (Ill.) | 5.84 |
| Life & Casualty (Tenn.) | 6.04 |
| Metropolitan Life (N.Y.) | 6.34 |
| Continental Assurance (Ill.) | 6.42 |
| American National (Tex.) | 6.58 |
| John Hancock (Mass.) | 6.63 |
| Republic National (Tex.) | 6.96 |
| Aetna Life & Casualty (Conn.) | 8.83 |
| *Participating policies surrendered at end of 20 years* | |
| Connecticut Mutual (Conn.) | $2.50 |
| Bankers Life (Iowa) | 2.60 |
| Home Life (N.Y.) | 2.64 |

**Bought by a man at age 25**

| Company | Interest-adjusted cost per $1,000 |
|---|---|
| Northwestern Mutual (Wis.) | $2.74 |
| Phoenix Mutual (Conn.) | 2.89 |
| National Life (Vt.) | 3.05 |
| Massachusetts Mutual (Mass.) | 3.19 |
| Sun Life (Que., Can.) | 3.20 |
| Provident Mutual (Pa.) | 3.21 |
| Confederation Life (Ont., Can.) | 3.23 |
| Guardian Life (N.Y.) | 3.27 |
| New England Mutual (Mass.) | 3.31 |
| Mutual Benefit (N.J.) | 3.39 |
| State Mutual of America (Mass.) | 3.43 |
| Lincoln National (Ind.) | 3.48 |
| Great-West Life (Man., Can.) | 3.49 |
| Canada Life (Ont., Can.) | 3.54 |
| North American Life (Ont., Can.) | 3.54 |
| New York Life (N.Y.) | 3.59 |
| Manufacturers Life (Ont., Can.) | 3.70 |
| Crown Life (Ont., Can.) | 3.82 |
| State Farm (Ill.) | 3.85 |
| Franklin Life (Ill.) | 3.86 |
| Continental Assurance (Ill.) | 3.88 |
| American United (Ind.) | 3.96 |
| Nationwide Life (Ohio) | 3.99 |
| Penn Mutual (Pa.) | 4.00 |
| Republic National (Tex.) | 4.00 |
| Jefferson Standard (N.C.) | 4.03 |
| Equitable Life (N.Y.) | 4.04 |
| Mutual Life (N.Y.) | 4.16 |
| Life & Casualty (Tenn.) | 4.25 |
| Metropolitan Life (N.Y.) | 4.49 |
| Prudential (N.J.) | 4.51 |
| American National (Tex.) | 4.56 |
| Occidental Life (Cal.) | 4.72 |
| Aetna Life & Casualty (Conn.) | 4.84 |
| John Hancock (Mass.) | 4.94 |
| *Nonparticipating policies surrendered at end of 10 years* | |
| Allstate (Ill.) | $3.98 |
| Life & Casualty (Tenn.) | 4.89 |
| IDS Life (Minn.) | 4.90 |
| Travelers (Conn.) | 4.91 |
| National Life & Accident (Tenn.) | 5.22 |
| Occidental Life (Cal.) | 5.26 |
| Southwestern Life (Tex.) | 5.36 |
| Crown Life (Ont., Can.) | 5.44 |
| Franklin Life (Ill.) | 5.72 |
| Continental Assurance (Ill.) | 5.74 |
| Provident Life & Accident (Tenn.) | 5.96 |
| American National (Tex.) | 5.98 |
| Life of Virginia (Va.) | 6.00 |
| Lincoln National (Ind.) | 6.01 |
| Liberty National (Ala.) | 6.14 |
| Jefferson Standard (N.C.) | 6.24 |
| Business Men's Assurance (Mo.) | 6.26 |
| Republic National (Tex.) | 6.31 |

| Company | Interest-adjusted cost per $1,000 |
|---|---|
| **Bought by a man at age 25** | |
| Aetna Life & Casualty (Conn.) | $6.32 |
| Connecticut General (Conn.) | 6.46 |
| United Benefit (Neb.) | 6.56 |
| *Nonparticipating policies surrendered at end of 20 years* | |
| Life & Casualty (Tenn.) | $4.13 |
| Allstate (Ill.) | 4.16 |
| Travelers (Conn.) | 4.37 |
| Southwestern Life (Tex.) | 4.63 |
| National Life & Accident (Tenn.) | 4.67 |
| Occidental Life (Cal.) | 4.75 |
| Republic National (Tex.) | 4.76 |
| Franklin Life (Ill.) | 4.95 |
| Continental Assurance (Ill.) | 4.99 |
| Crown Life (Ont., Can.) | 4.99 |
| Connecticut General (Conn.) | 5.00 |
| Provident Life & Accident (Tenn.) | 5.17 |
| IDS Life (Minn.) | 5.22 |
| American National (Tex.) | 5.31 |
| Jefferson Standard (N.C.) | 5.52 |
| Life of Virginia (Va.) | 5.54 |
| Lincoln National (Ind.) | 5.55 |
| Aetna Life & Casualty (Conn.) | 5.58 |
| Liberty National (Ala.) | 5.64 |
| Business Men's Assurance (Mo.) | 5.78 |
| United Benefit (Neb.) | 5.90 |

**Bought by a man at age 35**

| Company | Interest-adjusted cost per $1,000 |
|---|---|
| *Participating policies surrendered at end of 10 years* | |
| Bankers Life (Iowa) | $4.35 |
| Northwestern Mutual (Wis.) | 4.65 |
| Connecticut Mutual (Conn.) | 4.74 |
| Massachusetts Mutual (Mass.) | 5.16 |
| Provident Mutual (Pa.) | 5.30 |
| National Life (Vt.) | 5.40 |
| Mutual Benefit (N.J.) | 5.59 |
| Canada Life (Ont., Can.) | 5.67 |
| Phoenix Mutual (Conn.) | 6.07 |
| Confederation Life (Ont., Can.) | 6.08 |
| North American Life (Ont., Can.) | 6.09 |
| Sun Life (Que., Can.) | 6.16 |
| Great-West Life (Man., Can.) | 6.17 |
| New York Life (N.Y.) | 6.26 |
| Guardian Life (N.Y.) | 6.27 |
| Nationwide Life (Ohio) | 6.31 |
| State Mutual of America (Mass.) | 6.32 |
| New England Mutual (Mass.) | 6.34 |
| Jefferson Standard (N.C.) | 6.39 |
| Penn Mutual (Pa.) | 6.45 |
| Crown Life (Ont., Can.) | 6.51 |
| Home Life (N.Y.) | 6.57 |
| Manufacturers Life (Ont., Can.) | 6.82 |
| Occidental Life (Cal.) | 6.94 |

**Bought by a man at age 35**

| Company | Interest-adjusted cost per $1,000 |
|---|---|
| American United (Ind.) | $7.07 |
| Lincoln National (Ind.) | 7.07 |
| Equitable Life (N.Y.) | 7.20 |
| Mutual Life (N.Y.) | 7.24 |
| Franklin Life (Ill.) | 7.41 |
| State Farm (Ill.) | 7.45 |
| Life & Casualty (Tenn.) | 7.64 |
| Prudential (N.J.) | 7.74 |
| Continental Assurance (Ill.) | 8.13 |
| Republic National (Tex.) | 8.31 |
| Metropolitan Life (N.Y.) | 8.53 |
| John Hancock (Mass.) | 8.55 |
| American National (Tex.) | 8.56 |
| Aetna Life & Casualty (Conn.) | 10.61 |
| *Participating policies surrendered at end of 20 years* | |
| Northwestern Mutual (Wis.) | $4.13 |
| Bankers Life (Iowa) | 4.18 |
| Connecticut Mutual (Conn.) | 4.45 |
| Home Life (N.Y.) | 4.54 |
| National Life (Vt.) | 4.63 |
| Phoenix Mutual (Conn.) | 4.64 |
| Massachusetts Mutual (Mass.) | 4.72 |
| Sun Life (Que., Can.) | 5.01 |
| New England Mutual (Mass.) | 5.05 |
| Mutual Benefit (N.J.) | 5.09 |
| Guardian Life (N.Y.) | 5.10 |
| Confederation Life (Ont., Can.) | 5.12 |
| Provident Mutual (Pa.) | 5.15 |
| Manufacturers Life (Ont., Can.) | 5.18 |
| Great-West Life (Man., Can.) | 5.22 |
| Lincoln National (Ind.) | 5.23 |
| New York Life (N.Y.) | 5.24 |
| Canada Life (Ont., Can.) | 5.30 |
| State Mutual of America (Mass.) | 5.35 |
| North American Life (Ont., Can.) | 5.43 |
| Crown Life (Ont., Can.) | 5.61 |
| Nationwide Life (Ohio) | 5.61 |
| Continental Assurance (Ill.) | 5.62 |
| Penn Mutual (Pa.) | 5.67 |
| Republic National (Tex.) | 5.69 |
| Jefferson Standard (N.C.) | 5.72 |
| American United (Ind.) | 5.73 |
| Franklin Life (Ill.) | 5.80 |
| State Farm (Ill.) | 5.85 |
| Equitable Life (N.Y.) | 5.97 |
| Mutual Life (N.Y.) | 6.05 |
| Life & Casualty (Tenn.) | 6.13 |
| American National (Tex.) | 6.37 |
| Aetna Life & Casualty (Conn.) | 6.51 |
| Occidental Life (Cal.) | 6.58 |
| Prudential (N.J.) | 6.91 |
| Metropolitan Life (N.Y.) | 6.92 |
| John Hancock (Mass.) | 6.98 |

| **Bought by a man at age 35** | |
|---|---|
| **Company** | **Interest-adjusted cost per $1,000** |
| *Nonparticipating policies surrendered at end of 10 years* | |
| Allstate (Ill.) | $5.76 |
| IDS Life (Minn.) | 6.36 |
| Life & Casualty (Tenn.) | 6.57 |
| Travelers (Conn.) | 6.84 |
| Occidental Life (Cal.) | 6.91 |
| Crown Life (Ont., Can.) | 7.03 |
| National Life & Accident (Tenn.) | 7.15 |
| Southwestern Life (Tex.) | 7.28 |
| Republic National (Tex.) | 7.40 |
| Continental Assurance (Ill.) | 7.41 |
| Franklin Life (Ill.) | 7.45 |
| Jefferson Standard (N.C.) | 7.70 |
| Lincoln National (Ind.) | 7.72 |
| American National (Tex.) | 7.76 |
| Provident Life & Accident (Tenn.) | 7.80 |
| Life of Virginia (Va.) | 7.88 |
| Business Men's Assurance (Mo.) | 8.04 |
| Aetna Life & Casualty (Conn.) | 8.14 |
| Liberty National (Ala.) | 8.15 |
| Connecticut General (Conn.) | 8.22 |
| United Benefit (Neb.) | 8.36 |
| *Nonparticipating policies surrendered at end of 20 years* | |
| Life & Casualty (Tenn.) | $6.51 |
| Allstate (Ill.) | 6.63 |
| Republic National (Tex.) | 6.65 |
| Travelers (Conn.) | 7.05 |
| Southwestern Life (Tex.) | 7.20 |
| Crown Life (Ont., Can.) | 7.32 |
| Continental Assurance (Ill.) | 7.34 |
| Occidental Life (Cal.) | 7.34 |
| National Life & Accident (Tenn.) | 7.36 |
| Franklin Life (Ill.) | 7.38 |
| IDS Life (Minn.) | 7.48 |
| Connecticut General (Conn.) | 7.51 |
| Jefferson Standard (N.C.) | 7.78 |
| Provident Life & Accident (Tenn.) | 7.78 |
| American National (Tex.) | 7.93 |
| Aetna Life & Casualty (Conn.) | 8.07 |
| Lincoln National (Ind.) | 8.13 |
| Life of Virginia (Va.) | 8.17 |
| Business Men's Assurance (Mo.) | 8.36 |
| United Benefit (Neb.) | 8.41 |
| Liberty National (Ala.) | 8.44 |

| **Bought by a man at age 45** | |
|---|---|
| *Participating policies surrendered at end of 10 years* | |
| Bankers Life (Iowa) | $8.12 |
| Northwestern Mutual (Wis.) | 8.28 |
| Connecticut Mutual (Conn.) | 8.75 |
| Provident Mutual (Pa.) | 8.98 |

**Bought by a man at age 45**

| Company | Interest-adjusted cost per $1,000 |
|---|---|
| National Life (Vt.) | $9.06 |
| Mutual Benefit (N.J.) | 9.24 |
| Massachusetts Mutual (Mass.) | 9.45 |
| Phoenix Mutual (Conn.) | 9.50 |
| New England Mutual (Mass.) | 9.75 |
| Nationwide Life (Ohio) | 9.92 |
| Canada Life (Ont., Can.) | 9.94 |
| Sun Life (Que., Can.) | 10.01 |
| New York Life (N.Y.) | 10.07 |
| Great-West Life (Man., Can.) | 10.16 |
| State Mutual of America (Mass.) | 10.26 |
| North American Life (Ont., Can.) | 10.32 |
| Jefferson Standard (N.C.) | 10.41 |
| Crown Life (Ont., Can.) | 10.43 |
| Penn Mutual (Pa.) | 10.45 |
| Confederation Life (Ont., Can.) | 10.56 |
| Manufacturers Life (Ont., Can.) | 10.58 |
| Guardian Life (N.Y.) | 10.64 |
| Home Life (N.Y.) | 10.72 |
| Mutual Life (N.Y.) | 10.86 |
| Occidental Life (Cal.) | 10.91 |
| Lincoln National (Ind.) | 10.92 |
| American United (Ind.) | 11.18 |
| John Hancock Mutual (Mass.) | 11.57 |
| Equitable Life (N.Y.) | 11.64 |
| Franklin Life (Ill.) | 11.75 |
| Republic National (Tex.) | 11.97 |
| State Farm (Ill.) | 11.98 |
| Prudential (N.J.) | 12.26 |
| John Hancock (Mass.) | 12.79 |
| Continental Assurance (Ill.) | 12.93 |
| American National (Tex.) | 13.20 |
| Metropolitan Life (N.Y.) | 14.00 |
| Aetna Life & Casualty (Conn.) | 14.73 |
| *Participating policies surrendered at end of 20 years* | |
| Northwestern Mutual (Wis.) | $8.49 |
| Bankers Life (Iowa) | 8.53 |
| National Life (Vt.) | 8.75 |
| Phoenix Mutual (Conn.) | 8.86 |
| Home Life (N.Y.) | 8.97 |
| Connecticut Mutual (Conn.) | 9.03 |
| New England Mutual (Mass.) | 9.18 |
| Massachusetts Mutual (Mass.) | 9.47 |
| Sun Life (Que., Can.) | 9.53 |
| Manufacturers Life (Ont., Can.) | 9.54 |
| Mutual Benefit (N.J.) | 9.55 |
| Provident Mutual (Pa.) | 9.65 |
| New York Life (N.Y.) | 9.70 |
| Lincoln National (Ind.) | 9.77 |
| Republic National (Tex.) | 9.83 |
| Guardian Life (N.Y.) | 9.86 |
| Great-West Life (Man., Can.) | 9.88 |
| State Mutual of America (Mass.) | 9.92 |
| Penn Mutual (Pa.) | 10.07 |
| Aetna Life & Casualty (Conn.) | 10.11 |

**Bought by a man at age 45**

| Company | Interest-adjusted cost per $1,000 |
|---|---|
| Nationwide Life (Ohio) | $10.22 |
| Confederation Life (Ont., Can.) | 10.23 |
| North American Life (Ont., Can.) | 10.24 |
| Canada Life (Ont., Can.) | 10.26 |
| Crown Life (Ont., Can.) | 10.34 |
| Jefferson Standard (N.C.) | 10.38 |
| Continental Assurance (Ill.) | 10.44 |
| American United (Ind.) | 10.48 |
| Life & Casualty (Tenn.) | 10.58 |
| Mutual Life (N.Y.) | 10.61 |
| Franklin Life (Ill.) | 10.75 |
| Equitable Life (N.Y.) | 10.79 |
| State Farm (Ill.) | 11.15 |
| American National (Tex.) | 11.39 |
| Occidental Life (Cal.) | 11.39 |
| John Hancock (Mass.) | 11.48 |
| Prudential (N.J.) | 11.70 |
| Metropolitan Life (N.Y.) | 12.35 |
| *Nonparticipating policies surrendered at end of 10 years* | |
| Allstate (Ill.) | $9.90 |
| Life & Casualty (Tenn.) | 11.07 |
| IDS Life (Minn.) | 11.10 |
| Republic National (Tex.) | 11.39 |
| Occidental Life (Cal.) | 11.71 |
| Crown Life (Ont., Can.) | 11.81 |
| Jefferson Standard (N.C.) | 11.86 |
| National Life & Accident (Tenn.) | 11.92 |
| Southwestern Life (Tex.) | 12.04 |
| Continental Assurance (Ill.) | 12.09 |
| Franklin Life (Ill.) | 12.12 |
| Lincoln National (Ind.) | 12.14 |
| Travelers (Conn.) | 12.40 |
| Provident Life & Accident (Tenn.) | 12.57 |
| American National (Tex.) | 12.63 |
| Business Men's Assurance (Mo.) | 12.73 |
| United Benefit (Neb.) | 12.77 |
| Liberty National (Ala.) | 12.97 |
| Aetna Life & Casualty (Conn.) | 13.10 |
| Life of Virginia (Va.) | 13.19 |
| Connecticut General (Conn.) | 13.21 |
| *Nonparticipating policies surrendered at end of 20 years* | |
| Republic National (Tex.) | $11.70 |
| Allstate (Ill.) | 11.85 |
| Life & Casualty (Tenn.) | 12.02 |
| Southwestern Life (Tex.) | 13.02 |
| Franklin Life (Ill.) | 13.06 |
| Continental Assurance (Ill.) | 13.07 |
| Jefferson Standard (N.C.) | 13.11 |
| National Life & Accident (Tenn.) | 13.23 |
| Crown Life (Ont., Can.) | 13.28 |
| IDS Life (Minn.) | 13.32 |
| Connecticut General (Conn.) | 13.50 |
| Occidental Life (Cal.) | 13.54 |

**Bought by a man at age 45**

| Company | Interest-adjusted cost per $1,000 |
|---|---|
| Travelers (Conn.) | $13.63 |
| Provident Life & Accident (Tenn.) | 13.72 |
| Lincoln National (Ind.) | 13.81 |
| American National (Tex.) | 13.99 |
| Aetna Life & Casualty (Conn.) | 14.03 |
| United Benefit (Neb.) | 14.04 |
| Business Men's Assurance (Mo.) | 14.15 |
| Liberty National (Ala.) | 14.41 |
| Life of Virginia (Va.) | 14.72 |

Reading 82

# Insurance Needs Change As Family Grows Older

**Merle Dowd**

*Resources for generating income change as years progress—another reason for reassessing insurance programs.*

Time has a way of changing plans, dollar requirements and family situations. If you haven't examined your life insurance lately, why not make an insurance check-up now?

The first question: Do you have enough life insurance?

Rather than rely on old rules such as death benefits equal to four or five times annual income or provisions for income equal to 50, 60, or 70 per cent of your present income, calculate your family's cash requirements.

Without your regular paycheck, how much would your family need to continue living at an acceptable standard? Your family might need only one car instead of two, for example. Or a widow may prefer to live in an apartment rather than assume the responsibility for maintaining (and paying for) a house. A widow might work to supplement income.

All these factors affect how much insurance you should provide.

You'll want to plan a lump sum for your children's education. With college costs climbing even faster than inflation, you're shooting at a moving target on this one. With preschoolers or children in early elementary grades, think high—and you'll still probably undershoot.

Cash needed for final medical, burial and estate settlement often is overlooked. Net worth above $120,000 reaches into the lower brackets of the graduated estate and inheritance taxes—and these must be paid in cash.

Social security offers some protection for the widow with children under 18 in her care (up to 22 if in school). Benefit rates recently were increased and could constitute a major part of survivors' income. However, benefits cease for a widow when the last child in her care reaches 18 (22 if in school). A husband needs to look at the years between the youngest child's 18th birthday and the

From the *Seattle Times Magazine*, July 29, 1973, p. 12.

time his wife reaches 62. Either she works or the husband must provide an income for those years through insurance or investments.

When a man has determined his survivors' income and cash needs, he should examine resources for satisfying those needs. Life insurance, investments, applicable social-security benefits and work-related income are four common methods for meeting survivors' money needs.

Resources for generating income change as years progress—another reason for reassessing insurance programs. Typically, families progress through at least three stages:

**1** Young families need maximum insurance protection because insurance provides the biggest payoff for the least out-of-pocket cash. Insurance provides an "instant estate" to care for a widow with young children that require full-time care. Term insurance, automatically renewable and convertible, provides the most protection for the fewest dollars.

**2** Middle families will have had time to accumulate a varied bag of assets—investments, insurance protection and job skills. Equity in a house, mutual funds, stocks or real estate may supplant the younger family's reliance on insurance. Such a balance benefits a living breadwinner and provides family protection.

**3** Near or at retirement with children on their own, the husband and wife are looking for income—not protection alone. Insurance can provide for final medical and burial expenses, plus probate and estate-settlement expenses and taxes. But, major income must flow from investments and converted assets.

Are policy beneficiaries up to date? Would insurance benefits flow to children without legal complications if husband and wife should die in an accident?

Inflation continues to erode the value of fixed dollar investments and cash savings. Some cash should be converted to investments that give a fighting chance to keep up with inflation.

Reading 83

# Deceptive Sales Practices in Life Insurance

**Joseph M. Belth**

*When a life insurance advertisement or sales presentation is described as deceptive, it is not intended to suggest that the deception is necessarily deliberate on the part of the life insurance company or agent.*

Life insurance contracts generally are long-term financial instruments that perform useful functions in our society. These useful functions, however, sometimes are obscured because many of the sales practices of life insurance companies and their agents are deceptive. *The purpose of this article is to describe a variety of such practices.*

From the *Indiana Business Review*, July/August 1972, pp. 48–56.

At the outset, it is necessary to define the word "deceptive." As the word is used in this article, a presentation is deceptive if it tends to give the recipient an erroneous impression of important relationships. The emphasis in this definition is on the recipient. When a life insurance advertisement or sales presentation is described as deceptive, it is not intended to suggest that the deception is necessarily deliberate on the part of the life insurance company or agent.

## BACKGROUND

Except at very young ages, the likelihood of death increases, with increasing rapidity, as age increases. Life insurance sometimes is written on a one-year renewable term basis, with premiums increasing in a manner designed to offset the increasing likelihood of death. Under such an arrangement, however, the insurance company experiences a phenomenon called "adverse selection," in which policyholders with deteriorating health tend to renew their policies and policyholders in good health tend to discontinue their policies. This adverse selection leads to a deterioration in the "quality" of the group, and to a larger-than-anticipated number of death claims relative to premium payments. Attempts to anticipate the adverse selection by larger premium increases tend to aggravate rather than solve the problem.

Level-premium life insurance, under which the premium remains constant, is a technique adopted by the life insurance industry in an attempt to minimize adverse selection and at the same time make it financially feasible for policyholders to continue their protection even to advanced ages. Such an arrangement requires that the policyholder be overcharged (relative to mortality costs, expenses, and profit) in the early policy years to offset the inadequacy of premiums in the later policy years. As a result of these overcharges, level-premium policies provide for "cash values" to be paid to policyholders who discontinue their policies. The level-premium arrangement makes life insurance companies major financial institutions and transforms what otherwise would be an insurance transaction into a combination or package transaction involving both insurance protection and a savings medium.

Because of the package aspect of cash-value life insurance contracts, it is necessary to distinguish between the "premium" for the contract and the "price" of the protection element of the contract. To compute the price of the protection element, it is necessary to separate the protection element of the policy from the savings element, at least in a theoretical sense. Since the separation involves the making of assumptions, no single price figure can be established as *the* price; rather, any price figure must be accompanied by a statement concerning the assumptions used in computing that figure.

The nature of a life insurance price figure may be illustrated by an analogy. Let us say an individual is purchasing a package that consists of an item A and an item B. When only the price of the package is given, no single figure can be established as the price of either A or B alone. To calculate the price of A or of B, it is necessary to make an assumption about the price of the other item in the package. Any figure established as the price of A, for instance, must be accompanied by a statement about the assumed price of B, and vice versa.

In cash-value life insurance, the two parts of the package are protection and savings, and any figure established as the price of the protection element must be accompanied by a statement about the assumed rate of return on the savings element. Conversely, it is possible to make a statement about the rate of return on the savings element only if an assumption is made about the price of the protection element. In short, the price of the protection element and the rate of return on the savings element are two sides of the same coin, and either one can be used to make comparisons among policies.

## DECEPTIVE PRACTICES—CLASS A

For purposes of discussion, the various practices described in this article may be divided into three categories. *Class A deceptive practices* are those involving a misallocation of the interest factor. Since the complexity of life insurance is a major barrier to an understanding of the full implications of Class A practices, a simple analogy may be used to strip away the complexity and illustrate the fundamental problem.

Assume an individual puts $1,000 per year into a savings account, and that the account is credited annually with 5 percent interest. Consider the tenth year. The saver starts the year with $11,578 and adds $1,000 to it. At the end of the tenth year, his account is credited with interest of $629 (5 percent of $12,578), making his account $13,207. Of the $629 interest in the tenth year, $50 is attributable to the tenth year's deposit of $1,000 and the other $579 is attributable to the previous deposits made during the first nine years. *It is deceptive to state* or *imply that the full $629 of interest in the tenth year* is *attributable to the tenth year deposit of $1,000.* In other words, the rate of return here is 5 percent. A presentation is deceptive if it suggests the saver is earning 62.9 percent interest, rather than 5 percent interest on his tenth year deposit of $1,000. This form of deception is the basic characteristic of Class A practices.

In the February 1970 issue of *Life Insurance Selling* magazine, there is an article by Richard F. Harris, Jr., entitled "I Tell Corporations, 'Put the Difference in Permanent'." In that article, $989 per year is the difference in premiums between a policy with cash values and an otherwise similar policy without cash values. Mr. Harris attributes the full amount of the cash value increase in any given year to the $989 difference paid in that year. For example, in the tenth year, he shows an "annual increase in assets" of $1,427. He attributes that increase to the $989 difference paid in the tenth year, and then he shows the "annual % tax free profit" that year as 44.3 percent.

The cash value of the higher premium policy at the end of thirty years is $45,134. Implicit in the relationship between a $989 annual deposit and an accumulation of $45,134 at the end of thirty years is an annual interest rate of about 2.6 percent. If an adjustment were made for the different amounts of protection under the two policies, the implicit annual interest rate would be about 3.8 percent. Such rate-of-return figures are not mentioned in the Harris article. Instead, after a negative figure in the first year, the "annual % tax free profit" figures are given as ranging from 15.6 percent in the second year to 77.5 percent in the thirtieth year.

The rate-of-return figures in the Harris article correspond to the figure of 62.9 percent used in the savings account analogy. In this instance, the misallocation of the interest factor results in an overstatement of the rate of return on the savings element.

Many companies utilize the so-called ledger statement as a part of their sales material. In the typical ledger statement, the dividend for any given year and the cash-value *increase* for the year are subtracted from the annual premium in order to arrive at the price of the protection element for the year. In a 1971 ledger statement prepared by the Acacia Mutual Life Insurance Company, for example, the annual premium for a $100,000 straight life policy issued to a man aged 40 is $2,448. In the tenth year, the dividend is $435, the cash-value increase is $2,100, and the price of the protection element for the year is *minus* $87.

The effect of this presentation is similar to the effect of the Harris article described above. Actually, a portion of the $2,100 cash-value increase in the tenth year is attributable to interest on the savings element developed during the first nine years. When a reasonable allocation of the interest factor is made (by assuming 5 percent interest, for example), the price of the protection element in the tenth year is $880 rather than *minus* $87. Thus, the misallocation of the interest factor in the typical ledger statement results in an understatement of the price of the protection element.

## DECEPTIVE PRACTICES—CLASS B

Class B deceptive practices are those that involve comparisons based upon the simple addition of dollar amounts payable at different points in time. Here again an analogy may be used to illustrate the fundamental problem.

Let's assume that Jones retained Smith to do a particular job, with the understanding that upon completion Smith would be paid $1,000 per year for forty years, a total of $40,000. After the job is completed, Smith asks Jones to begin the payments, and Jones says:

> Smith, you've done such a great job that I'm going to pay you 10 percent more than we agreed upon. I'm going to pay you $600 per year for thirty years and then $2,600 per year for the final ten years. That's a total of $44,000, which is 10 percent more than the $40,000 I originally agreed to pay you.

Hopefully, Smith would note that Jones has failed to take interest into account. For example, the two payment plans may be compared with an assumed interest rate of 5 percent. The present value, or current lump sum equivalent, of the original payment plan ($1,000 per year for forty years) would be $18,017. The present value of the modified payment plan that Jones proposed, however, would be $14,562. It is deceptive to state, suggest, or imply that the original payment plan is 10 percent better than the modified payment plan. In other words, what Jones described as an arrangement providing 10 percent more for Smith actually provides 19 percent less, assuming 5 percent interest. This form of deception is the basic characteristic of Class B practices.

In September 1970, at the annual meeting of the National Association of Life Underwriters, Dilworth C. Brinton gave a talk on the advantages of straight life over term insurance. An article describing the talk appeared in the September 16, 1970, issue of *The National Underwriter.*

Mr. Brinton indicated that for a $100,000 straight life policy issued at age 25 and continued to age 65, the "net return over cost" is $30,923. Then he indicated that for a $100,000 one-year renewable term policy over the same period, the "cost of term insurance" is $34,579. Finally, he stated that the "total difference" in favor of the straight life policy is $65,502.

Mr. Brinton's analysis does not take interest into account. His straight life "net return over cost" figure was calculated by adding up the forty years' premiums, subtracting the simple total of the forty years' dividends, and subtracting the cash value at the end of the forty years. His "cost of term insurance" figure was calculated by adding up the forty years' premiums and subtracting the simple total of the forty years' dividends.

When an assumed interest rate of 5 percent is applied to this situation, the "cost" of the straight life policy in present-value terms is $9,163, and the "cost" of the term policy is $9,733. These figures still favor the straight life policy, but by $570, as compared with Mr. Brinton's figure of $65,502. The comparison used by Mr. Brinton fails to consider the interest factor, and the comparison thereby distorts the relationship between two markedly different kinds of life insurance contracts.

The most frequently used technique for illustrating the price of life insurance is the traditional net cost method. This method serves as the basis for the price information contained in the most widely disseminated volume of life insurance policy data—A.M. Best Company's *Flitcraft Compend.*

Frequently a twenty-year period of analysis is used. The simple total of the dividends for the twenty-year period and the cash value payable at the end of the twentieth year are each subtracted from the simple total of the premiums for the period. The remainder is divided by 20 (the number of years in the period of analysis), and the result is the twenty-year average net cost.

The method may be illustrated with the Acacia Mutual figures referred to earlier. The premiums for the $100,000 policy are $2,448 per year; thus the simple total of twenty years' premiums is $48,960. The simple total of the first twenty years' dividends is $8,441, and the cash value at the end of the twentieth year is $39,500. The twenty-year average net cost, determined by subtracting the dividends and the cash value from the premiums and dividing the remainder by 20, is $50.95, or 51 cents per $1,000 of face amount.

The traditional net cost method distorts the relationship among policies. Since the simple total of dividends is used in the calculations, companies are encouraged to "steepen" their dividend scales. A company is said to have a steeper scale than another company when the former pays smaller dividends in the early policy years and larger dividends in the later policy years than the other company. When a company steepens its dividend scale, it not only benefits from increased interest earnings by deferring the payment of larger dividends, but also from the fact that many policyholders will either die or discontinue their policies before receiving the larger dividends in the later years.

To illustrate the manner in which the traditional net cost method distorts relationships among policies, consider Table 1. Figures are shown there for

**Table 1 Traditional Net Costs and Interests Adjusted Cost for $25,000 Participating Straight Life Policies Issued in 1970 to Men Aged 35**
(Ranks from Low to High Shown in Parentheses)

| Company | Traditional net cost | | Interest adjusted cost (5%) | |
|---|---|---|---|---|
| Phoenix Mutual | $-3.46 | (1) | $6.34 | (7) |
| Metropolitan Life | -3.09 | (2) | 6.33 | (6) |
| Aetna Life | -3.00 | (3) | 6.66 | (9) |
| Mutual of New York | -2.92 | (4) | 6.43 | (8) |
| Confederation Life | -2.33 | (5) | 5.97 | (2) |
| Prudential | -2.22 | (6) | 7.17 | (10) |
| Bankers Life (Iowa) | -2.21 | (7) | 5.49 | (1) |
| Provident Mutual | -1.92 | (8) | 6.07 | (3) |
| Crown Life | -1.25 | (9) | 6.08 | (4) |
| Manufacturers Life | -1.19 | (10) | 6.31 | (5) |

$25,000 participating straight life policies issued in 1970 to men aged 35 by ten large companies. These policies were not chosen at random; they were selected because they tend to shift markedly in rank (either upward or downward) when moving from the traditional net cost method to the interest adjusted method. The only difference between the traditional net cost method and the interest adjusted method is that the latter takes account of interest. In this illustration, the assumed interest rate in the interest adjusted price calculations is 5 percent.

The policies of the five companies whose ranks improved when moving from the traditional net cost method to the interest adjusted method—Confederation Life, Bankers Life (Iowa), Provident Mutual, Crown Life, and Manufacturers Life—are characterized generally by relatively low premiums, relatively flat dividend scales, and relatively small cash values. The policies of the five companies whose ranks worsened when moving from the traditional net cost method to the interest adjusted method—Phoenix Mutual, Metropolitan Life, Aetna Life, Mutual of New York, and Prudential—are characterized generally by relatively high premiums, relatively steep dividend scales, and relatively large cash values. The traditional net cost method, which involves the simple addition of dollar amounts payable at different points in time, distorts relationships among policies.

## DECEPTIVE PRACTICES—CLASS C

Class C practices are those involving presentations that are simply false. Although they do not involve a misallocation or an omission of the interest factor, their falsity usually is difficult to detect because they are complex and tricky. Two examples of such practices are presented here.

In the November 1969 issue of *The Radiator* (the magazine of the Massachusetts Mutual Life Insurance Company), there is an article by Raymond L. Paul entitled "Why Get Complicated?" Mr. Paul suggests the following technique for handling the question of investment return when it arises in the sales interview:

> Ask the prospect what kind of return he would expect to get if he invested $1,000 a year. Assume he answers 8 percent. Then ask him what kind of return he would expect to get if he invested the $1,000 a year in a life insurance contract. Assume he answers 4 percent.
>
> What would it cost the prospect to buy the life insurance? Wouldn't it be the difference between what he would have earned on the 8 percent investment and what he would earn on the life insurance investment? This difference amounts to $40 a year.
>
> If the prospect invests $1,000 a year in a straight life contract at his age of 30, his family would get $50,000 when he dies. "Mr. Prospect, that's $50,000 of death protection for $40 a year. Can you really afford to invest in anything else?"

In his book *See You Next Week* (published by The Research & Review Service of America, Inc.), Wayne W. Wolfe suggests the following technique to persuade a term insurance policyholder to convert to straight life:

> Mr. Client, you have a lot of protection in that term policy for the $300 it costs. You know, of course, there is no cash value in it. It's the kind of policy you have to die to beat. Did you know, Mr. Client, that the permanent kind of life insurance can be so arranged that you eventually get all of your money back if you don't die? [Wait for answer.]
>
> Since you get all of your money back, the cost of permanent insurance is really just the interest on your money, isn't it? [Wait for answer.]

> Now, here's an intriguing point. Since the term premium pays just for the insurance, with no return, isn't that term premium just like interest on the permanent premium that buys the same amount of insurance? [Wait for answer. Repeat if necessary.]
>
> In that case, you are paying about 30 percent interest, Mr. Client. Let me show you what I mean. At your age of 30, your $50,000 term policy costs you $300 per year. Whole life, which would return all of your money eventually, would cost you $1,000 a year for the same amount. The term premium is interest on the permanent. That's where I got the 30 percent interest figure. Don't you think that is pretty high? Can you invest money anywhere for that much return? [Wait for answer.]
>
> Well, you can make just such an investment here, by coverting that term to permanent life insurance!

In the Paul article, the cost of the "$50,000 of death protection" is *not* $40 per year. In the Wolfe book, the "investment" does *not* produce a 30 percent rate of return. The flaws in these presentations, however, are extremely difficult to pinpoint. Their detection is left to the reader as an exercise in mental gymnastics.

## RECENT DEVELOPMENTS

Late in 1968, Senator Philip A. Hart, chairman of the Subcommittee on Antitrust and Monopoly of the Committee on the Judiciary, referred publicly to the possibility of "truth in life insurance" legislation. In a speech before a life insurance industry group, he made the following statements:

> Obviously, if it makes sense to tell consumers how much of what is in a package on a supermarket shelf, or how much interest they will pay for using someone else's money, it makes sense to tell them how much they are paying for death protection and how much they are saving when they plunk down a life insurance premium.
>
> Hopefully your industry will think so too—and start supplying the information.
>
> If not—watch for Truth in Life Insurance to follow Truth in Packaging and Truth in Lending through the legislative mill.
>
> Because that's the way people are thinking in consumerland.

Early in 1969, as a direct result of Senator Hart's admonition, three life insurance trade associations appointed a prestigious industry committee to look into the price disclosure problem. The report of the committee was released in May 1970. The major recommendation of the committee was that the interest adjusted method be used in making cost comparisons instead of the traditional net cost method. Thus, if the major recommendation of the report were implemented, a major step would have been taken in the direction of overcoming the problem of Class B deceptive practices.

Developments since the release of the industry report, however, suggest that whatever progress is made on a voluntary basis is going to be painfully slow. The three trade associations that formed the special committee "received" the report and authorized its publication. They did not approve or endorse the report, however, apparently out of a fear of violating the antitrust laws.

A major insurance trade publisher—The National Underwriter Company—developed a comprehensive volume of price information based on the interest adjusted method recommended by the committee. The other major insurance trade publisher—A. M. Best Company—apparently is planning to do nothing.

The recognition of the interest adjusted method by the life insurance companies has been slow. One company—Bankers Life (Iowa)—quickly supported the committee's recommendation by making interest adjusted costs for its policies available as a part of its sales material. A few other companies placed interest adjusted cost figures in their rate books. At the urging of Virginia H. Knauer, President Nixon's special assistant for consumer affairs, many more companies are planning to make interest adjusted cost figures available to their agents. Even so, many major companies apparently are still planning to do nothing.

Even if all companies were to make interest adjusted cost figures available to their agents, such information would not necessarily reach prospective buyers. Furthermore, the availability of interest adjusted cost figures would not eliminate the use of the discredited traditional net cost methods or other Class B deceptive practices.

The committee report is silent on the subject of price information for one policy year at a time—a problem even more serious than the one to which the committee addressed itself. In other words, the committee report is silent on what have been described in this statement as Class A deceptive practices. Furthermore, nothing in the committee report relates to the problem of Class C deceptive practices.

In February 1972, the Wisconsin insurance department promulgated an administrative rule to take effect June 1, 1972, relating to disclosure requirements and deceptive practices in the sale of life insurance. The rule defines deception in such a way as to appear to encompass many of the deceptive practices referred to in this article. The effect the rule will have on life insurance sales practices remains to be seen.

In March 1972, a task force on price illustrations was formed by the National Association of Insurance Commissioners (NAIC). The task force is considering the possibility of developing a model bill or model rule providing for disclosure of information on the costs and benefits of life insurance policies. What the task force will recommend, what the NAIC will do with the recommendation, and what the states will do subsequently even if the NAIC adopts a model bill or model rule remains to be seen.

In April 1972, the Wisconsin insurance department proposed another administrative rule. This rule would require that certain policy information, including interest adjusted cost figures, be furnished by each company *to its agents,* and that the information be furnished to any policyholder or prospective buyer *upon request.* The information which is the subject of the proposed rule would not constitute adequate disclosure even if the rule is put into effect. The provision that the information be furnished to prospective buyers only upon their request means that the proposed rule was emasculated even before it was disseminated to interested parties for comment. A hearing has been held, but what the Wisconsin insurance department will promulgate remains to be seen.

Also in April 1971, the Pennsylvania insurance department published "A Shopper's Guide to Life Insurance." The guide contains some suggestions for life insurance buyers and some premium and interest adjusted cost figures for certain policies issued by major companies operating in Pennsylvania. Although publication of the guide is a commendable effort by the Pennsylvania insurance department, the information is not an adequate substitute for required price disclosure to the consumer at the point of sales.

## CONCLUSION

Sales practices of the type described in this article are widespread in the life insurance industry. Material of the type illustrated by the Harris article, the Brinton talk, the Paul article, and the Wolfe book appears sporadically. Ledger statements are used by many companies. The traditional net cost method of illustrating the price of protection is widely used.

Knowledgeable people in the life insurance industry are aware of the deceptive practices described in this article. By and large, however, they seem willing to live with such practices. Among their rationalizations are the following:

**1** All the life insurance companies use these practices; therefore, we too must use them to stay competitive.

**2** Life insurance is a desirable service, and it is very hard to sell; we are justified in using these practices to get people to buy.

**3** The money a person puts into life insurance would otherwise be kept in a non-interest-bearing checking account or would be frittered away, so it is reasonable to ignore the interest factor.

**4** It would make the sales presentation considerably more complicated if we were to recognize the interest factor.

**5** There has been no discernible public demand for an abandonment of these practices.

**6** We are closely supervised by the various state insurance departments, but they have not challenged us concerning these practices.

These rationalizations add up to an abdication of responsibility by the life insurance industry and the state regulatory agencies. It is possible that either the industry itself or the state regulatory agencies could correct the situation, but to date there has been little progress. It is to be hoped that the recent development in the "truth of life insurance" area will result not only in required price disclosure to the consumer at the point of sale, but also in a sharp reduction in the use of deceptive sales practices.

# Savings, Investments, Estate Planning, Wills and Trusts

Reading 84

## How To Get More Interest on Your Savings

**Betty Furness**

*In addition to interest, would you like a toaster, clock, radio, blanket, cookware, carpet sweeper or steam iron for "nothing"?*

You know very well how much money you and/or your husband make. If you're smart enough to have some of the money stick to you and you put it in a savings account, do you also know exactly how much money your *money* makes? You do? You wanna bet?

If you think 5 percent interest is the same 5 percent interest the whole banking world over, guess again. I've just been pursuing my own ignorance on the subject and, after considerable tutoring, have emerged into the bright light of actually being able to tell the benefits of one account vs. another—and I can't wait to tell you what I've learned.

Two reasons for using a bank instead of a sugar bowl for savings are that you want your money to be safe, and you want it to grow. Safe is usually taken care of. Federally chartered commercial banks are required by law to belong to the Federal Deposit Insurance Corporation. State-chartered banks may voluntarily belong, as may mutual savings banks. Savings-and-loan associations are insured by the Federal Savings and Loan Insurance Corporation. Both organizations insure each depositor's account up to $20,000. Participating banks are eager to point out this safety feature. You'll find it in their window and ads—look for it.

Before we start growing our money, let's sort out the different kinds of banks. A commercial bank is where your checking account is. It also has savings accounts. A savings-and-loan is just what it says it is. It'll save, and it'll lend (its loans are largely restricted to real estate), but it is not permitted checking accounts. Mutual savings banks are largely found in Eastern states, where they are a holdover from the 1820s and '30s, when commercial banks didn't welcome small people's small money. These banks were "mutually" established to hold the money of farmers and carpenters and seamen. As a matter of fact, you'll still find a Seamen's Savings Bank right on Fifth Avenue in Manhattan. When people and money went West, the bankers and plowmen and future cowboys all got off the same covered wagon together, and the bankers there were well pleased to

From *McCall's*, August 1972, pp. 22–28.

bank the small funds of their new friends in commercial banks, eliminating the necessity for "mutuals."

The mutuals and savings-and-loans operate similarly from the savers' viewpoint, so consider them as one.

Enough history. Interest is what you're concerned about. One noteworthy point is that interest ceilings are established for all banks by the Federal Reserve Board, the amount varying from time to time according to the supply of money available in the economy. Right now, on regular savings accounts, commercial banks can pay no more than 4½ percent, and "thrifts" (the bankers' name for financial institutions such as savings-and-loans and mutual savings) can pay no more than 5 percent (except under certain circumstances, which we'll get to in a minute). Since all financial institutions are eager to borrow your money, there's no reason why you should lend it to them at less than the ceiling rate.

I asked an officer in a commercial bank why anyone should have a savings account there, since thrifts pay more interest. "Convenience," was his answer. One-stop banking. I would suggest, then, that if maximum growth is your aim, do your thrifting at a thrift.

You'd think that with your money insured, interest ceilings established and computers to do the arithmetic, it wouldn't matter much where you save. Not so.

A couple of years ago, at Kansas State University, a graduate student named Jackie Pinson got to wondering just how easy it is to compare different types of savings accounts. Her pursuit of this seemingly simple question ended up months later as a thesis on the subject, and the answer was "very hard." She began by creating a hypothetical savings account, complete with deposits and withdrawals. She then figured how much interest it would earn under the computing systems used by a variety of banks, all using the same declared interest rate over the same period of time. To her own amazement, she discovered that the difference between the highest-paying system and the lowest was 171 percent.

On the assumption that you prefer to earn the highest rate, let me try to acquaint you with some of the tricky facts of savings life and the ornate vocabulary pertaining to it.

The RATE is the percentage used to calculate interest. The ANNUAL YIELD (or ANNUAL RETURN or EFFECTIVE ANNUAL RATE) is the amount of interest you receive in one year's time. If a bank were to compute your interest yearly, the annual rate and the annual yield would be the same. But banks don't do that. They COMPOUND interest. If they compound quarterly, for instance, they figure out your interest at the end of three months, add that amount to your balance and compute the interest at the end of the next quarter on your balance, which now includes the previously earned interest. Not only is your money earning money, but the money it has *earned* is earning money, too.

Banks need your savings. The basic business they're in is borrowing peoples' money, on which they pay a given interest, to lend to other people at a higher interest. Since the interest rates they pay are limited by law, banks have had to devise other ways to compete for your dollars. One method they've worked out is to compute the interest on your account more often than semiannually or quarterly. With the aid of computers, many banks now compound interest daily. Some even claim to compound it every second, others "continuously." But the difference between daily compounding and continuous compounding is negligible; on $1,000 at 5 percent, it comes to one penny at the end of two years, and 6 cents at the end of ten years—no way to get rich. But daily compounding does beat quarterly. If you can put a certain sum of money in a savings account and just let it lie there nourishing itself, you have fewer decisions to make than if you're a money-in-and-outer. You might be well advised to have an account from which you agree not to make withdrawals for a prescribed time—varying, for example, from two to five years. This type of account, available at both commercial banks and thrifts, is called by several names: term savings, time savings, certificate of deposit, investment savings, investment certificate, savings certificate. I even found a "Big Bonus 6 Savings Certificate Account." These accounts require a substantial cash minimum—$500 to $1,000—and most can't be added to during the agreed-upon term. You'd have to start again, with another $500 or so. They do, however, pay more for the privilege of holding onto your money. That's where the Big Bonus 6 account got its name. These accounts pay 5¾ percent at commercial banks and 6 percent at thrifts. Compounded daily, 6 percent amounts to 6.18 percent annual yield.

A factor to consider in tying up money for a matter of years is that interest rates may change. A 6-percent savings-certificate account guarantees 6 percent—no more, no less—until the maturity date. If interest rates go down, you've got a good deal. But if they go up, you're stuck with the guaranteed amount.

If you're trying to hide money from yourself to keep from spending it, this type of account is a good substitute for personal discipline. But you should know that if you ask for principal before the maturity date, you may have to sacrifice up to ninety-days' interest to get your money out.

Active savings accounts offer more options, complete with more confusion. Currently there are two types of account being widely advertised. Both are PASSBOOK accounts. One, the old-fashioned kind, is called a REGULAR account (or DAYS OF GRACE or REGULAR GRACE DAY). Money deposited by the tenth of the month earns interest from the first of the month, meaning that for nine days you can earn interest on money that isn't yet in the bank. Money deposited after the tenth earns interest from that day on, and interest is usually compounded quarterly. The catch in a regular account is that money withdrawn before the end of the same quarter doesn't earn any interest at all.

There are also some regular accounts that, in addition to the ten grace days at the beginning of the month, allow you to withdraw funds with full quarterly interest during the last three days of the quarter. Grace-day accounts are of particular value to people who receive monthly pension or annuity checks after the first of the month and don't need to withdraw money until the end of the quarter.

Which brings us to the question of withdrawing *any* money. When you withdraw $50 from your account, which $50 are you taking out? If you think it's the last $50 you put in, you may be right. Banks call this transaction last in, first out, also known as LIFO. Federally chartered savings-and-loans use this, as do some other banks. But there are also banks that figure that the $50 you take out is the *first* $50 you put in, and they compute interest on the basis of first in, first out, or FIFO. To spare us the mathematics, take Jackie Pinson's word for it, FIFO pays less than LIFO.

Another way of computing interest in regular accounts is called LOW BALANCE, which turns out to be the worst deal of all because it pays interest on the lowest amount in the account during the quarter. Deposits made in that quarter are ignored and do not begin to earn interest until the beginning of the next quarter. Not good for our side.

For real money-in, money-out people, there are accounts computed from DAY OF DEPOSIT to DAY OF WITHDRAWAL (or DD-DW, or DAILY DIVIDEND, or DAILY INTEREST). The first name explains it best. Your money earns interest from the day it's deposited till the day it's withdrawn, with no penalties for depositing late (as in low-balance computing) or withdrawing early (as in most regular accounts). The interest rate is the same as that of the regular accounts, but the yield for active accounts comes out better. If you can get a DD-DW account with grace days, that's even better.

These DD-DW accounts are being widely advertised by both commercial banks and thrifts, but if you don't read ads, you may not know you have a choice of either a regular or a DD-DW, but be sure to ask if you're losing any interest by not waiting till the end of the quarter.

In addition to interest, would you like a toaster, clock, radio, blanket, cookware, carpet sweeper or steam iron for "nothing"? A lot of banks offer such premiums at the end of the quarterly-interest period, hoping to lure your money away from their competitors. The Federal Reserve Board and the Federal Home Loan Bank Board have limited the cost of these premiums to $5, leading to items like those listed or small pots of philodendron worth less.

But some state-chartered commercial banks suffer no such restrictions. In what amounts to a passionate plea for your money, some have offered what seem to be grand and glorious gifts *in lieu of interest.* Take Texas. For a thirty-month certificate of deposit of $1,800, a Dallas bank recently offered a $232 Browning automatic shotgun, or $225 in immediate cash. They even offered to lend you the money to purchase the certificate if you didn't have the cash! Last year in Boulder, Colorado, a bank offered a 1971 Ford Maverick or a vacation for two anywhere in the world (maximum of $2,500) *in advance* for a five-year $10,000 certificate of deposit. This makes a philodendron plant look pretty silly, but if you have $10,000 to tie up for five years, you can probably afford to buy your own philodendron.

The practice of offering small gifts has given birth to a breed of premium chasers who move their money from bank to bank, collecting electric shavers and alarm clocks en route. The banks have wised up to this game and now insist if you get your toaster, you'll have to leave the account intact for twelve or fourteen months. A bank in which I have some money feels the premium-type promotion is beneath their dignity, but they do want their share of attention. So in their lobby in the winter they have an ice skating rink with professional skaters performing during the lunch hour. In the spring they stage dog shows with champion dogs ... and dignity.

I've oversimplified the methods of calculation used by various banks in the "interest" of trying to make things clear, but Jackie Pinson's findings weren't simple at all. Using the hypothetical account she set up on paper, complete with deposits and withdrawals covering a six-month period, she used five methods of interest calculation and four other variables (frequency of compounding interest, frequency of crediting compound interest, number of grace days and possible penalty for an excessive number of withdrawals charged by some banks) and worked out the interest in forty model accounts. She then sent that material to eight savings institutions and asked them which system they used. If they didn't use any of hers, would they please do the calculations their way and advise. In no case did the six-month yield match any of the model systems, and no two savings institutions using the same nominal rate came up with the same yield. So it turns out that even if you've chosen the right type of account for your particular form of saving, you still can't know you're getting the best possible return. The American Bankers Association says that there are at least fifty-four widely used ways of computing interest. It's been suggested that there may be as many as a hundred.

Jackie Pinson and Professor Richard Morse, who is head of the Family

Economics department at Kansas State, reasoned that if a graduate student couldn't come up with precise information on which bank pays how much, the average saver couldn't either.

When we use a bank's money by borrowing it, the bank is required by the Truth-in-Lending law to tell us how much we're paying for that use, both in annual interest rate and in dollars. So why, ask Pinson and Morse, shouldn't the banks give us equally precise information when they use our money? How about Truth in Savings? The idea is now being considered by the Vermont State Legislature, and a bill has been introduced in Congress by Senator Vance Hartke (Ind.—D.) and Representative Bill Roy (Kans.—D.). In introducing their bills, both used Jackie Pinson's material.

We don't yet have such a law but in this day, when our young claim they can't make any impact on the "system," it's refreshing to know that the garden-variety curiosity of a young woman in Kansas may be responsible for a law that would make it possible for us all to be wiser . . . and richer.

In the meantime, here are some simple rules to follow:

**1** Don't settle for less than the maximum interest currently paid, in any type of account. Remember that in passbook-savings accounts, savings-and-loans and mutual-savings banks pay more than commercial banks.

**2** Look for the most frequent compounding of interest.

**3** For maximum interest on large amounts and minimum opportunity to spend the money, time savings or savings certificates pay more in any type of bank. But you are tying up your money.

**4** A DD-DW (day of deposit—day of withdrawal) account is best if you deposit and withdraw frequently.

**5** A regular (grace days) account is best if you deposit regularly after the first but before the tenth of the month and don't have to withdraw until the end of the quarter.

**6** If your banking options are limited, remember that the LIFO system (last in, first out) yields more than either the FIFO or the low-balance system.

**7** Don't be fooled by highly publicized premiums. They are not an indication of a bank's true service.

**8** If banks have both a regular account and DD-DW, they'll probably be willing to convert. Don't be shy about asking.

**9** Because banks are as eager to use your money as you are to save it, you have every right to ask your bank to explain its system. If it's one of the lower-paying varieties, shop around. Remember—it's your money.

Reading 85

# Savings Accounts Pay More Interest

**Morton C. Paulson**

*The rates were liberalized so that thrift institutions would be better able to compete with other bidders for savers' dollars.*

It's almost unheard of—7.35 percent, 8 per cent, 8.5 per cent interest on bank savings. But that's what you can get now from certain kinds of savings plans.

Even ordinary passbook accounts pay up to 5.25 per cent—and occasionally slightly more.

Why? Because the Government has raised the legal ceilings on interest that thrift institutions can pay their customers. Savings and loan associations (S&Ls) and mutual savings banks are now authorized to increase to 5.25 per cent the maximum they may pay on passbook accounts. Commercial banks may boost their rate to 5 per cent from 4.5 per cent. On 90-day notice accounts with S&Ls, the maximum permissible rate is now 5.75 per cent, up from 5.25 per cent. (In a 90-day account money must remain on deposit for that length of time to qualify for a specified interest rate.)

All three types of institutions are now allowed to offer more generous rates on various savings instruments, such as certificates of deposits (CDs)—that is, receipts for money deposited for a stipulated length of time. Additionally, interest limits were removed entirely from four-year, $1,000 CDs. A few institutions are paying as much as 8.5 per cent on these.

## COMPETITION FOR THE DOLLAR

The rates were liberalized so that thrift institutions would be better able to compete with other bidders for savers' dollars. Depositors were withdrawing substantial sums from savings accounts and putting the money in higher-yield investments, such as corporate bonds.

It's all a result of Government moves to corral inflation. The Federal Reserve System has tightened its reins on the supply of money in circulation, making loans more costly. Hence, the higher returns from bonds.

The new rules have resulted in a profusion of attractive but sometimes confusing savings plans. Several New York mutual savings banks (banks that are somewhat similar to savings and loan associations) are offering 7 per cent annually on four-year CDs. But the interest is compounded daily, so the customer actually gets an "effective annual rate" of 7.35 per cent.

The Virginia Savings and Loan Association of Fredericksburg, Va., gives customers a choice of "nine ways to save." They range from ordinary passbook accounts to 30-day, $100,000 CDs (which pay 7.75 per cent).

A few S&Ls chartered by states and not subject to Federal interest limits pay rates on passbook accounts that are somewhat above the new Federal limits. In Maryland the rate is 6 per cent. Deposits in these accounts are insured by a state-supervised corporation; they are not covered by Federally backed insurance.

From *The National Observer*, July 28, 1973, p. 8.

**New Maximum Rates**

| In savings and loan associations | per cent |
|---|---|
| Regular passbook accounts | 5.25 |
| 90-day notice accounts | 5.75 |
| 90-day CDs, $1,000 minimum | 5.75 |
| 1-to-2½-year CDs, $1,000 minimum | 6.5 |
| 2½-year CDs, $5,000 minimum | 6.75 |
| 4-year CDs, no minimum | 6.75 |
| 4-year CDs, $1,000 minimum | No limit |
| **In mutual savings banks** | |
| Regular passbook accounts | 5.25 |
| 90-day CDs, no minimum | 5.75 |
| 1-to-2½-year CDs, no minimum | 6.5 |
| 2½-year CDs, no minimum | 6.75 |
| 4-year CDs, $1,000 minimum | No limit |
| **In commercial banks** | |
| Regular passbook | 5.0 |
| 90-day CDs, no minimum | 5.5 |
| 1-to-2½-year CDs, no minimum | 6.0 |
| 2½-year CDs, no minimum | 6.5 |
| 4-year CDs, $1,000 minimum | No limit |

## MAXIMUM LOAN LIMITS

Yields on four-year CDs for $1,000 or more vary quite a bit from place to place. The Beverly Hills (Calif.) National Bank pays 7 per cent, while the First Federal Savings and Loan in Aurora, Ill., offers 8.25 per cent. Not to be outdone, several banks and S&Ls in New Orleans are offering 8.5 per cent.

David Gatto, president of New Orleans Federal Savings and Loan Association, reports that orders for these certificates have come in from many parts of the country as well as from local people. But his association has had to stop issuing them, at least temporarily.

Soon after the new interest schedules were announced, the Federal Home Loan Bank Board, which regulates S&Ls, decreed that these institutions could pay rates of 6.75 per cent or more on only 5 per cent of their total deposits. For New Orleans Federal, 5 per cent came to $1 million. "We sold that amount in CDs in just four days," Gatto said.

There was such a rush to buy 8.5 per cent certificates at New Orleans' International City Bank and Trust Co. that tellers' windows were kept open late for a week. Ray Samuel, senior vice president for marketing, doubts that the bank will be able to continue the offer "much longer."

If you have idle funds that you want to put to work, or funds that are producing below-average earnings, it will pay to shop around for the plan most suitable to your financial needs. Savings institutions aren't *required* to offer the new maximums; most of them seem to be doing so on the longer-term instruments but a few still pay 4.5 per cent on passbook accounts.

## GO OUT OF TOWN?

Since rates on savings certificates vary as much as 1.5 per cent from place to place, you may want to consider dealing with an out-of-town institution.

Can you cash in a savings certificate prior to the maturity date? Yes—but there's a heavy penalty. First, the interest rate will drop back to that of passbook accounts. Second, you'll lose three months' interest.

If you already hold CDs from a Federally regulated bank, ask whether the interest rate will be raised immediately to the new maximum. Banks were authorized to do this. S&Ls were not, although an increase may be made when the certificate matures. If you don't get an increase now, it may be advantageous to redeem your CDs and buy new ones. You'll come out ahead if the new yield is greater than the penalty you'll pay—the loss of three months' interest—for cashing in early.

You'll notice that many institutions advertise two rates. One is the official annual rate. The other is the "effective annual rate" that results from compounding interest daily.

For example, 5.25 per cent increases to 5.47 per cent with daily compounding; 6.75 per cent comes to 7.08 per cent. The effective annual rate is the important one, because that's what you get—provided, of course, that your money stays with the institution for the required length of time.

Reading 86

# Is Estate Planning Still with It?

**Walter J. Blum**

*Do we estate planners use enough four letter words and do we use them often enough?*

The whole world knows that students are displaying new and critical attitudes toward every norm and every institution accepted by society.

Estate planning is no exception. I do not mean to imply that militant students have tried to seize or fire-bomb estate planning institutes, or that they have tried to radicalize estate planners—although I thought I spotted one or two suspicious looking characters among my fellow guildsmen attending the technical planning sessions earlier today. All I mean to suggest is that the wave of unrest on campuses should cause us to pause and take a new look at the role we estate planners are playing in a troubled world. How do we stack up in the light of contemporary student values and questions? How do we rate in this Age of Aquarius? Is estate planning still with it?

## ESTATE PLANNERS: ESTATE OWNERS

I begin with a disturbing thought, if not a fact. Let us compare the total number of persons who attended known estate planning sessions during the year 1970 with the total number of persons who in that year died leaving estates of a size that probably warranted planning. My very preliminary and rough research reveals that the crowd of estate planners exceeded the estate owners by 25 per cent. These figures could be taken to mean that last year each estate planner got to plan only 80 per cent of an estate. To be sure, this is not the same as finding

From *Taxes*, November 1971, pp. 659-665.

that the average estate is only four-fifths as much planned as it should be. Nor do the figures tell us that there is a shortage of estate owners—a condition which in these times no doubt would call for the appointment of a Presidential commission of inquiry. They do suggest, however, that you ask yourself why you paid to get into this meeting.

But don't start to leave yet. These startling new statistics, which just might turn out to be correct, paint too dark a picture for those in the know. We in the trade probably can take comfort in the thought that some estate planning is done by a team of two or more estate planners, thereby increasing the average amount of planning done by each planner. (Incidentally, this upward averaging might well explain why teamwork is so very fashionable in estate planning.) The figures become even less distressing when we recall that some estates are planned two or more times before it is unfortunately too late to revise the plan again. And there is always the possibility that some planners are counted twice because they attend more than one seminar or institute on estate planning during a single year. For all these reasons, I am not at all disheartened to see so many estate planners here today.

## HOW DOES ESTATE PLANNING STACK UP?

I turn now to my main theme: what insight into the present and the future of estate planning may we gain by concentrating on the things which activist students have been saying and doing lately?

A logical place to begin is with language. In the vocabulary of activist students the touchstone words today always contain four letters. Do we estate planners use enough four letter words and do we use them often enough? Further, are the four letter words we use sufficiently expressive? We are, I submit, very strong on five letter words—witness such old standbys as "issue," or "trust," or "legal," or "death," or "money" or "taxes." But we are far less impressive in the four letter league. The best we can offer right now seems to be "fees," "heir," "have" and "hold." On the campus these are not likely to rate with the masterpieces. I am confident that all forward-looking estate planners listening now will get the message and will take the necessary steps to redress this impoverishment in our language.

Under the prevailing new student logic, the question which quite predictably follows next is, "What are estate planners doing about pollution?"

This is indeed a great challenge to estate planning. If it can be shown that our art is tied in with ecology, we might improve our image over night. And we might even attract a few of the new breed students into our lofty profession (most of whose members, please note, grew up at a time when it was the air that was pure and sex was dirty). I admit that the relationship between estate planning and ecology is not exactly obvious. But once noticed, it is not very likely to be forgotten soon. The unvarnished fact is that estate planners have always placed primary emphasis on things green. The real mark of success in our trade is the maximization of the green stuff. Was it not an estate planner who discovered that the green can be made to grow by adroit use of sprinkling trusts? Do not all of us try to make it grow all the more by using the pourover method when conditions are favorable? Surely there should be little doubt in your mind that a master estate planner well deserves to be called a "jolly green giant." It is indeed a shame that the current best seller, *The Greening of America,* is not a great saga on estate planning.

How do we stand on another matter of interest to students—the generation gap? I am happy to be able to report that here we indeed hold a winning hand.

For years every estate planner has recognized the great importance of skipping a generation or two! No competent estate planner believes that things of value should be handed down outright from one generation to the next. We have stressed this point so much that a man of property these days has no difficulty whatsoever reinforcing his natural feelings with powerful monetary reasons to favor not his children but his grandchildren or better yet, his great grandchildren. It is perhaps not too far off the mark to say that estate planners invented the generation gap!

Another favorite theme of activist students is that decisions should be arrived at through the workings of so-called "participatory democracy." To the casual outside observer this process sometimes seems indistinguishable from a mass talkathon. On the surface, nothing could appear to be more unlike the tidy process of estate planning. A more penetrating comparison, however, suggests that highly sophisticated estate planning has already embraced the key element of participatory democracy," and is continuing to do so at an accelerating rate. The essence of "participatory democracy" is that everyone wants to get into the act. In estate planning this goes under the name of "teamwork." Just count up the number of experts who have already been admitted to the "team." There of course are the old standbys—the lawyers, the accountants, the insurance agents, the trust officers and the typists. Ministers still qualify, but in some regions they apparently are being replaced by psychiatrists to deal with matters of conscience. Then there are actuaries, appraisers, investment advisors and bankers. When a client seems to be contemplating something, which from a tax viewpoint he shouldn't be thinking about at all, the "team" might pick up a physician or a travel agent. According to usually reliable reports, even a dentist and a woman of notoriously doubtful virtue have made it, very likely because of inferences we usually draw from such contacts. There is no need to expand this listing in order to establish my point. Estate planning done by teaming up on the client is indeed a version of "participatory democracy." Sometimes it seems that only the client is left out of the act.

A test which activist students now apply to all things is that of relevance. Is estate planning relevant? In an earlier day this question would have been met with the query: relevant to what? Today such a clarifying question would itself be regarded as irrelevant. Fortunately, estate planners can readily demonstrate that from innumerable points of view, estate planning is indeed relevant. Take, for example, the position widely shared by students that whatever students are interested in is relevant. Everybody understands that most students say they are intensely interested in curtailing military expenditures by the United States. A sure-fire way of accomplishing this is to reduce the total of resources available to the government. Can anyone doubt that this is exactly what estate planning has sought to accomplish ever since the advent of our income and transfer taxes! Now that these elements are put in correct perspective, I ask you, is there anything more relevant today than estate planning?

Another common concern of activist students is discrimination between the sexes. To appreciate the challenge to be found here, one must call to mind the rhetoric featured by various women's liberation groups. The main point of attack is not that women are as good as men, but that they are entitled to be treated as well by society. On this score modern estate planning appears to have been far ahead of its time. For many years estate planners, for one reason or another, have been contriving to put control of family wealth in this country in the hands of women. By honoring the fact that on an average women outlive men, and then combining it with a generous use of the gift and estate tax marital deductions, we estate planners have succeeded in bringing an increasing share of private wealth under the domination of females. The women's liberation movement might take note that through estate planning, men clearly are being liberated from their wealth!

And this trend is likely to become more pronounced. I cite only one straw in the wind. Many estate planners are now urging that the present marital deduction, with its 50 per cent limit, be replaced by total tax exemption for transfers of wealth between spouses. Certain geriatric experts are already predicting that such a change in our tax law would result in women outliving men by an even greater margin than that which they already enjoy.

Before leaving the battle of the sexes all of us might note that estate planning considerations are validating the advice given by an early American philosopher: "Every man should have a wife—preferably his own."

Account must also be taken of student attitudes towards what is called the "Movement." While the "Movement" is many things, in the main it seems to be a drift or a drive to the left. Activist students appear to accept the merits, if not the inevitability of this development. Can it be said that estate planners are similarly disposed? It almost is self-evident that estate planners are fond of movements. We invented such fine steps as throw-backing, crossing trusts, accumulating income, skipping generations and giving-in-contemplation-of-living. When it comes to moves, we can give chess players a fair workout. But can we creditably claim to be pointed towards the left? In a profound sense we surely are oriented that way. The central concern of every estate planner is with what is left! The fact is we try to minimize taxes in order to maximize that which is left. Out motto could well be borrowed from the wisdom of a great modern architect who, in explaining his starkly plain glass and steel rectangles, said: "Less is more." Or, better yet, our motto could be: "Only that which is left is worth leaving." Thus the thrust of all our moves seems compatible with that of the current "Movement" on campus, which shouts that left is right.

It is not difficult to imagine some activist students castigating estate planners because of the profession's preoccupation with the problems of the rich rather than with the problems associated with poverty. I must confess that for a time this thought had me worried, especially in view of my own close connections with estate planners. But then I realized that such criticism would be unfounded because it looks at world affairs in much too narrow a context.

An analogy might be instructive here: A physician who administers to the healthy through practicing preventive medicine is addressing the problem of health no less than his colleagues who attend the sick. A comparable observation can be made about estate planners. They too are attacking the problems of poverty. But they do so by trying to prevent the wealthy from becoming poor. In short, they are the practitioners of poverty prevention—and maybe they realistically should be thought of as the PPP Corps.

Another potential trouble point in responding to concerns of students is the relationship between estate planners and that thing called the "Establishment." Among activist students there is a widespread combination of beliefs that minority groups in our society deserve special protection, and that any alliance with the "Establishment" is suspect. Estate planners will not hesitate to express agreement with these views. They have long felt that their clients constitute a beleaguered minority. And they have traditionally regarded those in government as oppressors. What estate planner does not habitually consider Revenue Service personnel as the entrenched source of error? What estate planner, further, does not enjoy a confrontation with this enemy? I might add that most planners probably would love to have their own confrontations replayed on national television, especially now that lawyers are replacing doctors as heroes on tube shows. Certainly our trust experts would be able to provide the mass audience with plenty of tiers (of both the first tier and second tier variety) as well as plenty of gas!

Much of the contemporary student creed seems to deal mainly with matters of style. Often what counts is not what is done but how it is done. This outlook should be near and dear to an estate planner's heart. After all, who are the real masters at putting form over substance! It is sufficient for me merely to mention such marvelous estate planning conceptions as "the independent trustee," the "reasonably ascertainable external standard" and the "limited power of appointment." Furthermore, who would deny that most estate planners would be totally lost without their forms?

We estate planners even anticipated another, yet related, student value—that of "doing one's own thing." I refer not to "do-it-yourself estate planning" by clients, of which we have had an ample supply lately. Instead I refer to the hundreds of court cases which attest to the widespread temptation on the part of many estate planners to generate controversy by doing their own thing instead of sticking to tested and approved ways of planning an estate. The fact is that estate planners tend to be individualists even in using form books. Let me put the point in another way: Can you think of any estate planner who admits that he cannot improve upon the forms employed by another planner?

A wholly different type of student value to be faced is that of "involvement." The crux of it seems to be that, to do anything that is worthwhile, a person must get "involved." Here we estate planners are well ahead of the parade. Have you looked at the estate tax portion of the Internal Revenue Code recently? Or at the estate tax return? I ask you, can you put your finger on anything that is more involved? And, further, do you think that anyone who today tangles with taxation can avoid getting caught in its webs? Perhaps we are close to having a clue to the recent wisdom that goes: "God is not dead; he just doesn't want to get involved." I much doubt that he seeks to qualify for membership in our guild.

Student activists often proclaim that the fewer the man-made barriers between individuals the better the life. This notion gains expression in various ways. Included, for example, are a new emphasis on physical contact among persons and a sharing of burdens in communal-style living. Can estate planners lay claim to participating in values such as these? Surely a good case can be developed. Inter-person physical contacts are at bottom a matter of touch, as anyone can plainly see. Taxation in essence is the activity by which government officially puts the "touch" on people, and estate planners are those closely in touch with this most touching business. There occasionally are complaints that the planners thems [illegible] dminister a version of the touch. Of course I am referring here not to fees, but solely to the fact that planners sometimes rub clients the wrong way. As for encouraging a sharing of burdens, this is what sophisticated estate planning is all about. Every planner labors under the impression that only by minimizing taxes for his clients will others be forced to contribute their fair share to the common welfare. So who needs a commune to get across this simple truth?

At this point I would like to offer a conjecture. Heavy use of drugs has been reported among student and other groups, but there does not seem to be much drug consumption among estate planners. Assuming this to be correct, I believe I have the explanation. One who works constantly with the Internal Revenue Code does not need anything else to feel stoned. Should cynics tell us that we are foolish in not becoming acquainted with the joys of pot, we need not reach far for an answer. The naked truth is that the whole business of estate planning can simply be reduced to the game of dividing up the "pot." This is, I suppose, just another way of saying that though our grass is green, we know how to cut it.

Mention must also be made of the music which permeates the culture of the young. Rock and roll seems to be the thing. I doubt that estate planners dig rock and roll. We are happier dealing with larger numbers. Just give us a client with rocks and Rolls—especially a chauffeur driven one—and we will know how to dig him. Yes, rocks and Rolls have long made the music to plan an estate by.

Many students have shown a deep interest in mysticism. They reject reason as the means of solving problems, and instead turn to various aspects of magic and to supernatural phenomena. Estate planners will be quite comfortable playing on this circuit. Much estate planning contains a large ingredient of prophecy and sometimes even prayer. Most estate planners, moreover, rely heavily on ritual. One need only read the boilerplate clauses in estate planning documents to detect the liturgical and the incantational quality of the ultimate in our literature. A large part of our work, furthermore, turns on a faith in extrasensory perception. And as for magic, just recall how, through estate planning, death in the right sequence or at the right time can be turned into pure gold.

I must not ignore the phenomenon of alienation. Students repeatedly say they are alienated—and even when they do not say it, their elders do. Alienation in some student circles seems to be the mark of membership in a sort of club. We estate planners can hardly be strangers to alienation. Almost all estate planning rests on things being easily alienable; in fact, ever since the halcyon days of medieval England, estate planners have been busily engaged in alienating all things that can be labeled as property. Alienation in a sense is the very heart of our art. With us, a truly successful act of alienation has a neat double aspect: it operates not only to transfer wealth but also to alienate those who are the fiscal minions of government.

Some observers of the campus scene believe that activist students are seeking to bring about a revolution. The leaders of the movement are frequently described as children of wealth who affect a look of being poor in order to assuage a feeling of guilt which is generated by their affluence. Estate planners will find this syndrome most familiar. All too often a client tries to mislead his advisor into thinking he is poorer than he really is; and all too often the advisor in turn tries to convince Revenue Agents of the same thing.

And talk about starting a revolution. Clients of estate planners for years have professed that they are ready to revolt. History, moreover, is on their side. A goodly portion of all revolutions has been inspired by taxes. My guess is that unhappy taxpayers have far outdistanced unhappy students in dreaming about Utopia!

Finally, I call attention to the belief held by many activist students that our society is about ready for the Apocalypse. It is at this juncture that students and estate planners seem to have a vision in common. For who can live by planning estates without being aware that his work must always reach a dead end! Unlike student activists, however, estate planners have no need for an underground press. The truth is that estate planners constantly feel the press of the underground. In dealing with clients they understand completely what is implied in that old principle of "oneupsmanship": "If you are not one up, you are one down."

## CONCLUSION

My conclusion, if I have one, is simple. In this Age of Aquarius, estate planners can well stand up to the challenge of students. But can students in this Age of Aquarius stand the challenge of planning estates?

In short, we may still be with it, but are they still going to be with us?

Reading 87

# The Skillful Giver's Guide

**Robert M. Randall**

*Even a family with an income under $20,000 a year can build up a net worth of $200,000 or more—enough to make estate planning important.*

For reasons that have nothing to do with the Internal Revenue Code, Christmas comes almost at the end of the calendar year. But because of that coincidence, in a lot of families Christmas is much more than colored lights, candy canes and the usual plaid shirts, toy trains, electric blenders and tricycles stashed under the tree. Right now, some families—wealthy and not so wealthy—are planning gifts to each other and to close relatives of thousands of dollars worth of cash, stock, real estate and life insurance.

For the superrich, the strategy of giving has long been as important as the strategy of getting. John D. Rockefeller Jr.'s fortune was once estimated at $400 million to $700 million, for example, but he made many gifts to his family while he was still alive. After he died in 1960, his estate was appraised at $161 million, of which half went to his widow, half to the Rockefeller Brothers Fund. Federal taxes were $10 million. A middle-income family that has acquired substantial property can easily lose a bigger percentage of its net worth to estate taxes than Rockefeller did.

These days, a surprising number of families with comparatively modest incomes have acquired large estates—often as a result of company-paid group life insurance, increased land values, stocks that have grown enormously in price since the 1930s, and easier access to the market through such devices as the mutual fund. Banks seeking trust accounts of not less than half a million dollars now find it useful to advertise in general publications. Even a family with an income under $20,000 a year can build up a net worth of $200,000 or more—enough to make estate planning important. Yet many middle-class families, lulled perhaps by the mistaken notion that estate taxes seriously affect only the Rockefellers, have made no effort to save estate taxes.

The key to cutting estate taxes is to give some of your assets away before you die. That idea is harder to accept for someone who has accumulated a moderate estate slowly and by his own efforts than it is for a rich man accustomed to inherited wealth. But because the gifts a person makes while he is alive are taxed differently from the bequests he makes in his will, good planning can save an estate from being reduced to the point where it will not support the survivors in the manner to which they are accustomed.

Gifts can shift income to children or retired parents in lower tax brackets. Gifts can even cut the expenses of settling an estate, since probate costs and lawyers' fees are proportional to the size of the estate; those fees will be lower if the estate has been diminished by gifts made before death. However, even when the motive for giving is affection unalloyed by any intention of ducking taxes, the giver would be ill advised to go ahead without consulting a lawyer.

There are plenty of reasons other than taxes to be careful about giving assets away. No one should beggar himself by overplaying the role of benefactor. Amateur family philanthropy is dangerous: it can become needlessly expensive and hopelessly fuddled. Property given without strings can be squandered, while a gift ringed about with too many restraints can be impossible for anyone to use.

The gift tax has its oddities. For a start, it is the giver who pays it. Even if A gives B $1 million, it's A who pays the gift tax, not B, who is thus doubly lucky. At first A may feel, correctly, that this is double taxation, since he has probably already paid income or capital-gains taxes on that $1 million. The gift tax, though, is intended to keep people from avoiding estate taxes. If A left B that $1 million in his will, A's estate would have to pay taxes on it. So, by the inexorable logic of Internal Revenue, if A makes the gift while he is still alive, a gift tax is due.

Not every dollar of a gift or a bequest is taxable. Up to certain limits, what someone gives away or leaves in his will is tax free. That is a result of a number of exemptions and deductions written into the law:

**1** The *annual exemption* allows anyone to give away $3,000 a year to each of an unlimited number of individual recipients. This may be done repeatedly, every year. By signing a gift tax return together, a man and his wife may give $6,000 jointly to any one person, even though the money really belongs to only one of them.

**2** A *lifetime exemption* applies after the annual exemption is exhausted. Beyond the $3,000 a year tax free, over his entire lifetime anyone may give away a total of $30,000, all at once or spread over many years. The whole $30,000 may go to one person, or it may be split up among many. As with the annual exemption, a man and his wife can combine their lifetime exemptions, so they can give a total of $60,000 tax free. When tax-exempt gifts are made under the lifetime exemption, the giver must file a gift tax form so that the IRS will know how much of the exemption has been used. If the $60,000 exemption is to be claimed, both man and wife must file and each must sign both forms.

**3** In addition, for a married couple there is a *marital exemption* from the gift tax. If a man gave his wife a $100,000 diamond necklace, he would first take the marital exemption of 50%; that would leave $50,000 subject to tax. If he has not used any of his other exemptions, he could subtract $3,000 and then $30,000—leaving gift taxes due on only $17,000.

**4** A similar *marital deduction* applies to estate taxes. When one spouse dies, half of his or her estate (after deducting lawyers' fees and probate costs) goes tax free to the survivor. So, for example, if the husband dies first, his wife gets half of his estate free of estate taxes; that part of his estate will be subject to taxes only after her death. Unless she has remarried, her estate will not qualify for the marital deduction, so it would normally be much more heavily taxed. For that reason it's especially important for the survivor to understand how to save money for the children by giving them some property before death.

**5** Every estate is allowed a *standard exemption* of $60,000. It would be easy to conclude that a man and his wife together have a combined exemption of $120,000, but it doesn't work that way. Say the wife dies first. Her estate will be entitled to a $60,000 exemption, so in addition to the marital deduction her husband inherits $60,000 tax free. When he dies, that same $60,000—not an additional $60,000—will be tax exempt in his estate. The calculations on page 347 show several ways in which the marital deduction and the standard exemption apply to a $500,000 estate that could be amassed by a family with income under $30,000 a year.

No one can beat estate taxes by parceling out everything he owns with his dying breath. A gift made less than three years before the giver dies is presumed to have been made in contemplation of death and taxes—so for tax purposes it is considered still part of the estate. Recipients often challenge that presumption in court, sometimes successfully. Earlier this year the U.S. Tax Court saved the children of Hilda Beecher Stowe, a distant relative of the author of Uncle Tom's Cabin, some $187,000 by ruling that she did not have mortality on her mind when she made them a large gift less than three years before she died early in 1965. The court was much impressed by testimony that Mrs. Stowe had celebrated her 80th birthday on Oct. 11, 1963 by dancing at the St. Regis Hotel in New York with her sons until 2 A.M.

Complicated tax regulations make a distinction between unconditional gifts and those that have strings. The rule of thumb: if the giver keeps strings attached, the property will be taxed as part of his estate and probably will not qualify for the annual exemption. There is an important exception. A man may give the family house to his wife and still live there. Otherwise, if he gives property away, he must give it away completely. If he retains the income from it, for example, it remains his in the eyes of the IRS.

Just as reading a driving manual doesn't qualify anyone to race at Le Mans, getting the gist of the tax rules is not enough preparation for making decisions about the management of an estate. There are as many as seven different taxes to consider. In addition to the federal gift and estate taxes, estate planners have to know how to juggle federal income and capital-gains taxes; they must also know the effect of state gift, estate and inheritance taxes. (Inheritance taxes, unlike estate or gift taxes, are paid by whoever get the property, not by the giver.) Those state taxes vary from one state to the next. Some states do not have them; elsewhere, however, the rates have climbed high enough that they can no longer be ignored in planning an estate. To make things still more intricate, some states do not allow the same exemptions and deductions that the federal government does.

Each kind of property is surrounded by its own thicket of problems for anyone who tries to give it away. *Stocks,* for example, often get the giver and the recipient into tangles created by the tax laws affecting capital gains. When the recipient sells a gift stock, his capital gain is calculated from what the giver paid for it, not from what it was worth at the time the giver parted with it. Eastman Kodak recently sold for 140¾ a share. Suppose the parents bought it at the equivalent of 2¾ in 1938, allowing for splits, and gave it to their children in 1958, when it went for the equivalent of 15½. If the children sell it now, they must pay capital-gains tax on 140¾ minus 2¾—a thumping $138 a share. The tax rate on the first $50,000 of capital gains is 25% of the gain, or half one's regular income tax rate, whichever is less; someone in the 30% bracket would pay only 15% on such a capital gain. Over $50,000 the rate is half one's regular income tax rate. With inherited property, as distinct from gifts made by a living donor, capital-gains tax is due only on any increase in value from the time of inheritance to the time of sale. If those children had inherited their Eastman stock in 1958 instead of getting it as a gift, the taxable gain per share would be less: 140¾ minus 15½, or $125.25.

Families who don't fully understand how capital-gains taxes work may hang onto a stock that they don't really want. They do it because the stock has increased dramatically in value, even though it now pays a small dividend. If they can afford to give it to family members with relatively low incomes, taxes—even on the full long-term gain—would be smaller when it was sold. The proceeds could then be invested in a stock with higher yield or better growth potential.

Stocks in small businesses are a special case. Giving away shares in a family enterprise should be handled with care, since control of the company could well be affected in unexpected and uncomfortable ways.

Gifts of *real estate* can produce capital-gains complications similar to those raised by stocks. In recent years many landowners—especially farmers—have been caught up in a bittersweet land boom. They watched happily as land values rose, but then winced to discover that for estate taxation purposes, the IRS values land at its current market price. Long Island potato farmers, for example, complain that unless their acreage is valued at its worth as crop land, it will have to be sold to developers to pay estate taxes. One way to bypass that predicament, and escape the gift tax too, is to deed chunks of land away, though many localities have zoning laws that specify a minimum size for such subdivisions.

Even if there are no large land holdings, the *family house* can be divested. A husband may assume that since he holds a house jointly with his wife, he has already given her a half interest. That simply isn't so, because property held jointly will be taxed in the estate of the spouse who dies first, unless the survivor helped pay for the property and can prove it. Whether to give the house to one's wife depends, among other things, on the value of the house, whether the mortgage has been paid off—and the state of the marriage. In any case, the gift qualifies for the marital deduction, the annual exemption and any unused part of the lifetime exemption.

Just as a man may wrongly assume that he has given his wife a half share in the house, he may also mistakenly believe that his wife, or another beneficiary, will get his *life insurance* tax free. But no matter who the beneficiary is, life insurance proceeds are reckoned as part of the estate unless the insured has taken care to give the policy away. To do that, he has to give up all his rights, including naming the beneficiary and borrowing against the cash value of the policy. Even group life insurance paid for by an employer can be signed over. That requires the consent of both the employer and the insurer, which is normally routine. Insurance companies have special forms for giving a policy away irrevocably. The gift tax is figured on the policy's cash value. Term insurance has no cash value, so it can be given away tax free.

In small quantities, *cash* itself is probably the asset given away most often and least carefully. The trivial sums enclosed in a child's birthday card can be ignored as far as the IRS is concerned, but for larger amounts the rules get sticky. Both fairness and the Gifts to Minors Acts dictate caution. Beyond casual amounts, a parent's accounting for funds that he has given his child but still manages should have some formality; there are rights and responsibilities to being comptroller of the piggy bank. All money and property held for a child must be turned over to him when he comes of legal age. After that, he may sue to recover funds that were mishandled.

*Heirlooms* and *works of art* can be hard to part with. But giving them away saves estate taxes, and there is the further compensation of seeing others get pleasure from the family treasures. No one who gives away a painting should keep it on his own wall, though. If the heirloom or art object is valuable, the giver would be wise to accompany it with a letter explaining that the gift was made without strings. (Getting collections and heirlooms appraised for estate planning purposes, or simply for insurance, can be a problem.)

Protecting a gift can be as important as choosing it well. The trust fund is a flexible device that can be used to do two things important to the estate planner: it can make a gift irrevocable, and thus no longer part of a taxable estate, and at the same time it can impose conditions on the use of the gift. A trust may seem a mystery that yields its secrets only to the rich, but in fact it can be thought of as a simple form of management contract. Precursors of trusts were used in the Middle Ages, when the Crusaders picked men they had confidence in to watch over home and hearth while they went to reform the infidel. An agreement established what powers the stay-at-home manager was to have over the property and how he was supposed to tend it.

Trusts come in an infinite variety, but the basic permutations are fairly simple. They may be revocable—subject to alteration at will by whoever sets them up, or irrevocable—out of his control and irretrievable in the hands of the trustee. They may be established for a precise number of years, or to last a maximum of 21 years after the death of the last surviving beneficiary named in the trust. (That limit, called the rule against perpetuities, is designed so that dead hands cannot direct an inheritance forever.) A lawyer may suggest a "sprinkling" trust, under which the trustee may distribute income as he sees fit to suit the changing needs of children as they grow up. Or he may propose a trust that would give a surviving wife only the income, unless some of the principal becomes needed to pay for a serious illness. Some wealthy families may go so far as to set up a dozen separate trusts for each child; in others the parents may even retire to manage their children's trusts full time. Whether a family is rich or merely prosperous, it can use trusts to reduce estate taxes.

To show just how gifts and trust funds can cut estate taxes, Stephen M. Raphael, an adjunct law professor at New York University and a practicing attorney, put together the composite family history summarized in the calculations over-leaf. It is based on some of the strategies he has worked out for his middle-income Brooklyn clients—among them a roofer, a teacher and an ad man. Plainly, where there's a will there may be a better way than just leaving everything to a spouse.

Raphael's hypothetical family includes a 55-year-old husband, his wife and four children, aged 19 to 26; he earns $28,000 a year. His major assets:

- 100 acres of Vermont farm land, bought for $20,000 in 1957. It's worth about $1,500 an acre.
- A house in Brooklyn, bought in 1956 for $25,000, now worth $50,000.
- A mutual fund portfolio, accumulated over the years, now worth about $100,000.
- $75,000 worth of a data processing company stock that has nearly tripled in value since he bought it in 1960.
- A $100,000 life insurance policy, payable to his wife. Cash value: $40,000.
- Checking and savings accounts totaling $15,000 and personal property, including household furnishings and two cars, worth about $10,000.

Using a simple will, the combined taxes on their two estates—assuming that he dies first—would come to $144,096, more than a quarter of the principal.

Changing the will slightly to set up one trust fund cuts the tax bill nearly in half, to $86,400. The optimum solution is to combine the new will with a gift-giving program and one more trust fund that consists of the insurance policy. He deeds to his wife his $25,000 joint interest in the Brooklyn house. Under the marital exemption, that is counted for tax purposes as a gift of $12,500, which is covered by his $3,000 annual exemption and a $9,500 chunk of his lifetime exemption. Over four years the couple will give some of their Vermont acreage away to their children; at $1,500 an acre they can give each child four acres annually and still stay within the $6,000 annual exemption. (Each gift should be recorded by a separate deed, and each tract should be physically marked off from the rest of the parents' property.) One year, instead of farm land, they will give each child $6,000 worth of the data processing stock.

The first trust fund is set up with the $100,000 insurance policy. The wife gets the income for life, and the trustee may give her some of the principal if she becomes seriously ill; otherwise, the principal goes to the children when she dies. The $40,000 cash value of the policy would normally be subject to gift taxes, but if both the man and his wife sign the federal gift tax forms, that $40,000 can be subtracted from what is left of their combined $60,000 lifetime exemption.

Over a relatively few years, the man has given away $270,000 to his wife and children—more than half his estate—without paying any gift taxes and probably without seriously jeopardizing his financial security. The only income-producing asset he disposed of was $24,000 worth of the data processing stock. His retirement income should cover his needs adequately. In any emergency his wife can still borrow money on the Brooklyn house, or they can mortgage their remaining farm land. The plan can continue after he dies; using her $3,000 annual exemption, she can give the children a few more Vermont acres at a time, keeping 20 acres to live on. Using gifts and trust arrangements, this couple can cut $125,916 from its potential combined estate tax bill.

Stephen Raphael admits that the Scrooge instinct is difficult to overcome. "It's hard to make people who have spent their lives saving and being acquisitive think in terms of giving," he says. But self-interest is persuasive. Raphael explains: "When they see how much estate taxes can take from their hard-earned fortune, their interest in generosity increases." Indeed, he says, many clients—including those whose motives bear no resemblance to Scrooge's—come to recognize that "giving is just another form of saving."

**Three Fates for a $500,000 Estate**

| Simple will leaving everything to wife: | | | |
|---|---|---|---|
| He dies, leaving a | $500,000 | gross estate, | |
| less | 20,000 | in probate costs, lawyer's fees and other expenses. | |
| | 480,000 | | |
| Subtract | 240,000 | —half of his estate less expenses—as a tax-free marital deduction, | |
| leaving | 240,000 | | |
| Subtract another | 60,000 | for the standard estate exemption, | |
| and | $180,000 | is his taxable estate. | Federal taxes: $44,700 |

**Three Fates for a $500,000 Estate *(Cont.)***

| | | | |
|---|---|---|---|
| She inherits | $500,000 | | |
| less the | 20,000 | expenses | |
| | 480,000 | | |
| and less the | 44,700 | in federal taxes, which leaves | |
| | 435,300 | When she dies, there will again be | |
| | 20,000 | in expenses. | |
| | 415,300 | | |
| Subtract her | 60,000 | standard exemption, | |
| and | $355,300 | is her taxable estate. | Federal taxes: $99,396 |
| | | | Total federal taxes: $144,096 |

**Will leaving half to wife, rest in trust:**

| | | | |
|---|---|---|---|
| As before | $180,000 | is his taxable estate. | Federal taxes: $44,700 |
| But this time | 240,000, | his estate before taking the standard exemption, | |
| less the | 44,700 | in taxes, | |
| goes into a | 195,300 | testamentary trust fund. She gets the income for life. When she dies, the children get the principal without paying further tax. | |
| She inherits the remaining | $240,000 | via the marital deduction. At her death | |
| there will be | 10,000 | in expenses for settling her smaller estate. | |
| | 230,000 | | |
| Her estate will use the | 60,000 | standard exemption, leaving | |
| | $170,000 | as her taxable estate. | Federal taxes: $41,700 |
| | | | Total federal taxes: $86,400 |

**Estate reduced by two trusts and gifts:**

| | | | |
|---|---|---|---|
| He has a | $500,000 | net worth. | |
| He puts their | 50,000 | house in his wife's name, | |
| | 450,000 | | |
| gives | 96,000 | worth of farm land to his children, | |
| | 354,000 | | |
| along with | 24,000 | in stocks, | |
| leaving | 330,000 | He puts in trust fund A | |
| a | 100,000 | insurance policy, reducing his gross estate | |
| to | 230,000 | When he dies, | |
| there will be only | 10,000 | in expenses. | |
| | 220,000 | | |
| Subtract the | 110,000 | marital deduction, and | |
| his net estate is | 110,000 | | |
| Subtract the | 60,000 | standard exemption, and | |
| | $ 50,000 | is his taxable estate. | Federal taxes: $7,000 |

**Three Fates for a $500,000 Estate *(Cont.)***

| | | |
|---|---|---|
| Trust fund B gets the | $110,000 | net estate, |
| less | 7,000 | in taxes. |
| That leaves | 103,000 | with the income going to his wife for life, then the principal to his children. |
| She inherits the | $ 50,000 | house and |
| | 110,000 | tax free from his marital deduction, |
| for a total of | 160,000 | |
| She gives | 24,000 | in farm land to her children, |
| leaving | 136,000 | At her death, |
| there will be | 10,000 | in expenses. |
| | 126,000 | |
| Subtract her | 60,000 | standard exemption. |
| Her taxable estate: | $ 66,000 | Federal taxes: $11,180 Total federal taxes: $18,180 |

Reading 88

# Surprises for Widows: Banks Help Find Unknown Death Benefits

**Morton C. Paulson**

*Millions of dollars in Social Security, veterans' benefits, insurance, workman's compensation, pension money, profit-sharing proceeds, teacher annuities, railroad retirement funds and other benefits go unclaimed each year because the intended beneficiaries don't know they exist or have no idea how to go about claiming them.*

In Indianola, Miss., a widow happened to mention that her husband once worked for the Civilian Conservation Corps, the Depression-era agency that hired unemployed youths. As a result of her offhand remark, the woman received $800 in retirement funds accrued by her late spouse.

In Dallas a father whose working wife had died learned that Social Security would pay $400 a month to his four children—and that he could collect $1,700 from a long-forgotten insurance policy.

In Florida the widow of a former Italian Army soldier learned she could get a $20-a-month pension plus a $550 lump-sum payment from the Italian government.

All of these people obtained their windfalls through the persistent digging of a local bank. Thus far, some 300 of the nation's 14,000 commercial banks—plus 300 branches—have started helping people in their communities track down, apply for, and collect any benefits that may be due them. The service is free; often it's not even necessary to be a customer of the bank.

From *The National Observer*, Aug. 4, 1973, p. 9.

The 300 banks are affiliates of Special Organizational Services, (SOS) a Texas-based company that developed the concept and provides a blueprint for implementing it. Almost all of the people who are assisted by the banks are widow, widowers, or others who have survived the death of a close relative.

## SUSPECTING THE NEED

Millions of dollars in Social Security, veterans' benefits, insurance, workman's compensation, pension money, profit-sharing proceeds, teacher annuities, railroad retirement funds, and other benefits go unclaimed each year because the intended beneficiaries don't know they exist or have no idea how to go about claiming them. Those who do know often find themselves engulfed in bewildering paper work and red tape.

SOS's mission is to minimize the travail and make sure, as far as possible, that nothing a person may have coming is overlooked. The program was conceived by tall, affable James W. (Bill) Walker, Jr., 55, a former life-insurance agent from Athens, Texas. From contact with insurance clients, and from helping a friend's widow organize her affairs, Walker become convinced that such services would be widely welcomed.

"I've seen what people go through," he said in a recent interview. "It can be an agonizing experience. Our objective is to make things as easy as possible through organization and direction."

## HELP FOR TOUGH QUESTIONS

Banks become subscribers by paying SOS between $500 and $5,000 a year, depending on their size. In return, a bank gets exclusive rights to offer the program, which is copyrighted, in its area. SOS trains bank personnel in ways to search out potential benefits and in the procedures for collecting them. In addition, the organization supplies the banks with record forms, promotional tools, a monthly bulletin, and continuing guidance. When a bank employe involved in the program has questions or runs into an unusual problem, he can call SOS headquarters for help.

SOS banks have already turned up millions of dollars in benefits that recipients didn't know existed, Walker says. There was the young widow who found a sheet of paper with a series of numbers on it—nothing else—among her deceased husband's effects. An employe of a bank in Lubbock, Texas, did some digging and found that the number was that of a life insurance policy that the woman hadn't known about. The insurance company paid her $2,400.

Thanks to a bank in Jackson, Miss., a widow learned that she wouldn't have to pay the $300 balance due on a credit-card bill; her husband had credit insurance.

"We're turning up thousands of cases like that," asserts Walker. "Credit life policies aren't paid off unless a claim is made, and you'd be just amazed at how much insurance goes unclaimed because survivors have no inkling it's there and it doesn't occur to them to check."

What's in all this for the banks? Quite a lot—many of the people who are helped are so grateful that they become customers. "The benefits of SOS never cease to amaze us," exclaims John H. Morton, assistant vice president and SOS coordinator at the Louisiana National Bank in Baton Rouge. In eight months Louisiana National assisted 73 persons—and has received $994,104 in new business from them. The People's State Bank of New Port Richey, Fla., which added

$113,000 in new deposits during the last year as a result of SOS activities, acclaims the program as "our greatest source" of new customers.

E. L. Jory, president of the Albuquerque National Bank, reports that SOS has not only attracted new customers but has also "tied our old customers a lot closer to us." Echoes William T. Gordon, president of the Bank of Virginia-Central in Richmond: "It's probably the best public-relations program we've gotten into."

How does one find an SOS bank? Usually the banks advertise the service in local newspapers or other media. They also furnish details about the plan to local bar associations, executors of estates, and various official agencies. And many solicit business by culling obituaries and contacting survivors of the deceased.

In September SOS will publish its first national directory of member banks. You can learn which banks closest to you offer the service by writing to Special Organizational Services, P. O. Box SOS, Athens, Texas 75751.

Reading 89

# Yes, Amateurs Do Make Money in Real Estate

**Changing Times**

*If the enterprise is sucessful, the investor gets all the rewards.*

"They're making more people, but they aren't making any more land." This remark, attributed to an old Texan, sums up the attractiveness of acquiring real estate in growing areas of the country. And the motto of the founders of the King Ranch in Texas is said to have been, "Buy land and never sell," which indicates that over the long run, real estate bought and put to productive use leads on to fortune.

Certainly real estate is one of the oldest forms of wealth and has a solidity that sets it apart from the more intangible forms of ownership, such as stocks, bonds, bank accounts and insurance policies. But can the ordinary person get into it? Doesn't it take too much capital and too much know-how? Aren't there big risks of getting gypped or being foreclosed?

The answer to these questions if that ordinary people with relatively small amounts of capital can invest successfully in real estate in their spare time and are doing it every day. This does not mean buying stock in a big real estate investment company or in a REIT (real estate investment trust) or participating in a large syndicate set up by a professional syndicate manager. What is meant here is a grass roots enterprise in which an individual invests his own money and time or in which a few friends, neighbors or business associates get together to search out local opportunities and invest in them.

Of course there are risks, and it takes time and hard work. But the advantages are great. There is no big overhead expense and no one taking the cream off the top. If the enterprise is successful, the investor gets all the rewards. In addition, he has the satisfaction of having done the job himself.

A few real-life examples will illustrate the point and also some of the problems. Names of individuals are fictitious.

## A YOUNG MAN STARTING OUT

"I had always wanted to start some kind of investment program," says 29-year-old Paul Knowles of Spring Valley, just east of San Diego, "but because of a tight budget I knew that it would have to be something self-sustaining." He had married and gone to work right after high school and soon acquired two children. His job as a salesman for a wholesale grocery firm didn't provide him with much excess income.

Knowles got his first break simply by learning that FHA would insure loans up to $39,600 with only 3% down on a small building containing four apartments, known as a four-plex. Armed with this information, he began looking for a building that was basically sound but in need of modernization. The area he picked was East San Diego, which has good access to freeways and shopping and has been completely rezoned for apartments.

For several weeks he answered newspaper ads, read the Sunday paper listing of units sold with location and price paid, and spent much time examining apartments and talking to owners. When he finally felt he knew enough to make an offer, he bought a unit from an owner who was eager to sell because one sale had already fallen through when the buyer couldn't qualify for the FHA loan. The price was $39,000 and the down payment was $1,300. Knowles points out that FHA rules require that before it will insure a loan, the building must be appraised and meet requirements for construction, roof, drainage, plumbing, freedom from termites, etc. There is no guarantee, of course, that a building, even if sound, can always be kept rented and profitable.

When bought, the building was fully occupied except for the apartment reserved for Knowles, and there had been no rent raise for two years. Knowles announced a $10-a-month increase. (This occurred prior to rent controls.)

The difference between rental income and outgo, including insurance, taxes, interest (at 8½%) and principal, was $120 a month, which Knowles spent on renovating whenever an apartment became vacant.

A local firm installed carpet in the first vacant unit at a discount to get future business. Knowles did the painting himself and bought paint, draperies and floor tile at sales. "I worked two weeks in the evenings and on weekends, and, after checking rents of comparable units in the neighborhood, I easily rented it for $140 a month, a $20 increase over the original rate." Over the next seven months he renovated the other apartments as they became vacant.

At this point he decided to trade his property for a larger one, but an ad brought no response. He then offered the unit for sale. After showing it for two Sundays, he sold it for $47,000 to a retired couple who were able to assume the FHA loan. He then ran an ad in the paper saying "Private party wants 6 to 8 units from owner." The response was good, and he bought a three-year-old, eight-unit building, using his profit and assuming an 8¾%, 25-year conventional loan and giving the seller a small second trust. Now he has saved up enough to buy another four-plex, and he hopes to continue his program of trading up. His advice is to buy older units and fix them up, rather than paying more for new ones. He also says he saves $6,000 to $8,000 in commissions by buying property direct from the owner.

Knowles may well be on his way to making a fortune in real estate, assuming he keeps at it and makes no major mistakes. A man named William Nickerson acutally made several million dollars starting in the same way except that his first property was a duplex bought for $1,000 down. For more information read Nickerson's book, *How I Turned $1,000 Into Three Million in Real Estate in My Spare Time* (Simon & Schuster, $7.95).

## A NEIGHBORHOOD SYNDICATE

Several years ago a group of neighbors got into a larger and somewhat less successful transaction. A doctor with a good income had asked the local banker for investment suggestions. The banker eventually came up with a waterfront farm some 100 miles distant consisting of about 925 acres selling for nearly a quarter of a million dollars. This sounded completely out of reach until the banker explained the following facts:

- Down payment was $80,000.
- The seller was willing to take back a first trust of $175,000 on which only the interest would be payable for five years.
- The cleared part of the farm was leased to a tenant who farmed it.
- A local sawmill operator was willing to pay $40,000 over a ten-year period for timber rights.
- The income would carry the taxes and interest.
- The depreciation on the buildings would give the owners a tax loss that would be applied to their other income.

So a syndicate was formed with ten units costing $8,000 apiece. The doctor took seven, leaving three, one of which was offered to John J. Bowdoin, who took it and, in turn, split it among himself and two friends. Thus Bowdoin, for an investment of only $2,700 ($8,000 divided by three) received a stake in a relatively large venture.

For about three years everything went well. An additional $10,000 was contributed pro rata to purchase a bulldozer for clearing more land and for other expenses. After three years, however, the partners began to worry about what would happen when the "interest only" period elapsed and they would have to start paying down the principal of the mortgage. About this time they accepted an offer to buy the property for $361,000. This sounded good, but then began the trouble.

It seems that the doctor, although nominally managing partner, was extremely busy with his practice and was relying on the banker to handle the legal details of the transaction. The banker, also busy, was not aware of how much the doctor was depending on him. So the ball fell between them. The sales contract gave the purchaser the right to occupy the property as of June 30. The tenant had agreed verbally to vacate the farm by that time. But it soon developed that under state law, he could require 90 days' written notice, and if it were not given, he had the legal right to occupy the farm for another year. On local advice he decided to exercise this right and the partners had to buy him off. Likewise, the timber cutter demanded reimbursement for all the timber that he could have cut had his contract not been canceled. In addition to cash payments to settle these claims and avoid lawsuits, the partnership had to pay $15,000 to a local entrepreneur to handle the negotiations.

Somewhere along the line, Bowdoin discovered that the banker had been given a second trust note in the beginning representing a finder's fee of 10%, or $24,750, which was payable on sale of the property. As a result of all this, the capital gain was not as large as anticipated. But for each $9,000 invested, the partners received $13,338, representing a true annual growth rate of 10.3% compounded over four years. This return would not generally be considered adequate considering the risks involved.

Lessons learned:

- The managing partner, or at least someone, must be diligent in understanding every provision of every contract and making sure all loopholes are closed and all loose ends tied up. A lawyer should be in the group if possible.
- Each partner should read the original partnership agreement closely and understand every provision and every charge.
- No contract should ever be signed to sell a property until the seller knows he has all the legal documents signed and delivered guaranteeing that he can turn the property over to the buyer under the terms and conditions stated in the sales contract.

## A NEIGHBORHOOD REAL ESTATE COMPANY

Back in February 1960, ten men, neighbors and mostly members of the local Kiwanis Club, met with the idea of forming a small real estate investment company to take advantage of the rapidly increasing land values in two northern Virginia counties south of Washington, D.C. The group consisted of a lawyer, a local banker, a retired accountant, a county building inspector, a highway inspector and a general practitioner, who, whenever a specific piece of property was mentioned, was likely to say, "Yes, I know where that is. I delivered a baby there once."

The minimum investment decided on was modest, $250 in cash and $25 a month for ten months. The lawyer drew up incorporation papers authorizing 5,000 shares of stock, and each incorporator was required to subscribe to a minimum of 50 shares at $10 a share. By the time of the first meeting word had gotten around so that the corporation acutally began life with 27 shareholders who owned a total of 825 shares and had pledged to buy an additional 525 shares.

Those of the group who had free time began scouting around the countryside and examining maps and records in the county courthouse. One evening in the summer of 1960, following a supper meeting of the Kiwanis Club, such officers and directors of the corporation who happened to be present were bundled into a car by the retired accountant, by then treasurer of the company, and driven over back roads to a rather inaccessible bit of scrub woodland. He recommended the purchase of three tracts totaling five acres because they lay in the middle of or close to what would be an interchange of Interstate 95 when it was extended south of Washington toward Richmond. The projected course of the highway was no secret, but no one had yet bought these tracts, perhaps because the asking price of $16,000 was considered too high. As one member reported scornfully, "It's only a pig farm and you could have bought the whole thing five years ago for $1,000." This remark illustrates one of the greatest dangers in the investment business—looking back instead of ahead. Fortunately, the other directors saw the potential value and the property was purchased. These tracts were sold some years later for over $200,000.

To illustrate some other dos and don'ts in this kind of investment, here is an abbreviated log of the company's activities over several years of its early history.

*Sept. 1960:* Bought 5 acres expected to be on I-95 interchange. Price, $16,000.

*Dec. 1960:* Although somewhat off the real estate track, bought 100 shares of the small local telephone company at 17. Rumor had it that the commanding general of the Marine Corps base at Quantico, Va., enraged because he could not get an outside line, had ordered the switchboard yanked out and regular service taken.

*Apr. 1961:* Bought 24 more shares of telephone stock at 14 through rights offering.

*Mar. 1962:* Company permitted stockholders to buy more stock at $12, new net asset value.

*June 1962:* Bought 12 landlocked acres along Interstate 95 for $300 an acre, with thought that access could be worked out later.

*Oct. 1962:* Offered one-half acre on the I-95 interchange to several oil companies for $33,750. No takers.

*Jan. 1963:* Received a 10% stock dividend on telephone stock.

*May 1963:* Offered stock to existing stockholders and interested friends at net asset value of $15 a share.

*Dec. 1963:* Bought a house on 29 acres of land near Manassas, Va., for $17,000. Also bought two waterfront properties on the Eastern Shore of Virginia, one 60 acres and the other 150, on the theory that the bridge-tunnel complex being built across the mouth of Chesapeake Bay would open up the area to traffic from New York to Florida. Unfortunately, no big pickup in traffic ever occurred and eight years later the company still had the two properties and had paid off the mortgages and lost its leverage.

*Mar. 1964:* Through rights, bought 96 more shares of telephone stock for 24, it then being traded in the market at 31.

*May 1964:* Put a price of $80,000 on half-acre I-95 tract. No takers.

*Nov. 1964:* Increased authorized shares to 10,000 (since nearly 5,000 had then been sold) and set the net asset value at $20 a share.

*Feb. 1965:* Made first sale of property—house and 29 acres sold for $27,750 net, a capital gain of over $10,000. Big celebration.

*Apr. 1965:* Appraised net asset value at $30. Also bought an acre of land on a corner of U.S. 1 and Telegraph Rd.

*Aug. 1965:* Bought 77 more shares of telephone stock through rights offering at $40 a share.

At about the same time, the real estate company found it now had so many stockholders that it was necessary to apply to the Securities and Exchange Commission for registration of its shares before any more could be sold.

*Apr. 1966:* After eight months of dealing with the Securities and Exchange Commission, was able to offer shares to the public at $30. Sold only 200 shares.

*Sept. 1966:* Agreed to sell half-acre on I-95 to Atlantic-Richfield for $90,000 but received no cash at this time.

*Nov. 1966:* With only $12.40 in bank, necessary to float bank loan.

*Dec. 1966:* Atlantic-Richfield, trying to delay settlement until it was ready to build a service station, found an old unused county road on property. Since no title insurance had been obtained, it was necessary to go through time-consuming procedure of applying to the County Board of Supervisors to abandon the road.

*Mar. 1967:* Delay in settlement with Atlantic-Richfield forced company to borrow $50,000 from bank at high interest rate plus two points.

*Aug. 1967:* Settled with Atlantic-Richfield. Paid off bank loan.

*Dec. 1967:* A stockholder who had bought in at 10, 15 and 30 determined the true annual growth rate of his investment to have been 27% a year compounded annually.

From here on, the company found the going easier. Its accumulated telephone stock appreciated because the area was growing rapidly. It eventually was sold for over $15,000. The company split its stock four for three, re-registered with the SEC twice, selling shares first at $30 ($40 on the old stock) and recently at $50 ($67 on the old stock).

Lessons learned:

- It's easier to buy land than sell it.
- Real estate deals almost always take longer than expected.
- Title insurance should be obtained on every piece of property at time of purchase.
- A small real estate company should have (1) dedicated people who know the area and have time to search out bargains, (2) a lawyer, an accountant and, if possible, a securities man among the directors or officers, (3) a close association with one and preferably two local banks where lines of credit can be arranged.
- Many contracts to buy that real estate agents offer owners of property are phony. A typical provision in a contract says that the buyer is making an "earnest money" payment but this money is to be put in escrow with a lawyer until settlement. Probably the check would not even be cashed but simply put away and the purchaser would not put up real money at all. Another provision allows six months for settlement. Still a third states that if, prior to settlement, the buyer's engineers find the property "unsuitable," the deal is off and the so-called earnest money will be returned to the buyer. In other words, such a contract is nothing more than a free option for six months.

Other clauses sometimes found in purchase contracts offered to land owners provide that settlement will not take place until after rezoning has been obtained. There may not, however, be any provision that requires the purchaser to apply for rezoning at any given time, which could give him what would amount to a free option for several years.

The case histories given indicate that you can invest in real estate without much previous business experience and without a big pile of money. But they also indicate that you cannot do it successfully without a lot of hard work and without learning all you can about the area and the properties that are available.

# Expenditures and Taxes for Government Services

## Reading 90

## Assessing Your Tax Assessor

**Robert M. Randall**

*Even families that can pay the tax will find the property tax system a puzzlement.*

Unless you live year round in a tent in some place like Yellowstone National Park, you can't very well avoid paying property taxes in one form or another. Homeowners, businessmen, landlords and tenants will each ante up part of the record $45 billion in property taxes that will be collected this year. That's $2.5 billion more than last year, and the increase will be enough to put some businesses into the red and to force some homeowners and farmers to sell out because they can no longer afford the taxes. Even families that can pay the tax bill find the property tax system a puzzlement. Mystery envelops the process that assessors use to evaluate property for tax purposes, and confusion surrounds the way that tax rates are arrived at year by year.

One obstacle to making sense of the system is the sheer anarchy of it all. There's only one federal government and there are only 50 states to levy various sales and income taxes, but there are 14,000 different jurisdictions in the U.S.—counties, school districts, townships and so on—that have the power to impose property taxes. What's more, each of the 14,000 has its characteristic way of valuing property, keeping records and hearing appeals. As a result, though most Americans know their federal income tax bracket and have some idea what they pay in state sales taxes, few can quote their property tax rate and fewer still know how it's calculated. With a little homework, however, a homeowner can find out if he's getting equitable treatment from the tax assessors; if he discovers that he's being had, anything from a subtle protest to a frontal assault can help him get treated at least as fairly as his neighbors.

Fairness, of course, is the crux. The Advisory Commission on Intergovernmental Relations recently polled American attitudes toward taxes. To the question "Which do you think is the worst tax, the least fair?", some 45% picked the property tax. Many professional economists and tax reform specialists agree. For one thing, the property tax is not necessarily progressive like the income tax; measured as a percentage of total income, it can hit poor families harder than rich. For another, the system is subject to abuses and encrusted with quirks that make it the despair of anyone who cherishes consistency in government. One ten-bedroom antebellum mansion in New Orleans, which was sold recently for $225,000, is carried on the tax rolls at $14,000; the owner was a veteran, which

Reprinted from *Money*, August 1973, pp. 60-63, by special permission; © 1973, Time Inc.

qualified him under Louisiana law for a $5,000 deduction from his tax assessment, so he would up paying $416 a year in property taxes. One of his servants lived half a mile away in a $25,000 house assessed at $6,000; with a homestead deduction, he paid $185 in property taxes—almost half as much as his employer was paying on a house worth nearly ten times as much.

## WELCOME STRANGER

John B. Rackham, a District of Columbia assessment specialist recognized nationally as an expert, calls the property tax "a complicated system that has been allowed to go to seed." Corruption is widespread. Also, the New York State Board of Equalization and Assessment concedes that because of out-of-date procedures, inequities in local assessments range from minimal to monstrous. California, by contrast, is relentlessly up to date: in some areas officials inspect neighborhoods by helicopter. Some small New England towns have an institution known, a bit cynically, as the "welcome stranger" tax. Long-time residents know what everybody's property is worth, so the assessors normally have little leeway with them, but a newcomer may find that his property has been reappraised sharply upward. Equity isn't everything, however; people simply don't like to pay taxes. Even in the town of Ramapo, New York, which state officials regard as a model of fair assessment practices, 700 taxpayers lined up for a hearing on the most recent "grievance day."

The process of figuring tax rates is fairly straightforward, though the results are almost always presented to the public as a *fait accompli*. The way it works in Stratford, Conn., is typical. First, the town council fixes the budget for local services—schools, streets, sewers, police and fire protection and so on. In 1973 that budget was $21.9 million; grants and other revenues would be $6.7 million, leaving $15.2 million to be raised by property taxes. Stratford expects to collect taxes on property valued at a total of $340 million, so simple arithmetic indicates that each dollar of assessed valuation will have to bear about $^{15}/_{340}$ of a dollar's worth of the tax burden. As tax rates are commonly expressed, that worked out to $4.47 for every hundred dollars of valuation.

There's one important complicating factor. Houses in Stratford, like houses in most communities around the U.S., aren't carried on the rolls at market value. They are assessed at a fraction of market value, usually expressed as a percentage. Suppose that the fractional assessment rate in Stratford is 70%. A house that is actually worth $40,000 would then be assessed at $28,000. At $4.47 per hundred, the tax bill will be 280 times $4.47, or $1,251.60.

Fractional valuation comes about because there is often no direct way to deal with the fact that real estate values fluctuate. Although they rise or fall over the decades, assessments are not revised regularly to keep up. The disparity finally must be standardized in order to accommodate new property to the existing system. For example, if values have gone up to the point where older houses in a community are assessed at half what they would now sell for, and someone buys a new house for $40,000, the fair thing to do is to put it on the rolls at $20,000. Thus, in effect, the community has a fractional valuation rate of 50%.

In a single state the fractional valuation rates can range from a few percent to more than 100%. As a practical matter, though, it makes no difference whether a town has a high fractional rate or a low one, as long as market values are fairly and consistently appraised. Trouble is, the homeowner has no way of discovering whether or not his property is overassessed or underassessed unless he can find out what fractional value rate is supposed to apply to his area. The homeowner who thinks that he's getting a bargain on his taxes because his property is listed at less than what it's worth may be fooling himself. His $50,000 house may be assessed at $35,000, but his neighbor's $50,000 house could be down for only $32,000.

## OVERTAXED TENANTS

The first step in determining whether or not your assessment is equitable is to find out what the fractional valuation rate is in your community. An increasing number of states publish the fractional valuation rates used by localities, often because state aid formulas are based on a standard of property valuation that must be consistent statewide. Some localities publish an official fractional valuation rate and stick to it; others apply different rates to different types of property. Minnesota, for example, has a rate for each of 24 different classes of property. In states where the practice doesn't have the blessing of law, it may still have the sanction of custom.

In such situations, who gets overtaxed? Welcome-stranger assessments hit hardest at new houses or property that changes hands often. Neighborhoods that have a considerable number of rental properties are sometimes overassessed because the assessors expect the landlords to pass the tax on to their tenants without much complaint. Industry pays a scandalously small share of taxes in some communities, but in others it gets stuck with the highest fractional valuation rates. Middle-income neighborhoods are sometimes subsidized by poorer districts that have less political clout. But some studies indicate that the more residential property is worth, the higher the fractional valuation rate is likely to be: a $30,000 house could be assessed at 50%, or $15,000, while a $60,000 house could be assessed at 60%, or $36,000.

In many states one group or another pays a disproportionate part of the property tax, and doing something about it isn't easy. The politics of Cook County, Illinois, which includes Chicago, are Byzantine at best, and not unexpectedly the tradition carries over into tax assessments. The county assessors long proclaimed that industry was paying tax at a higher rate than homeowners; residential property got a 22% fractional rate, they said, while industry's assessments went at about double that. Then a civic group called the Citizens Action Program showed that some residential property was in fact assessed at more than 40% of market value. The citizens' group was also able to prove that houses in two neighborhoods were assessed at an average of 27% of their market values—one-fifth higher than the county assessors had originally claimed.

Armed with the true fractional valuation rates, county residents started appeals that won them tax rebates averaging $200; the maximum was $7,000. But discovering the real fractional valuation rate was only half the battle. Each homeowner had to prove what the market value of his house was. Some did that by showing what similar houses had recently sold for. Others hired independent professional appraisers, who normally charge as much as $200 to assess the market value of a house. The Cook County homeowners got a bulk rate of $25 to $35 per house, so that with the average rebate of $200 most of them came out well ahead.

The Cook County reform corrected inequities, but it did not do away with the need to collect taxes. Since the cost of local services continues to rise, towns can raise the needed money in one of two ways: they can increase the tax rates, or they can reassess property values upward. When updating the tax rolls is necessary, nowadays localities increasingly hire outside mass appraisal firms to do the job quickly and fairly.

In theory, an outside firm is less vulnerable to charges of favoritism than local assessors are. C. Lowell Harriss, a Columbia economics professor, likes to tell of the mass appraisal firm that did its job so well that the town fathers locked up the new tax rolls so no one would find out how shockingly out of whack the old ones were. The largest of the firms, Cole-Layer-Trumble of Dayton, Ohio, is currently working on 70 mass appraisals around the U.S. ranging in scope from small towns to large sections of a state. The firm has 800 full-time employees, but the actual job of looking over the property to be appraised is frequently done by temporary workers, often college students. The field workers are sometimes the only part of the appraisal team that the homeowner under scrutiny ever sees. Their function is to list on a record card for each house the outside measurements, number of rooms, fireplaces, outbuildings, additions and general condition. The actual value assigned to the property is worked out by a trained appraiser using various arithmetical formulas.

## CHUMS ON THE BOARD

The mass appraisal system has its drawbacks. Contracts to appraise communities are almost always awarded to the lowest bidder, so firms try to keep the cost of appraising each piece of property down. (In large communities the range usually runs between $6 and $8 per parcel.) Cutting costs by using college kids instead of trained appraisers to do the actual inspections probably contributes to one of the major complaints against mass appraisal firms: when they zip through a community they make a lot of mistakes.

As a result of one mass appraisal project, an Ohio man found that a tiny three-bedroom house that he bought 20 years before for $11,000 had been reappraised at $22,500. He was convinced that the real market value was more like $16,000, so he complained to the local assessor. A check of the records showed that no one from the appraisal firm had been inside the house, since the owner had been on vacation when the evaluator came around to look at the property. After several appeals, the owner won a reduction to $17,550. But his troubles with mass appraisers weren't over. By coincidence, the same firm also reappraised a county in another state, where the man owned a country place. There too he thought the firm had overvalued his property; again the record card showed that at best the appraisers had taken a hurried look. This time his objection was heard by boyhood chums on the local appeals board, and they revised his assessment downward.

Professionals level other serious charges against mass appraisal firms. Some 39% of the members of the International Association of Assessing Officers rate the quality of mass appraisers' work poor or very poor. David R. Reed, supervisor of assessment for New Castle County, Delaware (and an employee of Cole-Layer-Trumble before he jumped the fence to work for the county), suggests some of the reasons why:

- Instead of preparing an assessment system that the locality can update efficiently on its own in a few years' time, some mass appraisers do the job in such a way that they themselves will have to do it again.
- Mass appraisers may be unwilling to spend the necessary time and money to make an intensive independent appraisal of industrial property; instead, they may rely on self-serving information provided by the owner.
- Since lawsuits can take vast amounts of a highly paid professional appraiser's time, appraisal firms are eager to negotiate reductions with businesses, which can usually afford to take their complaints to court. On the other hand, the mass appraiser can be confident that most homeowners can't afford to sue.

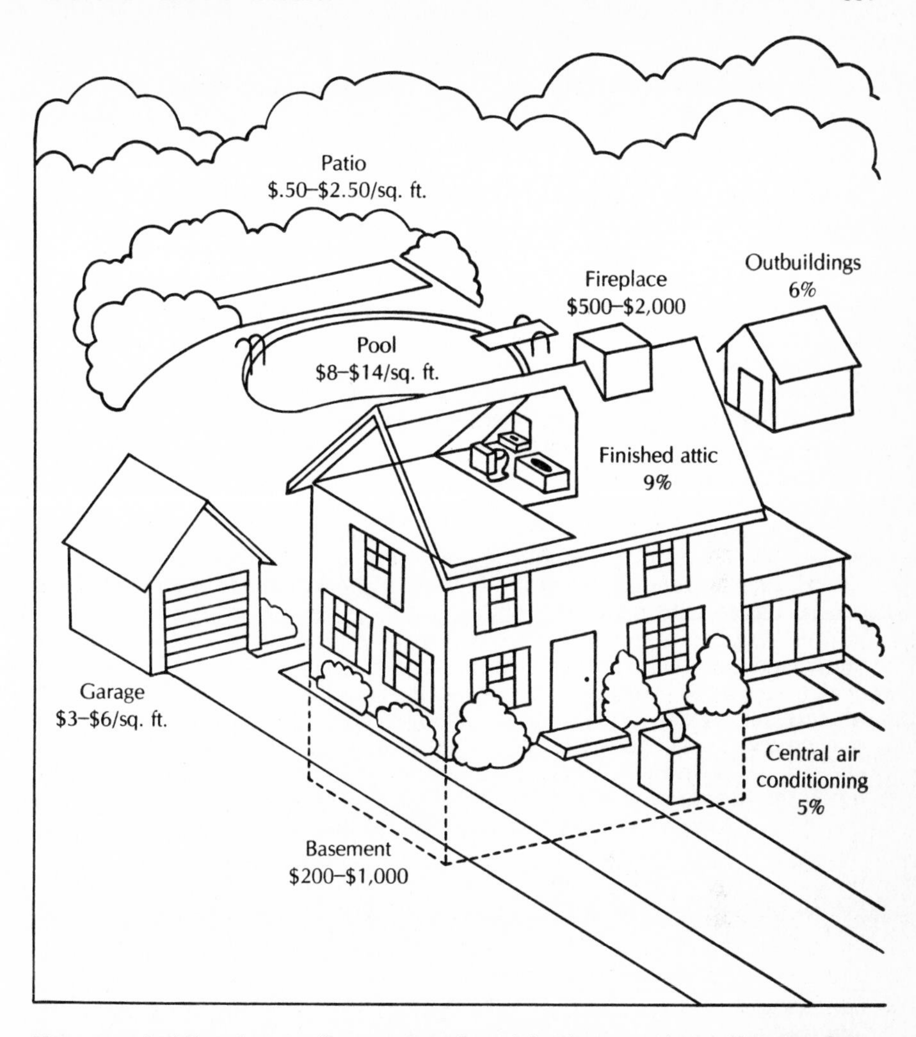


Mass appraisal firms have uniform systems for valuing large numbers of houses. Cole-Layer-Trumble, for example, starts by figuring the average value per square footage of each community's average, or "C grade" residence. This figure, multiplied by the square footage of any house, produces its base value. Some features of the house can add a percentage of the base to its value; an attic adds 6% to 19%, depending on whether it's unfinished or finished. Other features raise the base value by specific dollar amounts; a fireplace can add between $500 and $2,000. Outbuildings and improvements to the grounds add either a percentage or a dollar amount, as shown. Houses are also rated from AA+ to E, depending on the quality of materials and workmanship. An AA+ house is worth two and a half times as much as a C house, while an E house is worth only half as much. The appraisal firm figures that a house in excellent shape depreciates 20% in 24 years, while one showing normal wear depreciates 35% in that time.

Still, taxpayers who merely appeal assessments can do fairly well. One executive of an appraisal firm estimates that 10% to 20% who do so have good cases and actually win reductions.

There are plenty of ways to improve your chances of getting your assessment reduced whether a mass appraiser is involved or not. First, you should work out just how much you think the reduction should be. To do that, you need to know how much your property is worth. A real estate agent should be able to make a knowledgeable guess. Ask him or your assessor what the fractional valuation rate is; multiply that by your estimate of the market value. Then compare that figure with the assessment on your tax bill. (If it's not on the tax bill, you can get it from the bank that holds your mortgage.)

Suppose that your assessment is far enough out of line that getting it reduced to the amount you think is right would save you several hundred dollars a year or more. Whether you take your appeal to an informal hearing held by a mass appraiser's representative or to the regular local appeals board, the professionals offer these pointers:

- Don't miss the deadline for filing appeals. Even if the proceedings are very informal, try to get a definite appointment for your hearing.
- Prepare your case carefully. Be sure to check all the facts and arithmetic on the record card on your property, which is kept at the assessor's office.
- Write down the sale prices of as many as five houses similar to yours in your neighborhood that have changed hands in the past year. That's pretty good evidence of what your own house is worth. Your bank's mortgage appraisal, it it's recent, may also be acceptable. The appeals board may want to have an outside appraiser's figure. Find out ahead of time which kind of evidence your appeals board favors. If you use an outside appraiser, find out what kind of report the board requires and whether it must be certified.
- Use snapshots of any structural failures that have significantly lessened the value of the property to bolster your case for a reassessment. If outbuildings have been demolished, be sure that has been reported for the record. (In California, earthquake tremors often cause enough damage to send whole neighborhoods flocking to the assessor's office to file reports.)
- Make certain that improvements to the property have been valued at the amount they add to the market price of the house, not at what they cost you. A basement that has been converted into a $15,000 pleasure palace should add only a few thousand dollars to the total value of the property. (For some guidance on what various improvements can add to the market value of your house, see "Home Improvements for Love or Money," Reading 58.)

Some appeals boards are rubber stamps for the assessor or the appraisers. Worse, some states allow the assessor to sit on the appeals board. It's worth listening to local scuttlebutt to find out whether the appeals board has a reputation for petty tyranny, tough justice or openhandedness. Some boards respond more sympathetically than others to claims by veterans, the elderly, the unemployed or the poor; many will modify the effect of high tax rates by reducing assessments for people who can show that they are truly having a hard time paying their taxes. Other boards, however, quit paying attention when they hear a sob story.

If you don't feel you have been given a fair hearing by the local appeals board, you can always go to court to try to force a reassessment of your property. Rarely, however, does a homeowner stand to gain as much as a lawsuit will cost him. In addition to court fees and a lawyer, the homeowner has to pay for an expert witness, usually an appraiser. Even large corporations don't rush into court over property assessments. For them, it's standard practice to file petitions for review of assessment with the court for several years before asking for a trial. Instead of battling with a town year after year, corporation lawyers make their case once and ask for a retroactive reduction.

The property tax process seems grim and forbidding, but there's hope ahead for the hunkered-down taxpayer. To increase the professionalism of assessors, 15 states have begun training and certification programs in the past ten years. A minority of states have also introduced other reforms—separating the appeals function from the assessor's office, consolidating small assessment jurisdictions into bigger units and, in some cases, making the state responsible for assessments. In theory, at least, all of this makes assessment more uniform, less idiosyncratic and less susceptible to industry pressures.

Getting rid of fractional valuations would make assessment procedures a great deal easier for the average taxpayer to understand and cope with, but only five states have taken that relatively drastic step. John Shannon, assistant director of the Advisory Commission on Intergovernmental Relations, says that 14 states have adopted more consistent fractional valuation systems, which is at least a partial improvement; another 19 states have begun to take some steps in that direction.

Shannon thinks that property tax reform would be helped by a full disclosure policy that would enable each taxpayer to find out if he is being treated fairly in comparison with his neighbors. California now publishes all assessed valuations and estimated market values in the newspapers, which is an enormous help to the confused taxpayer. The ideal tax bill—a far cry from the typical variety —would list the assessor's estimate of full market value, the actual assessed value and the average fractional valuation rate for the tax district.

## THE WRONG KEYS

Another forthcoming reform is standardization of the process for giving tax relief to certain property owners—the elderly, the poor, farmers, the blind—who have previously had to plead individually with their local assessors in hardship cases. All 50 states now recognize the need for relief for one class or another. Some, like Louisiana, grant specific deductions from the assessed valuation of a property. Others tie relief to the taxpayer's gross income. In Michigan, for example, a senior citizen with a $4,000 annual gross income and a $400 property tax bill would get a $360 rebate; he would not be required to pay more than 1% of his gross income ($40) in property taxes.

Then too, the computers are coming. Some specialists say that only sophisticated computerized systems will be able to keep assessments in line with rising market values. A computer can be programmed to perform the hundreds of calculations necessary to determine the exact value of a house; it can check its memory of the prices of comparable neighboring houses when it prepares an assessment. Theoretically, a community with a computerized system could update its assessments every year, so it would never undergo the turmoil of an overdue mass reappraisal. Even if such systems can reduce inequity, they probably won't eliminate error. The computer system in Ramapo, New York, the most modern one in use, has managed to produce a number of mistakes in tax bills simply because somebody pushed the wrong keys.

Reading 91

# Closing Tax Loopholes—The Mills Plan

**U.S. News & World Report**

A bill introduced by Representative Wilbur D. Mills (Dem.), of Arkansas, chairman of the House Ways and Means Committee, proposes to repeal 54 sections of the income tax law that tend to reduce the tax bills of individuals and corporations. If the bill becomes law, 18 of these provisions will expire each year—among them the following:

| To expire on Jan. 1, 1974 | Annual taxes involved |
|---|---|
| Percentage depletion for oil, gas, other minerals | $1.0 billion |
| Rapid depreciation adopted in 1971 | $2.4 billion |
| Dividend exemption of $100 | $300 million |
| Capital gains taxed at reduced rate | $5.0 billion |
| Exclusion of company payments for employes' life insurance | $440 million |
| **To expire on Jan. 1, 1975** | |
| Deduction of personal interest | $4.5 billion |
| Deduction of State, local taxes | $8.5 billion |
| Sick-pay exclusion | $100 million |
| Deduction for research and development | $540 million |
| Deduction of intangible drilling and development costs | $325 million |
| Favorable treatment of capital gains at death | $4.0 billion |
| **To expire on Jan. 1, 1976** | |
| Investment credit | $3.9 billion |
| Deduction for charitable contributions | $3.8 billion |
| Deduction for medical expenses | $1.7 billion |
| Deduction for care of children, other dependents | $170 million |
| Lower tax rate on first $25,000 of corporation's profits | $20 billion |
| Exemption for State, local bond interest | $2.3 billion |
| Deduction for personal casualty losses | $80 million |

Note: "Taxes involved" are based on 1971 data.
Source: U.S. Treasury Dept., House Ways and Means Committee



Reprinted from *U.S. News & World Report,* June 19, 1972.

# Part Three

# Consumer Protection

This section is a logical continuation of the preceding one, "The Purchase of a Life Style."

From a realistic point of view the purchase should not take place until a buyer knows a considerable amount about his legal "rights," where to obtain information, and what agencies—both private and governmental—can be of assistance if help should be needed.

The first part of this section deals with buyer-seller communications. It contains readings dealing with the cost of product failure, phony repairs, and consumer satisfaction; in the next part of this section the dynamics of consumer protection of the federal, state, and local levels is discussed; and, finally, the international consumer movement is covered.

# Seller-Buyer Communications: Private Aids

Reading 92

## What To Do Until the Appliance Doctor Comes

**Grace Hechinger**

*Needless to say, the crucial part has not yet arrived from the factory which produced it, located clear across the country, if not in Tokyo.*

Scene I, A Home Appliance Showroom: We are knee-deep in wall-to-wall displays of refrigerators, washing machines, dryers and TV sets as far as the eye can see. An ingratiating salesman explains the revolutionary features of an endless variety of washing machines. He lingers lovingly in front of the super deluxe model while explaining all its "extras." The mind boggles at the rows of shiny buttons for every conceivable kind of laundry and even some inconceivable ones. And the machine only costs $90 more than the merely deluxe model. Really a bargain since you get all that technology for your money.

Scene II, At Home, Two Years Later: After three "no shows" a repairman finally arrives, timed perfectly to join the children as they come romping home from school. So after tossing the kids a snack, you show him where to turn off the water or the electricity or whatever (and hope that he will be able to turn it back on again at the end of his visit) and brace yourself for the bad news.

After much huffing and puffing, your friendly serviceman finally locates the source of the problem and is ready to deliver his diagnosis. "I'm afraid it's the decelerator . . ." (or the condenser or something equally mysterious), he announces with the solemnity of a doctor giving a negative prognosis. He adds that there has been a great deal of trouble with that part, particularly in this model. This is the very same machine that was only recently sold to you as another unsinkable Titanic. That super deluxe washing machine (or dishwasher or TV) you remember meeting in the showroom as the pride of American technology is now referred to by its "doctor" as a serialized lemon. Besides, you have had it for more than two years and are lucky to have escaped the consequences of its built-in "problem" for so long.

We know that he knows that we know nothing about the intestines of an appliance nor about the delicate "nerves" attached to its temperamental buttons and dials. How to know if it is worthwhile to invest another $40, let alone $80, for a cure or just shoot it like a lame horse? Of course, there is a guarantee on the new part that is currently prescribed for the machine's open-heart sur-

From the *Wall Street Journal*, Jan. 15, 1973. Reprinted with permission of the *Wall Street Journal*, 

gery, but how do you know that the "rotary up-take" or some other organ won't go next week? That is another part of the forest and would not be covered by the new guarantee. You do not understand this mysterious machine, but one thing is clear—its innards are paved with gold.

Needless to say, the crucial part has not yet arrived from the factory which produced it, located clear across the country if not in a suburb of Tokyo. "Don't call us, we'll call you, when it comes," is the familiar refrain. "You know how slow delivery is this time of year." (Winter, fall, spring or summer, there is no season for fast deliveries.) When the dashing machine surgeon departs, leaving despair and dirty footprints, you dissolve in tears.

There must be many households like ours who respond to the service muddle by avoiding all the super deluxe models like the plague. The more elaborate the gadgets, dials and buttons, the greater the odds that more will go wrong. And when it does, there will be fewer repairmen familiar with its complexities, fewer warehouses which stock the extra parts and fewer chances that the special gismo can be properly installed. The expense and inconvenience of it all has convinced us that what counts is the smallest number of moving parts and pushable buttons.

If a manufacturer wants me to put my faith in his more expensive, complicated machines, perhaps the way to woo my trust is by offering a longer free service period and longer parts guarantees. I realize that this would not cover the wide and vague range of damages resulting from external causes such as "abuse, misuse and acts of God." But I might at least be made to feel that the manufacturer himself has enough faith in the more expensive machines to make them seem worth the extra investment.

Even in the standard-priced appliances, greater interest by manufacturers in training manpower to service their product might be a simple matter of good business. Improved service might increase public confidence and thus willingness to buy. Salesmen, in turn, might be taught to give explicit maintenance details. The consumer movement has made many potential customers too knowing for the old sales pitch that considers it bad psychology to mention the possibility of a breakdown. A sophisticated interpretation of modern technology is not that nothing will go wrong, but rather that help will be available when it does. Repairmen should not only be initially well-trained, but given refresher courses to keep up with model changes.

Some companies now offer what is called a "service contract" which is like "life insurance" for your washing machine or dishwasher. But the costs are high, and they rise each year after you celebrate your machine's first birthday. You pay annually whether your machine is sick or not. Before you become eligible for such a policy, your machine must undergo a thorough physical examination—at your expense, of course.

To some extent, the service contract contradicts the image the company is trying to create; the need to insure against such expensive trouble can hardly inspire confidence in the appliance. Moreover, when you start to figure the odds, bear in mind that one expert theory has it that, without a service contract, any repair will cost between 20% and 40% of the machine's original price. It is not worth the company's trouble to repair it for less and few customers are willing to pay more than 40% on a continued gamble.

The gloom is not total, however. Some appliance manufacturers have installed a "hot line" telephone number for do-it-yourself advice in an emergency. In addition, a recent General Electric advertisement offers "Service by Appointment—Because General Electric knows your time is as important as ours." This "Customer Care Service" is a step in the right direction.

Perhaps GE has been spurred on by the consumer movement as well as by reports of the establishment of the nation's first successful TV repair cooperative. (The TV repair field is noted for its fraud and incompetence.)

Until there is concrete proof, however, that the gap between the sales pitch and the real-life kitchen is closing, we continue to rely on our private home remedy. Our present solution is a treasure named Eddie, an old-fashioned genius at repairs, who is rightfully proud of his craft. Eddie has assumed the stature of a trusted family retainer ever since the day he came to fix an ailing washing machine when I was imprisoned at home by a blizzard and two sniffling babies. Unfortunately, Eddie—a survivor of an endangered species—is beginning to talk of moving to sunnier climes.

So, we are left with a prayer for Eddie and two-and-a-half cheers for GE. We may be forgiven for some skepticism while we wait and see whether GE lives up to its service claims and how many other manufacturers of home appliances will be inspired to follow suit—service rather than soothing slogans. Perhaps some day I, too, will want that deluxe model and think of all those dials and buttons as something more than an IOU to the repairman.

**Reading 93**

# Consumer Costs in Product Failure

**John S. Berens**

*Many warranties do not even cover direct money costs associated with product failure.*

Exactly what is a warranty? The usual legal understanding is very clear: *a warranty is the assumption of responsibility, by the seller, for the quality, character, or suitablity of goods sold.*[1] A warranty may be *express* (an affirmation by the seller) or *implied* (recognized to exist at law even if a positive affirmation is not made by the seller). A majority of firms try to live up to these commitments, but to many, warranties are merely legal disclaimers of their clients' responsibility.[2] It is in this sense that many corporate lawyers appear to think of their clients' liability for products which are sold to the consumer either directly or through dealers.

That consumer also has his ideas about the meaning of a warranty. His conception is simply what the manufacturer will do for him in the event of product failure or defect. It is doubtful that consumers, in many cases, even attempt to read the precise legal circumscriptions in which the seller carefully restricts his liability to the performance of certain specifics. Instead, they tend to rely on the retail salesman's less technical statements such as "Guaranteed for five years!" or "This little baby carries a lifetime guarantee!" The average consumer probably feels that the manufacturer will take care of any defective product, up to the limit of actually replacing the same, for the duration of the express warranty period. The concept of implied warranty probably escapes the consumer's understanding even if he has heard somewhere of this legally recognized imposition of responsibility upon the seller.

From *MSU Business Topics*, Spring 1971, pp. 27–30. Reprinted by permission of the publisher, Division of Research, Graduate School of Business Administration, Michigan State University.

What manufacturers and the distributors of their products fail to realize is that even the best of warranties (in an express legal sense) only compensate the consumer for the direct money costs associated with product failure. That is, the manufacturer will *at best* restore the product to operative condition or will replace the product with another of like quality—hopefully, one which is in workable condition. In a technical sense these direct money costs are the dollars that the consumer would have to spend to repair or replace a defective product in the absence of the manufacturer's warranty, or those costs directly associated with product defects during the warranty period for which no compensation is paid.

Indirect money costs, on the other hand, are the net dollars a consumer must spend in his efforts to receive *service* on a product (such as phone calls, taxi fares when an automobile needs service, and so forth) or those which are incurred because the product is no longer perfoming its normal function (such as food spoilage due to a defective refrigerator or eating out when a cooking range is not operable). Other indirect money costs are incurred when one product's failure causes economic loss in other products, for example, when a defective phonograph needle ruins a record. In other words, indirect money costs are out-of-pocket costs to the consumer associated with and the result of product failure, but which are not directly spent to restore the unserviceable product to working order or to replace it.

## INADEQUACIES OF CURRENT WARRANTIES

Many warranties do not even cover direct money costs associated with product failure. For example, typical color TV warranties cover labor and parts for ninety days, parts but not labor for a period of one year, and the picture tube for two years, again without coverage of labor costs after the ninety-day period. In today's economy, parts manufacture is capital intensive while repair services are labor intensive. For example, a call to a TV repairman to replace an in-warranty, older-than-ninety-day, color TV tube can result in a charge of $40.00 for labor to replace the defective, but in-warranty, tube. Other warranties cover direct, but not indirect, money costs of the consumer. An example is the warranty of a leading film manufacturer who will replace defective film but who will not compensate a consumer who pays money for flash bulbs which did not fail but were used with the defective film and hence were an indirect money cost of product failure.

Some warranties are indeed ridiculous. A leading manufacturer of chocolate candy bars placed the following warranty on a five cent (⅞-ounce) candy bar: "We guarantee this bar to be of highest quality. If not, please return it to us; we will gladly replace." A consumer who buys a defective candy bar and makes a claim under the manufacturer's warranty is actually six cents poorer for going to the trouble of paying postage and returning the product.

Or consider the case of the ladies pendant watch distributor who offers a one-year guarantee on a five-dollar watch. You must return the watch along with a $1.50 handling charge to the distributor whose only identification is "Service Division" and an address. If the watch is beyond repair as determined by the service division it will be returned as received. If repairs are needed to parts found defective in materials and workmanship, repairs will be made at a predetermined labor charge—which is not stated in the "guarantee." If *during the warranty period* you choose not to have the watch repaired, after receiving word as to how much repairs will cost, they will return the watch to you along with replacements for the parts found to be defective in material and workmanship. In trying to use the warranty, the consumer has automatically lost the $1.50 handling charge. It is very possible—considering the hourly rate of competent watchmakers—that the total bill of handling and repairs would exceed the original price of the watch to the consumer. Note that the service division could find all returned watches beyond repair, return them without parts, and pocket the difference between their costs and the $1.50 received from the consumer. The service division's full responsibility under the warranty would be fulfilled by such action.

Bordering on the ridiculous are tire makers' warranties which offer a pro rata allowance based on useful remaining tread life of a defective tire. Sometimes the replacement price is set so high that the consumer pays as much as he would pay for a new tire which is generally available at less than list price, the price upon which the allowance is based.[3]

## THE BEST OF WARRANTIES DO NOT COVER ALL COSTS

Criticisms of the inadequacies of warranties in terms of their failure to cover direct and, to a certain extent, indirect money costs within the warranty period are legion. Criticism of the shortness of the warranty period itself is also common. But the failure of the manufacturer to provide coverage for certain other costs—time, energy, and psychic—is rarely discussed. Yet it is the existence of these very real costs which makes puny (in terms of a total cost picture) the current attempts to get manufacturers to do a better job with respect to coverage of direct and indirect costs. Some idea of their nature can be seen when we consider each of the following unrecognized costs:

*Time costs* result when a defective product causes a consumer to allocate his available time differently than he would if the product were not defective or were still in service. Examples of this cost would be time spent in negotiation with dealers over warranty obligations and the increased time needed to perform in a more primitive way a defective product's normal functions.

*Energy costs* refer to the reallocation of expenditures of energy or to the increased effort required when a product is not performing its normal function. Consider situations where the consumer, in pressing a warranty claim with a reluctant dealer, must make several trips through heavy traffic to the dealer's premises, or when a broken dishwasher requires a housewife to wash dishes by hand using this more primitive method until repair service can be obtained.

*Psychic costs* are those which result in an emotional drain or in changes in consumer well-being due to the failure of a defective product. This drain could be caused by the frustration of attempts to get recalcitrant dealers to live up to a manufacturer's warranty terms. Or they could be caused by changed relationships within the household, such as the annoyance caused by children when they are deprived of the electronic pacifier, television, for a period of time.

These costs are very real and should be considered in an evaluation of the warranty programs of a manufacturer. In fact, since the dealer is the contact between the manufacturer and the consumer, an analysis of his activities relative to warranty performance efforts should be included in any comprehensive attempt to evaluate a given manufacturer's program.

## POSSIBLE UNDETECTED SHIFTS IN CONSUMER FRANCHISE

Because of their failure to provide adequate compensation for direct and indirect money costs, manufacturers in general should not feel at ease and content with the typical warranties attached to their products today. When one considers the time, energy, and psychic costs of product failure, the level of discontent with warranties felt by consumers may be higher in many instances than most manufacturers suppose. This level of discontent may, and probably does, manifest itself in patronage shifts away from offending manufacturers' products and in poor recommendations of a particular manufacturer's product when other consumers indicate they are in the market for a product of that given type. The extent of these losses often is probably undetected unless the manufacturer has a continuous monitoring system which reports to him the extent of discontent with warranty service and resultant brand switching. That brand switching has reached a high level for many products and product classes is a well-documented phenomenon. For example, a recent study reported that one-third of the users of a product changed their brand every ninety days.[4] If by better warranties and warranty perfomance manufacturers can reduce this phenomenon, brand loyalty—a high level of which is desired by firms—can be increased.

## THE THREAT OF LEGISLATION

If manufacturers, either by themselves or through their dealers and trade associations, do not take action to increase consumer satisfaction with warranty coverage and administration, continued pressure in the city, state, and national legislative bodies is likely to result in laws under which the various affected industries will find it hard to operate. Several truth-in-warranty bills were under consideration by the Ninety-First Congress. Although none were passed, similar bills will be or have been introduced into the Ninety-Second Congress which began in January 1971. When one considers that many warranties fail to cover the direct and indirect money costs of the consumer, let alone provide coverage for time, energy, and psychic costs, the spectre of legislation looms even larger.

## SOME PROGRESS

A few firms today are compensating the consumer for indirect money, time, energy, and psychic costs associated with product failure. The common warranty practice as just pointed out is to pay all or part of the direct money costs. Indirect costs are rarely covered by warranty terms. The manufacturer cannot usually restore the time, energy, and psychic costs directly to the consumer although he could compensate the consumer for indirect money costs in such a manner. He can, however, provide money or other compensation to the consumer in lieu of direct time, energy, and psychic restorations in a manner similar to the damage awards of a court of law in liability actions. To date, the evidence does not indicate that specific monetary awards are being made for time, energy, and psychic losses, but the compensation plans for product failure of some companies are noteworthy in their implicit recognition of these losses.

The oldest of these more progressive plans is the double-your-money-back guarantee, which has been used for many products although it has been primarily employed with products of relatively low unit value. Also note that the General Electric Company in its warranty on photographic flash bulbs will replace each bulb which fails with four new ones. The Zippo lighter people will repair or replace a defective lighter at no cost to the consumer, and will return it with a small supply of lighter fluid and flint. Any return postage that the consumer may have sent with his lighter is refunded.

These efforts, though miniscule when considered in light of the overwhelming majority of inadequate warranties, are examples of movement in the right direction, that is, providing compensation to the consumer for some of the indirect money and other costs incurred by him in his experience with defective products. Other examples could be cited, but these serve to illustrate the direction in which manufacturers should be going with their warranty programs.

## CONCLUSION

Because of the generally inadequate coverage by warranties of direct money costs associated with product failure, let alone indirect money, time, energy, and psychic costs, the consumer probably should take the attitude that the best warranty is the one he never has to use. Since compensation for failure is so inadequate, the consumer should look for products which are not likely to need extensive warranty service. Perhaps the consumer overheard to say "I don't want a paint that's *guaranteed* to cover in one coat, I want a paint that *will cover* in one coat," has the best attitude, considering today's state of the warranty art. The time, energy, and psychic costs not covered by a paint manufacturer's warranty are too great for him to feel confident and secure with a one-coat "guarantee." If enough consumers adopt this attitude there will be additional (beyond the already present legislative) pressure on manufacturers to improve both product performance and warranty service.

## REFERENCES

1 Harold F. Lusk, *Business Law Principles and Cases,* Uniform Commercial Code Edition (Homewood, Ill.: Richard D. Irwin, 1966), p. 836.
2 George Fisk, "Guidelines for Warranty Service after Sale," *Journal of Marketing,* January 1970, pp. 63-67.
3 Consumers Union, "Guarantees and Warranties," *Consumer Reports,* December 1969, pp. 391-392.
4 "Brand Loyalty—A Sometime Thing," *Sign and Display Industry,* September 1969, pp. 21-23.

Reading 94

# The Critical Element: Consumer Satisfaction

**Elisha Gray, III**

*The average bank president doesn't stand in line to cash a check.*

Until recently, we Americans were mainly concerned with economic growth . . . with more jobs . . . higher wages . . . stronger lifetime security . . . a greater avalanche of products . . . an accumulation of private possessions . . . and an expanding Gross National Product. These are goals common to nearly all mankind, and we have attained them to a degree unmatched by any other people on earth. But now we want to go beyond the struggle to make a better living. We want to make a better life.

To my mind consumerism is part of this manifestation of our hopes. I don't believe that this attitude calls for radical changes in the thinking of the business community, but it does call for a new order of priorities and self-expectations and a recognition that consumer satisfaction is of paramount importance.

You who are home economists can make significant contributions to consumer satisfaction. To begin with you can help to intensify efforts to educate the young for their present and future roles as consumers . . . now when their minds are most receptive. To me it doesn't make sense to teach a student a foreign language, but not show him how to decipher the label on a can of soup . . . to teach him all about the body politic, but not about the nutrition he needs to keep his own body in good health . . . to teach him how the Egyptians built the pyramids and leave him ignorant of how manufacturers write their warranties . . . to prepare him for two score years of earning a wage and simultaneously neglect what he needs to know if he is to spend his wages wisely.

But America can't wait another generation to have a public that's educated for the marketplace. Today the consumer's job is much harder than it was in earlier years. He has many more decisions to make. The products we are turning out are more sophisticated, more complicated, more technologically advanced than ever before. Ultimately he must possess the knowledge and the willingness to protect himself by the vigilant exercise of his own good sense.

In the offices, factories, and board rooms of American industry the cause of consumerism must find recognition. Sometimes we businessmen get so caught up in the nuts and bolts of our enterprises that we almost forget our main objective. We scramble to get new supplies of raw materials. We worry about shipping dates. We run down to Washington to testify before just about every committee and commission in town. And once a year we go shopping for an armored suit to wear at the annual meeting of stockholders. It's easy to forget that we are all really in the same business: to satisfy customers. There is the further danger that men at the top will become too remote from the experiences of their customers. The average bank president doesn't stand in line to cash a check. The average head of an automobile company doesn't miss his weekend golf game because the garage failed to fix his car.

But as I go around the country I am heartened by the way leaders of busi-

From the *Journal of Home Economics*, vol. 64, October 1972, p. 22, copyright by the American Home Economics Association, Washington, D.C.

ness are trying to respond to the new consumerism—to improve their products and refine quality controls and to speed up the processing of complaints, and, more importantly, to do something about them.

I am very much encouraged by the work of the 150 Better Business Bureaus in America. The Council of Better Business Bureaus has launched a program to increase telephone capacity in all offices across the country with the ultimate goal of zero busy signals, for obviously, if consumers can't get through to make a complaint, we can't give them satisfaction.

Another sore point with Americans is unethical advertising. Therefore, the council has a far-reaching plan to monitor advertising so that it doesn't mislead people by promising something other than what the company is prepared to deliver. And if the council can't get reform through the gentle arts of persuasion, it is fully prepared to take whatever legal actions are necessary.

Perhaps the most promising endeavor of all is to establish panels of arbitration whereby a qualified and totally unbiased third party can settle a dispute between a business and a dissatisfied customer . . . without all the delay, expense, and nastiness of going to court. Support of the Better Business Bureaus provides an excellent way for home economists to carry on the vital work of educating the business community in better ways to serve the public.

The achievements of our economy are rooted in competition, but the aspirations of our society are founded upon cooperation. Ours should not be an adversary system that divides the populace into winners and losers. We are all consumers, and we stand to benefit from better values in the marketplace. We are all dependent on jobs; so we all stand to benefit from better conditions and rewards of work. We all share this economy together. It should be a judicious blend of competition and constraint that brings out the best performance from each of us in order to provide the greatest rewards for all of us.

## Reading 95

# Washington Pressures/Nader Network Switches Focus to Legal Action, Congressional Lobbying

**Theodore Jacqueney**

*"Nader and the other consumer groups are trying to get industry back to the free enterprise system."*

After less than two years, Ralph Nader is well into an effort to change his hallmark from press release to legal brief and from general muckraking to pinpoint pressure on Capitol Hill.

The change in style began with a major fundraising effort in mid-1971. The result is a network of fulltime lawyers, lobbyists, writers and analysts working in 19 organizations directly or indirectly associated with Nader and functioning—as one Nader associate put it—in an atmosphere of "creative anarchy."

From the *National Journal*, June 9, 1973, pp. 840–849, © 1973.

The familiar Nader exposes will continue, expanding earlier attacks on public and private handling of meat inspection, water pollution and auto safety to include reports on "think tanks" under federal contract, Washington law firms and science policy.

But the Nader network now is after bigger game than press clippings and more space on library shelves.

What began in 1968-69 as a largely volunteer consumer crusade with a $63,000 budget now includes Nader's first unit of registered lobbyists, a new legal-action unit and an expanding collection of Nader-style groups in states and communities, all operating on a combined budget approaching $2.6 million.

Their common goal, says Nader, is to move "beyond just exposing, to a more meticulous process of advocacy."

The new style was demonstrated on May 31 by a suit filed by Nader's Public Citizen Litigation Group in U.S. District Court for the District of Columbia to close 20 nuclear power plants across the nation on grounds they are unsafe.

A second phase of the new Nader approach will begin this summer when a dozen registered lobbyists will start working on Capitol Hill, pressing for creation of a Consumer Protection Agency and reforms in the procedures of Congress.

The nearly two years of transition have not been entirely painless for Nader.

In that time, Nader has disappeared from the list of the 10 most-admired American men compiled annually by the Gallup Opinion Index.

His most ambitious project—a study of 484 members of Congress and their methods of operation—was a critical dud, although Nader and his associates insist the project was the most useful study yet done.

But even Nader's most severe critics judge his operation effective, although many find fault with his methods.

"Nader obviously sticks in the craw of a lot of businessmen," said Edward Burling Jr., a founder of Covington & Burling, one of Washington's most prestigious law firms.

"Businessmen have reason to fear the Nader group, no question about it," he said. "Businessmen do. Clients do. Some of my partners do. They think he is a wild man stirring up a whole mess of trouble.

"But essentially, I think Nader is effective as hell," said Burling, stressing that he spoke only for himself and not for the law firm. "Personally, I think he is phenomenal. I think he has done more than anyone could have dreamed a young fellow starting out would do."

Nader's operation is typical of the population explosion among public-interest groups in Washington.

There are more people working for them than ever before: they are involved in more issues and sustained by more money and they are gaining in experience.

But Nader still contends that the public-interest groups are underdogs.

Public-interest groups, he says, are outnumbered both by business, lawyers and by corporate and trade association research.

"The thing that really worries me," he said, "is that the public-interest movement is given delusions of grandeur, and is made out to be far more powerful than it is."

## CONGRESS WATCH

The newest large-scale Nader group is Congress Watch, a combined lobbying and research operation which Nader said will have a budget "in the $100,000 range," and which will field up to 12 lawyer-lobbyists by mid-summer.

### Claybrook

The director of Congress Watch is Joan B. Claybrook, who supervised the production of profiles of Members of Congress for the 1972 Ralph Nader Congress Project.

Miss Claybrook is a former special assistant in the National Highway Traffic Safety Administration, a former Congressional Fellow, and a June 3 graduate of the Georgetown University Law School.

She earned a reputation among some 1,250 staff members and volunteers on the Congress Project as a tough taskmaster when she was working to make sure the reports were turned in by deadline.

"She can work consistently until one o'clock in the morning, or until five if she has to, and never complain," said one Nader associate who asked not to be identified by name. "Ralph likes this and trusts her."

### Issues

According to the registration form which Congress Watch has filed with the Clerk of the House of Representatives, the group will concentrate on consumer affairs, the environment, transportation, congressional reform, health safety and criminal law.

The form specifically named the Consumer Protection Act (S 707), which would create a Consumer Protection Agency and a President's council of consumer advisers, and the Auto Safety Recall Act (S 355) as legislation it would be trying to influence.

Creation of a Consumer Protection Agency will have first priority, Miss Claybrook said. "Ralph has worked on this for three years, so this is one thing that we will try to do."

Miss Claybrook said that her team might take on new issues as time goes on, but that Congress Watch "will try to concentrate on areas where other groups are not working."

A second priority target will be reform of Capital Hill procedures, she said. Specific goals will depend on recommendations to be released as part of the final publications of the 1972 Congress Project.

### Mandate

Miss Claybrook said her mandate may take Congress Watch beyond mere lobbying.

"We will not just have people walking around on Capitol Hill," she said.

Because the group will be "issue-oriented," she said, its members will be prepared to follow the issue wherever it takes them. If winning on the issue means "talking to Members, testifying before committees, consulting with staff—or litigating in court—we will do whatever is involved," she said. "A lot of our work will involve research and writing."

**Preview** Although Congress Watch did not exist at the beginning of the year when major reform battles took place, members of Nader organizations participated in an operation co-ordinated by the Committee for Congressional Reform. The committee is an ad hoc group put together by some 50 public-interest organizations.

Michael K. Beard, executive director of the committee, said that Nader representatives were "extremely helpful" in providing background information.

"If we wanted information on any Member of Congress, we could get it from their files," Beard said. "It was all in one place, well-organized and fairly up to date."

Beard said that Nader also talked with some Members on behalf of the committee.

**Backup** Miss Claybrook said that Congress Watch will not be the exclusive lobbying arm for the Nader network.

"Other Nader groups will be testifying before committees and consulting with Members and their aides," she said.

### Staff

Miss Claybrook already has hired five lawyers for her staff and two already are registered as lobbyists. She said she expects Congress Watch to be "operational" before the end of July.

She said she had interviewed about "150 people so far who want to come to work here. I spend about an hour to an hour-and-a-half with each of them. I consider the quality of the people we will have to be that important that I am willing to make this kind of investment in time."

**Experience** Miss Claybrook said that she is less interested in previous experience as a lobbyist or as a Hill staff member than she is in an applicant's involvement in political or social issues, an ability to articulate and a capacity to write under pressure.

**Effectiveness** Judgments about the probable impact of Congress Watch are divided.

One former Nader staff member, who asked not to be quoted by name, said:

"I just have to laugh at the idea that Joan Claybrook is going to weld a group of graduating lawyers with no Hill experience" into a lobbying force that can compete with professionals.

But Richard P. Conlon, director of the Democratic Study Group, offered another view.

"If Joan is representative of the quality of the (people in the lobby) operation, then there is no question in my mind that it will be an effective force.

"But it will all boil down to the kind of people that are involved. If you have a lot of inexperienced people who try to push people up here around with rhetoric, then it will not work."

## LITIGATION GROUP

A recent Nader spin-off group with a great potential impact on national and consumer affairs is the Public Citizen Litigation Group, which acts much as a private law firm for a variety of Nader causes.

Founded in February 1972, the organization operates from offices in the Dupont Circle Building in Washington on an annual budget of $75,000, all of it drawn from Public Citizen Inc. fundraising efforts.

### Staff

The litigation group has a staff of three attorneys who are involved in cases ranging from impoundment of highway funds to better federal treatment of Vietnam veterans.

**Morrison** Director of the law group is Alan B. Morrison, 35, a graduate of Harvard Law School.

Before joining Nader, Morrison spent nearly two years with the New York City law firm of Cleary, Gottlieb, Steen and Hamilton, and four years in the U.S. Attorney's office for the Southern District of New York.

"The last two years I was assistant chief of the civil division," he said, "which means I represented the government in the kinds of cases for which I am now suing them.

One of the highest-paid members of the Nader network, Morrison earns $16,500 a year.

**Bonner** Raymond T. Bonner, 31, joined the Nader group in July 1972. A 1967 graduate of Stanford Law School, Bonner practiced law in Hawaii before entering the Marine Corps in 1968. He spent a year in Vietnam as a captain and civic action officer.

Bonner collaborated in writing *Troubled Peace: An Epilogue to Vietnam,* a report issued by the Nader-founded Center for Study of Responsive Law in March 1973. The report charges that the Veterans Administration is short-changing Vietnam veterans and concentrating on veterans of earlier wars who "do not need or merit its help."

**Jacks** W. Thomas Jacks, 27, joined the Nader group in late 1972 after a year as clerk to Judge Roszel C. Thomsen of the U.S. District Court for the District of Maryland.

He is a 1971 graduate of the University of Texas Law School and specializes in laws governing the President's right to impound funds which are appropriated by Congress.

### Litigation

In addition to the nuclear moratorium case, the litigation group is involved in efforts to:

- remove Howard J. Phillips from his post as acting director of the Office of Economic Opportunity, on the grounds that he has not been confirmed by the Senate (plaintiffs are Democratic Sens. Harrison A. Williams Jr., N.J., chairman of the Labor and Public Welfare Committee, Claiborne Pell, R.I., Walter F. Mondale, Minn,. and William D. Hathaway, Maine, all members of the committee);
- force the Agriculture Department to rescind an increase in the support of milk prices that Nader lawyers claim was the result of "political considerations resulting from campaign contributions to the Nixon campaign and to Members of Congress . . . ;"
- challenge the legality of Presidential impoundment of Highway Trust Fund money through a friend of the court (amicus curiae) brief in *State Highway Commission of Missouri v. Volpe;*
- force the Securities and Exchange Commission, in a joint case with the National Committee for an Effective Congress, to require disclosure of the existence and operation of "voluntary" political funds;

- prevent the General Services Administration from giving away to private industry patents and innovations which are owned by the federal government;
- challenge minimum fee schedules for attorneys.

**Ethics** Morrison said the challenge to attorney fee schedules is part of a broader study of "whole ranges of cases involving claims of 'professional ethics' that are misused to adversely affect consumers.

"For example, there are laws that prohibit the advertising of prescription drugs in Maryland and Virginia, which may adversely affect a consumer's access to information about inexpensive drugs. We will file a suit in Maryland, and we are looking into filing a suit in Virginia, on behalf of consumer groups there."

### Letters

"Although we are in the business of litigating lawsuits," Morrison said, "we do not do this unless it is necessary.

"In most cases, we write letters first, because a lot of times it works. In some instances, the law requires it; this is the doctrine of administrative remedy. Also, I find that if you write a letter first and make factual assertions, if your facts are wrong they point it out to you. If our facts are wrong, we want it pointed out before we go too far."

A recent letter questioned whether naming Gen. Alexander M. Haig Jr. as White House staff chief succeeding H. R. Haldeman did not violate an 1838 statute that forbids military men to hold civilian government jobs. Morrison said the reply was unsatisfactory and on June 6 he filed suit, asking the U.S. District Court for the District of Columbia to decide whether Haig must resign his commission.

## FEDERAL DOCUMENTS

The Nader-allied *Freedom of Information* Clearinghouse is a one-man operation that exists to pry federal documents loose from reluctant government officials.

Although its director, attorney *Ronald L. Plesser,* shares space with the litigation group and has resorted to court action 16 times under the *Freedom of Information Act (80 Stat 250),* officially he is part of the pioneer Nader operation, the Center for Study of Responsive Law. Plesser began operations in April 1972 with a $25,000 grant from the Stern Foundation.

### Function

Plesser said in an interview that his "main function is to file suits to propogate" the *1966 Freedom of Information Act.*

Most of his 16 lawsuits, he said, were filed on behalf of "internal Nader groups who, in the course of their research, need access to information which government agencies are denying them."

**Litigation** One example of Plesser's court actions is *Schuck v. Butz,* which he said was filed to "obtain the audits of civil rights investigatory reports done by the Department of Agriculture."

"They have documents," he said, "that indicate that the extension services and the home loan banks have been operated in a racially-segregated manner, especially in North Carolina, Alabama and Mississippi.

"There are suits pending in these states right now. It is important, because the Department of Agriculture has great control of these funds programs. If we win this one, it will go a long way toward opening up all these civil rights documents that the government has and is not making available to the public."

**Saying the Word** An example of Plesser's technique for getting information without going to court involved the Nader study of Vietnam veterans, *Troubled Peace.*

The author, Paul Starr, 23, a graduate sociology student at Harvard University, said that at one point he was getting a "run-around" from Defense Department officials on "drug data."

"I went to the drug abuse office with Ron Plesser," Starr recalled. Only after Plesser cited the right provision of the act, Starr said, did Defense officials "reveal the information I wanted. If I had tried to do the same thing on my own, I would never have gotten the information.

"That is Plesser's job. Whenever anybody doing Nader research has any trouble getting government information, he goes with you."

Said Plesser: "We know where we stand. If a bureaucrat makes a statement, I know whether that statement can be backed up. In the case of Paul Starr's report, the guy told me we were on a fishing expedition. He said we had to ask for specific documents.

"The background to this was that the Department of Defense had said that 10 per cent of returning veterans from Vietnam were heroin addicts. We wanted the particular background facts. So I told Paul to ask for the specific information he wanted. Paul asked, and they replied, 'You fellows are on a fishing expedition.'

"I then said, 'Of course we are fishing. You will not tell us what information you have. There is a finite set of materials behind that 10 per cent figure that you are using, and that information is what we want. That is a sufficient test under the Freedom of Information Act.' "

### Press Center

Plesser said also that he is "broadening our work" in connection with a Press Information Center which Nader has established in partnership with the National Press Club.

The center's function is to file suits on behalf of journalists under the act.

*"The idea is to sharpen journalists' access to information through the use of the Freedom of Information Act requirements,"* Plesser said. "The tools provided by the act have just not been used. So we will litigate to get the tools we need and to create new law so that the use of the act is increased."

Plesser said that only 150 cases have been brought to court in the seven-year history of the act, most of them by corporations.

## GRASS ROOTS

Nader-style activist groups have been growing at the state and local level at a rate at least equal to the growth of the Washington operations.

One Nader aide said that the *Public Interest Research Groups, which are coordinated from Washington by the Citizen Action Group, are among the most important parts of the Nader network.*

"We have been trying hard for several years to encourage as much citizen activity as possible," said Theodore J. Jacobs, 39-year-old executive director of the Center for Study of Responsive Law and Nader's top aide.

"One of the basic things Nader believes in very strongly is that if what he has been doing will have any lasting meaning, it must become more widely developed as a career role, or at least a part-time role that citizens can engage in.

"The books and reports that we have done so far have been designed to document abuses. The steps we are engaged in now are attempts to give people the tools in becoming mini-Naders themselves. We particularly want to encourage activities on the state and local level."

## PIRGs

The director of the Citizen Action Group is *Donald Ross.* He and two staff organizers travel five or six days a week, organizing new groups and servicing old ones. Most groups are student financed, although Nader has provided money for a few. The local groups are staffed with lawyers, scientists and organizers, backed by student researchers.

The *first groups were founded in Oregon and Minnesota* during the 1970–71 academic year. Ross said that similar units now are active in New Jersey, Texas, Vermont, Missouri, North Carolina, Michigan, Massachusetts and Iowa, with total memberships of about 450,000 persons.

Ross estimated the total budget of the research groups at between $800,000 and $1 million, most of which is raised through student government donations. He said they employ between 50 and 60 fulltime personnel locally.

Ross's Washington office has a budget of $50,000, which is provided by Public Citizen. Ross, in keeping with Nader's claim that his is the "most frugal" public-interest group in Washington, estimated that he will spend only $30,000 this year. Ross's annual salary is $7,000. His two organizing staff associates get $5,000 each, he said.

## Ross

The 29-year-old Ross has worked for Nader for three years. An attorney, he previously served with the Peace Corps in Nigeria.

Ross characterizes the energy and zeal that is associated with the Nader orgainization. He said he spends "18 hours a day, seven days a week, living out of a suitcase and just talking, talking, talking. People do this when they work in a political campaign. But that has an end date; at a certain date, the project is ended, and usually it only requires six to eight weeks to work on a campaign. This goes on."

Ross described how he goes about his job:

"I can go into a town and, if people are interested in consumer protection, I can give them five projects to do in three hours. I can tell them how they can work to drive down food prices. I can tell them how they can work on employment discrimination against women, or how they can investigate property taxes, or how to investigate government inspection programs, or how to investigate government health-care services. All of these things tell people how they can work at being public advocates and, to use Ralph's phrase, 'public citizens.' "

## Books

In 1972 Nader and Ross published a book, *Action for a Change* (Grossman Publishers), which was written as a working handbook for this central Nader project. Now Ross has finished another book, scheduled for publication later this year, called *A Public Citizen's Action Manual* (Grossman Publishers) that he said "will give advice to citizens' groups on all sorts of how-to-do-it programs." The Nader organization will distribute 100,000 of these, he said.

## States

The quality of the work of the individual groups varies widely, Ross said. "Our groups are turning out 75 page reports. Some are very good, and some fairly shoddy."

**Minnesota** Among successful projects cited by Ross is the Minnesota Public Interest Research Group. He said it has a salaried staff of 14 and a current budget of $275,000. Ross said the Minnesota group has done "a very impressive study of occupational health hazards caused by asbestos spraying materials used on construction sites in the Minneapolis-St. Paul areas. This will be very relevant to future occupational-health-and-safety fights that occur nationally."

The Minnesota group recently won a suit against the Agriculture Department's Forest Service to stop timber cutting in the boundary water canoe area along the U.S.-Canadian border.

**Vermont** Another local Nader-style operation is the Vermont Public Interest Research Group, which is staffed with "three lawyers, two other staff persons, and is based in the state capital, one block from the state legislature," Ross said.

"The Vermont group illustrates perfectly what we are trying to do," he said. "They have more resources than any other citizens' group in Vermont. They've specialized in health care and environmental issues, and they are expanding. What other citizen organization has the resources to investigate state Blue Cross-Blue Shield plans?"

**Oregon** The Oregon Student Public Interest Research Group publishes eight-page magazines whose January and February 1973 issues included articles entitled, *Dangerous Toy Results, A Look at Federal Rent Controls, Timber Industry After Forest Park* and *Rock Mesa—Endangered Wilderness Area.*

**New Jersey** The New Jersey group has more than 100 students at three college campuses who were to receive credit for projects in the spring semester, according to a group press release. Their activities have included a November 1972 search of 10 large department stores for toys which had been banned by the Food and Drug Administration. Group members found three banned toys on sale in the state in what spokesmen called "large quantities."

## National Project

Although the Citizen Action Group emphasizes "building organizations autonomous of Washington," Ross said he is embarking on coordinated national projects. The first project will involve toy safety, according to Sandy Dement Sterling, a Ross associate.

Public-interest organizations in 18 states already have searched for banned toys. "In the 18 states that we looked at, we found at least one-third of the banned toys on store shelves," said Mrs. Sterling. "We filed three suits, using some of the state groups as plaintiffs, to get the FDA to issue the regulations that are required by law."

## Critics

Some of the local actions have prompted counter-suits by affected businesses. The Connecticut Citizens' Action Group was sued in April to stop distribution of a guide that rated prices in about 50 local drug stores as "good, average, poor or erratic." The suit charges that the publication of pharmacies' price lists was "done unprofessionally and unfairly hurt sales."

Christian S. White, a lawyer, worked for Nader for one year during 1970-71, much of that time with Ross. Now a special assistant to the director of the Consumer Protection Bureau of the Federal Trade Commission, he said that "Ross was dynamite at enthusing young students. He is effective at getting something happening. It was an evangelistic thing—Ross would go in and spread the gospel. He is an effective speaker, and effective at keeping the emotional level and commitment up."

But, said White, "I am very skeptical about what these groups are going to do. The conception is, if there is one good public interest research group in Washington, and there are massive problems around the country, then 30 more must be better.

"But are there enough good people that you can get to do this work for peanuts in the boonies? Still, if they can litigate some good cases, maybe some of them can work."

## NADER REPORTS

Nader's new focus on legal action and lobbying so far has not slowed down the publication of investigations of government and industry that have been his hallmark over the years.

Subjects covered by reports scheduled for release this year range from Maine's paper industry to the American Automobile Association and include critical looks at food advertising, the Veterans Administration and "company towns."

Also in preparation is a report entitled, *What Is Right With America,* which, according to Nader aide Jacobs, "is designed to come up with models of superb performance."

### Congress Project

Ten of the many Nader reports to be released this year will wind up the most ambitious, expensive and critically disappointing of all of Nader's efforts—the investigation of Congress in 1972.

Nader and his aides vigorously defend the quality of the profiles of Members of Congress which were released last October and of a 225-page paperback book, *Who Runs Congress?* (Grossman-Bantam), which resulted from the investigation. But Nader staff members who normally would be working in other areas are devoting much of their time to quality control of the new works which are based on the $450,000 Ralph Nader Congress Project Study.

**New Reports** Robert C. Fellmeth, director of the Congress Project, said he is hoping to publish, by November, six studies of congressional committees, two volumes on topic studies of the congressional process, and a private handbook for what he called "activist" Members of Congress.

The final volume will be a handbook for citizen organizations who want to influence Congress.

David E. Price, professor of political science at Yale University, who headed the study of the House Interstate and Foreign Commerce and Senate Commerce Committees, said his report will differ from earlier project material because it will be "more analytical."

"It is not the popularized stuff that *Who Runs Congress?* represented," he said. "Ours is more of a cross between an academic and a journalistic report."

Fellmeth said the handbook for "activists" will provide information "on how to draft and accomplish legislation. It will examine possible bases for legal suits against the executive branch. It will have tactics and rules for operating within the committee structure. It will be very detailed."

The Members' handbook, he said, will not be made available to the general public.

The handbook for citizen groups, he said, will provide eight or nine case studies of citizen influence on legislation, instructions for opposing incumbent Members in elections and advice for getting information from Congress that is being withheld.

Fellmeth plans to return to his native California when the Congress Project is completed to start his own grass roots public-interest group.

**Old Reports** Meanwhile, the controversy over the Congress Project reports which already have been published goes on.

Nader officials said in October 1972 that 55 per cent of the Members or aides who reviewed their profiles prior to publication commented favorably on the work. Nader aides still use that figure.

However, a set of figures supplied by Fellmeth in May 1973 shows that of 430 reviewing Members, slightly less than half commented favorably. Another 24 per cent were critical of the profiles and 27 per cent had no comment.

Members who declined to be interviewed or otherwise cooperate with the project were not shown their profiles prior to publication.

Rep. Benjamin S. Rosenthal, D-N.Y., normally a Nader ally, said in an interview that the profiles were not one of his (Nader's) glorious moments.

"The threat of the profiles probably had more impact on Congress than the profiles themselves," Rosenthal said. "But the fact is that the quality of the reporting was not high and—I hate to say this—but Ralph personally lost some clout around here."

Said Nader: "I think there are two real ways to evaluate these profiles. First, are they accurate repositories of relevant information, and, second, how do they compare with others?"

On the second score, Nader said, he did not think there was any comparison. "This is the first time this has ever been attempted. As such, I think it is pretty good. I think that it is a tremendous, comprehensive amount of information."

## Health

A 10-member staff of Nader's Health Research Group, directed by Dr. Sidney M. Wolfe, is monitoring a broad range of problems, including drugs, occupational health, health-care delivery systems and the Food and Drug Administration.

One example of their work is a March 1973 report charging that some electronic cardiac pacemakers could cease functioning without warning.

Wolfe said that medical devices such as pacemakers should "be covered by the same regulations that apply to drugs. There is no legislation now. There are no requirements of any kind for testing or pre-marketing clearance of medical devices. Only if the devices are proven dangerous are they taken off the market."

Other reports in preparation will cover community mental-health centers, the National Institute of Mental Health, and "brown lung" disease which affects textile workers.

Dr. Wolfe's group includes a physician, a biochemist, a public-health specialist and four lawyers.

The group's current budget is $110,000, not all of which will be spent because the project still is not fully staffed, Wolfe said.

Wolfe received his medical degree in 1965 from Case Western Reserve University, served his residency at Cleveland Metropolitan General Hospital and was on the staff of the metabolic disease branch of the National Institutes of Health before he joined the Nader organization.

### Think Tanks

A report on relationships between the federal government and private consulting firms will be released in a few months, according to the center's Jacobs.

Barry Willner and Daniel Guttman, both 25-year-old lawyers, have invested two years of research and writing in an 800-page document which will focus on the Rand Corporation, the MITRE Corporation, Booz, Allen and Hamilton Inc., and Peat, Marwick, Mitchell and Company.

Willner siad they will contend that there is no thought of "merit system" or conflict-of-interest reflected in government contracts for consulting services.

"It will also focus on case studies of a Defense Department weapons system, and it will examine professional research and development groups in the fields of housing, education and transportation," Willner said.

Again reflecting the new Nader focus, Willner said that the study will be followed up by litigation seeking "restitution to the government when the work of the professional consulting organization is worthless."

### CARG Reports

The Corporate Accountability Research Group, headed by Mark J. Green, has two reports scheduled for release.

**Monopolies, Law** One is *The Monopoly Makers,* to be published by Grossman, in which the group will cover "the economic policies of the (federal) regulatory agencies, and how they create monopolies rather than investigate them," according to Green.

Another report to be released this summer will cover Washington law firms, based on a study that has been in progress for more than three years.

The research group headed by Green has a $60,000 budget and a staff of four lawyers and one economist, with salaries ranging from $5,000 to $7,500 a year, Green said. He said that he and other group members supplement their incomes with outside speaking fees.

**Charters** In still another demonstration of the new Nader focus, Green said in an interview that his group now is concentrating on corporate charter practices.

"Writing books is easy," he said. "What we are trying to do is implement solutions into law.

"That is why we are now drafting federal chartering legislation" for corporations, he said. "We are arguing that state chartering has failed, and that federal chartering is viable. Our purpose is to draft it, and then lobby for it."

## APPRAISAL

There is almost universal agreement among Members of Congress, their staffs and members of the business community in Washington that Nader is an effective force in shaping federal policy.

Where they disagree is on whether that is good or bad.

### Facts

"A great many other public-interest lobbyists overlook this, but Ralph's first contribution has been to provide facts," said Gary B. Sellers, Nader's principal lobbyist from 1969 to 1972 and now legislative assistant to Rep. Phillip Burton, D-Calif.

Said Michael Pertschuk, chief counsel to the Senate Commerce Committee: "In given areas, Nader has people who have established their expertise, and within these areas these people become very influential, because there are not that many people who can provide these kinds of resources.

"They are available to congressional staffs as the staffs search for information. More and more, they are there as the legislation is being formulated—and that is the important time."

Pertschuk specifically mentioned Nader's antitrust specialist, Mark Green, as someone "our staff would feel confident in calling for information."

Rep. Rosenthal said "the quality of the Nader organization research is their basic strength. They make known here on the Hill things that were previously unknown."

Said Stuart M. Statler, minority counsel to the Senate Government Operations Committee's Permanent Subcommittee on Investigations: "Up on the Hill, we do not have the resources we need. Whatever outside research help we can get, whatever good, hard information we can come by, is awfully welcome. In my experience, some of the Nader people have been as good or better in this role than any other group I can think of."

**Media** Howard E. Shuman, administrative assistant to Sen. William Proxmire, D-Wis., added that Nader brings not only facts to Capitol Hill but media.

The Nader groups, he said, are effective because "they get good information to us, and, second, because Nader himself gets attention, and that helps to focus issues.

"When Nader testifies, the cameras show up, and the people get informed, and that comes back to Senators and Congressmen. They hear about it from the folks back home. And you do not get public interest change without arousing people."

**Doubts** Nader's reputation for marshalling facts is one of the reasons why attacks on the Congress Project reports have significance.

Even Pertschuk called the profiles of Members "spotty," and one former Nader aide said simply that Nader "fouled up on the Congress Project."

Said a Democratic House staff member, who works closely with Nader and who declined to be identified by name:

". . . the profiles were less gutsy than they were supposed to be. They were just sops, in a lot of instances. Some Members have told me that Nader said things about them that they would be embarrassed to say about themselves. The point of all this is that Nader's name had considerable potency up here in the past. Now he is seen in a different light by some Members of the House and Senate."

## Critics

Only one Washington representative of the business community interviewed by *National Journal* accused Nader of being anti-business.

Others, however, did criticize what they considered the one-sided approach that Nader takes in his campaigns.

**Kenna** E. Douglas Kenna Jr., president of the National Association of Manufacturers, said of the Nader network:

"Certainly the Nader groups have great impact. Without question, they have caused awareness in some areas that has not existed before, and this has been beneficial.

"But I think their general mode of operation is to call attention to isolated problems, without looking for solutions. They create situations where the particular issues they are interested in get out of focus, as far as the general public interest is concerned. There really is an imbalance."

**Markley** Rodney W. Markley Jr., vice president and Washington representative of the Ford Motor Co., said Nader's operations "are effective and they do have impact."

Nader, he said, "somehow finds very competent people to staff his organizations in various fields. He has a great capacity to get very competent people to come aboard."

"They are a challenge to business," Markley said, "but by and large it is a challenge that business can meet in getting its story across and answering the charges of the public interest groups. The important thing is that there are answers to these charges that Nader comes up with, and we will try to provide the answers."

**Bauer** Raymond Bauer, a professor at the Harvard Graduate School of Business Administration, said in an interview that "Ralph Nader is very good at raising issues, but he raises them in a vulgarized manner, and then someone has to come in to balance his views if you are going to get an accurate picture."

But, Bauer added, "Nader packs a wallop in the business world. I know a lot of corporations that are doing social audits now. Three or four have told me, 'We want to be prepared in case Nader descends on us.' I suspect they do not mean Nader specifically, but rather symbolically."

## Support

Mary Kay Ryan, consumer counsel for the Cost of Living Council, said that she believes "industry has over-reacted to Nader, and over-reacted to its own detriment."

Mrs. Ryan, saying that the view was her own and not that of the council, said:

"Nader and the other consumer groups are trying to get industry back to the free enterprise system. (They are) not antibusiness. Many of the principles that Nader fights for are simply good business.

"For example, I know that one Nader group is interested in toy product safety. I cannot fathom how industry could put out toy ovens that heated up inside to over 600 degrees, as the National Product Safety Commission said one does. Household ovens only heat up to 550 degrees.

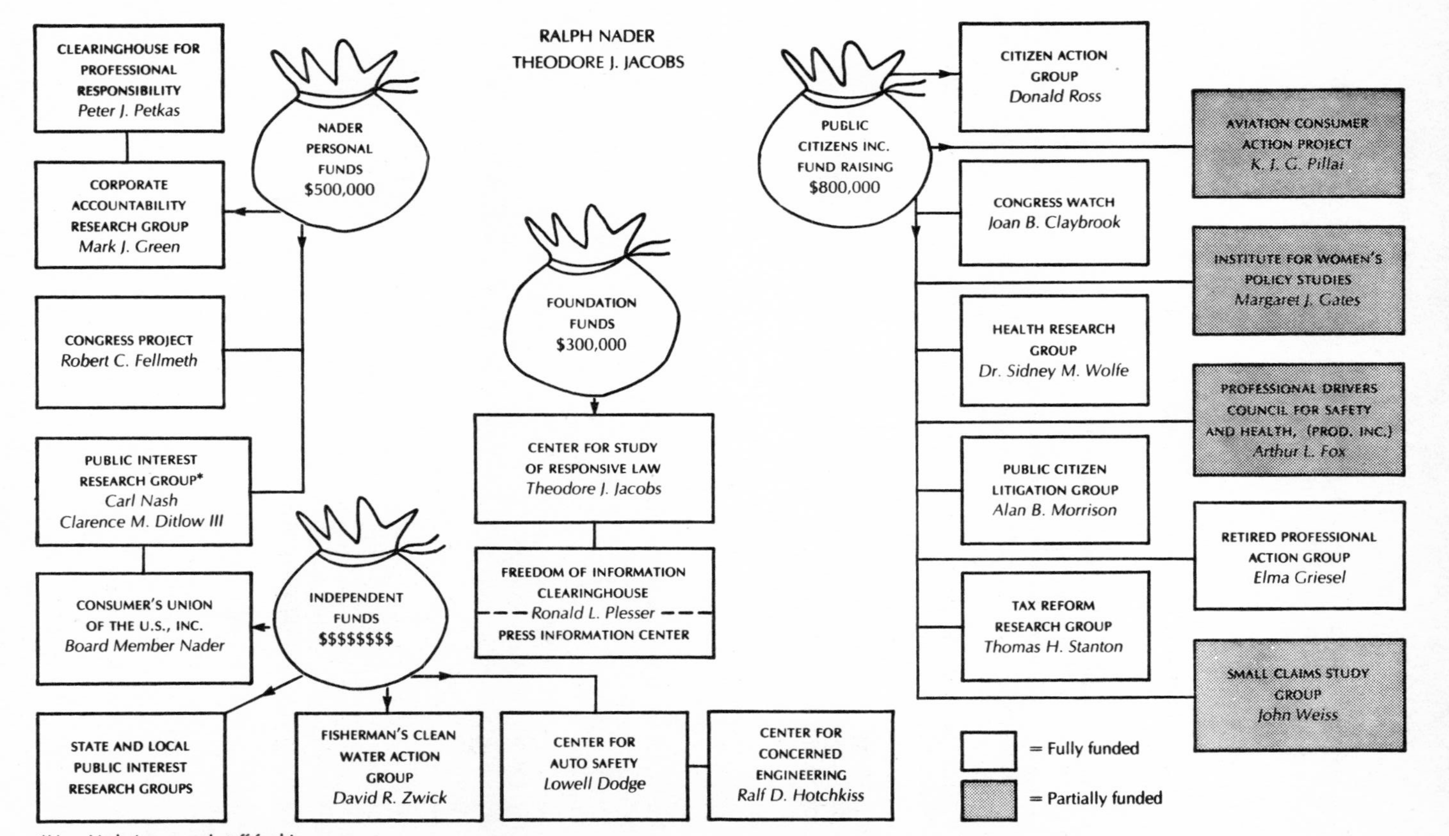


*Now Nader's personal staff for his role on Consumers' Union Board of Directors

**Nader network funding—1972.**

"That is what I mean when I say that Nader is not antibusiness. For the most part. Nader's interests and the business interests are interrelated. The consumer wants the best product that industry can produce, and that is what industry wants, too, I should think."

## NADER ORGANIZATION FUNDING: A COMPLICATED CASH FLOW

Ralph Nader's Washington network operated in 1972 on about $1.6 million, which came from public contributions, foundations, royalties from the sale of publications and money which Nader earned by writing and lecturing.

The budget figure does not include up to $1 million which was raised by state and local Public Interest Research Groups to finance their own activities.

The first effort to audit the Nader network now is underway. Nader said the audit probably would be published sometime this summer and would provide "more data than anybody wants to read."

In general, however, the cash flow for Nader's activities involves two formal organizations—the Center for Study of Responsive Law and Public Citizen Inc.—and Nader himself.

### Center

The center is the oldest of the Nader organizations. Established in 1968, it is the clearinghouse for major Nader studies and reports.

Theodore J. Jacobs, executive director of the center, said its 1972 budget was "close to $300,000."

Most of the money, Jacobs said, came from the *Stern Fund,* the Field Foundation and the Midas-International Corporation Foundation.

The center, in turn, makes grants to other Nader's organizations, among them the Center for Auto Safety.

Nader said the auto safety center received a grant "in the $8,000 to $10,000 range" from Jacobs in 1972.

Since 1970, the budget of the Center for Study of Responsive Law has declined as Nader changes his focus from expose to advocacy. The center's budget for its first year of operations, 1968-69, was $63,000. Jacobs confirmed that it went to $324,000 in 1970, to $320,000 in 1971, dropped to around $300,000 in 1972 and will run "more than" $175,000 in 1973.

Royalties from center-connected publications, he said, were $33,000 in 1971 and $28,000 in 1972.

Under Internal Revenue Service regulations, contributions to the center are tax-deductible.

### Fundraiser

Public Citizen was established in 1971 as the fundraising unit in Nader's network. Public Citizen is tax-exempt, but contributions are not deductible.

Public Citizen brought in about $1.1 million during the year ending June 1972 in response to three major solicitations by mail. The net income after mailing costs was about $800,000, according to one Nader aide, who asked not to be identified.

Full-page advertisements in newspapers also raised money for Public Citizen, Jacobs said. "One single ad in *The New York Times* brought in close to $60,000," he said.

**Grants** During 1973, Public Citizen is financing the total budget of six Nader organizations and parts of the budgets of four others.

Those fully financed are Public Citizen Litigation Group ($75,000); Citizen Action Group ($50,000); Tax Reform Research Group ($125,000); Retired Professionals Action Group ($45,000); Health Research Group ($110,000); and Congress Watch ($100,000).

Other groups that received Public Citizen funds in 1972 are the Aviation Consumer Action Group ($8,000); the Small Claims Study Group ($9,500); the Institute for Women's Policy Studies ($10,000); Professional Drivers Council for Health and Safety ($4,000); and one grass-roots organizations, the Connecticut Citizens' Action Group ($25,000).

**Contributors** The Nader organization recently changed its policy on disclosure of the names of persons who contribute more than $1,000 to Public Citizen.

Jacobs told *National Journal* that only three persons are in that category, all of whom contributed exactly $1,000. They are Ester Johnson, Aldwick, N.J.; Mark Swann, Morgan Guaranty Trust Co., of New York; and Henry A. Berg, New York City.

**Personal Funds**

Nader personally provides the rest of his groups' funds.

The operations which Nader personally financed in 1972 were the Congress Project, the Corporate Accountability Research Group and the Public Interest Research Group.

Asked about his income, Nader said: "You mean my personal deficit.

"I was tremendously in the hole in 1972," he said, because of the expenses of the Congress Project. Nader estimated his "personal deficit" at "close to $300,000," adding, "It will be a long time before I get out of this hole. Can you put in an appeal for funds?"

Although there have been periodic rumors about Nader's having investments in stocks, commodities and real estate, Nader said in an interview that all of his income is from "two sources—lecturing and writing, mostly writing."

In 1972, he said, that income ranged "between $150,000 and $175,000."

Later, in response to a question relayed through associate Jacobs, Nader dealt with a report that he held stock in the R.V. Weatherford Corp., an electronics manufacturer, by saying he does not now own stock in the firm.

Jacobs said that Nader's mother inherited 50 shares of Ford Motor Co., stock in the mid-1960s but that the shares were sold soon afterward.

Nader, whose lecture fees run as high as $3,000 for an appearance, said:

"I do not receive any salaries or expenses from any of the groups like Public Citizen or the center.

"If anything, it is the other way around," he said.

"The basic approach is that everything is spent, and more at times, except the few bucks that it takes to live on, and that is not much."

# Consumer Protection: The Federal Government, State and Local Levels

## Reading 96

## Consumer Protection Against—What*

**Helen F. McHugh**

*The punitive sanctions that government may levy against the business engaging in the injurious practice are so limited that the seller is in no way encouraged to reform.*

Recently the *Congressional Quarterly* published a summary of the responsibilities related to consumer affairs that are scattered among 39 federal agencies (1). From this list it appears that only 5 of these 39 accept consumer complaints and subsequently endeavor to do something about them, and that none offers the type of consumer protection intended to be remedial in nature. A discussion of the five agencies that receive consumer complaints follows.

### U.S. POSTAL SERVICE

A statute adopted in 1872 prohibits the use of the mails for fraudulent activity (2). Those using the mails to misrepresent their products are denied remittances for their products or services (3). The department is active in the prosecution of those using the mails to promote fraudulent activity.

Further, the Postal Reorganization Act is designed to cope with the problem of unsolicited merchandise. Probably each of us at some time has received such merchandise through the mails as, for example, keyrings with the individual license plate number, aprons, greeting cards. Section 3009 of the Postal Reorganization Act provides that unsolicited merchandise may be treated as a gift by the person to whom it is mailed (4). He may use it, or throw it in the trash, or give it to a neighbor's child, or dispose of it in any manner that he sees fit without any obligation to the sender. As a result of this particular section, the Federal Trade Commission dropped its proposed trade regulation rule on this same class of merchandise (5).

The Act makes no provision, however, for restoring value lost to anyone who has fallen victim to fraudulent activities promoted through the mails. For example, a consumer may be misled by deceptive advertising received through the mails and pay money for a product that turns out to be a hoax. He can complain to the U.S. Postal Service, but the law does not provide a means for him to recover the money he paid out. This situation of no provision for redress is not unique to the U.S. Postal Service.

*This article is based on a paper entitled "Status of Procedures for Consumer Recourse," which appears in *Proceedings: Second Annual Conference, Association for Consumer Research,* College Park, Maryland, September 1-3, 1971, pp. 157-163, (David M. Gardner, editor). Permission to use major parts of the paper is gratefully acknowledged.

From the *Journal of Home Economics*, vol. 64, May 1972, pp. 14–17. Copyright by the American Home Economics Association, Washington, D.C.

## FEDERAL TRADE COMMISSION (FTC)

From the Commission's inception, FTC took into account only those consumer complaints that served to document actions by businesses for which cease-and-desist orders were being prepared. The Commission responded to cases that involved interstate commerce or aroused significant public interest until the chairman of the FTC directed that all complaints be referred to someone who could do something about the matter (6).

Trade regulation rules issued by the FTC have given some protection to consumers. One of the more recent prohibited the mailing of unsolicited credit cards to individuals (7). In an effort to minimize the effect of the rule, one of the major oil companies recently sent out a simple form on which one had to list only his name and address, and the form thus filled in could then be construed as a request for the company's credit card. Presumably a boy or girl old enough to drive the family car might obtain a credit card without parental consent.

A position known as consumer protection specialist has been established by the agency to deal with consumer complaints, with consumer education, and with consumer counseling. The intent is to find the means eventually to resolve all types of consumer problems in their incipiency (8). Needless to say, that goal has not been reached. Literature of the agency describes it as the *fourth* line of defense for those who have been gypped (9). Other services parallel those of the Food and Drug Administration.

## FOOD AND DRUG ADMINISTRATION (FDA)

Similar to the actions already mentioned, the FDA accepts consumer complaints not to follow up on behalf of the consumer but rather as input for the investigations the agency carries out against manufacturers and processors. If violations of its regulations are found, the FDA refers the case to the Justice Department for prosecution or for injunctions against the violator (1). No action is taken to make restitution to the injured consumer although an injunction may prevent harm to others.

In an arrangement similar to that used by the FTC, the FDA has telephone numbers available in at least 8 cities through which complaints can be registered. Another service is recorded consumer messages available via telephone (1).

## FEDERAL HOUSING ADMINISTRATION (FHA)

In addition to providing advice to prospective purchasers of houses or of home improvements, the FHA is expected to investigate any consumer complaints that are registered. However, a study of the potential penalties leaves some doubt about the effectiveness of FHA efforts. If a complaint is found to be justified, the FHA requests the builder to correct the situation. If the builder fails to do so, he *may* be denied future FHA assistance (1). Again, the recommended action includes no requirement that restitution be made. In fairness to the agency, however, restitution is somewhat encouraged.

## FEDERAL COMMUNICATIONS COMMISSION (FCC)

By monitoring the activities of its licensees, the FCC is responsible for the holders of radio and television licenses who operate in the public interest. The FCC has the responsibility for investigating complaints from the public with respect to what is aired by these media. The agency's ineffectiveness has been documented (10, 11).

When it is recognized that a substantial number of messages received over the radio and television relate to our consumption activities, concern with what comes over the air waves is understandable. Indications are that claims of advertisers may be drawn under closer scrutiny in the future. However, this action is developing in part through the advertising industry itself (12).

## INTERSTATE COMMERCE COMMISSION (ICC)

Persons who have moved during the last half century can attest to the difficulties encountered by the householder who engages the services of a commercial mover. The charge given to the ICC is to assure reasonable transportation charges and efficient service. In carrying out this charge, the ICC (a) " . . . requires motor carriers to maintain insurance to cover . . . damage to goods, and (b) under the Truth-in-Lending Act of 1968, requires that ICC supervised carriers, when acting as creditors, inform their customers of all conditions of a credit arrangement" (1). Ironically, movers seldom grant credit to an individual being moved. The almost universal requirement to pay the bill in cash before the mover will even unload the goods leaves the consumer without leverage for the settlement of damage claims. The net effect is to diminish the value of the insurance protection that the carrier is required to maintain.

Of the agencies reviewed, then, five receive complaints but none can assess penalties to compensate the injured consumer. The punitive sanctions that government may levy against the business engaging in the injurious practice are so limited that the seller is in no way encouraged to reform. Governmental agencies have no power to act on behalf of individual consumers; business firms have sufficient power *not* to act if they so choose. This state of affairs requires adjustment. However, changes should not be made lightly. The government—and more particularly the Federal Government—is not the only avenue for protection of the consumer.

## COMPONENTS OF AN EFFECTIVE SYSTEM

Most students of consumer affairs agree that a system that truly protects consumer interests has three components: (1) an information and educational component, (2) channels in the market system through which restitution can be effected, and (3) market rules that encompass the legislative and regulatory aspects (13, 14). Adequate development of these three components depends upon allocation of resources consistent with the contribution that each makes to the overall protection of the consumer. The following elements relate to the above components and deserve closer study:

*The nature and magnitude of consumer complaints* Within the last 5 years, each of the three persons who have served the President as Special Assistant for Consumer Affairs has illustrated public statements with complaints received—and has selected the statements, seemingly, for their potential impact (15-17). None of these statements has included the frequency of the complaint or its economic magnitude. Searches of the literature have produced no other data. Change should not be predicated solely on the presence or absence of complaints but rather on the potential benefit to society as a whole. Although many believe that a need for redress exists, the " . . . need is neither well identified nor clearly defined" (18). It is imperative that research into these matters precede proposals for change, especially as the proposals may pertain to legislative action. It cannot be assumed that legislators have the appropriate information at hand for making these decisions.

Studies of the economic gains and losses that could evolve from proposed changes should provide information useful also to the business community in establishing policies of a voluntary nature.

*The potential within the business community.* The need for action in the business community stems from the present imbalance of power in favor of business and industry. The traditional avenues of recourse through business and industry have diminished in effectiveness with the changing character of the economy. Urbanization, the increasing size of economic units, and the complexity of the consumer goods market have contributed to the relative decline in the power of the consumer. The strength of competitive forces affects the degree of outside control that is necessary for an orderly market that assures economic justice.

The present void of avenues for redress through the market system means that stronger controls are required to effect a balance between the consumer and producer. Therefore, the business community stands to gain from its own efforts to develop avenues for informal resolution of disputes and grievances. Such developments would reduce the need for legislative reform. Although no data are available to support the contention, the directness of an approach through the business system should have cost advantages over the more circuitous legislative route. Furthermore, a problem resolved in the market should have educational value and the long-range impact associated therewith, whereas legislation has been likened to the shotgun approach (14).

*Investment in consumer education* is considered to be a long-range approach to the process of consumer protection. Education can be acknowledged as investment in the human agent (19). Consumer education, therefore, becomes an investment in the individual for his role as a consumer. There are many traditional interpretations of consumer education, but the focus here must be on the impact that the consumer can have on the market, for consumers *can* exert influence on market procedures. An understanding of economics and the market processes and structures should enable one to enlarge that influence. The theory of markets reveals that firms in the main are confronted with some form of imperfect competition—something less than free competition and something more than monopoly. Literature, especially that for lay consumption, abounds with the term "free enterprise" used as synonymous with free competition in describing our market system. Only when this misconception is corrected will consumers make full use of their market power.

Although investment in consumer education can have a social as well as a private return, no data have been generated to measure such returns. Measurement of returns on the investment would require that the investment itself be measured. Consumer education finds itself competing with general and vocational education for the resources of the individual. Priorities assigned to these categories of education will differ among individuals, but consumer education traditionally has not fared so well as vocational education. Indeed, the 1968 Amendments to the Vocational Education Act relegate consumer education to subcategory status (20).

Before any significant policies related to consumer education are undertaken, some input by the researchers is in order. It is through consumer education that the individual should become sensitive to the impact that his actions in the marketplace can have on competition that leads ultimately to a balance of power within the system. Further, the role that consumer education has to play takes on added importance when the influence of government is fully recognized.

*The impact of government rules.* Market regulations that evolve from legislative action or executive order derive power from the government. Because of this fact, market rules are unique. Their uniqueness results from the fact that, as Stigler points out, the government has " . . . the power to coerce" (21). This characteristic requires, therefore, that the power be used with discretion and fairness. Before changes are effected, however, information more accurate and more complete than now exists must be provided. The direction that changes should take cannot be determined without a factual basis.

By recognizing the unique quality of market rules, one is led to conclude that a balance among the elements is essential for effective protection of the consumer. To assure that the power is used with fairness, the judicial process stands in varying degrees of readiness.

*Judicial avenues.* Another device that can figure in the protection of consumers is the small claims courts. The statutory provisions outlining the judicial process for small claims determine whether such departments assist or deter consumer protection. For example, the small claims departments in the State of Oregon are required to handle all claims of $20 or less. Controversies involving greater amounts up to $200 may be handled through the small claims department; however, at the time of the hearing, the defendant may elect to have the cause tried in the district court (22). Furthermore, although Oregon law does not permit attachments (before hearing action) to be issued for small claims, a judgment can be issued and serviced for the payment of $1 if the case is decided in the plaintiff's favor (22).

Other states may permit claims of up to $500 to fall within the small claims category, but relatively narrow dollar limits for cases prevail. Other provisions of the statutes, along with the dollar limits, reduce the effectiveness of this mechanism. It has been contended that under current provisions, many " . . . small claims courts are simply collection devices for the easy credit merchants" (23).

Small claims and other "consumer" courts can be devised whereby a nonprofessional will find it possible to go before such a tribunal whenever his complaints have been substantiated. Such a device, which would not require the services of an attorney, would meet the criteria of economic feasibility. Adjustments in the structures of these bodies could result in a more workable avenue for recourse when the dollar amount in controversy does not warrant the services of an attorney. Without such devices, an imbalance of power exists, with the consumer once again in the disadvantaged position.

## RECOMMENDATIONS

The need for information to aid in establishing effective recourse for the consumer is overwhelming. Data are missing with respect to the effectiveness of existing laws. Costs and benefits of proposed actions have been neither identified nor measured. These measurements would have merit not only for the drafting of legislative proposals but also for the development of policies in the business community—an aspect important to the maintenance of balance among the components of consumer protection. Appropriate research should precede any substantial policy developments with respect to educational programs or revisions in the judicial process.

In light of the situation as it exists at the national level, a future course of action for effective protection of the consumer should include the following elements:

**1** Establishment of channels for the informal resolution of disputes and grievances through the market system

**2** An expansion of educational efforts to include an understanding of the consumer's ability to influence the market structure by his economic actions

**3** Changes in market rules in light of research findings, including cost and benefit estimates

**4** Modification of the judicial process so that the cost of adjudicating claims—even small ones—may be economically feasible

It is imperative that meaningful research be undertaken to generate data related to each of these items. Unless data are obtained, no basis exists for recommending changes or for judging the feasibility of changes recommended by others. Without the facts at hand, the matter of balance among the elements falls to chance.

## REFERENCES


1 Federal consumer responsibility is fragmented. *Cong. Quart.* (1969), pp. 2349-2359.
2 *U.S. Code, 4, 1964.* Title 18, Chapter 47, Section 1001; Chapter 83, Section 1691.
3 *U.S. Code, 8, 1964.* Title 39, Chapter 9, Sections 903-906.
4 *Federal Trade Commission News Summary,* 25 (October 1, 1970).
5 New postal law gives unsolicited merchandise gift status. *Women's Wear Daily* (September 14, 1970).
6 Williams, L. Telephone conversation, Federal Trade Commission Consumer Education Division, October 12, 1970.
7 Title 16—Commercial practices, Chapter 1, Subchapter D, Part 421, *Federal Register,* Vol. 35, No. 52 (1970), pp. 4614-4621.
8 Federal Trade Commission. Consumer protection specialist. Job description, no date.
9 Federal Trade Commission. *Fight Back: The Ungentle Art of Self-Defense.* Washington, D.C.: U.S. Government Printing Office, 1969, unnumbered.
10 Smith, D. American radio today: The listener be damned. *Harper's,* Vol. 229, No. 1372 (1964), pp. 58-64.
11 Gordon, L. J. Recent developments in consumer economics. Paper presented at 12th annual conference of the Council on Consumer Information, St. Louis, Mo., Apr. 20, 1966.
12 Admen set up their own watchdog. *Business Week,* No. 2150 (June 12, 1970), p. 56.
13 Carman, J. M. Research opportunities in consumer policy. In *Economics of Consumer Protection,* L. L. Mather (editor). Danville, Ill.: Interstate, 1971.
14 Uhl, J. N. Consumer education and protection: *A synergistic relationship.* In *Economics of Consumer Protection,* L. L. Mather (editor). Danville, Ill.: Interstate, 1971, p. 103.
15 Furness, B. Address to the Consumer Education Conference, Indiana University, Bloomington, Indiana. October 16, 1967.
16 Knauer, V. Remarks at the Southwestern Regional Conference on Consumer Affairs conducted by the Office of Consumer Affairs, Los Angeles, California, May 19, 1971.
17 Peterson, E. Remarks before the Texas Consumer Conference at Southern Methodist University. Dallas, Texas, September 29, 1966.
18 Anderson, D. E. Policy implications for consumer action groups. In *Economics of Consumer Protection,* L. L. Mather (editor). Danville, Ill.: Interstate, 1971, p. 136.
19 Schultz, T. W. *The Economic Value of Education.* New York: Columbia University Press, 1963.
20 Part F—Consumer and homemaking education. *Public Law 90-576,* 90th Congress, 2d Session, H.R. 18366 (October 16, 1968), p. 22.
21 Stigler, G. J. The theory of economic regulation. *Bell Journal of Economic and Management Science,* Vol. 2, No. 1 (1971), p. 4.
22 *Oregon Revised Statutes,* 1969, Chapter 46.
23 Dix. L. V. Personal communication, November 9, 1970.

Reading 97

# Does Antitrust Protect the Consumer?

**H. Michael Mann**

*Dr. H. Michael Mann, Director, Bureau of Economics, Federal Trade Commission says yes. And it could protect the consumer more if consumer organizations would give unstinting support to vigorous antitrust efforts.*

Below are some questions and answers derived from Dr. Mann's talk to the Association of Massachusetts Consumers, Inc., *("Antitrust and the Consumer: The Policy and Its Constituency",)* April 22, 1972. The views expressed are Dr. Mann's and do not necessarily represent the views of the Commission.

## WHAT IS A COMPETITIVE MARKET?

Two essential characteristics are: A market that is free from domination by a few firms. One that is not difficult for a new firm to enter. These conditions insure that consumers are really sovereign, that is, consumers receive the greatest range of choice at lowest prices.

## DOES ANTITRUST MAINTAIN COMPETITIVE MARKETS?

Originally it was designed to. Its approach was to emphasize business behavior—particular business practices that injured other businessmen. Most antitrust activity, still today, involves relatively unconcentrated industries.

Meanwhile many industries have become highly concentrated with substantial market power, the freedom to set prices unhampered by a threat that someone will cut prices below those established by the dominant sellers. These powerful firms escape antitrust liablity because the law does not reach noncompetitive price behavior if coordinated without meetings of the executives of the firms involved, a common way to conspire to fix prices.

## DOES MARKET POWER AFFECT CONSUMERS?

Economically, yes. When a handful of firms accounts for most of the output, monopolistic pricing tends to occur, and consequently, output is less than would be the case if the industry had more competitors. The reduction in output means that less is available than consumers could have, and could be produced and sold without loss to the producers.

## ARE THERE OTHER EFFECTS?

Yes. Social and political effects. The market gives corporate management the freedom to spend money on activities that it considers "good" for society. The power of corporate management is, in the political sense, irresponsible power, because it is answerable ultimately only to itself for the expenditures made in its name and frequently only for its benefit. Consumer sovereignty is nurtured by

From *FTC, Consumer Alert.*

competitive forces because consumers are guaranteed lots of choice among many competing producers who cannot afford to engage in any spending which does not ultimately benefit the consumer.

### CAN ANTITRUST CONSTRAIN MARKET POWER?

Only in a limited way. The law, in its present state, makes it difficult, if not impossible, to undermine high market concentration and high barriers to entry—the conditions which germinate market power.

### WHY DON'T MORE CONSUMERS VIEW ANTITRUST AS CONSUMER PROTECTION?

It is difficult for an individual consumer to perceive benefits from antitrust. The outcome of a single successful action is likely to mean only a few pennies to him and therefore, the individual consumer cannot perceive how antitrust helps. The fact that most antitrust action escapes publicity because of its complexity, that antitrust's beneficiaries, the consumers, are very large in numbers and unorganized, and that holders of monopoly power are few in number and more skilled in political expression, limits antitrust's effectiveness. These problems mean that even consumer organizations have tended to ignore antitrust matters.

Says Dr. Mann, "What is needed is an increased consumer consciousness that the benefit of procompetitive policies are substantial, a task which is clearly worth the effort of consumer organizations."

Reading 98

# The Fractured Legal Structure of Consumerism

**Morton J. Simon**

*It is even possible that Congress and the public agencies—unless they truly have an anti-business chip on their collective shoulder—will stop listening to the consumer activist when and if the direct-to-government public complaints begin to dwindle significantly.*

"The Boston Tea Party was America's earliest and best-remembered episode of consumer activism," someone said recently.

Perhaps so but it was a quite illegal, dark-of-the-moon, justified-only-by-Parson Weems, false-front escapade. Since then, however, consumerism has become more law abiding. In fact, it has become both a creature of the law and much-favored beneficiary of the law.

The federal and state fraud laws, the Interstate Commerce Act, the various food, drug and cosmetic acts, the Printers Ink statute and other deceptive adver-

Reprinted from *Public Relations Journal*, October 1971, p. 6, by permission. 

tising statutes, the Federal Trade Commission Act, the fur and textile acts, the various safety acts, the Fair Packaging Act, the obscenity laws, etc., etc. are all consumer-oriented—part of the consumer-protection matrix in which business and its communicators are set. We have even seen reruns of the chicken-and-the-egg act with the law taking the lead without any consumer/grassroots groundswell or even a weak-minority voice on the side of the alleged angels.

Whatever your personal or corporate views about the "consumer movement" or the "consumer revolution" or "consumer crisis"—its purposes, roots, aims, methods, strengths, weaknesses, or life expectancy—one thing is clear. As long as we have it with us, business and its public relations function are going to have to live with the law and lawyers—whether they like it or not.

Take the word of Betty Furness, one-time Westinghouse saleswoman and White House consumer aid, who said when she recently resigned as chairman of the New York Consumer Protection Board: "The next consumer watchdog should be a male lawyer who understands how legislators work." She may not have endeared herself to Betty Friedan, Gloria Steinem *et al.* but she certainly knew what she was talking about. Add to this the title of one of President Nixon's messages to the 1971 Congress: "Proposals For a Buyer's Bill of Rights."

Consumerism may seem monolithic in its philosophy but it most certainly is highly—and dangerously—fractured in both a practical and legal sense. When a client tells a PR counsellor "We have consumer trouble," he may mean a wide variety of things, including any of these:

- The FTC has begun an investigation of the company's product advertising.
- A local housewife group has complained about pollution from a company plant and is demanding action under the federal act of 1899.
- A Congressional committee has announced hearings into the entire industry's "cents-off" pricing practices.
- The FDA has implied—without actually charging or proving—dangers to children from a company product.
- A well-known university professor has held a press conference to protest the company's lobbying against pending consumer bills.
- A large number of individual, but similar, product complaints have suddenly come in from upstate New York with threats to write to congressmen, senators, Nader, Lefkowitz, Choate *et al.*
- OCTOPUS is demanding that the Securities & Exchange Commission investigate alleged fraud in the company's annual statement. (OCTOPUS? This is one of the many new, often-law-student-manned consumer splinter groups such as SOUP, ASH OR GASP. This particular accronym means Organized Consumers to Outlisten Pontificators Using Semantics).

The experienced PR practitioner would obviously react differently to each of these situations. So too does each require a different marshalling of legal skills and even attitudes.

Against this background of multifarious legal involvements—especially in the legislative sector—of consumerism, the current stature of public relations *per se* becomes important as both a threshold and continuing question.

PR is certainly the devil's advocate—using that term in the most pernicious sense—in the minds of the civilian activists. For example, when the Nader group recently took out after Citibank for, among many other things, an alleged policy of non-disclosure, the report conceded grudgingly that the bank "was eager to go into great detail about its transactions with black businesses . . . (but such) activities are primarily geared to public relations."

Once again—as with the politicos—we see high-test consumerist users of hard-sell public relations and publicity condemning the techniques which make their own progress possible. These proponents of the "Galbraith doctrine" of "exaggerated, dramatized and loudly and repeatedly asserted criticism" are grabbing every publicity ploy or opportunity they can find or manufacture.

This has perhaps reached such a plateau that *PR Reporter* recently predicted that Nader may be about to "publicize himself right into oblivion" and that the "crusader has turned into a zealot."

What about the stance of government? What do the senators, the congressmen, the administrative agency people and others in similar power positions think of public relations?

Consumerism undoubtedly has had a serious and adverse effect on the already-niggling attitude from government toward public relations itself—quite apart from government belittling of specific PR or publicity programs. This generally critical posture goes back to 1913 when Congress decided that "No money appropriated by any act shall be used for the compensation of any publicity expert, unless specifically appropriated for that purpose."

Not only do individual members of Congress and its committees follow this mandate but there seems more and more of a distinction being drawn between "information" and "public relations," the latter being equated with propaganda. We saw this in the 1970 Senator Fulbright charges against the military for the millions spent on publicity. This came to pointed public appreciation with the CBS-created Selling Of The Pentagon.

When a Federal agency issues a statement, it is proudly glorified as NEWS—in solid caps, in red letters more than 100 points high—and it emanates from an office of public information. When business seeks to answer this NEWS—perhaps to straighten out its misshapen facts—such releases or statements are downgraded as press agentry or propaganda.

In our opinion, PR is under greater government pressures today than paid advertising. Some critics—echoing what the late Senator Kefauver once said to us personally—say that advertising is out in the open and "there for all to see and skip," while publicity and public relations are, somehow, subliminal and covert.

All of this is part of the current climate to which consumerism and its parallel drives are contributing so much. Even new industries—spawned by the overall consumer-oriented thinking—are adding to this. For example, in April the SEC issued a Litigation Release describing the Complaint against Ecological Science Corporation. Among other things, the SEC charged the company with holding "meetings with numerous newspaper reporters to generate favorable publicity; and disseminating news releases . . . which served only to create an image of activity in pollution control by ECO."

The Federal Power Commission is taking hard looks at promotion and publicity costs in its rate cases. The Pennsylvania Public Utilities Commission ordered two utilities to file reports and prove they are not violating an earlier order against promotional activities. Applying the "fairness doctrine," the courts are opening the door to non-commercial broadcast answers to "controversial" commercial advertising, even against the policy of the individual stations and the FCC. The FTC and others are hammering at large companies as having too much promotional know-how which is said to contribute to monopoly.

We have heard at least two members of Congress—perhaps more history-conscious that their colleagues—apply to PR men and women generally the same epithet which Carl Sandburg applied to Ivy Lee: "paid liar."

This government thinking may not be too hard to understand when we find the image of public relations so low that a columnist on a major-city newspaper—in criticizing the mayor on lack of ghetto funds—writes:

> If the mayor needs money so badly for (other departments), how can he justify in this era $615,496 that goes to the city representatives office for publicity and public relations?

Despite consumerism's becoming such a pressing issue, some PR and publicity people still do not recognize that a company is just as responsible for deception in a news release as in paid advertising. This has led to some false feelings of security—indifference, as some insist. Yet some of the earliest FTC orders involved deception in publicity and public relations.

Furthermore—in the judicial arena—successful product liability suits are being premised on deceptive claims in releases. Little difference is being ascribed to misrepresentation in paid advertising, news release and product labeling. This is merely an acknowledgement of what financial PR people have known and feared for years: the legal exposures resulting from deception in a company release or in the speech of a top company official, as developed at length in the 1963 SEC investigation and report.

Consumerism is intensifying this. The law and the courts *do* read the newspapers and *do* feel the public pulse. We may expect a deepening concern and more action—not only where the release or photograph is deceptive but where it is ambiguous or incomplete. This latter will follow the current thrust, seeking more and better information for the consumer—thus, in theory at least, permitting a better-informed and more intelligent choice and buying decision.

It is something more than an educated guess to anticipate that the FTC will move against deceptive releases in appropriate cases. Thus far, the Commission's consumer shields have been able to find more than enough pure-advertising cases to keep them busy. Failing such paid claims in a specific case—deemed by the Commission to have sufficient public interest—we will see a proceedings based on news releases alone, especially if the releases get good and wide press treatment.

Writing in the June, 1971 *Public Relations Journal,* Edward L. Graf Jr. said:

> Generally, however, the need for similar cooperation (between PR counsel and legal counsel) in product publicity has not received as much attention. Consumerism and the growth of product liability suits promise to change this.
>
> The legal problems encountered in product public relations are similar to those faced in advertising. Both functions deal with product claims and include statements attributable to the manufacturer . . . .Finally, a public relations release may be subject to all of the common law theories of liability for disparagement of other products, passing-off one's product as that of another and deceit.

This stricture is likely to be extended beyond product publicity to such things as claims and statements about company function—as in the SEC Litigation Release referred to above—or about the company's competitive position and activity ("release language" has already been considered important in antitrust litigation) or to *collateral* company activity in the environmental and ecological areas (we already have a new word: ecopornographic).

At least one member of the FTC, Mary Gardiner Jones, has already commented on questionable material in what she calls "traditional commercial advertising designed to sell products which also contains public service oriented statements." While admitting to some doubts about First Amendment questions, the entire tenor of her remarks is clear for all to read: wisdom dictates that such claims had better be legitimate.

What can the PR practitioner do about this?

Obviously the first and most important approach is to make sure of the clear, demonstrable, factual basis for all releases or other company utterances. With this, don't retouch or "get cute" with publicity pictures. This is not enough, however, since so much depends on tests, studies, photographs, etc. made by outside sources and even the client—both of whom we may *assume* are honest.

The answer seems to be the same as that adopted by advertising agencies and departments on the basis of past FTC action: insist on affidavits by the fact-source and then adhere religiously to such affidavit-supported materials and data. Speaking at a recent NYU/PRSA-sponsored seminar on consumerism, Richard M. Detwiler, Batten Barton Durstine Osborn vice president for public relations, publicly recommended this procedure, after lamenting the indifference of many publicity people in such matters. His solution is sound.

An informed press is held to be as important in a democratic society as an informed public. More and more newspaper and broadcasting people are now seeking a broad grounding—perhaps even beyond normal journalistic needs—in the nuts-and-bolts of consumerism.

Furthermore, these educational forays seem invariably to include study of the relevant legal elements. Thus, Columbia University's Consumer Journalism Conference in New York and the Southern Newspaper Publishers Association's seminar on Covering Consumer News at the University of Tennessee College of Communication (both this past May) stressed such legal matters.

This is as might have been expected. So much of the consumer story is premised on the ever-growing mass of new protective laws. It is hard to imagine a reporter writing "consumer news" intelligently without a clear understanding of this new legislation. Furthermore, he is merely getting in step with his special-interest journalistic brother, the financial reporter or writer.

The PR man must match this special legal knowledge in dealing with the press. Ernest Little, public relations manager for Texaco Canada, put it this way: "The public relations man is required to keep on top of . . . legislative developments which can affect his company and his industry." A failure to do this is likely to meet a very critical—if not caustic—reception from a press which has done its homework better.

This enforced "legal literacy" may be a good thing. It is analogous to what Justice Brennan said of coverage of the Supreme Court:

> I think the best coverage is being given by those newspapers which afford reporters an opportunity for some special instruction in the work of the Court. Those reporters seem to . . . improve their understanding through intensive self-education.

The same is true of the well-informed and effective PR man or woman. It is for this reason that the more-thoughtful practitioner is coming to recognize the initial need for more interest in consumer law.

Notwithstanding government's "statutory distrust" (the term is ours) of publicity, we find all levels and sectors of government increasing its output. Much of this is being justified as "information." Whatever its rationale, a very large portion of the increase is keyed to consumerism.

Not only are existing channels and methods being exploited but entirely new consumer publications and organs have been developed. Last April the White House inauguarated a newsletter *Consumer News.* Its first issue proudly announced that it is "the first interagency newsletter of its kind to be published by the Federal Government." This year the FTC started distribution to a broad mailing list of a new periodical *Consumer Alert.*

Both of these are definitely more than information vehicles. They practically beg the public to "speak up." They do more. They spell out the precise channels for speaking up. This is likely to become boilerplate if we can judge by the first five issues of the White House publication. All repeat what looks like a standing story under the headline "Speak up & be heard."

Not satisfied with the increased quantity of its emissions, the FTC now has a "hotline" delivery service—the adjective is the Commission's—to speed its words to a waiting public and press. This "need for speed" again appears in the apparently continuing procedure (as in the *Metro-mail* case) to release adverse news about a Complaint or other action even before a copy is served on the respondent company. There has been one break in this technique. In the *Wonder Bread* case, the ITT-Continental Baking PR people were invited to the FTC's news briefing conference and then "permitted" to give their side of the story after the Commission's "information chief"—there's that word again—had finished. Thus both sides hit the wires together.

Catering to the consumer activist (we'll discuss at greater length later), the Commission has new Rules on consent orders. These usually result in at least a tripling of the publicity formerly generated by even a promptly-accepted consent order. Add to this, of course, the Commission's continuing monthly *News Summary* for some more exposure.

New sources of government publicity are being steadily created. Existing departments, bureaus, commissions, administrations, etc., are adding new functionaries, each of whom becomes another fountainhead. One of the latest seems to be the Post Office which now has a Consumer Advocate who will be, as the announcement headlined, "A New Voice for Postal Customers." Our personal "fairness doctrine" makes us hope that this gentleman may listen to the gripes of business as well as those of the housewife.

Beyond this, entirely new government-related groups are springing up. Among the most important are the Consumer Protection Committees organized under government aegis in various metropolitan areas. Amalgams of top consumer-protection brass from the federal/state/municipal government complex, these Committees may be expected to provide more grist for the anti-business, pro-consumer mill, no matter how balanced their members may try to be. In the August *Consumer News*, the White House announced that Federal Executive Boards—composed of top Federal officials in 25 major cities—are developing programs "to make the Federal Government more responsive to local consumer problems and to increase cooperation among Federal agencies . . ."

Company PR people must, therefore, be more alert for much more government publicity—possibly even completely unexpected—and must be prepared to counter it. It has been suggested that a company—even if caught flat-footed in such an unexpected situation—does itself a disservice with a "No comment" or a "We will have a statement after our counsel has had an opportunity to study the Complaint," or a "We will answer the charges at the hearing. We do not try our cases in the newspapers." Such a brief statement may actually be justified by the facts—especially if the government has jumped the publicity gun—but it is still pointless and meaningless.

Most Complaints are not issued in a vacuum. The company usually has some knowledge of what is going on —usually enough to issue a sensible and affirmative statement—if only to point out that the company has been constructively cooperating with the government and, perhaps, even making it clear that the agency *has* jumped the gun.

This increase in government-spawned publicity—especially when coupled with its almost frenetic cries for "more truth" and more and more information from the business sector—is leading to some criticism of the government's own tactics and output. The organized tobacco industry has been the leader in this. Some Senators have also criticized the unfair tactics. This has not brought much correction however. There also is growing criticism of the "lies, broken promises, false representation, unfounded breastbeating and similar semantic irregularities" so regularly engaged in by our politicians.

Virginia Knauer, White House consumer aid, is widely reported as being considerably concerned over similar charges, strongly addressed to her by a New Jersey advertising man.

Unfortunately the FTC has for many years—since the Rodale Press case (involving book advertising)—taken the position that its news releases are not "part of the record" and therefore a respondent has no standing to complain about any alleged unfairness or other irregularities in a Commission release. What can one say about such "official blindness" as to the marketplace impact of a release from the Commission?

The Commission is, at least, now pointing out in its releases that announcement of a Complaint is not a determination of fault but merely an indication that it has "reason to believe" that the respondent company has violated the law. This tentative concession to propriety probably had its genesis in some Congressional complaints about "regulation by publicity."

We have mentioned already the government's plea to the consumer to "speak up." This is an implementation of the fourth element of President Kennedy's "consumer rights": the right to be heard. From the business point of view, this may be the most important.

At the moment the principal channels for such speaking up—complaints, if you will—are the consumer's Congressmen, the Federal, state and local regulatory agencies or the consumer activist groups. The latter, in turn, are conduits to the wide-eared government people.

Business and its communicators must establish alternative channels—not only for its own informative play-back but to shunt aside the growing and officially-nurtured use of the government as a sounding board for the consumer.

When such messages reach government ears, they lead to more investigations, more bills, more hearings, more Rules, more Regulations, more agency orders, more floor speeches, more news releases from Washington and state capitals, etc. Furthermore, these complaints—even if they do eventually filter through to business—have by that time become so general or emotionally-charged that it is difficult to pin them down specifically and, above all, to do something about them.

Much effort is going into the creation of these consumer-business alternative channels. Some are company toll-free reverse WATS "hot lines." Whirlpool calls its own arrangement the "cool line." Some are consumer/business/media conferences or councils piloted by local newspapers. Some are industry-wide national programs undertaken by industry trade associations.

At the White House level, we have a new Presidentially-inspired National Business Council for Consumer Affairs. It is described as an "advance guard group" trying to identify and correct "potential" consumer-problem areas before they need regulatory-agency intervention. Promotion and advertising are among the important areas to be examined by one of the seven subcouncils.

The purpose of all of these is and must be the same: to try to get feed-back on public dissatisfactions directly from either the individual or locally-organized consumer in order to do something about it before the government—Federal or state—gets into the act. Call this self-regulation or intelligent self-interest, if you will. Whatever its definition, it probably is, in the long run, the most significant action business can and must undertake.

It is even possible that Congress and the public agencies—unless they truly have an anti-business chip on their collective shoulder—will stop listening to the consumer activist when and if the direct-to-government public complaints begin to dwindle significantly.

Unfortunately, government and the activists have sometimes taken a dim view of some of such efforts—sometimes with justification. Even trade sources and publications have joined in the criticisms on occasion. *Advertising Age,* for example, lifted an editorial eyebrow under the pregnant headline "Can you almost level?" The reason usually has been that a company has not acted promptly and intelligently on the complaints. Half-hearted or indifferent reaction merely compounds the accusation and makes the activists' case that much stronger. Real follow-through is needed. As the recently-deceased Ogden Nash put it:

*Auto people would be smarter if*
*they answered a complaint*
*About a self-starter with some*
*specific explaint.*

A promising experimental program of *voluntary* but *binding* arbitration of consumer complaints was started last July in Philadelphia. The Philadelphia Center for Dispute Settlement was worked out by the National Center for Dispute Settlement (Washington), the Pennsylvania Retailers Association and the Pennsylvania League for Consumer Protection. Based on two years of settling Philadelphia landlord-tenant disputes, the Center now arbitrates all kinds of disputes at the retail/consumer level. A similar program is to be set up in Harrisburg, Pennsylvania.

This and other approaches are sorely needed when we hear people like Joseph Martin—until recently the FTC general counsel—publicly urge that the consumer movement should develop "sophisticated political clout" and elect representatives and public officials who will "join those already engaged in the consumer crusade." Add to this the July 1st promise of Lawrence Meyer, director of the FTC Office of Policy Planning, as headlined in the Commission's own release: "FTC TO ACCELERATE ITS 'AGGRESSIVE AND HARD-HITTING' CONSUMER PROTECTION AND ANTITRUST ACTIVITIES."

It may be more than coincidence that House hearings were held this March on HR 5259: the Legislative Activities Disclosure Act. It departs significantly from the language and thrust of the 1946 Regulation of Lobbying Act and even the 1967 amendatory bill—never adopted—as to the tests for registration as a lobbyist.

If adopted, this bill might expose even the editor of a house organ to registration as a lobbyist if his publication happened to carry an article or comment about pending legislation. So concerned are communicators about this that PRSA recently filed with the Congressional Committee on Standards of Official Conduct a written protest and statement, pointing out the almost limitless net which might entangle PR practitioners.

To the PR man or woman this legislation—if adopted in its present form—would be extremely critical because of the plethora of consumer bills presently pending in Congress and the greater need for reaction thereto from the private sector. Apart from the need for registration, the new bill also contains onerous record-keeping and reporting requirements.

The FTC has assumed and is reaching out for new power. No longer may we assume quite legally that "every dog is entitled to its first bite." Now, through affirmative order and Rule, the Commission is seeking to create an entire dormitory of Procrustean beds in which business and its communicator must lie and toss—sleep being hardly possible under these circumstances.

Here are just a few examples: an attempt to make cigarette manufacturers devote a big chunk of their advertising to warnings about the built-in evils of their product; the support of "class action suits" by consumers, based on allegedly unfair or deceptive business practices; the demand for early injunction powers before final hearing; use of new and tougher forms of cease and desist orders; the demand for filing of test results on which advertising or other claims are to be based; the attempt in several cases to enforce *"mea culpa"* admissions in company advertising after an order is entered, sometimes referred to as "corrective advertising"; investigations into the effect of TV on the public; the requirement that entire industries submit substantiation of advertising claims even though there is absolutely no charge of deception involved; the drive for more product information; the campaign against "artificial product differentiation"; an inquiry into "non-verbal persuasion"; complaint about non-price competition; etc., etc.

One could go on almost endlessly in this vein. Every week seems to produce some new reaching-out by the Commission in its effort—as one trade paper recently editorialized—"to be well thought of by Ralph Nader and other consumerists." So dangerous have some of these FTC thrusts become that even Robert Choate, another highly-publicized consumerist, has objected. He points out that new FTC standards would render illegal matters which were previously quite acceptable and that the affected companies do not even have an iterim opportunity to correct their now-suddenly - rendered - illegal - by - FTC-mandate activities.

As long as this proliferation continues, the PR arm will be under constant and increasing pressure. Some thoughtful practitioners are becoming convinced that the volume and frequency—as well as differentiation—is becoming so substantial, that individual instances can no longer be handled on an *ad hoc* basis. Some are beginning to structure their tactics as to have readily available a "universal campaign" as one called it.

Probably the most accurate description of this turmoil is that the FTC and other government agencies are forcing on the company communicator a restudying of his hither-to accepted concepts and techniques relative to both the government sector and the various other publics which may be involved.

We find this "urge to splurge" evident with other arms of government also. We do not find as much restraint as in the past. If continued, this could involve business in such an extensive communications effort that it may become a core activity in some industries.

Typical of this lack of restraint is the recent outburst of Rhode Island Senator Claiborne Pell about an "unpublished Pentagon study" allegedly proving that certain toothpastes caused "painful gum inflammation." He himself admitted that the inquiry "may not be conclusive" and he was roundly rebuked by the American Dental Association which also accused him of a possible "serious disservice to the public health."

Consumerism has brought a very considerable increase in "public relations advertising." Once confined, perhaps, to strike situations or some low-key, institutional promotion, it has now developed into what is being officially described as "societal" advertising. Company activities in the pollution and environmental contexts are good examples. Almost every company which has a "we're doing something about pollution story" to tell is telling it.

Of course, members of government and the consumerist are already taking pot shots at this type of company program. Last May, the executive director of the FTC announced that it was "keeping close watch over ecological advertising" in order to make sure that "the public is not being misled." At the moment this Commission monitoring seems to be limited to product advertising.

In keeping with this current approach, the Commission has brought actions against Chevron and Crown gasolines, challenging claims for pollution reduction. A careful reading of the charges turns up a frequent FTC ploy: a charge that a claim is legally deceptive if the product will not perform in the indicated manner in *all* cases, even though it does so perform in many or even most cases.

The prospective scope of this inquisition is evident, however from this language in the Commission release: "What was formerly of no significance may now be highly material to their (the consumers') choices." The most menacing threat is found in these words of FTC's Basil Mezines: "This need (to redefine what constitutes fair advertising and promotion) exists virtually everwhere because of changes occurring in our society." He also pointed out that change "imposes new obligations upon the government to prevent unfair competitors from seizing business. . . ." This lip service to protection of competition—one of the FTC's basic purposes under its Congressional mandate—is not new. Much Commission consumerism activity has paraded in this cloak.

Speaking to the title "Public Service Advertising: a Regulatory Dilemma," Mary Gardiner Jones of the FTC last April dealt at length with the new importance of this subject. Recognizing the propriety of societal or public service advertising, Miss Jones—seemingly the most frequent unofficial FTC spokesman on consumerism and its various facets—admits that she has neither "the special expertise nor the inclination to analyze or predict the future course which the law may take in coming to grips with this type of advertising," referring to mixed product/societal communications.

It is significant that she also referred to S. 927 (now pending in the Senate) which would make it a *criminal offense* to make any false claims about prevention or control of air or water pollution. In such reference she quoted Senator Spong's statement that "many industries apparently are placing more emphasis on advertising their abatement activities than they are on abatement itself."

She may have given a fairly realistic indication of "official thinking" in Washington when she strongly suggested that companies would be safer if they used "a clear separation, if not total divorcement" of its commercial and societal messages. Otherwise, she continued, the company "runs the risk of having the entire message . . . subject, in all respects, to the commands of Section 5 of the FTC Act."

Make no mistake: such advertising is fast becoming a target for Congressional and agency scrutiny and attack. Not only must the PR practitioner worry about his company's or client's actual activities in these arcas but his is the problem of how to tell the world about them.

We have seen Michigan Senator Hart, in a letter to the FTC criticizing as allegedly deceptive Bethlehem Steel's "ecology advertising" about the company's restoration and reclamation efforts after its strip mining despite the company's denials.

Then too, an entirely new concept is being introduced here. The courts have now validated the right of consumerists, environmentalists, etc. to have access to the airwaves in order to give their side of the story in answer to paid product-advertising. The Federal Communications Commission was directed to give consideration to the demands of these "non-commercial" groups (such as Friends of the Earth) in order to assure balanced presentations on "controversial" matters. This is posited as an extension of the "fairness doctrine" as first applied in the realm of cigarette advertising on the air.

If this now-judicially-approved "counterbalance" doctrine is not overturned by the Supreme Court or Congress, a company's promotional efforts—in the broadcast media at least—could become a "shambles" as the National Association of Broadcasters has put it. There is hardly any product or service which could not be considered as "controversial" or an "issue of public importance" in the minds of *some* activist group.

To inject a bit of humor into this serious prospect, the situation to be avoided is the sort of thing described by S. J. Perelman in one of his trenchant "advertising pieces" back in 1947:

> Perhaps the most curious mutation of this corset advertising is the transformation or clinical type, consisting of two photographs. The first shows a rather bedraggled young matron in a gaping, misshapen girdle at least a dozen sizes too large for her, cringing under the cool inspection of a trained nurse and several friends. . . .The second photograph, naturally, depicts the miracles wrought by the proper girdle which, in addition to the benefits promised in the text, seems to have removed the crow's feet from under the subject's eyes, marcelled her hair, reupholstered the divan and papered the walls.

Routinely, the PR element in deciding corporate reaction to litigation is premised largely on whether or not "fighting the case" with its additional publicity is acceptable. The basic alternatives are "Kill it fast. We don't want any publicity." as against "Fight it. The publicity won't hurt us." This enforced choice is frequently troublesome.

Consumerism has introduced a new element—perhaps even a new dimension—in that a company may now be exposed to very intense and extended adverse publicity even though it does its best to avoid publicity by accepting immediately a consent order or similar adverse disposition. In short, the company may have less and less to say about it.

Thus, in FTC matters, acceptance of a consent order now means at least three FTC news releases because of a new Rule under which the order must stand on the Commission records for 30 days for public examination and potential protest. It was this which opened the door for SOUP to get into the act in the Campbell Soup case, resulting in several additional waves of publicity.

Also, on June 11th, the Commission announced that it was undertaking a new compliance review program covering all "consumer-oriented" orders entered since January 1, 1960. You may rest assured that if your company or client has done anything "the least bit out of line," it is likely to be investigated with, once more, the chances for more odious publicity.

Beyond all of this, the role of the activist will continue to be dynamic. Many FTC actions, of course, have their genesis in such sources but, even after what may seem like a "quiet" disposition, the activist role may continue to be very disturbing.

They may get behind a state prosecution of some kind—based on the same activity which you may have thought was now behind you because of the consent-order disposition with the FTC. This state or local action is even more "promising" in markets in which a Consumer Protection Committee is in operation. The consumerists have a way of using the "admissions" in a consent order against the respondent. Yet such orders quite clearly state that the respondent does not thereby admit to any violation.

All of these post-order developments must be kept in mind when seeking the public relations decision at the outset of the case. In close cases, it may well be that this potential proliferation of publicity will dictate "fighting the case."

All who have so far suffered their consumerism baptism agree that the solutions will not be easy and that progress is likely to be slow. Furthermore, even if the consumer demands are neutralized or reversed, the government's increased-publicity policy will continue and those new laws already on the books will stay there. Don't look for any repeals although there may be less obsessive enforcement.

The PR pressures will intensify in both marketplace and the legal arenas. As a curtain line at one discussion of these prospects, we heard a very knowledgeable and experienced practitioner declaim that the successful PR man or woman will need "the enthusiasm of a cheerleader, the self-assurance of a fiancee, the friendliness of a Russian in Cairo, the tenacity of a rainsoaked St. Patrick's Day parader, the diplomacy of a telephone company supervisor, the patience of a research chemist, the disposition of a selfless parent, the glibness of an M.C., the showmanship of a Barnum and, above all, the genius of an Einstein."

**Reading 99**

# The Glass Curtain Is Breakable

**Peter J. Celliers**

*The sour effect of an occasional defective product cannot be masked; it can only be modified by fast, concerned action to make good.*

Push-button practitioners of modern public relations target increasingly on "publics" and "markets"—forgetting that at the end of the line there's just one guy buying a product. Too few public relations people focus on this rather evident truth. Yet, if the buyer is pleased, he becomes our key to the biggest publicity medium of them all: word-of-mouth.

A soured consumer, on the other hand, is a festering focus of negative publicity. And not all the releases and position papers and special editorial placements, not all the big-name seminars and other devices created to improve the client image will repair the damage done to a company's reputation by one man's "Bah!"

The consumer who's been sold a "lemon"—be this a tangible product or a service—is a ticking bomb, primed to tell his story to anyone who'll listen. His woes trigger others to recall their experiences, often with the same brand product—all amplified in the context of mutual commiseration.

Reprinted from *Public Relations Journal*, June 1972, pp. 18–22, by permission. Copyright June 1972.

Whether personal or corporate, reputations are most immediately vulnerable to talk. (If neighborhood gossips are not example enough, think back to World War II propagandists who proved rumor more credible and faster spreading than traditional media—more so when the word was negative.) Yet public relations use of word-of-mouth techniques is rudimentary—whether in encouraging the spread of positive word or in guarding against negative.

To take just one example: the management of consumer complaints—one of the most immediate generators of word-of-mouth—is almost never delegated to the public relations department. It has, unfortunately, become an area of specialization in its own right.

Consultants and others in this field bandy techniques on conducting complaint interviews, create their own jargon about buy-back situations and repeater identification, nonwarranties and disclaimers—but no one talks much about the effect on public attitudes of defective products and the handling of complaints. So this key factor in a corporate reputation is casually left to disinterested dealers and indifferent complaint clerks following defensive routines determined by lawyers. The result, predictably, is an exacerbation of dissatisfaction, thus ensuring wider dissemination of negative word of mouth.

If proof were needed that the product itself is a matter for active public relations concern, consider only *Time's* cover story on "America the Inefficient," highlighting the increasing proportion of substandard or defective goods and service put on the market today by even the most reputable producers.

Turn to the headlines won by Ralph Nader and other champions of the consumer; it's not all hot air, much as we might like to think so. Note the publicity given, not by chance, to the appointment of ever more consumer protection authorities in state and Federal, even city government. Look even to the growing acceptance of populist concepts in our political life.

Along with this evidence of the mounting need for consumer protection—which should start within the producer company, for self-protection—see the proliferation of newspaper columns acting as intermediaries for unhappy and frustrated buyers who can get nowhere with manufacturers or service organizations—more percisely, who can't get past a do-nothing complaints section to someone who'll show real concern.

It's this factor of concern, so basic to soothing outrage, that points the problem squarely toward the public relations department. For the preservation of favorable word-of-mouth calls for much more direct action than do-good stands in favor of a balanced ecology or racially distributed employment practices.

Most publicity programs start from the assumption that the product is a good one and just needs to be known better or more widely used. Few programs involve public relations guidance to shape the product. Fewer still anticipate the occasional bad apple; that's left to someone else.

"The best public relations in the world," I wrote recently to the president of one of America's Top Twenty, "can only enhance a good reputation. And this is based in the first instance on a good product or service. The sour effect of an occasional defective product cannot be masked; it can only be modified by fast, concerned action to make good."

## CONCERNED ACTION MISSING

Recent eye-opening experiences with this and another major company make it clear, however, that fast, concerned action is the last thing that happens. And when a customer has gone 10 rounds with dealers and complaints clerks, so that at white heat he dashes off a letter to the president of the company X, as I did, he comes up against an impenetrable "glass curtain" that separates him from any corporate executive capable of taking meaningful action.

Knowing how much "yes-ism" usually insulates top management, I suspect that news of a product's inadequacy is often not allowed to filter up the executive floor. But still more often, I suspect, the real spooks are the company lawyers: "Admit even by indirection that the product's occasionally faulty and you're wide open to suit."

If the research department has access to complaint files—as in any well ordered company it must—then I say that public relations must insist on a parallel privilege . . . indeed on priority in this. Furthermore, I believe that any conscientious public relations chief will challenge unquestioning acceptance of the legal viewpoint. You can be so safe that you end up in the poorhouse. Having been involved in several such jousts, I can say that public relations doesn't win out over legal unless the top echelon is sold. And that can only be done by freeing-up communications, by letting customer complaints get through to where they belong as the single most critical market feedback—right at the top.

For evidence that top management is dimly aware that something should be done—but believes that the technicians are doing all that's needed—thus, need to be sold on the right approach—turn to the annual report of one of America's largest listed companies. There you'll find a page filled with addresses to which customers can turn for help with problems—all part of a nationally promoted campaign to convince buyers of the corporation's active interest in them. Certainly such management is convinced they're doing the right thing to judge from the promotional budget allocated in this activity.

## CASE HISTORY CHARTED

But consider, in lieu of what is promised, what actually happens for lack of assigned public relations participation:

Over a year ago, I bought one of the company's products. It was seriously defective. I took it back to the dealer. Instead of replacing it, he fixed it—company policy, he explained. A couple of weeks later, it went bad again. Back to the dealer. Eight months and a dozen inconvenient fix-ups later, the product was still not performing as warranted.

At this point, in desperation, I wrote the president of the company. I pointed out that my experience was far from unique, that this was giving the company a bad name, that the dealer's hands were tied and the customer relations group did nothing. I suggested that this was bad business and bad for business.

Result: three "there, there" letters from customer relations people telling me to take it easy . . . period. No exchange offered; no promise to do a real job of repair; no offer to extend the warranty; no talk of any action at all.

I have since written a total of 16 letters of reasonable, temperate, detailed complaint to six different officers in the company, specifically including the two top public relations men, one of whom (when I followed up by phone) explained:

"Oh, I never read copies of letters."

"Not even when the original's addressed to your president?"

"Why should I?"

Effective results of all my efforts: zero. Not an acknowledgement of receipt, let alone a word of concern from any top executive or his public relations people.

Eventually, a really shrill epistle brought a telephoned promise by a man who wouldn't give me his name to continue to fix the product—at constant inconvenience to me—without cost even after expiry of the warranty. Big, backhanded deal! Would they put that in writing? "You know we couldn't do that!" Because it would tacitly admit that the product was defective, and thus give me grounds to insist on a substitution? "Well, you're saying that, not we." (Yoohoo, corporate lawyers!)

In another similar situation, I was dealing with a giant service company. After five months and eight letters repeatedly requesting service, I received a bland unsigned form letter advising that my complaint had been noted . . . period. Short of marching into corporate headquarters with a gun or buying enough stock to force open a seat on the board of directors, the consumer ends up smack against a glass curtain.

## QUESTIONNAIRES IGNORED

Both these companies have full-fledged public relations departments headed by a VP. Both have substantial public relations budgets and considerable internal public relations staff. Both do a reasonably good job of positive public relations. One of them, indeed, is hipped on questionnaires: Every time you walk into a dealer, it seems, a questionnaire pops up in your mail two days later asking if you've had satisfactory service. Only thing is, no one reads them when they're returned. At least not the ones that say "No."

The incredible frustration of these experiences has not been totally wasted; it has led me to overhaul my handling of complaints. Right now, thank God, my volume of complaints is low; and we keep it that way by fast and positive attention to those we do get. But if ever the complaints increase, I'll quickly detach some of my best people from the market development work they're doing now to give personal attention to complaints. So doing, they'll be even more positively employed.

Specifically, as regards Mexico, we recognized years ago, when the Mexican National Tourist Council was first established, that word-of-mouth was our biggest potential. "Friends who've been there" represent up to 70 per cent of the push toward a first trip, and a satisfactory first trip leads to a 94 per cent return ratio.

But word-of-mouth was also our biggest peril—since first-time travelers tend to talk up the negative on their return home, as evidence of "an adventure." We judged, correctly, that the best defense is an education. Our primary public relations drive, consequently, is to ensure a full flow of accurate information—so prospective visitors would know what to expect, how to plan trips, how to avoid mistakes, which (humanly) they'd blame on everything except their own ignorance.

We didn't stop at that. Our efforts to shape the product—ensure that tourist facilities leave no room for criticism, support our projection of an image of sunny relaxation—include continual inspection of hotels, licensing of guides and similar supervision. Beyond this, we arrange meetings between leading representatives of the U.S. market and the facilities operators in Mexico to keep the Mexican services on their toes and fully conscious of the demands and expectations of U.S. tourists.

And in case a visitor has a legitimate gripe, the Government maintains a legal assistance section within the tourism department in Mexico City to provide 24-hour assistance—plus a complaints department which is empowered to bring suit, and has at times brought suit, against private commercial enterprises after all other forms of reasoning and persuasion have failed to clear up a valid tourist grievance.

As a foreign government public relations representative, my situation may be somewhat different. Adapting my experience to a tangible consumer-product—and applying the experience of a public relations company which specializes in actually handling complaints as a client service—I would suggest the following guidelines for any public relations practitioner, who agrees that customer complaints—and the resultant word-of-mouth—are a legitimate public relations responsibility:

- Public relations should sit on the product evaluation committee.
- Everyone from the president's secretary on down must have clear instructions on routing of complaint mail: (a) in a small company, such letters should go at once direct to the public relations staff; (b) in a large company, they go equally promptly to the complaints section—which should be responsible to the public relations department, not to sales.
- Copy of every complaint letter must additionally go to research, sales and service departments in a small company; in a large company, with a considerable volume of complaints, the complaints section circulates a weekly summary of complaints.
- Handling of complaints should be routinized as follows:

  **a** Problems for which there's a straightforward solution should be resolved and a reply sent out *that same day,* specifying what's been done to set matters right and *thanking* the writer on behalf of his fellow consumers and the company for helping maintain the quality of product service.

  **b** If the problem is larger, the complaints or public relations department has one day to determine a solution, one day to get a draft letter okayed by the legal department, *must* send out a reply on the third day specifically referring to the problem (as evidence that this is no form letter) and detailing what's being done to handle the complaint.

  **c** Such letters—which are okayed by legal, then returned to public relations—*always* take the position that the writer's doing the company an appreciated service, *never* challenge or deny the validity of the complaint (no matter what the legal department may say), always indicate that a solution is in the making and are always signed by an identifiable name with a title suggesting that a significant company officer is handling the matter.

  **d** Short of possible litigation or an insurance aspect, letters of complaint which cannot be handled as indicated above go to the head of public relations . . . who has authority in such cases to *demand* action from anybody in the company. Even here, however, an answer must go out within three days—so that the writer gets a reply within a maximum of one week even allowing for postal delays.

It all boils down to *demonstrating* the concern that any company should feel over a bad product and an aggrieved customer. If you have any doubts as to the overriding importance of public relations handling of complaints, just speak up at any cocktail party and mention a brand name.

Make it a question: "Know anything about XX gidgets?" Twenty to one you'll get a snarl from someone. And that, like it or not, is word-of-mouth—public relations' forgotten stepchild.

Reading 100

# Feel Ripped Off? Don't Suffer in Silence

**FTC Consumer News**

*Almost all the states have some form of small claims court, and procedures have usually been streamlined and simplified.*

What can a consumer do if he or she has been "ripped off" by an unscrupulous merchant?

The feeling of frustration that can result when one realizes he has been swindled does not have to be the only thing he is left with. There are a number of avenues to follow.

## COMPARE FIRST

Of course, the ideal solution is to shop and compare carefully in the first place. A consumer who is willing to shop for what he wants and who will take time to think realistically what quantity and quality he really should receive for his money is not an easy mark for the gyp artist. And reputable businessmen welcome the buyer who gives honest merchandising the careful consideration it deserves.

## BUT. . .

If a consumer does find himself on the losing end of a transaction that seems unfair or downright dishonest, or even if he has seen but avoided a trap set for the less sophisticated, there are things he *can* do if he has the courage to make himself heard. Certainly it is not enough to "chalk up to experience" a purchase about which he was misled, or simply to congratulate himself on not having been duped in the way others might have been. Gypsters thrive in an environment of inaction.

## GO BACK TO THE SELLER

A good starting point is to protest directly to the seller (if he can be found). Possibly the misrepresentation was done without his knowledge, in which case, he can take steps to insure against its repetition. There is even a chance he might square himself with the consumer. But if he doesn't, there are further lines of action.

## COMPLAIN TO MEDIA

If advertising was involved, the consumer can complain to the radio station, television station or newspaper that carried the ad. The complaint should be backed by as many *hard* facts as the consumer can amass. Truth in advertising is too important to these media to risk gaining a reputation for carrying phony ads.

From *FTC, Consumer Alert,* vol. 11, #8, September/October 1972, p. 1 and vol. 11 #4, April 1972.

## GO TO LOCAL AUTHORITIES

Another possibility is local government. This is particularly important because most of the things the consumer buys are marketed only locally, and the seller is not engaged in interstate commerce. The result is that the consumer has to depend not on the federal but on his city or state government for protection. Nearly all of the states have statutes aimed at misrepresentation of products and services. In many states these laws are enforced vigorously. (For a list of state and local consumer protection offices see page 417.)

## GO TO SMALL CLAIMS COURT

The dissatisfied consumer also has the small claims court in his area available to him for redress against the cheat. This avenue is all too often overlooked by the aggrieved consumer, so these Courts can end up more as debt-collection agencies than potential forums for the inexpensive vindication of wronged consumers' rights.

Almost all the states have some form of small claims court, and procedures have usually been streamlined and simplified. Generally the services of a lawyer are not a prerequisite to bringing an action, although legal advice would be of assistance if it could be obtained.

## WRITE THE FEDERAL TRADE COMMISSION

The FTC's fight against consumer deception is directed at gyp schemes that have an actual or potential impact on the public, as distinguished from actions to settle private controversies. In short, it has neither the staff nor the money to tackle cases that do not have sufficiently broad public impact. Also, the FTC concentrates its efforts on halting law violators who do at least some of their selling across state lines. Thus, while the FTC cannot undertake to settle private or purely local difficulties, it does stand ready to halt large-scale deception.

When writing a letter to the Federal Trade Commission, Washington, D.C. 20580, give as many facts as possible, including any evidence of the "rip-off", such as a copy of misleading advertising used to sell the product or the service. The consumer has the FTC's assurance that his identity will be protected.

The FTC provides the consumer with protection against many instances of deception in the marketplace. But he should remember that he can do a great deal for himself by following this advice:

**1** Shop around more before buying.
**2** Bring complaints first to the seller.
**3** Report false advertising to the media carrying it.
**4** Report deception to local organizations concerned with better business standards.
**5** Consider suing the seller in small claims court.
**6** Write the facts to the Federal Trade Commission.

To individual consumers and shoppers, this means that selection of products may be limited. Without discount stores, products of alternative quality and price may not be available. Consumers may also pay more for their goods. (By excluding certain retail sellers, the major tenants may deny the consuming public the benefit of lower prices.)

Should the FTC staff be successful in its litigation of these antitrust cases, legitimate business operations will be protected from a number of leasing practices which impinge on their freedom to compete freely in an open market. This, in turn, should provide consumers with comparative products at competing prices.

## 45 STATES HAVE ESTABLISHED CONSUMER PROTECTION OFFICES

Forty-five of the 50 States, the Commonwealth of Puerto Rico, and the Virgin Islands, now have a total of 70 specifically designated consumer offices. The responsibilities and powers of the offices vary widely. Some perform in an advisory capacity; others actually enforce consumer protection laws.

Twenty-seven of the States, the Commonwealth of Puerto Rico, and the Virgin Islands have such an office under only one branch of the government.

Thirty-nine States and the Commonwealth of Puerto Rico have a consumer fraud or protection agency or bureau in the Office of the Attorney General.

Nineteen of the States have two or more consumer offices with divided or coordinated responsibilities. Twelve States and the Virgin Islands have an independent consumer protection office or department of State Government.

Five have a consumer office under the Governor, five under the Department of Agriculture, two under the Department of Agriculture and Commerce (one department), four under the Department of Commerce, and one under the Department of Labor.

In addition, 53 cities and 18 counties have reported to the Office of Consumer Affairs, Executive Office of the President, that they have established consumer offices with varying responsibilities and powers. Seven cities have consumer protection co-ordinating committees in joint participation with the Federal Trade Commission, and other State, Federal, and local agencies.

Listed are the 45 States with codes showing where the consumer protection responsibility lies:

Alaska, Arizona, Arkansas, Colorado, Idaho, Illinois, Iowa, Kansas, Maine, Maryland, Missouri, New Hampshire, New Jersey, New Mexico, North Carolina, North Dakota, Ohio, South Dakota, Vermont, Washington, and Puerto Rico (AG only.)

California (AG—IND), Connecticut (AG—IND), Delaware (AG—IND), Florida (AG—AGR), Georgia (IND), Hawaii (GOV), Indiana (AG—CO), Kentucky (AG—IND), Louisiana (AGR), Massachusetts (AG—GOV—IND), Michigan (AG—GOV—IND), Minnesota (AG—CO), Mississippi (AG—AGRCO), Nevada (CO), Nebraska (AGR), New York (AG—GOV), Oklahoma (IND), Oregon (AG—CO), Pennsylvania (AG—AGR), Rhode Island (AG—IND), Texas (AG—IND), Utah (AG—IND), Virginia (AG—GOV—AGRCO), West Virginia (AG—L),Wisconsin (AG—AGR), Wyoming (IND), Virgin Islands (IND).

**Code:**

AG—Office of Attorney General.
AGR—Department of Agriculture.
AGRCO—Department of Agriculture & Commerce. (One Department.)
GOV—Office of Governor.
CO—Department of Commerce.
L—Department of Labor.
IND—Independent Office.

The County Consumer Offices are located in these counties: Humboldt, Santa Clara, Ventura, CALIF.; Dade, FLA.; Sedgwick, KAN.; Montgomery, Prince Georges, MD.; Silver Bow, MONT.; Camden, NEW JERSEY; Nassau, Orange, Rensselaer, Rockland, Westchester, NEW YORK; Multnomah, ORE.; Allegheny, Lackawanna, PENNA.; and Arlington, VA.

The City Consumer Offices are located in the following cities: Los Angeles, CALIF.; Jacksonville, St. Petersburg, FLA.; Atlanta, GA.; Chicago, ILL.; Indianapolis, IND.; Louisville, KY.; Boston, MASS.; Detroit, MICH.; St. Louis, MO.; Bayonne, Belleville, Berkeley Heights, Bloomfield, Cape May, Chatham, Clifton, Dover, Edison, Elizabeth, Fair Lawn, Freehold, Gloucester City, Hackettstown, Hamilton Township, Hammonton, Long Branch, Madison, Morristown, New Brunswick, North Bergen, Nutley, Paramus, Parsippany-Troy, Passaic, Paterson, Perth Amboy, Phillipsburg, Red Bank, Teaneck, Union, Union City, Weehawken, Willingboro, Woodbury, NEW JERSEY; Long Beach, Long Island, New York City, Schenectady, Yonkers, NEW YORK; Columbus, OHIO.; Philadelphia, PA.; Virginia Beach, VA.; and Seattle, WASH.

The seven cities in which coordinating committees have been formed are:

Los Angeles, San Francisco, CALIF.; Chicago, ILL.; New Orleans, LA.; Boston, MASS.; Detroit, MICH.; and Philadelphia, PA.

Reading 101

# The New Consumer Product Safety Act

**William G. Haemmel**

*Section 14 provides that a manufacturer must test and certify that the product has met the requisite standard and set forth the date and place of manufacture.*

Consumer products became subject to federal regulations under the new Consumer Product Safety Act, and the government will have the authority to set safety standards for products and to ban those products which present real hazards to consumers. Public Law 92-573 was signed by the President on October 27, 1972, and became operational on December 26, 1972.

A consumer product is any article or part of an article produced or distributed for sale for personal use, consumption or enjoyment in a household, school, in recreation or otherwise. "Consumer products include all retail products used by consumers in or around the household, except foods, drugs, cosmetics, motor vehicles, insecticides, firearms, cigarettes, radiological hazards, and certain flammable fabrics."[1]

The new Consumer Product Safety Act joins the growing list of consumer protection laws which reflect the nation's concern with its business environment. The list includes the National Traffic and Motor Vehicles Safety Act of 1966 (15 USC 1381), the Flammable Fabrics Act Amendments of 1967 (15 USC

[1]Final Report of the National Commission on Product Safety, 1, footnote.

1191), the Food, Drug and Cosmetic Act (21 USC 301), the Radiation Control for Health and Safety Act of 1968 (42 USC 262), and the Poison Prevention Packaging Act of 1970 (70 USC 1471) and others.

## THE NATIONAL COMMISSION ON PRODUCT SAFETY

Following the completion of a two year study by a seven-man, bipartisan National Commission on Product Safety in June, 1970, the Congress took up the task. New York City attorney, Arnold B. Elkind served as the Commission chairman. In its Final Report the Commission estimated that 20 million Americans were injured each year as a result of incidents connected with household consumer products; 30,000 were killed, 110,000 were permanently disabled and the annual cost to the nation was set at more than $5.5 billion. The Commission concluded:

"The exposure of consumers to unreasonable consumer product hazards is excessive by any standard of measurement."[2]

In hearings before the Senate Commerce Committee, Commission Chairman Elkind estimated that approximately 20 percent of the injuries could be prevented. He translated this into 6,000 lives, 22,000 permanent cripples, 4 million injuries and $1.1 billion saved. It was further estimated that the setting of product safety standards would save only five percent.[3]

## THE CONSUMER PRODUCT SAFETY COMMISSION

A new Federal independent regulatory commission, the bipartisan Consumer Product Safety Commission (CPSC) is created, to consist of five Commissioners, appointed by the President and confirmed by the Senate. The Commissioners have seven year terms and the President names the Chairman. CPSC will be advised by a 15-member Product Safety Advisory Council, appointed by CPSC and made up of five members from government, five from industry and five from consumer and community organizations.

In addition to a broad grant of new authority over products heretofore not subject to regulation, Section 30 transfers certain product regulatory functions from other agencies to CPSC. The Secretaries of Commerce and Health, Education, and Welfare and the Federal Trade Commission are relieved of responsibilities under the Federal Hazardous Substances Act (15 USC 1261), the Flammable Fabrics Act (15 USC 1191), and the Poison Prevention Packaging Act (70 USC 1471) and the functions are placed upon CPSC, among others.

The new agency will also collect and disseminate information relating to injuries and conduct continuing studies, investigations and tests relative to consumer products and make public disclosures of same, consistent with the Freedom of Information Act (5 USC 552(b)). The reach of CPSC in interstate commerce is as broad as possible; Section 3(a)(12) uses the "affects" commerce terminology.

## STANDARDS, BANS, AND RULES UNDER SECTIONS 7, 8, and 9

Section 7 deals with CPSC's development and promulgation of consumer product safety standards. Where a hazard of injury, illness or death exists, the stan-

[2]Ibid.
[3]Consumer Safety Act of 1972, Report, Senate Committee on Commerce, 2.

dard must issue a standard. If feasible, the standard must be set forth in performance requirements. Notice must appear in the Federal Register and CPSC can develop its own standards or accept an offer from a qualified standard developer.

Where CPSC finds an unreasonable risk exists and that no standards will provide protection, the agency can ban a consumer product. Section 9 sets forth the administrative procedure dealing with CPSC's issuance of consumer product safety rules. Interested parties are afforded an opportunity for written and oral submissions. The rule must spell out the risk which the standard seeks to reduce or eliminate and the basis and findings as regards the standards must be included. Section 9(a)(1) prohibits extra stockpiling of a product which is noncomplying before a standard becomes effective. Certain deadlines in multiples of months are provided in the several sections.

Section 10 allows any interested person, including a consumer or consumer organization, to petition CPSC to issue, amend or revoke a rule and requires a reply or action within 120 days. Section 10(e) provides for "mandamuslike" relief in that a suit will lie in a U. S. District Court to compel such action of CPSC. Similarly, Section 11 provides for judicial review of a consumer product safety rule by any person adversely affected, "or any consumer or consumer organization."

Where the Consumer Product Safety Commission determines that "an imminently hazardous consumer product" exists, Section 12 provides that the Commission can petition a U. S. District Court for an order declaring a product to be such a hazard, seizure and a mandatory notice calling for public notice, recall, repair, replacement or refund for such a product.

## CERTIFICATION OF PRODUCT AND ACTION

Section 14 provides that a manufacturer must test and certify that the product has met the requisite standard and set forth the date and place of manufacture. CPSC may require the use of and prescribe the form and contents of labels which set forth substantially the same information.

Section 15 calls for close and careful scrutiny by every manufacturer, distributor and retailer of a consumer product who obtains information that a product does not conform to a standard or contains "a substantial product hazard" and immediate notice to CPSC, unless there is actual knowledge that CPSC has been informed. Following a hearing, CPSC can require public notice of the existing hazard, and that the product be made to comply with the standard, or refunds or replacements.

Broad authority is granted CPSC under Section 16 as regards inspection and recordkeeping, within reasonable limits as to times and manner. Imported products are made subject to the new law and exports are exempted. Section 19 spells out certain prohibited acts, including failure to comply with the standards or rules or failure to keep or furnish certain information and for other acts or failure to acts.

## CIVIL AND CRIMINAL PENALTIES

Where any person knowingly violates Section 19 he can be subjected to a civil penalty of $2,000 for each offense with a maximum penalty of $500,000 for any related series of violations. Criminal penalties of $50,000, a year in jail, or both, can result where Section 19 is knowingly and willfully violated after having received notice of noncompliance. Under Section 22 either CPSC or the Attorney General can move in any U. S. District Court to restrain violation of Section 19 or restrain distribution of a consumer product which does not comply with a consumer product safety rule. The offending product can be seized in proceedings similar to in rem proceedings in admiralty.

### PRIVATE PARTY RIGHTS

In addition to the rights and powers vested in CPSC, the new Consumer Product Safety Act grants considerable power to private parties, both individually and in the form of consumer organizations. Section 10 authority to seek action by CPSC has already been noted above. In addition to the usual State court action based upon product liability, Section 23 provides that suit will lie in any U. S. District Court for a person injured due to a failure to knowingly observe a consumer product safety rule. The action must meet the usual $10,000 or more amount in controversy rule. Section 24 allows private enforcement of product safety rules and Section 15 orders. Thirty days' notice must be given to CPSC and if a CPSC action is pending, the private action cannot follow. Reasonable attorney's fees may be awarded the prevailing party.

Section 26 grants broad power to CPSC to preempt state or local consumer product safety standards, but allows the new agency to grant an exemption if the proposed local rule imposes a higher standard than the Federal standard.

It is readily apparent that the Congress has fashioned a powerful, far-reaching and important Consumer Product Safety Act and that its impact can be a profound one. Having found "an unacceptable number of . . . products which present unreasonable risks of injury" and product complexities which cannot be safeguarded against, and inadequate existing Federal, State and local authority, the Congress has mandated a sweeping change.

While the cynic may say that the new Consumer Product Safety Commission will soon become just another old and tired regulator and not an effective watchdog in the public interest, the new law does provide for action by consumers and consumer organizations in the public interest. The public interest groups have made themselves heard in the halls of the legislatures, in the courts and in the administrative agencies, and there is every reason to believe they will make their voice heard in the instant matter.

Reading 102

## Secret Kickbacks Boost Utility Rates

**Arthur E. Rowse**

*Many bank executives also serve as utility directors.*

Secret kickbacks to big banks by major utilities have cost consumers untold millions in padded power rates. *The backroom payments, primarily ties to expansion loans, have boosted effective interest rates in some cases above legal levels,* according to Arnold H. Hirsch, a Washington utility consultant.

The extra fees, known in financial circles as "compensating balances," have been around for some time. *But until now utilities have been able to hide*

From *Consumer Newsweek*, Oct. 25, 1971, p. 1.

*payments in inflated rates,* says Hirsch. "They've been getting away with murder," he says of the utilities.

When "compensating balances" are required by banks before making a loan, the borrower leaves a certain amount of money with the bank in a non-interest-bearing account. But interest is paid on the total amount of the note. The firm gets the use of only 80 to 90 per cent of the loan total, thus raising the interest rate by as much as 25 per cent.

*The role of "compensating balances" in utility dealings has surfaced in a case pending before the Federal Power Commission.* Great Lakes Gas Transmission Co., a firm that brings natural gas to the U.S. from Canada, borrowed $277,750,000 from a syndicate of five banks headed by the First National Bank of New York. The short-term cash was loaned at a floating rate 1.75 points above the prime rate. Interest averaged 8.98 per cent.

*But there was another cost hidden in the fine print.* Great Lakes agreed to maintain minimum balances in each of the five lending banks totaling 10 per cent of the loan, or $27,775,000. Since this money couldn't be used—except by the banks—it meant Great Lakes actually borrowed $259,975,000 but paid interest on $277,750,000. The effective interest rate was thus close to 10 per cent.

*Yet the company said its minimum balance requirements were less than normal.* They usually are 20 per cent, sometimes as high as 50 per cent.

*Bankers benefit doubly.* Beyond enjoying extra high interest rates, they can put the compensating balances to work for them in more loans or investments.

*Many bank executives also serve as utility directors. Two Great Lakes directors are board members of banks that profited from the loans.* Such potential conflicts of interest are common, according to Vic Reinemer, co-author with Sen. Lee Metcalf of "Overcharge," an expose of the electric industry.

Metcalf has introduced legislation, the Utility Consumers Counsel and Information Act, to give consumers a peek at what is under the table and get better representation for them at rate hearings.

## Reading 103

# Supreme Court Decision on Finance Charges

**Consumer News**

*The rule affirmed by the court was designed to prevent any evasion of the credit disclosure requirements of the truth-in-lending law.*

### SUPREME COURT DECISION ON FINANCE CHARGES

The Supreme Court's decision on April 24 (*Leila Mourning vs. Family Publications Service Inc.*) assures consumers of additional protection under the 1968 Truth-in-Lending Act. The decision, in favor of Mrs. Mourning, reinforces a basic intent of the law—a guarantee that when a consumer buys something on credit, he will receive from the seller or creditor a complete & detailed state-

From the Office of Consumer Affairs, *Consumer News*, vol. 3, no. 4, May 15, 1973, p. 1.

ment of finance charges & the total cost of the purchase. With this information, a consumer knows precisely how much it will cost him to buy on credit. The information also makes it easier for him to compare cash prices & credit costs for the same product or service available from other sellers.

The court's decision upholds the Federal Reserve Board's authority to require creditors to disclose all information required by the act, including the total purchase price, in all payment plans of 4 or more installments. The requirement, issued in 1969, is known as 4-Installment Rule of Regulation Z under truth-in-lending law. Under this rule, the disclosures must be made in each agreement involving 4 or more installments, even if an agreement appears not to involve a finance charge.

The rule affirmed by the court was designed to prevent evasion of the credit disclosure requirement of the truth-in-lending law. In the past, some creditors have tried to evade the requirement by making no reference to the existence of finance charges even though such charges were part of the installment payments. The hidden finance charges would make the total price higher, of course, than it would have been if the consumer had paid for the purchase in a single payment.

Before signing any installment-buying contract, read it to be sure it contains—& you understand—all information required by the truth-in-lending law:

- Is the purchase price clearly stated?
- Is the amount of the down payment or trade-in allowance (or both) clearly stated?
- What is the balance owed?
- What is the total amount to be financed? Is it the same as the balance owed? Or is it less than the balance (meaning that the last payment will be larger than the individual payments)?
- How many installments will you have to make? What is amount & date of payments?
- What is the finance charge in dollar terms?
- What is the finance charge in terms of an annual percentage interest rate?
- Is there an itemized list of all charges not included in the finance charge?
- Is there an explanation of penalties, if any, for late payments or other delinquency?
- If the creditor requires a security (such as title to your car, stocks or bonds) for the installment contract, is the creditor's security interest fully described?

Reading 104

# University Student Consumer Action

**Richard L. D. Morse**

*Students spend a lot of money and most feel they do not know how to spend it well.*

Student exploitation is nothing new. Students have been fair game for landlords experienced in renting shoddy accommodations to transient students. Insurance agents exploit the student's growing awareness of his need to assume the responsibilities of adulthood. Salesmen of cookware, china and table service convince them that these items are a necessary part of independent living. Some travel agents lure them with exciting holiday tours that prove disappointing. Students are also prey to service repairmen who know that students must accept their terms because of the limited time they have to shop around or to seek redress for any wrongs via the courts.

A student at the Kansas State University, Robert Flashman, while enrolled in a course in Family Economics, became aware of consumer organizations and activities. He recognized that students were having many of the same problems that the general consuming public faced, yet some problems were unique to students. He discussed what students might do about their problems with his professor, Mrs. Rasmussen. And Mr. William Fasse, an instructor in the Department of Family Economics, suggested that he read 'The Consumers Voice', a publication of the Consumer Education and Protection Association, because this is an action-oriented organization which seeks redress for consumer complaints of its members by direct negotiation. If negotiations fail, the offending establishment is picketed.

## FORMAL PROCEDURE

All of this encouraged Mr. Flashman to develop a formal set of procedures for handling student consumer complaints. Coincidentally, two Student Governing Association Senators had been making plans for improving relations between students and local merchants which they formalized in a bill they introduced in Student Senate. Their action prompted Mr. Flashman to meet with the Student Governing Association and the result was the development of a Consumer Relations Board with appropriate subcommittees. Furthermore, the operation as part of the Student Governing Association is provided office space, clerical and telephone services, part-time legal services as well as budgeted funds.

The design involved nine steps or procedures:

**1** Complaints will be submitted to CRB Grievance Committee for evaluation. (In cases where doubt or vagueness of the issue is at hand, an oral consultation with the consumer will be required.)

**2** CRB will make sure that all available avenues of grievance settlement between the merchant involved and the consumer have been attempted.

**3** Written notification of a complaint will be sent to the merchant by CRB organization in behalf of the consumer. A suggested solution will also be submitted with the notification. CRB will also request the merchant to return a statement of expected grievance settlement or alternate action.

From the *International Consumer*, Winter 1972–73.

**4** If written notification does not bring about settlement by a prescribed time, the CRB Grievance Committee will personally confront the merchant concerning matters for settlement of the consumer's grievance.

**5** If settlement is not reached at this time, letters will be written to the Better Business Bureau of Northeastern Kansas in Topeka, the Chamber of Commerce in Manhatten in behalf of the consumer.

**6** If settlement is not reached at this time complaint will be submitted to Arbitration Board.

**7** If results are not forthcoming, the county attorney will be notified of and briefed on the situation pending.

**8** If items 1-7 bring no results, the attorney general will be enlightened as to the situation at hand.

**9** If all other courses of civilized settlement fail a nonviolent informative picket will be established to publicly bring into view the complaint of the consumer.

The University newspaper, 'The Collegian' carried articles describing the venture and immediately student complaints began arriving. Many were of the expected sales and service kinds. But the University itself came under fire with objections about handling of enrolment fees, residence requirements in relation to fee schedules, and university housing. Each complaint was handled according to the plan of procedure. Not all of the complaints were found to be justifiable. However, by the end of the semester 35 complaints had been filed involving over 800 students and a saving of over $19,000. No case reached the step which required the services of the arbitration committee, nor was picketing ever necessary.

## WRITTEN REPORT

This significant record was documented in a term paper written by Mr. Flashman and later published by the Student Governing Association. A notice of the availability of this publication was mailed to all colleges and universities in the United States with enrolments of more than 10,000 students. The response from coast to coast reflected gratifying interest on the part of student governing bodies. The second year's experience was even more successful. Reporters for the student newspaper were by now more knowledgeable about consumer problems and were able to write with more professional competence due to their experience in writing about the activities of the Student Consumer Relations Board. For example, there were articles on the dangerous implications of 'holder in due course' doctrine on consumer credit contracts, the implications of wage-price freeze on rent, and on life insurance schemes for college students.

The number of students interested in becoming involved in consumer issues grew markedly as evidenced by the number who expressed willingness to serve on the Consumer Relations Board, the Grievance Committee which investigates complaints, the Research Committee and the Arbitration Committee.

Furthermore, the student governing associations at the four other state colleges and universities in Kansas were so impressed with the work done at Kansas State University that at the first year's end they were either considering establishing or had actually established consumer relations boards of their own.

The significance of this common concern is reflected in their sending delegates to appear at hearings of the State Legislative Committee which was considering additional consumer protection legislation for the State of Kansas.

Another indication of student support was the Student Governing Association's willingness to underwrite a national conference on consumer affairs in May of 1972 on the campus of Kansas State University. Representatives of student governing bodies throughout the nation were extended an invitation to attend, which resulted in attendance from each region of the U.S. The readiness with which speakers accepted invitations to address the students reflects their interest in supporting this kind of student activism. The keynote speaker was Miss Betty Furness, former White House consumer adviser. Proceedings of this national congress have been published in tabloid newspaper style and are available.

The participants concluded that no specific organizational format should be prescribed, but that each college or university should develop its own according to the dictates of the circumstances on their campuses. However, they did agree to hold a second national conference. This was held at Indiana State University, October 10–13, 1972.

It is clear that there is an identifiable consumer interest among students. The students are generally well organized in some form of governing body with some degree of authority for looking after the students' interest. Mr. Flashman's major contribution has been to enlarge the student governing association's concept of its responsibility to include specifically the consumer interests. IOCU members could lend their support by bringing to the attention of other student body leaders these documented experiences. At a time when students are seeking relevant activities, direction can be focussed on this area. It is also an ideal time to capitalize on the enthusiasm and blossoming capabilities of young people. The procedures used at Kansas State University are not proposed as a model, but a reporting of the experiences at Kansas State University may stimulate other students who are action-oriented and looking for ways to be helpful to their fellow students.

As a university professor and consumer advocate, I have been impressed with the resources students have at their command and their ability to function responsibly. In addition, since consumer interests cut across so many academic areas, it is gratifying to see students in architecture, engineering, statistics, accounting, psychology, as well as those in Family Economics and Home Economics identify with consumer interests and become aware of the need for their professional areas to join the ranks of consumer advocates.

Students are a special type of consumer and are worthy of IOCU attention.

Students spend a lot of money and most feel they do not know how to spend it well.

Students have questions, not only about the best buy and product quality, but about the fairness of their treatment by sellers and respect shown for their wanting to know the truth about what they pay for. Also they are questioning what is right and wrong about the system of economic distribution. They want to become responsible consumer citizens.

Students are professionally oriented, yet most will not have acquired a defensive attitude about their professions. In fact they are likely to be scrutinizing their curriculum and the future role of their profession in society. So the students who gain a consumer perspective can bring it into their profession and insist that it be included in the curriculum.

Students are an easily identified target for sellers and vulnerable because they are in a state of confusion and transition. Individually, they are virtually defenceless; collectively, they present a formidable power group.

Students will emerge from the universities as future subscribers and readers of consumer publications and become not only members but assume leadership in years to come. There is tremendous competition to gain favour of students so IOCU leaders cannot expect immediate acceptance. Yet IOCU represents so much that students want and need that IOCU members should give careful consideration as to how best to approach student groups in their countries.

### HOW MIGHT STUDENTS BE APPROACHED BY MEMBERS OF IOCU?

I recognize the fact that patterns of university and college organizations vary from country to country, as well as from institution to institution within any given country. Some colleges and universities may have no student organization. However, if there is any kind of student group at all concerned with student government or involvement, then I have some suggestions to make.

The leadership of the student body of the university should be contacted and inquiry made as to what provision, if any, is made in their organization for meeting the consumer needs of their students. If no provision is made for handling consumer complaints of students or representing their interests, describe briefly the successful operation of the Consumer Relations Board and offer to supply a set of the publications detailing the operation of the Consumer Relations Board. If the offer is accepted, mark the significant pages with brief translation. Also attach a note offering assistance, then leave the rest to the students. Repeat the procedure the following year if no activity results. The composition of student leadership changes quickly. Eventually the idea may fall into the hands of a student who has sensed the need for a consumer front, but had not realized its feasibility. Some student with ambition may be challenged by this opportunity to be innovative in creating a new and needed service for students. I am sure that members of IOCU who venture on this path will find working with students both stimulating and rewarding.

Reading 105

# Small Claims Courts Aren't Doing Their Jobs

**Changing Times**

*While the Small Claims Study Group found that in some courts it may take only a week or so to get a hearing, in most it may take weeks, even months.*

With consumers growing more aware of their rights, it's not surprising that one old arena for settling buyer-seller disputes—the small-claims court—is coming in for new attention. What investigation reveals about these courts, though, isn't entirely encouraging. Most individuals who wind up there are defending themselves rather than bringing suit against a company. The fact is that many small-claims courts have become mass-production collection agencies for landlords,

From *Changing Times*, The Kiplinger Magazine, April 1973, pp. 41–43. Reprinted with permission of The Kiplinger Washington Editors, 1729 H Street, Washington, D.C.

utilities and finance companies rather than the "people's courts" they were originally intended to be.

The problems don't end there, either, yet many people, including legislators, see a great potential for small-claims courts, and efforts are being made to improve them and make them more easily accessible.

The theory of small-claims courts is great. The first statewide systems were set up in the U.S. some 50 years ago following much effort by legal reformers who saw that justice was denied to many people simply because they couldn't afford it. The reformers wanted a system that would allow petty disputes to be settled quickly, simply and inexpensively without lawyers.

To illustrate, suppose a repair shop lost your $60 vacuum cleaner and refused to reimburse you. The court procedure should go something like this:

- You start action simply by paying a relatively small fee to file a claim with the clerk of the court, who then sets a hearing date.
- A summons is delivered to the shop owner either by mail or by an officer of the court.
- On the hearing date both you and the owner appear before the judge to explain the issue involved. The judge reads your claim and asks you for any supporting evidence—the claim check, for example. Then he asks the defendant what he has to say. The merchant might admit guilt but argue that the vacuum wasn't worth $60. The judge will ask you for proof.
- After hearing both sides and asking pertinent questions, the judge makes his decision on the spot or after a few days' further consideration. In any event, the entire procedure should only take a short time and be fairly free of legal formalities.
- If the judgment is against the defendant, you'll get the money plus court fees a few days later.

## BUT IT DOESN'T ALWAYS WORK

That's how it goes in theory, and, sometimes, in practice. Recent critics of the system have found that getting justice isn't always so simple.

One massive study, *Little Injustices*, by the Nader-backed Small Claims Study Group, headquartered in Cambridge, Mass., looked at such courts throughout the country. Not all states have small-claims courts by that name, but all have courts of limited jurisdiction to handle small cases, though some of these qualify only technically. The study group found that problems range from having difficulty locating the courts in telephone directories to finding yourself up against defense lawyers or court-wise representatives who are adept at tactics of delay. You could also find that winning in court doesn't guarantee that you collect. John Weiss, on the Harvard teaching staff and director of the study, wrapped up the problems in one sentence: "For the vast majority of American consumers, small-claims courts are either unavailable, unusable or invisible." The major criticisms of the courts come down to these points.

### It Isn't Simple

Just finding the proper court may be a problem. The courts that have jurisdiction in small-claims cases might be magistrate's courts or mayor's courts or even justice-of-the-peace courts.

Getting procedural information is hard, too. Some clerks and judges are reluctant to go into detail. How-to manuals are very scarce. And many of the courts have become quite formal and legalistic. Not understanding procedure can be disastrous since in some places there is no right of appeal from a small-claims court. Some cases have been thrown out simply because the plaintiff didn't use the exact corporate name in his claim. Inarticulate litigants have lost cases because they didn't present them clearly and, despite their obvious difficulties, got no help from court personnel.

### It Isn't Quick

While the Small Claims Study Group found that in some courts it may take only a week or so to get a hearing, in most it may take weeks, even months.

Part of the problem is crowded dockets. Few courts hold hearings every weekday; fewer still have night or Saturday sessions to make it easier for working people to appear.

Then, too, old-hand litigants know how to delay your day in court. They may refuse delivery of the certified or registered mail summons; avoid personal delivery of the summons by court officers; ask for a change of venue to a distant location, making it hard, if not impossible, for you to appear; seek and get continuance after continuance, often on the flimsiest of excuses; or countersue for an amount great enough to throw the case into the even more crowded docket of a regular civil court and make it necessary for you to get a lawyer. Eventually, the regular court may return the case to the small-claims court, but by then several more months may have passed.

### It Isn't Always Cheap

Cost of filing might range from a few dollars, as in Massachusetts, to as much as $20, as in some parts of Louisiana, though the usual fee is under $10. There may be additional fees. For instance, if the summons can't be delivered by mail, you may have to pay extra to have personal service made by an officer of the court. Should your case be fairly complicated or if you know you're going to be up against a lawyer, you may want to get legal advice of your own. Since most courts aren't open in the evenings or on Saturday, you will have the additional expense of losing at least part of a day's pay.

If you win but the defendant doesn't pay, you may have additional court costs to force payment. In some places the only way to get a corporation to cough up is to put the company into receivership, which usually takes several hundred dollars in bond.

And after considering all these potential problems, you might decide the limit on how much you may sue for just doesn't make it worth the bother. Highest recoverable amounts range from $100 to several thousand dollars, with small-claims courts in most states limited to cases involving a maximum of $200 to $500.

## IMPROVEMENTS ARE COMING

Not all of the courts suffer from all of these problems. In some areas court personnel go out of their way to see that inexperienced litigants get fair and just treatment. And, of course, the very fact that such a court is available probably does help to settle some disputes.

"We'll never know how many problems were settled out of court just because a small-claims court was there," said David Gould, project director of the National Institute for Consumer Justice in Ann Arbor, Mich. The institute, a nonprofit private organization working with a federal government grant, is preparing its own report, which is expected to include scores of proposals for court improvements.

Many of its recommendations are similar to those of the Small Claims Study Group. Among the recommendations of both: publishing good how-to manuals; using lay advisers to help people prepare cases; regular Saturday or evening sessions; requiring corporations to post bonds to ensure payment of judgments against them; using volunteer arbitrators with full court authority to help lighten case loads; and raising dollar limits of court jurisdiction.

Both Gould and the Nader group believe that federal funds should be made available to states to create more small-claims courts and to upgrade others. Legislation to do this was introduced in the last Congress by Sen. James Pearson (R. Kans.), and similar measures are expected sometime during this Congress.

## A SHINING EXAMPLE

At least one court has already become something of a model of what small-claims courts could be. New York City's Harlem Small Claims Court is advertised extensively in the community, is open for weekly night sessions, makes use of advocates from the community to advise litigants and depends heavily on volunteer arbitrators (lawyers all) who have full court authority. Litigants have the option of arguing their case before a judge or arbitrators, and despite the fact that there is no appeal from arbitrators' decisions, many choose to go before them. The court uses bilingual personnel, and its instruction manual, printed in English and Spanish, is acknowledged to be one of the best in the country.

Judges and arbitrators often encourage people to settle cases out of court. Some cases never get to court because the advocates try to track down the source of trouble and get it solved.

This, of course, is only one court in one community. Until more courts operate somewhat like the one in Harlem, getting fair treatment in many places will remain a difficult task for most people.

# The International Consumer Movement

Reading 106

## The Consumer and the Common Market

**Paul Kemezis**

*Despite the breakdown of traditional organizations in the nineteenth century, the spirit of the guilds never lost its hold on the merchant class.*

### I FROM SMALL SHOP TO CONGLOMERATE

Europe's drive towards the dream of material satisfaction may seem sporadic (numerous households in the Community have cars but no bathrooms) but its momentum cannot be denied. By the early Sixties, almost two-thirds of all European households owned washing machines, more than half owned television sets and refrigerators, and a third had a car.

As it moves into its American era, continental Europe has put its own stamp on the new way of life. Its cities do not taper off into American or British style suburbs with low-profile single-family houses. Instead, multistoried apartment buildings wander over city limits into cow pastures, bringing into sharp relief contrasting lifestyles.

In America, the single continental market and intense attention to marketing has generated huge manufacturing corporations and sales chains. Gigantic firms manipulate consumers and markets with massive advertising campaigns.

The creation of the European Community's continental market has quickened the growth of American style corporate society on the old continent. The transition from small, privately owned shops to multimillion dollar conglomerates, however, is far from complete.

#### Small Shops Abound

On the threshold of the supermarket age, Europe still has a formidable number and variety of small shops. Although all European cities sport big stores, the hold of the small specialty shops on most local commerce has been broken only in Germany and the Netherlands. Even in these countries there is still one small shop for each 90 to 100 inhabitants.

In France there is a specialty store for every 68 persons, in Italy for every 60. Belgium remains the shopkeeper's paradise with one such store for every 49 inhabitants; 74 per cent of these stores are operated by one person.

From the *European Community*, October 1972, pp. 19–23.

## Medieval Guild Mentality Lives On

Twentieth century Europe has inherited the conservative commercial mentality of the medieval guilds, encouraging the *status quo* instead of competition. A shopkeepers' revolt can still stagger governments in many countries, although the consumer boom and the European Community's widened horizons are weakening the system's inefficiency and extravagance.

Either extreme—the shopkeepers' guild mentality or the American giant corporation—shatters the economics textbook assumptions of a sovereign consumer voting for or against products with his pocketbook. The producer, always one step ahead of both textbooks and consumer, finds ways of keeping the demands of a free market economy from rocking his boat.

Medieval guilds have in fact, if not in name, survived in Europe. Officially these groups, which invented and nurtured the concepts of controlled markets, restricted competition, price-fixing, and oligarchical commercial control, lasted until the nineteenth century.

The industrial revolution destroyed the basis of the guild system. The local market system, where goods were produced by familiar craftsmen, was replaced by a national and sometimes international commercial network.

Before the industrial revolution, the local craftsman, though in no sense a free competitor, was at least bound to a high standard of quality because complaints about his goods might be delivered at his door.

Slowly, goods mass produced in distant industrial centers by powerful and unfamiliar manufacturers began to appear. The irreversible pattern of the present seller-dominated consumer society was set. More goods were available at low prices, but the consumer was more on his own than before. "Buyer beware" became the rule. Although nineteenth century liberalism theoretically guarded consumers' interests by the invisible hand of competition, its main effect was to temper the power of government controls, the consumer's only recourse against manufacturers.

Despite the breakdown of traditional organizations in the nineteenth century, the spirit of the guilds never lost its hold on the merchant class. The American writer, Edward McCreary, reports some modern examples of this mentality:

- Obtaining a license to dryclean clothes in Zurich is almost impossible unless one agrees to charge the standard price set by the drycleaners' association.
- Opening a supermarket in the Netherlands requires a sales license for several types of goods.
- Apples from Normandy still have to pass through the Paris fruit market to reach Norman consumers. McCreary estimates that the cost of getting goods to market in Europe is two or three times higher than in the United States.

## Corporate Collusion Restricts Competition

The guild mentality also survives in the realm of production. A report about American competition by the Union of Industries in the European Communities, cited in Jean-Jacques Servan-Schreiber's *Le Défi Américain*, says that "certain American firms are badly informed about European market price mechanisms which the different continental competitors try to respect. A common study of the methods applicable to establishing net costs has enabled us to get rules which, while safeguarding competition, are beneficial to all interested parties. We must not allow American firms . . . to provoke a price war that would cause serious difficulties in our markets."

Corporate collusion to restrict competition is not new in Europe. Cartels appeared almost simultaneously with the industrial revolution in Germany, and by 1914 a government commission counted 385 cartels and syndicates in the Reich. Then protectionism shot tariffs sky-high and kept them there through World War II.

### Restrictive Practices under EC Fire

With the establishment of the Community, all types of national protection are breaking down, and restrictive practices by firms are under fire. The Community is also opening doors to mergers on the European level to increase productivity and pool technological know-how. Although the idea of mergers may sound automatically bad for the consumer, the Community, under explicit Common Market Treaty provisions, seeks to ensure that the savings from such combinations are passed on to the public.

Perhaps European firms, following the American model, will gain the power to dictate consumer wants and set society's values by their own narrow standards of profitability. *Le Défi Américain* argues that huge Euro-corporations must be formed to beat the Americans at their own game in Europe. Whether dominated by Philips, the Dutch conglomerate, or IBM, the interests of the average consumer could be equally ignored.

Describing the "reversed sequence" in which the supposed sovereign consumer is controlled by manufacturers, economist John Kenneth Galbraith says: "It is true the consumer may still imagine his actions respond to his own view of his satisfaction, but this is the result of illusions created in connection with the management of his wants."

There seems no immediate danger that Europeans will be engulfed with advertising on the American scale. Although the amount spent on advertising in Europe rises yearly by at least 10 per cent, per capita expenditure has remained below the astronomical US levels. In addition, the European guild mentality is not yet as open to aggressive American-level advertising expenditures.

Beyond manipulation of the public stands the further danger of non-accountability. America's leading consumer watchdog, Ralph Nader, finds that US corporate neglect of the public interest through pollution, shoddy products, and fraud would normally amount to a crime. The vastness and anonymity of the corporate structure, however, plus the difficulty of determining the precise effects of the practices, make correction difficult.

In the United States the unification of corporate charters under federal government control has been suggested as a means of improving supervision, while Europe is on the verge of creating the "Eurocompany" charter. Europe's need to consolidate and harmonize national tax systems, health and safety standards, pollution laws, and many other business standards to create a real common market offers a broad field for regulating arbitrary corporate power.

But perhaps, as Galbraith suggests, the high-consumption society has an inexorable logic dictating that over-sized corporations must exist and manipulate consumers to buy more and more goods of less and less real value to keep the entire economy from collapsing. In that case, the only answer may be Commission President Sicco L. Mansholt's February 1972 proposal: finding a "satisfactory" level of consumption and using public coercion to adjust production to that level, making sure that the goods produced do not represent any unavoidable loss of resources.

This concept of limited growth may seem inimical to consumer freedom; but if the consumer is not free anyway, it might help turn more attention toward the essentials of a healthy, satisfying life, and away from glittering and costly appearances.

## II THE RISE AND FALL OF EUROPEAN CONSUMER GROUPS

As the European and American industrial systems steamed ahead in the early twentieth century, flying the banner of "the public be damned," consumer protection was spawned in their wake.

In America, a great wave of protest prodded the government into its first hesitant actions to regulate industry. In Europe, despite the lack of an American-style moral crusade, legislators and labor unions pushed through rules to protect consumers.

As America moved toward a high-consumption society, protection groups, especially the powerful Consumer's Union, began helping citizens to pick their way through the jungle of mass advertising to the best buys. Individual crusaders, like Ralph Nader, appeared to force change through the channels of US civil law. Aided by two other characteristically American institutions, an outspoken press and the free-wheeling investigative authority of the US Congress, individuals and groups produced striking successes such as massive recalls of defective cars and the banning of cigarette advertising on television.

### Europeans Leave Initiative to Government

In Europe, private pressure groups are important, but European society has so far tended to let government take the initiative in righting social wrongs.

In the non-governmental sector, consumer protection has long been an objective of European labor unions, cooperatives, and other social groups. Born in the working-class ferment of the early twentieth century, these movements have lost impetus in Europe's new prosperity. The cooperatives, for example, which are now hard to distinguish from commercial firms, failed in their aim of bringing essential goods to working-class families at lower cost by avoiding middlemen.

In the post-World War II period, independent consumer groups began to grow in Europe. Some groups concentrate on product testing, publishing results, while others take on a Nader-type role, applying political pressure for change. In the six Community member states and Britain, the groups publish numerous consumer periodicals, 11 of them with a circulation of at least 10,000. The biggest are the powerful British Consumer's Association *Which* (600,000) and the German *DM* (500,000).

### Sweden's "Market Court"

Consumer protection provided by governments in Europe varies. Protection is best in Sweden where a consumer's ombudsman system, begun in 1971, hears complaints, investigates, and can take a producer to a "market court." Such a system would be helpful in other countries, since an individual consumer's appeal to the civil courts can often be more trouble than it is worth. In Europe, the burden of proof of unfair commercial practices generally rests on the person making the complaint.

In most European countries the means to enforce consumer protection rules are inadequate. Consumer-oriented test laboratories, though much improved during the last 10 years, are still small and understaffed compared to industrial research labs.

According to Belgian consumer expert Paul Richely, many countries' traditional systems prevent rigorous inspection. Until recently in Belgium, for example, firms would be warned in advance of inspection visits. In Italy there is the time-honored art of killing the spirit of consumer protection laws (which have suddenly flourished in the last decade) by burying them under mountains of legal interpretation. Everywhere in Europe, the legally prescribed danger limits are softened by unofficial tolerances granted by government departments, frequently more attuned to the problems of businessmen than of consumers.

Responsibility for consumer protection is frequently divided between numerous government agencies; there is no central office where the consumer can bring problems. The purity of milk, for example, might come under either the agricultural or public health ministry. Once reported, the complaint is likely to be shunted back and forth between ministries. In one European country, a major exporter of dairy products, the foreign trade bureau checks the purity of exported dairy products more carefully than other departments check dairy products sold on the home market.

As the European Community integrated its members' economies, the consumer's viewpoint became increasingly important to Community officials. In the early Sixties, the Community began considering the technical problems involved in removing trade barriers in Europe. At the same time, Europe's industrialists, recovering from the initial shock of lower tariffs, established powerful industrial lobbies in Brussels. When Commission officials, adrift in a flood of technical details, asked for advice, industrial experts hastened to offer clear, concise, and producer-oriented suggestions.

In 1961 Sicco L. Mansholt, at that time Commission member responsible for agriculture, finally asked the inevitable. Who speaks for the consumer? Commissioner Mansholt's call for a clear consumer's voice led to the foundation in June 1962 of the Consumers' Liaison Committee.

### Common Consumer Viewpoint Presented

The Liaison Committee brought together five European-wide organizations to pool consumer views for the Commission. These were: the European Community of Consumers' Cooperatives, representing 12 national organizations; the two labor federations—the European Confederation of Free Trade Unions and the European Secretariat of the World Confederation of Workers—which preserved separate identities; and the Committee of Family Organizations of the European Bureau of Consumers' Unions (BEUC) speaking for nine politically active national consumer groups. Although the two groups are independent, members of the European Bureau are also affiliated with the International Organization of Consumer Unions in The Hague.

The Liaison Committee examined Commission projects in their early stages and created a common consumer position. Committee members sat on Commission advisory boards, and the group was considered the legitimate voice of European consumers.

During its 10 years of activity, the Liaison Committee moved from general opinions toward more specific views as it gained experience in detailed problems. In agricultural policy, it called for low price levels as the common farm policy was established, and later took up the call for a strong structural policy to shift the Community out of what is regarded as a protectionist agricultural *status quo.*

As early as 1964 the group pushed for action on firms' exclusivity clauses and abuses of dominant positions. On food laws, the Liaison Committee took the position that the best national law in each sector should serve as the model for Community regulations. Eventually, it participated in shaping the laws, with varying degrees of success.

### The Commission Gets into the Consumer Act

The Commission in 1968 established inside its competition division a special consumer unit to act as a central contact point between the Commission and the Liaison Committee. This consumer unit runs a public information campaign, holds conferences, and arranges consumer exhibits and television shows. So far, the small size of its staff and its peripheral place in the Community bureaucracy have prevented the unit from keeping fully informed on the vast range of Community activities.

Despite its vigorous activity, the Liaison Committee had deep flaws. Composed of diverse groups, it had difficulty reaching a common consensus. For example, union representatives were not eager to hold down prices if it meant wage demands would go unanswered. The group's decision-making procedure was cumbersome; Commission suggestions has to go through the Committee to the five European-level groups and then on to the national groups. In the end one opinion was given, but its formulation was a long hard pull.

Lack of financial support, the paramount weakness, finally brought the Committee to an end in February 1972. Providing an alternative to industrial advice took in-depth research in specialized fields, an overwhelming drain on the Committee's meager resources.

No one knows where Community consumer cooperation will go now. This spring, the BEUC was joined by the dynamic British Consumers' Association, whose head, Peter Goldman, quickly outlined a three-point action plan calling for

- a full Commission directorate for consumer affairs
- a new, adequately funded body to represent consumers at the European level
- more consumer representation on Community committees.

Other BEUC spokesmen urge that a consumer affairs directorate be placed directly under the Commission President's authority, an arrangement similar to the American system of having a special presidential advisor on consumer affairs.

In June 1972 the Commission said it wanted to improve contacts with European consumer organizations. It plans to reestablish regular contacts with the five consumer organizations of the disbanded Liaison Committee. About $200,000 will be earmarked next year for campaigns and research designed to promote the consumers' interests and EC contact with consumer organizations. The Commission staff devoted to consumers' interests will be increased.

The entry of Norway, Denmark, and Britain, which have made great advances in consumer action, could give greater weight to the consumer viewpoint in the work of the Commission and the Council. Things may be looking up for the EC consumer.

## III WHY MAYONNAISE LABELS MATTER

Fourteen years after the Common Market Treaty, the most qualified person to assess the effects of European integration is the Continental housewife.

When she buys clothes, her chances of buying goods from another country are four times greater than in 1958. Because of increased specialization among national industries, high quality men's clothes are likely to be made in Germany, women's clothes in France, and everyday work clothes in Italy.

Her refrigerator is twice as likely to have come from another Community country and represents a smaller portion of her budget than it did 14 years ago. Although basic food prices may be higher, such "luxury" products as quality cheeses are now easy to find and reasonably priced. Some housewives now buy products they did not recognize 14 years earlier. The Common Market, for example, taught many Germans that artichokes are a food, not a flower.

The European car buyer in 1972 is four times more likely to buy a car from another Community country than in 1958. Improvements introduced by one European manufacturer, such as disc brakes or fast delivery, are soon copied by all. While facing generally higher prices due to inflation, the European consumer has increased his rate of real consumption by about 72 per cent in 14 years; total consumer spending has risen 92 per cent in the Community, compared with a 35 per cent rise in US private consumption, 38 per cent in Britain.

## Benefits Increased as Tariffs Decreased

The quality of goods improved and relative prices declined as intra-Community tariffs were eliminated during the first 10-year stage of Community development. European markets were formerly divided by tariffs averaging 11 per cent on semi-finished goods and 17 per cent on finished goods and food. By 1968, when these barriers had disappeared, intra-Community trade had quadrupled, and the proportion of a normal European household's expenses spent on Community goods had risen from 14 per cent to 20 per cent. The selection of goods expanded, quality rose, and prices fell or rose more slowly as specialization took effect.

Despite vast improvements, however, the European consumer has by no means reached the millenium. A study made by the Commission in late 1970 revealed large price differences in stores throughout the Common Market. Price disparities result from the jungle of restrictions on distribution, protective government regulations, and differing tax levels.

The Common Market objective of injecting a massive dose of competition into Europe by eliminating all public and private trade barriers remains far from achieved. Therefore, even before the job of tariff cutting was complete, the Community turned to solving non-tariff barriers in the consumer's interest. As tariffs gradually disappeared in the Sixties, technical and legal regulations, less obvious than tariffs and quotas but equally damaging to trade, emerged like rocks left behind by the tide.

National technical specifications affect practically every product's makeup, size, shape, weight, wrapper, or label. All regulations aim to preserve public health and prevent fraud, but philosophies and means of achieving these goals vary widely. Differences in national regulations force Community exporters to vary their products depending on destination, thereby increasing production costs and raising prices. For example, member states' lists of acceptable additives among the thousands of chemicals for preserving or coloring foods are notably different. Thus, a German canned goods exporter might have to use one preservative in a product destined for Italy and another in the same product exported to the Netherlands. The thoroughness of inspection procedures and punishments for fraud also change drastically just one step across a border.

## All Food to Be Treated Equally

In the area of food law, the Commission decided on a two-part program to ensure public health and promote free trade. The first step was to harmonize laws horizontally, approving specific preservatives, colorants, and other food additives. The Commission also tackled the problem vertically, establishing individual criteria for each product type. The first areas chosen for examination were processed meats, chocolate, and jams. Now, practically every item on the grocer's shelf is either awaiting or undergoing study.

Countries often ban products out of habit or protective instinct. German and French ice cream may not contain vegetable fats, and German beer must be made from pure malt rather than raw grains. In such cases where health is no factor, the solution is usually to abolish national barriers against non-conforming products and establish rigorous labeling laws to let the consumer choose between the national good, made in the traditional way, or the product from a partner state.

The Commission took its first major step in harmonizing labels in 1969 when it sent the Council a draft directive on textile labels designed to help the buyer know his purchase. Cutting through the jungle of such words as "pure," "virgin," "artificial," and "natural," the rules say a fabric made entirely of one fiber will be labeled "pure." Otherwise, the label must define its makeup in percentages—"Wool 80 per cent, Acrylic 20 per cent." Where fibers are known by brand names that differ in each country, a common term, such as "polyester" will go beneath the brand.

Other labeling initiatives by the Commission include laws on giving information in plain language about a product's "life." Often such information is coded and can be understood only by the dealer. Labels would have to include clear storage instructions and indicate whether the products contained such additives as colorants. When the directives are passed, a European mother will know how much of her child's orange juice is real or artificial.

The Commission has already produced results on common features for cars and has prepared directives on fertilizers and detergents.

## Competition Affects Consumers

In addition to technical harmonization, the second major Commission activity for consumers is enforcing the Common Market Treaty rules of competition. If left uncontrolled, businesses could divide the Common Market into compartments with artificially different and, of course, high prices. In 1964 the Commission made a landmark ruling against the German radio firm, Grundig, which had given exclusive sales rights for its products to a single firm in France, thus distorting prices. In the 1971 Deutsche Grammophon case, the Commission decided against another widespread practice—banning the re-export of products so that exported goods could be sold at a low price abroad and at a high price at home without fear of competition from re-exports. By the firm's rules, dealers were being prevented from taking advantage of a $2 price difference between the cost of the same record in France and Germany. According to the German Government, these two rulings have brought price cuts of 30 per cent for color television sets and 6 per cent to 11 per cent for certain phonographic equipment in Germany.

The Commission also deals with patent rights, monopolies, and the very flexible concept of abuse by a firm of a dominant market position.

The reverse side of the Community's competition policy, which encourages firms to cooperate to improve productivity or technology while maintaining a fair degree of competition, ensures that gains from industrial cooperation are passed on to the consumer.

The Community has almost accomplished a general application of the value added tax (VAT), a tax on a product at each stage of production and distribution, and hopes by the end of the decade to harmonize both VAT and excise tax rates. Similar tax systems and levies will help make price differences an accurate measure of producer efficiency and an effective guide for consumers choosing between national and other member states' products.

The public may find it comical that the Community spends as much energy discussing mayonnaise labels, the fat content of ice cream, or re-export bans as it does on world monetary problems. The public, however, is the first to benefit from the lower prices, wider selection of goods, and clearer consumer choices.

## Reading 107

# Consumerism in Canada

**Jacob S. Ziegel**

*Jurisdictions in Canada in questions affecting the consumer's welfare are more or less evenly divided between the provinces and the federal government.*

As in the United States, the *consumer protection* movement sometimes disparagingly referred to by its critics as *consumerism* has grown rapidly in Canada. But it is a mistake to assume that the phenomenon began with Ralph Nader and will only survive as long as his remarkable career. The truth is that consumerism is as old as the recorded history of civilized society. The biblical references to the evils of usury and the enjoinder to merchants to observe honest weights and fair measures are early examples; consumer protection legislation in Western Europe can easily be traced back to the middle ages; and in Canada most of the pre-confederation provinces, including Lower and Upper Canada, found it necessary to enact legislation to protect the consumer against adulterated food products and to impose standardized bread sizes. This historical continuity merely illustrates the simple proposition that consumerism is no exotic cult of academia or the sublimation of frustrated spinsters (as a Canadian senator once claimed) but fulfills one of the elemental needs of any organized community.

Still it is true that the movement has made greater strides in the last ten years than during any other decade in this or any other century. A number of factors explain this intensive burst of activity. One is the rapid urbanization of Canadian society and the growing complexity of everyday household products. The typical grocery before the war carried about 1,500 different items; the average supermarket today contains not less than 7,500 items and, thanks to the new technologies, new products are being introduced at the rate of over 1,000 a year. Almost invariably they come pre-packaged and pre-labelled and the consumer must accept the producer's word that the contents conform to their description and that the goods will do what is claimed for them.

From *The Canadian Banker*, vol. 78, no. 6, November-December 1971, pp. 4-6.

Another factor, paradoxically, is the growing affluence of many Canadians. The steady growth in discretionary income since the end of the war has made it possible for millions of Canadians to become owners of automobiles and a wide range of household appliances. The ready availability of consumer credit has vastly accelerated this process. The volume of outstanding consumer credit has grown from $835 million at the end of 1948 to over $11 billion at the present time—a twelvefold increase. But the perils of consumer credit are almost as great as its undoubted benefits and the "Buy now, Pay later" syndrome has spawned many abuses. Consumer dissatisfaction with the quality of some of the new durables, including, particularly, automobiles, has grown apace and imaginative fly-by-night artists have not been slow to separate the consumer from his money in many new directions.

But the overriding factor (and the unifying one) is the overwhelming disparity in sophistication and bargaining power between the consumer and the professional supplier of goods and services. Written agreements are almost invariably standardized—usually to the consumer's disadvantage—and even the rare consumer who understands their contents has no option but to accept them. The businessman relies on a battery of experts to counsel him in his affairs; the consumer is expected to fend for himself, and by himself. Such an unequal confrontation can have only one outcome.

The consumer's problems are by no means confined to the conventional trading patterns. Almost every level of government today exercises a wide array of powers whose effects may have far-reaching repercussions on the consumer's welfare and life style. Public power and the optimum allocation of economic resources are not necessarily co-extensive. A public monopoly may be as unresponsive to the consumer's needs as a private one. Increased tariffs and production quotas may protect domestic producers but they also increase prices for the consumer. Governments must serve a plurality of interests. The consumer's complaint is not that this is wrong but that in the balancing of competing factors his interests are often ignored. The long imposition of a discriminatory tax on margarine (happily now repealed) is a classical case in point. The moral is that the consumer's voice needs effective representation in the counsels of government; for far too long the largest of all constituencies has been disenfranchised.

## THE GOVERNMENTAL RESPONSE

Jurisdictions in Canada in questions affecting the consumer's welfare are more or less evenly divided between the provinces and the federal government. The provincial jurisdiction is derived from the provinces' generic power to regulate "property and civil rights"; the federal sources are more specific and include such heads of power as the right to regulate banks and banking, interest, weights and measures, bankruptcy and insolvency, and—the most potent power of all—the right to outlaw fraudulent and deceptive practices via the criminal law.

Both levels of government have indicated an increasing willingness to exercise their powers, though the degree of activity varies considerably from jurisdiction to jurisdiction and much remains to be done to give consumer interests the same weight as is accorded to the other major components in Canadian society. What has been accomplished to date can best be subsumed under several of the major rubrics listed in President Kennedy's famous Consumer's Bill of Rights message of 1962.

## THE RIGHT TO SAFETY

Historically, this is among the oldest of the state's concerns and its lineage is reflected in the federal Food and Drugs Act. The proliferation of modern drugs and the introduction of literally hundreds of food additives has greatly enhanced its importance and the need for a constant updating of the Act. Canada's Act and its administration are reputed to be among the best in the Western world, but the time lag is painfully evident in such illustrations as the thalidomide tragedy of the early sixties and the licensing of cyclomate which was subsequently discovered to contain dangerous carcinogenic properties.

Until 1969, neither the provinces nor the federal government exercised any general jurisdiction over dangerous products which were not designed for human consumption or medical purposes. The gap was bridged that year by the adoption of the federal Hazardous Products Act. This important measure empowers the federal government either to prohibit outright the sale or distribution of dangerous products or to impose restrictions on their distribution. So far the powers have been exercised sparingly. Their most important use has been with respect to the introduction of a series of mandatory labels to warn of the dangers associated with various types of products. The single most important weakness in the administration of the Act has been the absence of an adequate research arm so that dangerous products can be eliminated from the marketplace before they can cause serious harm. Happily, steps are now afoot to remedy this weakness.

## PROTECTION AGAINST FRAUDULENT AND DECEPTIVE PRACTICES

This right is so self-evident that its inclusion in a consumers' charter must appear almost trite. The facts are quite different. Fraudulent and deceptive practices of all kinds are very widespread and range from the blatantly criminal to the pseudo-legitimate, so common as almost to have acquired an aura of respectability.

Among the latter, false or deceptive advertisements are currently attracting the most attention. Here too federal initiative has led the way. In 1960 Section 33C was added to the Combines Investigation Act to prohibit deceptive pricing practices. In 1969 Section 306 was transferred from the Criminal Code (where it had long lain dormant) to become Section 33D of the Act and thus to enable the federal authorities to prosecute other forms of deceptive claims. While the total number of prosecutions is still small their impact has been considerable, if one may judge by the noisy reactions of the advertising industry. Both Sections 33C and 33D rely for their enforcement on the criminal law and like most criminal processes it is often painfully slow, and sometimes unfairly stigmatizing for the defendant. The most urgent need however is for broad provincial involvement in the form of a general injunctive power to prevent deceptive practices since even under the most optimum conditions it is neither desirable nor possible for the federal government to prosecute every deceptive practice, however local in nature.

## WARRANTY PROBLEMS

Another group of problems, which fall within the provincial jurisdiction, are also the focus of increasing attention. These encompass the area of unconscionable bargains or contracts which though generally perfectly legitimate contain unfair elements. Two familiar examples are the contract of sale which substantially excludes or minimizes the retailer's or manufacturer's responsibility for defective goods and the one-sided consumer credit agreement. The vice in both cases is that the consumer has to submit to terms which usually he does not understand and would be powerless to alter if he did. The phenomenon of this type of imposed consent is a common one and affects many everyday consumer transactions.

Federal and provincial legislation has attempted to redress the contractual imbalance in a number of ways. In the consumer credit area a federal act, the Small Loans Act, regulates the cost of loans up to $1,500 (a ceiling which is now much too low). A provincial act, known in many provinces as the Unconscionable Transactions Relief Act, and incorporated in Quebec in Articles 1040c-d of the Civil Code, empowers the court to re-open any lending transaction if, in the court's opinion, the cost of the loan is excessive and unconscionable. A wide variety of provincial provisions also deal specifically with other types of consumer credit abuses. Unfair warranty provisions have recently been dealt with in several provinces, including Ontario, British Columbia, and Manitoba by prohibiting retailers from excluding the much more stringent requirements of the provincial Sale of Goods Act. It is doubtful whether this is a sufficient answer to the problem.

## THE RIGHT TO KNOW

A free marketplace is meaningless unless the consumer can make an informed judgment about the price and quality of competing products and competing services. Business itself has been slow to provide the consumer with the essential information without which an intelligent choice is impossible. What is supplied is often irrelevant or seriously incomplete. As a result it has been left to legislation to make good the deficiencies of Main Street. The movement has been strongly contested but progress has been made. All the provinces and the federal government (in the case of bank loans) now require the disclosure of the cost of consumer credit in terms of the annual effective percentage rate as well as in dollars and cents. This is the so-called Truth in Lending legislation.

Early in 1970, the federal government adopted the Textile Labelling Act, which is designed to breathe some sanity into the chaotic nomenclature of synthetic textiles. Still more important is the recently enacted Consumer Packaging and Labelling Bill which has three major goals: first, to introduce a uniform system of disclosure of the quantitative and qualitative contents of household products; second, to reduce the proliferation of package sizes and weights to facilitate cost comparison between different sizes and different products; and, finally, to prevent deceptive packaging and labelling and "cents off" pricing practices. Regrettably the federal government failed to add a unit pricing requirement. Still more regrettable is the inactivity of the provincial governments in this area. Surprising as it may seem, there is still no law which requires a retailer to mark the prices of the goods on his shelves.

## THE RIGHT TO BE HEARD

The undoubted progress that has been made in making the consumer the conscious goal of legislative solicitude could not have been achieved without parallel progress at the executive level. Despite their large numbers Canadian consumers are pathetically unorganized, financially weak, and lacking in skilled leadership. The only consumer organization that has national roots, the Consumers' Association of Canada, still only has about 70,000 members and relies almost entirely on voluntary help. What was needed was a voice within government that would represent the consumer constituency with the same resources and funds as are available to other cabinet ministers.

Two important events which coalesced in the mid-60s brought about the critical breakthrough, and as a result have placed Canada well in the forefront of consumer progress in the Western world. The first event was the recommendation in the report of the Ontario Select Committee of 1965 that the provincial government establish a Consumer Protection Bureau. The recommendation was adopted by the government in 1966 and its initiative has since been copied by most of the other provinces. The second equally decisive event was the establishment in 1967 of the Federal Department of Consumer and Corporate Affairs. Under the energetic and able leadership of Ron Basford, its present Minister, the Department has proven an important catalyst for sparking action at the provincial as well as the federal level.

All this is not to suggest, as some business spokesmen would have us believe, that the politicians have sacrificed consumer expediency for solid free enterprise principles. Consumerism is not a monolithic power, no relentless engine, that sweeps everything before it. Some important victories have been won but many more battles loom ahead in the 70s. In a sense they will be more difficult struggles because they will challenge more strongly entrenched interests and require a much more sophisticated examination of our communal structures. Procedure, no less than substance, will be in issue. But it remains true to say that the consumer has obtained a firm foothold on our collective conscience and that the future looks much more promising than it did even ten years ago.

**Reading 108**

# CAC Prods Government

**Mary Kehoe**

*The Consumers' Association of Canada had its origin during the Second World War when women's organizations co-operated with the federal government to maintain the price ceilings established by the Wartime Prices and Trade Board.*

The ban on deceptive packaging enacted at the 1971 session of the Parliament of Canada can be traced to a series of well-documented presentations to the government by the Consumers' Association of Canada. So can the establishment of the Department of Consumer (and Corporate) Affairs, and standard sizes for children's clothing. The achievements of the CAC include stricter inspections of abbatoirs and of the manufacture of dairy foods.

From *Canadian Labour*, vol. 16, no. 9, September 1971, pp. 5–7ff.

The Consumer Packaging and Labelling Act, unanimously approved by the House of Commons in March 1971, has two main objectives:

- to ensure that every packaged item contains a clear statement of the net weight of its contents; the name and address of the manufacturer; and a list of the ingredients, if so required by government regulations.
- to prevent false or deceptive labelling practices, such as "slack-filling" of containers and "cents-off" promotions. For this purpose the government may regulate the shapes and sizes of containers. (Slack-fill containers are larger than the contents require.) Price-discount regulations are expected to limit the use of such claims to real reductions in prices within a specified short period and require that the regular price also be shown.

The CAC brief to the House of Commons' Committee on Health, Welfare and Social Affairs that examined the packaging and labelling bill made specific recommendations on: lists of ingredients, with warnings where appropriate; standard weights and measures; product performance and country of origin.

"It was the culmination of more than 50 resolutions from the association dating back to the 1950s", explained CAC Executive Secretary Frances Balls, in a recent interview in Ottawa.

The CAC commended the Minister of Consumer and Corporate Affairs for the bill's requirement of a dual system of weight-listing. The use of both metric and foot-pound systems in labels "will allow price comparisons in either system and will help those who are no longer in school to familiarize themselves with the metric system", the brief noted.

The wide variation in package sizes has made it difficult for a prospective purchaser to figure out which product was less costly, the CAC said, in welcoming the possibility of standardization of package sizes. "This problem is particularly frustrating when the largest package is labelled 'Giant Size' or 'King Size' and, after the buyer has gone through all the mental gymnastics, it becomes apparent that the smaller package is the more economical one." Standard package sizes "will also allow manufacturers to compete in the marketplace on the basis of the quality of each product rather than on the basis of the size of the package which contains the product."

The Consumers' Association first requested that a prominent warning be displayed on labels of products containing injurious substances in 1962; notification of recommended antidotes to poisons and instructions concerning disposal were recommended in 1963 and 1967. Because shampoos and other cleansing agents are sources of some allergies, the labels of such products should have some appropriate warnings, the CAC pointed out. And all ingredients of packaged foods should be listed, legibly, on the labels.

The 1971 brief regretted that the packaging bill did not require "code dating of good products ... in a manner which can be easily understood by consumers".

Earlier warnings about the hazards to health of food that has been refrozen after thawing were repeated. Uniform standards for fresh fish and canned salmon again were recommended.

Previously the CAC had requested that labels providing accurate information on performance characteristics be required for wigs, hair pieces, hearing aids, scuba and skin diving gear. Because of safety factors, comparable labels should be mandatory for tires, paint and floor coverings.

In 1967 and 1968, the association protested inaccurate "Made in Canada" labels, which often indicated the actual country of origin obscurely. "Another method commonly used is to label a product as Canadian when one component of a product is Canadian or when an imported product is reworked or reconstituted in Canada," the brief noted.

The CAC endorsed the penalty provisions of the Consumer Packaging and Labelling Act: maximum fines of up to $3,000 and maximum one-year jail sentences for convictions of some false-label offenses, such as "cents-off" claims; and maximum $10,000 fines for other offenses.

Products previously covered by other legislation, such as that administered by the Department of Agriculture of the Department of National Health and Welfare, are to be gradually "phased into" the new packaging law.

The Department of Consumer and Corporate Affairs ruled that products with major hazards, such as aerosols containing petroleum solvent, drain cleaners and model airplane cement were to conform to the new regulations by June 1, 1971. Less hazardous products, such as antifreeze and bleaches, were given the same deadline for relabelling at point of manufacture; but were given an extension, until February 28, 1972, for new labels at the retail level.

The Consumers' Association of Canada had its origin during the Second World War when women's organizations co-operated with the federal government to maintain the price ceilings established by the Wartime Prices and Trade Board. The CAC was formally established in September, 1947, "to develop a more enlightened opinion on economic affairs and consumer interests, and to express this opinion in such a way as to benefit the home, the community and the nation." The present name of the association dates from 1962, when a national office was established. Previously all work was voluntary.

Mrs. Balls, a home economics' graduate of the University of Saskatchewan, was appointed executive secretary in 1967. The same year, Eric Luxton, who resigned recently, was appointed editor of *The Canadian Consumer* and public relations director of the CAC.

Chiefly resulting from a membership drive conducted last year in co-operation with the Consumers' Union of the United States, CAC membership has grown to 70,000. Prior to this campaign, there were 23,000 members.

One consequence was the start of a testing program, in January 1971, following the appointment of a testing program manager, Conrad Harris, who is a graduate of the University of Manitoba. Before joining the CAC staff, he was the director of technical services for interprovincial Co-operatives, Winnipeg, Man.

As volunteers, CAC members may spend up to three hours a week in preliminary surveys of a product to be tested. For the report on reconstituted fruit juices published earlier this year in *The Canadian Consumer*, members initially were asked to advise the CAC testing program manager of the brand names of orange, apple, grapefruit and orange-grapefruit juices available in supermarkets in their cities. From these, the most generally available brands were selected for testing by a private laboratory. The samples of the designated brands were purchased by CAC members in Vancouver, Calgary, Winnipeg, Waterloo and Halifax, and forwarded to the national office, in Ottawa, which sent them to the testing laboratory.

Within the next few months the CAC expects to publish reports on comparison tests of tiretreads, men's shirts, light bulbs and household appliances.

## CU-CAC TESTING PROGRAM

The Canadian Association also is involved in joint testing of certain products with the Consumers' Union. Canadian models of television sets, washing machines, electric drills and AM clock-radios have been shipped to the United States for inclusion in the Consumers' Union testing programs.

CAC members who are well-informed on a particular topic, or others who may be persuaded to contribute their services, also compare products or analyze services in articles in *The Canadian Consumer*. Examples this year include reports on camping trailers, life insurance, studded tires and wills.

The annual membership fee for adults is $4; the student rate is $2. Those who wish to receive the Consumers' Union monthly magazine, *Consumer Reports*, as well as *The Canadian Consumer* or *Le Consommateur canadien*, each bi-monthly, pay $10.

Because the work of the association can help all consumers, the CAC receives an annual grant, currently $100,000, from the Department of Consumer and Corporate Affairs.

Although about a fifth of the CAC members are men, they seldom are involved in testing programs, because of the time required for comparison shopping during ordinary business hours. A few are involved in consultative committees, such as the preparation of the policy statement on the White Paper on Taxation.

In some areas, credit unions encourage members to take joint action as consumers, by distributing the leaflet "CAC and what it can do for you . . ."

Future goals of the CAC include: a ban on candy-flavoured headache tablets; standard sizes for adult clothing; improved safety standards for motor vehicles and tires; and enforcable standards for flammable fabrics.

Because the cost of attempting to sue a company for a faulty product or service is prohibitive for an individual, delegates to the 1971 annual meeting of the Consumers' Association of Canada called for legislation permitting "class action"—a joint submission by consumers with similar complaints against the same company.

"In a mass transaction society, it is becoming increasingly unlikely that consumers can seek effective redress in the courts of this land because they are individually at a disadvantage on a case-by-case basis against better organized and better represented business interests", the CAC resolution pointed out. Thus provincial affiliates of the association were encouraged to request provincial governments to introduce legislation to permit "consumer class actions as a form of recognized procedure permitting consumers with similarly-based complaints against the same business interest to proceed together in one action giving maximum redress to consumers and allowing for the public enforcement of consumer protection laws".

As yet, government regulations concerning the dating of food and drugs are inadequate, the 1971 annual meeting declared. Current practices of dating perishable foods are intelligible only to manufacturers and retailers, the CAC said, calling for the establishment of a system of open dating "showing expiry date on all packages where such is important to the quality of the product". Because treatment for accidental poisoning from a prescribed drug can be initiated more quickly if the name of the drug is known, such identification on the label, as well as the recommended dosage, should be mandatory, under regulations of the Food and Drug Directorate.

Most car seat belts currently available for young children are unsafe, the national convention noted. Thus the CAC requested that the Ministry of Transport develop, and subsequently enforce, mandatory standards "for the design, construction and performance of devices which are intended to safeguard children from birth to eight years when riding in a motor vehicle, and to require satisfactory performance under dynamic test procedures as well as under static tests as a requirement for certification".

On pollution, the CAC urges business and industry to increase their recycling of waste materials; local associations to request municipal governments to arrange for regular collections of reclaimable waste materials; and the provision of non-smoking areas in public transport vehicles.

Some achievements of the Consumers' Association of Canada have been the result of persistent prodding, in briefs to parliamentary committees and members of the federal cabinet, and public discussion on deceptive packaging or labels lacking essential information. Thus, the removal of red stripes from packages of bacon, by government order in 1953, was the climax of a long campaign by the CAC. So was the recent decision of manufacturers of children's clothing to adopt Canada Standard Sizes (CSS). Other improvements in food processing for which the CAC can claim credit include: minimum standards for industrial milk used to manufacture dairy by-products; a ban on the sale of meat from dead animals; stricter inspection of abbatoirs; and expiry dates on vitamin preparations.

With the new testing program and the increase in the number of alert, price-and-quality-conscious members of the CAC, the list of achievements can be expected to multiply in the next few years.

Reading 109

## Consumerism Factfinder

**Anne McMahon**

*Consumerism covers the methods of educating the consumer; consumer guides; private and governmental guards against dangers to health, safety, or economic well-being; and consumer behavior and its relation to marketing policy.*

Books dealing with consumerism are listed by subject in the card catalog. Look for the subjects:

Consumer credit
Consumer education
Consumer protection
Consumers

Books

Historical background of consumerism can be found in:

Campbell, Persia. *Consumer representation in the New Deal.* New York, AMS Press, (1940), 1968.

Mark V. Nadel, *The politics of consumer protection.* New York, The Bobbs-Merrill Company, Inc., 1971.

Sorenson, Helen. *The consumer movement, what it is and what it means.* New York, Harper, 1941.

Frequently mentioned current books include:

Aaker, David A. *Consumerism: search for the consumer interest.* New York, The Free Press, 1971.

Buckhorn, Robert F. *Nader, the people's lawyer.* Englewood Cliffs, New Jersey, Prentice-Hall, 1972.

Green, Mark J. *The closed enterprise system, Ralph Nader's study group report on antitrust enforcement.* New York, Grossman, 1972.

McCarry, Charles. *Citizen Nader.* New York, Saturday Review Press, 1972.

Taylor, Jack L. Jr. and Arch Trolsrop. *The consumer in American society: additional dimensions.* New York. 1974.

## THE DIRECTORIES

Directories on many subjects can be found in:

Klein, Bernard. *Guide to American directories.* 8th ed. Rye, New York, B. Klein Publications, 1972.

*Public Affairs Information Service.* Monthly with quarterly and annual cumulations. The subject heading "Directories" lists hundreds of directories under over 100 subheadings including "consumer protection."

Some useful sources of information on people and organizations include:

*The book of the states.* Lexington, Kentucky. The Council of State Governments, Annual.

*Congressional staff directory.* Annual. Washington, D.C., The Congressional staff directory.

*Consumers directory.* International Organization of Consumers. Biannual.

*Directory of government agencies safeguarding consumer and environment.* 4th ed. 1972-73. Alexandria, Va., Serina Press, 1971. Includes state and federal agencies.

*Encyclopedia of associations.* Detroit, Mich., Gale Research, 1972.

*Guide to federal consumer services.* Washington, D.C., U.S.G.P.O., 1971.

*Standard directory of advertisers.* Skokie, Ill. National Register Pub. Co., 1973.

*State consumer action: summary '71.* Washington, D.C., U.S. Government Printing Office, 1971. Summarizes activities of the states and lists consumer offices and personnel.

*United States Government Organization Manual,* 1972-73. Washington, D.C., U.S. Government Printing Office, 1972.

To start your own consumer organization, see:

Knauer, Virginia. *Forming consumer organizations.* Washington, D.C., U.S. Government Printing Office, 1972.

## DISSERTATIONS

*Dissertation abstracts international.* The retrospective index, volumes for social sciences and psychology/sociology, political science, list doctoral dissertations under the subject heading: Consumer.

## BIBLIOGRAPHIES

Herrmann, Robert O. *The consumer behavior of children and teenagers: an annotated bibliography.* Chicago, American Marketing Association, 1969.

*Consumer education bibliography.* Washington, D.C., U.S.G.P.O., 1971.

*Consumer information.* Washington, D.C., U.S.G.P.O., 1971. Lists popular pamphlets.

*Consumer product information, an index of selected federal publications on how to buy, use, and take care of consumer products.* Pueblo, Colorado, Consumer Product Information, Public Documents Distribution Center (Quarterly)

*Newsletter.* American Council on Consumer Interests. See section "Consumer resource materials."

## PERIODICAL INDEXES AND ABSTRACTING SERVICES

*Business Periodicals Index*
*Index to Legal Periodicals*
*Public Affairs Information Service Bulletin*
*Reader's Guide to Periodical Literature*

Indexes to the newspapers:

*The New York Times*
*The Wall Street Journal*

Abstracting services:

Portland Oregon. International organization of consumers unions. The Hague, Netherlands.
*Consumer Review*. Bimonthly. International Organization of Consumers Union. The Hague, Netherlands.
*Journal of Marketing*. Chicago, American Marketing Association. See section "Marketing abstracts," also current awareness source.

## NEWSLETTERS AND REPORTING SERVICES

*Consumer alert*. U.S. Federal Trade Commission. Monthly.
*Consumer legislative monthly report*. Washington, D.C., U.S. Executive Office of the President, Office of Consumer Affairs. Lists current bills by subject.
*Consumer News*. U.S. Executive Office of the President. Office of Consumer Affairs. Virginia H. Knauer, Director. Monthly.
*Consumer Newsweek*. Washington, D.C. Consumer News. Weekly reports on hearings, legislation, etc.
*Consumer trends: An Independent Newsletter on Consumer Credit and Financial Affairs*. St. Louis, Missouri, Consumer Trends. Semi-monthly.
*Consumerism, New Developments for Business*. Chicago, Commerce Clearing House. Weekly. Reports legislative, regulatory, and judicial actions. Includes cumulative subject index. Subjects indexed include: advertising, boycotts, class actions, publications, etc.
*Newsletter*. American Council on Consumer Interests. University of Missouri, Columbia, Mo. Includes "council business," "federal, state and local consumer action" and "consumer resource materials." Published 9 times a year.
*Of consuming interest*. Arlington, Va. Federal-state reports. Biweekly.
*Transportation Topics for Consumers*. Washington, D.C. Department of Transportation. Semiannual.

## SOURCES OF TRADE, INDUSTRY, AND OTHER JOURNALS

*Ayer directory of publications*. Annual.
Katz, William. *Magazines for libraries*. New York, Bowker, 1972. 60,000 titles by subject with critical comments.
*The standard periodical directory*. New York, Oxbridge, 1973.
*Ulrich's international periodicals directory*. A classified guide to current periodicals, foreign and domestic. New York, Bowker, 1972.

## TRADE JOURNALS

Many trade journals are the original sources for the tables which appear in *Statistical Abstracts.*

*Advertising Age.*
*Automotive News.* Annual almanac issue published in April contains statistics on automobile industry.
*Modern Photography.* December issue has annual guide to top cameras.
*Progressive Grocer.* April issue has annual report on the grocery industry.
*Quick Frozen Foods.*
*Supermarketing.* September issue has the annual consumer expenditures study.

## OTHER JOURNALS

Standard consumer guides:

*Changing Times.*
*Consumer Bulletin.* Has annual edition.
*Consumer Information Series.* Washington, D.C. General Services Administration, Irregular.
*Consumer Reports.* Has annual buying guide issue.

Journals worth knowing about:

*Business and Society Review/Innovation.* Monthly.
*Economic Priorities Report.* Published by the Council on Economic Priorities. Bimonthly.
*Family economics review.* U.S. Dept. of Agriculture. Monthly.
*International consumer.* International Organization of Consumers Unions. Quarterly.
*The Journal of Consumer Affairs.* Quarterly.
*Journal of Home Economics.* American Home Economics Association. Monthly.
*Media and Consumer.* Media and Consumer Foundation. The June 1973 issue has *the consumerist reading list,* a critical guide to more than 100 books and publications you should know about.
*Money.* Time, Inc. A monthly for the discerning consumer.
*The Washington Monthly.* Discusses politics, bureaucracy, and the consumer.

## GOVERNMENT DOCUMENTS AND CONGRESSIONAL HEARINGS

*The monthly catalog of U.S. government publications* is the index to publications of the Superintendent of Documents. The December issue has an annual index.

House and Senate Hearings are indexed in *The Monthly Catalog of U.S. Government Publications.* Some examples:

*Diet pill industry,* hearings, 1968.
*Consumer protection act of 1970,* hearings.
*Consumer safety act of 1972, hearings.*

To keep up with Congressional actions see:

*Congressional Record.* Daily with bimonthly index. Covers debate, action, texts, supplementary documents, and reprints of articles.

*CQ Weekly Report.* Washington, D.C. Congressional Quarterly.

To keep up with federal agency regulations and Presidential proclamations see:

*Federal Register.* Daily, Monday through Friday. This supplements the *Code of Federal Regulations.*

This factfinder is intended to help you obtain the most recent materials on the subject to augment a bibliography which is no longer current after the date of publication.

*Notes:*

________________________________________

________________________________________

________________________________________

________________________________________

________________________________________